D0949008

NO LONGER
the property of
Whitaker Library

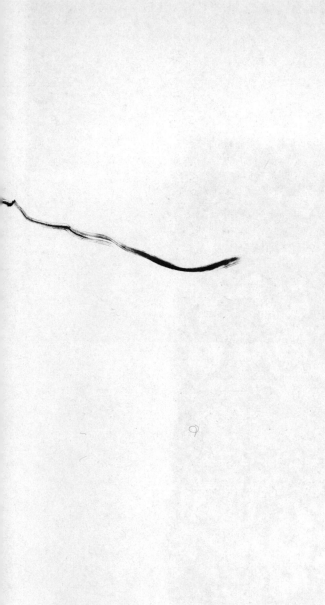

Utopia and the ideal society

Utopia and the ideal society

A study of English utopian writing
1516–1700

J. C. DAVIS

Senior Lecturer in History, Victoria University of Wellington

CAMBRIDGE UNIVERSITY PRESS

Cambridge
London   New York   New Rochelle
Melbourne   Sydney

73297

Published by the Press Syndicate of the University of Cambridge
The Pitt Building, Trumpington Street, Cambridge CB2 1RP
32 East 57th Street, New York, NY 10022, USA
296 Beaconsfield Parade, Middle Park, Melbourne 3206, Australia

© Cambridge University Press 1981

First published 1981

Printed in Great Britain by
Western Printing Services Ltd, Bristol

British Library Cataloguing in Publication Data
Davis, J. C.
Utopia and the ideal society.
1. Utopias
2. Political science – England – History
I. Title
321'.07   HX806   80-40743
ISBN 0 521 23396 8

TO MY MOTHER AND FATHER
AND TO THE MEMORY
OF JAMES ARTHUR STIRK

Contents

Preface

This book has been many years in gestation. In the course of that long period I have incurred innumerable debts and obligations. It is impossible to mention by name all those who have assisted the work in its progress. Many of them are referred to in the text or footnotes. Others will know who they are and will perhaps accept this general acknowledgement.

In particular, however, I am indebted to Werner Stark, Donald Pennington and Brian Manning for their early encouragement and interest; to J. H. M. Salmon for support and encouragement when the project could have foundered; to Professor S. T. Bindoff, Maurice Goldsmith and John Morrill for allowing, and even encouraging me, to inflict earlier drafts of part of this on their students and colleagues. I am grateful to John Pocock for his reading and criticism of a draft of my chapter on Harrington and for much else besides. Geoffrey Elton will, I hope, know how much his encouragement has meant to me and how much it is appreciated. My friends and colleagues, especially Miles Fairburn and Peter Webster, have endured much in the name of utopia and have never failed in interest, enthusiasm and support. Most of these good people would, no doubt, blench at large parts of what follows and are, of course, in no sense responsible for any of its shortcomings.

I have been assisted by research grants from the University Grants Committee of New Zealand and from the internal research committee of Victoria University, Wellington. I am also indebted to the Master and Fellows of Corpus Christi College, Cambridge for their hospitable tolerance when I was visiting scholar with them in 1976. Many libraries in England, Scotland, Ireland and the United States have advised me, assisted me with information and made material available to me but I would like particularly to acknowledge the help of two New Zealand libraries: the Victoria University of Wellington library and the librarian and staff of the Alexander Turnbull Library, Wellington. Margaret Smith, with inexhaustible patience and good humour, has typed all of this more than once. At Cambridge University Press Bill Davies and Elizabeth O'Beirne-Ranelagh have, with their care and good counsel, begun to make this appear a work of scholarship.

Finally, my wife and two daughters, Sandra, Laura and Kate, have sustained me with their own kind of ideal society and have somehow come to comprehend my wrongheaded absorption with these issues outside of it.

J.C.D.

Wellington, October 1979.

Introduction

The initial premise of this book is that a serious study of the political thought of early modern utopias is warranted and in some respects over due. The reader must decide for himself whether the text validates that assumption. But a study of ideal-society literature inevitably imposes an awareness of form as well as content, of approach as well as substance. What methods are to be used and to what end? And, arising out of the methods deployed, what form has the analysis taken? What questions has it sought to answer?

During the last ten or fifteen years a great deal of attention has been focussed on the issue of methodology in the study of the history of political thought, and great claims have been made for a methodology 'derived' from Thomas S. Kuhn's paradigmatic analysis of scientific revolutions.[1] The thrust of this new approach has been to push historians of political thought away from concerns with coherence, more appropriate to philosophers and literary critics, to a more truly historical emphasis on relating the material studied to its contemporary context. That context is seen primarily in terms of paradigms (structures of theory and their maintenance in traditions of intellectual activity) and the language through which they are transmitted, amended and ultimately displaced in what amount to revolutions in political thought paralleling those which Kuhn has schematised in the history of scientific thought. In more general terms what is studied is the linguistic context in which the act of political thinking takes place, and by which it is seen to be necessarily shaped, or the

---

[1] J. G. A. Pocock, *Politics, Language and Time: Essays on Political Thought and History* (London, 1972), especially Chapter 1: 'Languages and their Implications: The Transformation of the Study of Political Thought'. It should perhaps be pointed out that Kuhn has not always been happy with the way in which his name has been invoked in the application of paradigmatic analysis in fields other than the history of science. Thomas S. Kuhn, *The Structure of Scientific Revolutions* (2nd edition, Chicago, 1970), Postscript. For a somewhat sharper cautioning see Paul A. Feyerabend, 'Consolations for the Specialist', in I. Lakatos and A. Musgrave (eds.), *Criticism and the Growth of Knowledge* (Cambridge, 1970), p. 198.

relationship between ideology and linguistic context and their interaction in the evolution of thought.[2]

While this particular methodology insists, against Marxists and sociologists of knowledge, on the autonomy of thought (or at least of language), and rejects the present-centredness of Whig historiography, it does share with the latter a way of seeing past thought in terms of self-conscious traditions. Just as Kuhn's paradigms of scientific thought helped to define (and indeed to create) a self-conscious scientific community and in some respects to allocate intellectual authority within that community, so the paradigms of political thought, deployed by practitioners of this methodology, distinguish the members of a particular tradition of thought and allocate authority amongst them as a consequence. What is seen is the transmission through time of various presuppositions about man and society, man and history, meaning and morality and so on. These presuppositions, and the language through which they are expressed and related one to another, emerge, are clarified, modified and ultimately displaced in a process whereby the paradigms or linguistic contexts of political thought are created, evolve and meet their fate in extinction, anachronism, obsolescence or transformation. That process is seen as a self-conscious one in which thinkers are aware of their predecessors, of the nature of the paradigm or linguistic context in reference to which they operate, and of its implications. Status is conferred on those who are seen to be aware of that process and, at least retrospectively, of their place in it. The modifications they make to the paradigmatic frame of reference are conscious choices of critical significance. Participants in these traditions are then self-conscious authors reading each other's work and transmitting their ideas in a common and evolving language and tradition of concern. An already classic study in this *genre* is John Pocock's *The Machiavellian Moment*, which traces the evolution and modification of a particular paradigm, that of classical republicanism, through from the ancient Greeks to the American Revolution.

These paradigmatic approaches and linguistic preoccupations have not been adopted here. This is not because of methodological belligerence or repugnance on my part, nor because I regard these methods as entirely inappropriate to the study of utopian thought. A history of utopian thought

---

[2] Pocock, *Politics, Language and Time*, p. 25. 'The historian's first problem, then, is to identify the "language" or "vocabulary" with and within which the author operated, and to show how it functioned paradigmatically to prescribe what he might say and how he might say it.' See also John Dunn, 'The Identity of the History of Ideas', *Philosophy*, 43:164 (1968), pp. 85–104; Quentin Skinner, Meaning and Understanding in the History of Ideas', *History and Theory*, 8 (1969), pp. 3–53; 'Conventions and the Understanding of Speech Acts', *Philosophical Quarterly*, 20 (1970), pp. 118–38; 'On Performing and Explaining Linguistic Actions', *Philosophical Quarterly*, 21 (1971), pp. 1–21.

which related it to mainstream traditions of non-utopian thought would be both possible and desirable. But utopian thought itself is not a tradition in the sense outlined above. This is because of the nature both of utopian thought and of many of those who practise it. Its practitioners are not always aware of those utopian writers who have preceded them. In fact such awareness is very rare indeed. Until very recently utopians have not seen themselves as transmitting, extending or transforming a tradition of thought. In that respect the greater number of utopian writers have been unselfconscious. To illustrate: it is inconceivable that James Harrington could have written his *Oceana* in the 1650s without having read and absorbed the writings of the Florentine republicans of the late fifteenth and early sixteenth centuries and in particular those of Machiavelli. Thus Harrington's *magnum opus* may be described as 'a Machiavellian meditation upon feudalism' and his thought may be related to the evolution of the paradigm of classical republicanism.[3] However, it is also possible and of some significance to note parallels between the structure of the ideal society envisaged in *Oceana* and that depicted in Sir Thomas More's *Utopia*. Harrington may have read and been influenced by the *Utopia*. We do not know. Nonetheless, it can be argued that Harrington's classical republicanism was of a different order to his utopianism. In relation to the former he was taking certain concepts – *virtu, fortuna*, the one, the few, the many, balance, corruption – which had been linked by his predecessors in a paradigm of explanatory and prescriptive force to analyse the politics of the Roman republic or late renaissance Florence, and he applied that paradigm to explain and offer solutions to the dilemmas of English politics in the 1650s. In the process he modified a tradition and transmitted it for further modification through the neo-Harringtonians to the Augustans and the republicans of eighteenth-century America. His utopianism, on the other hand, cannot helpfully be analysed in terms of a tradition, paradigmatically defined, which Harrington self-consciously commented on, amended and transmitted to equally self-conscious successors. His *Oceana* is not in this sense a commentary on a tradition stemming from More and evolving in a continuous and self-conscious way through the seventeenth century and beyond. And yet as structures of thought, as designs for an ideal society, *Oceana* and the *Utopia* have much in common. They are both examples of a type of ideal-society thought.

In the same way it is doubtful whether John Bellers had read or even knew of the existence of Andreae's *Christianopolis*, and yet his *Proposals for Raising a Colledge of Industry* bear marked similarity to it. We do not

---

[3] J. G. A. Pocock, *The Ancient Constitution and the Feudal Law: A Study of English Historical Thought in the Seventeenth Century* (Cambridge, 1957), p. 147. Cf. *The Political Works of James Harrington*, edited by Pocock (Cambridge, 1977), p. 15.

know whether Gerrard Winstanley had read any of the utopian works discussed in this book and yet his *Law of Freedom* and the society he depicts there conforms to a pattern of ideal-society thinking which may be defined as utopian. What men like Gott and Bacon, Bellers and More, Harrington and Andreae have in common is not self-conscious membership of a developing intellectual tradition but subjection to a common mode of social idealisation and its consequences. For, when the choice of the utopian mode is made, a shift in the configuration of possibilities within a political theory has to be accepted. Utopia does not offer *carte blanche* to the political imagination, for, in choosing it, the writer is rejecting other possible forms of ideal society. Utopian writing is *not* a tradition of thought, although it has usually been treated as one – with disastrous results. Rather, it is a mode or type of ideal society, and what utopian writers have in common is not common membership of a tradition but their subjection to a common mode. This explains the similarities to be found in the utopian works of writers of diverse traditions. 'Traditions' and 'modes' should perhaps complement each other but, in this work, I have been intent on establishing the latter.

The modes of thought I am describing and (I hope) discovering here are not, as I have said, dealt with in terms of reference to the history of paradigms or the recovery of linguistic context. The principal reason for this is that I am attempting to look at the structures of these ideas from the inside, modally, instead of from the outside and in terms of the flow of tradition, paradigmatically. What I am asking is what people are deciding to do when they write out their vision of an ideal society and, secondly, how it is that we find certain consistencies of internal structure in the resultant blueprints. Two consequences stem from this, both of which may be distressing to some readers. First, because we are not dealing paradigmatically or in terms of tradition with utopian thought, there follows no distribution of authority amongst the practitioners of the mode. Major and minor figures in the intellectual traditions of early modern England must serve equally well as illustrations of the nature and shape of a particular type, or set of types of social thinking. I have chosen, therefore, as far as I am able, to treat both famous and obscure figures with equal attention and respect. Secondly, in order to allay the suspicion that I am simply imposing categories upon the material, most of the utopias dealt with here have been described in exhaustive detail, as have the problems of those confronted by choices between ideal-society types. What I am hoping to induce on the part of the reader is an act of recognition, a perception that amongst the detail may be perceived the lineaments of the ideal-society types which I have distinguished. This may irritate those who feel that knowledge may be assumed in the case of the famous like More and Bacon, or those who do not wish to wade through the details of the obscure and sometimes, it must be admitted, dull writings of 'minor' figures. The case for the latter has been made. My exhaustive treatment of the famous must be defended on the grounds of the confusion with which their utopianism has been treated and the hope that my approach may help to clear away some of that confusion. More modestly, it must be said that no great claims are being made for the methodology used here – if in fact it may be dignified with that name. It represents no more than a conservative and cautious resort to old-fashioned 'close textual analysis'. Nor, in rejecting other approaches, do I intend to disparage them. What is appropriate in the study of ideal-society thought may not be so in relation to other forms and *vice versa*.

If we mean by history in the realm of thought the development of paradigms and the substitution of one paradigm for another, then there is perhaps no history of utopian thought to be written. This book could claim only to be an historical examination of a relatively unchanging phenomenon. Utopia would ironically be out of time, not only in the sense that it represents an escape from history as the flow of contingency, but also in that it escapes history as a discipline, as the study of the patterns discernible in that flow. Is utopia a paradigm? No. For a paradigm is partly defined (although its precise meaning and characteristics tend to remain obscure) by its capacity for structural flexibility and transformation, its capacity to sustain, direct and finally succumb to evolving tradition. But utopia as a structure of thought is relatively unchanging. It is its sameness, its constancy which must be emphasised. The bold claim might be made that utopia as outlined here has barely changed in the last four and a half centuries. Of course, details have varied. Modes of transport, dress, communications, economic organisation, technology, leisure pursuits; these things change as envisaged in the ideal society, but the structure by which the deficiencies of man and of nature are contained remains comprised of the same elements – institutional, legal, educational and bureaucratic devices and their sanctions. As a mode of visualising an ideal society utopia has remained relatively constant.[4]

[4] It has been suggested to me that Robert Nozick in his *Anarchy, State and Utopia* (Oxford, 1974), Part III has outlined a form of utopia which is entirely new and therefore stands outside my definition of the type and simultaneously undermines my insistence on the constancy of the utopian mode. Nozick in fact uses utopia as a subjective, philosophical category. It is its intention which defines it. Therefore because it is good it can be used to test the goodness or deficiencies of Nozick's minimal state. He is able to defend his minimal state as a framework for utopia in which a whole variety of utopian communities may co-exist and utopian experiments may take place without ever describing the structure of one of them. This notion of utopia defined by intention (i.e. good) is set against a market society analysis so that we have a consumer's view of utopia and a vague image of the consensus utopia emerging from a limitless series of free experiments. Material or natural restraints on this process are not referred to. As a

It will be, then, one of the principal arguments of this book that there are various modes of ideal society; various types of answer to the question, 'What is the shape of my ideal society?' And, secondly, that once a specific mode has been chosen, or, to be more precise, once the necessary assumptions have been made (regarding the nature of man, and of man in society, and of the relationship between men, the natural world and time), then a mode of visualising an ideal society has been chosen and certain elements in a political configuration will follow. The available modes are five: utopia, millennium, arcadia, cockaygne and perfect moral commonwealth. Once the choice has been made the exigencies or constraints of the mode are such that the ideal society depicted will end up with certain features or structures common to all ideal societies of that mode. Given a certain set of assumptions, answers to the question 'What is my ideal society?' will invariably end up looking alike. That is why a nineteenth-century utopia like Edward Bellamy's *Looking Backwards* shares common features and structures with More's *Utopia*; not because they belonged to a common literary or philosophical tradition, but because they made similar assumptions and came to similar conclusions; because they chose a common mode of ideal society. It need hardly be said that these modes or types are themselves no more than heuristic devices, useful, I hope, for explanatory and analytical purposes. In practice, as we shall see, the modes may interlock or overlap in the thought of individuals. And equally we shall see, as in the case of Francis Bacon, the mode may impose demands which a particular thinker may not wish to meet but from which he can only escape by breaking off the exercise.

When I began the serious study of utopian thought over a decade ago I was willing to accept that there existed a degree of consensus regarding the definition of utopian, and most of the secondary writers I read on the subject wrote as if this were indeed so. My readiness to accept that we knew what it was that we were talking about may have arisen in part from my innocent but ardent desire to get beyond semantics and problems of definition to explain the social origins and implications of utopian writing. Why did some people or groups in society abandon reality in order to engage in utopian dreaming? What sorts of social frustration, blockage, aspiration and dysfunction did their work represent? What sort of function did their activities have for society as a whole? How did their blueprints balance between reflection and rejection of the social realities around them and what in turn did this tell us about their social rôle? How did the evolution of these patterns correspond with social change? I

method used in a philosophical enquiry into the ethical bases of the state and its limits this may be perfectly justified, but as a definition of utopia for historical purposes it will not do. We need a definition in terms of structure, not intention, and this Nozick is not concerned with. See my discussion below, Chapter 1.

wanted, in other words, to study early modern utopianism as an exercise in the sociology of knowledge.

I look back now on that aspiration and those questions with sympathy but also, unwillingly, with a tinge of embarrassment. They were so presumptuous. I became increasingly uneasy about the simple antithesis of social realism versus utopian dreaming. Those margins of mental inconsistency in which we spend most of our existence and which we tend to call realism frequently seemed evasive, cosily self-congratulatory as compared with the hard-headed, rather pessimistic preoccupations with practicality that I sometimes found in the utopian writers I studied. More distressing still, I could not find any social consistency amongst the authors I studied. Their backgrounds – even sometimes their identities – were shrouded in obscurity. Where they were not, it was increasingly difficult to find common features of social origin, situation or aspiration. I was struck by their diversity, as paradoxically I came more and more to see striking common features in their utopian visions. And moreover as I read their works I found that frequently they were men who visualised not one form of ideal society but several, that they were comparing and contrasting one form of ideal society with another and experimenting with those forms. Were all these forms utopian or only some, and, if the latter, how was utopia to be distinguished from other forms and what was the significance of these distinctions? On the one hand, I could observe striking similarities, on the other, diversity. How were these to be reconciled? Again, from the point of view of social analysis, the ideal-society thinkers I studied were seldom solely that, seldom men whose whole lives were devoted to a single vision. They were also courtiers, lawyers, diplomats, academics, country squires, administrators, small or large merchants, soldiers, physicians and, sometimes, political intriguers. To attempt to relate their utopian vision to their social position was to take merely one aspect of their activity and treat it as typical, and the justification for this seemed less and less convincing.

By the time I had pulled together my findings in answer to my original questions, and written a 'history' of utopian thought in seventeenth-century England, I was profoundly dissatisfied. Not only would the material I examined not yield answers to the questions I had set but it was clear that the questions themselves were the wrong ones. This was not simply because those questions did not 'fit' the data available but also because those questions were based on assumptions that were unwarranted. Basic to that was an assumed definition of utopia which was vague and imprecise and to some degree subjective, a category which did not enable the historian to discriminate between utopia and various other forms of ideal-society thought, nor, with any precision, to identify the utopian amongst the plethora of political writings generated by the past.

In other words, I did not know what utopia was and had to begin again. What some wide reading in the literature of the field had given me, with assistance from some of the more perceptive commentators, was an awareness that there was not simply one form of ideal-society thought, the utopian, but several, and that analytical progress could not be made until the distinctions between them were clarified. To some extent the forms of ideal-society thought were incompatible with one another. They offered, as it were, critiques of each other.

This book begins with the task of distinguishing the utopian from other forms of ideal society. In Chapter 1 a set of typologies, heuristic devices, are outlined. These are offered as means by which utopian material may be selected and by which the confrontation between varieties of ideal-society thought in the writings of one individual or of various individuals through time might be analysed. It will be argued that once a particular type or mode of ideal society has been adopted the writer is perforce committed to the elaboration of a particular structure of ideal society. In Chapters 2 and 3 the emergence of a modern utopian tradition in the work of Sir Thomas More and the writings of some continental thinkers is examined in this light. Thereafter follow a series of case studies from seventeenth-century England to illustrate both what I have called 'the exigencies of the mode', the analytical value of the typology which I have adopted and the diversity of content which utopian thought can embrace. Only in Chapter 11 is there an attempt to deal with what might be regarded as a tradition of utopian writing, and this might be allowed to pass as a justification for that chapter's inordinate length. The full-employment utopians of seventeenth-century England are bound in a tradition not because of their utopianism but because of their attempt to tackle a common problem – that of full employment – by means of a common mode – utopia. I know of no comparable group in seventeenth-century England.

Having made some effort to justify the form of this work and the approaches used in it – or the non-utilisation of other approaches – perhaps I could be permitted a word of justification for the content of it. Why, after all, spend so much time and devote so much space to the chimaera of utopian speculation? In the first place, what makes the study of ideas of these ill-assorted few worthwhile is that they stand at the fountainhead of a long and dominating political process. In the second place, they help to reveal something fundamental about the nature of political idealism. The process to which I refer is the growth of the centralised, bureaucratic, sovereign state with its impersonal, institutional apparatus. It is arguable that the development of this Leviathan has been the most important political development of the last four hundred years and also the most universal. The comprehensive, collective state with its assumption of obligations in every area of human life, from health to employment, education to transport, defence to entertainment and leisure, is a feature of every advanced state, whether of the East or the West, and of the aspirations of most Third World governments. Curiously, both revolutionaries and reactionaries, by their demands that the state more closely control social processes, have furthered the growth of Leviathan. It is a development beside which Marxism, Capitalism, Liberalism and Socialism pale in significance and become almost petty ideologies. And the utopian's significance is that he prefigured this development and, in a sense, prepared the language and conceptual tools to accompany its emergence. Modern utopianism begins in the sixteenth century in a world of weak governments with limited aspirations extending principally to defence and foreign policy and the maintenance of a degree of law and order at home. Even these limited goals were only infrequently sustained in a world of personal administration, amateur and fitful 'bureaucracy' riddled with inconsistencies, irrationalities and privileges – the world of the *ancien régime*, a world in which the language of politics was virtually indistinguishable from the language of private morality. Into this world of chaos, confusion, irregularity and incipient disorder the utopian injects images of a total and rational social order, of uniformity instead of diversity, of impersonal, neutrally functioning bureaucracy and of the comprehensive, the total state. He provides the imagery for the process which, I have suggested, has dominated social evolution for the last four centuries and shows no signs of losing its dominance now. If we wish to understand that process and its significance, it may be worthwhile to look at him.

However few of us sketch out a detailed ideal-society blueprint, all of us, in deciding our political preferences or defining our political prejudices, or simply in conceptualising the kind of political change we would like to see, make reference, implicitly if not explicitly, to a model of assumed social perfection. However vague and inchoate that model may be, it is with reference to it, even unconsciously, that we justify our own political principles, axioms and judgements. Utopia, though perhaps the socially dominant model of the recent past, is only one form that this ideal-society model can take. The fact that we expect institutions, new or reformed, legislation or educational programmes, to solve, or at least cope with, most of our social problems owes much to that tradition of thought. But in a more general sense it may be of some importance to recognise the nature and functioning of ideal-society models in a wide range of political discourse. Even short-term solutions to short-term problems frequently have long-term social consequences. The choice between alternatives is often justified on the basis of a vague, unarticulated concept of an ideal society. We use justificatory terms like 'fair', 'just', 'reasonable', even 'efficient', with this inchoate perfect society as our model of reference.

Some at least of the confusion of political debate, the inexactitude of terminology, the unexpectedness of policy results may well arise from our unwillingness to consider these normative ideal societies and even from our ability to confuse what are basically incompatible ideal societies.

This study has not been written with the intention of showing how ideal-society concepts have influenced political history. The aim here is rather more modest and consists of a preliminary and, I believe, necessary attempt to clarify our understanding of utopian and other ideal-society forms and to illustrate the value of those distinctions in application to an important body of ideal-society writing between about 1516 and 1700. As an historian, I naturally hope that the work will help towards a greater understanding of that period, and, in particular, of some aspects of the social thought of the era.

I

Utopia and the ideal society:
in search of a definition

If it were possible, I would have such priests as should imitate Christ, charitable lawyers should love their neighbours as themselves, temperate and modest physicians, politicians contemn the world, philosophers should know themselves, noblemen live honestly, tradesmen leave lying and cozening, magistrates corruption, etc.; *but this is impossible*, I must get such as I may.

Robert Burton, *The Anatomy of Melancholy*
(6th edition, 1651),
'Democritus Junior to the Reader'

'Human nature must have changed very much', I said. 'Not at all', was Dr Leete's reply, 'but the conditions of human life have changed and with them the motives of human action.'

Edward Bellamy, *Looking Backward*
2000–1887 (1888)

... certainly there must be some unity in a state, as in a household, but not an absolute total unity. There comes a point when the effect of unification is that the state, if it does not cease to be a state altogether, will certainly be a very much worse one; it is as if one were to reduce harmony to unison or rhythm to a single beat.

Aristotle, *The Politics*, Book II,
Chapter 5

This book must begin with a paradox. It may not be resolved but we had better be aware of it from the very beginning. My initial object in studying utopian thought was to find out why people wrote utopias, and what the social significance of those curious essays in the rejection of social reality might be. But the historian has to select his examples, case studies, data from the welter and confusion of records, documents, publications and artefacts that the past has bequeathed to us. He needs a principle of selection, a guide as to what to leave in and what to leave out. So that, whatever my initial desire, an initial problem proved more pressing in its immediacy. From the profusion of political programmes, social commentaries and fanciful ephemera that had been thrown up by a century or so, how was I to select the utopias? The paradox was clear: in order to study what utopias are, it is necessary to know what they are. This book has obviously been written in the belief that we can get beyond this paradox, but we have to be aware of the difficulty, and the problem of defining utopianism – a tiresome task – must command our careful attention. We shall not be concerned with utopian experiments in themselves, but with the appeals and programmes behind such experiments as well as with utopian schemes which were divorced from activism of any kind. How are we to distinguish and identify these amongst other forms of political and social commentary?

Perhaps the simplest and most common concept of utopia, one with which a recent writer began, is that which sees utopias as 'man's dreams of a better world'.[1] This definition is more complex than might appear at first glance, but, for the purpose of selection, it remains too vague to be

---

[1] Nell Eurich, *Science in Utopia: A Mighty Design* (Cambridge, Mass., 1967), p. vii. Mrs Eurich also defines utopias as 'fictional, imaginative stories of ideal people living in better societies that exist only in the writer's mind, at least at the time of recording', *ibid.*, p. 5. For another example of emphasis on the dream as the distinguishing quality of utopia see V. Dupont, *L'Utopie et le Roman Utopique dans la Littérature Anglaise* (Toulouse, 1941), p. 9: 'L'histoire de l'Utopie est en somme celle d'un rêve, persévérant des hommes. Si l'on croit à l'avancement de notre espèce par sa volonté et par ses travaux, ce rêve pourra indiquer dans quel sens ont été accomplis les efforts et conquis le progrès.'

useful. In the period of the English Civil War, for example, many men were capable of thinking of a 'better world' than that of the chaos in which they lived. Does this mean that Thomas Hobbes, William Prynne, Oliver Cromwell, Charles I and the Fifth Monarchists should be viewed as utopians? Under this definition, every man becomes his own utopian and a comprehensive history of utopianism in the seventeenth century would become a comprehensive history of political thought in the seventeenth century.

Just as the concept of 'better' is too imprecise, vague and subjective, so the emphasis on 'dream' carries with it difficulties of its own. For it can ambivalently mean fictional, unreal or impractical. None of these concepts are self-defining and they can all be interpreted in subjective ways. Irving D. Blum, in his attempted bibliography of early modern English utopias, suggested three defining characteristics. (1) Utopias were 'permeated with the feeling that society was capable of improvement'. (2) A utopia was 'composed, at least in part, of plans for improving society, and (3) formed of proposals that are impractical at the time of its writing'.[2] The question is, of course, by whom and in what manner are these criteria to be applied? To take the last one, for example, how is impracticality to be defined? Is it only those schemes not adopted for implementation which are impractical? But do not many programmes which are adopted and implemented prove hopelessly impractical? Who is to be the judge of the scheme's practicality – the historian or the original author? It is not surprising that Blum ends up with a debatable list. Even under his own criteria, Bodin, Hobbes and Filmer may look unlikely utopians.

Nevertheless these same elements within this simple definition of utopia as 'man's dreams of a better world' have provided the basis for a much more serious discussion of utopianism. The concept of 'dream' is related to the fictional aspect of utopias, and the concept of 'better' is related to the idea of perfection in utopias. The visualisation of a better world is in part a subjective process. What will be seen as better depends, to some extent, upon the individual. At the same time, however, it is a reflection of existing circumstances, since visions can only be said to be 'better' by reference to some pre-existing standard or condition. This envisaged 'betterness' can thus be seen as one of three things: a passive indulgence or escapist dream, designed to provide a mental refuge from an unattractive reality; a satiric reflection of what exists, designed to highlight the abhorrent in the status quo, and lastly a blueprint for action, providing a model of what should replace the existing state. The last of these is very closely related to Mannheim's definition of utopianism as the disruptive,

[2] Irving D. Blum, 'English Utopias from 1551 to 1699: A Bibliography', *Bulletin of Bibliography*, 21:6 (1955), pp. 143-4.

challenging force in intellectual history,[3] and all three approaches to the idea of betterness implicitly reject the status quo.

If the concept of 'betterness' leads us to see utopianism as implicitly or explicitly a rejection of the status quo, the problem remains as to whether all rejections of the status quo are utopian, or only some, and if the latter how we are to decide which are utopian and which are not. For example, in the seventeenth-century movements for law reform, the abolition of tithes, the curtailment of monopolies, and the reform of the church were all, in a sense, rejecting aspects of the status quo. Are they then to be considered utopian? The problem is not only what to leave out and what to include, but also when to include what we are going to include, for some programmes are by this definition utopian at one period, ideological at another. Royalism has to be seen as utopian during the Interregnum, ideological at any other time. Presbyterianism was utopian in the early seventeenth century and became ideological in the 1640s. Thus the qualities of 'betterness' or 'disruptiveness' are of no great assistance in isolating what might be considered specifically utopian material. The field of consideration might be narrowed by substituting the quality of 'perfect' for that of 'better'. Most men can think of a better world; surprisingly few make the effort to visualise their perfect world and set their vision down on paper. Moreover this quality of perfection has the advantage of being related to the other aspect of the simple definition we began with, the dream. If social perfection existed, the utopian would not be prompted to write. He begins as a critic. But the standard of criticism, the perfection, exists in the mind. It is a fiction, a thing feigned or imagined, and the utopian takes the unusual step of forming his imaginary vision on paper.

The fictional element in utopian writing has been most emphasised by Friedrich Engels, Karl Marx and their followers. For Marx and Engels utopian writing was a purely mental exercise in which 'Reason became the sole measure of everything.'[4] It was a search for absolute truth 'independent of time, space, and of the historical development of man'.[5] Certainly it did not have the 'real basis' that their socialism was, in their view, to have. Judith Shklar, much more recently, has reiterated the view that what she calls 'classical utopianism' has no historical basis. 'Utopia is nowhere, not only geographically, but historically as well. It exists neither

---

[3] Karl Mannheim, *Ideology and Utopia* (London, 1960); Mannheim, 'Utopia', in E. R. A. Seligman and A. Johnson (eds.), *Encyclopaedia of the Social Sciences* (London, 1935).

[4] Friedrich Engels, 'Socialism: Utopian and Scientific', in K. Marx and F. Engels, *Selected Works* (Moscow, 1958), vol. II, p. 166; see also *ibid.*, pp. 116–28, and Marx and Engels, 'Manifesto of the Communist Party', *ibid.*, vol. I, pp. 61–4.

[5] Engels, 'Socialism: Utopian and Scientific', p. 128.

in the past nor in the future.'[6] Thus, 'Rousseau was the last of the classical utopists. He was the last great political theorist to be utterly uninterested in history, past or future, the last also to condemn without giving any thought to programs of action.' 'The utopian form was ideally suited to convey his concern for the contrast between what is and what ought to be. With it came the characteristic indifference to history.'[7] The 'classical' utopia as presented here is pure fiction, a Platonic model, designed for contemplation only and not for action. It transcends time and place.[8] Therefore when political programmes become identified in time, when they become 'activist' or when an attempt is made to translate fiction into fact, they cease to be utopias.[9] Hence the nineteenth century, when schemers like Owen and Cabet endeavour to translate theoretical fictions into experimental facts, witnesses the end of the classical utopia. Harrington and Hartlib are seen not as utopians but as educational reformers. However, somewhat uncomfortably, Winstanley and the Diggers are to be seen as 'partial exceptions' to the rule that 'classical' utopians cannot be activists.[10] Yet more recently, Elizabeth Hansot has produced a variation on this theme. She distinguishes between the classical utopias of such as Plato, Thomas More and Johann Andreae, and the modern utopias of Bellamy, Wells and Howells. The classical utopia is seen as 'unconcerned with actualisation in time'. It offers an unchanging standard by which individual men might be changed. The modern utopia, by contrast, seeks primarily to change social arrangements, only thereby changing man, and furthermore it seeks to incorporate a capacity for change within the model society. The seventeenth and eighteenth centuries are seen as a critical period when the classical mode began to give way to the modern utopia. As with Engels and Shklar, the fictional element in utopianism is emphasised, presumably by contrast with more 'realistic' forms of political writing. Utopias are 'totally fictive constructions or reconstructions of society'.[11]

The difficulty here is that while fiction may be a necessary condition

[6] Judith Shklar, 'The Political Theory of Utopia: From Melancholy to Nostalgia', in Frank E. Manuel (ed.), *Utopias and Utopian Thought* (Boston, 1966), p. 104. See also my criticism of this view, J. C. Davis, 'Utopia and History', *Historical Studies*, 13:50 (1968), pp. 165–76.

[7] Judith Shklar, 'Rousseau's Two Models: Sparta and the Age of Gold', *Political Science Quarterly*, 81:1 (1966), pp. 26, 27.

[8] But note here M. I. Finley's caution, 'Utopia transcends the given social reality; it is not transcendental in a metaphysical sense.' M. I. Finley, 'Utopianism Ancient and Modern', in Finley, *The Use and Abuse of History* (London, 1975), pp. 180–181.

[9] Shklar, 'The Political Theory of Utopia', pp. 106–7.

[10] *Ibid.*, p. 107.

[11] Elizabeth Hansot, *Perfection and Progress: Two Modes of Utopian Thought* (Cambridge, Mass., 1974), p. 3 and Chapter 1 for the general argument.

for utopia (as it may be for any form of political theory) it is by no means a sufficient one. It defines utopia in terms of perfection without enabling us to distinguish between various forms of social perfection. If classical utopia is defined simply as a standard of judgement, we must ask why one standard rather than another is chosen. Again, if More, in particular, is to be seen as a classical utopian, it becomes difficult to see the classical utopia as primarily directed at individual rather than social change.[12] Beyond this lies the questionable assumption that there is a mode of political writing free of fiction which may be contrasted with a utopian form 'marred' by fiction, or, to put it another way, that there is a known and identifiable political reality to which realistic political writing adheres and from which utopian writing deviates.

Two scholars to whom all students of utopianism owe a great deal, Glenn Negley and J. Max Patrick, have attempted to overcome this problem by broadening the defining criteria. They suggest that utopian writing may be distinguished by three characteristics. It is fictional, it describes a particular state or community and its theme is the political structure of that fictional state or community. This is certainly an improvement on the definitions already looked at and is useful in its emphasis on the political concern of the utopian writer. Nevertheless, for the purposes of selection, problems remain and many of these arise out of the vexed issue of fiction, the importance of which Negley and Patrick are at some pains to emphasise. 'This primary and necessary discrimination eliminates from utopian literature all speculation the form of which indicates that it should properly be designated political philosophy or political theory.'[13] The objections to this are numerous. In the first place, what do Negley and Patrick mean by fiction? They might mean that, to qualify as a utopia, a work must have an imaginative, narrative setting – an imaginary dialogue, the recollections of an imaginary traveller, a journey to imaginary lands or a trip to the moon, something of this sort.[14] However, they again include as utopian the work of Gerrard Winstanley, who adopts no such narrative devices, but makes his proposals directly, in a matter-of-fact way.[15] Equally, it does not seem reasonable that every political discussion using such fictional

---

[12] See below Chapter 2.

[13] Glenn Negley and J. Max Patrick, *The Quest for Utopia* (New York, 1952), p. 3. See also Glenn Negley, *Utopian Literature: A Bibliography* (Lawrence, Kansas, 1977).

[14] For the problems of defining the genre of the imaginary voyage see Philip Babcock Gove, *The Imaginary Voyage in Prose Fiction* (New York, 1941).

[15] Negley and Patrick, *Quest for Utopia*, pp. 288–9. For a discussion of Winstanley's utopianism see below Chapter 7. Cf. Angele B. Samaan, 'Utopias and Utopian Novels 1516–1949: A Preliminary Bibliography', *Moreana*, 31–2 (1971), pp. 281–93. Here again great stress is laid on the fictional form but Winstanley is included.

devices and concentrating on a particular community should be described as utopian. Negley and Patrick were aware of this problem. 'The fictional nature of utopia', they wrote, 'does not, however, give complete license to the imagination; there is a point at which sheer fantasy ceases to be utopian in any definable sense.' Thus a limit is set to the range of the utopian imagination and this limit is that 'utopia will bear some resemblance to the existing state of society of the utopist'.[16] Utopian writing becomes a blend of fact and fiction but we are really no nearer to an adequate criterion for distinguishing utopias from other forms of political speculation combining fact and fiction. On one level 'fiction', as a standard of criticism of political writing, is an emotive concept. Those views which we reject as untrue, we also see as fictional or unrepresentative of the real situation. On another level all political philosophy deals in fictions — 'sovereignty', 'the dialectic', 'general will', 'separation of the powers', 'public opinion', 'common good'. Fiction then may be seen as an attribute of utopian writing only in the same sense that it is an attribute of all political theorising; although literary devices of a fictional or imaginative kind might be exploited with greater frequency in the utopian tradition. The threefold criteria of Negley and Patrick are all applicable to the nature of utopia, but they are not adequate. They do not provide a sufficient basis for selection. Moreover all the criteria considered so far – 'better', 'perfect', 'fiction' – are, to a degree, subjective. What is better, or perfect, or fictional (in the broader sense) to one person, need not be so to another.

The difficulty that we are labouring under at the moment is that the adjective 'utopian' is being used as a catch-all label for all forms of ideal society.[17] Two problems may and do arise from this. The first is that contradictory statements are made about utopia by authors who are examining different forms of ideal society. Thus we may be told that utopianism is an expression of great optimism, or of profound pessimism;

---

[16] Negley and Patrick, *Quest for Utopia*, p. 4.

[17] A number of examples of the undifferentiated definition of utopia as ideal society may be given, although it should be recognised that some of the authors cited have in practice been more discriminating. V. Dupont, *L'Utopie et le Roman Utopique*, p. 13: 'Utopia: (1) tableau de société idéale; (2) pays fictif ou regne cette perfection idéale.' Fred L. Polak, *The Image of the Future*, 2 vols. (Leyden, 1961), vol. I, pp. 171, 383–420, 437, where utopia is defined as perfection on earth. Rosabeth Moss Kanter, *Commitment and Community: Communes and Utopias in Sociological Perspective* (Cambridge, Mass., 1972), p. 3. 'Utopia is the imaginary society in which humankind's deepest yearnings, noblest dreams, and highest aspirations come to fulfillment, where all physical, social and spiritual forces work together, in harmony, to permit the attainment of everything people find necessary and desirable.' Peyton E. Richter (ed.), *Utopias: Social Ideals and Communal Experiments* (Boston, 1971), Introduction; Thomas Molnar, *Utopia: The Perennial Heresy* (New York, 1967).

that utopia enables men to live naturally, or that it is designed to subdue and discipline human nature; that in utopia the state withers away, or that it becomes more complex and comprehensive, even that state and society become coincident; that utopia begins with ideal men, perfect human beings, or that it assumes that unrighteous and recalcitrant people will be its raw material. This last has perhaps been the most serious stumbling block of recent years where commentators have identified utopia with a denial of original sin,[18] while amongst utopians themselves we find a frequent insistence that, as James Harrington wrote, 'It is the duty of a legislator to presume all men wicked.'[19] The second difficulty arising from or associated with the use of 'utopia' in the undifferentiated sense of ideal society is that it encourages a subjectivism of approach, some aspects of which we have already noted. The commentator, drawing on a variety of ideal societies, endorses what is 'good' in 'utopia' as what corresponds to his or her own preferred values. Casting his net wide he almost always finds what he is looking for and utopia becomes all things to all men. 'It is an image of the future systematically constructed and synchronised with the continuous course of history, depicting a totally different, ideal society, just and worthy of humanity.'[20] It is the last qualification to which objection may be made, for, of course, what is just and worthy is open to debate. In the same way, the insistence that utopia always represents an exercise in the reconciliation of individual self-expression and social cohesion reveals nothing more than a particular liberal-conservative bias in the commentator concerned.[21]

Two different approaches to the problem can overcome these difficulties. First, it can be helpful to distinguish utopia as a programme from

---

[18] See, for example, Roger L. Emerson, 'Utopia', in Philip P. Weiner (ed.), *Dictionary of the History of Ideas* (New York, 1973), vol. IV, pp. 458–65; David Lodge, 'Utopia and Criticism, The Radical Longing for Paradise', *Encounter*, 32:4 (1969), p. 72 (quoting G. K. Chesterton); Constantinos A. Doxiadis, *Between Dystopia and Utopia* (London, 1968), p. 53; J. L. Talmon, 'Utopianism and Politics', in George Kateb (ed.), *Utopia* (New York, 1971), pp. 93–4; W. W. Wagar, *The City of Man, Prophecies of a World Civilisation in Twentieth Century Thought* (Boston, 1963), p. 15. A. Rupert Hall's categorisation of pre-twentieth-century utopianism as concerned with moral rather than technical problems may be seen in a similar light. A. Rupert Hall, 'Science, Technology and Utopia in the Seventeenth Century', in P. Mathias (ed.), *Science and Society 1600–1900* (Cambridge, 1972), pp. 33–53.

[19] James Harrington, 'The Commonwealth of Oceana', in *The Oceana and Other Works, with an account of his life by John Toland* (London, 1771), p. 152. See also Davis, 'Utopia and History', p. 171.

[20] Polak, *Image of the Future*, vol. I, p. 437. Cf. the subjectivism of Rosabeth Kanter's 'deepest yearnings, noblest dreams and highest aspirations'. Kanter, *Commitment and Community*, pp. 1, 3.

[21] Talmon, 'Utopianism and Politics', pp. 92, 96.

other types of ideal society.[22] Utopia is but one type of a form, the ideal society. Secondly, it is necessary to recognise the other aspects of the utopian vision which are bound up with the perfection but escape its subjectivism. These are the totality of the change envisaged, its closed-society nature, and the order or stability of the new establishment.

All visualisers of ideal societies are concerned to maximise harmony and contentment and to minimise conflict and misery; to produce a perfected society where social cohesion and the common good are not imperilled by individual appetite. By looking at the way in which they deal with a basic source of conflict and misery, it is possible to distinguish between utopias and other forms of ideal society. All ideal societies must solve the problem of relating the existing and changing supply of satisfactions, some of which are by nature limited in supply to the wants of a heterogenial group, the desires of which will be, in some respects, unlimited. To adapt Herbert Marcuse's terms, satisfactions may be limited by both material and sociological scarcities.[23] The material scarcity of satisfactions consists, for example, in there being only a given number of fertile pieces of land, only one best horse, only a given number of beautiful women or men, and only one specific example of each. Sociological scarcity arises out of the hierarchical distribution of these satisfactions (some men have more than others) and the existence of specific socially derived satisfactions (there are only so many places on the committee, only a limited number of holders of a certain title of honour, only one king or only one seat of power). Given a certain supply of satisfactions, with given levels of both material scarcity and sociological scarcity, and a given size of community, problems can be seen to arise in a number of ways. In the first place wants can quantitatively outstrip the supply of satisfactions: people want more. Secondly, there can be a presumed qualitative deficiency: people want better, or different satisfactions. Thirdly, people can be dissatisfied with the social distribution of material scarcity: resenting others who have more or better, striving to get more or better, or simply coveting specifics possessed by others. Fourthly, people can be dissatisfied with the distribution of socially derived satisfactions, wanting greater power, prestige and so on, or resenting the greater power and prestige of others.

This 'collective problem', a paucity of satisfactions weakly co-ordinated with the desires and aspirations of a community of individuals, is one fundamental cause of conflict and social tension. Hence an ideal society must be based on some attitude, implicit or explicit, to the 'collective problem'. We can distinguish utopia and four alternative types of ideal society by the way in which they deal with this issue. These types of ideal

---

[22] Davis, 'Utopia and History', pp. 169–74. The distinctions made here are heuristic devices and not intended as descriptions of mutually exclusive realities.

[23] Cf. Hansot, *Perfection and Progress*, p. 125.

society are not in practice mutually exclusive, although their premises make them logically inconsistent one with another. The four alternatives to utopia will be called, for convenience, the Land of Cockaygne, arcadia, the perfect moral commonwealth and the millennium. The first two, Cockaygne and arcadia, solve the collective problem by envisaging a drastic change in the supply of satisfactions. They differ markedly, however, in their attitude to human appetites.

COCKAYGNE

The Land of Cockaygne tradition was strongest in late medieval Europe but its themes have been expressed from ancient times and in many cultures.[24] It has remained active as a target for satire from the seventeenth to the twentieth centuries,[25] and formed a feature of such activities as the Feast of Fools and the Lords of Misrule, the Saturnalia still popular in the early modern period.[26]

---

[24] See A. L. Morton, *The English Utopia* (London, 1952), Chapter 1; also Morton's version of the Cockaygne poem in modern English which has been used here, *ibid.*, pp. 217–22; Robert C. Elliott, *The Shape of Utopia: Studies in a Literary Genre* (Chicago, 1970), Chapter 1; Arthur O. Lovejoy and George Boas, *Primitivism and Related Ideas in Antiquity* (Baltimore, 1935; reprinted New York, 1965), pp. 40–1 for Teleclides' (*fl. c.* 440 B.C.) version: 'First there was peace among all things like water covering one's hands. And the earth bore neither fear nor disease, but all needed things appeared of their own accord. For every stream flowed with wine, and barley cakes fought with wheat cakes to enter the mouths of men, pleading to be gulped down if they loved the whitest. And fishes, coming to men's houses and baking themselves, would serve themselves upon the tables . . . and roasted thrushes with milk cakes flew down one's gullet.' Cf. a very similar version by Pherecrates, *ibid.*, pp. 38–9. For later examples see George Boas, *Essays on Primitivism and Related Ideas in the Middle Ages* (Baltimore, 1948), pp. 154–74. For similar elements within the Buddhist tradition see Jean Chesneaux, 'Egalitarian and Utopian Traditions in the East', *Diogenes*, 62 (1968), pp. 90–2, 100. Here 'All the material needs of men will be covered by "wishing trees" from the branches of which hang clothes and jewels for the inhabitants of the island. The tree stretches forth its branches when the people wishes something and nobody need work.'

[25] See, for example, Joseph Hall, *Mundus Alter et Idem*, translated by John Healey, edited by Huntington Brown (Cambridge, Mass., 1937), especially pp. 177ff.; George Orwell, *Animal Farm* (London, 1951), p. 13.

[26] Charles Pythian-Adams, 'Ceremony and the Citizen: The Communal Year at Coventry 1450–1550', in Peter Clark and Paul Slack (eds.), *Crisis and Order in English Towns 1500–1750* (London, 1972), pp. 57–85; Natalie Zemon Davis, *Society and Culture in Early Modern France* (Stanford, Calif., 1975); Peter Burke, *Popular Culture in Early Modern Europe* (London, 1978), Chapters 7 and 8.

In Cockaygne there were satisfactions enough to satiate the grossest
appetite.

> Ah! those chambers and those walls!
> All of pasties stand the walls,
> Of fish and flesh and all rich meat,
> The tastiest that men can eat.
> Wheaten cakes the shingles all,
> Of church, of cloister, bower and hall.
> The pinnacles are fat puddings,
> Good food for princes or for kings.
> Every man takes what he will,
> As of right, to eat his fill.
> All is common to young and old,
> To stout and strong, to meek and bold.
>
> Yet this wonder add to it –
> That geese fly roasted on the spit,
> As God's my witness, to that spot,
> Crying out, 'Geese, all hot, all hot!'
> Every goose in garlic drest,
> Of all food the seemliest.
> And the larks that are so couth
> Fly right down into man's mouth,
> Smothered in stew, and thereupon
> Piles of powdered cinnamon.
> Every man may drink his fill
> And needn't sweat to pay the bill.

Needless to say, in Cockaygne women are always sexually promiscuous
and men may forever remain at the age of thirty by drinking at fountains
of youth. Compared with its abundance of every sensual satisfaction,
Paradise itself seems to the poet a poor prospect.[27] Conflict is eliminated,
not by changing the character of man nor by elaborate social rearrangement, but by the fullest private satisfaction of men's appetites. The only
direct social comment on the theme is a gratuitous reversal of the social
order. While peasants were to arrive freely at the Land of Cockaygne,
their lords and ladies were to struggle chin-deep in the filth of the farm-
yard, before they could reach its pleasures.

[27] Morton, *English Utopia*, p. 217:

> Though Paradise is merry and bright
> Cockaygne is a fairer sight.
> For what is there in Paradise
> But grass and flowers and greeneries.

Whoso will come that land unto
Full great penance he must do,
He must wade for seven years
In the dirt a swine-pen bears,
Seven years right to the chin,
Ere he may hope that land to win.
Listen lords both good and kind,
Never will you that country find,
Till through the ordeal you've gone
And that penance has been done.

It was a penance that the peasant had already performed.

ARCADIA

The arcadian tradition, also apparently universal in its appeal, represents a more complex approach to the collective problem.[28] While it is assumed that satisfactions, at least material ones, are more abundant, they are not grossly so, as in Cockaygne. Nature is generously benevolent rather than hostile to man, but at the same time men's desires, in particular sociological ones, are assumed to be moderate. There is thus a harmony between man and nature in Arcadia which parallels a social harmony between men of moderation. Arcadians tend to assume that, if the problems of material scarcity are resolved in a world of men of moderation, problems of sociological scarcity will also cease to exist.

This was a common theme in Hebraic prophetic writings and in Greek thought.[29] To take an example from Hesiod's *Works and Days*:

First of all the deathless gods having homes on Olympus made a golden race of mortal men. These lived in the time of Cronus when he was king in heaven. Like gods they lived with hearts free from sorrow and remote from toil and grief; nor was miserable age their lot, but always unwearied in feet and hands they made merry in feasting, beyond the reach of all evils. And when they died, it was as though they were given over to sleep. And all good things were theirs. For the fruitful earth spontaneously bore them abundant fruit without stint. And they lived in ease and peace upon their lands with many good things, rich in flocks and beloved of the blessed gods.[30]

[28] For an examination of the relationship between the utopian and the arcadian traditions see Northrop Frye, 'Varieties of Literary Utopia', in Manuel (ed.), *Utopias and Utopian Thought*, pp. 41–9.

[29] For examples, see Lovejoy and Boas, *Primitivism in Antiquity*, pp. 25–7, 46–7, 86–8, 292–393; Boas, *Primitivism in the Middle Ages*, pp. 72–5, 157–9, 164, 166–7; Eurich, *Science in Utopia*, Chapter 1; Polak, *Image of the Future*, vol. 1, pp. 96–117; Elliott, *Shape of Utopia*, Chapter 1; Chesneaux, 'Utopian Traditions in the East', p. 83.

[30] Lovejoy and Boas, *Primitivism in Antiquity*, pp. 25–7; cf. Elliott, *Shape of Utopia*, p. 4.

As Lovejoy and Boas wrote of this feature of classical thought, the golden age 'was enjoyed by a different breed of mortals in a different condition of the world'. Each sense may be satisfied in natural abundance but 'the flesh restrained itself within the law'.[31] In Arcadia, unlike Cockaygne, men work, but the burden is light and easy; they age and die, but it is a peaceful, almost pleasant process; they live in comfort and ease, not in excess. Indeed, one of the primary characteristics of Arcadia is ease, a state of contented rest. In Gabriel de Foigny's *On Life and Death Among the Australians* (London, 1693) this reaches an extreme in the Australians' imagined preference for death over life because it represents to them an idealised state of rest.[32]

Perhaps the best known early modern version of the arcadian vision is that of another Frenchman, Michel de Montaigne. His essay, 'Of Cannibals', consciously contrasted a society of happy savages with the ancient utopian tradition.

I am sorry that Lycurgus and Plato did not have this knowledge; for it seems to me that what we actually see in these nations surpasses not only all the pictures in which poets have embellished the golden age, but all their ingenuity in imagining a happy state of man, but also the conceptions and very desire of philosophy...This is a nation, I should say to Plato, in which there is no sort of traffic, no knowledge of letters, no science of numbers, no name for a magistrate or for political superiority, no custom of servitude, no riches or poverty, no contracts, no successions, no partitions, no occupations but leisure ones, no care for any but common kinship, no clothes, no agriculture, no metal, no use of wine or corn.

On the one hand, Montaigne's cannibals enjoy a temperate, healthy climate, a natural abundance of food and drink, and a relaxed, leisurely style of life. On the other hand, their desires are moderate or 'natural'. 'They are still in that happy state of desiring only as much as their natural needs demand; anything beyond that is superfluous to them'; 'they have no lack of anything necessary, nor yet lack of that great thing, the knowledge of how to enjoy their condition happily and be content with it'.[33]

This theme of moderate men set in a world of natural bounty was one that was exploited in the seventeenth century by both colonial entrepreneurs and millenarian speculators. The New World was frequently offered as a natural paradise only requiring to be adorned by men of

---

[31] The last quotation is from the *Hexaemeron* of Ernaldus of Bonneval, cited in Boas, *Primitivism in the Middle Ages*, p. 74, and in general pp. 72–5.

[32] This tract is partially reprinted in Frank E. and Fritzie P. Manuel (eds.), *French Utopias: An Anthology of Ideal Societies* (New York, 1966).

[33] Michel de Montaigne, *Selected Essays*, translated by Donald M. Frame (New York, 1943), pp. 78, 79, 86.

simplicity and good will.[34] Equally those who visualised a pre-lapsarian state restored as preliminary to, or immediately following, Christ's second coming were able to visualise it in arcadian terms.[35] An English example of the arcadian cultural primitivism implicit in Montaigne is a little-known, anonymous tract entitled *A Paradox: Proving the Inhabitants of the Island, called Madagascar or St. Lawrence (in Things temporal) to be the happiest People in the World*.[36] The author pictured the islanders as enjoying a carefree, primitive, natural and happy life which he vigorously contrasted with the anxieties, strains, crises, artificiality and decadence of contemporary European society. He ended by praising 'the mercies of God towards this People, whose simplicity hath herein made them more happy than our too dear bought knowledge hath advantaged us'.[37]

As Northrop Frye has pointed out, arcadia has two characteristics which distinguish it from utopia. First, arcadia emphasises the integration of man and nature. Utopia, on the other hand, seeks to illustrate man's capacity to dominate nature. Secondly, the arcadian simplifies human desires and at the same time throws great stress on their satisfaction.[38] Utopia, by contrast, seeks to act out a pattern of restraint. In addition, it might be said that the arcadian tradition is much more radical than the utopian. It not only rejects, as here, the institutions of an acquisitive society, but it rejects all institutions whatsoever and so highlights the institutional preoccupations of the utopian.

A final example, chosen because it illustrates well the tensions between arcadia and utopia, may be taken from the work of James Harrington's friend and collaborator, Henry Neville. In June and July of 1668 Neville anonymously issued in four parts a work claiming to consist principally of the report of a Dutch sea captain on his discoveries on an island near to Madagascar. *The Isle of Pines*, as it was entitled, proved to be one of the

---

[34] For examples, see Vernon Louis Parrington, *American Dreams: A Study of American Utopias* (Providence, R.I., 1947), pp. 5–6.

[35] For only two examples amongst the many possible see the Rosicrucian documents, *Fama Fraternitas* (1614) and *Confessio Fraternitas* (1615), appended in translation to Frances A. Yates, *The Rosicrucian Enlightenment* (London, 1972). See also my discussion of millenarianism below.

[36] Reprinted in *The Harleian Miscellany* (1744), vol. 1, pp. 256–62. Although undated the tract may have been published in the 1630s or 1640s. At that time the names 'St Lawrence' and 'Madagascar' were being used interchangeably. There was considerable English interest in the island in the later 1630s and the myth of Madagascar as a natural paradise was current then and in the early 1640s. Eliot Warburton, *Memoirs of Prince Rupert and the Cavaliers*, 3 vols. (London, 1849), vol. 1, pp. 59–61; Richard Hakluyt, *The Principal Navigations, Voyages, Traffiques and Discoveries of the English Nation*, 10 vols. (London, 1967), vol. IV, pp. 238, 245, 254.

[37] *A Paradox*, p. 262.

[38] Frye, 'Varieties of Literary Utopia', p. 41.

most remarkable publishing sensations of the seventeenth century and, according to Owen Aldridge, was 'one of the most successful literary hoaxes in the English language'.[39] Within six months of its English publication, three Dutch, two French, an Italian, an American and four German editions had appeared. It was republished in many European editions for a full century. Following hard on its first appearance came a succession of attempts to impugn its veracity, in themselves bearing witness to its success as a hoax.[40]

Neville's story took the form of a report by Henry Cornelius van Sloetten of a voyage which had taken him to an island two or three hundred leagues northwest of Cape Finisterre. Here he found a community of about two thousand naked people of English tongue and descent. Their leader, William Pine, gave an account of the community's evolution since his grandfather, George Pine, and four women had been shipwrecked on the island. George Pine had left an account of his experiences in which he recalled the arcadian impression which the island had first made upon him: 'the country so very pleasant, being always clothed in green, and full of pleasant fruits, and variety of birds, ever warm and never colder than England in September; so that this place, had it the culture that skilful people might bestow on it, would prove a paradise'. Very soon he was indulging in a set pattern of polygamous sexual activity with the women.

Our family beginning to grow large, and there being nothing to hurt us, we many times lay abroad on mossy banks, under the shelter of some trees, or such like, for having nothing else to do, I had made me several arbors to sleep in with my women in the heat of the day, in these I and my women passed the time away, they never being willing to be out of my company.

Within fifty-nine years, George Pine's progeny numbered 1789.[41] However, the arcadian existence which George Pine had enjoyed was undermined for his descendants by the pressure of numbers which he himself had helped to create: 'in multitudes disorders will grow, the stronger seeking to oppress the weaker'. Men competed for what was now in short

[39] A. Owen Aldridge, 'Polygamy in Early Fiction: Henry Neville and Denis Veiras', in *P.M.L.A.*, 65 (1950), p. 465. For evidence of Neville's authorship see Anna Maria Crino, 'Lettere inedite italiane e inglesi di Sir Henry Neville', in *Fatti e Figure del Seicento Anglo-Toscana*, Biblioteca dell'Archivum Romanicum, 48 (Florence, 1957), pp. 203–4. There is an edition of the *Isle of Pines* in the Everyman series but unfortunately this consists of only a part of the work. See Philip Henderson (ed.), *Shorter Novels: Jacobean and Restoration* (London, 1930). The only complete modern edition is *The Isle of Pines 1668: An Essay in Bibliography*, edited by W. C. Ford (Boston, 1920).

[40] Ford (ed.), *Isle of Pines*, pp. 13–19, 42.

[41] Aldridge, 'Polygamy in Early Fiction'; Ford (ed.), *Isle of Pines*, pp. 66–8, 70.

supply and in so doing abandoned moderation: 'whoredoms, incests and adulteries' soon led to civil war and out of this arose the need for a harsh code of laws and a government strong enough to implement them.[42] When nature's bounty is insufficient or when men abandon moderation, arcadia is unattainable and those in search of social perfection must seek other means.

The arcadian tradition thus solves the collective problem by postulating both an abundance of satisfactions and a moderation or simplification of desires to a 'natural' level.[43] So it forms a half-way house between the Land of Cockaygne, with its emphasis on gross abundance, and the perfect moral commonwealth, with its insistence upon men's reconciliation with the status quo, upon moral conformism; but it forms a blend quite unlike either of the two alone.

PERFECT MORAL COMMONWEALTH

Two categories of ideal-society thought which early modern Europeans probably regarded as more serious or realistic than the escapism of arcadia or the grosser indulgence of Cockaygne were the idealisations of the perfect moral commonwealth and the millennium. Both were rooted in contemporary views of history and its capacity for moral meaning. The millenarian expectation was sustained by the sense of history as a meaningless flow of contingencies in which significance could only be attached to particulars by reference to universal and eternal values which, in Christian Europe, meant in relation to providential history.[44] This scheme empha-

---

[42] Ford (ed.), *Isle of Pines*, pp. 71–4.

[43] In this sense William Morris' *News from Nowhere* is an arcadia rather than a utopia. Man's innate sociability, good sense and will to work is released through a process of revolution involving the abandonment of cities and commercial life. The stripping away of capitalism's artifice reveals a natural man on whom can be built a naturally harmonic society. 'The art or work-pleasure, as one ought to call it, of which I am now speaking, sprung up almost spontaneously, it seems, from a *kind of instinct* amongst people, no longer driven desperately to painful and terrible overwork, to do the best they could with the work in hand – to make it excellent of its kind; and when they had gone on for a little, a craving for beauty seemed to awaken in men's minds . . .' *News from Nowhere*, edited by G. D. H. Cole (London, 1948), p. 125. My italics.

[44] John Pocock sometimes seems, by implication at least, to suggest that a paradigm which saw history as a meaningless flow was the only one available in medieval Christendom, to the extent that the erection of the classical republic as a means of overcoming contingency had to be seen as either paganism or an act of apocalyptic drama. *The Machiavellian Moment* (Princeton, 1975), Chapter 1 and pp. 31–3, 43, 47, 80, 84–5. The Christian time-scheme 'denied the possibility of any secular fulfillment' (*ibid.*, p. vii). However, there exists a whole literature which gave meaning to the history of individuals in the achievement of sainthood, or to the history of communities in the achievements of saintly princes or

sised the focal points of creation, fall, incarnation, resurrection and second coming of the Son of God. In the second view of history, moral meaning could be given to human life on earth in terms of order, stability, justice and happiness by the moral effort of individuals in emulation of the exemplars provided by Jesus, the Son of Man, or by the saints, or, in a broader context, by social improvement in the reigns of monarchs of great Christian virtue. This view nurtured that form of ideal-society thinking for which I have used the name 'perfect moral commonwealth'.

The perfect moral commonwealth tradition accepted existing social arrangements and political institutions. Society is to be made harmonic by the moral reformation of every individual in society, and hence of every class and group. Most writers within this tradition tended to concentrate on the 'moral rearmament' of kings, nobles, magistrates, priests, and gentlemen largely because these literate groups formed their audience.[45] Nevertheless, some extended their survey to the whole range of society. A. B. Ferguson has seen this sort of approach as a characteristic of the pre-Tudor period:

government remained for most of the commentators of this period personal rather than institutional – personal, that is, in the sense that it depended on the moral nature of men running it, not in the sense, more typical of renaissance thought, that it depended on the dynamic personality of the artist in politics. They found it consequently hard to discern the mechanism of social forces, of impersonal causes to the modern eye more susceptible of manipulation by legislation or by administrative policy.

The medieval view of public life 'remained limited by the fixed horizons of a prescribed moral order and a providential history'.[46] It was by means of a renewal of the observance of this prescribed moral order that the writers of the perfect moral commonwealth tradition sought their ideal society, and their efforts to achieve this in that way continued into the early modern period.

Although Ferguson may be right about a growing preoccupation with institutions from the Tudor period, the perfect moral commonwealth and

monastic houses. The issue is perhaps primarily that of the distinction between providence acting mediately or immediately in the affairs of men and human societies.

[45] See, for example, L. K. Born, 'The Perfect Prince: A Study in 13th and 14th Century Ideals', *Speculum*, 3:4 (1928), pp. 470–504; Erasmus, *The Education of a Christian Prince*, edited by L. K. Born (New York, 1965); Felix Gilbert, 'The Humanist Concept of the Prince and *The Prince* of Machiavelli', *Journal of Modern History*, 9:4 (1939), pp. 449–83.

[46] A. B. Ferguson, *The Articulate Citizen and the English Renaissance* (Durham, N.C., 1965), pp. 33, 91. Cf. Donald W. Hanson, *From Kingdom to Commonwealth: The Development of Civic Consciousness in English Political Thought* (Cambridge, Mass., 1970).

the perfect prince remained powerful images throughout it and beyond. Both Erasmus and Luther gave renewed vigour to it at the beginning of the sixteenth century.[47] The assumptions behind Sir Thomas Elyot's *The Book Named the Governor* (1531), as behind many similar works, were those of the perfect moral commonwealth tradition, though here the examination of a moral education is restricted to that fitted for the governing class.

For as much as all noble authors do conclude and also common experience proveth that where the governors of realms and cities be found adorned with virtues and do employ their study and mind to the public weal, as well to the augmentation thereof as to the establishing and long continuance of the same, there a publique weal must needs be both honourable and wealthy.[48]

Seventy years later Thomas Floyd published *The Picture of a Perfit Commonwealth*, which was heavily indebted to Elyot, and reiterated the theme that the realisation of a perfect commonwealth was dependent on the morality of princes and magistrates.[49] Still later, Sir John Eliot's *The Monarchie of Man* cast the theme on the wider basis of society as a whole. Eliot, despite his reputation as a 'parliamentarian', found the English form of monarchy the best but its perfect realisation depended on the performance of their duty by all men. 'The King is to command; the subject to obey; both with like readines in their places, and like affection to each other.'[50]

In *A Comparative Discourse of the Bodies Natural and Politique* (1606), Edward Forset had argued in a very similar fashion while shifting the emphasis from rulers to the ruled. Kings had great power but they ought to exercise it virtuously and for the good of all. The virtuous exercise of power would involve kings in calling parliaments but the powers of those bodies would be severely limited: 'both the ruler should wholly indevour of his people, and the subject ought (as in love to his owne soule) to conforme unto his soveraigne'. The obligation of subjects was more completely set out, however. Forset held that, as regards subjects, there were four elements of the body politic as of the body natural.

---

[47] Erasmus, *Education of a Christian Prince*; Luther, 'Secular Authority, To What Extent it should be Obeyed', in John Dillenberger (ed.), *Martin Luther, Selections from his Writings* (New York, 1961).

[48] Sir Thomas Elyot, *The Book Named the Governor*, edited by S. E. Lehmberg (London, 1962), p. 15.

[49] 'The Picture of a Perfit Commonwealth 1600', edited by D. T. Starnes, *University of Texas Studies in English*, 4 (September 1931), pp. 32–41. Listed as a utopia in Negley, *Utopian Literature*, p. 45 (no. 357).

[50] Sir John Eliot, *The Monarchie of Man*, edited by A. B. Grosart (London, 1879), p. 13. *The Monarchie of Man* was probably written in the 1620s but was not published until 1879. A manuscript copy exists in the British Museum, Harleian mss. 2,228.

First, the generous, to advance and mainteine the state with their well deserving actions: Then the learned, to instruct and direct with skill in cases of consultation: Thirdly, yeomen with their labour to produce and worke the commodities of the land: and lastly Trafiquers which may both vent out by exportation what may be spared, and bring in the necessaries that shall be wanting.

In order for the name 'commonwealth' to be applied, 'the whole wealth, wit, power and goodnesse whatsoever, of every particular person must be conferred and reduced to the common good'.[51]

In the Elizabethan period the popular writer, Thomas Lupton, published two dialogues on the imaginary land of Mauqsun (Nusquam) which he used as a standard of criticism for contemporary England and in which he deployed images of a perfect moral commonwealth.[52] Life in his imaginary kingdom is marked by

the marvellous maners, the honest behaviour, the faithful friendship, the curteous conditions, the commendable customes, the plain meaning and true dealing, the Lords liberalitie, the Ladies great curtesie, the husbands fidelitie, the wives obedience, the maydens modestie, the maisters sobrietie, the servants diligence, the Magistrates affabilitie, the Judges equity, the commons amitie, the preferring of publique commoditie, the generall Hospitalitie, the exceeding mercie, the wonderful Charitie, and the constant Christianity of that Countrey . . .[53]

There, landlords would never think of racking their rents, nor tenants attempt to enhance the prices of their produce.[54] It was a land of 'godly lawes, politike orders, righteous Rulers, merciful Magistrates, just Judges, loving Lawyers, pitifull Phisitians, zealous Husbandes, obedient wives, dutifull Children, trustie Servants, good Landlords, honest Tenanntes, curteous Gentlemen, vertuous Gentlewomen, charitable Neighboures and faithful Subiects'.[55] The recurrent catalogues of appropriate virtues for each circumstance rapidly become tedious but they illustrate well the conservative element within the perfect moral commonwealth tradition. The structure of society is unchanged; each man becomes good, functions perfectly, in his station.

As a mode of criticism, the model could be inverted and contemporary society condemned by describing it in terms of the vices peculiar to each social group or category as, for example, in William Perkins, *A Treatise*

[51] Edward Forset, *A Comparative Discourse of the Bodies Natural and Politique* (London, 1606), pp. 16–18, 3, 38, 48.
[52] Thomas Lupton, *Sivqila, Too Good to be True* (1580); Lupton, *The Second Part and Knitting Up of the Boke Entituled, Too Good to be True* (1581). Listed as a utopia in Negley, *Utopian Literature*, p. 87 (no. 713).
[53] Lupton, *Sivqila*, 'Dedicatory Epistle', see also 'Preface'.
[54] Lupton, *The Second Part*, pp. 26–7.   [55] *Ibid.*, p. 203.

of Vocations (1612). On the other hand, it was difficult to criticise the model itself without appearing to impugn either society's capacity for moral renewal or the efficacy of Christian moral standards. John Carpenter's late-sixteenth-century assault on the pride of perfect moral commonwealth theorists (and other ideal-society thinkers) for thinking that man might overcome his imperfections was unusual in both its breadth and its savagery.[56]

The tradition flourished into the seventeenth century and beyond, appealing to writers of very different persuasions.[57] Bishop Joseph Hall, who satirised the Land of Cockaygne, found his ideal in the perfect moral commonwealth. In *Solomons Politicks of Commonwealth* (1627) he set out in a great paradigm the justification for a hierarchical society and its various degrees. He then proceeded to prescribe the moral duties of men in every rank, so that the commonwealth would be perfected, if each man in his station were to do his duty.[58] Yet this innately conservative theme appealed to 'puritan' preachers as well as to anglican bishops. Richard Bernard's immensely popular allegory, *The Isle of Man*, described an England perfected because it is populated by perfect Englishmen. 'They runne all one course, and as true Israelites, *quod vir unis*, for publike good. Therefore doe the people live in peace, the Land prospereth, Justice flourisheth, vertue is exalted, vice suppressed, and the enemies at home and abroad made to feare.'[59]

---

[56] John Carpenter, *A Preparative to Contention* (1597): 'As if (forsooth) it were not onely lawfull for men to make, alter, and change lawes and reforme al things at their own pleasures: but also, that it were possible themselves could reforme all, and constrain every action of man to answer to right perfection in this world, wherein the very best things that be, do savor of imperfections...'

[57] For a continental example, which is sometimes described as a utopia, see Kaspar Stüblin, *De Eudaemonensium republica* (1553). The capital of the island of Macaria is pictured as a city of elevated civic morality where the public interest is preferred to private interest and where harmony is based not on equality but on rigorous ethics. See Luigi Firpo, 'Kaspar Stiblin, Utopiste', in Jean Lameere (ed.), *Les Utopies à la Renaissance*, Travaux de l'Institut pour l'Etude de la Renaissance et de l'Humanisme (Paris and Brussels, 1963), pp. 107–33. For a similarly confused ascription see another work sometimes described as a utopia, Antoine Le Grand, *Scydromedia seu sermo quem Alphonsus de la Vida habuit coram comite de Falmouth* (London (?), 1669). The ills of England attributed here to the moral and political failings of her citizens are corrected by their conversion to virtue and political wisdom. See also, J. Max Patrick, '*Scydromedia*, a Forgotten Utopia of the 17th Century', *Philological Quarterly*, 23:3 (1944), pp. 273–82, especially pp. 281–2. For a discussion of the theme in seventeenth-century New England see T. H. Breen, *The Character of the Good Ruler: Puritan Political Ideas in New England 1630–1730* (New Haven, 1970).

[58] Joseph Hall, 'Solomons Politicks of Commonwealth and First his King', in *The Works of Joseph Hall* (1628), pp. 229–39.

[59] Richard Bernard, *The Isle of Man, or the Legall Proceedings in Man-Shire against SINNE* (1635). This is the tenth edition. The work appears to have been

Thus in the perfect moral commonwealth the collective problem was solved, not by increasing the range or quantity of satisfactions available, but by a personal limitation of appetite to what existed for every group and individual. The emphasis was upon duty, loyalty, charity and virtue practised by each individual as a precondition of society's regeneration. Only the new man can produce the new society; or rather, the old society made good. Of course, there were problems with the perfect moral commonwealth but few of its advocates recognised them. One was that, in a world of perfect morality, magistrates might appear to be redundant. The political order then might be dissolved by this essentially conservative intention. As Luther had once pointed out, 'If all the world were composed of real Christians...no prince, King, lord or sword would be needed...'[60] Secondly, it was possible to see competition in Christian charity leading to strife over doing good. Thomas Lupton was aware of this potential for irony. In Mauqsun, servants could quarrel over who should help a decayed master, or gentlewomen over which amongst them should care for a foundling, or citizens over who should assist a debtor.[61]

MILLENNIUM

The fourth alternative to the utopian solution of the collective problem is that offered by the millenarians, although, by and large, the millenarians concentrate on the process of solution, the second coming, and pay little detailed attention to what will emerge from the cataclysm. For many of them it is a perfect form of time that is at issue rather than a perfect form

first published in 1626 and went through eleven editions by 1640, and seventeen editions altogether in the seventeenth century. The problems of the perfect moral commonwealth could become acute for mid-seventeenth-century thinkers faced with the shattered institutional structure of England. Republicans saw that in a society of free and equal citizens much would depend on the capacity of individuals to act morally and conscientiously in pursuit of the public good. For widely differing results see, [Marchamont Nedham], *The Excellencie of a Free-State: Or, The Right Constitution of a Commonwealth* (1656); Robert Norwood, *A Pathway Unto England's Perfect Settlement* (1653) and *An Additional Discourse Relating unto a Treatise lately published by Capt. Robert Norwood* (1653). Even for Thomas Hobbes, the power and authority of sovereign institutions was in the last resort dependent on the capacity of citizens to respond morally to the covenants and conditions which they had imposed upon themselves.

60 Luther, 'Secular Authority', pp. 368–9. Cf. The description of the Isle of Bragman in Sir John Mandeville, *The Blessed Isles of Prester John* (1356). Here is a perfect moral commonwealth in which morality is seen as dissolving social structure. 'Judges need us none to have among us, for none of us does til other but as he would have were done til him,' in Manuel and Manuel (eds.), *French Utopias*, p. 20.

61 Lupton, *The Second Part*, pp. 185–201.

of society. We must be careful, however, not to oversimplify. As recent scholarship has been at pains to point out, early modern millenarianism was a complex phenomenon.[62] Despite these difficulties, Norman Cohn has managed to produce a working definition of millenarianism which would appear to be acceptable. He sees the term as embracing any religious movement with a phantasy of salvation which is to be collective (enjoyed by the faithful as a group), terrestrial, imminent, total (utterly transforming life on earth, not merely to improve but to perfect) and accomplished by agencies which are consciously regarded as supernatural.[63]

Since the time of St Augustine, the Catholic orthodoxy had been turned against this forward-looking millennialism, in favour of an amillennial approach which saw the thousand years of scriptural prophecy as referring to a period of years from the life of Christ onwards, or a specific 'thousand' years (in the sense of a perfect period of time) of the span of time since Christ. In that way the millennium could be viewed as past or passing and its radical energies defused. The belief in a *future* millennium was throughout the medieval period confined to a populist tradition centred around such fabrications as the *Sibylline Oracles* and the activities of figures like Joachim of Fiore and their followers. The early protestant reformers tended to follow St Augustine in his rejection of an earthly millennium and his insistence on an amillennial interpretation of the scriptures, but there was sufficient ambivalence in their notions of divine history and the rôle of Anti-Christ to allow scope for reinterpretation by their followers. At the end of the sixteenth century and the beginning of the seventeenth, such a revision was taking place as to make belief in a future millennium not only possible but a kind of orthodoxy for men of differing shades of opinion, and especially in England.

Thomas Brightman in *A Revelation of the Revelation* (1615) offered a reinterpretation of history in the light of scriptural prophecy which envisaged a future millennium when the converted Jews would return to

---

[62] See, for example, E. L. Tuveson, *Millennium and Utopia: A Study in the Background of the Idea of Progress* (Gloucester, Mass., 1964; reprint 1972); Peter Toon (ed.), *Puritans, The Millennium and the Future of Israel: Puritan Eschatology 1600–1660* (Cambridge, 1970); B. S. Capp, *The Fifth Monarchy Men: A Study in Seventeenth-Century English Millenarianism* (London, 1972); William Lamont, *Godly Rule: Politics and Religion 1603–1660* (London, 1969). A recent and valuable corrective to some interpretations of the development of apocalyptic thought in Britain is provided by Katherine R. Firth, *The Apocalyptic Tradition in Reformation Britain 1530–1645* (Oxford, 1979). See also Paul Christianson, *Reformers and Babylon: English Apocalyptic Visions from the Reformation to the Eve of the Civil War* (Toronto, 1978).

[63] Norman Cohn, 'Medieval Millenarism: Its Bearing on the Comparative Study of Millenarian Movements', in Sylvia L. Thrupp (ed.), *Millennial Dreams in Action* (The Hague, 1962), p. 31.

the Holy Land and God's saints would reign on earth. He was a post-millennialist, in the sense that he believed that Christ's second coming in judgement would take place after the setting up of an ideal state on earth.[64] While Brightman's work was very influential, it was possibly the work of a leading continental Calvinist divine which opened the floodgates of chiliastic interpretation. In 1622 Johann Heinrich Alsted published his *Theologia Prophetica* in which he abandoned his earlier adherence to Augustinian views in favour of a belief in a future millennium. Five years later in *Diatribe de Milleannis Apocalypticis* he adopted a full post-millennialist position, in which he saw the rule of resurrected martyrs and converted Jews preceding the last judgement and commencing in the year 1694.[65] Further impetus to the acceptance of millenarian expectancy was given in the same year, 1627, by the publication of Joseph Mede's *Clavis Apocalyptica*, a translation of which was authorised by the Long Parliament in 1642. Mede appears to have been a hesitant pre-millenarian, although in the revised edition of the *Clavis* of 1632 his hesitancy was weakening. The destruction of the Papacy, he believed, would be followed by the thousand year rule of Christ and his resurrected martyrs. Christ would be present in his kingdom, but in what sense was not made clear.

The influence of these and allied writings in England was immense. It is no exaggeration to say that they affected the thinking and aspirations of a whole generation – the generation coming to maturity in the 1640s. The belief in a latter-day glory, a coming period when men's dominion over nature would be restored to its pre-lapsarian completeness, in the Great Instauration (to use the term adopted by Charles Webster), was very widespread.[66] With the collapse of control over press and pulpit in the 1640s, these themes were taken up by men and women who did not share the scholarly reserve of writers like Brightman and Mede. Not only did some extremists emphasise a pre-millennial interpretation of an imminent apocalypse, but in addition they urged the abandonment of expectant waiting in favour of a radical activism to assist King Jesus in the realisation of his purposes. What had been scholarly argument in the hands of men of learning in the time of James I had become popular activity with revolutionary potential by the late 1640s. Amongst and through the Fifth Monarchists these radical notions continued to have influence down to the

---

[64] For the distinction between pre-millennial and post-millennial, see George Shepperson, 'The Comparative Study of Millenarian Movements', in Thrupp (ed.), *Millennial Dreams*, p. 44.

[65] An English translation by William Burton was published in 1643 under the title of *The Beloved City*.

[66] See Charles Webster, *The Great Instauration: Science, Medicine and Reform 1626–1660* (London, 1975), Chapter 1. The phrase is, of course, taken from Sir Francis Bacon.

1680s.[67] The seventeenth century thus saw a fundamental change in the nature and significance of a form of thought extremely widespread in England.

Clearly, views on what constituted the ideal society to be realised in the millennium differed, just as millennialism itself was a very diverse phenomenon. Nevertheless some conceptions of ideal societies were involved in millenarian processes of thought and some general observations may be made about them. First, the emphasis with the vast majority of millenarians was on the process, the *coming* of a new dispensation, rather than on the detailed description of the new social order. Their inhibitions with regard to visualising the new society might be readily explained. It was, after all, God, the literal *deus ex machina*, who was to bring it about. The design might therefore be thought to be in his hands.

The coming in of the Kingdom of God shall not be by the arm of flesh, nor shall it be the product of the strifes and contests of men which are in the world ...it is not the sons of men, that by outward force, shall build the new Jerusalem: that comes down from heaven adorned as a bride for Christ, fitted and prepared by himself.[68]

It followed for many that in view of the process of its inception, the new order was not even a subject of valid enquiry. 'The formall world is much affrighted, and every form is up in Arms to proclaim open wars against it selfe: The Almighty power is dashing one thing against another, and confounding that which he hath formerly faced with the glory of his own presence: He setteth up and casteth down and who shal say, what does thou?'[69] Secondly, and especially for pre-millenarians who saw Christ coming in person not only to inaugurate but also to preside over his kingdom on earth, it seemed an act of impiety to prejudge the Son of God's actions. Even the Fifth Monarchists were, as Bernard Capp has written, 'reluctant to set down the details of the millennium, feeling they ought "rather to leave the Ordering and Management thereof" to Christ and his immediate subordinates'.[70]

Nevertheless, there were those who, despite the risks, did set out to

---

[67] B. S. Capp, 'Extreme Millenarianism', in Toon (ed.), *Puritans, the Millennium and the Future of Israel*, Chapter 4; Capp, *Fifth Monarchy Men*, Chapter 9; Louise Fargo Brown, *The Political Activities of the Baptists and Fifth Monarchy Men in England During the Interregnum* (London, 1911).

[68] John Owen quoted by Peter Toon, 'The Latter-Day Glory', in Toon (ed.), *Puritans, the Millennium and the Future of Israel*, p. 38.

[69] Joseph Salmon, *Heights in Depths and Depths in Heights* (1651), in Norman Cohn, *The Pursuit of the Millennium* (London, 1962), p. 347.

[70] Capp, 'Extreme Millenarianism', p. 72. Cf. Savonarola's insistence, in this respect, that the spirit was more important than any form. Donald Weinstein, 'The Savonarola Movement in Florence: Millenarianism in a Civic Setting', in Thrupp (ed.), *Millennial Dreams*, p. 192.

describe the coming kingdom in all its perfection. Curiously, inhibitions tended to remain. Notwithstanding promises to the contrary, the picture remained blurred. In a sermon preached originally in Holland in 1641, Thomas Goodwin offered *A Glimpse of Syons Glory*, and a glimpse indeed it remained. Christ would reign personally on earth with his saints, the church would be purified and delivered from its enemies, the Jews would be converted and many prophecies fulfilled. No social context was given to any of this. Goodwin asked if there would be need of ordinances any more; but his imagination fails. He was not sure but it appeared probable.[71] Henry Archer in *The Personall Reign of Christ Upon Earth* (1642) likewise promised a full description of the coming kingdom. It would be universal, spiritual and 'Monarchicale'; 'hee will governe as earthly *Monarches* have done' but with honour, peace and riches.[72] Tantalisingly unspecific as this may be, we have to be satisfied with it. When Archer pushes beyond government to society, we are offered as the new society a combination of arcadia and perfect moral commonwealth. On the one hand, original sin is so tamed 'as that it shall get little or no ground of them'. The children of the saints prove, conveniently, to be saints also. There is a 'generall holinesse in all persons'. On the other hand, there is an abundance of all material things. There is no sickness, no violent or untimely death, no infant mortality. Men live to a ripe old age, without bodily troubles, enjoying 'all fulnesse of all temporal blessings, as peace, safety, riches, health, long life, and whatsoever else was enjoyed under any Monarchy, or can be had in this world'.[73] For more radical millenarians the vision of the new society began to break down to a list of reforms which were felt to warrant divine sanction: decentralisation, codification, simplification and laicisation of the law; or the conversion of copyhold to freehold; the abolition of a national church and tithes; or schemes for setting the poor to work. The comprehensive view of a changed society was lost in a welter of partial schemes and fragmentary reforms. For most of the radicals the new society remained, as Capp says, a hazy world, 'always summer, always sunshine, always pleasant'.[74] Those

---

71 [Thomas Goodwin], *A Glimpse of Syons Glory: Or, The Churches Beautie Specified* (London, 1641), especially pp. 26–7. For Goodwin's authorship see the case made by A. R. Dallison in Toon (ed.), *Puritans, the Millennium and the Future of Israel*, Appendix 2. For a counter-ascription to Jeremiah Burroughs see Christianson, *Reformers and Babylon*, Appendix 11.

72 Henry Archer, *The Personall Reign of Christ Upon Earth* (1642), pp. 1–3.

73 *Ibid.*, pp. 29–30, 30–2. A similar pattern of great promise and vague performance seemed to attend attempts to describe paradise lost, as well as paradise regained. Cf. John Salkeld, *A Treatise of Paradise And The Principall Contents Thereof* (1617).

74 Capp, *Extreme Millenarianism*, pp. 72–6. Although such works as William Aspinwall's *A Brief Description of the Fifth Monarchy, or Kingdome, That*

who saw a millennium being established before Christ's second coming, the post-millennialists, might feel less inhibited about visualising the new dispensation but, on the whole, they appear to have been more conservative, both socially and theologically, than their pre-millennial counterparts. However that may be, on the comparatively rare occasions when sustained attempts were made at social description, the result tended to be, as in the case of Henry Archer, a combination of perfect moral commonwealth and arcadia. This was because the hold of original sin over both men and nature was held to be inconsistent with the reign of Christ. As Thomas Burnet wrote later in the seventeenth century,

The present constitution of Nature will not bear that happiness that is promis'd in the Millennium, or is not consistent with it. The diseases of our Bodies, the disorders of our Passions, the incommodiousness of external Nature; indigency, servility and the unpeaceableness of the World; These are things inconsistent with the happiness that is promised in the Kingdom of Christ. But these are constant attendants upon this life, and inseparable from the present state of Nature.[75]

The millenarian's solution to the collective problem is then, in the main, the product of a *deus ex machina*. It is thus not secular in concern and so cannot readily involve the visualisation of the arrangements which will replace the world of the Beast, since this is a matter that the millenarian has already consigned out of his own hands and out of the hands of men. In this case the ideal society is left as a vague, tenuously perceived goal and neither in its conception nor its realisation can it be described or analysed. It does not have the 'blueprint' quality of the utopia. Where, despite this, visualisation of the new society is undertaken by millenarian writers, it tends to assume changes in nature and man which lead to arcadian or perfect moral commonwealth images or a combination of both. Utopia, by contrast, accepts recalcitrant nature and assumes sinful man.

UTOPIA

Utopia can therefore be distinguished from four types of ideal society by means of their various approaches to the collective problem: the reconciliation of limited satisfactions and unlimited human desires within a social context. The millenarian shelves the problem by invoking a *deus ex*

shortly is to come into the World (1653) contained some references to the continued necessity of civil government and the kind of apparatus that would be required to maintain it.

[75] Thomas Burnet, *Theory of the Earth*, quoted in Tuveson, *Millennium and Utopia*, p. 180. Cf. the views of Irenaeus (quoted, *ibid.*, p. 11) and the Joachimites as represented by Cohn, 'Medieval Millenarism', p. 36.

machina. Some force or agency from outside the system will miraculously alter its balance and functioning. In the perfect moral commonwealth tradition, the necessity for a prior change in the nature of man, his regeneration, and hence in the nature of men's wants is assumed. Men's desires become limited; limited, in fact, to the satisfactions, both material and sociological, that exist, as a whole and for particular groups or classes. In the Land of Cockaygne precisely the reverse happens. Material and sociological scarcities are wished away. Men's appetites remain unlimited but satisfactions multiply, on the material level especially, for their accommodation. Satisfactions are private rather than communal. Arcadia is found somewhere between these last two. Satisfactions are abundant but it is men's 'natural' rather than their conventional desires which are most apparent. Thus the arcadian tampers with both aspects of the collective problem.

The utopian is more 'realistic' or tough-minded in that he accepts the basic problem as it is: limited satisfactions exposed to unlimited wants. He seeks a solution not by wishing the problem away nor by tampering with the equation. He does not assume drastic changes in nature or man. In most utopias, indeed, the problem is never resolved completely on an individual level and has to be dealt with by the restraint or punishment of recalcitrant individuals. The utopian's concern is rather to control the social problems that the collective problem can lead to – crime, instability, poverty, rioting, war, exploitation and vice. None of these evaporate in utopias.[76] They are controlled and where possible eliminated, and the utopian is concerned to show how. Utopia is a holding operation, a set of strategies to maintain social order and perfection in the face of the deficiencies, not to say hostility, of nature and the wilfulness of man. The

[76] The significance of these distinctions might be readily grasped if we compare them with some recent definitions. (1) 'Utopia is a society planned without restraint or handicap of existing institutions and individuals. The utopist may populate his fictional state with a race of men wiser, healthier, and more generous than any society has ever seen.' Here utopia and the perfect moral commonwealth are confused. Negley and Patrick, *Quest for Utopia*, p. 4. (2) J. K. Fuz, *Welfare Economics in English Utopias* (The Hague, 1952), pp. 3–4, distinguishes between utopias of realisation and escape (confusing utopias and arcadias) and utopias of men and of measures (confusing perfect moral commonwealths and utopias). (3) J. O. Hertzler, *The History of Utopian Thought* (London, 1923), pp. 2–3, confuses perfect moral commonwealth and utopia. On the other hand some commentators have made valuable attempts to distinguish utopia clearly from other forms. See, Elliott, *Shape of Utopia*, pp. 65–6 (distinguishing between utopia and ideal societies based on the moral renewal of individuals); M. I. Finley, 'Utopianism Ancient and Modern' (distinguishes utopia from millennium and arcadia); George Kateb, 'Utopias and Utopianism', in David L. Sills (ed.), *International Encyclopaedia of the Social Sciences* (n.p., 1968), vol. XVI, pp. 267–75 (distinguishes utopia and arcadia).

utopian's method is not to wish away the disharmony implicit within the collective problem, as the other ideal-society types do, but to organise society and its institutions in such a way as to contain the problem's effects. The perfect moral commonwealth tradition idealises man. The Land of Cockaygne idealises nature, in an admittedly gross way. In arcadia, too, nature is idealised but at the same time man is naturalised. In utopia, it is neither man nor nature that is idealised but organisation. The utopian seeks to 'solve' the collective problem collectively, that is by the reorganisation of society and its institutions, by education, by laws and by sanctions.[77] His prime aim is not happiness, that private mystery, but order, that social necessity.

Utopias are sometimes given the forms of literary fiction but not always. Like other forms of ideal society they are always conceived as total schemes, something which distinguishes them from other forms of political writing. They are concerned to project a total social environment.[78] From this arises the utopians' preoccupation with detail, which, in turn, is one reason why the fictional narrative approach is so frequently suitable to their purpose. The new environment should create, within the observer, awareness of change in every facet of life, and the fictional narrator reporting his day-to-day experiences is a useful way of illustrating this. The totality of the utopian vision is part of the perfection, the order of the utopia. It stems from the urge, not merely to improve, but to perfect.[79] These three – totality, order, perfection – are cardinal characteristics of the utopian form. They are so interrelated, in this context, as to appear aspects of the same phenomenon. The order of 'a Perfect and Immortal Commonwealth' must be complete, perfect in itself, and total. Campanella, in his *City of the Sun* (1623), has magistrates not only for criminal and civil justice but also for the supervision of magnanimity, fortitude, chastity, liberality, sagacity, truth, beneficence, gratitude, cheerfulness, exercise and sobriety. His Solarians thus find that they can be accused of 'ingratitude

---

[77] Cf. François Bloch-Lainé, 'The Utility of Utopias for Reformers', in Manuel (ed.), *Utopias and Utopian Thought*, pp. 205–29. See p. 206: 'Serious utopianism ... deals with things as they are: the nature of man, who is neither angel nor beast – this excludes utopias founded on angelic natures in a universe where everyone would always be good and pure – and the nature of the material world, a hard world where the easy life will not arrive tomorrow – which also excludes utopias characterised by such an abundance of material goods that everyone might soon be satisfied without threatening his neighbours.'

[78] Cf. Polak, *Image of the Future*, vol. 1, p. 432. Utopia 'offers a total plan, a complete system, for another world, which in its intricately balanced structure encompasses the whole of human relationships in society and on earth'. See also Kanter, *Commitment and Community*, pp. 237, 241.

[79] Cf. Norman Cohn's characterisation of the millennium, in this respect, as envisaging total transformation. Cohn, 'Medieval Millenarism', p. 31.

and spite (when one person denies another proper satisfaction), of indolence, surliness and anger, and of scurrility, gloominess, and lying, which
last they abhor more than the plague. And the guilty ones as punishment
are deprived of the common table or intercourse with women or other
honors for such time as the judge deems suitable for their correction.'[80]
Almost by definition, then, the perfection of utopias must be total and
ordered; the totality, ordered and perfect. In order to achieve this, without
denying the nature of man or society, there must be discipline of a totalitarian kind. 'There must be suitable Laws for every occasion and almost
for every action that men do.'[81]

I believe, that the utopian writings of early modern England will illustrate this well, but are we seeing no more than a self-justifying process of
definition and selection in operation? The definition of utopia as a type of
ideal society to be distinguished by its approach to the collective problem
and its vision of a total, perfect, ordered environment must be validated
by its correspondence to the classic sources of the utopian tradition. In
Chapters 2 and 3 the sources of the modern utopian tradition in More's

---

[80] Negley and Patrick, *Quest for Utopia*, pp. 323–4.

[81] Gerrard Winstanley, *The Law of Freedom in a Platform* (1652) in G. H. Sabine
(ed.), *The Works of Gerrard Winstanley* (New York, 1941), p. 528. There is
another form which is based on a certain type of perfection, or, rather, stability in
time the republic of the Aristotelian/Polybian type redesigned by the Florentines and continuing through an Atlantic republican tradition in the seventeenth
and eighteenth centuries (Pocock, *Machiavellian Moment*; see also J. H. Hexter's
review essay in *History and Theory*, 16:3 (1977), pp. 306–37). The essence of
this exercise is to achieve stability in order that the citizen may realise his full
humanity as *zōon politikon* through the exercise of civic virtue, giving meaning
to civic morality. In this tradition, as isolated by Pocock, that situation or
moment is achieved by the balancing of the one, the few and the many. Most of
its practitioners appear to be pessimistic about the permanence of what might be
achieved by these constructs and this is understandable given that the aim of the
exercise is the participatory republic. Since action, participation and decision by
free citizens is the aim rather than subjection, obedience and imposed discipline,
all depends on the achievement of a degree of political morality by those citizens,
and the antithesis of corruption and stability remains a feature of that tradition.
Those who are not pessimistic about the achievement of stability in the republic
must either stress the moral capacities of the participating citizen, thus pushing
in the direction of the perfect moral commonwealth, or must look very hard at
the manner of citizen participation, at the restraints upon it and the mechanisms
by which it might be conditioned. Harrington is the classical republican most
obviously preoccupied with the latter set of solutions and so comes closer to the
utopian, but there remains, as we shall see, a tension in his thought between the
free citizenship of the participatory republic and the totalitarian discipline of
utopian subjects. The classical republic seeks to create a situation in which
citizens may act morally in governing themselves. Utopia reduces men to subjects, in a system the moral efficiency of which is guaranteed, but whose opportunity for personal morality is nullified.

Utopia and a number of continental writings of the sixteenth century will be examined in this light. What, very briefly, of the ancient utopian tradition?

Aristotle's criticism of Plato's *Republic* illustrates the points I have been trying to make. The keynote of Plato's (or Socrates') ideal state for Aristotle is its unity; a unity which to Aristotle is bad because it becomes total, perfect. 'The cause of Socrates's error lies in his false premise about unity; certainly there must be some unity in a state as in a household, but not an absolute total unity.'[82] Indeed, unity is *The Republic*'s self-possessed ideal: 'Is there anything worse for a state than to be split or disunited? or anything better than cohesion or unity?' The ideal state for Plato is an organism of total unity such that 'the whole is aware of the feeling of the parts'.[83] The elaborate and detailed regulation of the relations between the Guardian class and the rest of society are designed to promote, and are only justified by the promotion of, this perfect, total unity or order.

[82] Aristotle, *The Politics*, Book II, Chapter V, translated by T. A. Sinclair (London, 1962), p. 65. See also K. R. Popper, *The Open Society and Its Enemies*, 2 vols. (London, 1945). Popper's distinction between utopianism and 'piece-meal social engineering' throws into relief the utopian's preoccupation with a total reshaping and total order. See especially, *ibid.*, vol. I, Chapter 9: Popper, 'Utopia and Violence', *Hibbert Journal*, 46 (1947–8), pp. 109–16. Plato's totalitarianism is well illustrated by his insistence on the primacy of military discipline even in peace. 'The greatest principle of all is that nobody, whether male or female, should ever be without a leader. Nor should the mind of anybody be habituated to letting him do anything at all on his own initiative neither out of zeal, nor even playfully... For example, he should get up, or move, or wash, or take his meals... only if he has been told to do so... In this way the life of all will be spent in total *community*.' *Laws*, 942 a,f. Popper, *Open Society*, vol. II, p. 103.

[83] Plato, *The Republic*, translated and with an introduction by H. D. P. Lee (London, 1955), pp. 219, 218–22.

The re-emergence of utopia:
Sir Thomas More

If anyone doubts the truth of my story, let him put off passing judgement until all reports of wanderings and sea travels have been made.

J. V. Andreae, Christianopolis (1619)

What argument, then, remains for preferring justice to the worst injustice when both common men and great men agree that provided it has a veneer of respectability, injustice will enable us, in this world and the next, to do as we like with gods and men?

Plato, *The Republic*

Outside Utopia, to be sure, men talk freely of the public welfare – but look after their private interests only. In Utopia, where nothing is private, they seriously concern themselves with public affairs. Assuredly in both cases they act reasonably.

Sir Thomas More, *Utopia* (1518)

Amongst the dramatic shifts and challenges in European religion, thought and culture in the late fifteenth and early sixteenth centuries, one of the more surprising is the rather abrupt re-emergence of the practice of utopian writing. For a thousand years, perhaps longer, no European had conceived of a utopia and committed it to paper, or, if they had, it did not survive.[1]

The explanation of the re-emergence of utopia is in part, of course, an explanation of its absence in the middle ages. It has been argued that we may assume a medieval world-view which was focussed on the divine and eternal rather than the human and earthly.[2] Men lived in a world where circumstances were so vitiated by contingency that it was necessary for them to accept the impossibility of meaning in secular life and, therefore, to resort to the contemplative or the apocalyptic if their lives were to have moral meaning. History could have no meaning unless touched by divine grace or divine providence. The appropriate mode of ideal-society thought for Christians would be millenarian rather than utopian.[3] This view was being challenged in the late fifteenth and early sixteenth centuries by the

---

[1] See, for example, J. O. Hertzler, *The History of Utopian Thought* (London, 1923), p. 123; A. L. Morton, *The English Utopia* (London, 1952), p. 34; Glenn Negley and J. Max Patrick, *The Quest for Utopia* (New York, 1952), p. 258; Fred L. Polak, *The Image of the Future*, 2 vols. (Leyden, 1961), vol. 1, pp. 183–7, Chapter 9. Cf. also F. Graus, 'Social Utopias in the Middle Ages', *Past and Present*, 38 (1967), pp. 3–19. Graus' discussion is not concerned with utopias in the sense of my definition. He discusses rather the Land of Cockaygne and the perfect moral commonwealth traditions. The danger of typifying these as utopian is that in elaborating the differences between what he sees as medieval and modern utopias, Graus obscures the continuation of the Cockaygne and perfect moral commonwealth traditions. Separate terms are therefore preferable.

[2] H. S. Herbrüggen, *Utopie und Anti-Utopie* (Bochum-Langendreer, 1960), pp. 43, 115, 209. J. G. A. Pocock, *The Machiavellian Moment* (Princeton, 1975), Part 1.

[3] There are problems with insistence on the dominance of this paradigm or world-view through the middle ages. For example, one must ask why millennialism was so associated with heresy in medieval Europe if the paradigm of orthodoxy repeatedly pushed men in that direction. I have already suggested the pervasiveness of another mode, the perfect moral commonwealth, in medieval Christian thought.

revival of classical republicanism conducted by the Florentines, Giannotti, Guicciardini and Machiavelli. By means of a carefully constructed Polybian balance of the one, the few and the many – of monarchy, aristocracy and democracy – stability might, under favourable circumstances, be brought to the republic and the degeneration of pure forms be avoided. This stability was necessary to create a framework in which the actions and words of citizens participating in ruling themselves could be given meaning and thereby a latent history. But it was a 'this-worldly' history and classical republicanism long confronted the dilemma of whether its capacity to give meaning to history was in essence secular and pagan or apocalyptic. The framework, the constitutional machinery, of classical republicanism existed to enable men to realise their full humanity as participating citizens, but the concomitants of participation were freedom and the possibility of that failure of civil morality which came to bear the name corruption. The stability of the classical republic, essential to its ultimate purpose, was forever vulnerable to the misuse of the freedom wherein that purpose consisted. The republic would always be threatening its own integrity, if not existence, by extending to citizens a freedom which could undermine its stability.

It is worth having in mind the revival of classical republicanism in this period because it bears so many points of contact with the contemporaneous revival of utopian thought, and yet in substance the two are resolutely opposed; their priorities almost the reverse of each other. For example, in the name of participation and the freedom necessary to it the classical republican risks corruption and thereby instability, but to avoid corruption and achieve permanence the utopian, by contrast, tends to reject participation and risk freedom. Just as Machiavelli was elaborating a classical republicanism in which *fortuna* might be conquered by *virtu*, so More was depicting a world of stability, rationality and moral meaning with a secular history (or historical myth) of that meaning; a world which was neither apocalyptic nor classical republican. In doing so he recreated a mode of ideal society and gave it a name, utopia.

Thomas More in 1515 was a Londoner of some standing. Son of a prominent common lawyer, who was soon to be made a Judge of the Common Pleas, he himself had been educated in the law, had lectured on the law and since 1510 had held the quasi-legal office of an Under-Sheriff of London. Yet there is little evidence to support the descriptions of him as a lawyer 'engaged as counsel in every case of importance'[4] or even as

---

[4] Sir Thomas More, *Utopia and a Dialogue of Comfort Against Tribulation*, edited with an introduction by John Warrington (London, 1951), p. vii. Nevertheless for the general significance of lawyers see William J. Bouwsma, 'Lawyers in Early Modern Culture', *American Historical Review*, 78:2 (1973), pp. 303–27.

'a rising barrister, much employed in commercial cases'.[5] More's legal work prior to his appointment as Under-Sheriff seems to have been more as adviser, lecturer or orator than as a practising barrister. As Under-Sheriff More held a court every Thursday morning. Between 1510 and 1515 he was employed on a variety of negotiations as an arbitrator, on committees for sewers and the maintenance of London Bridge. In 1511 and 1515 he was again reader in law at Lincoln's Inn.[6] Very little is known about More's business activities before 1515.[7] He may have been admitted to the Company of London Mercers in March 1509, although this is open to doubt.[8] The evidence for identifying him with 'the class of rich London merchants'[9] is slight and tenuous. Certainly More represented the city of London on several important occasions. In 1509 he was sent as one of their burgesses to Parliament. In 1512 he was a member of a city delegation which waited on King Henry VIII. He appeared on occasion before the House of Lords and before the Privy Council on behalf of the city. In 1514 he welcomed the Venetian ambassador in the name of London and in May 1515 he went to Flanders (where he wrote part of the *Utopia*) as a spokesman for city interests. Nevertheless it would be rash to see More as an important or even influential leader of city politics before 1515. On the one occasion on which we know he participated in a crisis in the city he was singularly ineffective.[10] He was agent and mouthpiece rather than magnate.

In the *Utopia* More attacked not only the values of the aristocratic classes of his day but also the practices of lawyers and the ethics of mer-

---

[5] J. H. Lupton (ed.), *The Utopia of Sir Thomas More* (Oxford, 1895), p. xxi. Legal business is conspicuously absent from More's correspondence, see *The Correspondence of Sir Thomas More*, edited by Elizabeth Frances Rogers (Princeton, 1947). On More as lecturer see Nicholas Harpsfield, 'The Life and Death of Sir Thomas More, Knight', in E. E. Reynolds (ed.), *Lives of Sir Thomas More* (London, 1963), p. 44. Margaret Hastings, 'Sir Thomas More: Maker of English Law?' in R. S. Sylvester and G. P. Marc'hadour (eds.), *Essential Articles for the Study of Thomas More* (Hamden, Conn., 1977), pp. 92–103; Richard O'Sullivan, 'St. Thomas More and Lincoln's Inn' in *ibid.*, pp. 161–8.

[6] Russell Ames, *Citizen Thomas More and his Utopia* (Princeton, 1949), pp. 186–8. More was not, as sometimes stated, commissioned as J.P. for Hampshire in 1510. He may, however, have been a justice for Middlesex in 1509 and for Kent from 1518. See E. E. Reynolds, 'Which Thomas More? A Retraction', *Moreana*, 4:13 (1967), pp. 79–82.

[7] Cf. Ames, *Citizen Thomas More*, pp. 39, 59–60, 64.

[8] *Ibid.*, pp. 184–6. John Colet, Dean of St Paul's, was admitted to the Mercers Company but could hardly be described as a 'rich London Merchant'. See Lupton (ed.), *The Utopia*, p. xxv. Also Lupton, *A Life of John Colet, D.D.* (London, 1909).

[9] Morton, *English Utopia*, p. 37.

[10] Martin Holmes, 'Evil May Day: The Story of a Riot', *History Today*, 15:9 (1965), pp. 642–50; Ames, *Citizen Thomas More*, Appendix E.

chants. He was free to do so because he saw himself as neither businessman nor lawyer but as a scholar. More's services were valuable to his
employers more frequently because of his talents as grammarian and
rhetorician than as lawyer or businessman.[11] The *Utopia*, with its panoply
of prefaces and appendices written by some of the leading scholars of the
day, self-consciously proclaimed itself to be an important product of
northern humanism.[12] More, however, was a special type of scholar. Not
only a scholar with experience of the worlds of politics, law and business
but above all a member of an informal fraternity of Christian humanists.[13]
With his friends More was committed to a revival not only of Christian
spirituality but also of Christian morality and its effectiveness in ordinary
lives and society in general. For four years he had lived with the monks of
the Charterhouse. He wore a hair shirt and practised self-flagellation. He
admired Pico della Mirandola who, like himself, sought to live the
disciplined life of a monk without the buttressing of monastic institutions.[14]

More wrote the *Utopia* in the period between May 1515, when he left
England as a member of an English mission sent to renew amity and commercial treaties with Flanders, and September 1516, when he sent the
completed work from London to Erasmus in Antwerp.[15] He was a minor
figure involved in a side issue to the complicated diplomacy surrounding
the allegiances of the Emperor and the kings of France and England.
Even the question of state service around which his masterpiece in a sense
revolves[16] was not an issue facing More on that scale at that time. He did

[11] William Nelson, 'Thomas More, Grammarian and Orator', *P.M.L.A.*, 58 (1943),
pp. 337–52. For examples of More's work as orator see *Calendar of State Papers,
Venetian* vol. iii (1520–6), 1037; vol. iv (1527–33), 70, 385, 386.

[12] Peter R. Allen, '*Utopia* and European Humanism: The Function of the Prefatory
Letters and Verses', *Studies in the Renaissance*, 10 (1963), pp. 91–107; J. H.
Hexter, 'Thomas More: On the Margins of Modernity', *Journal of British Studies*,
1 (1961), p. 23. On the *Utopia* as a humanistic linguistic exercise see H. W.
Donner, *Introduction to Utopia* (Uppsala, 1945), pp. 8–9.

[13] St Thomas More, *Utopia*, edited by Edward Surtz, S. J. and J. H. Hexter, in
The Complete Works of St. Thomas More, vol. iv (New Haven and London,
1965), 'Introduction, Part i' by J. H. Hexter. This work is henceforth cited as
the Yale *Utopia*.

[14] G. G. Coulton, *Medieval Panorama* (Cambridge, 1943), Chapter 22; Vittorio
Gabrielli, 'Giovanni Pico and Thomas More', *Moreana*, 4:15/16 (1967), pp. 43–
57; E. E. Reynolds, *The Field is Won: The Life and Death of St. Thomas More*
(London, 1968), pp. 32–3.

[15] See J. H. Hexter, *More's Utopia: The Biography of an Idea* (2nd edition, New
York, 1965).

[16] J. C. Davis, 'More, Morton and the Politics of Accommodation', *Journal of
British Studies*, 9:2 (1970), pp. 27–49. Cf. Ed Quattrocki, 'Injustice Not
Councillorship the theme of Book One of *Utopia*', *Moreana*, 31/32 (1971),
pp. 19–28.

not become a royal councillor until August 1517, did not take up regular
duties at court before the spring of 1518 or receive a royal pension until
June 1518.[17] His preoccupation with the humanist's rôle in politics was
probably triggered by conversation with such humanist-courtiers as
Tunstall, Giles, and Busleyden whilst in Flanders, rather than by any
peculiar pressure upon himself. The 'Discourse of Utopia', More's description of his ideal state, must be seen in the context of the whole book of
which it forms only a part. The description of Utopia takes up almost the
whole of Book II but the island is only fleetingly referred to in Book I,
which contains important references to three other model imaginary
societies. In addition, both books are embedded in an apparatus of pre-
faced and appended letters and verses. 'Thus the world of Utopia becomes
an incident in a long discussion; it is not a separate book but the central
subject of the conversation – a rather lengthy anecdote told to a group of
humanists, all of whom listen to it and comment on it.'[18] In order to grasp
the significance of the anecdote one has to follow the conversation rather
carefully.[19]

Three forces may be seen as inducing men to behave in a socially
acceptable way or in a way conducive to a stable and healthy society. They
are law and the sanctions behind it; informal social pressure, in the shape
of public opinion, accepted norms of behaviour and fashion; and conscience, the small voice within, be it the voice of God or the voice of
society internalised. Trouble arises when these forces are in conflict one
with another or when they are threatened by necessity. More was concerned in Book I of the *Utopia* to demonstrate a social malaise caused by
the malfunctioning of these pressures. He described a Western Europe in
which socially accepted acquisitiveness and conspicuous expenditure were
undermining public law and morality, where the appeal of Christ to men's
consciences had to be accommodated to the patterns of behaviour to which

---

[17] E. M. G. Routh, *Sir Thomas More and his Friends 1477–1535* (New York,
1934), p. 92, n. 3. He was certainly not an important figure at court in a political
sense until about 1526 or 1527. In 1525 More was described by a foreign
ambassador as 'now coming into repute with the King' but he was considered a
person to whom gifts rather than a pension, should be offered. *Calendar of
State Papers Venetian*, vol. IV (1527–33), p. 294. Cf. also F. L. Baumann, 'Sir
Thomas More: A Review Article', *Journal of Modern History*, 4:4 (1932), pp.
604–15. G. R. Elton, 'Thomas More, Councillor', in Richard S. Sylvester (ed.),
St. Thomas More: Action and Contemplation (New Haven, 1972), pp. 88–90.

[18] Allen, '*Utopia* and European Humanism', pp. 99–100.

[19] What merit the following analysis may possess owes much to two suggestive
essays: J. H. Hexter, 'The Loom of Language and the Fabric of Imperatives:
The Case of *Il Principe* and *Utopia*', *American Historical Review*, 69:4
(July 1964), pp. 945–68; E. Harris Harbison, 'Machiavelli's *Prince* and More's
Utopia', in William H. Werkmeister (ed.), *Facets of the Renaissance* (New
York, 1963), pp. 41–71.

society was reconciled. In his famous analysis of theft and enclosures in contemporary England, More illustrated how law (in the shape of 'unjust acts'), socially accepted behaviour (in the form of ruthless acquisitiveness, war and the evil of retaining), and above all the 'terrible necessity' of hunger drove men both into crime against conscience and into retribution against conscience, through a penal code which defied the laws of Moses, Christ and reason. In the end law had become an instrument of socially condoned oppression and corruption.[20] This theme of the clash between conscience and law, conscience and social conformity, crops up repeatedly in More's writings, thought and life.[21] He used his own refusal to attend the coronation of Anne Boleyn as an illustration of it,[22] and, of course, More was well aware of the dangers of a clash between conscience and law:

as for the law of the land, though every man being borne and inhabiting therein, is bounden to the keping in every case upon some temporall paine, and in manye cases upon paine of Goddes displeasure too, yet is there no man bounden to swere that every law is well made, nor bounden upon the payne of Goddes displeasure, to perform any such poynt of the law, as were in dede unleafull.[23]

Conscience, however, for More was not a subjective thing but a positive, an institutional, factor. His conscientious refusal of the oath of supremacy was not the product of an agony of spirit like Luther's, but a reasoned willingness to defy one set of institutions in order to serve a greater and more universal; a denial of the part in order to serve the whole.[24] In his reply to charges against him at his trial he implicitly denied freedom for the individual conscience, defending himself on the grounds that he had committed his conscience to a higher and more competent authority than that which he had offended:

this Indictment is grounded uppon an acte of parliament directly repugnant to the lawes of god and his holy churche the supreme gover[n]ment of which,

20 See e.g. the Yale *Utopia*, pp. 61, 63, 67, 69, 73–5, 241.
21 See Margaret Roper to Alice Alington, Aug. 1534, *The Correspondence of Sir Thomas More*, edited by Elizabeth Frances Rogers (Princeton, 1947), pp. 521–3.
22 William Roper, *The Lyfe of Sir Thomas Moore, Knighte*, edited by E. V. Hitchcock (Early English Text Society, Original Series no. 197, 1935), pp. 57–9. For a further example see Sir Thomas More, 'A Dialogue of Comfort Against Tribulation', in *Utopia and a Dialogue of Comfort*, edited by John Warrington (London, 1951), pp. 284–5, where More warns against the social pressures on men in office.
23 More, *Correspondence*, p. 524.
24 See J. Duncan M. Derrett, 'The Trial of Sir Thomas More', *English Historical Review*, 79 (1964), pp. 468–73. On More's view of the unity of Christendom see Franklin le Van Baumer, 'The Conception of Christendom in Renaissance England', *Journal of the History of Ideas*, 6:2 (1945), pp. 137–8.

or any parte whereof, may no temporall prince presume by any lawe to take uppon him, as rightfully belonging to the Sea of Roome, a spirituall preheminence by the mouth of our Sauiour hymself, personally present uppon the earth, [only] to St. Peeter and his successors, Byshopps of the same sea, by speciall prerogative graunted; It is therefore in lawe amongest Christen men insufficient to charge any Christen man.[25]

The *Utopia* is concerned with how this malaise of warring pressures upon men and within society can be cured; in other words with how a good social order can be arrived at and maintained. For More this meant a social order in which harmony was ensured in such a way that law and social pressure confirmed the dictates of conscience. This theme was first developed in the debate taking up almost the whole of Book 1. Hythlodaeus acted as the spokesman of Christian conscience. He was 'desirous neither of riches nor power'. He repeatedly demanded the application of the gospel standard. He insisted on speaking the truth. 'To speak falsehoods, for all I know, may be the part of a philosopher, but it is certainly not for me.'[26] The debate developed two ideas; the idea of Hythlodaeus as a conscientious man and the related idea of his unwillingness to compromise with the pressures of politics.[27] In opening the debate Giles and More urged Hythlodaeus to enter the service of a prince on the grounds that this would enable him to advance his family and friends. Hythlodaeus replied that he had already benefited them by distributing his property amongst them. Moreover, far from benefiting himself, such service would rob him of his personal freedom. More then suggested that Hythlodaeus ought to enter public service for the public interest even if it involved personal disadvantage. Hythlodaeus denied his own ability in a purely formal gesture and argued that the effect of life at court would so disturb his equanimity as to render him incapable of service to the public interest. Kings were devoted to the pursuit of war in which he had neither interest nor ability. Their courts were permeated by flattery and the pursuit of status, deaf to wisdom. Hythlodaeus recalled a visit to the household of Cardinal Morton principally to illustrate the pressure of the curial milieu against conscience. In the course of this episode More introduced his first imaginary society, the commonwealth of the Polylerites, to illustrate the possibilities of a rational penology.[28]

At the end of this long excursion More returned to the debate on public

[25] Roper, *Lyfe of Sir Thomas More*, pp. 92–3.

[26] Yale *Utopia*, pp. 57, 101.

[27] For a fuller interpretation of the debate and the suggestion that the whole of the *Utopia* is a debate on counsel, see J. C. Davis, 'More, Morton and the Politics of Accommodation', pp. 27–49.

[28] Yale *Utopia*, pp. 55–85. For a legislative attempt to couple slavery with poor law reform in the manner of the Polylerites see the Act of 1547, Anno Primo, Edw. VI, c.3.

service with the argument from reference to Plato that it is the duty of a philosopher to enter the service of a prince. Hythlodaeus' answer was to show that kings and their courts are impervious to the appeals of conscience and reason.[29] Their 'crafty machinations' in pursuit of territorial advantage or pecuniary profit make goodness to them appear folly. 'If I proposed beneficial measures to some king and tried to uproot from his soul the seeds of evil and corruption, do you not suppose that I should be forthwith banished or treated with ridicule?'[30] Hythlodaeus illustrated this idea with respect to both foreign policy and currency manipulation and into both examples he introduced a fictional society, in the first case that of the Achorians, in the second that of the Macarians, to demonstrate that rational and good arrangements were not inconceivable. To all this, he held that kings and their courts would be deaf and More agreed with him. However, the fault lay as much with Hythlodaeus as with the princes. For if he was to make an impact he would have to abandon his academic approach in favour of a more practical one. In order to succeed he would have to accommodate his advice to the play in hand. Hythlodaeus rebutted this argument in favour of accommodation, in a most elaborate reply.[31] In twisting what he had to say from what he believed to what others would be prepared to hear, he would add to the madness of courts rather than cure it. Christ had demanded conduct the reverse of this. The advice was impractical in that it involved a deception impossible to carry through in the close confines of a court. In adjusting his message Hythlodaeus would either leave it substantially the same, in which case it would have no impact, or alter it in the direction of others' opinions, in which case he would be left with no integrity. But, beyond all this, even were he to win the ear of a prince and be instrumental in framing new laws, laws and good advice in themselves were not enough. Law in a corrupt and vicious society was ineffective. One had only to observe 'the many nations... ever making ordinances and yet never one of them achieving good order'.[32] The root cause of the inefficacy of law was the system of private property.

When every man aims at absolute ownership of all the property he can get, be there never so great abundance of goods, it is all shared by a handful who leave the rest in poverty...I am fully persuaded that no just and even distribution of goods can be made and that no happiness can be found in human affairs unless private property is utterly abolished.[33]

While such a system remains, law can be at best only a palliative but it will always be merely a partial remedy and may exacerbate the evil in

29 Yale *Utopia*, pp. 87–97.
31 *Ibid.*, pp. 97–107.
33 *Ibid.*, p. 105.
30 *Ibid.*, p. 87.
32 *Ibid.*, p. 103.

other areas. It is in order to demonstrate this, and the corollary that there can be a cured society if private property and the price mechanism are abolished, that the description of Utopia is introduced. Thus Utopia appeared as the climax of a sequence of imaginary states, the Polylerites, Achorians and Macarians, used by Hythlodaeus to illustrate a position he was taking in the debate on counsel. That debate was concerned with the issue of whether goodness, moral wisdom, conscience could be effective in politics. Utopia therefore illustrated how and under what conditions conscience could be so effective. It showed a society in which law, social pressure and conscience converged in the direction of goodness, but it was a standard of goodness which was pre-ordained, not chosen by the inhabitants of that society, and to which their wilfulness was made to conform.

'But suppose', said Budé in his letter to Lupset,

we were to estimate laws by the standard of truth and the command of the Gospel to be simple. Anyone with a spark of intelligence and sense would admit, if pressured, that there is a vast difference between the principles of Christ, who established the moral law, and the conduct of His disciples and the opposing doctrines and tenets of those who regard the golden heaps of Croesus and Midas as the ultimate goal and the essence of happiness.[34]

In Utopia, or Hagnopolis,[35] as that holy community was also called, the distinction between law and morality, between good citizen and good man, have disappeared. The crescent-shaped island of Utopia is divided into fifty-four city-states, joined together through a representative council[36] for matters of concern to the whole island and important issues of external relations, but otherwise independent. The Utopian family or household is the basic, almost the only, purely social unit.[37] It provides the organisation for the pursuit of agriculture, industry and trade. It is the basic unit of both military and political organisation. 'The family provides a powerful cohesive force for the whole commonwealth both as a coercive institution and as a training place for citizens. It is one of the means by which Utopians counteract the possible disruptive effects of their egalitarianism.'[38] Nevertheless the individual family or household is not sacrosanct. Households are maintained at a certain size by the constant redistribution of adults, and rural households are constantly being reformed by the drafting of urban dwellers into the country for farm service and the return to the towns of those who have fulfilled this obligation.[39] The territory of each

---

[34] *Ibid.*, p. 7.   [35] *Ibid.*, p. 13.
[36] For the council of the whole island see *ibid.*, pp. 113, 125, 153.
[37] On the importance of the Utopian family see J. H. Hexter's introduction to the Yale *Utopia*, pp. xli–xlv.
[38] *Ibid.*, p. xlii. Cf. Peter Laslett, *The World We Have Lost* (London, 1965), p. 79.
[39] Yale *Utopia*, pp. 115, 135.

city-state includes an area of at least twelve miles radius from the city proper, and More is careful to distinguish between the organisation of urban and rural households.[40] No rural household numbers less than forty adults[41] (in addition to two serfs) and no children are mentioned. The rural household consists of drafted labour from the towns conscripted for two years' farm service, half of every household returning to the town each year. There may be a number of men who choose to stay in the country and obtain leave to do so but the rural household is a rather unstable institution, which cannot be based on a blood relationship and which is substantially changed in personnel every year. The urban households, on the other hand, 'as a rule are made up of those related by blood'. The number of adults is considerably less, never being more than sixteen or fewer than ten, and it is expressly stated that there are no limits on the number of children. However, the limits on adult numbers are carefully maintained as is the total number of households in each city (six thousand) by transferring individuals between families and between cities or by colonial expansion or withdrawal.[42] Authority within the households is based on age and sex.

In the towns every thirty households annually choose an official to govern them, called a phylarch or syphogrant. In the country also every thirty households are ruled over by a phylarch but there is no mention of any household choice here and this may be because of the relative instability of the rural household.[43] In the town every ten phylarchs and their households have set over them a protophylarch (or tranibor). All the phylarchs of the town, two hundred in all, take part in an election, by secret ballot, of a city governor from amongst four candidates selected by the four quarters of the city and approved by the senate. It appears that the rural households take no part in this process and have no representation in the election of a governor.[44] The governor holds his office for life 'unless

---

[40] On the population of Utopia, see *ibid.*, pp. 414–15. Each city is a day's journey from the next. As Fernand Braudel points out, 'The whole order would have changed if transport had accelerated, however slightly.' Fernand Braudel, *Capitalism and Material Life 1400–1800* (London, 1973), pp. 393–4.

[41] 'Nulla familia rustica in uiris mulieribusque pauciores habet...' Yale *Utopia*, p. 114.

[42] *Ibid.*, pp. 135–7. It is clearly misleading to identify the Utopian family or household as a simple kinship group. Cf. Gerard Dudok, *Sir Thomas More and his Utopia* (Amsterdam, 1923), pp. 131–2; Martin N. Ratiere, 'More's *Utopia* and *The City of God*', *Studies in the Renaissance*, 20 (1973), pp. 156–7.

[43] Yale *Utopia*, pp. 115, 123.

[44] This must be so since the electoral college consists of two hundred phylarchs, and as 'there are six thousand... households in each city, apart from its surrounding territory' (Yale *Utopia*, 135–7), and a phylarch represents thirty families, the city alone will have two hundred phylarchs and the surrounding territory must therefore be unrepresented.

ousted on suspicion of aiming at a tyranny'. The protophylarch's tenure of office is renewed annually but he does not lose his position without good reason. The phylarchs and other officials hold their places for one year only. Day-to-day city government is carried on by a senate consisting of the twenty protophylarchs, the governor and two phylarchs, a different pair being chosen every day. This body deals with disputes between citizens and the administration of punishment for offences against the law. More important matters are referred to an assembly of the two hundred city phylarchs, who may inform their groups of families, take a decision and report to the senate.[45] It is important to note that what has been described so far refers only to the governments of individual city-states and that from the representative system within those city-states, such as it is, rural households are excluded.[46] Utopia is a republican league of city-states.[47] The only central organisation Utopia has consists of a council of the whole island. This meets once a year and is made up of 'three old and experienced citizens' from each city-state. How they are chosen we are not told. The council deals with some important internal matters if they are laid before it by the assembly of a city-state and with the distribution of surpluses between city-states, but it is chiefly concerned with Utopia's external relations.[48]

Through these institutions a system of law and public administration has been developed that is all-embracing in its totality. The uniformity of life in Utopia has often been commented on. Behind it lies a discipline amounting to regimentation. Every aspect of the Utopian's daily life is subject to some form of regulation. Their cities are 'identical in language, traditions, customs and laws. They are similar also in layout and everywhere as far as the nature of the ground permits similar even in appearance.' The streets are laid out in long, continuous blocks of houses similar in appearance and absence of privacy. There is no allowance for idiosyncracy or individuality in Utopian architecture or civic planning. The cities that exist are based on lines laid down by Utopus himself 1760 years before. Each is divided into four equal zones, with a carefully regulated

---

[45] *Ibid.*, pp. 123, 125, 191.
[46] H. W. Donner, and a number of other writers, have been at pains to emphasise the democratic nature of Utopian government. Donner, *Introduction to Utopia*, p. 37. Donner miscalculated the number of phylarchs admitted to the senate and confuses the phylarch's right to inform his household of matters before the assembly with a right to debate such matters with them. This is expressly forbidden in the *Utopia* (Yale *Utopia*, p. 125). Service in the country would have involved disenfranchisement but beyond this we are not told how households choose their phylarchs. Thus there is a representative system but how far it extended, even within the towns, we are not told.
[47] Cf. Russell Ames, *Citizen Thomas More*, pp. 86–8, 161.
[48] Yale *Utopia*, pp. 113, 125, 147, 153.

market building placed in the middle of each zone. Communal dining halls are situated at fixed and equal distances one from another. The homes of the Utopians conform to a standard pattern of three storeys with a flat roof. In the same way their clothes are uniform except for distinctions between the married and unmarried and between the sexes. The allocation of the day's time is not subject to individual choice but regulated to a standard pattern – three hours' work before noon, two hours' rest, three hours' work, bed at eight o'clock, and eight hours' sleep. No one is free to withdraw or refuse his labour. 'The chief and almost the only function of the phylarchs is to manage and provide that no one sit idle. . . ' Very few are licensed from manual work and amongst those are numbered the higher officials. Phylarchs, although technically licensed from work, are nevertheless expected to work with the rest. The work that men and women do is also subject to control. It has already been mentioned that town dwellers are drafted into the country for two years' farm service. Both men and women, without exception, are trained in the pursuit of agriculture. In addition everyone is taught 'one particular craft as his own'. This will be the craft pursued by the individual's father. Only by special permission will he be allowed to pursue another and he will be transferred to another household to learn it. 'The intervals between the hours of work, sleep, and food are left to every man's discretion', but at the same time a range of leisure pursuits is prohibited and the principle is laid down that leisure must be used purposively, for 'the freedom and culture of the mind'. Political discussion outside the senate is prohibited as a capital offence. A man may only travel outside his city with the permission of phylarch and protophylarch. He must travel in an official party and return by a fixed date. Even within his city's territory he may only travel with permission of his wife and father. If he stops longer than one day in a place he must take up the work of his trade. The punishment for non-observance of these regulations is severe and for a second offence the penalty is slavery. Seating in the dining halls and in the temple is subject to regulation. Lawyers are forbidden and the number of priests is fixed at thirteen per city. The number of adults per family is limited and any above the prescribed limits may be transferred to another household. Women may only marry after the age of eighteen, men after the age of twenty-two. Sexual intercourse before marriage is a serious civil offence. One is only permitted to commit suicide with the approval of the priests and the senate.[49]

Now you can see how nowhere is there any license to waste time, nowhere any pretext to evade work – no wine shop, no alehouse, no brothel anywhere, no

[49] *Ibid.*, pp. 113, 121–3, 125–7, 129, 131–3, 135–7, 139, 141, 145–7, 187, 195, 227, 233–5.

opportunity for corruption, no lurking hole, no secret meeting place. On the contrary, being under the eyes of all, people are bound either to be performing the usual labour or to be enjoying their leisure in a fashion not without decency.[50]

There is thus no privacy in Utopia. The individual is under the constant pressure of law, socially accepted standards and, given the Utopians' view of religion and the pursuit of pleasure,[51] of conscience to conform. All three pressures converge to produce the same kind of behaviour. While it is true that Utopians regard as valid only those laws 'ratified by the common consent of a people neither oppressed by tyranny nor deceived by fraud',[52] they have accepted a discipline which is totalitarian in its scope and denial of human individuality. If we mean by moral behaviour a free choosing of the good rather than the bad when both alternatives are available, the Utopian's area of choice is so limited that he is almost incapable of moral behaviour. In Utopia the bad alternative is, as far as possible, unavailable. Even the much vaunted religious freedom of the Utopians is a freedom which if indulged in can lead to the deprivation of civil rights. Those who choose not to believe in the immortality of the soul or in a providential judgement are deprived of public rights and respect on the grounds that the pressure of conscience within them towards obedience to the laws is considerably weakened.[53]

What we have called the collective problem is solved in Utopia neither by the idealisation of men (perfect moral commonwealth) nor by the idealisation of nature (arcadia), but by the twofold disciplining of men. First, although they are not fond of work, the Utopians are inured to it by their upbringing, social attitudes and structure and the supervision of the phylarchs. This intensive use of all Utopia's labour resources results in the prevention of scarcity.[54] Secondly, this produce appears sufficient because the Utopian's demands are minimal, his wants conditioned by the society in which he lives, its laws and customs. The structure of Utopian society militates against acquisitiveness and ostentation. Uniformity of dress, housing, dining facilities, supervised travel and leisure make the pursuit of status by material ostentation impractical.

One of the great contrasts in the *Utopia* is that between the Utopians' restrained and disciplined behaviour at home and their amoral, free-wheeling conduct in foreign relations and in particular in war. J. H. Lupton, one of the great editors of the *Utopia*, was shocked and puzzled

[50] *Ibid.*, p. 47.   [51] *Ibid.*, pp. 161–79.
[52] *Ibid.*, p. 165.
[53] *Ibid.*, pp. 221–3. On the Utopian religion as hermeticist see Frances Yates, *Giordano Bruno and the Hermetic Tradition* (London, 1964; reprint 1971), pp. 185–7, 233.
[54] Yale *Utopia*, pp. 181, 129–31.

by their unchivalrous conduct in foreign affairs. The Utopians loathe war
but prepare for it constantly. They never make treaties. They prefer cunning to bloodshed and that mercenaries or neighbours should if possible
do their fighting for them. In their enemies' territory they seek to encourage treason and sedition, regicide and assassination. They take 'more
care to avoid danger than to win praise or fame'. They are prepared to
pursue colonial expansion by aggressive methods when they themselves
have a surplus of population and when they find land unused or deficiently
exploited.[55] All this contrasts rather oddly with the Utopians' domestic
attitudes and with More's membership of a group opposed to wars of
territorial expansion, militarism and the employment of mercenaries.[56]
Even odder is the arrangement whereby citizens of Utopia unused by
their environment to ostentation and luxury are despatched as 'Financial
Agents' to confiscated estates in conquered territory, there to live 'in great
style and to play the part of magnates'.[57] The key to the explanation of
these oddities is to be found in a passage at the very end of the description
of Utopia. As he concludes his discourse Hythlodaeus explains why Utopia
is not only the best state but 'the only one which can rightly claim the
name of a commonwealth. Outside Utopia, to be sure, men talk freely of
the public welfare – but look after their private interests only. In Utopia,
where nothing is private, they seriously concern themselves with public
affairs. *Assuredly in both cases they act reasonably*.'[58] Thus the socially
destructive egotism of men outside Utopia is not altogether irrational, for
the social arrangements under which they live do not ensure the com-
patibility of public and private interest. Indeed, given private property,
the two are almost bound to be mutually exclusive: 'outside Utopia, how
many are there who do not realize that, unless they make some separate
provision for themselves, however flourishing the commonwealth, they
will themselves starve? For this reason, necessity compels them to hold
that they must take account of themselves rather than of the people, that
is, of others.' Equally the rationality of the Utopians is to a degree egotistical. For 'where everything belongs to everybody, no one doubts, provided
only that the public granaries are well filled, that the individual will lack
nothing for his private use'. Again the Utopians believe that, as long as
public laws are not broken, 'it is prudence to look after your own interests,
and to look after those of the public in addition is a mark of devotion'.[59]

55 Lupton, *The Utopia*, pp. xlvi–xlvii. Cf. Dudok, *More and His Utopia*, pp. 147–9.
For a discussion of this problem and a solution alternative to the one presented
here, see Shlomo Avinieri, 'War and Slavery in More's *Utopia*', *International
Review of Social History*, 7 (1962), pp. 260–90. Yale *Utopia*, pp. 137, 197–209.
56 See Robert P. Adams, *The Better Part of Valor: More, Erasmus, Colet and Vives
on Humanism, War and Peace 1496–1535* (Seattle, 1962).
57 Yale *Utopia*, p. 215.
58 *Ibid.*, pp. 237–9 (my italics).   59 *Ibid.*, pp. 165, 239.

More's recognition of the fact that most men will pursue their own interests (*commoda*) is the key to his Utopia and to his utopianism. He does not say that all men will act so, for even in Utopia there are groups of men who put service before interest,[60] but, by and large, he holds that most men will pursue their interests as they are defined by the circumstances prevailing at a particular time and, moreover, that they will be acting rationally to do so.

This explains or at least provides a key to More's emphasis on environment and on legal/institutional reform.[61] More did not envisage the Utopians as ideal men or even as eminently reasonable men. They are capable of falling from grace and punishments including slavery and death are provided to condition and control behaviour. The eternal supervision under which the Utopian lives suggests that More had little faith in the average human being's propensity to civilised social behaviour. Just as the defects of the land of Utopia are made up by diligence[62] (i.e. it is not an arcadia) so the continuing defects of the nature of Utopian men and women are contained as far as possible by law, social arrangements, supervision and education. Nevertheless there are Utopians who 'having had an excellent rearing to a virtuous life,...still could not be restrained from crime'.[63] They have to be punished most severely. As Hexter has argued,

Utopia implies that the nature of man is such that to rely on individual conscience to supply the deficiencies of municipal law is to embark on the bottomless sea of human sinfulness in a sieve. The Utopians brace conscience with legal sanctions. In a properly ordered society the massive force of public law performs the function which in natural law theory ineptly is left altogether to a small voice so often still.[64]

More, then, appears to be saying that men will always act reasonably in following their interests and that those interests will be defined in accordance with circumstances. Therefore, since contemporary circumstances produced evil behaviour, circumstances must be altered to induce men to act well. So that, for example, in Utopia marriage was so arranged as to

---

[60] *Ibid.*, pp. 225–7.
[61] Cf. Hexter, 'Thomas More: On the Margins of Modernity', pp. 30–7.
[62] Yale *Utopia*, p. 179.   [63] *Ibid.*, p. 185.
[64] Hexter, 'Thomas More: On the Margins of Modernity', p. 31. Cf. Elizabeth Hansot, *Perfection and Progress: Two Modes of Utopian Thought* (Cambridge, Mass., 1974), pp. 49, 56. Herbrüggen's argument that utopian ideality is founded on the ethical capacities of the citizens, i.e. their natural ability to construct a rational society, founders on this very point. Rationality for More here consists in reasonable behaviour in accordance with circumstances. Just as men outside Utopia are capable of acting rationally so it is the changed circumstances of Utopia, not the ethical capacities of its citizens, which make action of a different order rational. For a convenient English translation of Herbrüggen's remarks on this point see Sylvester and Marc'hadour (eds.), *Essential Articles*, pp. 251–62.

minimise the risk of dissatisfaction and to make faithful monogamy in the individual's interest.[65] Whereas the classical republicans envisaged, in a carefully balanced constitution, the merging of the interests of groups and individuals into what might be seen as the general interest, More began with a given notion of the collective good and sought to create social circumstances such that the individual would be led reasonably to identify his particular interest with that collective good and its maintenance. To put it in political terms, More suggested that in contemporary Europe political 'realities' ruled out certain forms of conduct for the man who was reasonably concerned with his own interest, and would appear absurd and futile in the 'idealist'. The conduct Hythlodaeus was discussing in Book 1 was ruled out by the political and social structure and direction of early-sixteenth-century society. The answer implied by the *Utopia* was that the political realities must be changed in order to free men for a different order of political rationality in desirable conduct, and to rule out those forms of conduct which were at present sanctioned but which were found reprehensible. Seeing the pursuit of interest as the key to More's *Utopia* also explains the problem of the contrast of the Utopians' behaviour in dealings amongst themselves and in dealings with other states. Within Utopia they are honest, direct, open. In their external relations, particularly towards enemies, they are Machiavellian. In both circumstances their conduct is reasonable. Within Utopia their good behaviour accords with circumstances and the conditioning of their interests to social harmony by law, institutional provision and education. But their Machiavellian behaviour outside Utopia is equally appropriate to a world of lawlessness – a Hobbesian state of nature. In the same way it is useless to expect Utopian behaviour of the 'Financial Agents' posted overseas. They are removed from the influence of Utopian institutions and arrangements, and can only be expected to pursue their interests as appropriate to their new environment. They are therefore expected to live in style as magnates, something which would have been a source of amusement within Utopia.

Thus More emphasises his concern with the institutional/legal/educational pressures on men and with the need for their rearrangement if law and social pressure are to be confirmatory of conscience. What would have seemed remarkable to More's contemporaries, however, was not the battery of almost universal regulation to which the Utopians were subjected. They were used to the sound of legal regulation of dress, trade, housing, work, city planning, restricted travel and recreation. Rather more surprising to them might have been that such regulations in Utopia were *enforced*.[66] The striking thing about Utopia is not the laws but their

[65] Yale *Utopia*, pp. 187–91.
[66] Yale *Utopia*, p. 103. Cf. Erasmus, *Praise of Folly*, translated by Betty Radice with an introduction by A. H. T. Levi (London, 1971), pp. 150–1.

effectiveness, and this was due to what Jean Desmarais called 'their system of public administration'.[67] The lynchpin of this is the officials who run it. Utopia, said Jerome Busleyden, 'has devoted its energies not so much to framing laws as to training the most qualified officials. It has not done so without reason, for otherwise, if we are to believe Plato, even the best laws would all be counted dead.'[68] The phylarchs, of course, whose main responsibility is for work discipline are elected annually and may only hold office for one year. We are not told how the managers of dining halls or the supervisors of the sick are selected but all other officials –ambassadors, priests, protophylarchs and the governor – may only be chosen from the leisured class, the intellectuals.[69] This scholar class from which the higher administration of the Utopian city-states is selected sets a tone of open-mindedness and disinterested effectiveness which permeates Utopian society. None of their official distinctions or offices are hereditary. Protophylarchs and the governor have reasonable security of tenure but the former can be deprived for soliciting votes and the latter for 'aiming at a tyranny'.[70] Above all they have nothing to gain beyond the performance of their duties. They can operate the system but hardly exploit it. There can be no bribery, no clientage, no faction in Utopia. The fawning flatterers of European courts with their endless factional intrigues and power struggles have been displaced. With their undivided loyalties the Utopian officials foreshadow the modern ideal of the bureaucrat. Like Hythlodaeus himself they are desirous neither of riches nor power.

More in the *Utopia* was claiming that community pressure could be made to correspond to and to endorse conscience and that the way to achieve this was through institutional and legal regulation, supervision and control. Moreover, he was aware of an environment in which exactly this was done, the environment of the monastery. More's use of the monastery as a model or of features of monastic life in his description of Utopia has frequently been noted.[71] The absence of pomp; devotion to

[67] Yale *Utopia*, pp. 27–9.

[68] *Ibid.*, p. 35. More himself was frequently represented as a model official. See, for example, William Roper, 'The Life of Sir Thomas More, Knight', in Reynolds (ed.), *Lives of Sir Thomas More*, pp. 20–3.

[69] Yale *Utopia*, pp. 127, 139, 141–3.

[70] *Ibid.*, pp. 123, 193. See, Lee C. Khanna, '*Utopia*: The Case for Open-Mindedness in the Commonwealth', *Moreana*, 31/32 (1971), pp. 91–105; Alan F. Nagel, 'Lies and the Limitable Inane: Contradiction in More's *Utopia*', *Renaissance Quarterly*, 26:2 (1973), pp. 173–80.

[71] See, e.g., Donner, *Introduction to Utopia*, p. 80; W. H. G. Armytage, *Heavens Below: Utopian Experiments in England 1560–1960* (London, 1961), p. 3; P. A. Duhamel, 'The Medievalism of More's Utopia', *Studies in Philology*, 52 (1955), p. 119; R. W. Chambers, 'The Saga and the Myth of Sir Thomas More', *Proceedings of the British Academy*, 12 (1926), pp. 202–6; Hexter, *Biography of an Idea*, pp. 85–94.

work, study, prayer; the uniformity of dress; the general austerity; the contempt for gold; the communion of property; the communal meals taken 'with some reading which is conducive to morality':[72] all these echo the cenobitic way of life. More himself in a letter to Erasmus written in December 1516 described the Utopian dress as 'a Grey friar's cloak'.[73] In certain respects the way of life of the Utopians bears more than a passing resemblance to that of the Carthusians, an order whose discipline More shared for four years.[74] Like the Carthusians, the Utopians enjoy a combination of public and private ritual worship, unusual in most monastic institutions.[75] The *conversi* in the Carthusian order were never allowed to grow beyond a fixed number nor were they allowed to occupy responsible administrative positions. Their vocation was the cultivation of the land and the performance of heavy manual tasks in order to free the monks for study. In this sense they resemble the mass of Utopians in their relationship with those licensed from work.[76]

The monasticism of the high middle ages had represented, in some respects at least, an attempt to erect communities free from the play of *fortuna*, in which moral effort could be made effective and time be given meaning in terms of the eternal. It is not surprising, therefore, that *Utopia* should reflect the monastic model. How does it compare with the other model which early modern men were elaborating in their struggle to dominate *fortuna*? How does the utopian republic of city-states compare with the classical republic?

In the classical republic the object is civic participation in order that men might realise their full humanity in the exercise of civic virtue. John

[72] Yale *Utopia*, p. 145.

[73] *The Epistles of Erasmus*, translated and edited by F. M. Nichols, 3 vols. (New York, 1901), vol. II, p. 443.

[74] R. W. Chambers, *Thomas More* (London, 1963), p. 72. For Erasmus as an occasional admirer of the Carthusians see his colloquy, 'The Soldier and the Carthusian' (1523), in *The Colloquies of Erasmus*, translated by Craig R. Thompson (Chicago, 1965), pp. 127–33. For Erasmus' changing attitude to monasticism see *ibid.*, pp. 99–103.

[75] Yale *Utopia*, p. 233. For the Carthusians see Dom David Knowles, *The Monastic Order in England, a History of its Development from the Times of St. Dunstan to the Fourth Lateran Council 943–1216* (Cambridge, 1950), p. 378.

[76] Knowles, *The Monastic Order*, p. 379. Cf. James Kelsey McConica, *English Humanists and Reformation Politics under Henry VIII and Edward VI* (Oxford, 1965), p. 19. 'Erasmus sees a properly conducted Christian city fulfilling the same spiritual purpose as a monastery, with the additional merit of being more useful to society as a whole.' See also Hexter's remarks regarding the resemblances of More's *Utopia* and Calvin's *Geneva* and the common ambivalence towards monasticism. J. H. Hexter, *The Vision of Politics on the Eve of the Reformation: More, Machiavelli and Seyssel* (London, 1973), pp. 107–17. D. B. Fenlon, 'England and Europe; *Utopia* and its aftermath', *T.R.H.S.*, 5th series, 25 (1975), pp. 115–35.

Pocock has suggested that in the Polybian system corruption could be identified with subjection, the rule of some who are citizens over others who are also citizens, rather than participatory citizenship. For Machiavelli the dependent individual becomes incapable of identifying his particular good with the good of all. He sees only those to whom he is subject and in whose decisions and actions he has no say.[77] In Utopia, however, there is a very important sense in which all men are subjects, none citizens. For citizens in the classical republic participate in order that, in some sense, they may rule themselves and in ruling themselves they may change the very form of the republic, hence the ever-present danger of corruption. In Utopia the form is forever unchanging. Utopians are ruled by laws, institutions and officials and are made to conform to them, pursuing their own interests as defined by a set of circumstances created for them. What the utopians gave up were the freedoms of participating citizens – to discuss, to choose, to act, to change – and in return they gained the defensive freedoms of subjects in a well-ordered society – freedom from the arbitrary, wilful, wicked acts of others and themselves, freedom from uncertainty and in the end freedom from change. More, in fact, looked very hard in his 'Dialogue on Counsel' (Book 1 of the *Utopia*) at the form of participatory politics with which he was most familiar – curial politics – and found it wanting.[78] Men will always pursue what their reason tells them to be in their own interests. More did not have the classical republican's faith that simple constitutional constructs and balances could lead men to regard the common good. Rather their interests and society's, he implied, could only be made to coincide by a total restructuring of the latter and by continuous coercion, education and scrutiny. Stability and permanence may only be possible in the classical republic if all men are virtuous.[79] To some, the extension of this might be that the republic is only possible, in the long term, by divine grace; only in the commonwealth of saints is the republic fully realised. But what if, like More and other utopians, we assume that all men are wicked? Then we are left with two alternatives: monarchy, in which some wicked men may be given full rein for their appetites and arbitrariness (a situation defensible for Sir Robert Filmer and other *jure divino* monarchists as a scourge visited by God on fallen men),[80] or a republic of subjects, not citizens, and this is what the *Utopia* offers.

Thus in contrast to a contemporary Europe of 'disasters, devastations,

---

[77] J. G. A. Pocock, *Politics, Language and Time: Essays on Political Thought and History* (London, 1972), p. 88.
[78] J. H. Hexter, Review Essay, *History and Theory*, 16:3 (1977), p. 308.
[79] Pocock, *Politics, Language and Time*, p. 99.
[80] Cf. the remarks of Martin Ratiere, 'More's *Utopia* and *The City of God*', pp. 144–68.

destructions and calamities', with 'the great cities laid waste, the states destroyed, the commonwealths overthrown, the villages fired and consumed', Utopia promises a 'commonwealth eternal'.[81] It does so not because it is peopled with gods, nor because of an unnatural material abundance. Utopian stability is founded on the constant and total disciplining of men.[82] The emphasis is thus upon rules, laws, the institutions associated with the promulgation and administration of law, and on the men who will operate those institutions and who are themselves conditioned by the nature of the new society. The concern throughout is with moral certainty, with the desire to make conscience effective, to ensure that between intention, deed and effect there are unbroken links. The desire is to bring an end to moral uncertainty and to the fear that history must be an endless and meaningless flux, a moral chaos. None of these was, of course, new or unique in More. What was original in his *Utopia* was the mode by which he chose to resolve these problems. He enquired as to the capacity of institutional, legal, educational and bureaucratic arrangements to give to man and society a sense of moral effectiveness and certainty. Paradoxically, what he risked in his construct was that in preventing uncertainty by restricting the freedom of men to an extreme degree, he might jeopardise their whole status as moral agents. Just as More must be the defining source for the modern utopian tradition, so too he defines that tradition's major and most intractable problem.

[81] Yale *Utopia*, pp. 35–7.
[82] R. S. Johnson has seen the totalitarian implications of utopian society but uses them, in my opinion without warrant, to argue for More's non-seriousness. See Johnson, 'The Argument for Reform in More's *Utopia*', *Moreana*, 31/32 (1971), pp. 123–34.

3

The re-emergence of utopia:
the European experience 1521–1619

Alas Jove, everything is despicable, everything is mixed up, confused, and turned upside down.

Anton Francesco Doni, *I Mondi* (1553)

My friend, you have undoubtedly come here under the leadership of God *that you might learn whether it is always necessary to do evil* and to live according to the custom of barbarians.

Johann Valentin Andreae, *Christianopolis* (1619)

Therefore wisdom should be sought in the whole book of God, which is the world, where more wisdom always may be discovered. It is to this book and not to the little books of men that Scripture sends us.

Tommaso Campanella, *The Defense of Galileo* (1622)

That nothing approaches nearer God than Unity, nor recedes further from him than dissonancy, the consciences and experience of all men do sufficiently evince. . .

Johann Valentin Andreae, *A Modell of a Christian Society*, translated by John Hall (1647)

Since Thomas More invented the term 'Utopia', it seems reasonable to look to him for its meaning, but the question then remains as to whether that meaning is singular or general. Did More invent a book, a unique work which others might read and variously interpret, or did he also define a genre, a way of looking at society and its political and moral problems which others too might adopt?

This problem in the re-emergence of utopian thinking is highlighted precisely by the fact that there were other writers in sixteenth- and seventeenth-century Europe who either, ignorant of More's work, pursued an orientation very similar to it, or, knowing it, seized upon its pre-occupation with morality and society and upon its recourse to institutional, legal, educational and bureaucratic solutions. Observations on the nature of utopianism *via* the *locus classicus* of the modern tradition need to be fleshed out by comparison with other works produced against a similar or contemporary background. Accordingly, four European 'utopias' of the sixteenth and early seventeenth centuries will be briefly examined in this chapter. They represent a group chosen for their variety of approach and style, but the lineaments of the utopian type may be clearly observed in them. Two of those chosen are German, two Italian. Two, Eberlein and Doni, are minor figures. The others, Campanella and Andreae, are much better known.[1] The first of our sample, like the last, was a Lutheran but almost a hundred years separates their writings. Whilst Eberlein's *Wolfaria* (1521) was written against the tension and uncertainties of Luther's stumbling towards open defiance and finally full separation from the Roman church, Andreae published his *Christianopolis* (1619) in an age when orthodox Lutherans might well be concerned that their church

---

[1] It has frequently been asserted that modern utopianism, at least until the end of the nineteenth century, was an Anglo-French phenomenon. This is certainly not true of the sixteenth and seventeenth centuries. The first French utopia, *Histoire du Grand et Admirable Royaume d'Antangil*, did not appear until 1616 and it was not until the work of d'Allais towards the end of the seventeenth century that the French began to make a contribution to the European tradition of utopian writing. See, Frank E. and Fritzie P. Manuel (eds.), *French Utopias: An Anthology of Ideal Societies* (New York, 1966), pp. 1, 35–42.

had become too comfortable and that its members had lost their social vision.[2]

Johann Eberlein von Günzburg's *Wolfaria* was first published in 1521 as the tenth and eleventh in a collection of fifteen pamphlets.[3] There is no evidence that the author knew of either More or his *Utopia*. Eberlein was born in a poor and backward area of Swabia, probably in or about 1460. Very little is known about his life. He studied theology at Ingolstadt, Basle and Freiburg, where he was registered as a student in 1493. Subsequently he became an observant friar of the Franciscan order, working as lector, preacher and confessor. In 1521, at the age of sixty-one, Eberlein broke with his past, leaving the Franciscans to follow Luther. He travelled to Wittenberg in order to study with him. It was at this moment, when his life was uprooted at the beginning of old age, that Eberlein produced his utopia. In 1524 he married and the following year obtained an appointment as evangelical pastor to Count George II of Wertheim am Main, and superintendent of twenty parishes in the region. When Count George died, in 1530, his Catholic successor dismissed Eberlein. Seventy years old and with a wife and four children, Eberlein sought refuge with friends in Ansbach. A living was found for him at a small village nearby and he died in 1533.[4]

Wolfaria, like the *Utopia*, was written in two sections but in this case the sections dealt one with spiritual, the other with secular government. Indeed, if the work has any consistent main theme it is its preoccupation with the relationship between secular and spiritual and what Eberlein saw as the related problem of social stability. Eberlein had relatively little to say about government within Wolfaria. The elected, salaried public officers were obviously of focal importance but no information was given as to how they were to be elected or what exactly their powers were. Clearly, however, they were intended to be administrators, bureaucrats, rather than legislators or policy makers, for Eberlein himself sought to lay down the law and to define the limits of policy as they were to be applied in his ideal society. Here we have once again, as in the *Utopia*, an attempt to create a total environment, to all intents complete and relentless in pursuit of its purpose. Law itself was to be simplified, codified and fixed. 'Everyone shall know the public law, so that he may know what he may do and what he may not do.' Given this, the legal profession was to be

---

[2] Cf. Gerald Strauss, 'Success and Failure in the German Reformation', *Past and Present*, 67 (1975), pp. 30–63.

[3] In the collection *Fünfzehn Bundsgenossen* (Fifteen Confederates). I have followed Susan Groag Bell's treatment of the work in, 'Johan Eberlin von Günzburg's *Wolfaria*: The First Protestant Utopia', *Church History*, 36: 2 (1967), pp. 122–139.

[4] Bell, *ibid.*, pp. 123–4.

discouraged as an unnecessary promoter of discord and disunity. Trades and professions were to be strictly regulated, with no provision for luxury. 'There shall be no honest work or means of livelihood other than agriculture. All the nobility shall live by agriculture.' The professions of both lawyers and merchants were to be discouraged. The master-servant relationship was to be governed by law. The care of the sick and the education of the young were to be publicly provided for. Usury was abolished as was the indiscriminate minting of coin. Prices were to be controlled, begging discouraged, timber, game and fish to be common to all. Serfdom was to be abolished. 'At the appointed time everyone shall be free.' City planning was subject to close regulation concerning the width of streets, functional zoning and restraint and economy in public construction. Public baths were to be provided on a separate basis for the two sexes. Even entertainment was to be publicly sponsored and organised. 'Every month there shall be a friendly modest public entertainment – this shall be seen to by the authority of all places. No entertainment shall last more than a half day.' This last provision brings us back to the utopians' typical concern with detail, the urge to have *everything* under control. Eberlein, like so many other utopians, insisted on uniformity of dress, only the sexes being distinguished. Or again, 'All men shall have long beards – strictly enforced, none shall have a smooth face like a woman – all men shall have their hair trimmed short.' 'All youths shall be forbidden to play cards or dice for money...the old ones may play at appropriate times, but never gamble for more than a penny.'[5]

The distinguishing feature of Eberlain's utopia, however, is his concern with ecclesiastical problems and the violence of the sanctions he suggests for the enforcement of his proposed regulations: 'all canon law and decretals shall be publicly burned'. Just as priests and laymen were to wear the same dress, so they were to obey the same law. The mendicant orders of friars were to be eliminated by execution. 'All begging monks shall be done away with by loss of life.'[6] But Eberlein was significantly ambivalent in his proposals for dealing with the monasteries. They were to be converted for use as schools and as shelter for the poor and aged. At first Eberlein suggested that all monks be allowed freedom of choice as to whether they remained at or left the monastery. Later he appears to have changed his mind, stipulating that no more than ten souls be allowed to remain and that there should be no recruiting of novices for ten years. Similarly, Eberlein outlawed the wearing of the monastic habit but in a sense he put the whole community into a modest, monastic uniform.[7] The secular clergy were not to be allowed any civil authority and were to be subject to careful supervision and the same laws as everyone else. Priests

[5] *Ibid.*, pp. 126, 131–3.   [6] *Ibid.*, pp. 130, 133–4, 136.
[7] *Ibid.*, p. 126.

were to be appointed by parochial election, subject to the confirmation of 'sheriff, court and bishop'. 'Every priest shall receive two hundred gulden from the common purse of his parish and no more.' 'Priests shall receive no tithes.' They were permitted to marry but were to be accorded no special privileges or respect. There were to be fewer holy days and sacraments, and a reformed liturgy. To back up this battery of regulations, Eberlein called for a severity of punishment verging on the hysterical. 'Those who marry secretly shall be drowned.' 'We order that all public adulterers shall be executed.' 'All public drunkards shall be drowned.' 'We forbid, by hacking off of head, that the people be taught any prayer but the Lord's prayer.'[8]

There is much that is crude, confused and even contradictory in Eberlein's *Wolfaria*, yet it shares common features with the sophisticated *Utopia* of More. They are both concerned to erect a regulation and supervision covering in detail the life of the individual without the community. They have both accepted sinful, not to say criminal, man as their raw material and they both direct their ideal states towards morally ordered ends. The common features they share are the characteristics of the utopian tradition.

Anton Francesco Doni not only knew of More but had collaborated with Ortensio Lando in the preparation of the first Italian edition of the *Utopia* published in 1548.[9] Doni was born in May 1513, the son of a Florentine scissors maker. He entered the monastery of Annunziata in his native city, a foundation supported by the Medici, and was eventually ordained. In 1540 he left the monastery and Florence to wander Italy, occasionally engaged in the study of the law. In the mid-1540s he returned to his native city, setting himself up as a printer. Thence, in 1547, he travelled to Venice, the city which was to be the scene of his major literary output. In the freedom of republican Venice, Doni joined a group of popular writers, Aretino, Lando, Nicolo Franco, the *poligrafi*, writing for a popular, vernacular audience in racy, witty and critical style. Between 1551 and 1553 Doni published nine books including his *I Mondi* (1553) in which his utopia appeared. From the later 1550s he was under increasing pressure from the authorities as a renegade priest. In 1562, possibly to reinstate himself, he wrote attempting to prove that Luther was the great Beast of the Apocalypse, but, as far as his own fortunes were concerned, to no avail. He left Venice in 1567, retiring to Monselice, and died seven years later.

---

[8] *Ibid.*, pp. 128, 130, 131.

[9] See P. F. Grendler, *Critics of the Italian World (1530–1560): Anton Francesco Doni, Nicolo Franco and Ortensio Lando* (Madison, Wis., 1969), p. 32. For Doni's life see *ibid.*, pp. 49–65. It is worth noting that Lando was also a former monk.

Doni's utopia appeared as the sixth of seven worlds in his *I Mondi* (1553). It is the subject of a dialogue between two characters, Savio and Pazzo, in the course of which Savio describes an ideal state revealed to them both by Jove and Momus. There can be no doubt that the work was influenced by More, but other, Italian, influences were equally strong and Doni's fertile imagination was quite capable of moulding all he had read and experienced to his own purposes. The Italian interest in city planning evident in Alberti's *De Re Aedificatoria* and Filarete's *Sforzinda* is clearly reflected in Doni's ideal city, and he may well have been aware of other contemporary ideal-society writings by his countrymen.[10] By and large the *poligrafi* conveyed a deeply pessimistic view of sixteenth-century Italy, as a world out of joint, lacking moral goals and incapable of self-renewal. In *I Mondi* Doni told of how Jove embarked on a scheme to reform the world by sending souls down from heaven. The only one willing to go was that of a prince. Jove admonished him to pursue moral perfection as a ruler, an admonition straight out of the perfect prince tradition. The prince, in response, only laughed – he would not be a prince if he did not do as he liked, 'the precepts of good government did not alter the conduct of princes'.[11]

It is out of this bitter pessimism that Doni's utopia springs. Once again his ideal state reveals an attempt to visualise the total regulation of life within a community and the typical utopian emphasis on society as a convention. Since out of a sour and corrupted nature nothing good could come, nature in both man and his environment had to be tamed and disciplined. Wisdom could not prevail in the world as it was. Doni's utopia is a city-state, the only city in a province the size of Lombardy, Tuscany or the Romagna. It is built in the shape of a star, and at its centre stands a temple with a hundred doors, from which radiate a hundred streets to a hundred gates in the city wall.[12] The rigidity of the city stands as a symbol of the total discipline imposed upon the community. In every street are located two related crafts. For example, one street is devoted to millers and bakers. No one is allowed to sell produce and as far as possible goods are made to order, thereby avoiding waste. The countryside outside the city walls is made highly productive by means of peasant specialisation and the growth of crops suited to the land. Money, weights and measures,

---

[10] *Ibid.*, pp. 162–6. See also, Grendler, 'Utopia in Renaissance Italy: Doni's New World', *Journal of the History of Ideas*, 26:4 (1965), pp. 479–83; John M. Berdan, 'Doni and the Jacobeans', *P.M.L.A.*, 22 (1907), pp. 291–7. See also Helen Rosenau, *The Ideal City: Its Architectural Evolution* (2nd edition, London, 1974), Chapter 3; W. Houghton-Evans, *Planning Cities* (London, 1975).

[11] Grendler, *Critics of the Italian World*, pp. 14, 79–80.

[12] Grendler, 'Utopia in Renaissance Italy', p. 488. Note also Doni's pessimism about the value of learning. Grendler, *Critics of the Italian World*, pp. 142–6, 171.

and lawyers are not allowed. Homes and furniture are kept simple and, as far as possible, uniform. This uniformity of life reaches out in many directions. Dress too is uniform except for variations of colour to distinguish various age groups. At mealtimes the populace resort to a street of inns where they consume identical food in identical surroundings. In extension of this pursuit of uniformity and control, women are held in common. The family is abolished. Deformed children are thrown at birth into a well. When healthy children are old enough they are taken from their mothers and raised in common. Every seventh day is given up to religious ceremonial. On other days services are held before and after the day's labour to encourage the people to 'make a feast of their work'. No provision is made for the defence of the community since the inhabitants assume that no one would wish to attack a people as frugal and dull as they. Similarly, Doni makes no mention of governmental system or élite since he saw himself as the final legislator leaving a system that needed no amendment.[13]

The emphasis in *I Mondi* is not on social happiness but on security and morality. Like More, Doni saw contemporary society as a conspiracy of rich against poor where lawyers, doctors and scholars studied how to cheat and rob and soldiers knew only how to kill and ruin. In Doni's pessimism no solution to these ills was perceived save that of putting all men in the same condition and firmly holding them to 'a life without aspiration'. As in most utopias, we are presented in *I Mondi* with 'a rational, even geometrical organisation of the physical environment and a highly regimented life for the inhabitants'. The problem of men's propensity to choose wrongly was to be solved by the use of structural, institutional and legal devices aimed at severely limiting their choices. In 1564 Doni tried the experiment again. Significantly, the ex-monk chose to attempt the depiction of an ideal religious order, *La Religione del Colbella* (The Order of the Knife), and once again detail, rigidity, uniformity and discipline are the keynotes of the exercise.[14]

Another Italian, who showed interest in Doni's *I Mondi*, was that strange and tortured figure, Tommaso Campanella.[15] The defender of empirical and open-minded scientific research as exemplified by Telesio and Galileo, Campanella was also the protagonist of universal Catholic monarchy under the Papacy, Spain or France, the upholder of sacerdotalism. Campanella was born at Stilo in Calabria in September 1568, the son of a shoemaker. In 1582 he entered a Dominican order and having something of a reputation for a prodigious memory probably shared the

---

[13] Grendler, 'Utopia in Renaissance Italy', pp. 489–91.
[14] *Ibid.*, pp. 495–6, 492, 483; Grendler, *Critics of the Italian World*, pp. 133–4, 210.
[15] For Campanella's interest in Doni see Grendler, 'Utopia in Renaissance Italy', pp. 493–4.

Dominicans' interest in memory systems or mnemonics. He was sent to Cosenza in 1588 to study theology and here he became interested in Telesio and developed a distaste for Aristotle. In 1589 he began surreptitiously to write a defence of Telesio and his insistence on the validity of empirical observation. Having left the monastery and travelled to Naples, in 1592 he was denounced and ordered to return. However, he chose to defy the order and went on to Rome, Florence and Padua where he became acquainted with Galileo. Finally, in 1594, he was arraigned before the Holy Office in Padua and sent to Rome where he was examined under torture. He was released on condition of his return to Calabria but now, alongside his scientific concerns, Campanella was developing a politically embarrassing doctrine of Papal world supremacy. In 1599 he was committed to a Neapolitan prison on charges of heresy and conspiracy. He was to remain in confinement for the next twenty-seven years, tried on numerous occasions, four times tortured and finally feigned madness in order to obtain release. During these years Campanella wrote many works including his *Città del Sole* (City of the Sun) and his defence of Galileo. In 1626 he was released to live in a Dominican monastery in Naples, but his freedom was illusory. Constantly under pressure and afflicted with uncertainty, Campanella at last, in 1634, fled Italy for France and the patronage of Louis XIII and Richelieu. Here he spent the last years of his life working for the conversion of the Protestants and trying to prolong his own life by astrology. He died in 1639.

The *City of the Sun* has a complex bibliographical history. An Italian manuscript version was first produced in 1602. A revised version of this manuscript was written by Campanella in 1611. During the following two years he worked on a Latin manuscript version and these various manuscripts seem to have circulated widely. In 1623 an edition of the Latin version was published in Frankfurt. Four years later an alternative Latin version was published in Paris.[16]

[16] J. E. G. Gardner, *Tommaso Campanella and his Poetry: The Taylorian Lecture 1923* (Oxford, 1923), pp. 7–9; F. Grillo, *Tommaso Campanella in America: A Supplement to the Critical Bibliography* (New York, 1957), p. 15. There is no adequate English edition of *The City of the Sun*. I have used the translation in Glenn Negley and J. Max Patrick, *The Quest for Utopia* (New York, 1952), pp. 314–44. A partial text will also be found in Charles M. Andrews (ed.), *Famous Utopias* (New York, n.d.). On Campanella's thought see, Friedrich Meinecke, *Machiavellism: The Doctrine of Raison d'Etat and its Place in Modern History*, translated by Douglas Scott (London, 1957), Book 1, Chapter 4; Bernardine M. Bonansea, 'The Political Thought of Tommaso Campanella', in John K. Ryan (ed.), *Studies in Philosophy and the History of Philosophy* (Washington, 1963), vol. II, pp. 211–48; Bernardine M. Bonansea, *Tommaso Campanella: Renaissance Pioneer of Modern Thought* (Washington, 1969); Nell Eurich, *Science in Utopia: A Mighty Design* (Cambridge, Mass., 1967), pp. 108–20, 290–1.

Campanella believed that in order to avoid social chaos there had to be an assigning of functions to every individual. Politics was seen as a branch of ethics. Law performed for society the rôle that virtue performed for the individual. Since there was no distinction, or possibility of distinction, between the good man and the good citizen, the civil magistrate could act as confessor. But because evil men did not respond even to the fear of punishment in the afterlife, the law was not simply a guide but must also be used as an instrument of discipline and social regulation.[17] The City of the Sun is a city-state ruled by a chief magistrate called Sol or Metaphysic who is aided by three officers: Power, who is concerned with the military arts; Wisdom, whose province is the liberal and mechanical arts, and Love, who supervises human reproduction. Beneath these are ranged a group of specialist magistrates dealing not only with criminal and civil justice but also policing the morality of the citizens in a specialist way, as categorised by their titles – Magnanimity, Fortitude, Chastity, Liberality, Sagacity, Truth, Beneficence, Gratitude, Cheerfulness, Exercise and Sobriety. The necessity for this close moral supervision stems from Campanella's pessimistic view of the nature of man: 'there is much corruption abroad in the world, men are not governed by true and higher reasons. . .the good are tortured and are not listened to. . .the bad have the rule'. Thus, 'All the higher magistrates are priests, and it is their duty to purge consciences.'[18]

The corruption of natural man is compounded in a system of private property.

From this arises selfishness; for in order to raise a son to riches and honors and leave him as heir to much wealth, each of us becomes either desirous of seizing control of the state (if power or wealth or descent has enabled him to throw off timidity) or greedy, contriving, and hypocritical (if he has little strength, a slender purse and mean ancestry).

Therefore the Solarians are given by Campanella a system of communal property, including community of women. This he defended by arguing that the initiative of self-interest could be replaced as a drive by love of country and that friendship was not a relationship dependent on a private property system.[19]

[17] Bonansea, *Tommaso Campanella*, pp. 268, 273, 279–82; Bonansea, 'Political Thought of Campanella', pp. 215, 220. For a millenarian element in Campanella's thought see Campanella, *A Discourse Touching the Spanish Monarchy* [translated by Edmund Chilmead] (1654), p. 9. In the same work he adopted a perfect moral commonwealth approach to the problems of the Spanish monarchy and its world mission. See *ibid.*, Chapter 8.

[18] Negley and Patrick, *Quest for Utopia*, pp. 319–23, 340–4.

[19] *Ibid.*, pp. 322–33. The City of the Sun has been characterised as a natural law society; the best form of society that could be achieved by the light of reason

The cenobitic characteristics of the community's administration of morals and communal property are reinforced by the uniformity of dress and communal refectories which Campanella compares directly with those of a monastery. In several places he portrays the Solarians as monks in a monastery.[20] The most striking transference of monastic features in this utopia, however, is the provision for tests on entry. Those who wish to become citizens of the City of the Sun must serve a kind of novitiate: 'they are first tested for a month on a farm and then for another month in the city after which time a decision is made, and they are accepted with certain ceremonies, oaths, etc.'. As in a monastery, the community is morally directed and a total discipline is striven for. Work, dwelling places and recreation are all assigned and controlled from above. Trading is only allowed at the gates of the city and, within the city, the work the citizens do is closely supervised. All head artisans are judges with power to punish recalcitrant workers by exile, flogging, dishonour, exclusion from the common table, from worship, or from the women. Daily military practice and bi-monthly exercises are held in which all must take part. Those who show fear are punished severely.[21]

'They have an abundance of things, because each wants to be first in his work, because it is slight and rewarding, and because they are all quite obedient.' But the collective problem is tackled from the side of consumption as well as that of production. Diet and dress are carefully regulated and the family, which Campanella saw as the primary source of status consumption, is abolished. The family, as a property relationship, could only, like private property itself, lead to social atomism. Therefore, 'the begetting of offspring is managed as a religious affair for the good of the state and not of individuals'. The chief magistrate, Love, 'sees to it that men and women are so mated as to produce the best offspring'. Detailed arrangements are delegated to a First Master of Reproduction and mating takes place in accordance with astrological rules. There is not so much a community of women in the City of the Sun as a surrender of sexual individuality to the state in the name of eugenic rationality.[22]

In its scientific aspects, the Sun City represents an attempt to create a

alone, without benefit of Christian revelation. The difficulty here is that the Solarians do appear to have some knowledge of Christ, the Christian martyrs and the apostles. See Bonansea, *Tommaso Campanella*, pp. 274–8; 'Political Thought of Campanella', pp. 226, 228–9 especially n. 73, p. 229.

[20] Negley and Patrick, *Quest for Utopia*, pp. 333, 328. Cf. Bonansea, 'Political Thought of Campanella', p. 233, n. 83; *Christianopolis an Ideal State of the Seventeenth Century translated from the Latin of Johann Valentin Andreae with an Historical Introduction*, edited by F. E. Held (New York, 1916), pp. 23–4. Hereafter cited as *Christianopolis*.

[21] Negley and Patrick, *Quest for Utopia*, pp. 327, 333, 335, 338, 334.

[22] *Ibid.*, pp. 336–7, 329–31, 322.

civic memory system, inspired by the hermetic dreams of Giordano Bruno (also a Dominican) and, in turn, stimulating the pansophist aspirations of people like Jan Amos Comenius in the early seventeenth century.[23] On the seven concentric walls of the city are portrayed all known phenomena; knowledge complete and frozen in an immutable orthodoxy. In the same spirit, one book is held to contain all that is known of the liberal and mechanical arts. There are no laboratories, only museums. As Judah Bierman has pointed out, 'throughout this city, dominated by its walls, there is no place for exploring new knowledge; in effect, knowledge is fully known, codified and exhibited'. Campanella thus sought to create a mental uniformity paralleling the physical, environmental uniformity of his city-state.[24]

The last of the utopias to be considered here, in relation to the main features of More's *Utopia*, is Andreae's *Christianopolis*, which was first published in 1619.[25] The more detailed and sophisticated presentation of government structure in *Christianopolis* may be due to the influence of More on Andreae,[26] who also admired Campanella as an anti-Aristotelian, translated several of his sonnets and dedicated two apologues to him in the *Mythologia Christiana*.[27]

Johann Valentin Andreae was born in 1586, the son of a Lutheran cleric, and grandson of an important Lutheran theologian, Jakob Andreae (1528–90). Andreae and three of his brothers became Lutheran pastors. True to his background, he remained a defender of orthodox but enlightened Lutheranism for the whole of his life.[28] In 1601 his father died

---

[23] Frances Yates, *The Art of Memory* (London, 1969), pp. 289, 363, 372–3; Yates, *Giordano Bruno and the Hermetic Tradition* (London, 1964; reprint 1971), pp. 367–72; Yates, *The Rosicrucian Enlightenment* (London, 1972), p. 137; Wilhelmus Rood, *Comenius and the Low Countries* (Amsterdam, 1970), p. 123; Allen G. Debus, *Science and Education in the Seventeenth Century: The Webster–Ward Debate* (London, 1970), p. 9.

[24] Negley and Patrick, *Quest for Utopia*, pp. 317–20; Judah Bierman, 'Science and Society in the *New Atlantis* and other Renaissance Utopias', *P.M.L.A.* (1963), p. 495.

[25] See *Christianopolis*.

[26] For Andreae's formal avowal of indebtedness to More, see *Christianopolis*, p. 141. A German translation of the *Utopia* was published in 1612.

[27] *Christianopolis*, p. 21; Eurich, *Science in Utopia*, p. 134.

[28] The best study of Andreae in English is now J. W. Montgomery, *Cross and Crucible: Johann Valentin Andreae (1586–1654) Phoenix of the Theologians*, Archives Internationales d'Histoire des Idées 55, 2 vols. (The Hague, 1973), vol. 1. Montgomery lays to rest the ghost of Andreae's heterodoxy, in particular the suggestion, made repeatedly of recent years, that Andreae was behind, or involved in, the Rosicrucian ferment of the early seventeenth century. Cf. Frank E. Manuel, 'Pansophia: A Seventeenth Century Dream of Science', in Manuel, *Freedom from History* (New York, 1971); Allen G. Debus, *The Chemical Dream of the Renaissance*, Churchill College Overseas Fellowship Lecture no. 3

and the family moved to Tübingen where Andreae became a student at the university and where he took his M.A. in 1605. At Tübingen he developed a friendship with Michael Maestlin, the teacher of another famous Lutheran, Johann Kepler. Andreae left Tübingen in 1607 to spend the next seven years wandering through Germany, Switzerland, France, Austria and Italy. Although he disliked Calvinism, the discipline and order of Geneva left a significant and indelible impression upon him. In February 1614, having returned to Tübingen, he was ordained into the Lutheran ministry and spent the rest of his life in pastoral activities and writing. During his preparation as an ordinand, Andreae made the friendship of Wilhelm Wense, who in turn became acquainted with Campanella. Wense was a prime stimulant to Andreae's idea of a Societas Christiana, a society of men from many walks of life dedicated to the moral and social reform of European society. In addition Wense put Andreae in touch with Tobias Adami, who was introducing Campanella's ideas into German circles and also became a supporter of the idea of a Societas Christiana.

In 1614 Andreae became pastor in the area of Vaihingen, northwest of Stuttgart, and in the same year he married. During the next six years he produced almost twenty works, including *Christianopolis* and a series of social satires in the Erasmian/Lucianic tradition. *Christianopolis* was dedicated to Johann Arndt, an orthodox Lutheran theologian. But, in addition to his intellectual interests, Andreae had severely practical problems to deal with. The town to which he ministered was twice ravaged by fire, in 1617 and 1618, and Andreae worked hard to organise its rebuilding. Between 1620 and 1639, he was chief pastor (*Specialsuperintendent*) at Calw, a Black Forest town not far from his birthplace. Here he seems to have attempted to organise groups of families to work together for mutual assistance and social purification. The impact of what we know as the Thirty Years' War and the recession of the 1620s prompted him to publish two editions, one Latin, one German, of Juan Luis Vives, *De subventione pauperum*. In 1634 and again in 1638 Calw was severely sacked, almost destroyed, by passing armies. The year after the second attack, Andreae became consistorial councillor and court preacher in service to Duke Eberhardt III and published, in 1639, a compilation of church regulations and discipline designed to counter Satan's efforts to substitute anarchy for order in church and state (*Cynosura oeconomiae ecclesiasticae*). The war and its effects had deepened Andreae's lifelong fear and horror of disorder. In *Vox libera* (1642) he attacked popular degeneracy, opulent power, hypocrisy, tyranny and confusion in church

(Cambridge, 1968), p. 18; Debus, *Science and Education*, p. 22; Yates, *Rosicrucian Enlightenment*, Chapters 3–5; Yates, *Art of Memory*, pp. 372–3; Eurich, *Science in Utopia*, pp. 120–9.

and state. For the last four years of his life he supervised a Lutheran school at Bebenhausen on the outskirts of Tübingen. He died in June 1654.

Christianopolis is a city-state situated on a small island named Caphar Salama. Andreae's description of it is broken down into exactly one hundred sections. The city is built in an exact square seven hundred feet in length, 'well fortified with four towers and a wall'. Distributed between the four corner towers stand eight other big towers and sixteen smaller ones: 'the citadel in the midst of the city is well-nigh impregnable'. Indeed, Christianopolis would have appeared more like a small-scale fortress than a city.[29] Around the community stands a moat, stocked with fish, and beyond that are open spaces in which wild animals roam. At its centre stands a great temple. The remainder of the buildings are of a uniform pattern, all three storeys high. 'Things looked much the same all round. . .'[30]

Andreae laid great emphasis on the importance of officials. His *Modell of a Christian Society* is almost dedicated to the proposition that perfect officials can produce a perfect society. Like More, he was aware of the inefficacy of law in contemporary society and linked this to the lack of good bureaucratic officials. 'Excellent laws stand out to view; but if anyone would urge their enforcement he would be ridiculed.' In Christianopolis the hereditary principle is eliminated from the administration. 'In this republic no value is set on either succession of title or blood apart from virtue.'[31] Despite some confusion and vagueness the main outlines of the governmental structure of Christianopolis are reasonably clear. A legislative body or council meets periodically in a council hall situated above the temple. Its twenty-four members are 'chosen equally from the three orders', but how they are chosen and what the three orders are Andreae does not specify. The men chosen are examples of virtue and can be displaced. The council's functions are twofold. They supervise the operation of the community, examining 'the present according to models, and if they find that they are deteriorating a single bit, they repair the matter'. Obviously they are not expected to legislate in a positive or sovereign manner but only within the limits of the original utopian blueprint. Secondly, they select the chief officials, the bureaucrats who adminis-

[29] *Christianopolis*, p. 149. On the 'town planning' aspects of Christianopolis see Patrick Abercrombie, 'Ideal Cities: no. 1. Christianopolis', *Town Planning Review*, 8 (1920), pp. 99–104. Abercrombie gets involved in a number of confusions by treating Christianopolis as a city rather than a household.

[30] *Christianopolis*, pp. 149–50.

[31] *Ibid.*, pp. 237, 165; G. H. Turnbull, 'Johann Valentin Andreae's *Societas Christiana*', *Zietschrift für Deutsche Philologie*, 73 (1954), pp. 407–32 and 74 (1955), pp. 151–85. For John Hall's translation of *Christianae Societatis Imago* see *ibid.*, 74 (1955), pp. 151–61.

ter the implementation of the blueprint. At what might be described as the executive level of the bureaucracy stand a triumvirate of officials – a Presbyter, a Judge and a Director of Learning. The Presbyter is the chief priest of the city-state and gives himself up to living as an example to the community and preaching once a week. As his assistant he has a Diaconus who is concerned with education and the performance of church services and the administration of the sacraments. The Judge, the 'PATER FAMILIAS of the city', supervises not only weights, measures, and numbers but also the individual citizens. 'Whatever methods they exercise in taming their passions and in thoroughly overcoming Adam, these he considers his sphere and he regulates everything with a view toward life eternal.' He is assisted by a 'state economist' who not only supervises the distribution of supplies amongst individuals but also guards against any over-indulgence. The third triumvir, the Director of Learning, supervises 'the sphere of human learning' while insisting that Christ is the real book of knowledge. He administers the college, of which more later. Operating in conjunction with these officials is a chancellor about whose functions Andreae is rather vague but who appears to have been a kind of presidential figure. He seems to have had some responsibility for the reception and departure of strangers but his main function was the promulgation of public decrees. The triumvirate have separate responsibilities but are in constant collaboration: 'all consult together in matters that concern the safety of the state. Each has a senate but on fixed days they all meet together that decision in the most important matters may be reached with common consent.' At these meetings 'questions of the truth of the Christian religion, the cultivation of virtues, the methods of improving the mind; also the need of treaties, war, negotiations, buildings and supplies are deliberated upon'. Beneath the triumvirate, the city is administered by eight men, living in the larger towers, and eight subordinates, distributed through the smaller towers. Their duties seem to be mainly those of economic regulation and the supervision of production, but Andreae has nothing to say about their selection. Again the relationship of the housing inspectorate to this structure is not defined.[32]

In terms of economic activity the city is divided into four zones, buildings on each of the city's four sides being allocated to one group of activities. Agriculture is carried on on the eastern side with fourteen buildings as well as land allocated to its pursuit. 'Here there is no rusticity, but the agriculture of the patriarchs is reproduced, the results being the more satisfactory, the closer the work is to God and the more attentive to natural simplicity.' On the southern side of the city there are seven mills and seven bakeries, but these buildings are also reserved for anything of a

[32] *Christianopolis*, pp. 266–7, 179–83, 185–9, 278, 174–5, 166–7, 160–1, 170.

mechanical nature and for the storing of wine and oil. The northern side of the city is devoted to slaughter houses and warehouses of provisions. To the west are seven workshops concerned with the forging and moulding of metals and a further seven occupied with the manufacture of salt, glass, brick and earthenware. All these activities required heat and here also a kind of Paracelsan scientific enquiry is pursued: 'a testing of nature herself'. 'Unless you analyse matter by experiment, unless you improve the deficiencies of knowledge by more capable instruments you are worthless.' The science pursued in Christianopolis is a 'practical' science more closely akin to technological development than to pure scientific research.[33] Production is closely supervised. The workers are allowed a free hand so long as there are sufficient materials in the stores. No money is permitted except in the community treasury and only selected individuals are allowed to engage in commerce. Begging is not tolerated and material assistance is only given to the poor after careful examination. 'If a person is physically strong, he is never permitted to deny the republic his efforts.' From time to time the citizens may be obliged to do compulsory work on the roads, in collecting the harvest, in maintaining the city's defences and sometimes even in the factories. Since all are willing and take pleasure in their work, few hours each day are needed to produce the required output. 'You will be surprised how a supply of provisions, not at all very great, can be made to suffice for temperate habits in everything.'[34]

Andreae is emphatic upon the artisan quality of his citizens: 'the whole state is one of artisans', 'the whole city is, as it were, one single workshop, but of all different sorts of crafts'. He even itemises what those crafts are: 'workers in brass, tin, iron; knife makers, turners, makers of jewel-cases, of statuary, workers in gypsum, fullers, weavers, furriers, cobblers; and among the nobler crafts, sculptors, clock-makers, gold-smiths, organ-makers, engravers, gold-leaf beaters, ringmakers, and other innumerable trades not to be despised. Tanners, harness-makers, blacksmiths, wagon-makers, all these you will find here.'[35] The lists of carefully chosen tradesmen represent an attempt to produce a balanced and integrated economy. Given the narrow home market for Christianopolis and the rather austere habits of its citizens, Andreae must have visualised most of this produce going for export to enrich the city's treasury and enabling it to pay tribute to foreign powers and to hire mercenaries when necessary.[36] However,

---

[33] *Ibid.*, pp. 150–5. On the rôle of science in Christianopolis see Bierman, 'Science and Society', pp. 496–7; Eurich, *Science in Utopia*, pp. 120–34. On Andreae's Paracelsan background see Montgomery, *Cross and Crucible*, vol. I, pp. 13–16, 25–6, 28–9; Debus, *Chemical Dream*, pp. 19–20; Debus, *Science and Education*, p. 23.

[34] *Christianopolis*, pp. 160–1, 153, 272, 168, 152.

[35] *Ibid.*, pp. 171, 160, 157.   [36] *Ibid.*, pp. 195, 246.

Andreae sets a very high value on these crafts in another sense. They are pursued not merely for necessity but also 'in order that the human soul may have some means by which it and the highest prerogative of the mind may unfold themselves through different sorts of machinery'. God himself is seen as the 'supreme Architect', the universe as a 'mighty mechanism'.[37]

At the centre of the city stands a building described as 'The College'. This four storey building is the most imposing in Christianopolis. On the ground floor are 'The Twelve Halls of the Citadel'; these are part classroom, part museum, part laboratory, part workshop. They are the Library, the Armory, the Archives, the Printers (which also acts as an office of censorship), the Treasury, the Laboratory (concerned with the investigation of the properties of nature 'for the use of the human race and in the interest of health'), the Pharmacy, a hall of Anatomy, a Natural Science Laboratory (which is mainly an exhibition hall), an Art Gallery, a Hall of mathematical instruments (which contains amongst other things 'the very valuable telescope recently invented'), and a Mathematical Laboratory (mainly concerned with astronomy and problems of motion). On the first floor of the college are the eight lecture halls of the school. At the age of six, children go into the care of the state. They are housed on the second and third floors of the college and educated on the floor below. Only the wisest and most virtuous are allowed to act as teachers. The priorities of education in Christianopolis are as follows: first the worship of God, second the pursuit of the best and most chaste morals, and third the cultivation of the mental powers; as Andreae points out, 'an order reversed by the world'. This involves a religious education, a controlled and limited education and constant moral supervision: 'youths the most valuable asset of the republic are molded and trained to God, nature, reason and public safety'. The content of their education is subservient to these ends: 'there are many things which it is expedient not to know in this life'. Above all, men must not be taught to aspire to things beyond their reach; 'we will always be in need, as long as we desire what we cannot obtain'. In this respect no one is left free of that part of the educational function which consists in moral supervision: 'the boys are so associated with those who are grown up, and the adults so observed by the married men, and the inspection is so carefully carried out all around, that to the utmost possible extent, moral corruption of the youth is avoided'. Nevertheless, there are still occasions when severe discipline is required. 'Punishments are inflicted with fasting and work; if there is need, with whipping; in extreme cases, though rarely, by imprisonment.' The boys are taught in the mornings, the girls in the afternoons and by women as well as men teachers. Time

[37] *Ibid.*, pp. 157–8, 221–2. Compare Pico della Mirandola's description of God as 'the best of artisans' in his *Oration on the Dignity of Man*.

out of the classroom is spent on manual training or 'honorable physical exercises'. The children are divided into three age groups and proceed through the eight classrooms or departments in sections according to age. The departments are as follows: Grammar and languages (which consist of Hebrew, Greek and Latin), Logic, Arithmetic, Music, Astronomy (which embraces astrology), Natural Science (which embraces history), Ethics and Theology. Four rooms are left on the first floor, two of which are devoted to the study of medicine and two to the study of jurisprudence. The latter is purely an academic exercise since there is no need for lawyers in Christianopolis.[38] All through his discussion of education Andreae emphasises the primacy of religion. In logic, for example, the students are taught 'not to subject all things to it especially not God'. Mathematics, astronomy, music all lead to contemplation of the divine. The highest study of all is theology, where 'though they love to hear the name of Lutheran, yet they strive first of all to be Christians'. In his section on natural science Andreae explains that 'the inhabitants of Christianopolis make everything in this world second to the church'. The judges of this ideal state punish in declining order of severity offences against God, against man and against property; again an order of priorities which Andreae saw reversed in the world around him.[39]

It is when one remembers the size of the population of Christianopolis, a mere four hundred, that the influence of the monastic model becomes once more apparent. It is a household rather than a city. 'About four hundred citizens live here in religious faith and peace of the highest order.' They are uniformly dressed in white or ashen grey, age and sex being distinguished by the style of the uniform. Their communally owned dwellings are small cell-like quarters, austerely furnished. Their leisure or 'vacation periods' consist of quiet contemplation. They worship every morning, noon and evening, and 'No one may be absent from these prayers, except for the most urgent reason. . . ' As in any monastic institution tests are imposed on those who wish to enter. Although presented in different guises, all three examinations employed in Christianopolis are moral in character. 'He asked me. . . to what extent I had learned to control myself and to be of service to my brother. . . ' For all his discipline and single-minded effort the citizen of Christianopolis expects no earthly rewards: 'it is glory and gain enough for him to please God'.[40]

of penalties, there is no use of these in a place that contains the very sanctuary of God and a chosen state, in which Christian liberty can bear not even commands, much less threats, but is borne voluntarily towards Christ. Yet it must be confessed that human flesh cannot be completely conquered anywhere.

[38] *Christianopolis*, pp. 174–5, 190–248.   [39] *Ibid.*, pp. 216, 241, 233, 164–5.
[40] *Ibid.*, pp. 150, 171, 156, 170, 162–3, 158, 145–8.

And so if it does not profit by repeated warnings (and in case of need, serious corrections) severer scourges may be used to subdue it.[41]

Thus, just as in the monastery and in the other utopias we have looked at so far, a total control is sought. Where this cannot be internalised, and this is always in doubt, self-control is supplemented by minute regulations and full provision of the means of enforcement. As article VIII of the Christianopolitan creed has it, 'We have gone from freedom to doing good.'[42] In Christianopolis the community lays down rules of dress, marriage, family size, work, leisure, consumption and religious observance. The community is a shining example of efficient planning. Andreae emphasised its neatness. The uniform homes of its citizens, completely lacking in individuality, 'are kept up at the expense of the state, *and provision is made by the carefulness of inspectors that nothing is thoughtlessly destroyed or changed*'. Their education is controlled for municipal and religious purposes and their reading is carefully censored. Two tablets set up on the wall of the college prescribe a communally endorsed orthodoxy of religious belief and social behaviour. At night the streets of Christianopolis are brightly lit to remove 'the veil which our flesh is so anxious to throw over license and dissoluteness'. As far as possible conscience, social pressure and the law are made effective against deviance or sin.

Against backsliders, especially those who remain stiff-necked after the vain warnings of brothers, fathers and civil authorities, they pronounce the wrath of God, ban of the Church, disgust of the state and abhorrence of every good man, with such success that it seems as if they had been shut off from the universe, that is, all the creatures of God. They consider this more severe than death and they all make a great effort for the recovery of such a man. If at last he continues to resist and is stubborn they expel him from the republic. Before this is done they tax him with the most extreme and debased labours or even with blows, by which means they prefer to punish the sins, than spill his blood, as far as this is permitted.[43]

Andreae defined history as 'a rehearsal of the events of the human tragedy'. Like Doni, he saw the world around him as a world out of joint. 'For whether we look at the churches, the courts, or the universities – nowhere is there a lack of unscrupulous ambition, greed, gluttony, license, jealousy, idleness, and other mastering vices at which Christ violently shuddered, but in which we chiefly delight'; 'hypocrisy has undertaken and violently usurped the protection of religion, tyranny that of civil

[41] *Ibid.*, p. 164.
[42] Montgomery, *Cross and Crucible*, vol. I, p. 128.
[43] *Christianopolis*, pp. 171, 159–60, 151–7, 168, 272, 162–3, 186, 258–9, 158, 170, 194, 175–8, 172, 257.

authority, quibbling that of letters'.[44] In this world of inverted values Andreae, like More, believed that all the pressures on men were against virtue. 'Everyone carries with him domestic, rustic or even paternal and inborn wickedness, and communicates these to his comrades, with so poisonous a contagion that it spares not even those who ought to be consecrated entirely to God...' Evil, again as in More's analysis, becomes a necessity and Christianopolis exists specifically to answer the question 'whether it is always necessary to do evil and to live according to the custom of barbarians'.[45] What had impressed Andreae on his visit to Geneva had been that municipality's attempt to mould, not to say dragoon, its citizens into virtue: 'the harmonious unity of their customs and morals'. In his autobiography he wrote,

While I was at Geneva, I noted something of great moment which I will remember with nostalgia till the end of my days. Not only does this city enjoy a truly free political constitution; it has besides, as its particular ornament and means of discipline, the guidance of social life. By virtue of the latter, all the mores of the citizens and even their slightest transgressions are examined each week, first by neighbourhood supervisors, then by aldermen, and finally by the senate itself, according to the gravity of the case or the obduracy and insolence of the offender...The resultant moral purity does so much honour to the Christian religion, is so consistent with it and so inseparable from it, that we would shed our bitterest tears that this discipline is unknown or completely neglected in our circles; all men of good will ought to labour for its restoration. Indeed if religious differences had not made it impossible for me, the harmony of faith and morals at Geneva would have bound me there – and so from that time I have striven with all my energy to provide the like for our churches.[46]

In *A Modell of a Christian Society*, Andreae argued 'That nothing approaches nearer God than Unity, nor recedes further from him than dissonancy...' While each man pursued his own divergent interest only moral weariness and misery could ensue.[47] As in *Utopia*, so in *Christianopolis*, the function of a perfect state is to make it the rational self-interest of every man to pursue the public interest.[48] Social arrangements are designed to reinforce private morality.

We are dealing here, of course with two aspects of morality and the writers we discuss are not always ready to distinguish between them. On the one hand, there is the individual-centred aspect which emphasises the

---

[44] *Ibid.*, pp. 232, 135–6.   [45] *Ibid.*, pp. 248, 146.

[46] Montgomery, *Cross and Crucible*, vol. 1, pp. 43–4; *Christianopolis*, pp. 13, 27–8. Cf. Hexter's remarks on the affinities between More's *Utopia* and Calvin's Geneva. J. H. Hexter, *The Vision of Politics on the Eve of the Reformation: More, Machiavelli and Seyssel* (London, 1973), pp. 107–17.

[47] Turnbull, 'Andreae's *Societas Christiana*', p. 152.

[48] *Christianopolis*, p. 178.

relationship between morality and choice. When the individual acts well it is because he has chosen wisely. If we take away his freedom of choice we also impair his moral capacity. On the other hand, there is the aspect of social morality which emphasises performance, not choice, and which assesses that performance in terms of what is seen to be an independently existent moral code, not in terms of the will and wisdom of choice of the individual. We behave well when we do as we are told by the moral code, not when we take risks with it by indulging in choice. A good society is one which achieves the full standard of the code and the question as to whether that performance is a result of the choices of the members of that society or a result of the coercion of them may be seen as secondary. In the process 'a truly free political constitution' may leave only the freedom to do that which is right in accordance with a pre-ordained moral standard, and, in the other moral sense, it may be doubted whether that is a freedom at all. Unity, order, moral efficiency are all.

Thus we are brought back to More and the common features of the utopias so far examined. They are preoccupied with dragooning men, far from ideal, into righteousness; with breaking out of the vicious cycle of pernicious social and political influences on weak men, into a situation where the pressures of institutional, legal and educational arrangements all lead in the direction that a rightly informed conscience should move anyway. But such is the nature of man and such are the depths to which necessity and disposition have brought him, that governance, control, supervision must be as complete as possible, total. Both at the levels of intention and of effect society must be made morally efficient. Clearly monastic life had always sought to erect such a degree of control, and the four men considered in this chapter, like Sir Thomas More, were influenced by the model offered by it. In the medieval world men had sought to realise a form of social and moral perfection in, to use Ernst Troeltsch's term, a sect-type withdrawal from the world. Such a withdrawal left a gap between the achieved standard of goodness and the greater society which, for reasons not yet fully understood, was no longer tolerable to some men by the sixteenth century. The demand for the full application of received moral ideals to the world of reality could only be met by two visions: the millenarian cleansing of the earth or utopia.[49] It is no accident that men who had aspired to the monastic ideal were engaged with this latter vision, nor that they carried to it many of the structures and devices of the monastic world.

[49] Cf. Martin Fleisher, *Radical Reform and Political Persuasion in the Life and Writings of Thomas More*, Travaux d'Humanisme et Renaissance, 132 (Geneva, 1973), p. 57. For a discussion of Thomas Münzer's millenarianism in these terms see, Sanford A. Lakoff, *Equality in Political Philosophy* (Cambridge, Mass., 1964), pp. 54–8.

Above all these utopians were rebelling against Aristotelianism, as they knew it, on two counts. They rejected both the idea of the state as a natural phenomenon and the distinction between good man and good citizen. According to Aristotle, 'It is evident that the good citizen need not necessarily possess the virtue which makes him a good man.' This was the alternative to a world of moral efficiency, a world in which good intention leading to good deed was followed by good effect, a world in which men pursued a consistent morality in both their private and public capacities. In this other world of unideal reality either good intention was absent or a shadow fell between intention and deed, between deed and effect. In this world men might accept a distinction between good man and good citizen which enabled one to discuss the world as it was rather than as it should be. Aquinas, like Aristotle, could make the distinction: 'It sometimes happens that someone is a good citizen who has not the quality according to which someone is also a good man, from which follows that the quality according to whether someone is a good man or a good citizen is not the same.'[50] But Campanella, like his fellow utopians, could not accept the distinction and he saw the source of it. In *The Defense of Galileo* he attacked the subjection of Christianity to an outsider like Aristotle, insisting that 'Aristotle's Averroism was the cradle of Machiavellism'.[51] For, by the beginning of the sixteenth century, the distinction between good man and good citizen was being broadened into an abyss by the work of writers, of whom Machiavelli was only an extreme example, who emphasised the amoral nature of political activity, or rather that politics was an activity in which men could realise their full humanity as moral agents by civic participation, rather than by conformity to a pre-ordained moral standard. The utopians were engaged in attacking this development. For them, not only were good citizens expected to be good men, but the whole apparatus of the state was to be refined as an instrument primarily devoted to producing men of virtue defined in accordance with a pre-ordained standard of perfection.

[50] Aristotle, *The Politics*, Book III, Chapter IV; Aquinas, *Selected Political Writings*, edited by A. P. D'Entreves (Oxford, 1948), pp. 117–19, 135, 147–9, 175.

[51] Thomas Campanella, 'The Defense of Galileo', translated and edited by Grant McColley, *Smith College Studies in History*, 22:3–4 (1937), pp. 33, 42. Andreae in turn admired Campanella as a struggler against the heathen Aristotle. *Christianopolis*, p. 21.

4

Robert Burton and the anatomy of utopia

How happy might we be, and end our time with blessed days and sweet content, if we could contain ourselves, and, as we ought to do, put up injuries, learn humility, meekness, patience, forget and forgive, as in God's Word we are enjoined, compose such small controversies amongst ourselves, moderate our passions in this kind, 'and think better of others', as Paul would have us, 'than of ourselves: be of like affection one towards another, and not avenge ourselves but have peace with all men'. But being that we are so peevish and perverse, insolent and proud, so factious and seditious, so malicious and envious, we do *invicem angariare*, maul and vex one another, torture, disquiet, and precipitate ourselves into that gulf of woes and cares, aggravate our misery and melancholy, heap upon us hell and eternal damnation.

> *The Anatomy of Melancholy* (6th edition, 1651), Pt 1, Sec. 2, Mem. 3, Subs. 8

. . . it is not houses will serve, but cities of correction.

> *The Anatomy of Melancholy*, 'Democritus Junior to the Reader'

No other English writer of the seventeenth century brought more clearly and relentlessly into focus the image of the world as a moral chaos, *fortuna*'s realm, than did Robert Burton. His *Anatomy of Melancholy* has recently been depicted as an essay in profound pessimism, 'a self-consuming artifact', repeatedly rekindling hope in the reader only to douse and extinguish it. In this view, his utopia is merely another illusion, mocking the incapacity of a flawed human nature ever to erect a society in which humanity and social life might be given meaning. The world is mad and the madness is universal. There is no escape from it.[1]

Yet such an interpretation misses the point in relation to both Burton and the nature of utopia. Madness does prevail in the nightmare world which Burton depicts, but it is not universal, for, if it were, how would we be able to distinguish it? There must be a standard of sanity by which madness may be recognised as such. Every delineation of the disease reflects a conceptualisation of health. The diagnosis of the world's madness presupposes – even if only in the mortician's mind – a sanity which is repelled, dismayed and downcast by it. And in his *Anatomy* that mind seeks to depict a sane alternative world. What is of import here is that Burton, examining several alternatives, sifts through ideal-society modes, illuminating and discarding them, only to settle finally on utopia. Stanley Fish has characterised that utopia as a self-consuming device which mocks its own pretensions, since 'if human nature enters, all that the Utopia was designed to exclude enters with it'.[2] But this is to conflate utopia and the

---

[1] Stanley E. Fish, *Self-Consuming Artifacts: The Experience of Seventeenth Century Literature* (Los Angeles, 1972), Chapter 6. A new interest in Burton's utopianism was stimulated by the following studies: J. W. Allen, *English Political Thought 1603–1644* (London, 1938), Part III, Chapter 8; V. Dupont, *L'Utopie et le Roman Utopique dans la Littérature Anglaise* (Toulouse, 1941), Section II, Chapter 4; B. Evans, *The Psychiatry of Robert Burton* (New York, 1944); J. Max Patrick, 'Robert Burton's Utopianism', *Philological Quarterly*, 27:4 (1948), pp. 345–58. Patrick emphasised the neglect of Burton's utopia and claimed that it 'is the first proper utopia written in English by an Englishman'. See also Pierre Mesnard, 'L'Utopie de Robert Burton', in Jean Lameere (ed.), *Les Utopies à la Renaissance* (Paris, 1963), pp. 73–88.

[2] Fish, *Self-Consuming Artifacts*, p. 326.

perfect moral commonwealth, a distinction which is insisted upon by Burton himself. His utopia is not premised on the sanity of its inhabitants, rather it is like an asylum which seeks to restrain and constrain its patients, to create a world of stability and 'normalcy' in which, and through which, they might be healed.

Despite the fame, even notoriety, of his work Burton remains an obscure figure. Apart from the unreliable gossip of sources like Wood and Fuller, we know little of his life beyond the bare details and what Burton chooses to tell us himself. He was born in 1577, the fourth of nine children, into a moderately prosperous and long-established family at Lindley in Leicestershire. In the *Anatomy*, Burton claims to have been 'a grammar scholar' at Sutton Coldfield in Warwickshire, but he evinced no relish for recollections of his schoolboy days.[3] He received his B.A. from the University of Oxford after a strangely prolonged undergraduate career and after transferring from Brasenose to Christ Church in 1599. Christ Church, in fact, became his home and he lived there until his death in 1640. There could hardly have been a more settled existence. After graduation he was made a Fellow of his college and supplemented his income with a couple of ecclesiastical livings. He enjoyed a comfortable, quiet and secure way of life.[4] The fact that he was three times appointed clerk of the market in Oxford hardly makes him 'a man of affairs'. He was a scholar, a bibliophile, an academic. He published a number of Latin verses in various volumes put out by the college or university of which he was a member. In 1606 he wrote a play, *Philosophaster*, which was acted at Christ Church in 1617 but it was an event which scarcely breached the walls of Burton's chosen community. The play was not published until 1862. But in 1621, at the age of forty-four, Burton published his *Anatomy of Melancholy*. It was an immediate and enormous success and he devoted the rest of his life to its revision and expansion. The work became over half as long again as its original form. Five editions came out in the twenty years before his death, and a further three in the later seventeenth century.[5]

[3] Robert Burton, *The Anatomy of Melancholy*, edited with an introduction by Holbrook Jackson, 3 vols. (London, 1932), vol. II, p. 63. This Everyman edition still provides the most useful text of the *Anatomy*. It is based on a collation of the fifth and sixth editions and incorporates the work of A. R. Shilleto in his edition of 1893 and the corrections of Edward Bensly.

[4] A copy of Burton's will can be found in F. Madan (ed.), 'Robert Burton and *The Anatomy of Melancholy*', *Oxford Bibliographical Society Proceedings and Papers*, 1, part 1 (1922–6), pp. 218–20.

[5] For the development of the work over its various editions, see Sir William Osler, 'Robert Burton – The Man, His Book, His Library', in Madan (ed.), 'Burton and *The Anatomy of Melancholy*', pp. 161–71; Edward Bensly, 'Some Alterations and Errors in Successive Editions of *The Anatomy of Melancholy*', in *ibid.*, pp. 198–215; Edward Gordon Duff and F. Madan, 'Notes on the Bibliography of the Oxford editions of the *Anatomy*', in *ibid.*, pp. 191–7.

Neglected in the eighteenth century except as a source for plagiarists, the *Anatomy* enjoyed a revival of interest in the 1800s which has never diminished. Since 1800 there have been over sixty more editions and reprints of the work. 'Scarce any book of philology', wrote Thomas Fuller of it, 'in our land hath in so short a time passed so many impressions.' According to Anthony Wood, the original publisher 'got an estate by it'.[6]

Part of the success of Burton's *Anatomy of Melancholy* must be attributable to the fashionable nature of the affliction in the late sixteenth and early seventeenth centuries. He 'offered a book on melancholy to a melancholy generation'.[7] But this is by no means a complete explanation for there were several other studies of melancholia available to the interested, and indeed Burton must be seen as heavily indebted to writers in this tradition such as Timothy Bright, Thomas Wright and Thomas Adams.[8] Moreover, his was a radical and satirical redefinition of a fashionable affliction as madness. A great deal of Burton's popularity is attributable to his skill as a writer of prose; more, perhaps, to the breadth and curiosity with which he approached his topic. For him, melancholy was more than a disease, it was a universal affliction, an index of the human condition. So that, in his study of the causes, symptoms and cure of melancholy, Burton offered his reader a survey of the physical and spiritual condition of man, a description of the state of society, and what amounted to a framework for the interpretation of history. Above all, while rejecting panaceas he never failed to leave his reader with some shred of comfort. Palliatives were always at hand. The whole thing was wrapped up in an astonishing display of erudition. Burton offered multiple authorities for every statement, however grotesque, and by his own standards there had hardly been a better authenticated textbook.

In the section of his work devoted to defining melancholy,[9] Burton offered a variety of definitions without seeming to fix on any particular one. He certainly associated its physical manifestations with 'black choler' and its psychological with fear or sorrow 'without a cause'. Earlier in the work, when dealing with bodily humours, Burton wrote, 'Melancholy, cold and dry, thick, black and sour, begotten of the most feculent part of

---

[6] Thomas Fuller, *The Worthies of England*, edited by John Freeman (London, 1952), p. 321; Anthony Wood, *Athenae Oxonienses*, edited by Philip Bliss (London, 1813), vol. II, p. 653.

[7] Lawrence Babb, *Sanity in Bedlam: A Study of Robert Burton's Anatomy of Melancholy* (Michigan, 1959), p. 3. See also the same author's *The Elizabethan Malady: A Study of Melancholia in English Literature from 1580 to 1642* (Michigan, 1951). The explanation of the malady's fashionableness lay partly in its association with genius.

[8] William R. Mueller, *The Anatomy of Robert Burton's England* (Berkeley and Los Angeles, 1952), Chapters 2 and 3.

[9] *Anatomy*, vol. I, pp. 169–70.

nourishment, and purged from the spleen, is a bridle to the other two hot humours, blood and choler, preserving them in the blood, and nourishing the bones.'[10] This is impossible to translate into modern terms. Lawrence Babb's definition of the renaissance view of melancholy as 'a psychiatric term denoting a morbid depression of mind'[11] is too limited. As Burton's study makes abundantly clear, melancholy was for him a physical as much as a psychological phenomenon. The important thing, perhaps, is that, in terms of symptomatology, it remained an elastic term.

Burton's analysis of the human condition began conventionally enough with the fall of man. Man, 'the most excellent and noble creature of the world', was now 'so much obscured by his fall that (some few relics excepted) he is inferior to a beast'. 'The impulsive cause of all these miseries in man, this privation or destruction of God's image, the cause of death and diseases, of all temporal and eternal punishments, was the sin of our first parent Adam, in eating of the forbidden fruit, by the devil's instigation and allurement.' In this sense, the whole work should be seen as a study of one aspect of the consequences of original sin and the fall of man. For Burton, melancholy 'is the character of mortality'. Moreover, as man through sin has corrupted the universe, so melancholy afflicts not men alone but 'vegetable and sensibles', 'Kingdoms, provinces, and politic bodies'.[12]

Having established the 'impulsive cause' of melancholy, Burton turned to the instrumental causes. These he found

as diverse as the infirmities themselves; stars, heavens, elements, etc., and all those creatures which God hath made, are armed against sinners. They were indeed once good in themselves and that they are now many of them pernicious unto us, is not in their nature, but our corruption, which hath caused it. For, from the fall of our first parent Adam, they have been changed, the earth accursed, the influence of stars altered, the four elements, beasts, birds, plants, are now ready to offend us.

The bulk of the *Anatomy* was given over to tracing as many of these causes of melancholy in men as possible and to finding defences against them. There is some reference, for example in his discussion of envy and emulation, to the social consequences of the disease, but in the main Burton was concerned with the individual causes, individual symptoms and individual treatment of melancholy in men.[13] It was only when he

---

[10] *Ibid.*, vol. I, p. 148.
[11] Babb, *Sanity in Bedlam*, p. 1. Other definitions are offered by Evans, *Psychiatry of Burton*, p. 62; Osler, 'Burton – Man, Book, Library', pp. 1–3. One of the secondary aspects of melancholy was its association with strong imagination. *Anatomy*, vol. I, p. 159.
[12] *Anatomy*, vol. I, pp. 79, 130–1, 144.
[13] *Ibid.*, vol. I, pp. 266–9; vol. II, pp. 186–9.

came to write the preface to his work that he returned to a discussion of the social manifestations of *melancholia* and their cure.[14]

In the preface, 'Democritus Junior to the Reader', Burton sought to justify and defend his work. The main theme of this justification is the universality of melancholy:

if thou shalt either conceive or climb to see, thou shalt soon perceive that all the world is mad, that it is melancholy, dotes...you shall find that kingdoms and provinces are melancholy, cities and families, all creatures vegetal, sensible and rational, that all sorts, sects, ages, conditions, are out of tune...who is not a fool, melancholy, mad?[15]

In this way Burton returned to the social and political manifestations of melancholia. The origins of his concern in this respect were twofold. In the first place 'kingdoms and provinces' were afflicted on the same basis as any other part of the natural, but degenerate, order. Secondly, however, the melancholic disorder of society intensified the misery of the melancholic individual. The social manifestations of the disease increased the individual's awareness of his alienation, anomie, deepened his melancholy. Whereas More saw the pressures of a maladjusted society compelling men to behave in a way counter to conscience, anti-socially, but still rationally, Burton saw a maladjusted society forcing men to act contrary to reason, as enemies to themselves and ultimately as self-torturers and self-destroyers.

In his discussion of symptoms Burton had suggested, almost off-hand, that melancholy itself might be a symptom – a symptom of sickness in society. As he proceeded with his work, this apparently casual idea seemed to assume more and more importance in his mind, until, by the time he had finished it, it had become one of his dominant thoughts and led him, as a summing up of the whole matter, to propose, in his address to the reader, a remodelling of the whole of society, in the interests of mental hygiene.[16]

His utopia, therefore, sprang out of his concern with melancholy as a universal affliction.

Men could take precautions to protect themselves against the hostility of the natural world which the fall had engendered. Far more difficult to deal with were the mutual hostility and self-destructiveness of men.

We can most part foresee these epidemical diseases, and likely avoid them. Deaths, tempests, plagues, our astrologers foretell us; earthquakes, inun-

---

[14] Babb, *Sanity in Bedlam*, p. 15. Babb suggests that 'the writing of the satirical preface probably did not occur until the *Anatomy* of 1621 was near completion'. The way in which Burton, as Democritus Junior, discussed the main text in his preface would seem to bear this out.

[15] *Anatomy*, vol. I, p. 39; see also, vol. I, pp. 49, 52, 120.

[16] *Evans*, Psychiatry of Burton, p. 91; see also pp. 77, 110; Mueller, *Anatomy of Burton's England*, pp. 9, 25, 33.

dations, ruins of houses, consuming fires, come by little and little, or make some noise beforehand; but these knaveries, impostures, injuries, and villainies of men no art can avoid. We can keep our professed enemies from our cities by gates, walls and towers, defend ourselves from thieves and robbers by watchfulness and weapons; but this malice of men, and their pernicious endeavours, no caution can divert, no vigilancy foresee, we have so many secret plots and devices to mischief one another ... And last of all, that which crucifies us most is our own folly, madness, weakness, want of government, our facility and proneness in yielding to several lusts, in giving way to every passion and perturbation of mind: by which we metamorphose ourselves and degenerate into beasts.[17]

Burton's analysis of the triumph of passion over reason and its effects upon men and the societies in which they live produced some of his most brilliant and incisive writing. Emulation, envy, hatred and faction were endemic to human society.

Every society, corporation and private family is full of it, it takes hold almost of all sorts of men from the prince to the ploughman, even amongst gossips it is to be seen; scarce three in a company but there is siding, faction, emulation betwixt two of them, some *simultas*, jar, private grudge, heart-burning in the midst of them. Scarce two gentlemen dwell together in the country (if they be not near kin or linked in marriage), but there is emulation betwixt them and their servants, some quarrel or some grudge betwixt their wives or children, friends and followers, some contention about wealth, gentry, precedency etc. ...they will stretch beyond their fortunes, callings, and strive so long that they consume their substance in lawsuits, or otherwise in hospitality, feasting, fine clothes, to get a few bombast titles, or *ambitiosa paupertate laboramus omnes*; to outbrave one another they will tire their bodies, macerate their souls, and through contentions or mutual invitations beggar themselves. Scarce two great scholars in an age, but with bitter invectives they fall foul one of the other, and their adherents; Scotists, Thomists, Reals, Nominals, Plato and Aristotle, Galenists and Paracelsians, etc., it holds in all professions.[18]

The dialogue between Democritus and Hippocrates was introduced to provide illustration of the anti-social nature of men's conduct and the conclusion that their behaviour was worse than the instinctive behaviour of animals. 'There is no truth or justice found amongst them, for they daily plead one against another, commit all unlawful actions, condemning God and men, friend and country.' This aggressive competitiveness, malice and self-seeking invaded the fabric of all relationships:

look into courts or private houses. Judges give judgement according to their own advantage, doing manifest wrong to poor innocents to please others. Notaries alter sentences, and for money lose their deeds. Some make false moneys; others counterfeit false weights. Some abuse their parents, yea, corrupt

[17] *Anatomy*, vol. I, pp. 135–6.   [18] *Ibid.*, vol. I, pp. 69–70, 74, 160–2, 267.

their own sisters; others make long libels and pasquils, defaming men of good life, and extol such as are lewd and vicious. Some rob one, some another; magistrates make laws against thieves, and are the veriest thieves themselves. Some kill themselves, others despair not obtaining their desires.

Even love, the basis of civilised life, which 'first united provinces, built cities, and by a perpetual generation makes and preserves mankind, propagates the Church', was debased and corrupted by passion. 'It subverts kingdoms, overthrows cities, towns, families, mars, corrupts, and makes a massacre of men; thunder and lightning, wars, fires, plagues, have not done that mischief to mankind, as this burning lust, this brutish passion.'[19] Thus, even the best of things were turned sour and evil by the wickedness and lack of moderation in men.

In his preface, Burton drew a series of sketches – of, for example, contemporary religion, war, lawyers, hypocrisy, snobbery, ambition, gluttony and faction – to demonstrate the baleful social consequences of the malignity of men. Religion had become an empty profession, devoting its resources to the conflict of bigoted and ignorant extremists. War, initiated by the worst of men for the basest of reasons, had become an accepted part of life: 'nothing so familiar as this hacking and hewing, massacres, murders, desolations; *ignoto coelum clangore remugit*, they care not what mischief they procure, so that they may enrich themselves for the present; they will so long blow the coals of contention, till all the world be consumed with fire'. Soldiers would always be necessary to protect Christian civilisation but thieves, murderers and rapists were not soldiers, not was the glorifying of slaughter martial virtue.

A poor sheep-stealer is hanged for stealing of victuals, compelled peradventure by necessity of that intolerable cold, hunger, and thirst, to save himself from starving: but a great man in office may securely rob whole provinces, undo thousands, pill and poll, oppress *ad libitum*, flay, grind, tyrannize, enrich himself by spoils of the commons, be uncontrollable in his actions, and after all, be recompensed with turgent titles, honoured for his good service, and no man dare find fault, or mutter at it.[20]

This inversion of natural justice was reflected in social attitudes to wealth and poverty. The rich were fawned upon, the poor scorned, irrespective of their personal merits. Lawyers, those 'gowned vultures' as Burton called them, did nothing to redress the balance. 'To see so many lawyers, advocates, so many tribunals, so little justice; so many magistrates, so little care of common good; so many laws, yet never more disorders; *tribunal litium segetem*, the tribunal a labyrinth, so many thousand suits in one court sometimes, so violently followed.' The innocent were condemned under sentence of the guilty. The law was altered under

---

[19] *Ibid.*, vol. I, pp. 49, 51; vol. III, 49.   [20] *Ibid.*, vol. I, pp. 54–6, 59–60, 62.

interpretation. Sentences were prolonged and changed. Offences were excused in great men, while poor men and younger brothers were compelled by hardship to steal and were then executed for it. Men's commercial relations, characterised by social atomism and aggressive competition, typified their relations in general.

What's the market? A place...wherein they cozen one another, a trap; nay, what's the world itself? A vast chaos, a confusion of manners, as fickle as air, *domicilium insanorium*, a turbulent troop full of impurities, a mart of walking spirits, goblins, the theatre of hypocrisy, a shop of knavery...wherein every man is for himself, his private ends, and stands upon his own guard. No charity, love, friendship, fear of God, alliance, affinity, consanguinity, Christianity can contain them, but if they be anyways offended, or that string of commodity be touched, they fall foul... In a word, every man for his own ends. Our *Summum bonum* is commodity, and the goddess we adore *Dea Moneta*, Queen Money, to whom we daily offer sacrifice, which steers our hearts, hands, affections, all...[21]

Hypocrisy, greed, savagery, conformity, gluttony, snobbery, villainy, sloth, ignorance and waste; these characteristics of men were perennial:

our times and persons alter, vices are the same, and ever will be; look how nightingales sang of old, cocks crowed, kine lowed, sheep bleated, sparrows chirped, dogs barked, so do they still; we keep our madness still, play the fool still, *nec dum finitus Orestes*; we are of the same humours and inclinations as our predecessors were; you shall find us all alike, much at one, we and our sons...

In this world values were inverted; the good abhorred, the worthless desired; 'wise men degraded, fools preferred'. It was not virtue, courage, wisdom, integrity or religion, but wealth, fame, place and dignity which were honoured amongst men. History in these circumstances became a mere welter, a confusion of events. Nothing impresses in Burton more than this sense of the passage of time as a disorder of happenings without pattern, purpose or merit.

I hear new news every day, and those ordinary rumours of war, plagues, fires, inundations, thefts, murders, massacres, meteors, comets, spectrums, prodigies, apparitions of towns taken, cities besieged in France, Germany, Turkey, Persia, Poland, etc., daily musters and preparations, and such-like, which these tempestuous times afford, battles fought, so many men slain, monomachies, shipwrecks, piracies, and sea-fights, peace, leagues, stratagems and fresh alarums. A vast confusion of vows, wishes, actions, edicts, petitions, lawsuits, pleas, laws, proclamations, complaints, grievances are daily brought to our ears. New books every day, pamphlets, currantoes...

And so it goes on. In a day of mass media and global communications, we

[21] *Ibid.*, vol. I, pp. 62–3, 64, 65.

are perhaps familiar with the sense of moral hopelessness engendered by
the chaotic disorder of this kind of continuum, but the image here is that
familiar to Burton's contemporaries of a secular world in which *fortuna*
alone held sway:

the world itself is a maze, a labyrinth of errors, a desert, a wilderness, a den of
thieves, cheaters, etc....in perpetual fear, labour, anguish, we run from one
plague, one mischief, one burden to another...Our towns and cities are but so
many dwellings of human misery...Our villages are like mole-hills, and men
as so many emmets, busy, busy still, going to and fro, in and out and crossing
one anothers projects, as the lines of several sea-cards cut each other in a globe
or map.[22]

It was the necessity to escape this process of time, which, with its disorderly press of confused events, left foolish men no opportunity of learning wisdom, that impelled Burton along the road to his ideal society. He
specifically rejected any attempt to progress by accommodation with the
inverted values of this world.

'Tis an ordinary thing with us to account honest, devout, orthodox, divine,
religious, plain-dealing men idiots, asses, that cannot or will not lie and dis-
semble, adapt themselves to the station in which they were born, make good
bargains, supplant, thrive, fawn upon their patrons, learn the usual methods of
getting on, be scrupulous in the observance of laws, manners, customs, praise
in glowing terms, defend with vigour, adopt others' opinions, doubt nothing,
believe everything, endure everything, resent nothing, and do all the other
things which lead to promotion and safe position, which make a man fortunate
beyond all question and truly wise according to our nations...

But these 'Herodian temporizing statesmen, politick Machiavellians', are
condemned by God and scripture.[23]

The immediate context of Burton's utopian design was thus the discussion of melancholy in 'Kingdoms, provinces, and politic bodies'.[24] But
in approaching his utopian cure for this disorder he was inevitably led to
face alternative forms of ideal society. Unlike Bacon, his choice was clear
and uncompromising. His opening insistence on the fall led him to see
fallen nature as so degenerate that an arcadian vision of natural harmony
was out of the question for him.[25] At the same time Burton's work is
almost devoid of millenarian anticipation. Just before he began the description of his utopia he dismissed the notion of social salvation at the hands
of a *deus ex machina*. 'It were to be wished', he wrote, in a mood of
reverie,

[22] *Ibid.*, vol. I, pp. 18–19, 53, 54–67, 68, 274; vol. II, 190–2.
[23] *Ibid.*, vol. I, p. 42. See also, vol. I, pp. 54, 281; vol. II, pp. 191–2.
[24] *Ibid.*, vol. I, pp. 79–107.
[25] *Ibid.*, vol. I, pp. 130–6; vol. II, p. 189. Cf. Dupont, *L'Utopie et le Roman
Utopique*, p. 159.

we had some visitor, or, if wishing would serve, one had such a ring or rings as Timolaus desired in Lucian, by virtue of which he should be as strong as ten thousand men, or an army of giants, go invisible open gates and castle doors, have what treasure he would, transport himself in an instant to what place he desired, alter affections, cure all manner of diseases, that he might range over the world, and reform all distressed states and persons, as he would himself.

Burton played around for some time with the miracles of statesmanship which might be achieved under the aegis of such a wonder-worker, but in the end he brings us down to earth again. 'These are vain, absurd, and ridiculous wishes not to be hoped: all must be as it is.'[26]

Since 'we converse here with men, not with gods', Burton also rejected the perfect moral commonwealth solution and he did so repeatedly and explicitly.

In fine, if princes would do justice, judges be upright, clergymen truly devout, and so live as they teach, if great men would not be so insolent, if soldiers would quietly defend us, the poor would be patient, rich men would be liberal and humble, citizens honest, magistrates meek, superiors would give good example, subjects peaceable, young men would stand in awe: if parents would be kind to their children, and they again obedient to their parents, brethren agree amongst themselves, enemies be reconciled, servants trusty to their masters, virgins chaste, wives modest, husbands would be loving and less jealous: if we could imitate Christ and his apostles, live after God's laws, these mischiefs would not so frequently happen amongst us; but being most part so irreconcilable as we are, perverse, proud, insolent, factious, and malicious, prone to contention, anger and revenge, of such fiery spirits, so captious, impious, irreligious, so opposite to virtue, void of grace, how should it otherwise be?[27]

Having disposed of alternative ideals Burton proceeded then to build his utopia. Admitting the anti-social behaviour characteristic of men, their folly and their misery, Burton declared, 'I will yet, to satisfy and please myself, make an Utopia of mine own, a New Atlantis, a poetical commonwealth of mine own, in which I will freely domineer, build cities, make laws, statutes as I list myself.'[28]

Bad location was one of the factors which Burton saw as causing melancholy in kingdoms. Poor soil, bad climate, aggressive neighbours could all induce misery in a state. He therefore suggested, in half-serious tone, that his utopia should be founded in any one of a number of remote or mysterious places – *Terra Australis Incognita*, on an island in the South Pacific, in the American interior or in northern Asia – but that it must be

26 *Anatomy*, vol. I, pp. 96–7. Cf. Fish, *Self-Consuming Artifacts*, p. 348.
27 *Anatomy*, vol. I, p. 106; vol. II, p. 202. See also, vol. I, pp. 102, 269.
28 *Ibid.*, vol. I, p. 97.

about forty-five degrees latitude to enjoy a temperate climate. The utopian state was to be divided into twelve or thirteen provinces. At the centre of each province a metropolis was to be set up, commanding a provincial area of some twelve miles radius. No village was to be allowed within six to eight miles of the city, unless it was a port. All necessaries were to be sold in the metropolis. There were to be 'no market towns, markets or fairs, for they do but beggar cities'. Moreover, the siting, layout and function of the cities were subject to a uniform pattern of regulation. All the cities were to be built on waterways: 'and for their form, regular, round, square, or long square, with fair, broad and straight streets, houses uniform, built of brick and stone'. Burton listed exhaustively the public buildings and facilities with which such towns were to be provided – churches, cemeteries, prisons, market places, courts of justice, public halls, armouries, public gardens, theatres, recreation areas and hospitals. There were to be few or no suburbs and only coastal or frontier towns were to be fortified.[29] We see at once the utopian's concern with order, neatness, uniformity and completeness and, less typically, an interest in the economic viability of towns large enough to function as civilising centres.

William R. Mueller has remarked that 'Burton does not have much to say about the political organisation of his Utopia'.[30] This is neither true nor false, because it misses the point. In Burton's utopia, as in others, there is no 'political organisation' because there are no politics. Laws are not made and changed in utopia. All necessary law is incorporated in the original design. Burton himself was the sufficient lawgiver.[31] On the other hand, like other utopians, he realised that law and disorder were not mutually exclusive and that, for disorder to be overcome, law had to be administered and enforced effectively. Consequently he has a good deal to say about the administrative organisation, the bureaucracy, of his utopia.

Basic to the administrative system are what Burton calls 'public governors', appointed in each city. Amongst them are 'treasurers, aediles, quaestors, overseers of pupils, widows' goods, and all public houses, etc.'. These people were to render annual accounts of their performance, expenses and receipts. Only 'fit officers to each place' were to be chosen. Above this administrative task-force were set the 'higher officers and governors of each city'. These were not to be 'poor tradesmen and mean artificers, but noblemen and gentlemen, which shall be tied to residence in those towns they dwell next, at such set times and seasons'.[32] At first

---

[29] *Ibid.*, vol. 1, pp. 80, 98–9. Burton was particularly contemptuous of English towns. See, *ibid.*, vol. 1, pp. 91–2.

[30] Mueller, *Anatomy of Burton's England*, p. 45.

[31] Cf. J. W. Allen, *English Political Thought*, pp. 90–1. 'He does not tell us how law is made in his commonwealth; and there was no need to say. He was, I imagine, well aware that he himself was its only possible lawgiver.'

[32] *Anatomy*, vol. 1, pp. 99–100.

glance, this might be regarded as simply an endorsement of social hier-
archy and conventional status structures. In fact it was almost the reverse.
Burton's emphasis was hierarchical but not in the conventional sense.
Status was in large part to become a function of merit and not *vice versa*.
He was insisting that municipal affairs must not be looked down upon by
a country-based élite but that they must take their full part in town life.
The terms upon which they did so, however, would not be the old ones.
Magistrates, and indeed all officials were to be chosen from amongst those
qualified by examination: 'and such again not to be eligible, or capable
of magistracies, honours, offices, except they be sufficiently qualified for
learning, manners, and that by strict approbation or deputed examinations'.
Moreover, scholars were to be given priority over soldiers. All officials
were to submit annual reports and could lose office for misbehaviour.
They were to inspect each others' work in order to prevent bureaucratic
oppression. There was to be no holding of offices in plurality and no
deputising of the performance of duties. Above all, merit and good
performance were to be the criteria of reward: 'let him be of what condition he will, in all offices, actions, he that deserves best shall have best'.[33]

Burton dismissed the 'utopian parity' espoused by Andreae, Campanella,
Bacon and Plato, as 'a kind of government to be wished for rather than
effected'. He proposed instead 'several orders, degrees of nobility, and
those hereditary'. Younger brothers, of whom, of course, Burton was one,
were to be provided for by pensions or 'so qualified, brought up in some
honest calling, they shall be able to live of themselves'. Baronies were to
be related to the ownership of land. Those who lost their land, lost their
title, which went to the new holders of the land. While some titles were to
remain hereditary, others were to be disposed of by election or gift:

given to the worthiest and best deserving both in war and peace, as a reward of
their worth and good service, as so many goals for all to aim at...and
encouragement to others. For I hate these severe, unnatural harsh, German,
French and Venetian decrees, which exclude plebeians from honours; be they
never so wise, rich, virtuous, valiant and well qualified, they must not be
patricians, but keep their own rank; this is *naturae bellum inferre*, odious to
God and men, I abhor it.

Burton emphatically believed in social hierarchy as both natural and
divine, but in the critical tradition of renaissance humanism he held that
a truly natural hierarchy must be based on virtue and merit.[34]

Of central government, Burton indicated a monarchical form but it is
clear, from what is omitted rather than from what is said, that the monarch

---

[33] *Ibid.*, vol. i, pp. 103–4, 106. Burton believed that he was following Chinese and
Venetian practice in the appointment of public officials.
[34] *Ibid.*, vol. i, p. 101; vol. ii, p. 170.

is a mere figurehead. The main function of central government appears to be the management of the national economy. Officials, known as supervisors, were to prepare a national plan for land utilisation and be responsible for its implemention. Apart from this, most of the functions of government were to be conducted on a local level. This was certainly true of judicial administration. Judges and officers, sitting three to a bench, were to act as arbitrators in each village, town and province. They were chosen by lot and not allowed 'to continue still in the same office'. Anyone bringing a suit had to deposit a pledge which was forfeited if his action was shown to be wrongly or maliciously brought. Alternatively, the suitor could have his case submitted to a committee with power to approve the issue for consideration in the courts. All parties' names were normally to be suppressed by the court and no case was to be pending for over a year. Burton was clearly aware of how existing legal procedures, technicalities and sheer delay could be used to wear down opponents and pervert justice. There were to be 'Few laws, but those severely kept, plainly put down, and in the mother tongue, that every man may understand.' As far as possible, every man was to plead his own cause. Lawyers, regarded by Burton with the highest suspicion, were not to exceed a certain number and were 'to be maintained out of the common treasure, no fees to be given or taken upon pain of losing their places; or if they do, very small fees, and when the cause is fully ended'.[35]

One of the most striking things in Burton's utopia is his insistence on the full utilisation of all economic resources and the erection of an apparatus of economy management in order to accomplish this. Certainly, the maximisation of available utilities was a more clear-cut theme with Burton than it was with Bacon. Earlier in the preface, Democritus Junior had deplored the economic backwardness of England, manifest in the paucity and meanness of her towns and attributable to the idleness of her people.[36] 'I will not have a barren acre in all my territories, not so much as the tops of the mountains: where nature fails, it shall be supplied by art...' All land was to be enclosed, 'for that which is common, and every man's, is no man's'. But this was to be accomplished without depopulation or oppression. The process was to be in the hands of supervisors 'that shall be appointed for that purpose'. Their first function was to draw up a scheme for employing the land to maximum advantage, 'to see what reformation ought to be had in all places, what is amiss, how to help it. *Et quid quaeque ferat regio, et quid quaeque recuset*, what ground is aptest for wood, what for corn, what for cattle, gardens, orchards, fish-

---

[35] *Ibid.*, vol. I, pp. 100–3. The last provision also held good of physicians and surgeons.
[36] *Ibid.*, vol. I, pp. 86–93. On Burton as a full-employment utopian see Pierre Mesnard, 'L'Utopie de Robert Burton', p. 84.

ponds, etc.' The same officials were then to make a 'charitable division' of land in every village, to apportion land for the lords' demesnes, to allocate tenancies, to arrange the particular functions of specific pieces of land, and to lay down the precise details of how that land was to be managed. Tenancies were to be arranged on long leases with certain fines and rents to encourage tenants to improve their lands.[37] Burton's sweeping proposals, while technically appearing to preserve the position of the landlord, so fundamental to the nature of seventeenth-century society, would in fact have destroyed their influence by placing all questions of land tenure and management in the hands of an official, bureaucratic class. In this respect Burton's utopia was far more radical than some commentators have suggested and it is interesting that he should have made his most radical proposals in the name of economic efficiency.

Burton recognised that there was little point in increasing output without adequate transport facilities to promote marketing and exchange. Consequently, 'All common highways, bridges, banks, corrivations of water, acqueducts, channels, public works, buildings, etc., out of a common stock, [were] curiously maintained and kept in repair...' Standard weights and measures were to be established. Prices of all commodities, including corn, were to be regulated and private monopolies were forbidden. In the towns each trade was to be confined to a certain district. In addition, 'Every city shall have a peculiar trade or privilege by which it shall be chiefly maintained.' Parents were to bring their children up in their own trade and trading companies and fraternities were approved of. In these ways Burton sought for stability and balance in employment patterns. As regards foreign trade, he proposed that there should be no duty on imported necessities and heavy duties on imported luxuries.[38]

Brokers, takers of pawns, biting usurers, I will not admit; yet because...we converse here with men, not with gods, and for the hardness of men's hearts, I will tolerate some kind of usury. If we were honest, I confess, *si probi essemus*, we should have no use of it, but being as it is, we must necessarily admit it.

Accordingly, only orphans, maids and widows were allowed to take interest on the use of their money, and, even so, were only allowed to lend through a municipal bank, 'and those so approved, not to let it out apart, but to bring their money to a common bank which shall be allowed in every city'. The maximum rate of interest was set at eight per cent, but the rate on particular loans was to be set by 'the supervisors'. On the other side, borrowing was restricted to 'merchants, young tradesmen, such as

[37] *Anatomy*, vol. I, pp. 100–1. On Burton's managed economy compare Dupont, *L'Utopie et le Roman Utopique*, pp. 162–3.
[38] *Anatomy*, vol. I, pp. 100, 102, 106.

stand in need, or know honestly how to employ it'. Again their applications must be approved by 'the supervisors'.[39] Faced with a social evil Burton's approach was not evasive nor exhortatory but regulatory.

As material resources were to be fully utilised and accounted for, so were people. 'I will suffer no beggars, rogues, vagabonds, or idle persons at all, that cannot give an account of their lives how they maintain themselves.' The impotent poor were to be maintained in 'several hospitals'. The married but infirm were to receive outdoor relief but the able bodied poor were to be 'enforced to work'.[40] On the other hand, while work, for those able to perform it, was obligatory, provision was made for leisure, although once more in a noticeably controlled way. 'As *all conditions shall be tied to their task*, so none shall be overtired, but have their set times of recreations and holidays, *indulgere genio*, feasts and merry meetings, even to the meanest artificer, or basest servant, *once a week* to sing or dance (though not all at once), or do whatsoever he shall please. . .'[41]

Surgeons and physicians, like lawyers, were to be maintained at public expense and not normally allowed to take fees. Similarly the provision of public hospitals for children, orphans, old people, the sick and the lunatic, was to be made out of the public purse and not left to the whims of private benefactors. In addition, these welfare facilities were to be universally available to all who stood in need. Accordingly, the state took over responsibility for its citizens' physical as well as legal and economic welfare. It provided clean water, 'common granaries', relief for the poor, aged and sick, employment opportunities and a reasonable standard of living for all. It was, in a very real sense, a welfare state.[42]

Apparently, in utopia, the church would be set in charge of its own house once more. There was to be an episcopalian hierarchy for the maintenance of ecclesiastical discipline, but there were to be no impropriations and no lay patrons. No parish was to contain over a thousand 'auditors' and the rectors of benefices were to be chosen by examination 'out of the universities'. Burton was a cleric and scholar who at times resented his lack of preferment and it is not surprising that he should have held such views. He was extremely critical of the church, its methods of preferment and the generally poor quality of the clergy. The latter he saw as a product of the failure of the universities and of the educational system generally.

[39] *Ibid.*, vol. I, p. 106.

[40] *Ibid.*, vol. I, p. 104. Burton was almost obsessed with idleness which he regarded as a national curse and 'the badge of gentry'. See, e.g., vol. I, pp. 88, 242, 244; vol. II, p. 70. For the ambivalence of Burton's attitude to poverty see Mueller, *Anatomy of Burton's England*, Chapter 4.

[41] *Anatomy*, vol. I, p. 105. My italics.

[42] *Ibid.*, vol. I, pp. 99, 103. Impressive as Burton's welfare state was, I cannot find that he provided for the payment of old age pensions. Cf. Osler, 'Burton – Man, Book, Library', p. 174.

In his utopia, universities were not mentioned at all; instead he proposed a substantial expansion of tertiary education with the establishment, in every town, of colleges of mathematicians, musicians and actors, alchemists, physicians, artists, 'that all arts and sciences may be sooner perfected and better learned'. Public historiographers were to be 'informed and appointed by the State to register all famous acts, and not by each insufficient scribbler, partial or parasitical pedant, as in our times'. In addition public schools 'of all kinds, singing, dancing, fencing, etc.' were to be set up. In them grammar and languages, taught by conversation, were to be a principal part of the curriculum. Also, perhaps as part of the public education system in its widest sense, Burton, like Bacon, suggested, 'I will have certain ships sent out for new discoveries every year, and some discreet men appointed to travel into all neighbour countries by land, which shall observe what artificial inventions and good laws are in other countries, customs, alterations, or aught else concerning war or peace, which may tend to the common good.'[43]

The provision of education, work and a reasonable standard of physical and material security were clearly instrumental in preserving social order. Beyond this, however, Burton provided specific rules for the repair and maintenance of social discipline. Drunkards were forbidden wine or strong drink for a year. Bankrupts were publicly shamed. Debtors were to be imprisoned for one year and, if they remained in debt at the end of that period, they were to be hanged. Those who committed sacrilege would lose their hands; perjurers and false witnesses their tongues. Murderers and adulterers should suffer the death penalty. Thieves would only be punished with death for persistent offences, otherwise they would be condemned to service in the galleys or the mines or to personal slavery. The concern for social order behind these repressive measures naturally extended beyond merely dealing with crime. No man was to be allowed to wear weapons in the city. This could clearly be justified in terms of law and the prevention of physical violence but it also overlaps into Burton's insistence on uniformity of dress. 'The same attire shall be kept, and that proper to several callings, by which they shall be distinguished.' Similarly, he prohibited conspicuous expenditure, particularly on lavish funeral display. It was both a foolish form of ostentation and a source of social friction.[44]

Utopian marriage arrangements were treated by Burton in the context of population control. People were another economic resource which had to be managed if maximum economic benefit were to be realised. No man

[43] *Anatomy*, vol. 1, pp. 99, 102.

[44] *Ibid.*, vol. 1, pp. 105–6. For conspicuous expenditure on early-seventeenth-century funerals see, Lawrence Stone, *The Crisis of the Aristocracy 1558–1641* (Oxford, 1965), Chapter 10.

was to marry until he was twenty-five, no woman until she was twenty, unless a dispensation was granted. When they reached marriageable age poverty was to be no bar to matrimony, 'but all shall be rather enforced than hindered'. The deformed and those likely to transmit hereditary diseases were forbidden to marry but for all others marriage was encouraged. Existing dowry customs were scrapped and dowries were only to be paid on the authority of the supervisors. The operative principle here was designed to balance out natural inequalities and make all females equally attractive. The 'foul' were to have large dowries, the fair none at all. On the death of one of the marriage partners, the other was not allowed to remarry for six months. Surplus population was to be siphoned off by colonisation.[45]

Whilst a great critic of warfare, as initiated and conducted in contemporary Europe, Burton was by no means a pacifist. He believed that a war in defence of Christian civilisation would be justifiable. In his utopia, men, money and naval forces were set in continual defensive readiness. They were put into action only 'upon urgent occasion'. Offensive wars were only waged if 'the cause be very just', and in all warfare the utopian armies were to proceed with moderation. There is a good deal that is question-begging and unsatisfactory in this and it has been remarked, with some justice, that Burton's utopian remarks on war fall decidedly flat after his brilliant and incisive critique of contemporary warfare.[46] In fact there were no utopian arrangements for warfare in the first edition of the *Anatomy*. The section was developed in the second and third editions.

Whatever our sense of dissatisfaction with this section of the utopia, it was at this point that Burton broke off. 'To prosecute the rest', he explained, 'would require a volume.' And he turned from the question of melancholy in kingdoms and states to a discussion of melancholy in families. Burton, then, suggested that his utopian design was unfinished but it remains far more complete than the longer fragment left by Bacon. The utopian section is the most sustained piece of non-derivative writing in the whole of the *Anatomy of Melancholy*. It is the longest section in which Burton communicated his own thoughts in his own words without dependence on the support of a multitude of authorities. What is equally significant, perhaps, is that for such a garrulous writer the description of his utopia is a model of succinctness. He has packed such a considerable amount of information into so few pages, that it is difficult to paraphrase; impossible to condense.

Burton was certainly preoccupied with his utopian design and gave considerable attention to its revision. Between the first (1621) and the

---

[45] *Anatomy*, vol. 1, p. 105.
[46] *Ibid.*, vol. 1, pp. 106–7. See also, for example, vol. 1, pp. 55–62.

fifth (1638) editions, he increased the text of the *Anatomy* by almost two-thirds, but over the same time he almost tripled the length of the utopian section. In other words, the relative importance of the utopia to the work as a whole grew.[47] Moreover, Burton was conscious of conducting his ideal-society exercise within a utopian tradition. He referred to the works of Andreae, Campanella, Bacon and More in establishing his intellectual patrimony. More in particular meets with his approval on numerous occasions and Burton belongs rightly in the Lucianic-Erasmian tradition of renaissance humanism which fostered More and Andreae.[48] Yet there are signs that his utopia was more than merely an intellectual or literary device. He believed that there were periods and nations in which the social aspects of melancholy had been overcome, and that, on occasion, this had been the result of abrupt and radical change. In such a way had England been brought from barbarity to civility by the Romans, and, in the same way, Burton suggested that the English could, if they were willing, bring civility to Ireland and Virginia. The Low Countries offered him a contemporary example of what could be achieved by intelligence and industry in the most unpropitious of circumstances. By contrast, the English exhibited lethargy, indolence and lack of imagination and the result was meanness, misery and melancholy.[49]

It must not be forgotten, of course, that the context of Burton's utopian design was the problem of melancholy in states and nations. The perfect society, as visualised by Burton, was designed to combat the causes: the litigious depredations of corrupt lawyers, the ostentatious display of wealth, the vagaries of an open market, the frustrations of unrewarded merit, the depressing effects of grinding poverty, disease and insecurity; all these were curbed, checked and eliminated in utopia. Even the hereditary transmission of mental and physical disorder was, as far as possible, ended through the regulation of marriage. But, in his search for a solution to the social aspects of *melancholia*, Burton made a clear choice of utopia. He rejected arcadia, the perfect moral commonwealth, and a *deus ex machina* in favour of a managed society, a utopia. The managed society he designed had a planned economy, a controlled and supervised market, public provision against personal misfortune, elaborate civic amenities, and state control of leisure, marriage, dress, and work. Moreover, the provision of an efficient and effective bureaucracy, particularly in the shape of supervisors and governors, meant that, whereas in England good regulations lapsed, in utopia they were enforced. 'We have excellent laws enacted,

[47] Patrick, 'Burton's Utopianism', pp. 348–9.
[48] Cf. Babb, *Sanity in Bedlam*, pp. 52, 108; Douglas Bush, *English Literature in the Early Seventeenth Century 1600–1660* (2nd edition, Oxford, 1962), p. 301; Mesnard, 'L'Utopie de Robert Burton', p. 88.
[49] *Anatomy*, vol. I, pp. 86, 88–9, 94; vol. II, p. 80.

you will say, severe statutes, houses of correction, etc., to small purpose it seems; it is not houses will serve, but cities of correction.'[50] Of course, this extension of social discipline until it embraced the whole of men's lives involved an almost complete loss of liberty.[51] To Burton this was rather illusory than lamentable. 'Servitude, loss of liberty, punishment, are no such miseries as they are held to be: we are slaves and servants the best of all...'[52] Freedom from disorder and sloth, the twin causes of social melancholy, might well be paid for in the coin of personal liberty.

[50] *Ibid.*, vol. I, pp. 90, 92–3.
[51] Cf. J. W. Allen's description of Burton's utopia. 'Everything in his Utopia is closely and governmentally regulated: not only the use of land and the conditions of its holding, but trade and prices, buying and selling, lending and borrowing, profession and occupation, marriage and even dress.' Allen, *English Political Thought*, p. 92.
[52] *Anatomy*, vol. II, p. 173.

Sir Francis Bacon and the ideal society

We were come into a land of angels, which did appear to us daily and prevent us with comforts, which we thought not of, much less expected.

Bacon, *New Atlantis* (1627)

We live not in Plato his Commonwealth, but in times wherein abuses have got the upper hand.

Bacon, *Speech upon the case of Sir Thomas Parry* (1614)

The subtlety of nature is greater many times over than the subtlety of the senses and understanding; so that all those specious meditations, speculations, and glosses in which men indulge are quite from the purpose, only there is no one by to observe it.

Bacon, *The New Organon* (1620) Book I, x

'Ambivalence' has been seen as one of the central characteristics of the social thought of Sir Francis Bacon.[1] He is the 'preremptory royalist' who helped to provide an intellectual basis for 'the English Revolution'; the scientific modernist consigning all past philosophy to oblivion yet unable to shake off the mental habits of the scholastic, the jargon of the alchemist and magician; the analyst of the imperfections of the human mind, carefully planning the retrieval of its dominion over nature; a constructer of self-consuming artefacts; pessimistic and optimistic, conservative and radical, timid and bold, a schemer tainted with corruption and yet possessed of a kind of integrity; Bacon, it appears, was all these things. So, likewise, his *New Atlantis* contains a central ambiguity: a society dominated by scientists who have the duty and the right to decide what information shall be made available to the state, but yet cannot be trusted not to lie and distort. The *New Atlantis* has the assured tone of Bacon's most confident works and yet he never completed it. His preoccupation with ideal-society images and with utopian notions remained so extremely ambivalent that it enables us to see at once the limitations of our ideal-society types, the way in which in practice they may overlap, the use to which they can be turned in analysing the complexities of his social thought, and the exigent nature of the commitments imposed by the choice of a particular mode of ideal society.

Although the *New Atlantis* is well known as a 'utopia', it will be necessary to describe the work in considerable detail. There are two reasons for this somewhat arduous procedure. The first is that most commentaries have been unbalanced in their emphasis on the 'scientific' aspects of Bacon's ideal society. A detailed consideration of the work will show that Bacon's visualisation of an ideal society was not merely intended to serve as a backdrop to an imaginative description of his scientific schemes. The second reason is that only through a detailed consideration of the *New*

[1] For ambivalence as the key theme see, Anne Righter, 'Francis Bacon', in B. Vickers (ed.), *Essential Articles for the Study of Francis Bacon* (Hampden, Conn., 1968); Hiram Haydn, *The Counter-Renaissance* (New York, 1960), Chapter 4. See also Stanley E. Fish, *Self-Consuming Artifacts: The Experience of Seventeenth Century Literature* (Los Angeles, 1972), Chapter 2.

Atlantis can both the scope and the crucial limitations of Bacon's approach to his ideal society be made clear.

Like More's *Utopia*, the *New Atlantis* may usefully, but somewhat arbitrarily, be seen in form as a drama.[2] This approach has been used here because, although in some ways unwieldly, it does enable the work to be broken down into clear phases. Seen as a drama, the work may be divided into a Prologue and two Acts, as follows:

I. *Prologue* – the voyage to New Atlantis

II. *Act One* – New Atlantis and the outside world

    i. Scene one   –   initial reception

    ii. Scene two   –   the visit of a person of place, conditions of entry fulfilled

    iii. Scene three   –   the Stranger's House

    iv. Scene four   –   the narrator's address to his fellow travellers

    v. Scene five   –   the first interview with the governor of the Stranger's House

    vi. Scene six   –   the second interview

    vii. Scene seven   –   the third interview

III. *Act Two* – New Atlantis described

    i. Scene one   –   the Feast of the Family

    ii. Scene two   –   Joabim the Jew

    iii. Scene three   –   the arrival of the Fellow of Salomon's House in Bensalem

    iv. Scene four   –   interview with the Fellow of Salomon's House

In the Prologue the narrator describes how he and his fifty companions arrived at the island of New Atlantis. Having sailed from Peru for China and Japan, they had encountered such contrary winds for so long a period that they had consumed their twelve months' supply of victuals without sighting land and gave themselves up for lost. In despair they prayed to God 'that as in the beginning he discovered the face of the deep and

---

[2] The *New Atlantis* was first published in 1627, the year following Bacon's death, by William Rawley, his chaplain. It appeared, in accordance with Bacon's design, in harness with his essay in natural history, the *Sylva Sylvarum*. It was described, both in its title and in Rawley's preface, as 'A Worke unfinished'. In citing the *New Atlantis*, I shall refer always to the first edition: *New Atlantis: A Worke Unfinished written by the Right Honourable Francis Lord Verulam, Viscount St. Alban* (London, 1627), which was printed and bound with the 1627 edition of the *Sylva Sylvarum*. All other references to Bacon's works will be to James Spedding, Robert Leslie Ellis and Douglas Denon Heath (eds.), *The Works of Francis Bacon*, 14 vols. (London, 1868–1890), hereinafter cited as *Works*. For the *New Atlantis* as a play see Howard B. White, *Peace Among the Willows: The Political Philosophy of Francis Bacon* (The Hague, 1968), p. 191.

brought forth dry land, so he would now discover land to us that we mought not perish'. On the following day they made landfall, and it is not without significance that Bacon emphasises that it was 'a kind of miracle' that had secured their delivery.[3]

With the mariners' arrival at New Atlantis, the Prologue ends and the first Act begins. The theme of Act One is that of the New Atlantans' relations with the outside world.[4] The paradox throughout is that the New Atlantans have knowledge of the affairs, learning and nature of the rest of the world, while the rest of the world remains in ignorance of them. They know without being known. In the first four scenes the difficulties and preconditions of access to New Atlantis are emphasised. 'A kind of miracle' is required to arrive there. Only in necessity, through sickness and lack of victuals, is humanitarian consideration given to the possibility of the mariners coming ashore. Before doing so, they must attest to the Christian faith, and abjure themselves of piracy and acts of violence. On disembarking, they are confined for three days under close scrutiny. Even when this confinement is relaxed, they are not allowed to travel over a mile and a half (a karan) from the city walls of Bensalem and their stay is subject to licence. These tests and restrictions on entry testify to the closed community nature of New Atlantis; only a certain type of individual is acceptable there.[5]

The three remaining 'scenes' of the first 'Act' all take place within the Strangers' House in the form of interviews between the governor of the Strangers' House and a number of travellers. In the first of these, the governor, who was also a Christian priest, informed a delegation of six of the travellers that, their period of confinement having ended, the state had given them a licence to stay for a further six weeks and that extensions of this might be permitted. In the meantime, they were to enjoy the facilities of the Strangers' House which was richly endowed, as it was thirty-seven years since its facilities had last been used. They were to be permitted to trade merchandise either for silver and gold or in barter for other goods, but they were still forbidden to travel over a mile and a half from the city wall without special leave.[6]

Next morning, the governor visited them again. This time he talked with ten of the travellers; 'the rest were of the meaner sort, or else gone

[3] *New Atlantis*, pp. 1–2, 7.

[4] *Ibid.*, pp. 2–7.

[5] Cf. Howard B. White, 'Political Faith and Francis Bacon', *Social Research* (1956), pp. 343–66. White emphasises the voyage and the easy arrival at New Atlantis as pointing to 'the triumph of science, as analogous to the triumph of navigation which conquers geographical remoteness'. This overlooks the miraculous nature of the discovery of New Atlantis and the restrictions and tests on entry.

[6] *New Atlantis*, p. 8.

abroad'. His theme was a paradox of knowing without being known: 'by meanes of our solitary situation; and of the Lawes of Secrecy, which we have for our Travellers; and our rare Admission of Strangers; we know well most part of the Habitable World, and are ourselves unknowne'. Within this context, priority was given to the question of how the Christian faith had been made known to the New Atlantans. The answer was by a miracle. Twenty years after the ascension of Christ, a pillar of light had been seen over the sea off the east coast of the island. On top of it stood a great cross of light. Boats were sent out but some mysterious force prevented them from approaching closer to the column than a distance of sixty yards. In one of the boats was a Fellow of Salomon's House, who offered prayer to the 'Lord God of Heaven and earth'. In this prayer, he noted that one function of his 'order' was 'to discern (as far as appertaineth to the generations of men) between divine miracles, works of nature, works of art, and impostures and illusions of all sorts'. And, in accordance with that function, he acknowledged what was happening before them to be 'a true miracle' and begged God to grant them the interpretation of the miracle. At this, his boat was allowed to approach. The pillar and the cross disappeared, leaving 'a small Arke, or Chest of Cedar, dry and not wett at all with water, though it swam'. When taken from the water, the ark opened to reveal a book and a letter. The book contained the Old and New Testaments, including those 'Bookes of the New Testament, which were not yet written'. The letter was from one Bartholomew who revealed that he had been commanded by God to launch the ark and its contents. Although there were Hebrews, Persians and Indians in New Atlantis, as well as the native population, they were all able to read the works in their own tongue.[7]

A number of points are worth noting about this account. The first is the priority and emphasis accorded to it by Bacon. The most important aspect of the New Atlantans' relations with the outside world, and, in particular, with their European visitors, is their common Christian faith. This is the first issue that the visitors raise in their dialogue with the governor of the Strangers' House, and he comments on the appropriateness of their priority.[8] It reflects both the seriousness with which Bacon held his own Christian faith and his belief in the Christian religion as a good guarantee of social order.

The second point worth noting is the miraculous course of the conversion of New Atlantis. It is beyond doubt, irrational and complete. Faith, not reason, is the only means by which it can be interpreted. And this, of course, is a typical reflection of Bacon's distinction between faith as a means of knowing God and reason as a means of interpreting nature. But like

---

[7] *Ibid.*, pp. 9–12.		[8] *Ibid.*, pp. 9–10.

Bacon himself, the Fellows of Salomon's House take all learning, and not merely what we would describe as natural science, for their province. Hence their duty of discerning 'between divine miracles, works of nature, works of art, and impostures and illusions of all sorts', and the Fellow's ability to certify this particular event a miracle. This ability is dependent upon his recognition of the peculiar basis of knowledge of the divine.

On the following day the travellers were once more visited by the governor who was again charged to explain how the New Atlantans could know so much of Europe whilst remaining unknown to Europeans. This interview, or 'scene', is taken up with an historical explanation of the seclusion enjoyed by the island. The governor first explained why other nations had no communications with New Atlantis. Three thousand years before, the island had been part of a worldwide network of traffic on a scale far greater than existed at the end of the sixteenth century. Their nearest great neighbour, Atlantis, on the American mainland, had launched two expeditions: one to the Mediterranean, from which no one had returned, and the other to the South Seas and the island of New Atlantis, where they were decisively outmanoeuvred by King Altabin. Less than a century after these events, Atlantis was visited by divine retribution for these 'proud enterprises' and destroyed in a great flood. As a result, the natives of America, descendants of the Atlantans, remained a primitive people. In addition, the basis of commercial relations between New Atlantis and their closest neighbour, America, had collapsed. At about the same time, there had been a great decline in navigation elsewhere. Partly this was caused by war, partly 'by a naturall Revolution of Time' (from which, apparently, New Atlantis was immune), and partly by the development of vessels unsuitable for long voyages.[9]

The problem remained as to why New Atlantans had accepted this isolation, for their shipping capacity and navigational skill had remained unimpaired. The answer, according to the governor of the Strangers' House, lay in decisions taken by King Solamona who had reigned about 1900 years before. Solamona viewed his country as self-sufficient. The island was large, fertile, and offered sufficient opportunities for its shipping in coastal trade, fishing and traffic to some nearby islands.

And recalling into his memory, the happy and flourishing Estate, wherein this land then was; So as it mought bee a thousand wayes altered to the worse, but scarce any one way to the better; thought nothing wanted to his Noble and Heroicale Intentions, but onely (as farr as Humane foresight mought reach) to give perpetuitie to that which was in his time so happily established.

Thus, unlike Utopus, Solamona was no great state maker. He found a

9 *Ibid.*, pp. 14–17.

society which had every appearance of felicity, and sought to perpetuate that happy state by securing it from 'Novelties, and a Commixture of Manners'. Accordingly, he stopped the free entrance of strangers and the free exit of New Atlantans and made his policy of seclusion part of the 'Fundamentall Lawes' of his kingdom.[10]

The governor contrasted the isolationist policy of New Atlantis with that of China. The former still admitted of humanity to strangers. Unlike the Chinese, the New Atlantans detained no one against their will, although they sought to make continued residence as attractive as possible, and, in fact, only thirteen visitors had ever chosen to leave.[11] Finally the Chinese were freely allowed to travel abroad, but this was forbidden to the New Atlantans, with only one exception. 'Now for our travelling from hence into parts abroad, our Lawgiver thought fit altogether to restrain it...But this restraint of ours hath only one exception, which is admirable; preserving the good which cometh by communicating with strangers, and avoiding the hurt.'[12]

The exception completes the explanation of the paradox of the isolation of New Atlantis, and, with it, what I have called Act One. It explains how the New Atlantans, unknown to others, know them so well. It also introduces what most commentators have seen as the key feature of Bacon's ideal society, Salomon's House or the College of the Six Days' Work:

amongst the Excellent Acts of that King, one above all hath the preheminence. It was the Erection, and Instillation of an Order, or Society, which wee call Salomon's House; The Noblest Foundation, (as wee thinke), that ever was upon the Earth; and the Lanthorne of this Kingdome. It is dedicated to the Study of the Works, and Creatures of God.

Every twelve years, two ships were sent out from New Atlantis, each carrying a mission of three Fellows of Salomon's House. They were commissioned to investigate assigned countries, 'And especially of the Sciences, Arts, Manufactures, and Inventions of all the World; and withall to bring unto us, Bookes, Instruments, and Patterns, in every kinde.' The ships returned immediately after landing the Fellows, who continued *incognito* their intellectual, technical and cultural espionage until the next

[10] This dating, of course, makes Solamona's reign prior to the conversion of New Atlantis to Christianity and, indeed, prior to the birth of Christ. *Ibid.*, pp. 17–18.

[11] *Ibid.*, p. 18. The attractiveness of New Atlantis to Europeans is revealed almost as soon as this interview closes. 'But when it came on amongst our people that the state used to offer conditions to strangers that would stay, we had work enough to get any of our men to look to our ship and to keep them from going presently to the governor to crave conditions.' *Ibid.*, p. 20.

[12] *Ibid.*, pp. 18–19.

expedition came twelve years later and picked them up.[13] So the explanation of the paradox is complete. New Atlantis possessed full knowledge of the outside world without being corrupted by it. Of course, this places a heavy burden on the integrity of the Fellows of Salomon's House. For twelve long years, as they search for knowledge to take back with them, they are exposed to the corrupting influences of the world outside. Bacon did not discuss the point. He would appear to have assumed that they were capable of sustaining the burden. This silent assumption, as we shall see, is not without its significance.

With the opening of the second 'Act' the scene shifts from inside the Strangers' House to the society outside. The period of confinement had ended and the visitors now wandered freely in Bensalem and became acquainted with residents of the city, though 'not of the meanest Quallity'. As the scene shifts so the topic of concern changes from the relationship between New Atlantis and the outside world to the society of New Atlantis itself: 'continually we mett with many things, right worthy of observation & Relation: As indeed, if ther be a mirrour in the World, worthy to hold Mens Eyes, it is that Countrey.'[14] The Act falls into four scenes: the Feast of the Family, the dialogue with Joabim the Jew, the arrival of the Fellow of Salomon's House, and, finally, his discourse on the work of that institution.

One day, two of the visitors were invited to a celebration of the Feast of the Family. 'A most natural, pious and reverend custom it is, showing that nation to be compounded of all goodness.' Any man living to see thirty persons descended from his body, alive and over three years old, might hold this feast at the cost of the state. Two days before the Feast, the father, or Tirsan as he was now to be known, with three friends and the assistance of the governor of the city or place, held council with all the members of the family. At this meeting, quarrels were settled, the distressed were relieved, the vicious reproved and disciplined and marriage plans arranged. The governor was prepared to use his public authority to enforce the decrees of the Tirsan, though this was seldom necessary, 'such reverence and obedience they give, to the Order of Nature'. Discipline and harmony having been established, the Tirsan chose one man from amongst his sons to live with him and this individual was known thereafter as the Son of Vine. The Feast day itself began with divine service which was followed by a procession honouring the Tirsan. In the course of this, heralds arrived bringing a royal charter conveying

---

[13] *Ibid.*, pp. 19–20. Compare these arrangements with Bacon's statement in *The Parasceve*: 'the materials on which the intellect has to work are so widely spread, that one must employ factors and merchants to go everywhere in search of them and bring them in'. *Works*, vol. iv, pp. 251–2.

[14] *New Atlantis*, p. 21.

privileges and rewards to him: 'the King is Debter to no Man, but for Propagation of his subjects'. Then followed a ceremonial feast in which the Tirsan was waited upon by his family, sharing his magnificence only with such of his children as happen to be Fellows of Salomon's House.[15] This celebration of propagation, fecundity and longevity involves a sharp contrast with what we know of the evanescent nucleated kinship group of Bacon's own day.[16] Still more significant, perhaps, is the disciplinary and conflict-resolving function accorded to the patriarchal family, for, apart from this reference, there is no discussion of how conflict and social disorder are dealt with in New Atlantis. Bacon shared, somewhat in-cipiently, the patriarchalist attitudes common in his day. The Feast itself was accompanied by a hymn celebrating Adam, Noah and Abraham, 'whereof the former two peopled the world, and the last was the Father of the Faithful'. Elsewhere in his works, Bacon employed the patriarchalist's parallels between the authority of father over family, king over country and God over creation. He was also of the opinion that parricide was a form of treason and should be treated as such at law.[17]

The second scene of this second Act continues the examination of the New Atlantan family. In it, the narrator makes the acquaintance of Joabim, who was a Jewish Merchant.

For they have some few Stirps of Jewes, yet remaining amongst them, whom they leave to their owne Religion. Which they may better doe, because they are of a farre differing disposition from the Jewes in other Parts. For whereas they hate the *Name* of Christ; And have a secret inbred rancour against the People amongst whom they live; These (contrariwise) give unto our Saviour many high Attributes, and love the Nation of Bensalem, extreamely.

Joabim, for example, acknowledged Christ's virgin birth and that he was more than a man and is now God's ruler of the seraphims. He saw the laws of Bensalem as Mosaic in origin. This moderate semitism was neces-sary to enable Jews to meet Bacon's tests on entry to his ideal society, and also to provide against conflict between Christian and Jew, but more broadly significant is the connection between this image of a Christian-ised Jewry in an ideal society and the notion of the conversion of the Jews

[15] *Ibid.*, pp. 21–5.
[16] See Peter Laslett, *The World We Have Lost* (London, 1965); *Household and Family in Past Time* (Cambridge, 1972). Gildo Massó's view that Bacon, in the *New Atlantis*, described the home in accordance with customary and statutory enactments seems to me to have very little warrant. Gildo Massó, *Education in Utopias* (New York, 1927), p. 34. For Bacon's emphasis on the family and on sheer size of family see also, J. O. Hertzler, *The History of Utopian Thought* (London, 1923), pp. 148–9.
[17] 'The Argument of Sir Francis Bacon ... In the Case of the Post-Nati', *Works*, vol. VII, pp. 644–5; 'A Preparation Toward the Union of Laws', *Works*, vol. VII, p. 737. On supporting parental authority see also *Works*, vol. VIII, p. 340.

as a precursor of the latter day glory and, accompanying it, the Great Instauration, or restoration of man's pristine dominion over nature. We shall see this juxtaposition of themes most fully developed in Samuel Gott's *Nova Solyma*.

Bensalem, according to Joabim, is 'the Virgin of the World': 'there is not under the Heavens, so chast a Nation, as this of Bensalem. Nor so free from all pollution or foulenesse.' There are 'no Stewes, no dissolute Houses, no Curtisans, nor anything of that kind'. Homosexuality is unknown.[18] By contrast, Joabim noted, in Europe single men were impure; marriage was 'but an office', most frequently merely a commercial bargain; the married were indifferent to the procreation of children; adultery was common.[19] Not only is this critical analysis of sexual mores and marriage the single aspect of European life discussed in the work, but, apart from Salomon's House, marriage and the family are the only features of New Atlantan society dealt with in any detail. In New Atlantis polygamy was forbidden. No couple could marry or make a contract until one month after their first meeting. Curiously, in relation to Bacon's emphasis on patriarchal authority elsewhere, marriage without parental consent was not void, but the children of such marriages were not allowed to inherit above one-third of their parents' inheritance. The New Atlantans had explicitly rejected More's utopian device for direct naked viewing of the betrothed, as possibly hurtful to anyone spurned. Instead, because of 'many hidden defects in men and women's bodies', they had instituted a more indirect system of examination on a non-obligatory basis.[20]

The third scene described the entry into Bensalem of one of the Fellows of Salomon's House. Joabim had secured a good vantage point for the narrator who describes in detail the magnificence and pomp with which the Fellow's entry was made. The latter sought 'to avoid all tumult and trouble' but, perhaps because this was the first view of a Fellow to Bensalem in the last dozen years, there was an elaborate procession in which all the officers of the City Companies appeared. The discipline of the people lining the streets was carefully noted. 'The street was wonderfully

---

18 *New Atlantis*, p. 26. This is difficult to reconcile with the reproof and censure of those 'subject to vice', which precedes the Feast of the Family. *Ibid.*, p. 21. For the conversion of the Jews and its millenarian associations see Peter Toon (ed.), *Puritans, the Millennium and the Future of Israel: Puritan Eschatalogy 1600–1660* (Cambridge, 1970), Chapters 2, 7. For Bacon's belief in an ancient Hebrew science and technology see Charles Webster, *The Great Instauration: Science, Medicine and Reform 1626–1660* (London, 1975), pp. 327–9.

19 Cf. 'Valerius Terminus', *Works*, vol. III, p. 232, where Bacon compares learning and sexual intercourse, both of which are cursed with sterility if pursued for pleasure and not fruit. Like Henry Neville, Bacon was childless; like him also, there is a preoccupation in his works with sexual fruitfulness.

20 *New Atlantis*, pp. 27–8.

well kept; so that ther was never any Army had their men stand in better Battele-Array, then the People stood. The windowes likewise were not crowded, but every one stood in them as if they had been placed.' So the importance and prestige of the Fellows of Salomon's House and the good order of the people were underlined.[21]

The fourth and final scene takes the form of a meeting between the narrator and the Fellow of Salomon's House and the Fellow's discourse describing the work of the foundation. Once more Bacon emphasised the status of the Fellow.

He was sat upon a low throne richly adorned, and a rich cloth of state over his hand, of blue satin embroidered. He was alone save that he had two pages of honour, on either hand one, finely attired in white. His undergarments were the like that we saw him wear in the chariot; but instead of his gown, he had on him a mantle with a cape, of the same fine black fastened about him. When we came in, as we were taught, we bowed low at our first entrance; and when we were come near his chair, he stood up holding forth his hand ungloved, and in posture of blessing; and we, everyone of us stooped down, and kissed the hem of his tippet.

The Fellow, speaking in Spanish, informed the narrator that he was going to give him his 'greatest Jewell', a description of Salomon's House and its works. The description is broken into four sections. First, 'The End of our Foundation is the knowledge of Causes, and Secrett Motions of Things: and the Enlarging of the bounds of Humane Empire, to the Effecting of all Things Possible.'[22] Then follows a very long section detailing the foundation's arrangements for the study of natural phenomena. Included in this most familiar part of the *New Atlantis* are mines, towers, zoological and botanical gardens, lakes, furnaces, perspective and sound houses, engineering shops, a 'Mathematicall House' and 'Houses of Deceits of the senses'. Most of the effort here appears to be employed in the compilation of what Bacon would have described as a natural history. Such discoveries as had immediate application were put into use throughout the kingdom, but the emphasis is upon the collection of data. Objectivity and scrupulousness are at a premium: 'wee doe hate all Impostures and Lies: Insomuch as wee have severely forbidden it to all our Fellowes under paine of Ignominy and Fines, that they doe not shew any Naturall Worke or Thing, Adorned or Swelling; but onely Pure as it is, and without all Affectation of Strangenesse'.[23] The third section of the Fellow's discourse deals with the 'Employments and offices of our Fellows'. Their duties

[21] *Ibid.*, pp. 28–30.   [22] *Ibid.*, pp. 30, 31.
[23] *Ibid.*, pp. 31–43. For possible sources of Bacon's model of Salomon's House see, Rosalie L. Colie, 'Cornelis Drebbel and Salomon de Caus: Two Jacobean Models for Salomon's House', *Huntington Library Quarterly*, 18:3 (1955), pp. 245–60.

were arranged so that data was collected, used to furnish axiomatic conclusions and so to direct further investigation. Twelve of the Fellows were
engaged on overseas expeditions and the rest of them were divided into
groups of three. The 'Depredatours' collected experiments from books and
the 'Mystery-Men' collected them from mechanical arts, liberal sciences
and elsewhere. Another trio, the 'Pioneers or Miners', performed new
experiments, while the 'Compilers' drew the information so far gathered
into convenient form. Out of this collection, three fellows called 'Benefactors' culled anything of immediate use in practice or theory. As a
result of continual reviews of the current state of knowledge, three fellows,
known as 'Lamps', were able to direct new experiments, which were
carried out and reported on by the 'Inoculators'. Finally three 'Interpre-
tators of Nature' induced from all this information 'greater observations,
axioms, and aphorisms'. In addition the college housed novices and
apprentices and a great number of servants.[24] The disposition of the
knowledge acquired in this way appears to be quite firmly in the hands of
the Fellows. 'We have consultations, which of the inventions and experiences which we have discovered shall be published, and which not: and
take all an oath of secrecy, for the concealing of those which we think fit
to keep secret: though some of those we do reveal sometimes to the state,
and some not.'[25] Bacon was well aware that technical skill and knowledge
could be put to evil, as well as good, uses.[26] Here he chose to place the
moral responsibility in the hands of the men of learning rather than in
those of the state.

The fourth and final section of the Fellow's discourse deals rather
sketchily with what are described as the 'Ordinances and Rites' of
Salomon's House. They had a museum consisting of two galleries. One
contained patterns and samples of the best inventions known to them.
The other housed statues of discoverers, like Columbus, and of the inventors of such things as music, gunpowder, letters, observations in
astronomy, printing, glass, metal and bread. Every day the Fellows gave
thanks to God for his 'Marveillous Works' and implored his aid in illuminating their labours and turning them to use. Periodically, they under-
took tours to inform the cities of New Atlantis of new and profitable
discoveries, and also to assist them with preparations against illness and
natural disaster. Judging from the fact that Bensalem had not seen any of
the Fellows for twelve years, Bacon did not intend this education function
of the foundation to be taken too seriously. So, with the Fellow's blessing

---

[24] *New Atlantis*, pp. 44–5.
[25] *Ibid.*, p. 45. The Latin text here is: *Ersi nonnulla ex iis, cum consensu, interdum Regi aut Senatui revelemus: alia autem omnino intra notitiam nostram cohibemus.*
[26] See, e.g., *De Sapientia Veterum*, xix, 'Daedalus; or the Mechanic', *Works*, vol. vi, pp. 734–6.

and a gift of a thousand ducats, the interview and the description of New Atlantis ends.[27]

About a third of the book is thus taken up with the treatment of relations between New Atlantis and the outside world. The same space is required for a description of the work of Salomon's House. The rest is given over to a discussion of the family and marriage, and to general support material. It is, perhaps, a testament to Bacon's literary skill that we first read the New Atlantis without realising how little he has in fact told us about his ideal society and its institutions. There is no description of the island itself, so that we have no idea of its size, population or the number of cities on it. It was a monarchy but beyond that we know virtually nothing of its governmental institutions.[28] Bacon clearly believed that factional politics was inevitable in an aristocratic society, but he offered no explanation of the elimination, or otherwise, of faction in New Atlantis.[29] There were social gradations in the ideal society but what they were and whether there was an hereditary nobility we do not know. Similarly we are not told how the island was defended, nor what its military organisation was. There is no mention of any judicial organisation beyond the exceptional jurisdiction exercised over a limited field by the Tirsan. Production and distribution of goods, land settlement, provision for the poor; none of these topics, all of which Bacon showed interest in elsewhere, are dealt with in the New Atlantis.[30] In the 1590s Bacon had written, 'Trust not to your laws for correcting the times, but give all strength to good education; see to the government of your universities and of all seminaries of youth, and to the private order of families,

---

[27] *New Atlantis*, pp. 43–7.

[28] The notion that, in the New Atlantis, Bacon 'carefully preserves existing institutions and instead of advocating revolution or radical change, superimposes science and advanced knowledge on a society that was essentially Jacobean England' just will not bear close scrutiny. Bacon provided too little information on both institutions and society in New Atlantis for it to have any validity. The presence of linguistic groups of Persians and Indians and the official toleration of Jews, for example, makes it difficult to reconcile with the society of Jacobean England. Glenn Negley and J. Max Patrick, *The Quest for Utopia* (New York, 1952), p. 360.

[29] See, *Essays*, LI, 'Of Faction', in *Works*, vol. IV, pp. 498–9; *New Atlantis*, p. 21.

[30] Cf. Christopher Hill, *Intellectual Origins of the English Revolution* (Oxford, 1965), p. 126. 'Bacon's House of Salomon has controlled the economy and the whole social order.' There is no evidence to support this in the *New Atlantis*. The same verdict must apply to the description of it as 'a capitalistic utopia'. Negley and Patrick, *Quest for Utopia*, p. 360; R. W. Gibson and J. Max Patrick, 'A Bibliography of Utopiana', in Gibson, *St. Thomas More: A Preliminary Bibliography of his Works and of Moreana to the year 1750* (New Haven and London, 1961), p. 312.

maintaining due obedience of children towards their parents, and reverence of the younger sort towards the ancient.'[31] The Feast of the Family
is in part, at least, an arrangement to comply with the second part of this
advice, but nothing is known of the educational institutions or arrangements of the New Atlantans. Finally, what religious settlement existed in
the ideal society? We know that there were priests and that Jews were
tolerated but, apart from this, nothing. Are the Fellows of Salomon's
House, who clearly played an important part in the religious life of New
Atlantis, also priests? Bacon provided no answer. Perhaps most astonishing of all is our lack of knowledge of the House of Salomon. Bacon
described in great detail the *work* of the foundation but said very little
about its *organisation*. How were Fellows recruited? What were their
conditions of service? How were they controlled and allocated their work?
How was the foundation financed and what determined its relationship
with society at large? That we know so little about the institution on
which Bacon lavished most attention in his short fiction must form a key
to any valid interpretation of the work as a whole.

The fact that Bacon left so many questions unanswered obviously
makes it difficult to characterise the work. A number of apparently
utopian elements appear in his description of the ideal society of New
Atlantis. Amongst the institutions mentioned or implied are the Strangers'
House, the Infirmary, Salomon's House, the City Companies and the
municipal government. The difficulty is that many of these are merely
mentioned and we are given very little, if any, idea of their organisation,
purpose and rôle in relation to the rest of society. The same may be said
of the handful of officials referred to.[32] Mention is made of 'Fundamentall
Lawes' but, beyond restrictions on the entry of foreigners, no details are
given.[33] There is, as we have seen, a disciplinary and conflict-resolving
function allocated to fathers preparing for the Feast of the Family, but,
given infant mortality rates and life expectancy, this can hardly have been
expected to provide the basis for a general social order. Apart from this,
the only general regulations that appear are the inheritance restrictions on
the offspring of marriages without parental consent, the injunction against
this, and one against deception by the Fellows of Salomon's House.[34] It

---

[31] *Works*, vol. VIII, p. 340.
[32] These are: the 'immigration official' who first communicated with the travellers, the 'person of place' who negotiated the conditions for their disembarkation,
the notary, the Conservator of Health, the governor of the House of Strangers
who is also a Christian priest, the governor of the city, the king and the Fellow
of Salomon's House. Perhaps the Tirsan and the Son of the Vine should also be
seen as taking on official status and function as a result of the Feast of the
Family.
[33] *New Atlantis*, p. 18.
[34] *Ibid.*, pp. 21–2, 28, 43.

may be this very lack of institutional and legal completeness, verging on confusion, which has led some commentators to characterise the New Atlantis as a realisable ideal.[35]

The crucial problem, however, is the nature of that ideal. For, while there are elements of discipline by regulation and bits and pieces of what might be an institutional and bureaucratic apparatus, the description of New Atlantis is too superficial for it to be labelled utopian in the sense already elaborated. There are, moreover, hints that we are dealing with a community of self-regulating individuals, with a community of moral paragons, a perfect moral commonwealth:[36] 'we were come', the mariners decided, 'into a land of angels, which did appear to us daily and prevent us with comforts, which we thought not of much less expected'; 'we were apt enough to think there was somewhat supernatural in this island; but yet rather as angelical than magical'; 'there is not under the Heavens, so chast a Nation, as this of Bensalem. Nor so free from all pollution or foulenesse. It is the Virgin of the World.' The basis of this unrivalled chastity are the New Atlantans' twin maxims: 'That whosoever is un-chaste cannot reverence himself'; and, 'That the Reverence of a Mans selfe, is next Religion, the chiefest Bridle of all Vices'. In the Tirsan's preparations for the Feast of the Family, provision was made for the city governor to give substance to his authority, but this was seldom needed, 'such reverence and obedience they give, to the Order of Nature'. New arrivals were carefully screened to maintain this general sense of moral responsibility.[37] There is a sense in which, as Harold Osborne remarked, the social institutions of New Atlantis were rather expressions of the character of the people than formative of it.[38]

But this is not the complete picture, for, while such emphasis was placed upon *self*-respect, *self*-control, internalised moral authority, nevertheless, some, admittedly very limited, social discipline and regulation was en-visaged. The laws which limited the rights of those who defy patriarchal authority and marry without parental consent assumed that such defiance would and did take place. There is no nation on earth as chaste as Ben-salem and yet it remains a function of the Tirsan to suppress vice in his

[35] Cf. Joseph Anthony Mazzeo, *Renaissance and Revolution: The Remaking of European Thought* (London, 1967), p. 224. 'In this respect Bacon's ideal Commonwealth is more truly a "Utopia" than most of its predecessors, if we give the term its usual modern meaning of an ideal society set some time in the future which men of the present may achieve through their own efforts.'

[36] Cf. V. Dupont, *L'Utopie et le Roman Utopique dans la Littérature Anglaise* (Toulouse, 1941), p. 132. Dupont describes Bacon, in the *New Atlantis*, as counting on Christian morality to make his citizens good.

[37] *New Atlantis*, pp. 9, 13, 26, 27–8, 22.

[38] Harold Osborne (ed.), *Bacon 'New Atlantis'* (London, 1937), p. xviii.

family. Throughout the *New Atlantis* run contradictory suggestions of moral perfection and moral failure, suppression unnecessary and suppression in operation. In other words, the *leit-motif* pervading the work is the unresolved tension between perfect moral commonwealth and utopian ideals.

It has been shown that implicit in Bacon's vision of a new learning was an alteration in the conception of the learned man. The virtues of this ideal were not purely intellectual. Indeed Bacon attacked reliance on pure intellect. As the fatal sin remains pride, so the key virtue is charity. 'The identification of scientific truth with use and therefore with charity, with power and therefore with pity, is fundamental to Bacon's conception of true learning.' 'Bacon often leaves the impression that the career of science is something of a religion in its selflessness and sense of dedication, and he at times spoke of the future scientists as though they were a priesthood.'[39] This saint-like image of the man of learning is clearly apparent in Bacon's treatment of the Fellows of Salomon's House and the relationship between them and society at large. The Fellow who paraded through the streets of Bensalem had 'an Aspect as if he pittied them' and while he arrived in great state he was careful to 'avoid all tumult and trouble'. 'He held up his bare hand as he went, as blessing the people, but in silence.'[40] The Fellows of Salomon's House appear as a species of moral superman. While their fellow citizens are carefully shielded from the corrupting influences of the outside world, they, as we have seen, are deemed capable of withstanding them on their twelve year long expeditions of enquiry. Again, Bacon was well aware of the corrupting influence of power,[41] but his learned paragons exercise it in high degree without deleterious effects. The philosophers in New Atlantis may not rule in any clearly expressed sense, but, as Mazzeo has pointed out, they retain the power of technological innovation and with it the capacity to alter the conditions of life, if not the structure of society.[42] Their collective moral responsibility even extends to deciding what knowledge shall be passed on to society at large. In New Atlantis the philosophers exercised a benevolent censorship even against the state, and Bacon appears to have assumed away the wider problems of political control under cover of the perfect moral character of the scientist. One is almost tempted to describe the result as a perfect moral commonwealth under the guidance of a benevolent, but unrestrained, moral élite, the Fellows of Salomon's House. Bacon's image of them has

[39] Moody E. Prior, 'Bacon's Man of Science', in Vickers (ed.), *Essential Articles*, pp. 147, 155.
[40] *New Atlantis*, p. 30.
[41] See e.g. the origins of tyranny as described in *De Sapientia Veterum*, II, 'Typhon; or the Rebel', in *Works*, vol. VI, p. 703.
[42] Mazzeo, *Renaissance and Revolution*, p. 222.

been described by one authority as 'possibly too flattering to human nature'.[43]

But even here Bacon hesitated and drew back. The optimism of the *New Atlantis* is not entirely 'unguarded', Bacon's faith in human rationality, human goodness not quite 'unbounded'.[44] He admitted that the Fellows of Salomon's House might be tempted to lie about and to distort what they had learned; that their integrity was vulnerable. It was necessary to legislate accordingly. 'But wee doe hate all Impostures and Lies: Insomuch as wee have severely forbidden it to all our Fellowes under paine of Ignominy and Fines, that they doe not shew any Naturall Worke or Thing, Adorned or Swelling; but onely Pure as it is, and without all Affectation of Strangenesse.'[45] Once, however, Bacon had admitted the moral fallibility of the Fellows in one thing (particularly in such an important thing as this) then he had raised the question of it in all things. If the Fellows could be motivated to deceive and distort, why could they not be tempted to exploit?

Bacon left so many loose ends[46] in the *New Atlantis* that it is tempting to return to the explanation that it was 'A Worke unfinished', half thought out, hastily executed, never intended for publication. Unfortunately there are difficulties here too. Partly these arise from the vexed question of when the work was written. Here the commentators are in considerable disarray. They fall basically into two groups: those who see it as a product of Bacon's last years, after his fall from office,[47] and those who would attribute

---

[43] Prior, 'Bacon's Man of Science', p. 161. On the social responsibilities of the 'scientist' in New Atlantis see, Robert Adams, 'The Social Responsibilities of Science in *Utopia, New Atlantis* and After', *Journal of the History of Ideas*, 10 (1949), pp. 374–98; Margery Purver, *The Royal Society: Concept and Creation* (Cambridge, Mass., 1967), p. 53; Judah Bierman, 'Science and Society in the *New Atlantis* and other Renaissance Utopias', *P.M.L.A.* (1963), pp. 492–500.

[44] Cf. Adams, 'Social Responsibilities', pp. 390–1.

[45] *New Atlantis*, p. 43.

[46] A final loose end in the *New Atlantis* concerns the history of Salomon's House. It was founded, according to the narration, about 1900 years before. Now, as is well known, Bacon repeatedly in his works suggested that, if his methods were adopted, the work of compiling a complete natural history would take only a few generations. The problem remains why, after so long, the work of compiling a natural history still goes on in New Atlantis, and why, indeed, so little technological innovation is evident there. Cf. Frank E. Manuel, 'Toward a Psychological History of Utopias', in Manuel (ed.), *Utopias and Utopian Thought* (Boston, 1966), p. 77.

[47] The following dates have been suggested by commentators in this group: 'the last five years of Bacon's life', G. C. Moore-Smith, 'The Date of the *New Atlantis*', *The Athenaeum*, 3771 (1900), pp. 146–8; 'the last two or three years of Bacon's life', J. W. Adamson, *Pioneers of Modern Education 1600–1700* (Cambridge, 1905), p. 54; shortly after Bacon's fall, J. G. Crowther, *Francis Bacon, The First Statesman of Science* (London, 1960), p. 128; H. Ross, *Utopias*

it to an earlier period of his life.[48] An intelligent compromise suggestion has been that Bacon first drafted the work in the period 1614–17
and revised it for publication in, or about, 1623.[49] Clearly, if the *New
Atlantis* was subject to a process of revision it becomes impossible to
explain away its inconsistencies, its unresolved problems, in terms of the
author's haste or his unwillingness to put his work before an audience.[50]
Whatever the date at which the *New Atlantis* was written, and it is doubtful whether this can be established with any precision, the significant point
is that the cardinal ideas of the work had engaged Bacon's mind for a
period of over thirty years of his life. In 1594, for the Christmas revels at
Grays Inn, he composed a number of speeches as part of a masque in
which counsellors addressed a mock monarch. The second counsellor
advised the study of philosophy and commended four principal works or
monuments. The first was 'the collecting of a most perfect and general
library, wherein whatsoever the wit of man hath heretofore committed to
books of worth be they ancient or modern, printed or manuscript, European or other parts, of one or other language, may be made contributory
to your wisdom'.[51] Second, came a garden of all plants, a collection of all
rare beasts and birds, and two lakes, one of salt water and the other of
fresh: 'in small compass a model of universal nature made private'.[52]
Next was 'a goodly huge cabinet, wherein whatsoever the hand of many
by exquisite art or engine hath made rare in stuff, form or motion; what-

Old and New (London, 1938), p. 64; '1622', Hertzler, *Utopian Thought*, p. 146;
'1624', Osborne (ed.), *New Atlantis*, p. xviii; Eleanor Dickinson Blodgett,
'Bacon's *New Atlantis* and Campanella's *Civitas Solis*: A Study in Relationships',
P.M.L.A., 46 (1931), p. 764; Harold Child, 'Some English Utopias', *Transactions
of the Royal Society of Literature*, 3rd series, 12 (1933), p. 38.

[48] Examples here are: '1614–17', S. R. Gardiner, 'Francis Bacon', *Dictionary of
National Biography*; Fulton H. Anderson, *Francis Bacon: His Career and His
Thought* (Los Angeles, Calif., 1962), p. 287. 'Some time before 1618', Catherine
Drinker Bowen, *Francis Bacon: The Temper of a Man* (London, 1963), p. 131.
'Sometime after 1609', Fulton H. Anderson, *The Philosophy of Francis Bacon*
(Chicago, 1948), p. 24. On p. 42 of the same work Anderson dates *New Atlantis*
in the period 1608–20.

[49] Mazzeo, *Renaissance and Revolution*, p. 221. F. H. Anderson also appears to
have considered the possibility of this solution. Anderson, *Philosophy*, p. 24.

[50] Rawley tells us in his life of Bacon that the *New Atlantis* was one of the works
his master had planned to translate into Latin 'for the benefit of other nations'.
Works, vol. I, p. 10. Spedding's opinion was that 'The *New Atlantis* seems to
have been written in 1624, and though not finished, to have been intended for
publication as it stands.' *Works*, vol. III, p. 121. R. P. Adams also adopts the
position that the *New Atlantis* was left in the form in which Bacon had intended
its publication. Adams, 'Social Responsibilities', p. 385.

[51] Cf. the work of the 'Depredatours' in Salomon's House, *New Atlantis*, p. 44.

[52] Cf. the lakes, orchards and gardens, zoos and aviaries of Salomon's House, *ibid.*,
pp. 33–5.

soever singularly chance and the shuffle of things hath produced; whatsoever Nature hath wrought in things that want life and may be kept; shall be sorted and included'. The last of the four works was the construction of 'such a stillhouse, so furnished with mills, instruments, furnaces, and vessels, as may be a palace fit for a philosopher's stone'.[53] The parallels between these four works or monuments and the 'Preparations and Instruments' of Salomon's House are too obvious to require much comment. Even more significant in this context is that, along with this, in the address of the Fifth Counsellor, Bacon coupled an appeal for governmental perfection, for 'Virtue and a gracious Government'. The prince was urged to seek inward peace; to visit all parts of his dominions, setting wrongs right; to check the faults of his great servants; to advance men of virtue and to repress faction; to reform the law, purging it of multiplicity and obscurity, and ensuring its execution; to back up the authority of the laws with good education in universities, schools and the home; and, finally, to seek prosperity.[54] Thus, as early as 1594, the institutional advancement of learning and the notion of political perfection were linked by Bacon in a single design. The civil model of New Atlantis, as well as the intellectual, was prefigured. In July 1608 Bacon spent seven days on a detailed review of his affairs. Again, the twin projects of a new type of learned institution and political reform were in his mind at the same time. In his notes for 26 July, he wrote, 'Foundac. of a college for Inventors. 2 Galeries w[th.] statuas or bases for Inventors to come. And a Library and an Inginary.' He went on to make sketchy remarks about the rules, allowances, and secrecy necessary in connection with such an establishment. Two days later he was making notes of a scheme for the drafting of new laws and the amendment of old, towards the compilation of an ideal code of law.[55]

Whenever the *New Atlantis*, as we know it now, was written, the point that needs to be repeated is that what Rawley considered to be the two cardinal features of the work,[56] the scientific institution and the ideal society, were linked in Bacon's thought and writing over a period of at least thirty years.[57] Given the longevity of the idea in Bacon's mind, it becomes difficult to accept the suggestion that the inconsistency and lack of development in the *New Atlantis* are entirely attributable to lack of

[53] Cf. the various departments of Salomon's House for the study of the contrivances of human art and the gallery housing patterns and samples of the best inventions. *Ibid.*, pp. 36–43, 45.

[54] The speeches of the 'counsellors' may be found in *Works*, vol. VIII, pp. 334–40.

[55] *Works*, vol. XI, pp. 66, 74, 76.

[56] See Rawley's preface, *New Atlantis*, 'To the Reader'.

[57] For this reason it is difficult to accept Eleanor Blodgett's argument that Bacon's *New Atlantis* was substantially influenced by the 1623 edition of Campanella's *Civitas Solis*. Blodgett, 'Bacon and Campanella'.

thought, care and time. Moreover, if one relates this issue to the way in which he dealt with different types of ideal-society notions in his works, one becomes aware of a profound unwillingness, on Bacon's part, to be committed to any form of ideal society. Four of our ideal society types – the millennium, arcadia, the perfect moral commonwealth and utopia – impinged upon Bacon's thought and the impact of the last two was particularly strong. Yet in the end he remained aloof, detached from all of them. He was torn between an impulse to idealise and a scepticism about, if not a distaste for, the ideal. Whenever he committed himself to one of the ideal-society modes available to him, Bacon encountered amongst its exigencies features unacceptable to him and this was particularly so with the utopian mode. It is this which provides the most probable explanation of the problems of the *New Atlantis*.

Bacon's chiliastic references were tantalisingly scant and perfunctory. He used Daniel's prophecy, that learning would increase in the autumn of the world, to bolster an optimistic view of intellectual progress, and commented on the predictability of religious controversy in these 'latter days'. As we have seen in the *New Atlantis*, he played with the juxtaposition of a Christianised Jewry, a Great Instauration, and, by inference, a latter-day glory. These were hardly more than early-seventeenth-century conventionalities. Nowhere does Bacon set out systematically to examine millenarian ideas and their implications.[58] Much more important and central to his thought was an arcadian strain arising out of his view of the ethico-religious end of the advancement of learning. As 'the proud knowledge of good and evil' had brought about the fall of man, so, Bacon argued, 'the pure knowledge of nature and universality' would lead to man's recovery of his original command over the creation.[59] Thus, 'natural philosophy proposes to itself; as its noblest work of all nothing less than the restitution and renovation of things corruptible'.[60]

And therefore it is not the pleasure of curiosity, nor the quiet of resolution, nor

---

[58] 'Valerius Terminus', *Works*, vol. III, p. 221; 'The Advancement of Learning', *Works*, vol. III, p. 340; 'Advertisement touching the controversies of the Church of England', *Works*, vol. VIII, p. 74. For Bacon's conventional division of the history of the world into four ages culminating in the end of the world, see 'A Confession of Faith', *Works*, vol. VII, p. 221. Cf. Webster, *The Great Instauration*, pp. 23–4. There can be no doubt of the importance of Webster's theme of the fusion of millenarian and scientific endeavours in mid-seventeenth-century England, but he does not seem to me to have established its centrality in Bacon's own thought. Cf. Katherine Firth's categorisation of Bacon as a 'cautious moderate' in relation to apocalyptic tradition, *The Apocalyptic Tradition in Reformation Britain 1530–1645* (Oxford, 1979), p. 205.

[59] 'The Advancement of Learning', *Works*, vol. III, pp. 264–5, 296. Cf. 'Valerius Terminus', *Works*, vol. III, p. 217.

[60] *De Sapientia Veterum*, XI, 'Orpheus; or "Philosophy" ', in *Works*, vol. VI, p. 721.

the raising of the spirit, nor victory of wit, nor faculty of speech, nor lucre of profession, nor ambition of honour or fame, nor inablement for business, that are the true ends of knowledge; some of these being more worthy than other, though all inferior and degenerate: but it is a restitution and reinvesting (in great part) of man to the sovereignty and power...which he had in his first state of creation.

It was Bacon's truly astonishing claim that it was the business of learning to undo the consequences of the fall of man.[61] He was not always prepared to see this as a possibility of *complete* recovery. In *Valerius Terminus* he wrote,

It is true, that in two points the curse is preremptory, and not to be removed; the one that vanity must be the end in all human effects, eternity being resumed, though the revolutions and periods may be delayed. The other that the consent of the creature being now turned into reluctation, this power cannot be otherwise exercised and administered but with labour...[62]

Later, in more optimistic vein, Bacon argued that, as a result of the fall, man lost both his innocence and his dominion of the creation, but that he might recover 'the former by religion and faith, the latter by arts and sciences'. Labour would remain indispensable to progress in the arts and sciences but the inevitability of vanity was not mentioned.[63] This recovery of human innocence and command of nature could clearly lead to an arcadian view of the ideal society as the Garden of Eden regained. At least one commentator has seen the *New Atlantis* in this light as an evocation of 'the happy existence of mankind before the Flood'.[64] Unfortunately there is little to justify this and little of the Arcadian in Bacon's social thought. He never examined in any systematic way what the recovery of a pre-lapsarian state would mean in terms of men's mastery over themselves and over each other. At times he even permitted himself to doubt whether man could attain to knowledge of the highest laws of nature and hence to complete command over the natural universe.[65]

On the other hand, Bacon frequently used the language and forms of the perfect moral commonwealth tradition. A good illustration of this may be found in the New Year letter he wrote to James I in January 1618.

I do many times with gladness and for a remedy of my other labours, revolve in my mind the great happiness which God (of his singular goodness) hath

61 'Valerius Terminus', *Works*, vol. III, p. 222. Cf. R. L. Ellis, 'General Preface to Bacon's Philosophical Works', *Works*, vol. I, p. 58; Haydn, *Counter-Renaissance*, p. 261; Hill, *Intellectual Origins*, p. 89; Anderson, *Francis Bacon*, p. 7.

62 'Valerius Terminus', *Works*, vol. III, pp. 222–3.

63 'The New Organon', *Works*, vol. IV, pp. 247–8.

64 Paolo Rossi, *Francis Bacon: From Magic to Science*, translated by Sacha Rabinovitch (London, 1968), p. 130.

65 'Advancement of Learning', *Works*, vol. III, p. 356.

accumulated upon your Majesty every way; and how complete the same would
be, if the state of your means were once rectified, and well ordered. Your
people militar and obedient; fit for war, used to peace. Your Church illightened
with good preachers, as a heaven of stars. Your judges learned, and learning
from you; just, and just by your example. Your nobility in a right distance
between crown and people; no oppressors of the people, no overshadowers of
the crown. Your Council full of tribute of care, faith, and freedom. Your
gentlemen and justices of the peace willing to apply your royal mandates to
the nature of their several countries, but ready to obey. Your servants in awe of
your wisdom, in hope of your goodness. The fields growing every day by the
improvement and recovery of grounds, from the desert to the garden. The
city grown from wood to brick. Your sea-walls or *pomoerium* of your island
surveyed and in edifying. Your merchants embracing the whole compass of the
world, east, west, north and south. The times give you peace, and yet offer you
opportunities of action abroad. And lastly, your excellent royal issue entaileth
these blessings and favours of God to descend to all posterity.[66]

Of course, there is a strong element of flattery in this, but the approach
employed is significant. Moreover, the flattery motive cannot have been a
serious factor in shaping the description of Elizabeth I's reign which
Bacon published in *The Advancement of Learning* two years after her
death. Here again 'the conjunction of learning in the prince with felicity
in the people' is the theme. Elizabeth's rule, according to Bacon, was
marked by a period of constant peace and security, when the truth of
religion was established, justice administered well, the prerogative used
with discretion, learning flourished, both crown and subject enjoyed a
'convenient estate and means', and obedience became habitual.[67] The idea
that a happy and harmonious society could be achieved by the conscientious
pursuit of civil morality by rulers, officials and subjects is quite clear here,
as it is in Bacon's long letter of advice to George Villiers, when first he
became favourite of James I.[68]

Bacon's defence of learning hung in part on the conviction that learning could play a key rôle in the attainment of civil morality and social
harmony. The learned man was a man equipped for conscientious morality
and self-improvement. 'For the unlearned man knows not what it is to
descend into himself or to call himself to account, nor the pleasure of that
suavissima vita, indies sentire se fieri meliorem.'[69] Men are governed by
two faculties, force and reason: 'the one is brute the other divine.'[70]
Learning, by fostering the rational in man, as opposed to the brute, makes

---

[66] *Works*, vol. xiii, pp. 452–3.
[67] 'Advancement of Learning', *Works*, vol. iii, p. 307.
[68] 'A copy of a letter conceived to be written to the late Duke of Buckingham',
    Works, vol. xiii, pp. 27–56.
[69] 'Advancement of Learning', *Works*, vol. iii, p. 315.
[70] *Works*, vol. viii, p. 334.

him amenable to government. 'And it is without all controversy that learning doth make the minds of men gentle, generous, maniable, and pliant to government; whereas ignorance makes them churlish, thwart and mutinous: and the evidence of time doth clear this assertion, considering that the most barbarous, rude, and unlearned times have been the most subject to tumults, seditions and changes.'[71] Though learned men, contemplative rather than active, may lack experience of '*ragioni di stato*', 'yet on the other side, to recompense that, they are perfect in those same plain grounds of religion, justice, honour, and moral virtue; which if they be well and watchfully pursued, there will seldom be use of those other, no more than of physic in a sound or well-dieted body'. Indeed, it was no more difficult for the learned man to pursue true virtue than it was for the politician to adhere to reason of state. If learned men had any fault, in this respect, it was that 'they contend sometimes too far to bring things to perfection, and to reduce the corruption of manners to honesty or precepts or examples of too great height'.[72]

The perfect moral commonwealth element in Bacon's thinking was then closely associated with his conception of the man of learning, and, as we have seen, this carries over into the *New Atlantis*. But, as before, Bacon could not go the whole way. He did not commit himself. Even while speaking of the moral appeal and potency of learning, he had to admit the tenuousness of its hold:

the nature and condition of men; who are full of savage and unreclaimed desires, of profit, of lust, of revenge, which as long as they give ear to precepts, to laws, to religion, sweetly touched with eloquence and persuasions of books, of sermons, of harangues, so long is society and peace maintained; but, if these instruments be silent, or that sedition and tumult make them not audible, all things dissolve into anarchy and confusion.[73]

There were limits to men's capacity for self-control and self-discipline. 'Nature is often hidden; sometimes overcome; seldom extinguished'; 'let not a man trust his victory over his nature too far; for nature will lay buried a great time, and yet revive upon the occasion or temptation'.[74] By the same token, even the best of monarchs could be 'depraved by the long habit of ruling'.[75] So man's vulnerability to temptation and to the corrupting influence of power remained, crippling Bacon's willingness to commit himself to the vision of a perfect moral commonwealth. In his advice to

---

[71] 'Advancement of Learning', *Works*, vol. III, p. 273. Cf., *ibid.*, p. 275: 'the felicity and delicacy of princes and great persons had long since turned to rudeness and barbarism, if the poverty of learning had not kept up civility and honour of life'.

[72] *Ibid.*, pp. 271, 456, 277.   [73] *Ibid.*, p. 302.

[74] *Essays*, XXXVIII, 'Of Nature in Men', in *Works*, vol. VI, pp. 469–70.

[75] *De Sapientia Veterum*, II, 'Typhon; or the Rebel', in *Works*, vol. VI, p. 703.

James I on the disposal of Sutton's estate, he pointed out that the will to
morality, good intentions, were not enough. Without 'such ordinances
and institutions as may preserve the same from turning corrupt, or at least
from becoming unsavoury and of little use', they were doomed to dis-
appointment.[76] Bacon was lifting his eyes from the vision of a society of
conscientiously self-disciplined men of good will, a perfect moral commonwealth, to the legal and institutional guarantees of the performance of
social good, that is towards utopia.

Bacon's interest in institutional methods of co-ordinating and controlling the behaviour of men is clearly apparent in his critical approach to
past philosophy. It suffered from self-indulgent individualism: 'one catches
at one thing, another at another; each has his own favourite fancy; pure
and open light there is none; every one philosophises out of the cells of his
own imagination, as out of Plato's cave'. To remedy this situation Bacon
provided his elaborate programme and method on the assumption that
'the mind itself be from the very outset not left to take its course, but
guided at every step, and the business be done as if by machinery'.[77] The
co-ordination of individual men's efforts was a key feature of his scientific
method. And it was the method itself which was to provide the unifying
force to which each worker must submit himself. In *Valerius Terminus*
he suggested that knowledge should be administered as the king of Spain
administered his dominions, with men absorbed in specialised or regional
duties but subject to central control and direction.[78] In the *New Atlantis*
we find the work of the Fellows of Salomon's House organised on this
kind of pattern. When he considered the advancement of learning, Bacon
accorded a place of priority to the institutional framework – 'foundations
and buildings, endowments with revenues, endowments with franchises
and privileges, institutions and ordinances for government' – without
which progress was impossible.[79] Again, this concern with academic
institutions is to be found clearly reflected in the New Atlantis and
Salomon's House. On the other hand, apart from some remarks on government by commission, Bacon showed little general interest in governmental
institutions.[80] He did not feel that any particular form of government was

[76] 'Advice to the King Touching Sutton's Estate', *Works*, vol. XI, p. 249.
[77] 'Natural and Experimental History for the Foundation of Philosophy', *Works*,
vol. V, p. 131. 'The New Organon', *Works*, vol. IV, p. 40. Cf. *Works*, vol. I,
p. 376.
[78] 'Valerius Terminus', *Works*, vol. III, p. 231.
[79] 'Advancement of Learning', *Works*, vol. III, pp. 322–5.
[80] See Bacon's memorandum to the king, January 1620, *Works*, vol. XIV, pp. 70–1,
where he suggests commissions for managing the cloth trade, controlling bullion
resources, grain supplies, 'introducing and nourishing manufactures', prevention
of depopulation, drainage of 'drowned lands', plantations in Ireland and defence.
Cf. also *Works*, vol. XIII, pp. 49, 52.

possessed of divine sanction. God allowed civil government (as he allowed ecclesiastical government)

to be varied according to time and place and accidents, which nevertheless his high and divine providence doth order and dispose. For all civil governments are restrained from God unto the general grounds of justice and manners, but that policies and forms of them are left free. So that monarchies and kingdoms, senates and seignories, popular states or communalities, are all lawful, and where they are planted ought to be maintained inviolate.[81]

In his discussion *Of the True Greatness of Kingdoms and Estates*, he followed Machiavelli in identifying greatness with capacity for war, but the key factors were population and spirit, not organisation or institutions.[82]

It might be expected that Bacon, as a professional lawyer, would have had a dynamic view of law as a means of moulding the will and behaviour of men. Certainly there were occasions when he expressed the opinion that the law could be used more vigorously. The education of youth was a topic upon which, as Bacon saw it, philosophy spoke too much and laws too little. What he most admired in Henry VII was his ability as a law-maker, an aspect of statesmanship which he found too often neglected by historians.[83] In discussing duelling, Bacon utilised the concept of law as a means of combatting the defects of man's nature. 'Revenge is a kind of wild justice; which the more man's nature runs to, the more ought law to weed it out.'[84] Perhaps the clearest discussion Bacon produced of the legislator's approach to a specific social problem was his essay 'Of Usury'.[85] Whilst usury had deplorable social effects, it had to be permitted because of the harshness of men's hearts, since without it they would not lend to those in need. The latter fell into two categories: those seeking relief from destruction, and those seeking commercial capital. Bacon therefore proposed that anyone might lend to the poor at a maximum rate of five per cent interest, while the supply of commercial capital should be at higher

---

[81] 'Certain Considerations Touching the Better Pacification and Edification of the Church of England', *Works*, vol. x, p. 107.

[82] *Essays*, xix, Of the True Greatness of Kingdoms and Estates', in *Works*, vol. vi, pp. 444–51; cf. 'Of the True Greatness of the Kingdom of Britain', *Works*, vol. vii, pp. 48–9.

[83] 'A Letter and Discourse to Sir Henry Savill', *Works*, vol. vii, p. 97. 'The Historie of the Raigne of King Henry the Seventh', *Works*, vol. vi, p. 97. It is worth noting Stuart Clark's comment that both Hall and Polydore Vergil had assessed Henry VII as a perfect moral prince, while Bacon saw him as a study in the interaction between character and circumstance in an amoral world. Stuart Clark, 'Bacon's Henry VII: A Case-Study in the Science of Man', *History and Theory*, 13:2 (1974), pp. 109–10.

[84] *Essays*, iv, 'Of Revenge', in *Works*, vol. vi, p. 384.

[85] *Essays*, xli, 'Of Usury', in *Works*, vol. vi, pp. 473–7.

rates and subject to licence. Astonishingly enough, for a man who was to be Lord Chancellor of England, Bacon showed no recognition of the practical and legal difficulties involved in a proposal of this kind. Yet he had complained, as early as the mid 1590s, of the multiplication of ineffective laws.[86] Moreover, this pessimism about law's potential for the production of clear-cut solutions to problems was much more typical of him. Law, he argued, might solve old problems but, in the very process of doing so, it tended to create new ones. 'For new laws are like the apothecaries' drugs; though they remedy the disease, yet they trouble the body. . . .' He saw no capacity in the law for eliminating envy, greed, ambition, faction, anger or the depredations of cunning and corrupt men. The baser side of human nature would find a way round institutional and legal obstacles for the working of its ill-will.[87]

Although Bacon maintained a lifelong interest in the compilation and amendment of English law it would hardly be correct to describe him as a law reformer. He was concerned rather with the clarity and expression of the law rather than with its substance: 'what I shall propound is not to the matter of the laws, but to the manner of their registry, expression and tradition: so that it giveth them rather light than any new nature'; 'the entire body and substance of law shall remain, only discharged of idle and unprofitable or hurtful matter; and illustrated by order and other helps, towards the better understanding of it, and judgement thereupon'.[88] Thus, his approach to legal science, like his approach to natural science, could be inductive.[89] His criticism of contemporary lawyers – 'they write according to the states where they live, what is received law, and not what ought to be law' – is almost a parody of his own professional attitude.[90]

Far more important than law itself in moving the will of men and influencing their behaviour was custom. It was 'the principal magistrate of man's life'.

Men's thoughts are much according to their inclination; their discourse and speeches according to their learning and infused opinions: but their deeds are after as they have been accustomed. And therefore as Machiavel well noteth (though in an evil-favoured instance,) there is no trusting to the force of nature or to the bravery of words, except it be corroborate by custom . . . insomuch as a man would wonder to hear men profess, protest, engage, give great words, and

---

86 'Maxims of the Law', *Works*, vol. VII, p. 315.
87 'Reading on the Statute of Uses', *Works*, vol. VII, pp. 417–18. See also *Works*, vol. VI, pp. 396, 462, 465, 498–9, 510–12; vol. XII, p. 189; vol. XII, pp. 7, 213.
88 'A Proposition . . . Touching the Compiling and Amendment of the Laws of England', *Works*, vol. XIII, pp. 63, 67.
89 Cf. Paul H. Kocher, 'Francis Bacon on the Science of Jurisprudence', *Journal of the History of Ideas*, 19 (1957), pp. 3–26. This article is reprinted in Vickers (ed.), *Essential Articles*.
90 'Advancement of Learning', *Works*, vol. III, p. 470.

then do just as they have done before; as if they were dead images, and engines moved only by the wheels of custom.

Custom alone was capable of altering and subduing men's natures, and, when socially endorsed, it was particularly strong: 'if the force of custom simple and separate be great, the force of custom copulate and conjoined and collegiate is far greater. For there example teacheth, company comforteth, emulation quickeneth, glory raiseth...Certainly the great multiplication of virtues upon human nature resteth upon societies well ordained and disciplined.'[91]

Herein, of course, lay the problem. Custom alone moulded the behaviour of men but how were good customs to be obtained and bad customs suppressed? Thought, persuasion, law were not enough. Bacon knew well enough that the problem was not to find models for the behaviour of men, but to find means of making men adhere to a good pattern of behaviour. In discussing the science of 'the Appetite and Will of Man', he wrote:

In the handling of this science, those which have written seem to me to have done as if a man that professeth to teach to write did only exhibit fair copies of alphabets and letters joined, without giving any precepts or directions for the carriage of the hand and framing of the letters. So have they made good and fair exemplars and copies, carrying the draughts and portraitures of Good, Virtue, Duty, Felicity; propounding them well described as the true objects and scopes of man's will and desires; but how to attain these excellent marks, and how to frame and subdue the will of man to become true and comformable to these pursuits, they pass it over altogether, or slightly and unprofitably.[92]

In the second Book of *The Advancement of Learning*, Bacon pointed again and again to the failure of moral philosophy. Virtue was known but how to be virtuous was not; or, at most, men had made the question a topic of conversation but not of scholarship. Of the determinants of men's behaviour two areas – nature and fortune – were beyond our command. It was necessary, if ever a science of moral philosophy were to be developed, for the distinctions of nature and fortune to be listed and examined in effects. The ancients had made observations of this type 'and yet nevertheless this kind of observations wandereth in words but is not fixed in inquiry. For the distinctions are found (many of them), but we conclude no precepts upon them...' There remained a third area of investigation: 'those points which are within our own command, and have force and operation upon the mind to affect the will and appetite and to alter manners: wherein they ought to have handled *custom, exercise, habit, education, example, imitation, emulation, company, friends, praise, reproof, exhortation, fame, laws, books, studies*'. Unfortunately Bacon restricted

[91] *Essays*, xxxix, 'Of Custom and Education', in *Works*, vol. vi, pp. 470–2; *Essays*, xxxviii, 'Of Nature in Men', in *Works*, vol. vi, p. 469.
[92] 'Advancement of Learning', *Works*, vol. iii, p. 418.

himself to a discussion of custom and habit, and this was merely a brief survey of a few commonplace precepts. There was, however,

a kind of Culture of the Mind that seemeth yet more accurate and elaborate than the rest, and is built upon this ground; that the minds of all men are at some times in a state more perfect, and at other times in a state more depraved. The purpose therefore of this practice is to fix and cherish the good hours of the mind and to obliterate and take forth the evil.

He concluded, somewhat lamely, that the best means towards this end were 'the electing and propounding unto a man's self good and virtuous ends of his life, such as may be in a reasonable sort within his compass to attain'. Finally, when it came to civil knowledge, Bacon declared that a knowledge of the means of moving men to conscientious behaviour was quite unnecessary: 'moral philosophy propoundeth to itself the framing of internal goodness; but civil knowledge requireth only an external goodness'. The sum of civil behaviour was 'to retain a man's own dignity without intruding upon the liberty of others'.[93] For the rest, Bacon concerned himself with the means to individual success and promised to treat government and law in a collection of aphorisms. Like much of his work, his discussion here of moral philosophy and civil knowledge was more valuable as criticism than for any positive contribution. He did little to make up for the neglect he found in others.[94]

The nearest Bacon came to a systematic discussion of the means whereby the will of man might be moved and moulded was in a work on quite another topic. *A Letter and Discourse to Sir Henry Savill, Touching Helps for the Intellectual Powers* was written early in Bacon's career.[95] In it, Bacon was concerned to show how capable of improvement the mental faculties of men were. His argument was that, of all creatures, man was 'the most susceptible of help, improvement, impression and alteration', and that, as this was true of his body, appetite and affection so it held good also of his power of wit and reason. Thus his discussion of the means

---

[93] *Ibid.*, pp. 432–5, 438, 441, 445, 446.
[94] Cf. the remarks to be found in George H. Nadel, 'History as Psychology in Francis Bacon's "Theory of History"', *History and Theory*, 5:3 (1966), pp. 283–5; Leonard F. Dean, 'Sir Francis Bacon's Theory of Civil History Writing', in Vickers (ed.), *Essential Articles*, p. 221; Haydn, *Counter-Renaissance*, pp. 255–256. Ronald S. Crane has shown how Bacon used the *Essays* to fill gaps in moral and civil knowledge delineated in the *Advancement of Learning* and the *De Augmentis*. Nevertheless, the work done there could hardly be seen as supplying the scientific approach to these disciplines that Bacon had called for. See, Ronald S. Crane, 'The Relation of Bacon's *Essays* to his Program for the Advancement of Learning', in *The Schelling Anniversary Papers* (New York, 1923), pp. 87–105; Fish, *Self Consuming Artifacts*, Chapter 2.
[95] 'A Letter and Discourse to Sir Henry Savill', *Works*, vol. VII, pp. 97–103. Spedding showed that the work was written between 1596 and 1604.

of influencing the will of man was a mere preliminary to demonstrating
how his intellectual, as opposed to moral, capacities might be improved.
'And as to the will of man', he wrote, 'it is that which is most maniable
and obedient; as that which admitteth most medecines to cure and alter it.'
The premier of these was religion; the 'most sovereign of all', 'able to
change and transform it in the deepest most inward inclinations and
motions'. (This was, of course, a priority reflected in the insistence on
Christian faith as a precondition of entry to New Atlantis.) Next came
'Opinion and Apprehension; whether it be infused by tradition and
institution, or wrought in by disputation and persuasion'. Third, was
example; fourth, 'when one affection is healed and corrected by another;
as when cowardice is remedied by shame and dishonour, or sluggishness
and backwardness by indignation and emulation; and so of the like'.
Lastly, 'when all these means, or any of them, have new framed or formed
human will, then doth custom and habit corroborate and confirm all the
rest'. These 'medicines' produced two kinds of cure: a true cure and a
'palliation'. The latter was 'more plentiful in the courts of princes, and in
all politic traffic, where it is ordinary to find not only profound dissimu-
lations and suffocating the affections that no note or mark appear of them
outwardly, but also lively simulations and affectations, carrying the tokens
of passions which are not'.[96]

What is revealing about this is that, even here, Bacon does not see the
state, its legal and institutional apparatus, as a means of influencing and
changing conduct on a mass basis. Moulding the wills of men remained a
question of individual influence, individual decision and individual will
rather than collective influence, collective decision and collective will. The
question then arises why, with these views as basic, Bacon's ideal society
was not a straightforward perfect moral commonwealth. The answer lies,
perhaps, in Bacon's profound pessimism about man – a pessimism which
left him, as we have seen, with a nervous hesitation over the invulner-
ability of his moral supermen, the Fellows of Salomon's House. Men were
imbued with a 'natural though corrupt' love of lies. Their rulers were
corrupt, their treaties acts of deceit. The people were a brute rabble,
'always swelling with malice towards their rulers, and hatching revolutions'. 'There is in human nature generally more of the fool than of the
wise; and therefore those faculties by which the foolish part of men's
minds is taken are most potent.' Holiness of life so far exceeded the
strength of human nature that it had to be regarded as a miracle.[97]

[96] *Ibid.*, pp. 100–1.
[97] *Essays*, I, 'Of Truth', in *Works*, vol. VI, p. 377. *De Sapientia Veterum*, II,
'Typhon; or the Rebel', in *Works*, vol. VI, p. 703; V, 'Styx; Of Treaties', *Works*,
vol. VI, pp. 706–7; IX, 'The Sister of the Giants or Fame', in *Works*, vol. VI,
p. 718. *Essays*, XII, 'Of Boldness', in *Works*, vol. VI, p. 402; LVIII, 'Of Vicissitude
of Things', in *Works*, vol. VI, p. 514.

Paradoxically, for a defender of learning and the contemplative life, Bacon held a deeply pessimistic view of the human mind and senses. In the *Novum Organon* he referred to the 'dulness, incompetency and deceptions of the senses'.[98] Elsewhere, he found the mind of man 'far from the nature of a clear and equal glass, wherein the beams of things should reflect according to their true incidence; nay, it is rather like an enchanted glass, full of superstition and imposture, if it be not delivered and reduced'.[99] It was against the shortcomings of the mind that Bacon warned men in his theory of the Idols of the Mind.[100] When these were added to the 'incapacity of the mind and the vanity and malignity of the affections', nothing was left but 'impotency and confusion'.[101] Consequently, the mind could not be left to itself but had to operate under the continuous guidance of method.[102] Only induction, sieved through exclusions, could lead man out of the darkness of his mind into the light of nature.[103]

This pessimistic view of the nature and mind of man was instrumental in preventing Bacon from visualising a perfect moral commonwealth. More than this, it nourished a basic political conservatism which inhibited him from committing himself to any form of ideal society. In so far as Bacon applied his system of induction to the kingdom of politics and law, as well as to the kingdom of nature, he was bound to end up a moderate conservative.[104] Hence his approach to ecclesiastical affairs was essentially

---

98 'The New Organon', *Works*, vol. IV, p. 58.

99 'Advancement of Learning', *Works*, vol. III, pp. 394–5; cf. 'Valerius Terminus', *Works*, vol. III, p. 245, 'That the mind of a man, as it is not a vessel of that content or receipt to comprehend knowledge without helps and supplies, so again it is not sincere, but of an ill and corrupt tincture.' In the *New Organon*, he referred to 'the ill complexion of the understanding itself, which cannot but be tinged and infected, and at length perverted and distorted, by daily and habitual impressions'. *Works*, vol. IV, p. 173.

100 For the Idols of the Mind see, 'The Great Instauration', *Works*, vol. IV, p. 27; 'The New Organon', *Works*, vol. IV, pp. 54–62.

101 'Valerius Terminus', *Works*, vol. III, p. 245. When he surveyed the state of knowledge Bacon found 'the information of the sense itself, sometimes failing, sometimes false; observation, careless, irregular, and led by chance; tradition vain and fed on rumour; practice, slavishly bent upon its work; experiment blind, stupid, vague, and prematurely broken off; lastly, natural history trivial and poor; – all these have contributed to supply the understanding with very bad materials for philosophy and the sciences'. 'The Great Instauration', *Works*, vol. IV, p. 28.

102 'The New Organon', *Works*, vol. IV, p. 40.

103 'De Principiis Atque Originibus', *Works*, vol. V, p. 463; cf. Ellis' preface, *Works*, vol. III, p. 69.

104 Anderson, *Francis Bacon*, pp. 118–31, 234–6; see also, Mazzeo, *Renaissance and Revolution*, p. 206; Kocher, 'Bacon on Jurisprudence'; Harvey Wheeler, 'The Constitutional Ideas of Francis Bacon', *Western Political Quarterly*, 9 (1956), pp. 927–36.

that of a *politique*. He could see good and bad in both bishops and puritans. No system of church government was divinely ordained. Altering the established system could only be dangerous.[105] Similarly, as he repeatedly said, he sought no innovation in English law but merely 'the better to establish and settle a certain sense of law which doth now too much waver in incertainty'.[106] In his great essay, *Of Innovations*, Bacon put forward a credo prefiguring the moderate conservatism of Edmund Burke. Innovations, he argued, are always misshapen but time itself is an innovator. It is necessary, therefore, for man to innovate according to time's pattern. 'It were good therefore that men in their innovations would follow the example of time itself; which indeed innovateth greatly, but quietly and in degrees scarce to be perceived.' In states experiments should be avoided, 'except the necessity be urgent, or the utility be evident'.[107]

The conservative view of politics, the pragmatic attitude to change, are amongst the most consistent features of Bacon's thought.[108] Elsewhere, he is hesitant, uncertain, ambivalent.[109] He occupied a 'curiously anomalous position as a herald of the new scientific age who is also an incorrigible addict of modes of thinking which his expressed programme would replace: allegory, myth, iconographical symbolism, alchemy'.[110] He was optimistic about the future of learning while retaining a pessimistic view

---

[105] *Works*, vol. VIII, p. 126. For Bacon's general position on ecclesiastical affairs see, 'Advertisement Touching the Controversies of the Church of England', *Works*, vol. VIII, pp. 74–95; 'Certain Considerations Touching the Better Pacification and Edification of the Church of England', *Works*, vol. X, pp. 103–14; 'A Copy of a Letter conceived to be written to the late Duke of Buckingham', *Works*, vol. XIII, pp. 30–2.

[106] 'Maxims of the Law', *Works*, vol. VII, p. 316. On his foreswearing innovation see, *Works*, vol. X, pp. 181–7, 380; vol. XIII, pp. 30–1, 63, 165–6; vol. XIV, p. 363.

[107] *Essays*, XXIV, 'Of Innovations', in *Works*, vol. VI, pp. 433–4. Cf. Farrington's translation of the 'Thoughts and Conclusions on the Interpretation of Nature', B. Farrington, *The Philosophy of Francis Bacon* (Liverpool, 1964), p. 79.

[108] His extraordinary declaration, 'Moderation, or the Middle Way, is in Morals much commended, in Intellectuals less spoken of, though not less useful and good; in Politics only, questionable and to be used with caution and judgement', is, so far as I know, without parallel in his works. *De Sapientia Veterum*, XXVII, 'The Flight of Icarus', also 'Scylla and Charybdis; or the Middle Way', *Works*, vol. VI, p. 754.

[109] For a comment, on Bacon's early work, to this effect, see Spedding, *Works*, vol. III, p. 173. See also, Haydn, *Counter-Renaissance*, pp. 10–11.

[110] Vickers (ed.), *Essential Articles*, p. xviii; cf. Rossi, *Francis Bacon*, Chapter 1; Harold Fisch, *Jerusalem and Albion; The Hebraic Factor in Seventeenth Century Literature* (London, 1964), pp. 82–6. Frances Yates, *Giordano Bruno and the Hermetic Tradition* (London, 1964; reprint 1971), p. 450; Yates, *The Rosicrucian Enlightenment* (London, 1972), Chapter 9; Webster, *The Great Instauration*, pp. 328–30.

of man's capacities as learner.[111] His view of history hovered uncertainly between his inductive approach to history as a branch of knowledge,[112] his dalliance with conventional cyclical theories,[113] and his concern with history as the fall of man and the recovery in which his scientific method was to be instrumental. That Bacon was frequently lacking in precision of thought can hardly be gainsaid. It was almost a part of his intellectual milieu.[114] But the problem goes deeper than this. Bacon, as Anne Righter has argued, was caught in a dilemma 'between the desire for truth and the distrust of certainty, the need to generalize and abridge and the fear of violating the individuality of facts'. He was the victim of a double impulse, 'a need to discover and establish truth on the one hand, and to prevent thought from settling and assuming a fixed form on the other'.[115] In a similar way, he acknowledged, but could never accept, the separation of the ideal and the actual.[116]

Bacon's scientific certainty, his optimistic faith in a method capable of coping with man's fallibility, led him to visualise a society exploiting those methods. But when it came to idealising that society in other respects he was caught in a dilemma. Possessed of the pessimism about man of the utopian and the pessimism about institutional innovation of the perfect moral commonwealth theorist, he was caught in the tentacles of his own conservatism and could not commit himself to either view of a society purged, changed and perfected.

Bacon wished to visualise an ideal society in which science was esteemed, scientists were of crucial importance and scientific results were effectively harnessed for social benefit. In the *New Atlantis* he tried to adapt the mode of Sir Thomas More to this purpose and found himself trapped. For, in choosing the utopian mode, he was committing himself to the assumption of deficiencies in both man and nature. The latter, deficiencies

---

[111] Cf. Prior, 'Bacon's Man of Science', p. 141. Virgil K. Whitaker, *Francis Bacon's Intellectual Milieu* (Los Angeles, 1962), p. 22; Karl R. Wallace, *Francis Bacon on Communication and Rhetoric* (North Carolina, 1943), p. 87; Rossi, *Francis Bacon*, p. 170.

[112] See, F. Smith Fussner, *The Historical Revolution: English Historical Writing and Thought 1580–1640* (London, 1962), Chapter 10; Dean, 'Sir Francis Bacon's Theory of Civil History Writing'.

[113] For an example of Bacon's espousal of cyclical views see, 'Advancement of Learning', *Works*, vol. III, pp. 378–9. For his rejection of the same see F. R. Jones, *Ancients and Moderns: A Study of the Rise of the Scientific Movement in Seventeenth-Century England* (2nd edition, St Louis, 1961), p. 45.

[114] Whitaker, *Bacon's Intellectual Milieu*.

[115] Righter, 'Francis Bacon', pp. 315–17.

[116] Haydn, *Counter-Renaissance*, Prologue, Chapter 4, Section 4. Cf. Theodore K. Rabb, 'Francis Bacon and the Reform of Society', in T. K. Rabb and J. E. Seigel (eds.), *Action and Conviction in Early Modern Europe* (Princeton, 1969), pp. 169–93.

in nature, were acceptable because science existed to remedy them. Indeed there would be no science in arcadia. The central problem lay in the utopian's assumption of human weakness and wickedness, for this meant that Bacon must assume the fallibility and corruptibility of his scientists. It followed therefore that, to prevent them from using their power to disorder society, he must restrain and control them and in so doing he risked destroying scientific freedom and with it the basis of the ideality of his society. Trapped in the exigencies of the utopian mode, Bacon exposes at once the problem and the impossibility of a scientific utopia. If science is to progress to the achieving of all things possible, minds, and to some extent actions, must be free of censorship and control. But scientific knowledge is power. It can, as Bacon knew, alter the material conditions of society and hence the structure of society itself. If we trust the scientist not only to pursue knowledge but to exercise his resultant power over society in a benevolent and enlightened way, then why may we not trust all men, particularly those not exposed to the temptations of scientific power? Why may we not, in other words, visualise a scientific perfect moral commonwealth? If, like the utopian, we cannot trust human nature, in scientists as well as others, how are we to have control without inhibiting freedom of enquiry? Bacon's failure to complete an ideal-society vision – his inability to assume either the automatic integrity of the scientist or to accept the stifling of free enquiry – is a great failure because it raises these still-unresolved issues at the moment of the conception of modern science.

Like More in Book 1 of the *Utopia*, Bacon faced the problem of the extent to which one is obliged to share true knowledge with those in power. More's problem here was solved in a perfect society because the knowledge he emphasised was moral knowledge which could be made consistent with, if it were not essential to, a stable and unchanging society. But Bacon's problem was not solved there because the knowledge he gave primacy to was technological knowledge. Behind it lay unanswered moral questions. Within it lay a capacity to produce instability and unknown social change.[117]

---

[117] Cf. Elizabeth Hansot, *Perfection and Progress: Two Modes of Utopian Thought* (Cambridge, Mass., 1974), pp. 72, 100.

6

Samuel Gott's New Jerusalem

... he only wrote what he hoped might be, and what he thought no one would take for truth. But whether the work is fact or fiction is a minor point compared with the intention of the book — that is, the right ordering of a Christian's life.

Samuel Gott, Nova Solyma (1648)

When any man becomes strictly honest and religious, he can hardly be suffered to breathe nor enjoy a common being among men.

Samuel Gott, An Essay of the
True Happiness of Man (1650)

... it is only by what they understand that people receive benefit, and every important truth needs frequent repetition and enforcement.

Samuel Gott, Nova Solyma

In 1642, baulked by the intransigent suspicion of his political opponents, Charles I spoke of the 'new Utopia of religion and government into which they endeavour to transform this Kingdom'.[1] Surprisingly often, historians, of rather different political persuasions from the king's, have shared his assumption: that there was in 1642, and perhaps long before that, a revolutionary programme in church and state; that the Puritan Revolution nursed in its bosom the Puritan Utopia. The king's prediliction for theories of well-laid conspiracy is perhaps more understandable than that of the historians. But, in any case these assumptions have, in the last twenty years or so, received a well-deserved battering. We are no longer persuaded that the English Civil War and its aftermath were the products of planned revolution. Accordingly we find it harder to discern the ideology and ideologists of such a revolution. The writers discussed in this chapter and the next – Samuel Gott and Gerrard Winstanley – have been seen as attempting to provide utopian goals for a Puritan Revolution, yet both viewed the events of the 1640s with great suspicion[2] and the label 'puritan' does not greatly enhance our understanding of either of them. It remains true, however, that the noise and confusion of civil discord set the background to their thought as, until recently, it set the seal on their obscurity.

Twenty years earlier, in the early 1620s, Robert Burton had, he believed, penetrated one of the causes of undeserved obscurity. The main reason 'that so many flourishing wits are smothered in oblivion, lie dead and buried in this our nation' was the unwillingness of the stationers to accept work for publication in Latin.[3] Latin was the language of fame, English that of obscurity. The experience of Samuel Gott would appear to suggest that, by the late 1640s at least, the reverse was true. His Latin work, *Nova Solyma*, published anonymously in 1648 and reissued in 1649, was immediately enveloped in an obscurity from which it was not

---

[1] John Rushworth, *Historical Collections*, 7 vols. (1659–1701), vol. 1, p. 727.
[2] For Gott's views see his preface to *An Essay of the True Happiness of Man* (1650), a4. For Winstanley see below Chapter 7.
[3] Robert Burton, *The Anatomy of Melancholy*, edited by Holbrook Jackson, 3 vols. (London, 1932), vol. 1, p. 30.

to emerge for two hundred and fifty years. Even then, in 1902, the excess of enthusiasm over discretion which tends to surround that which was lost and is found threatened to rob Gott of his work. The romance was diligently but incorrectly attributed to John Milton[4] and only eight years later was it restored to its rightful author.[5] The dispute over authorship, however, had the unfortunate effect of diverting attention away from the work itself and, once attributed to an unknown man, it could, perversely, be safely ignored again. The circle of obscurity was complete; or almost, since a few commentators, amongst whom Max Patrick is pre-eminent, have insisted on discussing Gott's work. And, to round out the ironies, we now, thanks to them, know more about the unheard of Gott than we do about the famous Robert Burton.

Gott was born in London in 1613, four years junior to Milton.[6] His father was a merchant, an ironmonger, probably with business connections amongst the gentry ironmasters of East Sussex, where he possessed land. He was a man of some eminence in his trade and in the life of the city.[7] Samuel was educated at the Merchant Taylors school and St Catharine's College, Cambridge, where he received a B.A. in 1632. The following year he embarked on a legal training and was admitted to Gray's Inn.[8]

[4] *Nova Solyma, The Ideal City; or Jerusalem Regained: An Anonymous Romance written in the Time of Charles I. Now first drawn from obscurity and Attributed to the Illustrious John Milton*, translated and edited by Walter Begley, 2 vols. (London, 1902). Most of Begley's editorial effort was directed to the proof of Milton's authorship and his translation presents serious difficulties. For a balanced assessment of it see C. H. Firth's review 'A Puritan Utopia', *Church Quarterly Review*, 57 (1903), pp. 101–30. Nevertheless, for want of a better, I have chosen to use it and throughout references to *Nova Solyma* will be to the Begley edition. Even earlier some unknown hand attributed the work to Emmanuel de Swedenborg. On the fly leaf of the British Museum copy (shelf mark: c62 a7) which was acquired in 1888, had been written, 'Swedenborg b. 1628, d. 1772'. Some later hand had added, in pencil, the comment 'Stuff'. The title page of the first edition reads, *Novae Solymae Libri Sex Londini, Typis Joannis Legati MDCXLVIII*. Begley's division of the six books into chapters was purely arbitrary.

[5] For Gott's authorship see, Stephen K. Jones, 'The Authorship of *Nova Solyma*', *The Library*, 3rd series, 1:3 (1910), pp. 225–38.

[6] Unless otherwise stated the details of Gott's life are taken from Jones, 'Authorship of *Nova Solyma*', and J. Max Patrick, 'Puritanism and Poetry: Samuel Gott', *University of Toronto Quarterly*, 8:2 (1939), pp. 211–26. See also J. Max Patrick, '*Nova Solyma*: Samuel Gott's Puritan Utopia', *Studies in the Literary Imagination*, 10:2 (1977), pp. 43–55.

[7] In 1640 his name appeared in a list of 'such inhabitants in tower ward as are conceived to be abilitie' to lend money to the king. Jones, 'Authorship of *Nova Solyma*', p. 227.

[8] J. Foster (ed.), *The Register of Admissions to Gray's Inn, 1521–1889, together with the Register of Marriages in Gray's Inn Chapel, 1695–1754* (London, 1889), p. 199, folio 895.

Both here and at Cambridge, Gott would have been exposed to the famous preacher, Richard Sibbes,[9] and through him, at least, to the influence of William Perkins. Their emphasis was on moral striving and social commitment in preparation for the coming millennium.[10] In particular, Perkins preached a latter-day glory to be presaged by the conversion of the Jews and their restoration to the Holy Land.[11] But this idea was by no means uncommon either at the universities or the Inns of Court. At Cambridge, Joseph Mede, who had stressed the conversion of the Jews and the two books, *Scripture* and *Nature*, as the keys to knowledge (both ideas attractive to Gott), enjoyed something of a vogue in the 1640s and 1650s.[12] Cambridge had since the mid sixteenth century been a centre of Hebrew studies and there can be little doubt that Gott studied and became a competent hebraicist there. It is likely that, because of his social, religious and educational background, Gott was acquainted with others working on the same problems, most particularly with the groups surrounding Milton, Dury, Hartlib, Theodor Haak, William Petty and linked through Comenius with Andreae.[13] He was certainly a friend of John Selden and Francis Goldsmith.[14] According to J. Max Patrick, 'Gott's intellectual

---

[9] Sibbes was preacher at Gray's Inn from 1617 to 1635 and commanded a large and influential following. In 1626 he became Master of St Catharine's Hall. See, *Dictionary of National Biography*; W. Haller, *The Rise of Puritanism* (New York, 1951), pp. 64–7; Wilfrid R. Prest, *The Inns of Court under Elizabeth I and the Early Stuarts 1590–1640* (London, 1972), pp. 18, 38, 189, 197, 207–8, 213–14.

[10] Christopher Hill, *Puritanism and Revolution* (London, 1962), Chapter 7, pp. 216–17, 273 n.2; Hill, *Society and Puritanism in Pre-Revolutionary England* (London, 1964), pp. 131, 140, 143, 179, 283, 315, 369; Perry Miller, *The New England Mind* (Harvard, 1954), p. 374.

[11] See Peter Toon (ed.), *Puritans, the Millennium and the Future of Israel: Puritan Eschatology 1600–1660* (Cambridge, 1970), pp. 6, 23–4. Katherine R. Firth, *The Apocalyptic Tradition in Reformation Britain 1530–1645* (Oxford, 1979), pp. 213–28.

[12] E. L. Tuveson, *Millennium and Utopia: A Study in the Background of the Idea of Progress* (Gloucester, Mass., 1972), pp. ix, 81, 85, 104; Toon, *Puritans, the Millennium and the Future of Israel*, pp. 23–4, 28–33, 117–18.

[13] See, J. V. Andreae, *Christianopolis*, edited by F. E. Held (New York, 1916), Preface, Chapter 4. Held's thesis that Gott was directly influenced by Andreae's *Christianopolis*, although endorsed by Harold Ross, is not proven. H. Ross, *Utopias Old and New* (London, 1938), p. 75. See also Patrick, 'Puritanism and Poetry', p. 212. For Gott as a supporter of the chemical philosophy see, Allen G. Debus, *Science and Education in the Seventeenth Century: The Webster–Ward Debate* (London, 1970), p. 34.

[14] For Gott's friendship with John Selden see Samuel Gott, *The Divine History of the Genesis of the World. Explicated and Illustrated* (London, 1670), a2. In 1652 he wrote commendatory verses for Francis Goldsmith's translation of Grotius. Goldsmith had also been a student at Gray's Inn.

milieu was...that of a broad and intelligent Puritanism. He himself was highly cultured: his reading in Latin literature seems to have been most comprehensive; his Latin poems are the productions of a versatile and well trained mind. And he was a capable Hebrew scholar.'[15]

On 23 June 1640, Gott was called to the bar.[16] His inheritance of his father's property in Sussex shortly thereafter may have diverted him from the practice of law but he maintained extremely close connections with the Inns of Court and with Gray's Inn in particular. In November 1657 he was elected Reader for Barnard's Inn and the following May he became an Ancient of Gray's Inn.[17] It would have been exceptional for a non-practising lawyer to have become an Inn of Chancery Reader and an Ancient.[18] But the Civil War had very serious effects on the Inns of Court. Gray's Inn, like the others, found its members dividing into two parties. For the first two years of the war it was almost closed down. Readings were not resumed on a regular basis until after the Restoration.[19] Gott's elevation to the positions of Reader and Ancient may thus have owed something to the necessities of the times. However that might be, he remained in some sense a lawyer through to his maturity and Gray's Inn was repaid with the attendance of his son and grandson.[20]

After his father's death in 1641 or 1642, Samuel settled on the family estates at Battle in Sussex. About the same time he consolidated his position in the county by marriage to the daughter of Peter Farnden of Seddlescombe, the head of a leading east Sussex family and also a prominent ironmaster.[21]

Gott's attitude to the struggles of the 1640s was that of a disenchanted neutral. In 1650 he deplored the previous decade as

an Age, wherein Letters are either neglected, or distasted. We have lately surfetted of knowledge, and now disgorge and nauseate it: or if any Books be read, they are only such as we disdain to read twice; Pamphlets and Stories of Fact, or angry disputes concerning the times. In times of Action whosoever

[15] Patrick, 'Puritanism and Poetry', p. 216. On Hebrew studies at Cambridge see Toon (ed.), *Puritans, the Millennium and the Future of Israel*, pp. 23–4.

[16] R. J. Fletcher (ed.), *The Pension Book of Gray's Inn*, 2 vols. (London, 1901–10), vol. 1, p. 339. See Wilfrid Prest, 'Legal Education of the Gentry at the Inns of Court 1560–1640', *Past and Present*, 38 (1967), pp. 20–39; Prest, *Inns of Court*.

[17] Fletcher (ed.), *Pension Book*, pp. 420, 422.

[18] I am indebted to Wilf Prest for advice on this point.

[19] Fletcher (ed.), *Pension Book*, pp. xxxiii, xliv–xiv; H. E. Duke and B. Campion, *The Story of Gray's Inn* (London, 1950), p. 23. Prest, *Inns of Court*, p. 135.

[20] Foster (ed.), *Register of Admissions to Gray's Inn*, p. 310 folio 1,266; p. 351 folio 1,366. As well as his son and heir, Peter, who was born in 1652, Gott also had a daughter born in 1644. Two other sons died in infancy.

[21] Anthony Fletcher, *A County Community in Peace and War: Sussex 1600–1660* (London, 1975), pp. 14, 19.

would appear considerable, and make any moment in Business, must pursue one of the Extremes, and desperately run up to the hight of it. . .[22]

In 1645 he was elected as a recruiter to the Long Parliament as an M.P. for Winchelsea. Three years later, at the end of the year in which he published *Nova Solyma*, he was amongst those excluded from Parliament in Pride's Purge.[23] In 1650 he wrote to his friend John Swynfen, the recruiter M.P. for Stafford who was also excluded in the Purge, wrestling in his conscience with the problem of the Engagement. Uncertain as he was, Gott felt an obligation to give *de facto* recognition to the new authorities in church, state and judiciary. Deplorable as the emergence of a republic was, for the 'preservation of men and humane society' obedience to it was necessary. Calvin himself had endorsed such a position. For his own part, Gott intended 'to live privately and out of business'.[24] He continued to play a part in local affairs. In 1654 he was appointed one of the commissioners for ejecting scandalous ministers in Sussex and in 1656 he was sitting on the assessment committee for that county. The same year he was elected M.P. for Rye, a town with which he already had associations,[25] and was refused admission to Cromwell's second Parliament. Since many of those so excluded were harmless, this does not necessarily mean that Gott or his views were in conflict with the Protectorate. In 1659 he was elected to represent Winchelsea and allowed to sit. Only one parliamentary speech was recorded of him, picturing Cromwell's second chamber as a necessary evil, for which he felt bound to plead 'as a lame man would for a wooden leg'.[26] This could hardly be described as a dogmatic position. He

---

[22] Gott, *An Essay of the True Happiness of Man*, a4.

[23] David Underdown, *Pride's Purge: Politics in the Puritan Revolution* (Oxford, 1971), pp. 212, 374. Fletcher, *County Community*, p. 293.

[24] [Gott] to Swynfen, [1650]: William Salt Library (Stafford), Salt Ms. 454 (Swynfen Mss.), no. [6A]. I owe this reference to Professor David Underdown. See also Underdown, *Pride's Purge*, pp. 56, 264; Blair Worden, *The Rump Parliament 1648–1653* (Cambridge, 1974), p. 85. On the Engagement controversy see John M. Wallace, *Destiny His Choice: the Loyalism of Andrew Marvell* (Cambridge, 1968), pp. 45–64.

[25] The manuscripts of Rye Corporation include a letter from the Mayor and Jurats to 'Samuel Gott at Seddlescombe'. The letter was dated 20 December 1655 and reads, 'We have taken opportunity by these to acquaint you that the middle aisle of the chancel here, which belongs to the parsonage of this parish, is very ruinous and one gutter, running between that aisle and the part enclosed by the use of the town, requires a mending. We have received much damage by the rain, and although, we have often solicited Thomas Morphet (who we understand doth hire the same of your Worship) that it might be repaired, yet he will do nothing, nor without your help is anything likely to be done.' *Historical Manuscripts Commission, Thirteenth Report, Appendix IV*, p. 226.

[26] Patrick, 'Puritanism and Poetry', p. 212. Fletcher, *County Community*, pp. 310, 315–16.

did not sit in either the Convention Parliament or that elected in May 1661.[27] In the autumn of 1661 he stood once more for election as M.P. for Rye in contest with Sir John Robinson. Sir John, Lieutenant of the Tower of London, was virtually a royal nominee. Gott, however, wrote in November to Rye Corporation expressing his respect for his opponent but refusing to stand down.[28] He was nevertheless defeated. After this Gott appears to have retired once more to the country. He wrote, studied, and worked on an 'artificial spring'. His intellectual isolation was irksome to him and he complained of it in his last work, *The Divine History of the Genesis of the World*, which he published in 1670.[29] In December of the following year he died at Battle.

In practice Gott's public life was far more limited than he had probably intended. As for many country gentlemen, there could be no wholehearted commitment to a régime which had broken with the ancient constitution and yet, in the cause of law, order and civility, obedience must be granted it. In consequence his life remained bounded by the local community, in which he lived and possessed a position of some importance, and the society of the Inns of Court with which he remained in contact until the Restoration. In parliamentary affairs he remained a peripheral and relatively unimportant figure.

Nova Solyma was first published in 1648 and a second issue appeared the following year. It is impossible to ascertain when it was written but the idea, derived from Begley, that Gott wrote it as a Cambridge undergraduate is rather weak. Gott left Cambridge at the age of nineteen and the work suggests greater maturity. The *Autocriticon*, which claimed that the novel was written in the heat of youthful ardour, was only appended to the edition of 1649 and is hardly a definite guide. Some of the ideas may have been conceived at Cambridge or the Inns of Court, but the work, which is long and in polished Latin, was most possibly a product of Gott's early retirement to Battle, between the years 1641 and 1645. In form, *Nova Solyma* is a philosophical romance most closely akin to works like John Barclay's *Argenis*, from which indeed Gott appears to have borrowed a number of devices.[30] As a philosophical romance *Nova Solyma*

---

[27] Patrick, 'Puritanism and Poetry', p. 213. Stephen K. Jones appears to be in error over Gott's membership of Charles II's first Parliament, 'Authorship of *Nova Solyma*', p. 228.

[28] Samuel Gott to the Mayor, Jurats and Commonalty of Rye, 19 November 1661. *Historical Manuscripts Commission, Thirteenth Report, Appendix IV*, p. 243.

[29] Gott, *The Divine History of the Genesis of the World*, a2.

[30] John Barclay, *Argenis, Translated out of Latine into English. The prose upon his Majesties Command: by Sir Robert Le Grys, Knight: And the Verses by Thomas May, Esquire* (London, 1628). For an example of possible influence compare *Nova Solyma*, vol. I, p. 83 with *Argenis*, p. 58. For other possible influences see Patrick, 'Gott's Puritan Utopia', p. 50.

exists on two levels. It is a baroque, picaresque fiction, a series of loosely related incidents wound together by a rather episodic thread of narrative. It employs a variety of literary forms and devices – fantasies, epic poems, lectures, dialogues, flashbacks and straightforward narrative. On the second level it remains a unity.[31] The main source of its cohesion is the theme that only the Christian faith offers an acceptable way of looking at the universe and a satisfactory way of life. Moreover, this unity or simpleness of purpose behind Gott's work is endorsed by his two other known, published works. In *An Essay of the True Happiness of Man* (1650) he sought to show that only the Christian faith offers men the possibility of true happiness. *The Divine History of the Genesis of the World* (1670) was dedicated to an attack on scepticism and proof of the credibility of a Christian account of the universe and its creation.

Gott's story began with the arrival at the city of Nova Solyma of two young Englishmen – Politian and Eugenius – in the company of Joseph, a citizen of that town. The strangers arrived on the day of the annual festival celebrating the founding of the city and the work recounts the story of the first year of their stay, ending, as it began, with the annual festival.

Nova Solyma depicts an ideal society created after the resettlement of the Jews in the Holy Land.[32] The prosperity and social harmony of the community are based on a conversion to Christianity and an expulsion of the Turk which had taken place fifty years before.[33] In this respect, the work is associated with that form of millenarian writing which, in its treatment of the latter-day glory, emphasised the preliminary conversion of the Jews. Thomas Brightman, for example, in *A Revelation of the Revelation* (1615), had predicted a future millennium when the Jews would return to the Holy Land and God's saints would reign on earth. Alsted in *Diatribe de Milleannis Apocalypticis* (1627) – a translation of which was authorised by the Long Parliament in 1642 – envisaged the rule of resurrected martyrs and converted Jews beginning in the year 1694 and preceding the Last Judgement. In Henry Archer's *The Personall Reign of Christ Upon Earth* (1642) the Jews were to be converted in 1650 or 1656 and Jerusalem was to become the most eminent city on earth.[34]

---

[31] Cf. V. Dupont, *L'Utopie et le Roman Utopique dans la Littérature Anglaise* (Toulouse, 1941), p. 197.

[32] The heroes were described as leaving Dover by ship for Joppa. The journey from Joppa to Nova Solyma took them one day on horseback. Joppa was thirty-five miles, or a good day's ride, from Jerusalem. Cf. Andreae, *Christianopolis*, ed. Held, p. 81. See also *Nova Solyma*, vol. 1, pp. 78–9, 86.

[33] *Nova Solyma*, vol. 1, pp. 88–9, 98, 99.

[34] Henry Archer, *The Personall Reign of Christ Upon Earth* (1642), p. 27; Cf. [Thomas Goodwin], *A Glimpse of Syons Glory* (1641), p. 21; Toon (ed.), *Puritans, the Millennium and the Future of Israel*, p. 34. Frances Yates, *The*

But, by the mid 1640s, the English atmosphere was full of references to this kind of expectation. As a new recruiter M.P., Gott may well have listened to two sermons preached to both Houses of Parliament on 26 November 1645, a day of public humiliation, and published early the following year. One was John White's *The Troubles of Jerusalems Restauration or the Churches Reformation*, the other John Dury's *Israels Call to March out of Babylon unto Jerusalem*, and both of them referred to the coming conversion of the Jews. It seems probable, however, that *Nova Solyma* was most closely connected with a work published in 1621 under the title *The World's Great Restauration or The Calling of the Jewes*. Its author was Sir Henry Finch (1558–1625), serjeant at law, client of Sir Francis Bacon, hebraicist and, like Gott, educated at Cambridge and a prominent member of Gray's Inn. Finch's book was an extraordinarily thorough textual analysis of all references in either Old or New Testaments to the conversion of the Jews, their overthrow of the Turk and their establishment of a world dominion based in the Holy Land. 'Wee need not be afraid', he wrote, 'to averre and maintcyne, that one day they shall come to Ierusalem againe, be Kings and chiefe Monarches of the earthe, sway and governe all, for the glory of Christ that shall shine among them.' According to Finch, the conversion of the Jews would come in 1650 and with it the decline of Turkish power, a process which would be completed, with the world domination of a Christianised Jewry, in 1695.[35] Gott's exercise in post-millennialist imagination might thus be read as an extension of Finch's work and one integrated to his time-scale. *Nova Solyma* remains outstanding, in this sense if no other, that it is one of the few attempts to visualise the social context of the latter-day glory. Yet there is little obtrusion of millenarian mechanics and strangely, as we shall see, men's hold on grace in the New Jerusalem remains uncertain. For these reasons *Nova Solyma* cannot simply be identified with the millenarian tradition.

Politian and Eugenius observed the educational system, the market,

Rosicrucian Enlightenment (London, 1972), p. 228. Margaret James, *Social Problems and Policy during the Puritan Revolution 1640–1660* (London, 1930), pp. 188–92; S. B. Liljegren, 'Harrington and the Jews', *K. Humanistiska Vetenskapssamfundet i Lund Arsberättelse*, 4 (1931–2), pp. 65–92; *Nova Solyma*, vol. 1, Excursus F, pp. 349–51. On Alsted see Firth, *Apocalyptic Tradition*, pp. 211–12.

[35] [Sir Henry Finch], *The Worlds Great Restauration* (1621), pp. 7, 59–60. I am indebted to Wilf Prest for his help on this point and also for an early copy of his essay on Finch. Wilfrid R. Prest, 'The Art of Law and the Law of God: Sir Henry Finch (1558–1625)', in D. Pennington and K. Thomas (eds.), *Puritans and Revolutionaries: Essays in Seventeenth-Century History Presented to Christopher Hill* (Oxford, 1979), pp. 94–117. See also, Patrick, 'Gott's Puritan Utopia', p. 51, n. 8. Finch's interpretation followed those of Brightman and Alsted.

the familial relations, the social conventions and the laws of their hosts. Above all, through lectures, discussions, and watching the spiritual struggles of certain central characters, Politian and Eugenius were witness to the religious principles of the Nova Solymans. They learned the illusory nature of romantic love and of the pursuit of sensory pleasure both through their own experiences and the adventures of others. And they found that true happiness could be gained only through patient, moderate and unflagging pursuit of the Christian religion. Interwoven with this didactic framework of the novel were illustrative and diverting tales of piracy, kidnap, thwarted or unrequited love, war, duels, dreams, bandits, suicide and infernal pacts. The novel ended one year after the Englishmen's arrival with the anniversary of the founding of the city. All was fulfilled. Politian and Eugenius married twin sisters. A commercial treaty was signed between England and Nova Solyma. Joseph experienced a vision of God and the Last Judgement, and the spiritual education of the two Englishmen was complete.

There is truth in the criticism that Gott's work reflects a period of uncertainty in the development of the novel. No doubt many of *Nova Solyma's* more absurd features could be explained in this way. Equally, it is incontestable that the work is possessed of considerable literary merit and interest. Gott was a skilful narrator, an accomplished poet, and a literary theorist of some significance. Even so his central preoccupations were not literary and his other, non-fictional, works bear this out. The main purpose of the work has to be seen as theological.[36] Its overriding concern was the intellectual respectability, or rather indispensability, of the Christian world-view. Gott attempted to show that reason, as well as faith, led to a necessary acceptance of a divine creator and a redeeming Christ. He explored this theme through a series of discussions and lectures on the validity of Christian theology and metaphysics and through the religious experiences of various characters in the novel. The Jews of Nova Solyma were led by reason, faith and experience to a full acceptance of Christianity.

Gott opened this theme with a discussion of the artistry of the natural universe and the question as to whether this was the result of accident or design.[37] Although Politian supported the notion of the universe as an accidental phenomenon, the argument was eventually resolved in favour of a divine creator. At this stage scriptural evidence was played down in favour of the arguments of reason. The finitude of all bodies in time and space was seen as suggesting a moment of creation. Similarly the pattern of cause and effect pervading the universe, and 'the drill and discipline of

---

[36] Cf. Dupont, *L'Utopi et le Roman Utopique*, p. 187. Sometimes the emphasis on Gott's religious purposes has led to a devaluing of his social and political proposals. Cf. A. L. Morton, *The English Utopia* (London, 1952), p. 69.

[37] *Nova Solyma*, Book II, Chapters 1 and 3, vol. I, p. 172.

the starry sky', were seen as placing the accidental theory out of court. The scientist, in consequence, enjoyed the advantage of systematically observing the handiwork of the creator: 'the special advantage of natural science is to rise from Nature to Nature's God, tracing his footsteps everywhere therein'.[38]

While arguing that reason itself was capable of leading men to the conclusion of a divine creator's existence, Gott was careful to warn that reason could not explain all the mysteries of God: 'you are greatly mistaken if you hold that our reason cannot rise to any knowledge at all of the Deity, or, on the other hand, expect a clear and perfect knowledge'. This was clearly not a prohibition on the use of reason in issues of theology but an attempt to establish a balance between the rôles of reason and faith.[39] However, the balance struck indicates a shift of emphasis, for,

[38] *Ibid.*, vol. I, p. 172, 184, 186. Cf. *An Essay of the True Happiness of Man*, p. 81. Gott has been seen justifiably as a Baconian (Christopher Hill, *Intellectual Origins of the English Revolution* (Oxford, 1965), p. 116). There is hardly space here to discuss Bacon's influence on Gott but perhaps a few remarks may be permitted. Gott had certainly read Bacon's works, including his *New Atlantis*, by 1670 (Gott, *The Divine History of the Genesis of the World*, pp. 12, 112–13) and probably well before that. He was a member of the Inn of Court in which Bacon had spent a great part of his life. He adopted Baconian attitudes to experiment and the value of the mechanical arts. (*An Essay of the True Happiness of Man*, p. 94; *The Divine History*, pp. 11–12.) Part of his later years he devoted to experiments with artificial springs, a subject which had interested Bacon. (Cf. Bacon, 'Sylva Sylvarum', in Spedding, Ellis and Heath (eds.), *The Works of Francis Bacon*, vol. II, p. 347.) However, both in the establishment of Christianity as a rational necessity as well as a revealed truth, and in subjecting cosmological theory to the test of scripture, Gott ran counter to Bacon's insistence on the separation of faith and reason. (Cf. e.g. *An Essay of the True Happiness of Man*, p. 142.) The description of *Nova Solyma* as 'a scientific utopia' has very little warrant. Cf. Glenn Negley and J. Max Patrick, *The Quest for Utopia* (New York, 1952), pp. 291–2.

[39] *Nova Solyma*, vol. I, p. 189. See also vol. I, pp. 189–92. As he grew older, Gott appears to have become increasingly impatient with the incursion of reason into theology and metaphysics. His *Divine History of the Genesis of the World* was both an attack on scepticism and cartesian system building and an attempt to re-establish the place of scripture in cosmology. 'For mine own part', he wrote, 'I must here profess that having long since studied Philosophy in the University, and read several philosophers both Antient and Modern, I could never find a satisfaction in any of them: and if I had not reflected on this Divine History, should have been tempted, as others, to invent some new philosophy suitable to mine own Fansy: For now he is no philosopher who will not attempt to make a new philosophical world, and produce his Module thereof; shewing how it might be best made, and with least charges: but certainly it is most Ridiculous and impious thus to presume that God must therefore have made the world according to our Module, because we judge it best; rather than acknowledge that to be best which he hath made, because he who made it is infinitely wiser than us.' *The Divine History*, p. 6.

having established the existence of a divine creator, Gott was beginning to approach the imponderables of that creator's will. While reason could help towards a definition of the problems it was ultimately faith alone which could resolve them. To illustrate the insufficiency of reasons and authority without faith, Gott introduced the story of Jacob's search for true religion.[40] Jacob insisted that the obligations of faith must be defined by the object of that faith, God. It was therefore divine will and not human reason or authority which was of crucial importance in the quest. Accordingly Jacob saw the rights and responsibilities of civil authority over religion as strictly limited:

in spiritual matters, by a parity of reasoning, the ordering and appointing is of God, and if any humanly authorised power denies or even strives against this principle, it is the people's duty to resist, and death itself is to be chosen in preference to such an unjust and monstrous tyranny. Nor are we morally bound to observe rites which do not owe their origin to that Deity...[41]

But the individualistic emphasis of Jacob's rejection of the right of secular authorities to prescribe religious doctrines and forms renewed the problem of fathoming the divine will as a personal and individual problem.

On the one hand, it had to be accepted that there was a purpose behind the creation and the only purpose which made sense was that God's creatures should enjoy immortal life. On the other hand, there appeared to be imperfections in nature, the elements warring against man, one species seeking the destruction of another.[42] How was this to be explained? The answer was through the doctrine of sin. While the origins of sin remained something of a mystery, its enormity and its disabling effects were readily apparent: 'he who sins wishes that God did not exist, or, worse still that he would be unjust'. In the fall of Adam we were all condemned. Theophratus, who had sold his soul to the devil, stood as a symbol of all men.[43] Given this condition, men had to give up all hope of reconciliation with God through their own merits. Just as it was God's grace alone which gave man knowledge of their sins, so it could only be God's sacrifice which could reconcile men to him. The redeeming Christ thus became a logical as well as a theological necessity.[44] Once the mechanism of election[45] and the need for perseverance[46] were made clear, Gott's

[40] *Nova Solyma*, Book II, Chapter 8.

[41] *Ibid.*, vol. I, p. 224. Gott saw the possibilities of the exploitation of religion for political ends but he denied that religion had originated in political necessity: 'religion seems innate in mankind', *ibid.*, vol. I, pp. 225–6. The problem of church and state does not arise in Nova Solyma principally because Gott makes virtually no provision for a church.

[42] *Ibid.*, Book IV, Chapter 3; Book IV, Chapter 5.

[43] *Ibid.*, vol. II, pp. 35, 55–9; Book II, Chapter 6; Book IV, Chapter 7.

[44] *Ibid.*, vol. I, p. 306, vol. II, p. 64; Book VI, Chapters 2, 4.

[45] *Ibid.*, Book VI, Chapter 5.   [46] *Ibid.*, Book VI, Chapters 9, 10.

picture was complete: 'at last the rays of Divine Light burst upon me, and taking away all my darkness and blindness, revealed to my eyes Jesus Christ, Messiah and Saviour, as well as Creator and God'.[47]

Closely related to this major theme of true religion is a sub-theme of true happiness. Gott portrayed the search for true happiness, and the dangers involved, in the actions and misadventures of various of his characters. True happiness was found to lie in moderate behaviour and the knowledge and love of God.[48] Thus, for example, he examined the love affairs of his characters to show how romantic passion was founded in illusion and fraught with anti-social consequences. Eugenius and Polician fell in love with the daughter of Zion and believing themselves in love with the same girl were driven finally to seek each other's elimination in a duel. Only the revelation that they were in love with twin sisters saved them from self-destruction.[49] Antonia's love for Philander was exposed as illusion when she discovered that Philander was in fact a woman disguised as a man. Philipina was destroyed by a love for Joseph which could never be requited:[50] 'no one can be in love and in his right mind at the same time'.[51] The madness that is romantic passion led, not to happiness, but to 'great disturbance in families...secret marriages, rapes, and even murder'. It was important therefore to avoid 'the clandestine amours of youth' and to give the leading rôle in marriage arrangements firmly to parents.[52] 'They lead the happiest married lives who avoid the romantic extremes of courtship, and let the strain of love pursue a quiet, even course, wherein it obeys its true law.'[53] True fulfilment, however, could only come with the Higher Love, the love of God, which left one, as it had left Joseph, invulnerable to earthly passion.[54]

The rejection of earthly love as man's true fulfilment, his true happiness, was but a part of a wider rejection of the satisfactions offered by the senses. This received its clearest expression in the episode where a nurse warned the children in her charge of the dangers and delusions of the kingdom of pleasure.[55] She described for them a world of natural harmony and sensual fulfilment, an arcadia.

All along the beach were shells glittering like precious stones, and the fine clean sand was the colour of gold. The open country abounded with the most beautiful trees, which, although they stood too thickly together for the soil to

[47] *Ibid.*, vol. II, p. 166.
[48] This is also of course, the conclusion of *An Essay of the True Happiness of Man.*
[49] *Nova Solyma*, vol. I, pp. 307–10, vol. II, pp. 23, 99–100, 102–11, 131.
[50] *Ibid.*, Book IV, Chapter 6; Book V, Chapter 1.
[51] *Ibid.*, vol. II, p. 109.
[52] *Ibid.*, vol. II, pp. 205–6. Cf. Dupont, *L'Utopie et le Roman Utopique*, p. 189.
[53] *Nova Solyma*, vol. II, p. 104.
[54] *Ibid.*, Book V, Chapter 2.
[55] *Ibid.*, vol. I, pp. 109–27.

bee cultivated, yet gave ample room for pleasant walks. There was everywhere cooling shade from natural arbours with their waving branches overhead, and yet light and sunshine withal. The perennial verdure had a most pleasing effect on the eye, and, embellished as it was with many a flower of varied hue dotted here and there, it recalled the brilliant canopy of heaven, and view with its many twinkling stars. Many shady alleys led in various directions, most pleasant for walking, for they were level and carpeted with the smoothest grass; but often they led nowhere, and there was no certain goal in any case – like a labyrinth, they misled by their devious twistings and turnings all who were foolish enough to wander through them.[56]

The lack of purpose in arcadian existence was seen as morally corrupting. As the dream went on the nurse developed her theme, moving from a world of natural harmony to one of excess, to a vision recalling that of the Land of Cockaygne tradition. Without temperance man became as a beast and the dream ended as they plunged into a cesspool beneath the palace of illusions.[57] Having accepted the doctrine of the fall and its universal effects, Gott was bound to see nature as degenerate, contaminated, and men's sensual experience as a snare.[58] As all men's faculties had been weakened by the fall, so had the relationship between sense and intelligence been dislocated. Men could not interpret their sensory experiences correctly. Indeed, Gott believed that it was one of the special functions of poetry to help re-establish the links between sense and intelligence.[59]

Just as man through his own fallen nature creates his own misery, so only in God is pleasure pure.

The true life that we should embrace is one of solid reality and severe earnestness; not a course of life that promises the greatest gain, or the most luxurious ease, nor yet one leading to mere fame or successful ambition, but rather that way should be chosen which, from a careful consideration of all things, seems most likely to tend to the glory of God and the service of our fellow citizens.[60]

The keynotes here were the defined ends and the cautious deliberative approach to means. This kind of life was only possible if man was capable of intelligent self-rule. The basis of self-rule had to be self-propriety, possessive individualism.[61] Accordingly God had given men in their minds' and souls' dominance over the body 'a Kingdom that is our private possession and we hold it on the freest of terms'. Yet, as had been shown,

---

[56] *Ibid.*, vol. I, pp. 109–10.   [57] *Ibid.*, vol. I, pp. 114–16.
[58] *Ibid.*, vol. II, pp. 55–9; Cf. *An Essay of the True Happiness of Man*, 243.
[59] *Nova Solyma*, vol. I, p. 296. For Gott's theory of the degrees of knowledge – matter, sense, fancy and intelligence – to which correspond degrees of happiness, see *An Essay of the True Happiness of Man*, pp. 8–13.
[60] *Nova Solyma*, vol. II, pp. 39–43, 96.
[61] For the background to what has been called possessive individualism, see C. B. MacPherson, *The Political Theory of Possessive Individualism: Hobbes to Locke* (Oxford, 1962).

the fall had damaged the relationship between mind and senses upon which such self-control was based. 'Our passions, indeed, affect our minds just as winds affect a ship. If the breezes are genial and moderated, the ship sails gallantly on; but when they are turbulent and contrary, there is constant risk of being wrecked.' Men were now capable of self-command but only with God's assistance.[62] Men's self-propriety, their rights in their own persons, became limited in accordance with the will of God. Specific limits were set to man's possessive individualism, first in regard to his own life and secondly in regard to the disposal of his own soul. Men could risk their lives only in the public interest or for the glory of God.[63] Gott examined the second query of man's rights over the disposal of his own soul, through the story of Theophratus. Theophratus as a young student of alchemy had entered into a compact with the devil whereby the devil was to take his soul in return for unlimited knowledge.[64] Theophratus was convinced that, as a result of the contract, he was damned. In other words, he took the view that his propriety in his own soul was complete and that he could therefore grant it away: 'a compact with the devil, however unfair its terms, is irrevocable. For as God requires our free vows and promises to him to be fulfilled as a sacred obligation due to Him, so in strict justice He allows the devil to claim his due, and exact the completion of our free compact with him.' Lucas, a friend of Theophratus, argued, on the other hand, that such a contract was invalid since the soul was not man's prerogative but God's: 'render unto God the things that are Gods'. Man's rights in his own soul were limited, leasehold rather than freehold. In fact it was this latter interpretation which in the end held good. Theophratus was saved on his deathbed. It was God, not the devil, who held title to his soul.[65]

In other respects, that is, exclusive of the right to surrender life and barter the soul, the full effect of the doctrine of self-propriety was felt. Alcimus, in a drunken stupor, was brought to sign a contract enslaving

---

[62] *Nova Solyma*, vol. II, pp. 121, 126. [63] *Ibid.*, vol. I, pp. 141–2.

[64] *Ibid.*, vol. I, pp. 212–13. As regards the Christian tradition the idea of the infernal pact goes back to the legend of Theophilus of Adana. Catholics solved the problem by appealing to the Virgin Mary, but for Protestants this was impossible and the diabolatry which flourished amongst early Lutherans was taken to mean eternal damnation for those involved. The spread of Johann Spies' *Faustbuch* of 1587 and the publication of Marlowe's *The Tragical History of D. Faustus* in 1604 may have brought the idea to Gott's mind. See also Norman Cohn, *Europe's Inner Demons* (London, 1975), pp. 233–4.

[65] *Nova Solyma*, vol. I, p. 210; vol. II, pp. 66–7. I have elsewhere argued for this limited view of self-propriety as a feature of the Levellers' political thought. J. C. Davis, 'The Levellers and Christianity', in B. S. Manning (ed.), *Politics, Religion and the English Civil War* (London, 1973), Chapter 6. Cf. C. B. MacPherson, *The Political Theory of Possessive Individualism: Hobbes to Locke* (Oxford, 1962), Chapter 3.

himself to Joseph and the contract was held to be good: 'surely it is not unjust that who cannot keep possession of his senses or his reason should come under some other authority than his own, as you have in your case'.[66] Gott clearly believed that those without material possessions were obliged to lose their possessive individualism in so far as they granted away command over their physical efforts. Indeed, he believed that wage labour, from this point of view, was virtually indistinguishable from slavery: 'such as have all their Estates in their own hands, that is live upon their daily labours, being slaves to every man who will hire them: which is a condition almost as servile as to be enslaved to one proper Master, the one being of Necessity, as the other of Compulsion'.[67] It followed that a limited self-proprietorship and a moral stewardship over life and the soul could only be fully exercised if men maintained their capacities for self-control. Gott had tried to demonstrate that a divine purpose ordered the universe, and that God wanted men's free submission to that purpose. However, self-possession was essential to voluntary submission. It was largely in order to facilitate the attainment of the degree of self-control, requisite for the fullest self-possession and the satisfaction of God, that he devised the elaborate educational provisions of Nova Solyma.

A full understanding of the significance of Gott's educational programme can, however, only be grasped if the distinction between elect and unregenerate, which runs through his social attitudes, is borne in mind. Education was of special importance to the elect for two reasons. Since Christianity was in part a rational creed its tenets could be taught. Secondly, the elect, weak like other men, needed to have instilled into them the strategies of faith and their moral obligations. Accordingly, the priorities of public education in Nova Solyma were set out as, first, the inducement of a religious habit of mind, second, the inculcation of ethical duties, and third, a 'liberal education, both literary and scientific'. Nevertheless, it was also important that the beneficent influence of education be extended to the degenerate. 'Although all do not attain unto eternal salvation, the religious influence imparted to them does certainly, through its elements of fear and reverence, make them inclined to a more respectable and honourable life.' Indeed, left to themselves, the damned could be a dangerous threat to the saved.

Some are so cunning that, were it possible, they would deceive the very elect, whence it can be seen how doubtful and difficult a thing it is to hold a straight

---

[66] *Nova Solyma*, vol. II, pp. 2–3.

[67] Gott, *An Essay of the True Happiness of Man*, p. 54. Gott did not view this condition as an especially miserable one, as long as working men kept their health and strength. 'Rich men need their Labors as much as they need their Riches. An Able Body may well earn its own Living.' *Ibid.*

and even course in religion, where there are so many rocks and stumbling blocks designedly placed in our way by malignant sophists, and so many quick-sands to swallow us up if we do not take care.[68]

The distinction between saved and damned is crucial not only to an understanding of Gott's emphasis on education but also to a grasp of his utopianism, for it offered one half of the explanation as to why the re-deemed Jews of Nova Solyma were not capable of a perfect moral commonwealth. The degenerate were not capable of the mutual love, without which 'a man may become to his fellow-man worse than a savage beast; he becomes full of hate, envy, fury, murder, yea, if he could he would follow up his vengeance to the depths of Hell itself'. The history of unregenerate man, if he were left unchecked, would become a story where

vast multitudes of men, sworn in under a deadly compact, fitted out with all the weapons of destruction, adorned with standards and banners, and marching in due rank and order, are led forth to lay waste a country, to burn its cities, and to slaughter its principal people; and the more terror they cause, and the greater the ravages they commit, so much the more do they boast and triumph in such deeds, and are handed down to posterity loaded with honours, this glorious tradition being kept up perhaps, to cover the vile atrocities of our ancestors from the researches of later generations, or to encourage posterity to rise to like wicked barbarity.[69]

The other half of the explanation of Gott's rejection of the perfect moral commonwealth lay in his belief that even the saved were morally vulner-able. Grace enabled men to live righteous lives but never perfect ones.[70] Thus, because of his views of both the elect and the condemned, education was seen by Gott as an indispensable instrument for the achievement and maintenance of social harmony. Religion may have been 'the foundation and cornerstone of society', but it was the rôle of education to make its precepts socially effective.

The founders of our republic, in their zealous enquiry how best to establish it on a sound basis, put the education of the rising generation in the very fore-front of all means to that end. They held the opinion that good laws, an effective army, and all other defences of the state were of comparatively no avail if obedience and benevolence and other virtues which tend to the well-being of mankind were not early planted in the minds of the young...[71]

---

[68] *Nova Solyma*, vol. I, pp. 239, 306; vol. II, p. 204.

[69] *Ibid.*, vol. II, pp. 37–8.

[70] *An Essay of the True Happiness of Man*, p. 248; *Nova Solyma*, vol. II, pp. 204, 210–21.

[71] *Nova Solyma*, vol. I, pp. 235, 239. Cf. vol. I, p. 90. It is important, nevertheless, to recognise that in Gott's view both learning and morality were subordinate to religion. 'Even as knowledge is the servant of morality, so both are true servants of religion.' *Ibid.*, vol. I, p. 306. On education as a means of social control in utopias see Gildo Massó, *Education in Utopias* (New York, 1927), pp. 21–3.

The educational system of Nova Solyma was designed to perform three main functions: to ensure maximum social advantage from the stock of human abilities available; to stimulate the highest fulfilment of the potential of gifted individuals; to internalise social, moral and religious discipline. In this last sense education paralleled social control by law and bureaucracy. In an illuminating analogy Gott even compared the school-teachers of Nova Solyma with magistrates.

For the Jews of Nova Solyma do not hold schoolmasters in contempt, as so many other nations do, nor do they class them simply as superior servants who have to see chiefly that the children are kept safe and do not get into mischief. On the contrary, they are classed with the chief magistrates of the nation, and especially are those schoolmasters held in honour who have the charge of the young and untrained, for they are invested with the order of the Sun, appropriately enough too, for the sun is the dispeller of all darkness, and renders possible the active duties of life.[72]

Primary education up to the age of ten took place in the home.[73] The teaching of mathematics and grammar began as soon as the child was able to talk. However, the main emphasis of the educational effort at this stage was on bodily fitness and self-discipline. 'We follow the glorious example of the old Greeks and Romans, and pay our regard to both mind and body.' This led to an unusual emphasis on exercise and the development of grace but even more surprising was the Nova Solyman's willingness to use the methods of selective breeding to ensure physical perfection.[74] The attempt to accustom children to physical hardness by exercise, endurance and frugality led naturally on to the inculcation of moral discipline.

Though it be granted that the soul is of separate origin and derived from God, yet it is closely connected with the body, and interacts upon it through the medium of the senses. We try to improve by art and culture in every way the gifts of body and mind with which kindly nature endows our race, in order that our children, both by their natural ability and the formative care they received when young, may strive onwards to the acme of human perfection... The earliest faults that show themselves in children are passion and over-readiness to cry and yell, and afterwards obstinacy, pride and envy. These are the vices we first of all try to master. We foster a voluntary habit of endurance and good temper, more by contrivance and the giving of prizes than moral precept.

---

[72] *Nova Solyma*, vol. 1, p. 234.

[73] *Ibid.*, vol. 1, pp. 90–7. For the absence of mathematical instruction in seventeenth-century English schools see W. A. L. Vincent, *The State and School Education 1640–1660 in England and Wales* (London, 1950), p. 13.

[74] 'Nor do we put aside those methods which breeders are so careful about with their dogs and horses.' *Nova Solyma*, vol. 1, p. 90.

In this way too children were taught kindness, liberality and humility. But the main emphasis was on the control of appetite.

Especially do we try to restrain the violent desires of our nature in the bonds of temperance and chastity. We put special restrictions on eating and sleeping too much; all must rise early and eat what happens to be set before them. Hardly ever do they get the chance of delicacies; but sometimes, to create disgust, we allow them to gorge to repletion.

Yet there was a creative as well as a repressive aspect to educational policy in Nova Solyma: 'our highest endeavour is to kindle into flame the spark of genius that may be latent in each, for we cannot hope that those who only follow the trite and vulgar pursuits of the mob can ever be so fired with enthusiasm as to dare...any truly great and noble act'. Gott defended the use of parable and myth in the education of the very young, as well as that of educational games, provided that they did not lead to idleness.[75] The unremitting struggles against idleness and dishonesty were, indeed, important features of the programme: 'hardly any portion of their daily life is allowed to lie fallow, but is so cultivated that each should bring forth the best fruit in due season'; 'We rank liars with those creatures that have not the use of speech, and treat them as equally unsuited for the society of articulately speaking men.'[76] There was no attempt to ensure equality of educational opportunity. The education of girls was not even mentioned. But Gott was concerned that all male talent, from whatever class it came, should be effectively utilised. 'Nor is anyone with natural endowments of a higher order allowed to remain unnoticed and neglected from the obscurity of his birth, as is so often the case elsewhere.' The extent to which this was a question of social, rather than individual, benefit was clearly revealed by Gott's suspicion of those whose claim to attention was purely that of ability. They were often, 'by their shortcomings in other matters', a cause of more trouble and inconvenience than their less able but more docile fellows. This contrast between the desire to exploit human intellectual resources to the full and the fear of overeducating representatives of the lower orders was something that recurred in Gott's development of his educational system.[77]

At the age of ten, children were accepted into the Public Academy

---

[75] *Ibid.*, vol. I, pp. 128, 129, 93.

[76] This emphasis was by no means unique in the 1640s. Samuel Harmar, for example, believed that universal and compulsory education with a schoolmaster in every parish could eliminate the three great evils of ignorance, prophanity, and idleness. Samuel Harmar, *Vox Populi or Glostersheres Desire* (1642); see Vincent, *State and School*, pp. 31–3.

[77] Cf. Vincent, *State and School*, p. 34. William Petty is an example of another contemporary theorist concerned that the talents of the poorer classes should not go unexploited.

where they would remain until they were seventeen.[78] Such an academy was situated in the principal town of every province, where it occupied an extensive group of buildings. It was virtually a closed community: 'the students here hardly ever return home til they have completed a full seven years' course'. It was difficult for outsiders to gain admission to the building, which was under the control of a porter. The students were thus protected from the less desirable influence of the town, and their familial relationships were suspended in the process. Great care and attention was bestowed on Public Academies. They were to provide an example and also an inspectorate for the work of other schools. All schools were subject to annual inspection. Once again the selection of pupils was based on social inequality modified by a desire not to waste talent. 'Our pupils are either lads of gentle birth, who by their position in life are likely to make a figure in State Councils, or else lads of great natural parts and good promise, admitted with the prospect of reaching the like honour.' The latter, if necessary, were supported financially by public scholarships. Those of the lower classes who were not intellectually equipped for a life of state service could nevertheless benefit from the state's educational provision. 'There are technical schools as well, and public workshops where the children of the poorer classes are taught the meaner occupations, or, if they show ability, are instructed in the mechanical arts and crafts. Others follow the trades by which they earn their livelihood in a private and more independent manner.' For these, 'the higher culture is considered out of place in their station in life, and even prejudicial, from its tendency to make the working classes dissatisfied with their humble duties, if once they have tasted the dignified "sweetness and light" of the "intellectual life"'. In addition to their craft or trade these pupils were taught 'reading, writing, arithmetic, with geometry and other such studies as are a help to the mechanical arts'. They also underwent military, moral and religious exercises which were standard for people of their age.[79]

In addition to this the educational élite received a literary education, a training in Latin, Greek, Hebrew, and a knowledge of modern languages, 'especially of those nations who trade with us, for the use of interpreters wastes time and hinders business'. Gott insisted on the value and status of trade. 'We regard trade with much favour; all classes of society engage in it. Merchants and farmers are under no social discredit; it is only the dishonest business people who are despised and disgraced.' Not only were his élite trained in commercially useful languages but they were also

---

[78] The Public Academies of Nova Solyma are described in *Nova Solyma*, Book III, Chapter 1.

[79] *Ibid.*, vol. I, pp. 238, 304. Here as elsewhere allowance has to be made for Begley's enthusiasms in translation.

taught the arts of business correspondence and negotiations.[80] It would be tempting but rash to interpret all this as a manifestation of bourgeois mentality. In fact it reflected fairly realistically the necessities of the existing social structure of seventeenth-century England. The gentleman merchant, the aristocratic businessman, were typical features of Stuart society. Gott, like Bacon, was merely insisting that the humanistic education received by these classes was not wholly suited to the kinds of life they led. His attitude was Baconian rather than bourgeois.

All these subjects of instruction remained subordinate to Gott's religious and moral ends. Much of his educational interest stemmed from the assumption that 'religion has always flourished most in a learned age'. As religion was the foundation and cornerstone of society so the priorities of the Public Academy were, first, religious habits of mind, secondly, the performance of duties, and only third, a 'liberal education'. Involved in this was the inculcation of citizenship. Students learned 'that habit of mind by which they would willingly, in their own interests, keep inviolate the laws of God and their country, and put the advantage of the republic before any private or personal benefits whatever'. It was the task of the Public Academy to repress the bad and encourage the good in all of its students. This task involved the educationalists of Nova Solyma in carefully devised schemes, designed to avoid the harmful effects of some of the more doubtful subjects in their curriculum. For example, against the abuse of rhetoric they had invented an anti-rhetoric capable of exposing oratorical sleight of hand. History was written so as not to be 'a mere recital of things', but to put in a bad light crimes and to extol good deeds. Particular problems arose in relation to drama. 'We do not...allow our pupils to personate a drunkard or a fool, nor yet to take the part of a parasite, adulterer, cut-throat, or blackguards of that sort; for to do this is unbecoming in a gentleman, nor can anyone do justice to such a character without a tendency to the vice in himself, either inherent or assumed.' Pupils were encouraged to greater effort and rewarded for attainment by the distribution of prizes. Gott discussed a particular form of prize, prize pens, largely to illustrate his own theories on the relative importance of various literary forms.[81]

From the age of seventeen to twenty, able students could attend courses in one of two lecture halls.[82] In the first they would receive general instruction in philosophy and civil prudence. In the other they would be prepared in theology, medicine and jurisprudence for entry into one of the learned professions. Not only were outsiders allowed to attend lectures at these institutions but

[80] *Ibid.*, vol. I, p. 242.
[81] *Ibid.*, vol. I, pp. 250–7, 297, 298, 305.
[82] *Ibid.*, Book IV, Chapter 2.

the students were given more liberty than in their previous years. Visits were allowed to the townspeople, and they might take part in the ordinary passing events, so as to gain some experience of the world before they made the sudden final plunge at the end of their students' course, the removal of too strict a discipline leading to license.[83]

Compared with his concentration on education and educational institutions, Gott provided only the sketchiest information about other aspects of his ideal society. This may well have been because the depiction of a utopia was secondary to his concern with Christian apologetics in the writing of *Nova Solyma*. Nevertheless he left sufficient information to make it clear that the good order of his fictional society was not dependent upon education, upon internalised social discipline, alone. Incidents of drunkenness, suicide, pacts with the devil and duelling illustrated the fact that the evil propensities of man had not been fully eradicated by the educational process and still had to be contained by social arrangements and discipline. In Nova Solyma the state laid down common standards of food and dress. Temperance was to be observed in both eating and drinking habits: 'the law is that each one's dress is to differ according to his rank and dignity, which is as strictly enforced as the distinction of dress between the sexes'. Luxury was subject to public censure. Pomp and ceremony, in festivals and funerals alike, was forbidden. Waste was not tolerated. 'He who wastes the means he has inherited, or as is less likely, acquired by himself, is obliged to send in his accounts not only to his creditors, but to the public censors.'[84] The cities of Nova Solyma were geometrically planned with streets of uniform buildings.[85] At the centre of the town was a public hall or merchants' exchange. 'In front a square tower rose from the roof, having on each of its four sides a clock face to draw attention to the passing hours, while the clock within ever and anon sounded forth the time for all to hear.' Time, like every other resource in Nova Solyma, was not to be wasted, but the symbol also perhaps conveyed temperance and the virtues of technology.[86]

'Arts, and crafts and husbandry are nowhere more diligently practised

---

[83] *Ibid.*, vol. ii, p. 7.
[84] *Ibid.*, vol. i, pp. 100–1, 106; vol. ii, pp. 132–4.
[85] *Ibid.*, vol. i, pp. 78–9.
[86] *Ibid.*, vol. i, pp. 201–2. On the growing demand for chronological precision in the context of an increasingly commercial society, from the end of the sixteenth century, see John U. Nef, *Cultural Foundations of Industrial Civilisation* (London, 1958), pp. 7–10; E. P. Thompson, 'Time, Work-Discipline and Industrial Capitalism', *Past and Present*, 38 (1967), pp. 56–97. On temperance and the image of the clock see Lynn White, Jr, 'The Iconography of *Temperantia* and the Virtuousness of Technology', in T. K. Rabb and J. E. Seigel (eds.), *Action and Conviction in Early Modern Europe: Essays in Memory of E. H. Harbison* (Princeton, 1969), pp. 197–219.

than with us.'[87] Indeed Gott was extremely suspicious of those without occupation. 'They who live without a calling and some constant Business', he wrote elsewhere, 'Wander up and down in the Wilderness of Vanity and Vice...'[88] Inessentials were exported, useful articles kept for home consumption. Thrift was encouraged, provided it did not degenerate into a miserly money-grabbing.[89] Charity to the poor was esteemed. 'What is asked of us for the poor is God's tribute money, and He has willed that the poor shall be ever with us as His tax-gatherers.'[90] On the other hand, begging was regarded as no better than theft: 'they who give alms to such do more harm than good'. A system of public collectors of charity had been instituted to prevent the abuses of private generosity and to distribute relief on a more effective basis.[91]

In Nova Solyma the duellist was held in worse repute than the public executioner, 'for the one acts against the authority of the state, and the other upholds it'.[92] If a man killed another in a duel, he was hung upside down as a symbol of his attempt to overturn justice. 'If both escape with their lives, they still do not escape punishment, for they are branded with a mark of ignominy so that all men can see it, and avoid them as they would dangerous goring beasts.' Issues of private honour could not be left in private hands for 'if a man were allowed to make a law for himself whenever he thought the established laws insufficient, you might just as well have no laws at all'. Accordingly it was the state which established honour and dishonour, branding the unworthy with 'the stigma of infamy' and the deserving with 'badges and orders of honours'. Some of their honourable awards were hereditary, 'and we make them so for the parents' sake, that the children may be educated up to their position, and possibly inherit the ancestral virtues'. However, should the recipient fail to live up to his title, he could be made to forfeit it. Gott wanted honour related to merit but with the advantages, as he saw it, of a hereditary system in so far as they were available. The parvenu was accorded the respect due to him for his self-advancement, 'for many a one has, likely enough, done as much for the good of the state in his single person as a dozen or more of the pedigree-family stamp'. True nobility did not arise from 'terrible and stirring deeds, not yet from tyrannical power, but from the shedding of a good influence everywhere, and from the copious flowing forth in daily life of all the higher qualities which mark a true gentleman'. Gott's emphasis here was a measure of his belief that a carefully

[87] *Nova Solyma*, vol. ii, p. 133.

[88] Gott, *An Essay of the True Happiness of Man*, p. 255.

[89] *Nova Solyma*, vol. ii, pp. 133–4. On Gott's attitude to money see also *An Essay of the True Happiness of Man*, pp. 52–60.

[90] *Nova Solyma*, vol. ii, p. 134.

[91] *Ibid.*, vol. i, pp. 238–9.

[92] For duelling and codes of honour in Nova Solyma see *ibid.*, Book iv, Chapter 5.

controlled system of civil honours was indispensable to the state that sought unity.[93]

Gott did no more than sketch the outlines of a legislative system in *Nova Solyma* and made no attempt at systematic discussion of legal matters. But the use of the law as a means of conditioning men's behaviour and the willingness to extend the law's operation into the most personal aspects of peoples' lives – selective breeding, dress, food, personal honour – reveal Gott's utopian approach. The treatment of governmental institutions, and of the officials who staffed them, was even more slight than Gott's description of the legal system of Nova Solyma. For example, he merely mentioned the existence of a Council of State but offered no explanation of its composition or function. At the end of the novel the annual election of magistrates took place. 'A general assembly was convened and the result was that Jacob, by a very large majority of all ranks,[94] was chosen to be the Father, or Chief, of the Senate, which is the highest honour in the city. Joseph was elected Leader, or Chief, of the young men, and Joanna was chosen to be daughter of Zion.' Unfortunately none of these offices or institutions was mentioned elsewhere in the novel. The same lack of information inhibits comment on the offices of Praefect of the Civic Guard, Negotiator, Public Censor, and Public Collector of Charity. Only in relation to public schools did Gott provide any framework for the rôles of the officials – headmaster, inspector, head tutor, schoolmaster, and porter[95] – to whom he referred.

The most serious discussion of an authority supplementary to that of the state concerned the position of fathers. Jacob compared the authority of fathers with divine authority. 'So great and so natural is the authority of parents over their children that no other human authority can be equal to it, not even the master over his servants, the king over his subjects, or the husband over his wife.' Indeed, in this sense, patriarchal authority was the highest of all authorities and a major prop of social discipline. Politian and Eugenius were rebuked for travelling abroad without their father's consent. Children were seen as the property of their parents, although parents did not have the power of life and death over them.[96] It was natural, for example, that parents should have control over their children's marriage arrangements, for it was not to be expected that God would approve a marriage made without their consent. But it was also

[93] Cf. *An Essay of the True Happiness of Man*, p. 67. 'Civill Honors are very necessary in a State, for thereby the State itself becomes more Honourable, & more compact within itself, by an orderly disposition of all the Members in their severale places and degrees.'

[94] Massó, *Education in Utopias*, p. 137, identifies this with democracy. On the basis of such scant information this can be seen as no more than an injudicious guess.

[95] *Nova Solyma*, vol. I, pp. 228, 236, 231, 233, 234, 238; vol. II, pp. 205, 222, 224.

[96] *Ibid.*, vol. I, p. 99.

socially convenient because the moderation of parents and the exercise of their authority prevented the anti-social consequences of the ardour of youth. A man was hardly fitted for rule, in the wider sense, unless he had graduated from the school of household government. Civil authority, in fact, had its origins in paternal authority.

The origin of kingly power is to be sought for in the patriarchal family life; and even nowadays single families are like so many provinces of an empire, each governed by its own paterfamilias, who rules in accordance with imperial policy. It is strictly a monarchy: one presides over the many, one is the ruling counsellor, and one provides the means – surely a noble and admirable arrangement.[97]

It was for this reason, perhaps, that the Chief of the Senate was also known as the Father. The significance of all this is that, whereas we see gaps in the institutional and bureaucratic apparatus of Nova Solyma, for Gott these were largely filled by patriarchal authority.

The other authority supplementary to that of the state in early modern society, the church, occupied very little of Gott's attention.[98] It might almost be said that the church did not exist in Nova Solyma. There was no reference to a priest throughout the work. The marriage ceremony was presided over by a public lecturer. Sacraments were reduced to a minimum – baptism and the Lord's Supper – and their efficacy was dependent on the faith of the recipient, not on the sanctity or ecclesiastical status of the celebrant. The principal religious observances of Nova Solyma were prayer and preaching, both of which were performed in a family context, as well as in larger groups. The people of Nova Solyma rejected Sabbatarianism, believing that there was 'no intrinsic sanctity in any particular day'. Nevertheless, they set aside one day when no work was done for religious observances, while insisting that this did not mean that religious observance should be neglected on other days.[99] This rejection of any intermediary between God and man was a reflection of the individualistic elements in Gott's religious thinking. For him, however, the corollary of an immediate relationship with God was that God should rule men's whole lives, worship and work: 'religion is meant for the whole man, body as well as soul'. It followed also that the interference of civil authorities in religious matters could not be tolerated. Having eliminated the

---

[97] *Ibid.*, vol. II, pp. 120, 205–6, 208. Cf. *An Essay of True Happiness*, p. 49. Here Gott suggested that the nearest men could come to realising the burdens monarchy imposed was in recalling those that fall on the father of a family.

[98] Cf. Massó, *Education in Utopias*, p. 47. Massó saw Gott as one of three utopians giving a commanding position to the church in their ideal society. The others were More and Andreae.

[99] *Nova Solyma*, vol. II, pp. 190–1, 198, 228. Cf. Hill, *Society and Puritanism*, Chapter 5; Hill, *The World Turned Upside Down* (London, 1972), pp. 287–8.

church, Gott was not about to accept the state as intermediary between
God and man:

in spiritual matters, by a parity of reasoning, the ordering and appointing is of
God and if any humanly authorised power denies or even strives against this
principle, it is the people's duty to resist, and even death itself is to be chosen
in preference to such an unjust and monstrous tyranny. Nor are we morally
bound to observe rites which do not owe their origin to the Diety...[100]

The problem thus arises as to how this check on civil authority is to be
equated with the total discipline characteristic of the utopian. The answer
lies in the theocratic nature of Gott's vision. Like Calvin in his *Institutes*,
Gott believed that he had revealed the unshakeable foundations of the
Christian faith with a clarity that made them unmistakable. Like Calvin,
in Geneva, he believed that a godly, an ideal society, had merely to act out
the pattern of life laid down in Christian doctrine. Like Calvin, he knew
not only the weakness of men's flesh but also the power of the creed
which he expounded. It was not necessary to develop a coherent theory of
politics. The state was merely a convenience, a device to contain the forces
of evil and to enable Christian doctrine and practice to do their work.
The utopian purpose was not central to Gott's work. Indeed he disavowed
it.[101] At the heart of any examination of Gott's thought must lie his continuing preoccupation, the establishment of Christianity as a rational
necessity as well as a revealed truth. It was the point at which the greatest
influence upon him, that of Francis Bacon, lapsed. Thus in *Nova Solyma*
he attempted to show how, while rational discussion could demonstrate the
existence of God, it failed to find an answer to the problem of evil. Only
faith could resolve this issue, and only the Christian faith offered men a
viable way of looking at the universe and an acceptable code of love,
morality and redemption. In *An Essay of the True Happiness of Man* he
argued that happiness was dependent on knowledge and that therefore no
happiness could arise from illusion or deception. Having shown that what
were conventionally considered to be forms of happiness were mere
illusion, and that classical philosophy offered no sound basis of knowledge
upon which to build true happiness, he turned once again to the Christian
religion. The greater knowledge was, the greater would happiness be. It

---

[100] *Nova Solyma*, vol. I, p. 224; vol. II, p. 199.
[101] See, *ibid.*, vol. I, p. 300, where Gott wrote of 'the impudent audacity of those
rash reformers who are for tearing up the old foundations, for putting civil and
political life on a new basis and for carrying out specious schemes which are as
costly as they are dangerous, in order to overturn what has stood the test of
many generations'. See also his statement in Parliament in February 1659 that he
could not 'look forward to *Oceana*'s Platonical Commonwealth, things that are
not, and that never shall be'. J. T. Rutt (ed.), *Diary of Thomas Burton*, 4 vols.
(London, 1828), vol. III, p. 144.

followed that the contemplation of God offered the greatest happiness but perfect knowledge of God was available only through the Christian faith. Twenty years later, in *The Divine History of the Genesis of the World*, he was still expounding the same themes. He dismissed the rationalist philosophies of past and present as purely mental schemes. His exegesis of the *Book of Genesis* sought to prove the importance of scriptural revelation in interpreting the universe. Although Gott offered a place to Baconianism, he sidestepped it by seeking the remarriage of faith and empiricism.

In *Nova Solyma*, as in his other works, his primary concern was not the visualisation of a utopian society, but an attempt to demonstrate the credibility of the Christian faith and the value of the Christian way of life. Having chosen a symbolic community of Jews to strengthen his argument, he had to show them in an ideal society. But this remained peripheral to his main concern and hence the picture was fragmentary. As the symbolism of the Jews, their conversion and reinstatement in the Holy Land arose out of the millenarian intellectual milieu and background of his day, it is surprising that the millenarian's framework of thought is not more apparent in his ideal society. Gott does not present an apocalyptic vision, but a society preoccupied with moral, spiritual and social improvement. Given his view of the fall and its consequences for man, Gott's rejection of arcadia and Cockaygne came almost automatically. Neither could he choose a perfect moral commonwealth. Only if he had believed in universal grace or an exclusive society could he have logically done that. Gott, however, took an élitist view of salvation, but was not prepared to recommend the withdrawal of the elect from a society of natural men. This was why the proof of his theology had to be rational as well as fideistic. It had to bind natural man as well as the man of faith. Moreover, even redemption, membership of the elect, did not guarantee perfect moral conduct. Yet his rejection of a perfect moral commonwealth was never entirely complete. He suffered the double vision of those who could not decide whether to keep their eyes on the elect or the unregenerate when contemplating society. He yearned for a society of morally committed men of grace but sought to come to terms with a society of the vicious, shiftless, faithless, and self-centred. Thus, for example, he gave great attention to the attractions of romantic love while suggesting that procreation should become a matter of state-managed eugenics. His educational system was built around the inculcation of a repressive moral conformity but also sought to stimulate creative individualism. He saw as desirable, and in this he reflected his social environment, the breakdown of familial relationships for those between ten and seventeen years old, and yet he lay great emphasis on the maintenance of the patriarchal family and patriarchal authority. All this was paralleled by a more fundamental dilemma: the knowledge that natural man was morally weak and the suspicion that all was not moral assurance even for the man of grace. Although his continuing theme was the basis of reason and faith upon which free men could act morally, Gott was never confident enough to assume that men would so act. Thus his utopianism, peripheral in terms of detailed provision, constantly insinuated itself into his decisions about and attitudes to his ideal society. The aim of the educational system, as of much else in Nova Solyma, was to subject individuals to a set of institutional pressures designed to produce simultaneously individual self-restraint and the creative pursuit of positive achievement. The possibilities of disharmony between these ends is readily apparent. To avoid discord it was necessary for Gott to dwell on the metaphysical assumptions behind the orthodoxy of educational practice and individual moral behaviour in Nova Solyma. Even so he was not prepared to guarantee the moral performance of the products of his educational system. Censorship, inspection, penalties, the proscription of the dishonest, and continuous vigilance remained necessary.

For puritans in England 1648 was a year of travail and anguish. The old church had fallen but the attempt to replace it had been frustrated by division. The godly were baulked by a set of political, religious and social dilemmas which appeared irresolvable. In 1648 all was in jeopardy as a godly, but alien, nation, the Scots, in league with a man of blood, turned to face a godly army, itself rent by faction, feud and distrust – most painfully of all by ideological difference. The outcome could only be the collapse of the ancient constitution. And at this moment of terrible necessity Gott published his New Jerusalem. To some it might appear the appropriate moment for a fusing of millennialism and classical republicanism. It might appear, in the multiple senses of that term, a Machiavellian Moment. Gott, millennialist and classical scholar, found such a moment not for him. A commonwealth of citizen saints ruling themselves eluded him. His work was not dedicated to virtue as discovered by man, the *zoön politikon*, exercising his capacities for moral choice by participating in the civic life of a well-balanced but free republic. Rather, virtue consisted in acting to accord with and attempting to realise the potentialities of a pre-ordained Christian moral standard. Gott showed no interest in the intricate balancing of forms, the political architecture of classical republicanism, for his overriding intention was not to erect a framework in which participating citizens would devise the codes of civic virtue appropriate to their particular commonwealth. His thought remained riven and tortured by tensions between self-rule and patriarchalism, between sainthood and the accommodation of natural man, between faith and reason. Like puritanism itself faced with the moment of revolution, he was torn between that pessimistic consciousness of the inescapability of sin which threw men in helpless dependence on the divine redeemer, and the optimism of a faith rooted in that dependence and the redeemer's boundless capacities.

Because his emphasis on individual morality was so strong, it was most difficult for Gott to reject the perfect moral commonwealth, but, in reality, he had little faith in the moral capacity of man. The unregenerate were weak, utterly dependent on the moral leadership of the elect. But even the latter were flawed, subject to doubt, despair and failure. Gott longed for a society of moral supermen, of saints, but he knew that even his elect, though their souls might be in the hands of god, had feet of clay. It was this which gave him his utopianism. 'To take away Affections is unnatural, but not to manage them rightly, is irrational . . . [102]

[102] Gott, *An Essay of the True Happiness of Man*, p. 120.

Gerrard Winstanley and the Restoration
of True Magistracy

And the plain truth is, theeves and murderers, upheld by preaching witches and deceivers, rule the Nations, and for the present, the Laws and Government of the world, are laws of darknesse, and the divells Kingdome, for covetousness rules all. And the power of the sword over brethren in Armies, in Arrests, in Arsons, in gallows, and in other inferiour torments, inflicted by some upon others, as the oppression of Lords and Mannours, hindring the poore from the use of the common Land, is *Adam* fallen, or *Cain* killing *Abel* to this very day.

> Winstanley, *A Watchword to the City of London and Army* (1649)

There must be suitable Laws for every occasion and almost for every action that men do; for one Law cannot serve in all seasons, but every season and every action have their particular Laws attending thereupon for the preservation of right order.

> Winstanley, *The Law of Freedom in a Platform* (1652)

. . . it would be a sin either for mating, or for anything else, in our ideal society to take place without regulation.

> Plato, *The Republic*

> Knowledg, why didst thou come, to wound, and not to cure?
> I sent not for thee, thou didst me inlure.
> Where knowledge does increase, there sorrows multiply,
> To see the great deceit which in the World does lie.

> Winstanley, *The Law of Freedom in a Platform*

Gerrard Winstanley's *The Law of Freedom in a Platform* is a work still remarkable for its singularity. What impresses is not so much Winstanley's communism, which was hardly as thoroughgoing a variety as is often supposed, but the fact that nothing else Winstanley wrote quite prepares one for his utopia.

In his early works the emphasis was millenarian. 'The swords and counsels of flesh shall not be seen in this work, the arm of the Lord only shall bring these mighty things to passe, in this day of his power...yet wait patiently upon your King, he is coming, he is rising, the Son is up, and his glory will fill the earth.'[1] In the beginning, he had waited on the Lord. At the end, in *The Law of Freedom*, he waited upon (and provided directions for) Oliver Cromwell. Then his attitude to civil authority had been ambivalent, verging on the anarchist. Now the state was the key instrument of social discipline and harmony. His early works are repetitive, mystical, vague; vague even in relation to the much-vaunted economic programme of the Diggers. It is impossible to find out from Winstanley's writings how the Diggers were organised, financed, employed and how their children were to be educated.[2] But *The Law of Freedom* is a model of organised clarity. In it, Winstanley's whole emphasis was on the detailed organisation of the new society. He offered a complete code of law and a paradigmatic view of the administrative establishment. There was no longer room for divine initiative. The cracks and interstices in the social fabric were to be filled, not by the holy spirit, but by the institutional

---

[1] Winstanley, 'The New Law of Righteousnes', in G. H. Sabine (ed.), *The Works of Gerrard Winstanley with an Appendix of Documents Relating to the Digger Movement* (New York, 1941), p. 153. Sabine's edition will hereafter, in this chapter, be cited as *Works*. Two important new works which came to my attention too late unfortunately to be used in this chapter are Olivier Lutaud, *Winstanley: Socialisme et Christianisme* (Paris, 1976) and T. W. Hayes, *Winstanley the Digger: A Literary Analysis of Radical Ideas in the English Revolution* (Cambridge, Mass., 1979).

[2] Cf. D. W. Petegorsky, *Left-Wing Democracy in the English Civil War: A Study of the Social Philosophy of Gerrard Winstanley* (London, 1940), p. 210. Petegorsky still offers the best historical account of the Digger movement.

agencies of man. 'And seeing we shall have successive Parliaments every year, there will be rules made for every action a man can do.'[3]

Of course, the contrast and singularity of *The Law of Freedom* should not be exaggerated. Many of its apparently surprising features can be traced through in Winstanley's other works. Nevertheless a significant contrast does remain. Winstanley's brief career as a writer can be wholly contained within the span of four years (1648–52). With the exception of *The Law of Freedom*, all his works were written in the first two and a half of these years.[4] His utopia was therefore published a year and a half after his previous work and after the collapse of the digging experiments. When it appeared, Winstanley's emphasis and the framework of his vision had changed. His early works had been afire with millenarian expectation, his social attitudes illuminated by the optimism of the perfect moral commonwealth theorist. In his last work he was a utopian.

Winstanley was born in 1609 in Wigan, Lancashire, an area with which he appears to have maintained close associations.[5] We know nothing

---

[3] Winstanley, 'The Law of Freedom in a Platform', in *Works*, p. 512.

[4] A number of chronological points may well be referred to here. We now know that *Fire in the Bush* was most probably published in March 1650. See Keith Thomas, 'The Date of Gerrard Winstanley's "Fire in the Bush"', *Past and Present*, 42 (1969), pp. 160–2; Christopher Hill, 'The Religion of Gerrard Winstanley', *Past and Present Supplement* 5 (1978), pp. 24–5. Although Winstanley refers to his having delayed publication only by a fortnight (*Works*, p. 445), it still seems to me probable that the work was written in February or March 1649. It expounds the theory of community in the earth, first announced in *The New Law of Righteousnes* (January 1649), but makes no mention of the diggings which began on 1 April 1649. It is difficult to accept that Winstanley wrote such a work between the collapse of the diggings and the publication of *The Law of Freedom*. Cf. Sabine's remarks in *Works*, pp. 443–4. Winstanley's comment in the prefatory address to Cromwell (dated 5 November 1651) that he had intended to put *The Law of Freedom* before Cromwell two years previously (i.e. in 1649) should not be taken too seriously. No doubt Winstanley was developing ideas at that time which were later to be found in his utopia. However, the work must have taken considerable preparation; Cromwell was a more obvious target of appeal in 1651–2 than in 1649 and Winstanley's own difficulties in 1649 preclude his having written such a work then.

The Saints Paradice had an undated title page and was incorrectly dated 1658 in the Thomason Catalogue and by Bernstein. The correct date of publication is most certainly 1648. Cf. Sabine, in *Works*, p. 91; Petegorsky, *Left-Wing Democracy*, Appendix 1; Eduard Bernstein, *Cromwell and Communism: Socialism and Democracy in the Great English Revolution*, translated by H. J. Stenning (London, 1930), p. 132.

[5] Unless otherwise stated, the details of Winstanley's life are taken from Sabine, *Works*, and Petegorsky, *Left-Wing Democracy*. In 1648 Winstanley dedicated what was probably his first published work, *The Mysterie of God Concerning the Whole Creation, Mankinde*, to 'My Beloved Countrymen of the County of Lancaster'. See, *Works*, p. 81.

of his early life or education.[6] His father was a burgess of Wigan and probably a trader in cloth and wool. In 1630 he had Gerrard apprenticed in London to Sarah Gater, the widow of a merchant tailor. Winstanley served his time and in 1637 became a freeman of the Merchant Taylors' Company. He seems to have made some progress and by 1640 was prosperous enough to marry a girl named Susan King. In 1643, however, the commercial difficulties brought on by civil war and possibly an over-extension of credit brought his business down in ruin.[7] His commercial failure at the age of thirty-four was clearly a traumatic experience for him and may have resulted in his antagonism to 'the cheating art of buying and selling'. The London trading companies and their organisation, however, retained his admiration.[8]

In 1643 he retired to live with friends in the countryside of Surrey and may have attempted to make a living pasturing the cattle of their neighbours. At some time in this period he appears to have become a Baptist, but by 1648 his connection with religious organisation of any kind was over. In his first work, *The Mysterie of God Concerning the Whole Creation, Mankinde* (1648), he preached universal salvation and the primacy of individual spiritual experience over all ecclesiastical institutions and doctrines whatsoever. He elaborated the same themes in his next three works[9] and suggested that God, working through individual men, was about to produce a new, collective harmony in English society, that England was 'the tenth part of Babylon that shall fall off first from the beast'.[10]

The first intimation of what the new England would be like came in January 1649 with the publication of *The New Law of Righteousnes*. But

---

[6] L. H. Berens' assertion that Winstanley 'received a good middle-class education' has no known warrant. Berens, 'A Social Reformer in the Days of the Commonwealth', *Westminster Review*, 164:3 (1905), p. 279.

[7] In 1660 Winstanley brought a petition in Chancery to protect himself against the executors of Richard Alsworth's will. Winstanley had broken off trading in 1643 in debt to Alsworth to the sum of £500. The executors claimed that this debt had not been paid; Winstanley that he had paid it in full but that the records had been lost. For the details see Richard T. Vann, 'From Radicalism to Quakerism: Gerrard Winstanley and Friends', *Journal of the Friends Historical Society*, 49:1 (1959), pp. 43–4; Vann, 'The Later Life of Gerrard Winstanley', *Journal of the History of Ideas*, 26:1 (1965), p. 134. Winstanley's move to Cobham parish after his business failure may have been due to the possession of property in the area by his father-in-law, William King. A London surgeon, King turned over this property to Winstanley and his wife in 1657. See, James Alsop, 'Gerrard Winstanley's Later Life', *Past and Present*, 82 (1979), pp. 74–5.

[8] See, 'The Law of Freedom', *Works*, p. 549.

[9] *The Breaking of the Day of God, The Saints Paradice*, and *Truth Lifting up its Head above Scandals*. In content and tone *Fire in the Bush* belongs with these works.

[10] 'The Breaking of the Day of God', *Works*, p. 87.

it remained the vaguest of clues. It was still necessary to wait upon the Lord for the coming of the third ministration, a purpose which God would achieve ultimately through the flowering of righteousness in every individual. The consequences of the rise of righteousness would include the end of property in the earth, the end of buying and selling, the end of dominion, a new status for the lowly, and a perfection which would permeate the very elements of the universe. In the meantime, Winstanley had received a vision pronouncing the words, '*Worke together, Eat bread together*', and forbidding men to work on the land for their social superiors.[11] This was the most nebulous of programmes and yet *The New Law of Righteousnes* represents a turning point in Winstanley's work. Prior to it his only concern was religious. He had expressed an extreme religious individualism, a profound anti-ecclesiasticism, a belief in universal salvation, and a millenarianism of a subdued and passive type. After this, while his religious concerns showed no signs of waning,[12] he added to his message the advocacy of communal working and eating and the withdrawal of hired labour as a means of overcoming the social alienation of man.

On this slender theoretical foundation the digging experiments began. The attempt to cultivate the unpromising waste land on St George's Hill, Walton-on-Thames began on 1 April 1649. Winstanley, Everard and twenty or thirty others dug the waste and planted vegetables. By mid April the Council of State, in receipt of complaints, was ordering Fairfax to disperse the Diggers. Fairfax and some of his junior officers, showed a tolerant, if bemused, sympathy with their activities and no effective action was taken.[13]

On 20 April Winstanley and Everard appeared before Fairfax at Whitehall and, on the same day, they and the other Diggers published *The True Levellers Standards Advanced*. This was an attempt to justify the digging and the theory of the earth as a common treasury. In *A Declaration from the Poor Oppressed People of England* (1 June 1649),

---

[11] 'The New Law of Righteousnes', *Works*, p. 190. Winstanley's italics.

[12] In *The New Law of Righteousnes* only two chapters (7 and 8) out of fifteen are even remotely concerned with the immediate social 'programme'.

[13] Some of the Diggers may well have been soldiers dismissed from Fairfax's regiments, Sabine in *Works*, p. 645n. Fairfax's sympathy for the Diggers comes clearly out in the sequence of events. An interesting sidelight on this is cast by the attitude of Andrew Marvell, who in 1650 was engaged as tutor to Fairfax's daughter. See, Bruce King, ' "The Mower against Gardens" and the Levellers', *Huntington Library Quarterly*, 33 (1970), pp. 237–42. The suggestion that the poor be set to work on the wastelands had been made in the Levellers' *Earnest Petition* of January 1648 and by Lieut.-Colonel Jubbes in December of the same year. See, H. N. Brailsford, *The Levellers and the English Revolution* (London, 1961), pp. 322–3, 433–4.

they denied the gentry the right to sell wood taken from the commons and published their own intention to avail themselves of that right. This may have been the final straw for the local populace who thereafter harassed the Diggers both physically, when they sometimes had the assistance of soldiers, and in the courts. Against this, in midsummer 1649, Winstanley wrote appeals to Fairfax, the House of Commons, the City of London and the army.

In the autumn, the Diggers temporarily abandoned their original project and moved into Cobham parish. Here they planted winter grain and built four houses. On 10 October the Council of State ordered Fairfax to support the local justices in action against them, and John Platt, who had an interest in the property of Cobham Manor, urged Fairfax to act vigorously. Towards the end of November, soldiers and local residents destroyed two of the Diggers' houses. The following month, Winstanley wrote protesting to Fairfax and again went to see him at Whitehall. In *A New Yeers Gift for Parliament and Armie* (January 1650) Winstanley appealed for tolerance on the part of landlords and the army and sought to defend, on historical and theoretical grounds, the right of the Diggers to cultivate commons and waste. He acknowledged the landlords' rights to their enclosures but insisted that they should recognise the common people's right to the commons.

An attempt to set the whole endeavour on a far more ambitious basis was made in the early months of 1650 when a group of Diggers visited the counties of Buckinghamshire, Surrey, Middlesex, Hertfordshire, Bedfordshire, Berkshire, Huntingdonshire and Northamptonshire, trying to raise support.[14] Though they were arrested in April, these agents seem to have had more success than has been generally supposed.[15] At Cobham, by April, the Diggers had planted eleven acres of grain and built six or seven houses, but they were indicted at the Easter quarter sessions and the experiment at Cobham collapsed.[16] What happened to the Diggers elsewhere is not yet known but it seems likely that faced with local hostility and official intransigence the experiments everywhere petered out in the course of 1650.

Winstanley tried, in *An Humble Request* (April 1650), to prove, to the satisfaction of the clergy, the universities and the Inns of Court, the scrip-

---

[14] See, 'A Letter Taken at Wellinborough', *Works*, pp. 439–41; reprinted from *A Perfect Diurnal*, 1–8 April 1650.
[15] Keith Thomas, 'Another Digger Broadside', *Past and Present*, 42 (1969), pp. 57–68. In early 1650, communities of Diggers were at work in Surrey, Northamptonshire, Kent, Buckinghamshire, Gloucestershire, Middlesex, Bedfordshire, Hertfordshire and Nottinghamshire.
[16] See Sabine, in *Works*, pp. 20–1; Paul H. Hardacre, 'Gerrard Winstanley in 1650', *Huntington Library Quarterly*, 22 (1958–9), p. 345.

tural basis of his beliefs, but by autumn he was winnowing a different kind of chaff. From August to December of 1650, he was engaged with some of his fellows in threshing wheat for Lady Eleanor Douglas, at Pirton in Hertfordshire. This employment led to an acrimonious dispute over payment and the survival of Winstanley's only known private letter.[17] Towards the end of the following year he was working on his utopian appeal to Cromwell, *The Law of Freedom*, which was published in February 1652.

After this, the glimpses that we catch of Winstanley are so fleeting that we cannot always be sure that it is him we see. On 4 April 1654 the Council of State received a petition for permission to import cumin wood to assist the poor of Lancashire, from a Mr Winstanley who was already engaged in the trade.[18] Whether it was Gerrard Winstanley there is no way of knowing. In 1660 Laurence Claxton, the one-time Ranter and Muggletonian, published an attack on Winstanley in which he accused him of being motivated by vanity in his activity as a Digger and of having retreated from his principles. The implication was that Winstanley had found it necessary to accept once more the commercial practices of the society in which he lived.[19] In 1660 Winstanley brought an action in Chancery against the executors of Richard Alsworth's will, who were still pursuing him for a debt which he claimed to have paid in 1643. Winstanley's wife, Susan, died in 1664 and his father-in-law bought out his interest in property in Cobham. A year later Gerrard reappeared in London married to Elizabeth, the daughter of Gabriel Stanley. His second wife bore him two sons; the first, Gerrard, in 1665 and the second, Clement, in 1670. With his wife, her two sisters and their husbands, Winstanley brought a second action in Chancery, in June 1675, against Ferdinando Gorges and John Holland for the recovery of a debt of £1850 and the payment of a £200 annuity.[20]

Winstanley's death, in September of the following year, was recorded by the Westminster Monthly Meeting of the Quakers. He was described there as a corn chandler. That he should have become a Quaker is hardly surprising, but that he should have adopted one of the most popularly

---

[17] Hardacre, 'Gerrard Winstanley in 1650', pp. 345–9. For the life of Lady Eleanor and her notorious prophecies, see Theodore Spencer, 'The History of an Unfortunate Lady', *Harvard Studies and Notes in Philology and Literature*, 20 (1938), pp. 43–59.

[18] *Calendar of State Papers Domestic 1654*, p. 73.

[19] Andrew Brink, 'Gerrard Winstanley', *Journal of the Friends Historical Society*, 49:3 (1960), pp. 179–180; Vann, 'Later Life of Gerrard Winstanley, pp. 133–4. Claxton's description of Winstanley as a 'Tithe-gatherer of propriety' may well have been metaphorical.

[20] For a skilful unravelling of these issues see Alsop, 'Winstanley's Later Life', pp. 76–80; Vann, 'Later Life of Gerrard Winstanley', pp. 134–5.

detested forms of buying and selling the fruits of the earth is rather more startling. As Richard Vann has remarked, the experiment in Digger communism appears to have come between failure as a merchant tailor and some success as a corn dealer.[21]

Winstanley's social theories were firmly set in the context of the interpretation of the history of the creation and the unfolding of God's purpose.[22] In the beginning 'the great Creator Reason' had made the earth as a common treasury, in which all men were to share equally and without dominion one over another. Selfish imagination and covetousness, however, made men dissatisfied with this. They began to seek a particular property in the things of the earth and a dominion over other men which would guarantee their possession and enjoyment of it. Man fell from the state of innocence and harmony in which he was created: 'by this imagination, mankind tears himself in pieces'.[23] By trickery and force men sought property and dominion and in so doing filled the world with division and conflict. Out of the conflict emerged the elder brother's usurpation of the younger; the establishment of kingly power whereby one group of men expropriated the rest and assumed tyrannical powers over the society in which they lived. In England the historical parallel to this universal conflict was the Norman Conquest.[24] As was the practice with the usurpers of creation rights elsewhere, the Normans on seizing power had laid claim to the land and introduced the art of buying and selling. This last practice endorsed and completed the expropriation of those robbed of their common rights in the earth. 'He that sels the Earth, and he that buyes, doth remove the land mark from the third person, because the land that is bought and sold, belongs to the third man, as well as to the other two that buys and sels.'[25]

To uphold these dubious claims to property the conquerors developed a system of law, encouraged a class of lawyers to grow fat on the system, and endowed a national clergy to preach up the establishment as God's will. But behind all this stood the power of the sword. Conquest right was by definition a product of force. It brought aggressive individualism,

---

[21] Vann, 'Later Life of Gerrard Winstanley', p. 136. For a dismissal of the accumulated evidence on Winstanley's later life see Christopher Hill (ed.), *Winstanley: The Law of Freedom and Other Writings* (London, 1973), pp. 32–3. Hill's revised opinion may be found in 'Religion of Gerrard Winstanley', p. 50.

[22] The references to his historical scheme are scattered throughout Winstanley's works. Perhaps the most convenient versions of his historical theory are to be found in *The True Levellers Standard Advanced* and *Fire in the Bush*.

[23] 'A New Yeers Gift for the Parliament and Armie', *Works*, p. 378.

[24] 'A Letter to Lord Fairfax', *Works*, pp. 286–8; 'An Appeal to the House of Commons', *ibid.*, p. 303; 'A Watchword to the City of London', *ibid.*, pp. 330–338.

[25] 'An Appeal to the House of Commons', *Works*, p. 309.

division and war in its train. Not only was the fall socially disastrous but it brought with it both personal and cosmic maladies. What Robert Burton called 'melancholy', and Winstanley 'the inward bondages of the mind', was caused, according to the latter, purely by 'the outward bondages, that one sort of people lay upon another'.[26] Moreover, the misery which afflicted man and society ultimately spread to the material universe, once Arcadian, now hostile, and presented man with an unremitting struggle against pestilence, tempest, drought and sterility.[27]

The fall was thus both a cosmic and a national disaster, but it was important to remember that it began as a personal and individual phenomenon. It was an experience in the life of every person, born in innocence, overcome by selfishness. By the same token, the work of redeeming the universe had to begin with the redemption of individuals. Ultimately all men and women would be saved. 'It is for the glory of God that he shall redeem not part but all mankind from death, for Christ gave himself a ransom for all.'[28] But salvation would not come through teaching, preaching or communal effort of any kind. It could only come through the spirit of God rising in every man, woman and child and overthrowing unrighteousness. Winstanley was convinced that he was living in an age and a nation where the rising of God's spirit in individuals could begin to affect society at large. Men could assist this development by acting 'according to your creation', by waiting, and by listening to those in whom the spirit had triumphed.[29]

Winstanley must have recognised that in terms of social activity this was not very helpful. In *The New Law of Righteousnes* he tried to set out the characteristics by which a society, wherein men had been redeemed by the spirit, might be known. There would be no private possession of the earth nor of any of God's creatures. There would be no buying and selling and no man would have dominion over another. Men would be satisfied with the necessities of life: meat, drink and clothes.[30] Finally, digging the commons and wastes was an anticipation of this new society. In *The True Levellers Standard Advanced*, Winstanley and his colleagues declared that they were digging the waste in order to 'work in righteousness, and lay the Foundation of making the Earth a Common Treasury for All'. The spirit had granted them a vision commanding them to embark upon the project of communal work and life upon St George's Hill. Scripture

---

26 'The Law of Freedom', *Works*, p. 520.
27 'The New Law of Righteousnes', *Works*, pp. 186, 200.
28 'The Mysterie of God Concerning the Whole Creation, Mankinde', *Works*, p. 81. This did not prevent Winstanley from believing in a present elect who could see and act righteousness. Cf. *ibid.*, p. 82.
29 'Truth Lifting up its Head above Scandals', *Works*, pp. 125–6.
30 'The New Law of Righteousnes'. *Works*, p. 184. Cf. *ibid.*, pp. 200–1.

showed that 'the Restauration of Israel' depended on making the earth a common treasury. They were encouraged in their work by their love for all men and by the knowledge that it was 'now in this Age of the World, that the Spirit is upon his Resurrection, it is likewise the Fulness of Time in a higher measure'.[31]

Particularly in his early works, Winstanley frequently employed millenarian language.[32] The present age was the dawning of the seventh dispensation.[33] The biblical span of six thousand years had passed since the time of Adam.[34] The mark of the beast, 666, was soon to be seen on English coinage.[35] The third ministration was at hand[36] and the prophecies of Daniel and the Book of Revelation about to be realised.[37] And yet Winstanley's millenarianism was of a very passive sort. There was to be no descent from on high, no apocalyptic slaughter. That the restoration of Israel would be God's work alone, there was no doubt,[38] but it would be accomplished through and in the spiritual reawakening of every person on an individual basis. As the fall was part of the spiritual history of every individual, so resurrection was an inward and individual process.

The enmity which burdens you is within, Even the Law of your members that wars against the law of your minde; so that the members are the creature; And that curse wars within them, and so troubles and enslaves the members. Therefore your Saviour must be a power within you, to deliver you from that bondage within. . . [39]

Even so the Spirit of love and blessing shall arise and spread in mankind like the Sun from East to West, and by his *inward power* of love, light, and righteousnes, shall let all mankind see the abomination of the swordly Kingly

---

[31] 'The True Levellers Standard Advanced', *Works*, pp. 257–63. It is noteworthy that the reasons for digging, given in a letter to Fairfax by a group of Diggers not including Winstanley, were somewhat different. The reasons they gave were: (1) 'the righteous law of Creation that gives the earth freely to one as well as to another without respect of persons'; (2) the victory over the king, being the overthrowing of the Norman yoke; (3) the hope that Parliament and army would make good their promises to the commoners; (4) necessity for food and clothing. 'To His Excellency the Lord Fairfax and the Counsell of Warre', *Works*, pp. 343–5.

[32] For an interpretation of Winstanley's thought as consistently millenarian see W. S. Hudson, 'The Economic and Social Thought of Gerrard Winstanley', *Journal of Modern History*, 18:1 (1946), pp. 1–21.

[33] 'The Mysterie of God', *Works*, p. 82.

[34] 'A New Yeers Gift', *Works*, pp. 376–7.

[35] 'A Declaration from the Poor Oppressed People of England', *Works*, pp. 270–1.

[36] 'The New Law of Righteousnes', *Works*, pp. 160–3.

[37] E.g., 'Fire in the Bush', *Works*, p. 496.

[38] 'The New Law of Righteousnes', *Works*, p. 186.

[39] 'Fire in the Bush', *Works*, p. 496.

power, and shall loath themselves in dust and ashes, in that they have owned
and upheld him so long, and shall fall off from him, loath him and leave him.[40]

The extraordinary inwardness of the process by which the millennium
was to arrive was reflected in the tolerance and pacifism of Winstanley's
early works. Since reformation was to be the work of the spirit within, no
man could teach righteousness to another.

And as for spirituall teachings, we leave every man to stand and fall to his own
Master: if the power of covetousnesse be his Master or King that rules in his
heart, let him stand and fall to him; if the power of love and righteousnesse be
his Master or King that rules in his heart, let him stand and fall to him, let the
bodies of men act love, humility, and righteousnesse one towards another, and
let the Spirit of righteousnesse be the Teacher, Ruler and Judge both in us and
over us; and by thus doing, we shall honor our Father, the Spirit that gave us
our being.[41]

Compulsion, likewise, was pointless. 'When this power riseth up to rule,
he doth not rule to enslave others to him by the murthering sword, but he
drawes all men in Love to him.'[42] Consequently, Winstanley repeatedly
disavowed the use of force. All men must be left free to respond to the
promptings of the spirit within them. Even the freedom of royalists, the
defenders of Norman tyranny, had to be respected.[43] Similarly, though
Winstanley roundly condemned the excesses of the Ranters, he would not
sanction their forcible suppression, 'for it is the work of the Righteous and
rational spirit within, not thy hand without that must suppresse it'.[44]

It would not require a great deal of imagination to see Winstanley's
position developing from here into that of an anarchist, and a number
of commentators have characterised his early writings in this way.[45]

[40] 'A New Yeers Gift', *Works*, p. 390. My italics. See also, 'The New Law of
Righteousnes', *Works*, pp. 175–6, 181–3, 186, 213, 216–19; 'The True Levellers
Standard Advanced', *ibid.*, pp. 255–7; 'Fire in the Bush', *ibid.*, pp. 454–5, 462;
'The Law of Freedom', *ibid.*, pp. 502, 534.

[41] 'A Letter to the Lord Fairfax and His Councell of War', *Works*, p. 283.

[42] 'Fire in the Bush', *Works*, p. 487.

[43] 'The Law of Freedom', *Works*, p. 542.

[44] 'A Vindication of those whose Endeavors is Only to Make the Earth A Common
Treasury', *Works*, p. 402.

[45] Cf. W. Schenk, *The Concern for Social Justice in the Puritan Revolution* (London,
1948), p. 104. Schenk's position was attacked by Walter Murphy who held that
Winstanley was opposed to the existing government, not to government in
general. Walter F. Murphy, 'The Political Philosophy of Gerrard Winstanley',
Review of Politics, 19 (1956), p. 227, n. 45. Perez Zagorin appears to adopt the
view that Winstanley was originally an anarchist but that his views were modified
by the violence meted out to the Diggers. P. Zagorin, *A History of Political
Thought in the English Revolution* (London, 1954), p. 55. I myself have
characterised the major shift in Winstanley's thought as that from anarchism to

Unfortunately the situation is rather more complicated than this, but its complications do have the virtue of once more illuminating our ideal-society types.

Winstanley made a number of statements which appear at first sight to have anarchist implications. For example, in *The New Law of Righteousnes* he declared, 'There shall be no need of Lawyers, prisons, or engines of punishment one over another, for all shall walk and act righteously in the creation, and there shall be no beggar, nor cause of complaining in all this holy Mountain.'[46] He disavowed 'imprisoning, punishment and killing', regarding even judicial execution as murder.[47] Yet in the same work he accepted slavery as a means of dealing with those who broke the laws of righteousness.[48] In *A Letter to the Lord Fairfax* he wrote, 'What need then have we of any outward, selfish, confused Laws made, to uphold the power of covetousnesse, whenas we have the righteous Law written in our hearts, teaching us to walk purely in the Creation.'[49] A few paragraphs later he was appealing to the law of contract and declaring his willingness to accept the existing enclosure laws.[50] 'If any man walk uprighteously towards his fellow creatures in civil matters', he wrote, in *Truth Lifting Up Its Head Above Scandals*, 'the Powers of a land must punish him, according to the nature of his offence, and so to be a terror to all unrighteousnesse.'[51]

The difficulties raised by these apparent contradictions can best be resolved by seeing Winstanley, in his early writings, not as an anarchist but as a perfect moral commonwealth theorist. He was not so much demanding the abolition of law as anticipating its almost complete performance (in so far as it was the law of righteousness). He was not denying

utopianism. I seek in this chapter to amend that characterisation. Cf. J. C. Davis, 'Utopia and History', *Historical Studies*, 13:50 (1968), p. 172.

   For the continuing dispute over changes in Winstanley's thought see George Juretic, 'Digger No Millenarian: The Revolutionising of Gerrard Winstanley', *Journal of the History of Ideas*, 36:2 (1975), pp. 263–80; J. C. Davis, 'Gerrard Winstanley and the Restoration of True Magistracy', *Past and Present*, 70 (1976), pp. 76–93; Lotte Mulligan, John Graham and Judith Richards, 'Winstanley: A Case for the Man as He Said He Was', *Journal of Ecclesiastical History*, 28:1 (1977), pp. 57–75.

   Much of the dispute to date has centred on Christopher Hill's treatment of Winstanley in *The World Turned Upside Down* (London, 1972) and *Winstanley: The Law of Freedom*. For Hill's reply to his critics see his 'Religion of Gerrard Winstanley'. I find no evidence in the tract itself to support his contention that *The Law of Freedom* was 'a more gradualist document', embodying a scheme of government intended to be operative only for 'a transitional period'. *Ibid.*, p. 41. Cf. 'Law of Freedom', *Works*, pp. 515, 527–8, 529, 534.

46 'The New Law of Righteousnes', *Works*, p. 183.
47 *Ibid.*, pp. 192–3.   48 *Ibid.*, pp. 185, 192.
49 'A Letter to the Lord Fairfax', *Works*, p. 284.   50 *Ibid.*, pp. 285–6.
51 'Truth Lifting Up Its Head', *Works*, p. 130.

the validity of government so much as foreseeing the obsolescence of its punitive functions and devices in a society of perfect civic morality:[52] 'you shall see these divisions swallowed up in love, so that magistrates shall love the people and the people shall cheerfully obey magistrates. God is working out an inward and an outward peace and liberty for all.' 'This does not mean that there will be no laws or government, but that magistrates will delight in doing justice for the good of the commonwealth.'[53]

Believing in the salvation of all men, Winstanley could envisage a society of men in each of whom the spirit of God had risen. Such a society would achieve harmony and peace. It would be a perfect moral commonwealth. 'When flesh becomes subject to the reason within it, it can never act unrighteously or trespass against others, but it does as it would be done by.'[54] In his thought this was closely linked with a millenarian expectancy, since God alone accomplished the triumph of his spirit within men. Thus the inauguration of the perfect moral commonwealth and its timing were in the hands of God, not men. It was necessary therefore to wait upon the Lord. The essential development in Winstanley's thought is, then, not that from anarchism to utopianism but the switch from this passive waiting, a blend of millenarian expectancy and the optimism of the perfect moral commonwealth theorist, to reliance on a dynamic secular state and its agencies in *The Law of Freedom*.

Even when he appeared to be attacking authority as such, his statements were far more limited than has always been recognised. In *Fire in the Bush*, for example, he raised the question whether Christ's coming 'will destroy all government, and all our Ministry and religion?' His answer was, 'it is very true; for all government and Ministry that is lifted up by Imagination, is to be throwne downe, and plucked up'.[55] The reference here was as much to ecclesiastical government as to secular government and the key words were, 'lifted up by Imagination'. Winstanley was commenting on the inevitable downfall of *unrighteous* government. One of the most quoted arguments for Winstanley's anarchism is the statement: 'every one that gets an authority into his hands, tyrannizes over others'. Insufficient attention, however, has been given to the rest of the sentence. It goes on, 'as many husbands, parents, masters, magistrates, that lives after the flesh, doe carry themselves like oppressing Lords over such as are under them; not knowing that their wives, children, servants,

52 Winthrop Hudson's verdict ('Winstanley's social optimism, it is obvious, rested ultimately upon an expectation that human nature would be completely transformed', Hudson, 'Economic and Social Thought of Winstanley', p. 6) has some application to these early works, but none to *The Law of Freedom*.
53 'The Breaking of the Day of God', *Works*, pp. 87, 90. For a fuller statement see, for example, 'The New Law of Righteousnes', *ibid.*, p. 159.
54 'The Saints Paradice', *Works*, p. 96.
55 'Fire in the Bush', *Works*, p. 471.

subjects are their fellow creatures and hath an equall priviledge to share with them in the blessing of liberty'.[56] Two points should be noted. First the qualification, 'after the flesh', implies that Winstanley was discussing the behaviour of the unrighteous. Secondly, if this is to be read as an attack on civil authority in general, then it should surely be regarded as an attack on patriarchal authority also. But this cannot be the case, since Winstanley had the highest respect for patriarchal authority. In his utopia he made it the basis of all civil authority.[57] The mysticism which made ecclesiastical institutions irrelevant for Winstanley seems never to have had the same effect on his attitude to political institutions.[58]

Winstanley's development from millenarianism to utopianism was a momentous change. He moved from extreme individualism, based on the expectation that men would be transformed from within, to an acceptance of the repressive functioning of the state, transforming men from without through an apparatus of totalitarian discipline. 'There must be suitable Laws for every occasion and almost for every action that men do.'[59] Although there is a sense in which it was a symbol of his impatience, his inability to go on waiting upon the Lord, such a change was not brought about by any single factor nor was it a sudden development.

Winstanley always had a respect for power and its personal and institutional manifestations. He was never an anti-authoritarian. Indeed almost all his works contained some sort of appeal to the established authorities or to those he believed to be in command of the power to achieve his purposes. When he called upon the army and the House of Commons, as he did repeatedly, to fulfil their obligations, he was by implication accepting their status and authority. 'Therefore you Parliament and Army that have power in your hands, reform the Law. . .'[60] In a recently discovered tract, *England's Spirit Unfoulded*, Winstanley argued in favour of taking the Engagement and in defence of the English republic. In 1650, as Professor Aylmer has remarked, Winstanley 'still regarded the republican regime as a possible, perhaps indeed the only possible, basis for further social advance'.[61] Time after time, he called to his defence the Acts overthrowing

---

[56] 'The New Law of Righteousnes', *Works*, p. 158.
[57] 'The Law of Freedom', *Works*, pp. 536, 538. See also the discussion of Winstanley's patriarchalism in Gordon J. Schochet, *Patriarchalism in Political Thought* (Oxford, 1975), pp. 161–2.
[58] Cf. Sabine's introduction to his edition of Winstanley's works.
[59] 'The Law of Freedom', *Works*, p. 528.
[60] 'A New Yeers Gift', *Works*, p. 362. Cf. 'The Saints Paradice', *ibid.*, p. 96; 'Truth Lifting Up Its Head', *ibid.*, p. 130; 'An Appeal to the House of Commons', *ibid.*, pp. 301–10; 'An Appeal to all Englishmen', *ibid.*, pp. 410–11; 'The Law of Freedom', *ibid.*, p. 507.
[61] 'England's Spirit Unfoulded', edited by G. E. Aylmer, *Past and Present*, 40 (1968), pp. 9–10.

'Kingly government' (i.e. the Acts abolishing the monarchy and the House of Lords and making England a free commonwealth) and their precursor, the Solemn League and Covenant.[62] Not only were the digging experiments warranted by scripture, 'but by the Law of the *Commonwealth* of *England* likewise'.[63]

Even in his early works, then, Winstanley was seeking to use, rather than to discard, those existing authorities and powers which he felt could be on the side of righteousness. He was prepared to endorse the legislative capacity of the House of Commons, demanding only that they enact equitable and reasonable laws.[64] Statutes meeting these requirements were already to be found in the existing corpus of law.[65] On one occasion he appealed even to the judgement of university-trained ministers and lawyers.[66] Both Fairfax and Cromwell were men of power whose sympathies he endeavoured to enlist and exploit. Winstanley was always more willing to accept the state, its agencies and its power than has been generally recognised.

The hostility with which the digging experiments were met, the beatings and the burnings, no doubt had their effect on Winstanley's final utopianism, although their influence has perhaps been exaggerated.[67] More important may well have been the effect upon him of the shock of the 'excesses' of the Ranters. He published two tracts in 1650 aimed at dissociating the Diggers from the Ranters. In *A Vindication* he stigmatised Ranting as a source of social disorder.[68] In *England's Spirit Unfoulded* he coupled a warning against the Ranters with support for the republic and 'An Incouragement to Take the Engagement'.

One specific, but fundamental, way in which Winstanley showed himself willing to come to terms with existing English law was over the question of enclosures. In his first defence of the digging experiment, *The True Levellers Standard Advanced*, he lay down a formula which was to be consistently repeated throughout his works; let the poor enjoy the commons, waste and confiscated lands and let the landlords enjoy their

---

62 E.g. 'The True Levellers Standard Advanced', *Works*, p. 257; 'A Declaration of the Poor Oppressed Commons', *ibid.*, pp. 275–6; 'An Appeal to the House of Commons', *ibid.*, p. 305; 'A Watchword to the City of London and the Armie', *ibid.*, p. 326; 'The Law of Freedom', *ibid.*, p. 507.

63 'An Appeale to all Englishmen', *Works*, p. 407 (title page).

64 'An Appeal to the House of Commons', *Works*, p. 308.

65 'A Watchword to the City of London and the Armie', *Works*, pp. 321–2.

66 'An Humble Request to the Ministers of Both Universities and to all Lawyers in every Inns-a-Court', *Works*, pp. 419–37.

67 Cf. Sabine, in *Works*, p. 59. Some account of the sufferings of the Diggers may be found in *Works*, pp. 284–5, 295–6, 392–3.

68 'A Vindication of Those Whose Endeavours is Only to Make the Earth a Common Treasury, Called Diggers', *Works*, p. 400.

enclosures.[69] Writing to Fairfax, he specifically accepted the obligation of the law and the army to defend enclosed land.[70] The formula was clearly expressed in *An Appeal to the House of Commons*. 'Therefore let the Gentry and Freeholders have their inclosures freed from all entanglements of Fines, Heriots, and other burdens, and let the Common people have their Commons and waste lands freed from entanglements of the *Norman* Lords of Manors.'[71] It reappeared in *A Watch-Word To the City of London*; 'Therefore as the Free-holders claime a quietnesse and freedom in their inclosures, *as it is fit they should have*, so we that are younger brothers, or the poore oppressed, we claime our freedom in the Commons...'[72] The classic statement, perhaps, came in *A New Yeers Gift to the Parliament and Armie*:

The Parliament, consisting of Lords of Manors, and Gentry, ought to have their inclosure Lands free to them without molestation, as they are freed from the Court of Wards. And the common-People, consisting of Souldiers and such as paid Taxes and Free-quarter, ought to have the freedom of all waste and common land, and Crown-land equally among them.[73]

In *The Law of Freedom* he appeared to challenge the general principle of property in land. It could not be possessed by 'creation right', for in the creation all were created equal. Nor could it be held by conquest right. Since the commoners had conquered the King, the land became common property.[74] However, the expropriation of the landed classes which Winstanley advocated was limited to the loss of tithes and copyhold services.[75] For the rest it was sufficient that the people should possess in common what he called 'the *Commonwealths* land', meaning by that commons, wasteland and land confiscated as a result of the Civil Wars.[76]

This formula on enclosures had also an historical dimension. Gentry and commoners had come together to fight for the overthrow of the oppressive monarchy of Charles I. The tacit understanding had been that, in the event of success, the gentry were to enjoy their land free of all

[69] 'The True Levellers Standard Advanced', *Works*, p. 260. In the same tract Winstanley came closest to attacking property as theft.

[70] 'A Letter to the Lord Fairfax', *Works*, pp. 285–6.

[71] 'An Appeal to the House of Commons', *Works*, p. 305.

[72] 'A Watchword to the City of London', *Works*, p. 326. My italics.

[73] 'A New Yeers Gift', *Works*, p. 371. The formula was repeated, *ibid.*, p. 373; 'An Appeale to all Englishmen', *Works*, p. 411.

[74] 'The Law of Freedom', *Works*, p. 508.

[75] *Ibid.*, p. 510. Significant numbers of the Diggers appear to have been copyholders. See Thomas, 'Another Digger Broadside', pp. 60, 67–8, nn. 22–31. Winstanley was concerned with the removal of the obligations of tenantry both here and in 'An Appeale to all Englishmen', *Works*, p. 412. For the anti-rent aspects of his work see below.

[76] 'The Law of Freedom', *Works*, p. 513.

obligations to the Crown, while the commoners were to have the free use and possession of the commonwealth's land. In 1650, 'Three Branches more of Kinglie power' remained to be uprooted. These were tithes, bad law, and the control of landlords over the commons and wastes.[77] The significant thing here is that the abolition of enclosures was not amongst the essentials for the overthrow of 'Kinglie power'.

The view that the activities of Winstanley and the Diggers were 'the last of a series of ineffectual attempts to overthrow enclosure' is thus a gross oversimplification.[78] There can be no doubt that Winstanley regarded the enclosing landlord as a manifestation of the covetousness which had poisoned the universe. There could be no place for him in the new society. The point, however, is that in the meantime Winstanley offered no challenge to the legal validity of enclosures. He had more to say against the payment of rent than against enclosures.[79]

The means of bringing down that symbol of covetousness and of the elder brother's expropriation of the younger, the enclosing landlord, was not an attack upon the legal validity of enclosures but a programme of labour withdrawal. In *The New Law of Righteousnes*, Winstanley first began the announcement of the digging experiments and the elaboration of a social policy. A key part of the programme was the withdrawal of the labour of the poor from the estates of the rich:

let the rich work alone by themselves, and let the poor work together by themselves; the rich in their inclosures, saying, *This is mine*; The poor upon the Commons, saying *This is ours*, the earth and fruits are common. And who can be offended at the poor for doing this? None but covetous, proud, lazy, pamper'd flesh, that would have the poor stil to work for that devil (particular interest) to maintain his greatnesse, that he may live at ease.[80]

The poor, indeed, had by their very labour upheld the system which expropriated them and sustained unrighteousness. It was incumbent upon

---

[77] 'A New Yeers Gift', *Works*, p. 357.

[78] Margaret James, *Social Problems and Policy during the Puritan Revolution 1640–1660* (London, 1930), pp. 101–2. Cf. Christopher Hill, *God's Englishman, Oliver Cromwell and the English Revolution* (London, 1970), p. 18. Cf. Hill, 'Religion of Gerrard Winstanley', p. 53. ('Winstanley wanted to throw down hedges in the field.') Bernstein clearly indicated in 1895 that a direct attack on enclosures was no part of the Diggers' programme. Bernstein, *Cromwell and Communism*, p. 106.

[79] See, for example, 'The Law of Freedom', *Works*, pp. 520, 529. In this work, Winstanley made no mention of enclosures. The only strong anti-enclosure language in the Digger canon comes in 'Light Shining in Buckinghamshire' and 'More Light Shining in Buckinghamshire' which are doubtful Digger material and in the preparation of which Winstanley had no hand. See, Sabine in *Works*, p. 605.

[80] 'The New Law of Righteousnes', *Works*, p. 196.

them to bring down that system by withdrawing the labour which supported it.

Divide *England* into three parts, scarce one is manured: so that here is land enough to maintain all her children, and many die for want, or live under a heavy burden of poverty all their daies: and this miserie the poor people have brought upon themselves, by lifting up particular interest, by their labours.[81]

The poor people by their labours in this time of the first *Adams* government, have made the buyers and sellers of land, or rich men, to become tyrants and oppressours over them. But in the time of *Israels* restoration, now beginning, when the King of Righteousnesse himselfe shall be Governor in every man; none then shall work for hire...[82]

Working for hire on the land of others had dishonoured the creation.[83] The hand of the Lord, it was revealed to Winstanley, would be upon those labourers who took such hire.[84] Their duty was now to seek the overthrow of kingly power and covetousness, not by the sword, but by withdrawal of their labour: 'the only way to cast him out, is, For the People to leave him to himself'.[85]

When this labour withdrawal took place the tenant and the enclosing landlord would be left with more land than they could work. Enclosures would cease because they would have ceased to be a practical proposition. The whole fabric of exploitation would collapse. One of the best descriptions of this process was given by Robert Coster in *A Mite Cast into the Common Treasury*. Significantly, he depicted the digging experiments as an alternative to wage labour for landlords. As a means of supporting those who withdrew their labour, digging and manuring the commons had the following advantages:

1. If men would do as aforesaid, rather then go with Cap in hand, and bended knee, to Gentlemen and Farmers, begging and intreating to work with them for 8d. or 10d. a day, which doth give them an occasion to tyrannize over poor people (which are their fellow-Creatures) if poor men would not go in such a slavish posture, but do as aforesaid, then rich farmers would be weary of renting so much land of the Lords of Mannors. 2. If the Lords of Mannors... could not let it out by percells, but must be constrained to keep it in their own hands, then would they want those great baggs of money (which do maintain pride, idleness, and fulness of bread) which are carried into them by their Tenants, who go in as slavish a posture as may be; namely, with Cap in hand, and bended knee, crouching and creeping from corner to corner, while his Lord (rather Tyrant) walkes up and down the Roome with his proud lookes, and with great swelling words questions him about his holding. 3. If the

[81] *Ibid.*, p. 200.   [82] *Ibid.*, pp. 190–1.
[83] 'The True Levellers Standard Advanced', *Works*, p. 258.
[84] 'The New Law of Righteousnes', *Works*, p. 199.
[85] 'A New Yeers Gift', *Works*, pp. 384–5.

Lords of Mannors and other Gentlemen, had not those great bagges of money brought into them, then down would fall the Lordliness of their spirits, and then poor men might speak to them; then there might be an acknowledging of one another to be fellow-creatures.[86]

Winstanley was even prepared to compromise with those 'great Ones of the Earth' who gave up the struggle and threw their possessions into the common treasury. They could share equally in the proceeds, without working themselves.[87]

The essence of the digging experiments was therefore the withdrawal of labour from employment on the estates of landlords and rich tenant farmers. No doubt this was at least as worrying to the gentry as an out break of anti-enclosure rioting would have been. The fact that the Diggers made no legal or violent challenge to private property merely made them more difficult to deal with in the courts. Winstanley may well have believed that a mass withdrawal of labour would lead to a rapid collapse of landlords and employing tenants. Once this had happened, the new society would be constructed, not only on the unpromising waste and commons, but on all the land. If he did envisage the digging of commons and waste as a temporary phase prior to the voluntary surrender of culti-vated land, his unwillingness to elaborate the social organisation of the digging communities becomes more understandable. By late 1651, how-ever, he must have known that it would be at best a long drawn out process. Accordingly, he made preparations in *The Law of Freedom* for the 'Commonwealth Lands' to be worked as if by a separate nation – commons, waste and confiscated lands were to be run under one system; freehold land, if its owners so chose, under another.

Yet I desire, that the *Commonwealths* Land, which is the ancient Commons and waste Land, and the Lands newly got in by the Armies Victories, out of the oppressors hands, as Parks, Forests, Chases, and the like, may be set free to all that have lent assistance, either of person or purse, to obtain it; and to all that are willing to come in to the practice of this Government, and be obedient to the Laws thereof: And for others, who are not willing, let them stay in the way of buying and selling, which is the Law of the Conqueror, till they be willing.[88]

---

86 Robert Coster, 'A Mite Cast into The Common Treasury', *Works*, pp. 656–7. Coster signed the 'Letter to Lord Fairfax and the Council of War' written in December 1649, 'An Appeale to All Englishmen' and the letter taken at Wellingborough, where his name appeared next to Winstanley's. On the Digger's policy of labour withdrawal see Petegorsky, *Left-Wing Democracy*, p. 147.

87 'The True Levellers Standard Advanced', *Works*, p. 266.

88 'The Law of Freedom', *Works*, p. 513. A function of Parliament in Win-stanley's utopia was to prevent the buying and selling of Commonwealth's land. It had no authority to prevent the sale of private land which remained under the old system. Cf. *ibid.*, p. 560.

It is important to recognise that Winstanley envisages only a partial communism, applied only to those inhabiting and working the commonwealth's land. There would be a system of law, a form of government, a type of economy, a way of life for them and an entirely different social system for those of their fellow Englishmen who were still addicted to the morality of buying and selling. Thus Winstanley's communism was limited and so was the basis of his new society. His adoption of these limitations was a reflection both of despair at full success through labour withdrawal and of a sense of urgency which made it impossible to wait passively for God's good time.

Winstanley's thought was always characterised by impatience at words without deeds, by a drive to act righteousness as well as to speak it. He condemned the teaching of the existing churches as a 'verball profession, without the pure righteous action'.[89] The redeemed were known by actions, not words: 'for this multitude of talk, and heaping up of words amongst professours shall die and cease, this way of preaching shall cease, and they that do worship the Father, shall worship him by walking righteously in the Creation, in the strength of the Law of Love and equity one to another'.[90] ' . . .everyone talks of freedome', he complained in *A Watch-Word to the City of London*, 'but there are but few that act for freedome, and the actors for freedome are oppressed by the talkers and verball professors of freedome'. In the same work he recalled how he was moved to embark on the digging experiments: 'my mind was not at rest, because nothing was acted, and thoughts run in me, that words and writings were all nothing and must die, for action is the life of all, and if thou does not act, thou dost nothing'.[91]

This theme, the futility of words without action, reappeared ever more frequently in his works. In *A New Yeers Gift For the Parliament and Armie* he wrote, 'Bare talking of righteousnesse, and not acting hath ruled, and yet does rule king of darkness in the creation; and it is the cause of all this immoderate confusion and ignorance that is in men.'[92] It was the 'badge of hypocrisie, for a man to say, and not to do'.[93] The people, he claimed, wanted only to realise that which they had been promised, 'for our freedome must not lye within the clasps of a Booke, in words that may be read, nor in the bare title of a Victory: but it must be freedome really enjoyed, or else it will do us no good'.[94]

---

[89] 'Fire in the Bush', *Works*, p. 445.
[90] 'The New Law of Righteousnes', *Works*, p. 185.
[91] 'A Watch-Word to the City of London', *Works*, pp. 317, 315.
[92] 'A New Yeers Gift', *Works*, p. 365. Cf. *ibid*., pp. 366, 381, 395.
[93] 'An Appeale to All Englishmen', *Works*, p. 409 margin. Cf. 'An Humble Request', *Works*, p. 434.
[94] 'An Humble Request', *Works*, pp. 429–30.

The same impetus for action and achievement which drove him to dig the commons finally drove Winstanley to appeal to Cromwell. Power *was* indispensable. *The Law of Freedom* was devised to demonstrate how the gap between profession and practice might be obliterated,[95] but Winstanley had not drawn it up as a paper exercise. If it were to be actualised, Cromwell had to be the agent. 'And now I have set the candle at your door, for you have power in your hand, in this other added opportunity to Act for Common Freedome if you will; I have no power.'[96]

In June 1649, a new argument was adopted to defend the digging experiments, that of economic necessity: 'seeing and finding our selves poor, wanting Food to feed upon, while we labour the Earth'.[97] From this time the appeal in terms of the economic necessity of the poor was a consistent feature of Winstanley's propaganda. It is, however, important to recognise that the argument was only introduced at a relatively late stage, certainly after the diggings had started.[98] 1649 was a year of chronically high food prices, which, coupled with the dislocation of war and high taxation, produced widespread and distressing hardship. If the spectre of mass famine did not take the stage of English life, it certainly hovered menacingly in the wings. In a petition to the House of Commons, actual starvation was reported in the area of Winstanley's home town, Wigan.[99] In *An Appeale to all Englishmen*, Winstanley and the Diggers blamed dearth and famine on the neglect of commons and wasteland.

---

[95] For Winstanley's comment on the contemporary gap between profession and practice see 'The Law of Freedom', *Works*, p. 509. It is noteworthy that, in Winstanley's utopia, hypocrisy was made a civil offence. *Ibid.*, p. 597, law 41.

[96] *Ibid.*, p. 510.

[97] 'A Declaration From the Poor Oppressed People of England', *Works*, p. 272.

[98] It seems to me that this should throw some light on the controversy as to whether Winstanley's communism was theologically or economically motivated. Before June 1649 the argument of economic necessity played no part; after that date it had, as I hope to show, a significant influence on the nature of his thought. For the view that Winstanley's motivation was primarily theological see Paul Elmen, 'The Theological Basis of Digger Communism', *Church History*, 23:3 (1954), pp. 207–18; W. S. Hudson, 'Gerrard Winstanley and the Early Quakers', *Church History*, 12 (1943), pp. 177–94; Hudson, 'Economic and Social Thought of Winstanley'; James, *Social Problems and Policy*, pp. 26–7. For the view that economic factors were the primary influence see Bernstein, *Cromwell and Communism*, p. 107; Petegorsky, *Left-Wing Democracy*.

[99] James, *Social Problems and Policy*, pp. 54–5. In August 1649 the Leveller news-sheet, *The Moderate*, reported that some men condemned to death for cattle stealing had justified themselves in terms of the economic necessity of their families and the evil consequences of the system of private property, which they thought the popular victory in the Civil Wars would have ended. *The Moderate Impartially Communicating Martial Affairs to the Kingdom of England*, 56 (31 July–7 August 1649). Quoted in Bernstein, *Cromwell and Communism*, pp. 167–8.

Their work was to be seen as a means of solving these problems. 'The wast and common Land being improved, will bring in plenty of all Commodities, and prevent famine, and pull down the prizes of Corne, to 12d. a Bushel, or lesse.'[100] The Diggers of Iver in Buckinghamshire had embarked on their experiment because they were 'resolved to pay no more Rent, things are so deare they cannot'.[101] Elsewhere, Fairfax was informed, 'wee digg upon the Common to make the earth a common treasury, because our necessity for food and rayment require it'.[102] Those who had done most to help Parliament, Winstanley claimed, 'have so wasted themselves, that now they can hardly get bread, but with great difficulty'.[103]

The argument from economic necessity may well have been the final factor pushing Winstanley over into utopianism. The millenarian, perfect moral commonwealth vision of his early works would solve the problem of social harmony through the rising spirit of God in every man. But it would not solve the collective problem, the shortage of satisfactions, in a world of dearth and economic injustice. Only a new basis of production and distribution could do that. The communist experiments, which began as part of a labour withdrawal programme, were finally developed, in *The Law of Freedom*, into a new system for the production and distribution of goods and services, a system placed in the context of a totally new and separate society.

To summarise, Winstanley was never an anarchist in the true sense of the word. He began as a millenarian, visualising the development of a perfect moral commonwealth through a divine act of spiritual and moral renewal taking place in every man. His own insistence on the test of action and pressure of the economic distress so evident in English society gave a new urgency to his concern with secular power. This respect for earthly power was always a feature of Winstanley's writings. What took place was a shift of emphasis. The key development in Winstanley's thought was the movement from a millenarian waiting upon the Lord to act from within, to an acceptance of the necessary subjection of men to external authorities. It is the moment when his millenarianism became a distant prospect rather than a present reality, and when his utopianism took over the realm of immediate policy.

Winstanley never attempted a systematic theory of the state, but in

100 'An Appeale to all Englishmen', *Works*, pp. 414, 408.
101 'A Declaration of the Grounds and Reasons', in Thomas, 'Another Digger Broadside', p. 65. Cf. Thomas' comment that this tract provides 'a much needed reminder that the aims of the Diggers were practical as well as symbolic'. *Ibid.*, p. 58. Cf. also the views of the Wellinborough Diggers, *Works*, p. 650.
102 'To His Excellency The Lord Fairfax and The Counsell of Warre', *Works*, p. 344. Cf. 'England's Spirit Unfoulded', ed. Aylmer, pp. 12–13.
103 'A New Yeers Gift', *Works*, p. 359. Cf. 'An Appeal to the House of Commons', *ibid.*, p. 306.

The Law of Freedom he made a number of attempts to provide theoretical justification for the subjection of men to the secular discipline of the state.[104] 'We must be subject to the Ruler; it is true', he wrote in his prefatory address to Cromwell,[105] and proceeded to offer reasons why this was so: 'because offences may arise from the spirit of unreasonable ignorance, therefore was the *Law* added'.[106] This 'unreasonable ignorance', or 'ignorant and rude fancy', as he calls it elsewhere,[107] is closely associated with the variousness of men, which also provides one of Winstanley's main justifications for the subjection of men to a system of law and authority. The ignorance he refers to is ignorance of the means of common preservation.[108] Because of their variety, their individuality, men in society are likely to become pursuers of self-preservation, rather than of common preservation. Consequently social conflict ensues: 'the body of the people are confused and disordered, because some are wise, some foolish, some subtil and cunning to deceive, others plain-hearted, some strong, some weak, some rash, angry, some milde and quiet spirited. By reason whereof offences do arise among brethren, and their common peace is broken.'[109] Amongst the consequences of this heterogeneity of men is the necessity of law.

And because the spirit in Mankinde is various within it selfe; for some are wise, some foolish, some idle, some laborious, some rash, some milde, some loving and free to others, some envyous and covetous, some of an inclination to do as they would have others to do them: but others seek to save themselves, and to live in fulness, though others perish for want. Therefore because of this was the Law added, which was to be a Rule and Judg for all mens actions, to preserve common Peace and freedom; as *Paul* writ, *The Law was added because of Transgression*, one against another.[110]

Law was necessary, then, because men were sinful and egotistical, pursuing their divergent self-interest, rather than common preservation. In *The Law of Freedom* this was seen as innate in fallen man, a consequence of original sin which had to be contained as far as possible by education and social discipline. Thus, 'Mankinde in the days of his

---

104 A number of commentators have held that Winstanley never accepted the fallen world as a permanent phenomenon, that he consistently anticipated a radical transformation of human nature or that he did not believe in original sin. While some of this may be true of Winstanley's early writings, it is not, as I hope to show, applicable to *The Law of Freedom*. Cf. Zagorin, *History of Political Thought*, p. 47; Hudson, 'Economic and Social Thought of Winstanley', p. 6; Murphy, 'Political Philosophy of Winstanley', p. 221, n. 21; Richard L. Greaves, 'Gerrard Winstanley and Educational Reform in Puritan England', *British Journal of Educational Studies*, 17:2 (1969), pp. 168–9.

105 'The Law of Freedom', *Works*, p. 508.

106 *Ibid.*, p. 515.   107 *Ibid.*, p. 526.

108 *Ibid.*, p. 537.   109 *Ibid.*, pp. 538–9.   110 *Ibid.*, pp. 535–6.

youth, is like a young Colt, wanton and foolish, till he be broke by Education and correction, and the neglect of this care, or the want of wisdom in the performance of it hath been, and is, the cause of much division and trouble in the World.'[111] For the same reasons, all officials were potentially corruptible.[112] Without compulsion, 'the spirit of rudeness would not be obedient to any Law or Government',[113] laws and officials existed to regulate the unrational covetousness to which all men are prone.[114]

Partly, perhaps, because he conceived of himself as the true heir of a revolution which had gone astray and whose leaders had reneged on their promises, Winstanley was very concerned in *The Law of Freedom* to establish correct definitions of true freedom, law and government. He began with the problem of freedom. 'The great searching of heart in these days is to find out where true Freedom lies that the Commonwealth of *England* might be established in Peace.' Freedom of trade he dismissed as freedom under the will of a conqueror, freedom of preaching as 'an unsetled Freedom', sexual freedom as the freedom of beast, and the freedom of elder brothers (i.e. the established system) as the beginning of all conflict. '*True Commonwealths Freedom*', he insisted, '*lies in the free Enjoyment of the Earth*'.[115] This relationship between man and the earth was seen by Winstanley as part of man's nature and as part of his history.[116] It followed that man could only be fully human, truly free, if he had rights in the earth and if he worked it or its products. Hence followed the communal ownership of land in his new society and his insistence that all men should be employed in manual work, engaged with the land or its products, until the age of forty.[117] Perhaps the crucial aspect of Winstanley's definition of freedom is its restrictiveness. It was based upon economic necessity, not upon individual worth or dignity.

Government, in *The Law of Freedom*, was defined as 'a wise and free ordering of the Earth, and the Manners of Mankind by observation of particular Laws or Rules, so that all the inhabitants may live peaceably in plenty and freedom in the Land where they are born and bred'.[118] The significant thing here is that the function of government has been extended from the 'ordering of the Earth', as it was in all of Winstanley's works after *The New Law of Righteousnes*, to control of 'the Manners of Mankind'. Whereas previously man had required no teacher and Winstanley had relied upon the moral renewal of men by the spirit working within them, so now he was concerned with their education, the laws controlling them and the overseers disciplining them. The control of men's manners had become a legitimate function of government.

There were only two types of government: Kingly Government and

---

111 *Ibid.*, p. 576. 112 *Ibid.*, p. 540. 113 *Ibid.*, p. 552. See also p. 562.
114 *Ibid.*, p. 583. 115 *Ibid.*, p. 519. Winstanley's italics.
116 *Ibid.*, pp. 520–2. 117 *Ibid.*, pp. 576–7. 118 *Ibid.*, p. 528.

Commonwealth's Government. Under Kingly Government the earth was ordered by the 'cheating Art of buying and selling' and the manners of men were governed by club law and covetousness. By Commonwealth's Government, on the other hand, the earth was disposed of without buying and selling and all were provided for. The behaviour of men was conditioned by 'the spirit of universal Righteousness dwelling in Mankinde, now rising up to teach every one to do to another as he would have another do to him'.[119] Although still using the language of his perfect moral commonwealth theories, Winstanley, as we shall soon see, was not prepared to leave social discipline in his utopia to the spirit within. His point at this stage was that while under Kingly Government men were governed by the laws of self-preservation, under Commonwealth's Government they had to behave in accordance with the requirements of common preservation.[120]

When Winstanley proceeded to analyse the meaning of 'government' he provided some of the classic evidence of the utopian type. There are, he argued, three essential parts of government: laws, officers and execution of the laws. In his view the scope of law had to be totalitarian. 'There must be suitable Laws for every occasion, and almost for every action that men do; for one Law cannot serve in all seasons, but every season and every action have their particular Laws attending thereupon for the preservation of right order'; 'true Government is a right ordering of *all* actions, giving to every action and thing its due weight and measure and this prevents confusion'. Good government also required a disinterested bureaucracy. 'There must be fit Officers, whose spirits are so humble, wise, and free from covetousness, as they can make the established Laws of the Land their will.' Finally it was requisite that there be enforcement of the laws.

There must be a faithful Execution of those Laws, and herein lies the very life of Government: For a right order in Government lies not in the Will of Officers without Laws, nor in Laws without Officers, nor in neither of them with Execution. But when these three go hand in hand, the Government is healthful; but if any one of these be wanting, the Government is diseased.[121]

Men in society would be subject either to the will of other men or to law. In the latter case, which was the preferable of the two, their rulers should also be subject to law.[122] But to what law should they be subjected? Winstanley defined law as 'a Rule, whereby Man and other creatures are governed in their actions, for the preservation of the Common peace'. These laws were of two types: unwritten, or natural law, and written, or positive law. Again each of these types could be further subdivided. The law of nature was either irrational, seeking merely the gratification of the

[119] *Ibid.*, pp. 529–34.   [120] *Ibid.*, pp. 537–8.   [121] *Ibid.*, pp. 528–9.
[122] *Ibid.*, pp. 507–8. On the necessity for legal reform see also *ibid.*, pp. 504–5.

animal desires of the body, or rational, avoiding excess and prejudice to oneself and to others. The latter Winstanley identified with conscience or the voice of God's spirit within men. Written law could either seek to sustain the rational nature of man, as did the Mosaic law, or, in upholding the will of a conqueror, like Kingly Government it could give free scope to the unrational law of nature.[123] Thus Winstanley sought a code of written law which would endorse the rational law of nature in the hearts of men, and which would contain and restrain men's unrational animal instincts.

For this purpose short and pithy laws were best and Winstanley provided a ready made code of sixty-two of these for his utopia.[124] Like other utopians he presented his ideal society as legislatively complete. The first group of laws (laws 1–9) dealt with the application of the law and judicial procedure. The bare letter of the law was to be applied with no elaboration. Those who distorted the law should lose office and be disqualified for life. Those who administered the law for profit were to suffer death. The laws were to be read four times a year to the people. Men could only be punished for a specific act, not for belief. They must be faced with their accuser and there must be adequate witnesses. False accusation was to be punished with the penalty for the crime concerned.

Penalties were set out for uncivil behaviour (laws 10–14). Violence was to be punished with the same degree of violence. Anyone striking an officer was to be made a bondman for a year. Gossips and those who spread false rumours were to be chastised. Those who used 'reviling and provoking words' would be admonished twice, once privately and once publicly, but if they continued they could be flogged and then, if necessary, put in servitude for twelve months. Anyone, not possessed of civil authority, seeking to dominate his fellows could suffer the same punishment.

Agricultural production was taken care of in two laws (laws 15 and 16). By the first, it was made incumbent upon every household to keep all necessary agricultural tools and to maintain them in good condition. A father failing to ensure this was liable to punishment. Secondly, every family was to assist in ploughing, digging, planting and reaping. Continued idleness would be dealt with by reproof, flogging and if necessary servitude (law 17).

The next group of laws (laws 18–21) dealt with the distribution of the goods and materials produced. Storehouses of two kinds were to be set up in every town and city. General storehouses would stock raw materials to be taken by every family as their work required it. The wasteful accumulation of goods from the storehouses was not allowed. The waiters who worked in the storehouses were obliged to deliver goods without payment, and neglect on their part was to be punished by the penalty of servitude.

[123] *Ibid.*, pp. 587–9. [124] *Ibid.*, pp. 590–600.

Another group of laws (laws 27–31) endorsed this system by making buying and selling illegal. Anyone engaging in such a transaction, either as buyer or seller, would be put to death, 'because it brings in Kingly bondage again: and is the occasion of all quarrels and oppressions'. Anyone enticing another to buy or sell would receive twelve months' servitude and the person who rebuffed such overtures would be publicly commended. Particular claims to the earth or to goods in the storehouses were prohibited. No one was to give or take hire for his work. Doing so involved loss of freedom and twelve months' servitude. In terms of overseas trade (law 32), buying and selling was permitted but only on behalf of, and to the profit of, the commonwealth as a whole. Goods exported should always be carried in English vessels. Gold and silver (law 33) might be used for foreign trade but domestically their only use was for the manufacture of household utensils. In Winstanley's utopia money had been abolished.

Two groups of laws dealt with state officials, the first group (laws 34–9) in general terms, the second group (laws 22–6) with the functioning of overseers. All state officials were to be elected annually. The reasons for this had been given earlier.

When publique Officers remain long in place of Judicature, they will degenerate from the bounds of humility, honesty and tender care of brethren, in regard the heart of man is so subject to be overspred with the clouds of covetousness, pride and vainglory, for though at the first entrance into places of Rule they be of publique spirits, seeking the Freedom of others as their own; yet continuing long in such a place, where honors and greatness is coming in, they become selfish, seeking themselves, and not common Freedom; as experience proves it true in these days...

Annual election of officials would, Winstanley believed, prevent the evil which befell corrupt officials, prevent oppression, benefit posterity, produce faithful officers, encourage civic virtue and furnish the commonwealth with able and experienced men. It was, in his eyes, a powerful device for the production of disinterested officials and public good.[125]

All men over forty years old were eligible for election, although younger men of exceptional ability or virtue could be chosen. Canvassing could lead to the disqualification of voter or candidate. Men over twenty were eligible to vote, except those convicted of a criminal offence. Two laws lay down the kind of men the electorate were to choose as officials. They were not to be turbulent, quarrelsome nor provoking men but 'rational men of moderate conversation' who were experienced in the laws of the commonwealth. Hypocrites were not allowed to bear office (law 41).[126]

[125] *Ibid.*, pp. 540–1.
[126] The character of men suitable for election had also been dealt with in greater detail earlier. Cf. *ibid.*, pp. 542–4.

The function of the overseers was to see the laws executed. On taking office their first task was to review the performance of their predecessors in order to check that they had performed their duties faithfully. They were to ensure that all families fulfilled their obligations to assist in agricultural production, to engage in trades and furnish the storehouses with their products, and they were also to see that the storehouses were efficiently run without buying or selling. Overseers who neglected to enforce the laws would be reproved by the courts and, in the case of a second offence, be expelled from office. All citizens were obliged to assist an overseer in the performance of his duties. Failure to do so could be punished by penalties ranging from a public reproof to servitude.

A considerable group of laws (laws 42–51) were given over to the regulation of servitude or bondage. The importance of this form of judicial slavery in Winstanley's ideal society should not be overlooked. The list of offences for which a person could suffer servitude is impressive. It includes the following: striking an officer, failing to assist an officer, acting in a socially disruptive manner, neglect of agricultural equipment, idleness, neglect of duty by a waiter in a storehouse, enticing others to buy or sell, claiming a property in the earth, giving or taking labour for hire, attempted abduction of another man's wife, and wastage of food. The minimum sentence of this type was twelve months' servitude. Bondage, it should be noticed, did not replace capital or corporal punishments, rather it supplemented them and offered a rigorous form of social discipline with the additional advantage of utilising the offender's labour resources. Bondsmen were clothed in a white uniform and had to work at the direction of the Taskmaster on any task he gave them. Their basic rôle would be as carriers or carters of goods but they would also be available to assist any freeman who convinced the Taskmaster that he had need of a bondsman's labour. The dependants of the bondsman would remain unaffected by his status. Bondsmen refusing to work would be flogged and put on coarse diet, 'to kill their Pride and Unreasonableness, that they may become useful men in the Commonwealth'. Should they revile the laws under which they suffered, they would be flogged. If they took weapons against them, they would be put to death. At the end of their period of sentence, they would be set free only if they expressed humility and respect for the laws of the commonwealth. Failure to do so would result in the renewal of their period of servitude.

The laws set out by Winstanley made no provision for a legally supported church. Indeed the only stipulation concerning religion was that preaching for hire should be a capital offence (law 40). Both marriage and burial were made simple civil ceremonies (laws 54 and 60). A final group of laws (laws 55–62) dealt with the family and marriage. No man should be a master or have charge of a household until he had served an apprenticeship of seven years. When he did set up a household the over-seers 'shall appoint him such young people to be his servants as they think fit, wherether he marry, or live a single life'. Thus in Winstanley's as in More's utopia the household was not simply a kinship group, nor was membership of it even a voluntary affair. Neither the master nor his dependants chose their association. Marriage, however, was to be a freely entered relationship. There was to be no impediment of birth or portion and men and women were to be free to marry for love. The exception to this was that a man impregnating a single woman was obliged to marry her. Rape was a capital offence. Surgeons and physicians were to attend any sick persons without charge, their maintenance coming out of the common stock (law 53).

There is a strong element of patriarchalism in Winstanley's approach to his ideal society. The origin of all magistracy is, in his view, to be traced to the position of the father in the family. In his utopia, the father is the basic state official. But the father, like other officers, has to be seen as a chosen or elected official. Winstanley's argument is that the father was chosen to exercise authority by the joint necessity of the children when young.[127] It was provided that 'all children shall be educated, and be trained up in subjection to parents and elder people more then now they are'.[128] As a state official, the father's duties were both educational and disciplinary. He was to teach the children reading, languages, the arts and sciences, to provide them with agricultural skills or a trade and to ensure that they were all possessed of 'a comfortable livelyhood'. At the same time, he was to prevent idleness by reproof or whipping and to instil order and social discipline into the children.[129]

The virtues of education were seen by Winstanley in strongly social terms: 'the neglect of this care, or the want of wisdom in the performance of it hath been, and is, the cause of much division and trouble in the world'.[130] It was required by law that all officers and overseers should assist fathers to educate children in good manners, a trade and the avoid-ance of idleness. Winstanley divided the population into four age groups: the first two, childhood and youth, should last until the age of forty; man-hood, forty to sixty, and old age, over sixty. Children were to be taught all arts and sciences in schools, of which, unfortunately, Winstanley gives us no details. He divided the curriculum into five subject areas: husbandry; minerology and metallurgy; animal husbandry; silviculture and wood-working; astronomy, astrology and meteorology. The emphasis here was on practical craft training and the approach was similar for girls. No group was to be brought up devoted to the study of books alone. All were to work manually until the age of forty. After this, those who chose to do

127 *Ibid.*, pp. 536, 538.   128 *Ibid.*, p. 515.   129 *Ibid.*, p. 545.
130 *Ibid.*, p. 576.

so could retire from manual work and devote themselves to state service. Officers would normally be elected from amongst those over forty, whilst those over sixty automatically became general overseers.[131]

A number of advantages were seen to arise from this system. Educationally it would produce men more capable of acting rationally, better citizens, and men capable of representing their country abroad.[132] But the work of all and the encouragement of invention would stimulate increased production. 'Every man shall be brought up in Trades and Labours, and all trades shall be maintained with more improvement, to the inriching of the Commonwealth, more then now they be under Kingly Power.'[133] It was on this basis that Winstanley confidently denied that his ideal society would be productive of poverty, idleness and conflict.[134]

The bureaucratic essence of the administrative system in Winstanley's utopia is well illustrated in his diagrammatic representation of the relationship between officials.[135]

In a private Family, a Father, or Master, is an Officer.

In a Town, City, or Parish
{
A Peacemaker
A four-fold office of Overseers
A Souldier
A Task Master
An Executioner
}

In a County or Shire
{
A Judge
A Peace-maker of every town within that Circuit
The Overseers and Soldiers attending thereupon
}
This is called either the Judges Court, or the County Senate.

In a whole land
{
A Parliament.
A Commonwealths Ministry.
A Post-master.
An Army.
}

After the fathers, the officials with whom the ordinary citizen was most likely to have contact were the peacemaker and the overseer. The number of peacemakers chosen would vary in accordance with the size of the parish or town. Together they sat in council to administer the affairs of

---

[131] *Ibid.*, pp. 576–80, 551. See also Greaves, 'Winstanley and Educational Reform', pp. 166–76.
[132] 'The Law of Freedom', *Works*, p. 576.
[133] *Ibid.*, p. 526. For the encouragement of invention see *ibid.*, pp. 512, 579–80.
[134] *Ibid.*, p. 513.   [135] *Ibid.*, p. 544.

the parish, to prevent trouble and preserve the peace. They endeavoured to reconcile disputants but those with whom they failed were sent to the Judges' Court. The peacemakers represented their community in negotiations with the outside world and acted as a check on the performance of their duties by other officials.[136] They dealt with any business referred to them by the overseers and in general acted as a kind of benign, elected J.P.

There were four types of overseer. The first acted as a peace officer, dealing particularly with disputes about private property (that is to say property taken from particular storehouses for the private use of households or persons). Any serious offence of this type had to be referred by him to the courts. The second type of overseers were those responsible for the management and supervision of production. They were to arrange the training of young people, the supervision of work, the transfer of youths from one trade to another (which normally meant their transfer from one household to another) and the distribution of youths from a household where the father had died. Each trade was to have a specialist overseer and in the country there would be overseers controlling the various branches of agricultural production. They were to keep all building and equipment in good repair and supervise the functioning of schoolmasters, postmasters and ministers. 'And this Office of Overseership keeps all people within a peaceable harmony of Trades, Sciences, or Works, that there be neither Beggar nor idle person in the Commonwealth.'[137]

As the second type of overseer had managed the production of goods, so the third type were responsible for the distribution of them. They took care of the supply of finished goods and raw materials and dealt with cases of negligence on the part of the storekeepers. Their activities extended to the maintenance of stables and herds of cattle and sheep.[138]

Lastly, all men over sixty became general overseers, functioning as a general inspectorate and calling to account any official or tradesman guilty of neglect or poor work. 'And the reason of all is this, That many eyes being watchfull, the Laws may be obeyed, for to preserve Peace.' These men, known as Elders, were to be respected by all and assisted by all. Like other officials they could be reproved or lose office for partiality.[139]

It is significant of the extent to which Winstanley saw his utopian state as locked in implacable battle with the socially disruptive aspects of man's nature, that soldiers, taskmasters, and executioners should be provided in every town and parish. 'A souldier is a Magistrate as well as any other officer, and indeed all State Officers are Souldiers for they represent power, and if there were not power in the hand of Officers, the spirit of rudeness would not be obedient to any Law or Government, but their own wils.' Each year a soldier was chosen to enforce the law, acting only upon

136 *Ibid.*, pp. 545–6. See also pp. 538–9.
137 *Ibid.*, pp. 548–50.   138 *Ibid.*, pp. 550–1, 581.   139 *Ibid.*, pp. 551–2.

instructions from the appropriate officer, bringing in offenders and protecting officials.[140] However, these 'soldiers' did not collectively make the commonwealth's army. This was based on a much wider obligation of all citizens to defend the laws and officers instituted for their common preservation. State officials would act as leaders. The rest of the people would make up the rank and file. This citizen militia stood behind the authority of the laws of the land and also acted in a military capacity to resist invasion, insurrection, or the threatened return of Kingly Government.[141]

The Judges' Court, which was clearly modelled on the quarter sessions, met four times a year in each county and was made up of a judge, peacemakers, overseers, and soldiers from the areas within the county. The court was to inspect the work of any officers within the county, to deal with grievances beyond the power of junior officials and, if law was wanting, to act subject to confirmation by the next Parliament. This last provision is a little difficult to reconcile with Winstanley's insistence that the judge was 'to pronounce the bare Letter of the Law'. No lawyers were allowed to appear before the court but each man was to plead for himself.[142]

Supreme above these institutions reigned the commonwealth's Parliament, the only body authorised to exceed the letter of the law in pursuit of its spirit. 'A Parliament is the highest Court of Equity in a Land, and it is to be chosen every year and out of every City, Town, and certain limits of a Country through the Land, two, three, or more men are to be chosen to make up this court.' Rather than be a device manipulated by the powerful, Parliament was to act like the father of a family, sustaining all and helping the weak and oppressed. It had four functions: commissioning officers and making general policy for the utilisation of commonwealth land; the abolition of all oppressive laws and customs and the removal of all burdens from the poor; the management of military activity; and the establishment of new law. It was to draw up laws based on reason and equity. These proposed laws were then declared to the people and one month was allowed for objections to be brought forward (although Winstanley does not explain what would happen in case of objection). This done, the statute was to be enacted as a binding law. Winstanley did not see this legislative function of Parliament as being particularly important. In the first place he had provided a ready-made code of law covering the main features of life in the new society. Secondly, there could be no disputing legality, since the choice was a simple, and not a multi-dimensional, one. 'There is but Bondage and Freedom, particular Interest, or common Interest; and he who pleads to bring in particular interest into a free

---

[140] *Ibid.*, pp. 552–3.   [141] *Ibid.*, pp. 571–5.   [142] *Ibid.*, pp. 554–6.

Commonwealth, will presently be seen and cast out, as one bringing in Kingly Slavery again.'[143]

The commonwealth's ministers were far removed from a sacerdotal caste. Their religious functions were negligible. Winstanley's main emphasis was upon their schooling the people in citizenship and their obligations and rights under the law. 'If there were good Laws, and the people be ignorant of them, it would be as bad for the Commonwealth as if there were no Laws at all.' It was for this reason, and for no religious purpose, that one day in seven should be set apart. The people could enjoy a day of rest, share fellowship with each other and be addressed by the minister. The latter was allowed to read three things to the people. First he should inform them of the affairs of the commonwealth as reported by the information service maintained by the postmasters. Secondly, he should instruct them in the law of the commonwealth, and presumably, although Winstanley does not mention this, inform them of legislative proposals. Thirdly, both for mental exercise and for pleasure, he was to give, and encourage others to give, speeches on history (stressing the advantages of Commonwealth's Government and the misery of Kingly Government), on the arts and sciences, or on the nature of man. 'And everyone who speaks of any Herb, Plant, Art, or Nature of Mankind is required to speak nothing by imagination, but what he hath found out by his own industry and observation in tryal.' Sometimes speeches were to be made in foreign languages to encourage the knowledge of them. Although these meetings had no liturgical content, they were not entirely without religious significance. 'To know the secrets of nature, is to know the works of God; And to know the works of God within the Creation, is to know God himself, for God dwels in every visible work or body.'[144]

Winstanley was clearly striving for an informed and conscientious citizenry, which would be the main source of his commonwealth's permanence. They would not only be capable of distinguishing 'bondage' and 'freedom' but would be sufficiently well informed to know that it was always in their interests to choose the latter. As an extension of this idea, Winstanley adopted a suggestion much canvassed in his day,[145] the establishment of a national information service. Two men were chosen every year in each parish to serve as postmasters. Every month they would send reports on the affairs and happenings of their parish to the chief city in their area. Here were two postmasters each for the north, south, east and west. They put together all the parish reports for their area and also

---

[143] *Ibid.*, pp. 556–62.
[144] *Ibid.*, pp. 562–9. For Winstanley as an intuitive Baconian see Charles Webster, *The Great Instauration: Science, Medicine and Reform 1626–1660* (London, 1975), pp. 367–8.
[145] See below, Chapter 11.

compiled a digest of the affairs of the whole nation which was distributed to every postmaster. The advantages of this system were that assistance could be speedily provided to areas of plague, famine, invasion or insurrection; information on accidents could help to prevent the same accident happening elsewhere, and the spread of new inventions and knowledge would be facilitated.[146]

Within the context of his ideal society, Winstanley had solved the problems of poverty, economic injustice and the socially disruptive effects of covetousness. In order to do so, he had devised a new system of production and distribution, a new code of law, and a new administrative system. He had moved from a rejection of the ability of one man to teach another,[147] to the establishment of a system for the indoctrination of children in citizenship by ministry, parents, all officials and schools, where the law itself was seen as an instrument of social education, reproving and punishing in order 'to Kill their Pride and Unreasonableness, that they may become useful men in the Commonwealth'.[148] From a denial of the necessity of 'Lawyers, prisons, or engines of punishment', he had come to the development of a society where every man was his own lawyer, schooled once a week in the law, where slavery replaced imprisonment, where flogging, judicial violence and torture, and capital punishment were accepted as essential parts of the machinery of social discipline. In his early works, Winstanley solved the problem of the disposition to tyranny of those in positions of authority by dispensing with such positions. In his utopia, positions of authority were accepted as inevitable. The guard against tyranny was in the form of regulation, impermanence of status and continuous inspection. In the legal code equal weight was given to the maintenance of bureaucratic integrity and to the punishment of crime.

In the middle of his code of laws Winstanley posed the question, 'What is Freedom?' His answer was,

Every Freeman shall have a Freedom in the Earth, to plant or build, to fetch from the Store-houses any thing he wants, and shall enjoy the fruits of his labours without restraint from any; he shall not pay Rent to any Landlord, and he shall be capable to be chosen any Officer, so he be above forty years of age: If he want any young men to be Assistance to him in his Trade or household employment, the Overseers shall appoint him young men or maids to be his servants in his family.[149]

To Winstanley the only freedom that mattered was freedom from economic insecurity. In the early years of the English republic the appeal of this was obvious. But to others the cost may well have appeared too high.

---

[146] 'The Law of Freedom', *Works*, pp. 570–1.
[147] 'The Saints Paradice', *Works*, pp. 93–6.
[148] 'The Law of Freedom', *Works*, p. 597.   [149] *Ibid.*

It meant a willingness to accept the disruption of the family as a kinship group, a system of unfree labour, a rigidly organised and centralised state, and the elevation of common human failings, hypocrisy, gossip and idleness, to the level of civil offences. When Winstanley appealed, 'Come change the heart of Man',[150] he also offered an apparatus by which that change was to be effected. 'Indeed covetous, proud and beastly-minded men desire more, either to be by them to look upon, or else to waste and spoil it upon their lusts; while other brethren live in straits for want of the use thereof. But the Laws and faithful officers of a free Commonwealth do regulate the unrational practice of such men.'[151]

[150] *Ibid.*, p. 600.   [151] *Ibid.*, p. 583.

8

James Harrington's Oceana

Give us good men, and they will make us good laws, is the maxim of a demagog, and is (thro' the alteration which is commonly perceivable in men, when
they have power to work their own wills) exceeding fallible. But give us good
orders, and they will make us good men, is the maxim of a legislator, and the
most infallible in the politics.

Harrington, *Oceana* (1656)

... as man is sinful, but yet the universe is perfect, so may the citizen be sinful,
and yet the commonwealth be perfect. And as man, seeing the world is perfect,
can never commit any such sin as shall render it imperfect, or bring it to a
natural dissolution; so the citizen, where the commonwealth is perfect, can
never commit any such crime as will render it imperfect, or bring it to a
natural dissolution.

Harrington, *Oceana*

The Cooks were all Cats and Kitlings, set in such Frames, so ty'd and so
ordered that the poor creatures could make no Motion to get loose, but the
same caused one to turn the Spit, another to baste the Meat, a third to scim
the Pot, and a fourth to make Green-Sauce.

If the Fram of your commonwealth be not such, as causeth every one to
perform his certain Function as necessarily as this did the Cat to make Green-
Sauce, it is not right.

Harrington, *A Discourse upon This Saying:
The Spirit of the Nation is not yet to be
trusted with Liberty* (1659)

... that government is not perfect which is not provided at all points.

Harrington, *Oceana*

In the last twenty years or so the stature of James Harrington as a political thinker and the study of his thought have been transformed. In the process an eccentric figure, associated somewhat obscurely with the rise of capitalism or market society, whose political thought stood awkwardly aside from contemporary traditions and founded no school, has been replaced by a seminal thinker, transforming a great European tradition of thought and enabling it to contribute to the ideologies of the emergent western world of the eighteenth century. This transformation has been largely the work of J. G. A. Pocock and it is a complex story that he tells.[1] Harrington's thought, in this account, ruralised and anglicised the classical republicanism of late renaissance Florence and made it available for transmutation into an Atlantic republican tradition in the eighteenth century. It dealt a blow to the pervasive English myths of ancient constitutionalism and the immemorialism associated with it, and provided a basis for the development of a sense of history and an incipient sociology of corruption.

All these claims we may let go uncontested; not least because there is considerable substance to them. We are concerned here rather with the status of Harrington's perfect and immortal commonwealth as an ideal society and with what that might tell us about the nature of his thought in general. As we shall see, however, the reinterpretation of Harrington's thought conducted by Pocock raises some difficulties for the solution of that problem.

It has been a persistent feature of Harrington scholarship to deny his *Oceana* (1656) – and the works he wrote in defence or elaboration of it during the subsequent four years – the character of a utopia. In the past,

[1] See J. G. A. Pocock, *The Ancient Constitution and the Feudal Law* (Cambridge, 1957); 'James Harrington and the Good Old Cause: A Study of the Ideological Context of his Writings', *Journal of British Studies*, 10:1 (1970), pp. 30–48; *Politics, Language and Time: Essays on Political Thought and History* (London, 1972), Chapters 3 and 4; 'Political Thought in the Cromwellian Interregnum', in G. A. Wood and P. S. O'Connor (eds.), *W. P. Morrell: A Tribute* (Dunedin, 1973); *Obligation and Authority in Two English Revolutions* (Wellington, 1973); *The Machiavellian Moment: Florentine Political Thought and the Atlantic Republican Tradition* (Princeton, 1975), Part 3; (ed.), *The Political Works of James Harrington* (Cambridge, 1977), Introduction.

this was either because utopia was misinterpreted as a category necessarily exclusive of all schemes intended for implementation in a real society,[2] or because Harrington was misinterpreted as a determinist thinker.[3] Neither of these misinterpretations need detain us now. The problem is to decide what status as an ideal society we shall ascribe to Harrington's perfect and immortal commonwealth, and that problem is complicated by the Pocockian reinterpretation of Harrington in two respects: Harrington's classical republicanism and his imputed millenarianism.

There can be no doubt that Harrington was, and aspired to be, a classical republican. Committed to the task of reconciling ancient and modern prudence, empire and authority, he saw his *Oceana* as an ambitious synthesis which would enable the principles of classical republicanism, hitherto applied only to ancient Rome or the city-states of sixteenth-century Italy, to be adapted for a substantial rural society whose political institutions, practices and traditions had collapsed in the aftermath of a bewildering civil war and an abortive revolution. Essential to those principles was the ideal of a republic in which the widest possible number of citizens participated, in some sense, in ruling themselves. Immediately we must observe that the value of participation and the individual freedom congruent with it is not rated highly by the utopian. The participatory citizens of the classical republic, exercising their civic virtue through freedom of choice, are replaced in utopia by subjects constrained, as far as possible, to act out a predetermined pattern of morality over which they have no control and which they may not change. There is, in other words, an antipathy between the classical republic and utopia. In the classical republic virtue and stability depended on: (1) the correct exercise of free will by all citizens; (2) the existence and observation of laws regulating the relationships between citizens; and (3) freedom from external contingencies.[4] The utopian assumes that the last of these can be resolved by isolation or by military strength, is prepared to sacrifice the participatory basis of the first, and, attaching primacy to the second, sets above morality in the civic sense order and the external observation of a pre-ordained moral code. It will be one of the arguments of this chapter that Harrington followed utopian impulses as well as classically republican aspirations and

---

[2] See, for example, G. P. Gooch, *English Democratic Ideas in the Seventeenth Century* (2nd edition, Cambridge, 1927), p. 251; R. H. Tawney, 'Harrington's Interpretation of his Age', *Proceedings of the British Academy*, 27 (1941), p. 11; Charles Blitzer, *An Immortal Commonwealth: The Political Thought of James Harrington* (New Haven, 1960), p. 32; W. H. Greenleaf, *Order, Empiricism and Politics: Two Traditions of English Political Thought 1500–1700* (Oxford, 1964), p. 237.

[3] Tawney, 'Harrington's Interpretation of his Age', p. 11.

[4] Cf. Pocock, *Machiavellian Moment*, pp. 75–6.

that the tensions in his thought cannot be fully appreciated unless the utopian dimension of it is acknowledged. The demonstration of this case must depend upon a close reading of his text, but because his utopianism has been an hitherto neglected and contested, if not despised, aspect of his thought some preliminary observations may be in order.

First, in relation to the dependency of republican stability on virtue in its citizens, on laws and on external security, which we have just looked at, it is worth noting how Harrington reacted in each case. External security was to be provided for by a massive military establishment and the creation of a commonwealth for expansion. Harrington was obviously preoccupied with laws and constitutional arrangements or what he called 'political architecture'. What is most revealing of the tension in his thought between the utopian and the classical republican are his doubts about the capacity of citizens to ever act virtuously. Those who debate the creation of a perfect and immortal commonwealth in *Oceana* seem to assume that 'it is the duty of a legislator to presume all men to be wicked'.[5] And throughout his work Harrington reiterates the proposition that a perfect commonwealth is not so much one that provides its citizens with opportunities for virtue, as one that is inviolable to their propensity to sin. When Valerius in his dialogue with Publicola is concerned with whether the senators in the new republic will be honest, he is reassured that the constitution is such that it allows no means by which they may be dishonest.[6] Now we might see this problem as overcome within the confines of the classically republican tradition by a careful consideration of those who should be admitted to citizenship, their moral capacities and the degree to which their interests may be reconcilable with the general good. The problem then would be the political architect's one of balancing limited groups of citizens and their interests so as to produce harmony. The paradox is, however, that, despite his pessimistic injunction to the legislator to assume the wickedness of men, in legislating himself Harrington adopts an astonishingly inclusive criterion for citizenship. It is instructive to compare him with the Levellers in this respect. In their second Agreement of the People (*Foundations of Freedom*, December 1648), written against the background of their last negotiations with the leaders of the New Model Army and in the shadow of an impending revolution, the Levellers proposed a franchise qualification excluding from citizenship not only women and children, servants and almstakers, but also royalists

---

[5] Harrington, 'The Commonwealth of Oceana', in *The Oceana and Other Works, with an account of his life by John Toland* (London, 1771), p. 152. This edition will be cited throughout this chapter as *Works*.

[6] 'Valerius and Publicola', in *Works*, p. 454. Cf. 'Political Aphorisms', *ibid.*, p. 483. 'Where the security is in the persons, the government makes good men evil; where the security is in the form, the government makes evil men good.'

and all those who would not subscribe to the second Agreement.[7] The logic behind this is clear. The viability of the republic where citizens ruled themselves was dependent on the capacities for self-rule which citizens brought with them. Women, children, wage-earners and almstakers were excluded because they were dependent on others and therefore incapable of self-rule. Royalists, by their acceptance of political subjection, were unfitted for citizenship,[8] just as those who were not committed to the republic, as embodied in the Agreement, could not be expected to participate in and for its preservation. Surprisingly, Harrington saw no need to exclude either of the last two categories from citizenship. Even if all the senators elected were royalists, the republic would have nothing to fear.[9] How was it that Harrington could ignore the threat of ex-royalists and other monarchists to the integrity of his republic in a way in which the Levellers could not?

The answer must surely lie in the nature of participation and citizenship in the Oceanic republic. In Oceana no citizen does anything in a fully moral sense and what he does do he doesn't do for very long. He never chooses by his own actions to prevent the corruption of the republic, for the republic is never in danger of corruption. The citizen participates in a set of rituals designed to reduce his moral responsibility rather than enhance it. The bicameral division of debate and resolution, discussion and decision which is an essential feature of the equal commonwealth is a good illustration of this, for, while the upper house may propose, it may not decide upon what it proposes, and while the lower house may decide, it may not decide what is to be proposed to it for decision. The secret ballot and rotation of office only heighten this sense of the limited public relevance of private capacities, and the proscription on political debate outside the senate and the limitations on property accumulation under the agrarian law serve to complete the picture. Participation in *Oceana* consists of the freedom to observe rituals and to accept predetermined limitations, the rejection of which would be folly, a self-destructive madness.

But perhaps the tensions observable in Harrington's thought and the status of his perfect and immortal commonwealth might be resolved by seeing a juxtaposition in his work, not of utopia and classical republic, but of millennium and classical republic; a juxtaposition which had been prefigured, for example, by Savonarola. John Pocock has argued strongly for a millennial, rather than utopian, element in Harrington's thought,

---

[7] Don M. Wolfe, *Leveller Manifestoes of the Puritan Revolution* (London, 1967), p. 297. Cf. the negative twist on these restrictions in the Officers' Agreement of 20 January 1649, in *ibid.*, p. 342.

[8] Cf. the Levellers' newspaper on this, *The Moderate*, 14 (10–17 October 1648), p. 2. I owe this reference to my student, Mrs Roberta Nicholls.

[9] 'Oceana', *Works*, pp. 203–4.

although he sometimes appears ambivalent about it. The argument here, complex sometimes to the point of obscurity, may, with temerity, be reduced to the following. To escape the world of *fortuna* in which all actions and hopes are seen as vitiated by the tarnished second nature of man, Christians may have recourse to grace, the direct assistance of God acting in an apocalyptic framework of providential history. The republic may only be inaugurated, and men may only escape the meaningless flux which is secular time, by divine participation, by grace, and the republic is therefore always millennial, not utopian. It is dependent on a divine initiative to recover the first nature, the *prima forma*, of men and hence functions as a community of saints.[10]

The basis of this contention may be summarised in the aphorism 'custom is King, if grace does not overthrow it', and can be traced to Pocock's deft analysis of Machiavelli's reflections on the problem of innovation.[11] Here political innovation in a world of flux is seen as so complex and difficult a problem that the innovator can only achieve stability with the aid of divine grace. This may well be the case in Machiavelli's thought and it may be the logical consequence of that thought, but it does not seem always to be the basis from which Harrington operates, nor are its assumed antitheses always shared by him. For example, by the mid 1650s, when Harrington began writing, custom and customary forms in England had collapsed. Monarchy, the ancient constitution, the Church of England and much else besides had abruptly gone. The point is that Harrington's explanation of all this remained basically secular, as his solutions remained secular, but we shall return to this argument in a moment. The more fundamental point is that the grace/*fortuna* antithesis did not have necessarily to be accepted by all Christians. It was possible for some of them to see time as having meaning independent of the direct intervention of God, both in the lives of individuals exercising free will in lives of moral effort, of redemptive and worshipful worth, and in societies exercising practical Christianity where men fed the hungry, clothed the naked, helped the fatherless and afflicted to create a better world by their own efforts. The politics of grace must either be the politics of saintly withdrawal (the monastery, the sect, the colony), or the politics of saintly totalitarianism (the Fifth Monarchists), or the politics of saintly expectancy (waiting on God for the coming kingdom). None of these approaches accords with Harrington's disposition in his writings, and the problem may be in part

[10] Pocock, *Machiavellian Moment*, Chapter 2; *Political Works of Harrington*, pp. 16–20, 26. For Pocock's incipient ambivalence see *ibid.*, pp. 27, 41 and *Machiavellian Moment*, pp. 170–1, 399–400.

[11] Pocock, 'Custom and Grace, Form and Matter: An Approach to Machiavelli's Concept of Innovation', in Martin Fleisher (ed.), *Machiavelli and the Nature of Political Thought* (New York, 1972), pp. 153–74, see especially p. 173.

resolved by bearing in mind the availability of a formula which allowed for God's interest in the government of men while allowing for human free will in the disposition of political forms. This is the formula which stated that God ordained government but not any particular form; that his influence in political constitutions was mediate rather than immediate. It was an argument frequently used against *iure divino* claims for particular constitutions or specific institutions.[12] God wished men to have an ordered life on earth and therefore approved of human government, but how the institutions necessary for this purpose were designed was left to human choice. Government, as opposed to anarchy, could be seen as having divine sanction, but the history of forms of government could be seen as a purely secular history free from divine intervention. It was precisely in this way that Harrington viewed and described English history. In his thought it is artifice which must control nature, not divinity control fortune, and the nature which is to be shaped is the second nature of men habituated to wickedness. There is no return to a *prima forma* brought about by divine grace; rather, virtue is ensured by 'providing it with an institutionalised structure of action'.[13] The political and the apolitical, reason and passion, remain in conflict within men and the situation is not redeemed by an apocalyptic reinstatement of the political but instead is contained by elaborately contrived institutions.

God ordains government but not any particular form of government. To say otherwise was to admit the possibility that human social history was constantly escaping the control of God, since history was a flux of forms, many lacking in moral authority and inherently unstable. But Harrington does not say this. His secular history of secular social processes is entirely compatible with the view that God, approving of government, had left men at liberty to devise its forms. Moreover, his history is not a meaningless flux presided over by *fortuna*. It has meaning and a key to that meaning is the relationship between empire, forms and authority. Changes in that relationship, the nodal points in Harrington's secular

---

[12] To take only three English examples: Francis Bacon, 'Certain Considerations Touching the Better Pacification, and Edification of the Church of England', *The Works of Francis Bacon*, edited by Spedding, Ellis and Heath, 14 vols. (London, 1868–90), vol. x, p. 107; John Goodwin, *Anti-Cavalierisme* (1642), p. 8; John Lilburne, *Strength Out of Weaknesse* (1649), p. 11. Harrington appears to argue that God works through second causes in politics although he is prepared to act immediately where human providence has failed. The point in Oceana is that it has not failed. Cf. 'The Art of Lawgiving', *Works*, pp. 364, 401, 442. Pocock sometimes appears to come close to an acknowledgement of the mediate/immediate distinction of the divine rôle in Harrington's thought. See, Pocock (ed.), *Political Works of Harrington*, pp. 78–80, 90–1, 94, 96, 109, 114, 120–1.

[13] *Ibid.*, p. 67.

history, are explained in secular terms. Thus the emergence of the Gothic balance is ascribed not to God but to flaws in the late Roman systems of landholding and to the elaboration of new forms of constitutional machinery to cope (albeit inadequately) with the new circumstances consequent upon the barbarian invasions. Similarly the Gothic balance in England began to deteriorate under the influence of actions taken by Henry VII and Henry VIII, neither of whom was seen as an agent of divine will. What was needed in the 1650s was a constitutional accommodation to the new circumstances, a political architecture appropriate to the new social foundations and the distribution of landed property on which they rested. What was different this time was, first, that a commonwealth, which was the system of greatest potential moral authority, could be erected, and, second, that with skill in political architecture the structure could be made immortal as well as perfect. This combination of immortality, high moral authority and perfection gave a twist to Harrington's proposals, particularly in respect to his attempts to reconcile his republic with the achievements and failures of that of Israel, that could lead to the adoption of a language of grace and almost of the millennium, but it was always momentary and never allowed to pervade the whole. There is, in other words, a minor tension in Harrington's thought between millennium and utopia, as well as a major one between utopia and classical republic, and the latter is never resolved. For his attempt to contain these tensions within a framework of artifice, of political architecture, we must turn to a detailed consideration of his work.

Fundamentally Harrington's ideal was a popularly based but aristocratically led society. The problem was to prevent both aristocratic domination, or oligarchy, and the anarchy of popular rule; in other words, to preserve a balance between aristocratic leadership and popular decision. Harrington's answer was what he called the 'equal commonwealth'. But he used the term 'equal' in a peculiar sense. By implication, he rejected the communist egalitarianism of Winstanley because, in his view, it was necessary to preserve the leisured and cultivated aristocratic class maintained by the existing social hierarchy. At the same time, he sought a system which, reaping the benefits of aristocratic statesmanship and political foresight, would yet not be dominated by the aristocrats. Enjoying to the full the benefits and qualities of aristocratic leadership, the people of his ideal society would always be free to determine how far, and in which direction, they would follow that lead. To prevent a general aristocratic dominance, Harrington devised the agrarian laws. To prevent factional dominance by the aristocrats he introduced the principles of rotation, ballot and the separation of the functions of debate and choice within a bicameral system. As he desired aristocratic leadership without dominance, so also he looked for popular deference without servility. The means towards this form of balanced constitution, this equal commonwealth which would rescue England from the disorder of Civil War and the lawless instability of the Interregnum, were institutional, legal and educational. In this sense then Harrington's formula for constitutional and political perfection was utopian.

The remedy for England's unhappy state in the 1650s lay not in waiting for the triumph of the inevitable but in an act of will, the adoption of a complete system of government, the parts of which were interdependent. To this end Harrington appealed for men of good will to rescue the people of England by such an act of leadership. 'If there be not men at the head of them', he wrote in 1659, 'who by introduction of a proper form, can clothe their nakedness, and reduce their passion unto temper, there is nothing to be expected, but darkness, desolation and horror.'[14] Like other utopians Harrington reduced the choice to the perfection of his ideal scheme or disorder, misery and anarchy without it.[15] Underlying his thought was the familiar utopian preoccupation with the polarities of order and disorder. Harrington's utopianism was further revealed in the means by which he suggested that men might prevent disorder and establish good order. Society would never be set right by the independent moral renewal of its citizens, but men had to be disciplined and their antisocial proclivities contained by institutional, legal and educational pressures.

Give us good men, and they will make us good laws, is the maxim of a demagog, and is (thro' the alteration which is commonly perceivable in men, when they have power to work their own wills) exceeding fallible. But give us good orders, and they will make us good men, is the maxim of a legislator, and the most infallible in the politics.[16]

It was the duty of the legislator to presume all men wicked.[17] The perversity of human nature was such that 'we are certain never to go right, while there remains a way to go wrong'. Consequently, in a rational

14 'A Discourse Shewing, That the Spirit of Parliaments, with a Council in the Intervals, is not to be trusted for a Settlement', *Works*, p. 577.

15 In *The Art of Lawgiving*, Harrington attacked an alternative constitution, the officers' *Agreement of the People* of January 1649, in a graphic picture of civil disorder. 'The Art of Lawgiving', *Works*, p. 405. For his identification of the ancient constitution with disorder see Judith Shklar, 'Ideology Hunting: The Case of James Harrington', *American Political Science Review*, 53 (1959), pp. 671–2; Pocock, *The Ancient Constitution*, Chapter 6; Pocock, 'Machiavelli, Harrington and English Political Ideologies in the Eighteenth Century', *William and Mary Quarterly*, 3rd series, 22:4 (1965), pp. 549–83.

16 'Oceana', *Works*, p. 70. Cf. *ibid.*, p. 44; 'A System of Politics', *Works*, p. 469.

17 'Oceana', *Works*, p. 152. There is little warrant for Gooch's view that Harrington maintained an optimistic view of the nature of man. Cf. Gooch, *English Democratic Ideas*, p. 255.

political order, 'it is not the people that are trusted, but the orders of the commonwealth'.[18] It was this recognition of the weakness and proneness to corruption of men which triggered Harrington's appeal to Cromwell to take on the mantle of legislator and introduce the utopian commonwealth. It was necessary that the legislator should be one man and that his scheme of government should be complete and introduced in one blow. Only in this way could men be made to conform to government, rather than their government conform to men.[19] Harrington sought perfect government and a perfect society through institutional, rather than personal, means. In this sense he was a utopian.[20]

The key concept in Harrington's design was not the agrarian law, important though that might be. It was rather the concept of the equal commonwealth, to which the device of the agrarian was subordinate. After having established the virtues of commonwealths in relation to other forms of government, Harrington went on to classify commonwealths according to three types of characteristic. They were either unitary or federal; designed for preservation or increase; equal or unequal. In reference to the last category, Harrington wrote, 'this is the main point'. The equal commonwealth was his supreme innovation, the point, he was forced to admit, at which his historical method broke down. He would have liked to have given an historical example of the working of such an equal commonwealth but he had to confess that there was no example. Venice, of all commonwealths, came the nearest, but even she was not equal enough.[21] The clearest and fullest definition of what Harrington meant by an equal commonwealth was given by him in *The Art of Lawgiving*. There he wrote:

An equal commonwealth is a government founded upon a balance which is perfectly popular, being well fix'd by a suitable *agrarian*; and which from the balance, thro the free suffrage of the people given by the ballot amounts in the superstructures to a senat debating and proposing, a representative of the people resolving, and a magistracy executing; each of these three orders being upon courses or rotation; that is elected for certain terms, injoining like intervals.[22]

---

[18] 'Valerius and Publicola', *Works*, pp. 455–6.

[19] 'Oceana', *Works*, p. 72.

[20] For an endorsement of my view that Harrington accepted man as a vicious and selfish creature and sought to contain these faults institutionally see J. A. W. Gunn, *Politics and the Public Interest in the Seventeenth Century* (London, 1969), pp. 115–17.

[21] 'Oceana', *Works*, pp. 50–1, 52.

[22] 'The Art of Lawgiving', *Works*, p. 370. Cf. the definition given in 'Oceana', *Works*, p. 51. 'An equal commonwealth . . . is a Government establish'd upon an equal Agrarian, arising into the Superstructures or three Orders, the Senate debating and proposing, the People resolving, and the Magistracy executing by

There were then four necessary features of an equal commonwealth: an 'equal Agrarian', the ballot, bicameral legislative (with functions of debate and decision separated and a dependent executive), and rotation of office. Only if all these institutional devices were met together could there be an equal, and therefore lasting, commonwealth.[23]

The importance of the concept of the equal commonwealth in Harrington's general political position and for his republicanism in particular could hardly be exaggerated. Because his method was largely historical and comparative he was forced to face up to the problem that historically commonwealths, like other forms of government, had failed. This came out quite clearly in his initial attack on monarchy and his attempt to prove the superiority of a popular commonwealth. He began by defining perfection of government as a situation in which no citizen could have an interest in, or the power to initiate, seditious activity. Monarchy, since it must be based on the support of independently powerful nobles, or on an army, would always be open to sedition and could never therefore be a perfect form. But Harrington's sense of the past was too strong for him not to admit that popular commonwealths too had been, and were, subject to sedition. Indeed he argued that they had only fallen in defeat to monarchies when they had been internally divided. If, however, commonwealths were subject to sedition as well as monarchies, how could they be said to be preferable or more perfect in form? It was at this point that Harrington rescued his republicanism by introducing the notion of the equal commonwealth. A commonwealth was

the government, which, *attaining to perfect equality*, has such a libration in the frame of it, that no man living can show which way any man or men, in or under it, can contract any such interest or power as should be able to disturb the commonwealth with sedition, wherefore an *equal commonwealth* is that only which is without flaw, and contains in it the full perfection of government.[24]

It is therefore both his utopianism and his republicanism which rest upon his concept of an equal commonwealth, that is to say upon the conjunction

an equal Rotation thro' the suffrage of the People given by the Ballot.' Confusingly, Harrington sometimes wrote as if only the Agrarian and rotation were necessary. See, 'Oceana', *Works*, p. 51; 'The Prerogative of Popular Government', *ibid.*, p. 282.

23 H. F. Russell Smith still gives one of the best analyses of this aspect of Harrington's thought. See, *Harrington and his Oceana: A Study of a Seventeenth Century Utopia and its Influence in America* (Cambridge, 1914), p. 23. Compare Eduard Bernstein's dismissal of the ballot and rotation as the most 'immaterial' institutions of *Oceana*. *Cromwell and Communism: Socialism and Democracy in the Great English Revolution*, translated H. J. Stenning (London, 1930), p. 200.

24 'Oceana', *Works*, pp. 49–50. My italics.

of the institutions of agrarian law, ballot, rotation and a bicameral legislative.

There is, however, a further point of significance in this position. As we have already seen, Harrington believed that there was no example of an equal commonwealth to be found in history. In this ultimate sense, both his republicanism and the character of his utopianism were without historical foundation. Like other utopias, Harrington's equal commonwealth stood outside and in conflict with all the known processes of history. It was therefore impossible for him to maintain his perfect and immortal commonwealth as inevitable or its adoption as historically determined. The balance of property in mid-seventeenth-century England might be favourable to the introduction of a commonwealth but it would not of itself determine the establishment of an *equal commonwealth*. The operation of the balance alone could not guarantee political and social stability. Harrington's utopianism, therefore, rested not on his theory of the balance of property, but on his concept of the equal commonwealth. While Harrington's *Oceana* stood outside time, it was dependent for its conceptualisation and hope of realisation on human, and not on divine, agency. Like the millennium, there had perhaps to exist for its inception a moment of grace, when a divinely inspired law-giver revealed the secret of the immortal commonwealth. There was, however, no *deus ex machina* on whom reliance for its establishment could be placed and moreover, while, in a millennium, the moment of grace inaugurated a continuum of grace, in *Oceana* the moment of grace occurred in what was otherwise a continuum of sin. The commonwealth could be perfected even though its citizens remained sinful. Good intentions could not be counted upon, and, even if they could, they would be insufficient. This was so because the problems of producing a stable society, an equal commonwealth, were not moral ones but structural and institutional ones, problems in political architecture. Harrington had recognised that history was not the blind play of *fortuna* but that the impersonal forces, of which man was both agent and victim, operated according to laws. With knowledge of these laws an equal commonwealth reconciling empire and authority, containing but not eliminating sin, could be produced.

The key rôle of the notion of the equal commonwealth in his political thought can be appreciated more fully when set in the context of Harrington's argument in the preliminaries of *Oceana*. He began by dividing governments, both theoretically and historically, into those of Ancient Prudence, ending with the rise of Caesar, and those of Modern Prudence. The latter subjected men to the rule of private interests and was typified as the rule of men rather than laws. Harrington rejected the governmental model of Modern Prudence as neither necessary nor desirable, as violent and unstable. In the second part of the preliminaries to *Oceana* he was concerned to analyse its historical progress in order to show its weaknesses and to demonstrate that the shift of the balance of property on to a popular basis made possible a return to the rule of laws rather than men. In the first part of the preliminaries he attempted to establish a theoretical ideal and to do so turned his back on Modern Prudence and followed the counsels of Ancient Prudence. Under Ancient Prudence government had been 'an art whereby a civil society of men is instituted and preserv'd upon the foundation of common right or interest; or. . .it is the empire of laws and not of men'.[25] This meant, as he remarked elsewhere, government under the form of a commonwealth rather than under king, Lords and Commons.[26] He self consciously followed the Ancients when he asserted that the 'principles of government are twofold: internal, or the goods of the mind; and external, or the goods of fortune'.[27] The former, the internal principle of government, was comprised of natural or acquired virtues such as wisdom, prudence and courage; that is, those things which conferred authority. The goods of fortune consisted of riches and were the basis of all power, or, as Harrington preferred to describe it, of empire. It was empire that he went on to describe and analyse next.

'To begin with Riches', he wrote, 'in Regard that Men are hung upon these, not of choice as upon the other, but of necessity and by the Teeth: for as much as he who wants Bread is his servant that will feed him; if a Man thus feeds a whole People, they are under his Empire.' Harrington's line of reasoning on empire was thus very simple. In a situation of scarcity men will tend to follow those who can provide for their wants. Riches, but above all land, therefore brought power. Land had two great advantages over other forms of property. It fed men and it was inexhaustible. Harrington could therefore conclude that, in most circumstances, 'as is the proportion or balance of dominion or property in land, such is the nature of the empire'.[28] But the balance of property determined the distribution of power, or empire, not necessarily the form of government. The theory of the balance of property rested ultimately on military and administrative considerations. Men would follow and fight for those who owned the land. If the balance was in one man, the situation would favour absolute monarchy; if in a few men, aristocracy or regulated monarchy; if in many, a commonwealth or popular government.[29] It is essential to grasp two points in respect of this. First, the disposition of the balance did

---

[25] 'Oceana', *Works*, p. 35.
[26] 'The Prerogative of Popular Government', *Works*, p. 221. On the importance of the classical theory of mixed government to Harrington's republicanism see Zera S. Fink, *The Classical Republicans: An Essay in the Recovery of a Pattern of Thought in Seventeenth Century England* (Evanston, 1945; 2nd edition 1962), Chapter 3.
[27] 'Oceana', *Works*, p. 36.   [28] *Ibid.*, p. 37.
[29] *Ibid.*; see also 'The Art of Lawgiving', *Works*, pp. 363–4.

not guarantee the existence or emergence of the appropriate form of government. Secondly, institutional adaptation to the balance did not necessarily guarantee political stability. There could be forms of government inconsistent with the balance of property. Such had been the situation in England since at least the reign of Elizabeth I. The balance of property had been popular but government had remained monarchical and aristocratic. Governments in such a situation oscillated between ineffectiveness and violence. In the long run they would fail, because in the long run men would obey those who could feed them. However, the long run could be very long indeed. No one, in the 1650s, was more conscious than Harrington of the possibility of an army-backed oligarchy seeking the indefinite perpetuation of aristocratic and monarchical forms by violence and against the balance of property.[30] An even more serious problem arose when the balance of property itself perpetuated instability. This could happen in two sets of circumstances: where the balance was equal and where the balance was in the few. When the balance was equal, as, for example, between nobility and people or between prince and people, the two sides of the balance would constantly be at war with each other in a struggle for supremacy. In such situations, Harrington said, governments 'subsist by confusion'. To fix such a balance by an agrarian law would be 'to entail misery'.[31] It was important therefore that there should be an overbalance of property in favour of one man, group or class, rather than an equal balance between an individual and a group, or between two groups. 'Imperfections of the balance, that is, where it is not good or down weight, cause imperfect government.'[32] An overbalance of property could be in one man, a few or the many. However, even where the case was one of an overbalance of property in the few, an unstable situation would subsist. The natural form of government to which an aristocracy, possessing an overbalance of property, would lean was a regulated monarchy. But 'a throne supported by a nobility is not so hard to be ascended as to be kept warm'.[33] The history of the Gothic balance was the story of exactly this situation and it was a tale of chronic instability. Only an aristocracy holding an *under*balance of property was a safe and desirable asset.[34] There

---

[30] See, for example, his brilliant analysis of the contemporary political situation in 'Oceana', *Works*, pp. 65–7, and in 'Pour enclouer le canon', *ibid.*, pp. 563–5. The idea that, in terms of provincial government, force could permanently override the balance of property is only partially true. The provincial balance could be overridden only on the basis of the possession of empire in the imperial state. Thus, in terms of provincial government, force could only permanently violate the balance provided it had a basis in empire of some kind. See, for example, 'Oceana', *Works*, p. 40.

[31] 'Oceana', *Works*, pp. 37–8.

[32] 'The Art of Lawgiving', *Works*, p. 364.

[33] 'Oceana', *Works*, p. 64.   [34] *Ibid.*, pp. 40, 124–5.

were then only two forms of overbalance of property which offered some hope of stability: overbalance in one person, leading to absolutism on the Turkish pattern, or an overbalance of property in the many, providing the basis for a popular commonwealth. What dissolved the charms of absolutism was the problem of external security. As Machiavelli had pointed out, once conquered an absolutist monarchy was easy to control and retain. It offered attractive prey to warlike and aggressive neighbours. To protect itself with a large standing army only added a further twist to the problem, for the army could provide a power base for usurpers or for those who might seek to maintain by violence a system contrary to the balance of property.

Thus the analysis of empire ended in the conclusion that a popular balance of property, as a basis for a popular commonwealth, was of all situations the most desirable. The problem remained, however, that a commonwealth must serve a general, rather than a private, interest, that it must be an empire of laws rather than men. England was fortunate in that the balance of property in her land had moved on to a popular basis. She could have a commonwealth without violence. Indeed, it was the only system that she could have without violence. But a wise and disinterested legislator was required if an appropriate and stable superstructure was to be raised. Accordingly, Harrington turned from his analysis of the principle of empire to that of the principle of authority.[35] But government, Harrington held, was analogous to the soul of man. As man could only be free if he acted rationally, so could the commonwealth only be free if governed by laws in the public interest and not tormented by the empire of private men pursuing personal ends. The problem was how to wed power and reason, empire and authority, dominion and legitimacy. Beyond this too lay the problem of how men, struggling with their own irrationality, could erect a system under which they could be governed rationally. How could they set up an empire of laws?[36]

In *The Prerogative of Popular Government* Harrington argued that

---

[35] The fact that Harrington was equally concerned with both empire and authority has not always been recognised. A. E. Levett saw that he distinguished between the two but asserted that he was only concerned with the former; 'James Harrington', in F. J. C. Hearnshaw (ed.), *The Social and Political Ideas of Some Great Thinkers of the Sixteenth and Seventeenth Centuries* (London, 1926), p. 188. There has been a general tendency to emphasise Harrington's analysis of empire at the expense of his treatment of authority. Amongst those who have insisted on their equal importance see, Greenleaf, *Order, Empiricism and Politics*, pp. 286–7; T. W. Dwight, 'Harrington and his Influence upon American Political Institutions and Political Thought', *Political Science Quarterly*, 2:1 (1887), p. 10.

[36] Cf. Blitzer, *An Immortal Commonwealth*, pp. 36–49; Gunn, *Politics and the Public Interest*, pp. 110–14.

law must proceed from will. Since the will in turn was moved by interest, the vital point was whether the law proceeded from the will of one man, a few men or a whole people. As the true nature of law lay not in partiality but in justice, the interest of a whole people was more just than that of a few.[37] In *Oceana* he developed a similar argument on slightly different lines. Here 'reason is nothing but interest' and, as the interest of the whole must be above the interest of the part, so the interest of mankind came nearest to right reason.[38] What could be done to make men give up private interest in order to pursue public interest, subdue their passions in order to act rationally in a social context? Harrington's answer was typically utopian: 'the safety of the people of *England*', he remarked in *The Art of Lawgiving*, 'is now plainly cast upon skill or sufficiency in political architecture; it is not enough therefore, that there are men addicted to all the good ends of a commonwealth, unless there be skill also in the formulation of those proper means whereby such ends may be attain'd'.[39] The harmonisation of interests would not occur naturally or spontaneously. It had to be engineered institutionally. Appeals to conscience or public morality would of themselves avail nothing:

unlesse you can show such orders of a Government, as like those of *God* in *nature* shall be able to constrain this or that *creature* to shake off that inclination which is more peculiar unto it, and take up that which regards the *common good* or *interest*; all this is to no more end, then to persuade every man in a *popular Government*, not to carve himself of that which he desires most, but to be mannerly at the Publick Table, and give the best from himself unto decency and the common interest.

Underlying Harrington's whole design was the conviction that 'such orders may be established as may, nay must give the upper hand in all cases to the common right or interest, notwithstanding the nearness of that which sticks to every man in private'.[40] It was Harrington's ambition to replace private interest by communal interest in the motivation and actions of men through the direction of a system of laws.[41]

The expression of the common interest had to be through representative institutions, but the formula 'vox populi, vox dei' was not enough. Unless 'invention' was used in the construction and procedure of popular assemblies, only chaos could result.[42] Two assumptions underlay Harring-

---

[37] 'The Prerogative of Popular Government', *Works*, p. 224.
[38] 'Oceana', *Works*, pp. 43–4.
[39] 'The Art of Lawgiving', *Works*, p. 367. In his preface to 'The Prerogative of Popular Government' (*Works*, p. 215), Harrington condemned the Grandees on the grounds that they did not have the intellectual capacity to solve England's problems.
[40] 'Oceana', *Works*, p. 44.
[41] Dwight, 'Harrington and his Influence', p. 11.
[42] 'The Prerogative of Popular Government', *Works*, p. 214.

ton's approach to the question of representative institutions for his ideal commonwealth. The first was that, while the interest and the empire of the commonwealth rested in the people, they had neither the leisure nor the wisdom to give adequate formulation to that interest. They could recognise the common interest when they saw it but they could not define it. The second assumption was that there existed a repository of political wisdom in those classes with education, leisure and wealth. They were able to define and distinguish the various interests at stake in any situation but they could not be guaranteed to pursue the common interest when they saw it. 'The *wisdom* of the few may be the *light* of mankind but the interest of the few is not the profit of mankind, nor of a commonwealth.'[43] Harrington's solution was the erection of a bicameral legislature composed of a senate with sole right of debate and proposal and a popular assembly with sole right of decision. The senate would be drawn only from the leisured classes. They would also be well represented in the popular assembly but the majority there would reside in the 'people'. '. . . the whole mystery of a Commonwealth', according to Harrington, lay 'only in dividing and chusing'.[44] As two girls, sharing a cake between them, would act reasonably if one girl divided the cake and the other chose how to distribute the pieces, so in such a bicameral system wisdom, reason, common interest and power would be reconciled. Moreover, Harrington believed that God had distributed into natural orders the determination of who should divide and who should choose in the body politic. There was a 'natural aristocracy diffused by God throughout the whole body of mankind of this end and purpose; and therefore such as the people have not only a natural but a positive obligation to make use of as their guides'.[45] He tended to assume that this natural aristocracy would be recruited from amongst the gentry. It was to be admitted that, even in an equal commonwealth, two or three men might rise to control the government, but, in those circumstances, their path to power could, he believed, only be the path of virtue. 'There is something', he added, 'first in the making of a Common-wealth, then in the governing of it, and last of all in the leading of its Armies; which (tho' there be great Divines, great Lawyers, great Men in all Professions) seems to be peculiar only to the Genius of a Gentleman.'[46] In Harrington's theory of leadership the desired qualities were to be found in an atmosphere of comfortable fortune, independence and cultivated leisure; exactly the atmosphere enjoyed, as he saw it, by the gentry of England. The division between senate and popular assembly was therefore based on social class.

Significantly, then, it was through his bicameralism that Harrington

[43] 'Oceana', *Works*, p. 45.
[44] *Ibid.*, p. 44. Cf. 'The Art of Lawgiving', *Works*, p. 419.
[45] 'Oceana', *Works*, p. 44.   [46] *Ibid.*, pp. 52–3.

reconciled authority and empire, reason and power, and therefore this, rather than the agrarian laws, must be seen as the lynchpin of his political system. The property-qualified senators had the leisure and wisdom to embody the community's reason, but, because they were a restricted class, without the balance of property, they were not representative of the community's interest or power. Their function was therefore restricted to debate and proposition. On the other hand, the popular assembly, representing the common interest and the balance of property or empire, were given the right of choosing between, or rejecting, propositions formulated by the superior wisdom of the leisured classes represented in the senate. In designing his legislature, Harrington was attempting to do more than merely give institutional expression to the balance of property. It was essential that, if the legislature was to be effective, it should respect that balance and the distribution of empire based on it. This Harrington's constitution did in according final powers of decision to the popular assembly. But he also based the legislature on a second principle, and that was the principle of reason and authority, the necessity for political wisdom and leadership. It was at this point that he 'contradicted' Machiavelli to assert the usefulness of a nobility or gentry 'in a popular government, not overbalancing it'.[47] By this token, leisure, as well as land, had become an important political factor. The balance of land lay in the sub-aristocratic classes. The sole claim of the aristocracy to even a subordinate place in the legislative process and to a monopoly of political discussion rested on the greater wisdom which their leisure, education and independence conferred. To his bicameralism, Harrington's theory of political leadership was as important as his theory of the balance of property. As previously argued, the basis of Harrington's utopianism was his concept of the equal commonwealth. Such a commonwealth to be perfect had to reconcile empire and authority. In his design, empire, the balance of property, was respected and stabilised through the agrarian laws. Authority, in the shape of disinterested government seeking the common interest, was sought through the ballot and rotation of office. But what reconciled empire and authority and gave perfection of form to Harrington's equal commonwealth were the bicameral institutions of senate debating and popular assembly resolving. For here both property and wisdom were respected and their proper rôles acknowledged.

Personal equality within the equal commonwealth was an intra-class equality, with the distinction of function between classes carefully maintained. In *A System of Politics*, Harrington described it as follows:

Equality or Parity has been represented as an odious thing, and made to imply the levelling of men's Estates; but if a Nobility, how unequal soever in their

---

[47] *Ibid.*, p. 40.

Estates or Titles, yet to come to the truth of Aristocracy, must as to their Votes or participation in the Government be pares regni, that is to say Peers, or in parity among themselves: as well likewise the People, to attain the truth of Democracy, may be Peers, or in parity among themselves, and yet not as to their Estates be oblig'd to levelling.[48]

This equality within classes was to be maintained by the ballot, rotation of office, and by the proscription of political debate outside the senate. By these means, Harrington believed, the formation of parties, whereby one group of men within a class could come to dominate the others, would be prevented. The relationship between classes would be maintained on its present levels by the agrarian laws 'An equal Agrarian is a perpetual Law establishing and preserving the balance of Dominion by such a distribution, that no one Man or number of Men, within the compass of the Few or Aristocracy, can come to overpower the whole People by their possession in Lands.'[49]

Harrington's constitutional respect for the balance of property was manifested not only on a national level but on a local level also. Indeed his treatment of local government is one of the most striking aspects of his utopia. Of the thirty orders or laws making up the constitution of Oceana, the first eleven were concerned with various aspects of local government. In fact, since in the seventeenth century almost all administration was through the organs of local government, the search for administrative effectiveness had to begin there. The principle underlying Harrington's approach to local government was that if the men of property would not obey and co-operate then neither would anyone else. They therefore had to be distinguished as a class and offered the opportunity of office and status in return for adherence to the system. The masses always had been, and always would be, deferential to their social superiors. In religion they would always follow them. In normal circumstances their politics would be absorbed from them, and, given the franchise, they would always elect them.[50] In the dialogue *Valerius and Publicola*, Valerius remarked, 'I am persuaded that the people, not under lords, will yet be most addicted to the better sort', and Publicola replied, 'That is certain.'[51]

The first four constitutional orders of Oceana distributed the people into categories or groups.[52] They were first divided into servants and freemen, and only the latter were regarded as citizens since servitude was

---

48 'A System of Politics', *Works*, p. 471. Cf. the depiction of Aristotle's views on political equality in Sanford A. Lakoff, *Equality in Political Philosophy* (Cambridge, Mass., 1964), pp. 17–18.
49 'Oceana', *Works*, p. 51.
50 'The Art of Lawgiving', *Works*, pp. 419, 420; 'Oceana', *ibid*.
51 'Valerius and Publicola', *Works*, p. 449.
52 'Oceana', *Works*, pp. 77–9.

'inconsistent with freedom or participation of government in a common-wealth'.[53] The second order divided citizens into youth (eighteen to thirty years old) and elders (over thirty years old). Harrington's immediate justification for this was military. The youth formed the marching armies, the elders the garrison forces of the nation. But, in fact, the distinction was more profound than this. Almost all political functions were confined to the elders. The political education of the youth was not considered complete until they had fulfilled their obligation to military service. Citizens were again divided into horse and foot. Those with an income of over £100 per annum from lands, goods or money were classed as the horse, those with an income less than this as the foot. The vague classification of 'gentry' was thus replaced by a class defined purely and precisely in terms of income and, as we shall see, with specific political privileges. Finally the administrative areas of England and Wales were geographically re-organised. The existing counties were broken up and redistributed into fifty tribes. Each tribe was composed of twenty hundreds and each hundred of ten parishes. There were thus ten thousand parishes.[54] In the next seven orders[55] Harrington worked upwards through the structure of local government, parishes, hundreds, tribes. Municipal government, except in the case of London and Westminster (for which separate provision was made),[56] was simply not recognised.

Once a year the elders of each parish were to assemble and elect a fifth of their number as deputies. On the list of those returned, members of the horse were to be given precedence. 'The first and second in the list are overseers by consequence; the third is constable, the fourth and fifth are churchwardens; the persons so chosen are deputies of the parish for one year from their election, and no longer, nor may they be elected two years together.' Given Harrington's assumption that he was dealing with a deferential society and the arrangements for the selection of these parochial officials, the dominance of the more substantial landowners in local affairs at the most basic level was made implicit in the constitution. Even should the men of substance neglect to take these parish positions, perhaps reserving themselves for higher things, their control over them was assured. For the rest Harrington made few changes in parish government

---

[53] This was a common attitude in seventeenth-century thought. The real problem is knowing what was included in the category of servant. See the discussion in C. B. MacPherson, *The Political Theory of Possessive Individualism: Hobbes to Locke* (Oxford, 1962) and Peter Laslett, *The World We Have Lost* (London, 1965). Wastrels and bachelors also suffered political disqualification in Oceana. See, 'Oceana', *Works*, p. 78.

[54] The number of counties and parishes corresponds fairly closely with the numbers for mid-seventeenth-century England. The point is that the relationship between them had been recast on a much more regular basis.

[55] 'Oceana', *Works*, pp. 78–90.   [56] *Ibid.*, pp. 157–9.

except to reduce the independence of the clergy yet further. A parson appointed to a parish, through the medium of the universities, had to receive, at the end of his first or probationary year, the support of two-thirds of the elders of his parish, expressed in a ballot. He had to conduct his services according to a directory approved by the legislature and accept the freedom of worship of all others, 'being not Papish, Jewish, or idolatrous'.

Every year the deputies of each parish were to assemble in the hundred to which their parish belonged. Here they were to elect out of their number four officers from the horse (a justice of the peace, a juryman, a captain and an ensign) and three from the foot (a juryman, coroner and a high constable). The hundred, therefore, served to provide a basis for the judicial and military organisation of the tribe. Through the hundred there would be provided twenty J.P.s and forty jurymen for each tribe. Not only was this adequate for the purposes of judicial administration but it shifted the basis of administrative responsibility. The J.P., the administrative workhorse of early modern England, owed nothing, in Oceana, to the national or central government. His dependence and answerability were purely local. These elections in the hundred were one of the pivots around which Harrington swung his decentralisation of English government.

As the deputies of every parish met annually in their hundreds so likewise they met in the tribe to elect both county officials and parliamentary representatives. By a complicated indirect ballot they elected the six major officials of the tribe. These were the Lord High Sheriff (who was both commander of the county militia and the first magistrate of the tribe), the Lord Lieutenant, Lord Custos Rotulorum and the Conductor (subordinate magistrates and military commanders) and two censors, who were to supervise the operation of the ballot and control the clergy. Harrington denied the possibility of 'men of more inferior rank' being elected to these positions. These magistrates of the tribe together with the J.P.s and the jurymen from every hundred (a total of sixty-six, no more than twenty of whom were expected to be recruited from the foot) made up a council called the phylarch or prerogative troop of the tribe. This body was to act as an intermediary between the local community and central government. They were charged with administering the military and electoral organisation of the county, with holding quarter sessions in their traditional form and with rendering assistance, military if necessary, to the itinerant judges. Petitions from county to Parliament had to be drawn up by the phylarch and approved, clause by clause, 'by the ballot of the tribe'. On the other hand, all commissions from Parliament had to be addressed through the phylarch. Parliament, for example, levied taxes on the phylarchs, who were left to raise the revenue through the hundreds and parishes. Given certain principles, respecting tax relief for those with children and penalties for those without, the question as to how the phylarch raised the required money was left open.

A number of commentators have suggested a lack of originality in Harrington's programme for local government, that it was merely an adaptation of what already existed. There is truth in this – justices, quarter sessions, constables, Lord Lieutenants all reappeared – but the structure was subject to subtle changes which indicate Harrington's principle of the equal commonwealth in operation. The centre of gravity of local administration has become purely local. None of the officials, including Lord High Sheriff and J.P., were selected by the national government. All were chosen locally. In this way and through his proposals for county government, Harrington produced a system of government basically federal in character. Within local government the propertied were clearly to be dominant. Most dramatic of all, the municipal boroughs, with their jealously guarded privileges, and hard-won charters, were swept away, absorbed into the county, hundred and parish structure. The balance of property principle operated here more clearly than it did in the agrarian law. Those with the capacity to feed were possessed of local power. The country dominated the towns. Equally clearly the ballot, rotation of office and the proscription of any form of political discussion[57] worked to prevent the formation of competing groups of county notables.

The deputies assembled in tribes to elect not only county officials but also national representatives.[58] This time Harrington could not allow social deference to do its work unaided, because he had to distinguish the capacity of the leisured for political wisdom and leadership from that of the masses for detecting the common interest. Accordingly, a senate of three hundred members had to be elected out of the horse. The functions of this body were to elect a national magistracy and executive Councils of State, and to debate and formulate proposals for submission to a second and popular assembly, to be known as the Prerogative Tribe. This popular assembly consisted of four hundred and fifty deputies elected out of the horse and six hundred out of the foot. Debate was restricted to the senate and prohibited in the popular assembly, which existed purely to vote on proposals submitted to it by the senate and on issues of judicial review. Members of both senate and the Prerogative Tribe held their seats for three years, after which they were obliged to stand down for the same period. A third of the members of both houses reached the end of their period of tenure every year. There was, therefore, an annual replenishment of members and the assemblies were never dissolved. The perpetual existence of the legislature was seen by Harrington as a major advantage of his system of rotation.

Democracy in Harrington's utopia was thus very indirect and guarded.

[57] For the proscription of political discussion at a local level see *ibid.*, p. 90.
[58] *Ibid.*, pp. 91–2, 104–49.

All officials and representatives were elected by the deputies, that is by one-fifth of the citizens over thirty years old.[59] Moreover both at county and at parliamentary levels their choice was in some respects restricted to certain classes. His bicameralism, based on both class and functional division, was an attempt to wed empire and authority. He saw the distribution of seats in the Prerogative Tribe as a means of protecting the mass of citizens against the consequences of a natural deference carried too far. 'Otherwise the people, beyond all manner of doubt, would elect so many of the better sort at the very first, that there would not be of the foot or of the meaner sort enough to supply the due number of the prerogative tribe, and the rest of the magistracys...'[60] Candidates for the senate had to be elders of the horse who had satisfactorily completed their military obligations and were married.[61] This too may be seen as a check on the deferential tendencies of the people. Apart from the overtly class basis of representation and the much enlarged assemblies, the most striking aspect of Harrington's proposals was the demise of the parliamentary borough. London and Westminster would be represented but as counties. The rest of the boroughs would be absorbed into their rural hinterlands. Once again this must be seen as securing the unequivocal political dominance of the landed classes, those classes which Harrington was convinced were best fitted for political and military leadership. The check upon this situation degenerating into sectional rule was the franchise in the hands of the 'people' and their majority in the popular assembly.

All officials of central government were elected from the senate.[62] They included the Lord Strategus, who acted as president of the senate and general of the army; the Lord Orator, vice-president of the senate and responsible for its good order; and two censors, who acted as chancellors of the two universities, presidents of the Council of Religion and supervisors of the ballot in the senate. All these were annual magistrates elected for one year of office and having to stand down the following year. In addition there were three commissioners of the seal, who acted as judges in Chancery, and three commissioners of the treasury, who acted as judges in Exchequer. These commissioners had a three year term of office, one of each standing down each year and replacements being elected out of the newcomers to the senate. The Lord Strategus and the six commissioners were *ex officio* members of all the councils of the senate. There were four

---

[59] Cf. MacPherson, *Political Theory of Possessive Individualism*, p. 183. MacPherson claims that the senate and popular assembly were elected by 'the whole people'. Cf. 'Oceana', *Works*, p. 91; 'The Art of Lawgiving', *ibid.*, p. 411.

[60] 'The Art of Lawgiving', *Works*, p. 419.

[61] Cf. Russell Smith, *Harrington and his Oceana*, p. 47.

[62] For the description of the executive which follows see, 'Oceana', *Works*, pp. 114–23.

of these councils elected by the senators from their number and subject to the same triennial rotation. They dealt with day-to-day administration and with the preparation of material for introduction into the senate. The largest of them, the Council of State, dealt with foreign affairs and provincial government. It also considered laws to be enacted, amended or repealed. Where secrecy was required it was expected to manage affairs without reference to the senate and the Prerogative Tribe, but it had no power to engage in war without authority from the senate. It administered the navy and arsenals and kept records of military activity. The Council of State was, in addition, commissioned to punish any who sought to introduce debate into a popular assembly or acted seditiously in any other way. The Council of War was a subcommittee of the Council of State. As its name implies it was responsible for military affairs and the waging of war. In a state of emergency, the senate could elect nine additional knights to the Council of War. This enlarged body was empowered to act as dictator for a period of up to three months. During that time they could levy men or money, make war or peace, and enact laws which would be valid for one year. The dictatorship was Harrington's attempt to avoid the danger to commonwealths, arising from what he called 'the slow pace of their orders', without precipitating the establishment of a permanent oligarchy.

Both the established national religion and liberty of conscience were to be sustained under the management of the Council of Religion. A national religion was to be practised in accordance with a directory made and published by Parliament.[63] For the rest there was to be a toleration of alternative religious practice, provided it was Christian and did not owe any foreign allegiance. Given this, Harrington recognised that full toleration meant the award of full civil rights. He gave this principle clearest expression in *The Art of Lawgiving*:

That no religion, being contrary to or destructive of Christianity, nor the public exercise of any religion, being grounded upon or incorporated into a foren interest, be protected by or tolerated in this state. That all other religions, with the public exercise of the same, be both tolerated and protected by the council of religion; and that all professors of any such religion be equally

[63] The most serious discussion of Harrington's religious views is still J. W. Gough, 'Harrington and Contemporary Thought', *Political Science Quarterly*, 45:3 (1930), pp. 395–404. Gough argued that Harrington was an Independent, and suggested that his agrarian law owed much to the Diggers. This last idea will not bear examination. Douglas Bush has also queried the notion of Harrington as a purely secular thinker; *English Literature in the Early Seventeenth Century 1600–1660* (Oxford, 1945), p. 254. For Harrington's attitude to the Jews see, S. B. Liljegren, 'Harrington and the Jews', *K. Humanistiska Vetenskapssamfundet i Lund Arsberättelse*, 4 (1931–2), pp. 65–92.

capable of all elections, magistracys, preferments, and offices in this common-wealth, according to the orders of the same.[64]

Unlike other utopians (for example, Burton and Hartlib), Harrington did not wish the clergy to combine their ministerial functions with any other employment. He was concerned to contain the divisive effects of religious controversy and to avoid the political consequences of religious fervour which he had observed in his own lifetime. To this end it was necessary to control the clergy: 'if you know not how to rule your clergy, you will most certainly like a man that cannot rule his wife, have neither quiet at home nor honour abroad'.[65] In order to keep the clergy out of politics it was important that they should be stipendiated and not landed.[66] At the same time Harrington proposed that the income of all benefices be improved to the value of £100 per annum. He feared the poor, ignorant preacher more than the comfortable and cultivated cleric. The university convocations were to act as arbitrating bodies in all religious disputes and to supervise all religious assemblies and discussion. In addition to its other functions the Council of Religion received all petitions addressed to the senate. Only such as it thought fit were actually referred to that body.

The Council of Trade was dealt with much more sketchily. Harrington promised to give more details later, a promise which he never fulfilled. In the meantime it was possessed of a general commission to control external trade to the benefit of the nation. Separate provision was made for ambassa-dorial representation abroad.[67]

Each of the four councils nominated three members to serve for a week at a time on a Council, or Academy, of Provosts. This body held a kind of open salon for the discussion of political matters. It represented 'the affability of the commonwealth', an attempt to give a sense of the open-ness of the central government to ideas from outside.

Harrington had devised an executive, which was recruited solely from the senate, but which was also heavily dependent on that body and changed in composition every year. There was little opportunity for a professional element to develop in the formulation of policy. The relationship between the executive and the class from which it was drawn was close and con-stantly renewed. The landed classes collectively administered the country and its affairs on a day-to-day basis. Should they, however, wish to initiate a new line of policy or legislation they were obliged to refer it to the popular assembly and were dependent on its decision.

As the civil organisation of the state was based on institutions operated by election from amongst the elders, so the military organisation was

[64] 'The Art of Lawgiving', *Works*, p. 423.   [65] 'Oceana', *Works*, p. 169.
[66] 'A System of Politics', *Works*, p. 475.
[67] See, 'Oceana', *Works*, pp. 116–17.

based on the youth. Harrington estimated the youth of England and Wales (i.e. the non-servant class aged between eighteen and thirty) at half a million in number. They were to meet annually in parishes and elect a fifth of themselves as deputies. From this hundred thousand, a full-time army of forty thousand (ten thousand horse and thirty thousand foot) was elected. The troops selected their own officers but supreme command was vested in the officers of the senate. Harrington went into considerable detail on the way in which the army could be mustered, trained, financed and used for national defence, conquest and the control of provinces.[68] It was a citizen militia, locally based, locally raised and locally organised. It confirmed that the centre of gravity of government in Oceana was local and regional. But it was also designed to produce an army capable of sustaining imperialistic expansion. This was vitally important for Harrington's whole scheme. The last law of the Oceanic constitution provided for the division of the spoils of successful conquest. A commonwealth for increase provided the means of satisfying the land hunger of those restricted by the limitations of the agrarian laws.

'The Center, or Basis of every Government', Harrington declared, 'is no other than the Fundamental laws of the same.'[69] In his ideal constitution he provided for two sets of fundamental laws: those relating to the ballot (under which term he included the rotation of office) and the agrarian laws. Every public office in Oceana was elective or subject to confirmation by secret ballot. Equally, every office, except clerical office, was subject to a limited period of tenure and a compulsory vacation from office on the termination of that period.[70] The purpose of ballot and rotation was to prevent the emergence of factional or party pursuit and manipulation of office. By keeping access to office open, Harrington hoped that politics would never become a mere struggle for power. 'Equal Rotation', he wrote, 'is equal vicissitude in Government, or succession to Magistracy confer'd for such convenient terms, enjoying equal vacations, as take in the whole body by parts, succeeding others, thro' the free election or suffrage of the people.'[71] The openness of the rotational system is then one of the devices designed to prevent those who think themselves entitled to office from having an interest in subversion. If we accept Harrington's own estimate of the number of elders per tribe at ten thousand, or half a million elders in the nation, then a hundred thousand

---

[68] See *ibid.*, pp. 163–78; 'The Art of Lawgiving', *Works*, pp. 423–4, 430. In defence of the homeland the military organisation of the youth could of course be supplemented by that of the elders.

[69] 'Oceana', *Works*, p. 94.

[70] *Ibid.*, pp. 94, 104–12. The terms of operation of the ballot and rotation relative to specific offices are scattered through the work.

[71] *Ibid.*, p. 51.

deputies would be elected.[72] Merely on the level of parish offices there would be fifty thousand positions to fill (five offices for each of ten thousand parishes). Over two years, given the system of rotation, a hundred thousand men would occupy these positions. That is to say that in the course of two years, all the deputies, that is one-fifth of the adult male citizen population, would have been presented with the opportunity of office on a parish level. For the citizen youth this kind of availability of office was paralleled in the militia. Harrington's system of rotation was, like many other aspects of his utopian design, complex in its purposes. It took into consideration both the aspirations of those without office and the effect of power on those with it. Like the Levellers, he was sceptical of men's ability to withstand the corrupting influence of power. He defended the triennial limitation of tenure in the following way.

The term in which a man may administer government to the good of it, and not attempt upon it to the harm of it, is the fittest term of bearing magistracy; and three years in a magistracy describ'd by the law under which a man has liv'd, and which he has known by the carriage or practise of it in others, is a term in which he cannot attempt upon his government for the hurt of it. . . [73]

Divines, physicians and lawyers were excluded from office because they began with a partiality imparted to them from the nature of their professions and from which the system of rotation could not defend the state.[74]

In recent years, perhaps unfortunately, much of the discussion of Harrington has centred on the nature of his agrarian laws.[75] 'An equal Agrarian' he defined as: 'a perpetual Law establishing and preserving the balance of Dominion by such a distribution, that no one man or number of Men, within the compass of the Few or Aristocracy can come to overpower the whole People by their possession in Lands'. The purpose of the agrarian laws was therefore to prevent the balance of property or empire slipping from a popular basis to an aristocratic one, to keep the balance of

[72] Cf. *ibid.*, p. 154.
[73] 'A System of Politics', *Works*, p. 471.
[74] 'Oceana', *Works*, p. 169. In November 1649 an unsuccessful attempt was made, on similar grounds, to bar lawyers from sitting in the House of Commons. See, Stuart E. Prall, *The Agitation for Law Reform during the Puritan Revolution* (The Hague, 1966), pp. 34–5.
[75] See, MacPherson, *Political Theory of Possessive Individualism*, Chapter 4; J. F. H. New, 'Harrington, A Realist', *Past and Present*, 24 (1963), pp. 75–81; MacPherson, 'Harrington as Realist: A Rejoinder', *Past and Present*, 24 (1963), pp. 82–5; New, 'The Meaning of Harrington's Agrarian', *Past and Present*, 25 (1963), pp. 94–5; Greenleaf, *Order, Empiricism and Politics*, Appendix. Christopher Hill has made the point that, in advocating an agrarian law, Harrington was 'only summing up a tradition'. Hill, *The World Turned Upside Down* (London, 1972), pp. 92–3.

lands in the hands of the many rather than of the few. Now Harrington clearly defined what he meant by the 'few'. It was any number less than five thousand. If the land of England fell into 'fewer than five thousand hands, it is swerving from a commonwealth'.[76] The use of the number five thousand has been traced to classical sources, but perhaps more pertinent was the regional basis of Oceana's government. The distribution of territory in that number of hands would mean, on average, one hundred large-scale landowners in every county or tribe. On such a basis the domination of county government and hence of national government by small, self-centred and dependent cliques remained inconceivable. Harrington could still visualise disinterested, non-party government with land confined in the possession of a number as small as five thousand equal magnates.

The problem of the agrarian law was how to legislate so as to prevent the number of landowners falling below that number. Harrington estimated that the gross national income from land was about £10 000 000 per annum.[77] To prevent the ownership of land being restricted to less than five thousand individuals, all that was necessary was to make it impossible to possess an estate worth over £2000 per annum. It was accordingly made illegal to accumulate such an estate by way of purchase. Harrington dismissed the possibility of such accumulation by donation as being too slight to warrant legislation. There remained two means of accumulation: marriage and inheritance. The first he dealt with severely by limiting dowries to a maximum capital sum of £1500. At a return of five per cent per annum on land this represented a potential income of £75 per annum.[78] The crucial issue was accumulation by inheritance and Harrington was delicate in his dealings with it, because it touched upon the central core of the English gentleman's political outlook, the sanctity of property, and because he wished, while preventing their domination, to preserve the English aristocracy.[79] In Oceana, the agrarian law merely established two categories of men having more than one son and over £2000 per annum in land.[80] In the first category men who could distri-

---

[76] 'Oceana', *Works*, p. 51. 'The Art of Lawgiving', *ibid.*, p. 367.

[77] 'Oceana', *Works*, pp. 154–6.

[78] 'The Art of Lawgiving', *Works*, pp. 427, 407.

[79] In Scotland where the Agrarian was fixed at £500 per annum, he deliberately sought to destroy the aristocracy.

[80] In *The Art of Lawgiving* this was extended to include daughters. The two principal versions of the Agrarian are as follows: 'That every man who is at present possest, or shall hereafter be possest of an estate in land exceeding the revenue of two thousand pounds a year, and having more than one son, shall leave his lands either equally divided among them in case the lands amount to above 2000 l. a year to each; or so near equally in case they come under, that the greater part or portion of the same remaining to the eldest, excede not the value

bute at least £2000 per annum to each son were obliged to divide their estates equally between them. Thus, for example, a man with two sons and £5000 per annum in land had to leave £2500 per annum to each of his sons. It should perhaps be noted that individuals holding land in multiples of £2000 per annum would be very few indeed. Harrington believed that there were no more than three hundred families in England with over £2000 per annum in land.[81] In cases where these families with gigantic holdings had a number of sons, the estate could be rapidly broken down, *without the property right of the family being invaded*. In this way the agrarian law operated over a long term to break up exceptionally large estates and to prevent their accumulation. In other words, it acted as a check on any tendency for the balance of property to move from a popular to an aristocratic basis. The more fertile such families were in the production of male heirs the more effective and rapid would be the process, and *vice versa*. In the second category came men who possessed over £2000 per annum in land, but not sufficient to distribute over £2000 per annum to each heir. In this case a maximum limit was set on the inequality of inheritance of £2000 per anum. Thus, for example, a man with two sons and £2500 per annum in land could not leave more than £2000 to the favoured son. He could, of course, leave less, and it is even possible that Harrington would have preferred him to leave equally to all his sons, but, in this respect, there was no compulsion. The effect again of the provisions of the agrarian law was, if not to make it impossible, still to set up obstacles to the accumulation and retention of estates worth over £2000 per annum in land. The more optimistic the view one took of the philoprogenitive capacities of the rich, the more effective would the check be felt to be. The law said nothing to limit the inheritance of only sons and nothing on the disposition of estates of less than £2000 per annum in land. In *The Art of Lawgiving*, Harrington sought to extend the law to cases where there were no sons, only daughters, and provided that where there were sons, the eldest could not inherit more than £2000 per annum in land. Men

of two thousand pounds revenue.' 'Oceana', *Works*, p. 95. 'That everyone holding above two thousand pounds a year in land, lying within the proper territory of the Commonwealth, leave the said land equally divided among his sons; or else so near equally, that there remain to the eldest of them not above two thousand pounds a year in land so lying. That this proposition be so understood, as not to concern any parent having no more than one son, but the next heir only that shall have more sons; in such sort, as nothing be hereby taken from any man, or from his posterity, but that fatherly affection be at all points extended as formerly, except only that it be with more piety, and less partiality. And that the same proposition, in such familys where there are no sons, concern the daughter or daughters in the like manner. That no daughter, being neither heir nor co-heir, have above fifteen hundred pounds in portion, or for her preferment in marriage.' 'The Art of Lawgiving', *ibid.*, p. 408.

81 'Oceana', *Works*, p. 100.

were also permitted to accumulate *additional* estates in the provinces of Scotland and Ireland up to the value of £500 and £2000 per annum respectively. The provincial opportunities for exceeding the limits of the Agrarian were one of the bases upon which Harrington believed that he was proposing the establishment of an imperialistic commonwealth. He clearly wished over the long term to produce an upper limit on landed estates within England and Wales of £2000 per annum, but he would not proceed by confiscation,[82] nor by insisting upon equal inheritance. His object was to prevent domination by an aristocracy while preserving aristocrats and their capacities for political and military leadership.

There has been a good deal of mathematical analysis of Harrington's agrarian laws, particularly from the point of view of all land falling into the hands of only five thousand men. The point is that it is quite possible to make nonsense of the mathematical provisions of his system.[83] For example, were all land to fall into the possession of five thousand proprietors, it would be impossible to work the rotational system of office-holding without assuming a commercial interest capable of providing a balance equal to that from land. If the possession of land were restricted to five thousand then that number, by definition, would be the only recipients of income from land over £100 per annum. They would therefore form the whole equestrian class, in respect of income from land. Assuming that no parish offices were taken by the horse (although Harrington elsewhere suggested that this would not be the case),[84] there would yet remain over 5050 offices to be filled by the horse.[85] Given the system of rotation and vacation from office this means a requirement of at least 10 100 potential office holders from the horse. As the landed were limited to five thousand, this would presuppose a greater number, 5100, being drawn from other sources. Moreover, as Harrington had prohibited divines, physicians and lawyers from holding political office, the majority of office

---

[82] See his expression of the object behind the Agrarian, *ibid.*, pp. 99, 189; although the agrarian law did provide that 'whosoever, possessing above the proportion allowed by these laws, shall be lawfully convicted of the same, shall forfeit the overplus to the use of the State'. *Ibid.*, p. 95.

[83] Harrington himself denied the validity of the mathematical approach to politics and to the universe; see, 'The Prerogative of Popular Government', *Works*, pp. 247–8. This was, of course, directed against Hobbes.

[84] 'Oceana', *Works*, pp. 79–80.

[85] Made up as follows: four offices in every one of a thousand hundreds (4000); six offices in every one of fifty counties (300); senators (300); deputies from the horse in the popular assembly (450). In addition there were a small number of ambassadorial and extraordinary functions which might be performed by members of the horse. Also to be taken into account are the position of minors amongst the five thousand landowners and those of them who exercised the profession of cleric, lawyer or physician.

holders would have to be drawn from purely commercial interests. But it is quite clear that Harrington would contemplate no such state of affairs. He denied that the Agrarian could tip the balance from gentlemen to merchants.[86] He was almost excessively suspicious of the instability of fortunes based on money and not on land. 'Commonwealths upon which the City life has had the Stronger influence, as Athens, have seldom or never been quiet. . .'[87] There were only three cases where 'balance in mony may be as good or better than that in land', and none of them applied to Oceana.[88] The numerical possibilities to which his system was left open could, if pushed to extremes, produce almost the reverse of what Harrington intended.

Two points are worth making in relation to this. In the first place, Harrington's figures, his numerical exactness, his statements of precise salaries, costs of implementation, numbers of officials, urns, pellets and so on, are *not* part of a mathematically perfect system. They are the obsession with detail, the dotting of i's and crossing of t's of the utopian mentality.[89] The second point is that most recent academic criticism has been directed at this situation where five thousand hold all the land. But this was so extreme a possibility as to exist for Harrington only as a point of theoretical reference. He believed that when he was writing there were not three hundred with an income of over £2000 a year from land. To reach the extreme situation 4700 had to acquire estates of £2000 to the exclusion of all others, except the original three hundred, from landownership. How were they to do it? Acquisition of such estates by purchase or gift was illegal. By marriage the process could take up to thirty generations unless one married a childless widow, but her infertility, and the heavy taxes associated with it,[90] might discourage such a match. The only clear method was by inheritance from more than one source and such good fortune was not normally in the control of the recipient. It would be, as Harrington intended, far more attractive for those ambitious for lands to throw themselves into imperialist activities.

A man is a spirit rais'd by the magic of nature; if she does not stand safe, and so she may set him to some good and usefull work, he spits fire, and blows up castles: for where there is life there must be industry or work; and the work of idleness is mischief, but the work of industry is health. To set men to this, the commonwealth must begin betimes with them, or it will be too late: and the

[86] 'The Prerogative of Popular Government', *Works*, p. 280.

[87] 'Oceana', *Works*, p. 33.

[88] 'The Prerogative of Popular Government', *Works*, p. 228.

[89] Charles Blitzer has seen this obsession as a psychological symptom of Harrington's preoccupation with stability. Blitzer, *An Immortal Commonwealth*, p. 219.

[90] A man over twenty-five years old, married for three years and with no children was liable to double taxation. 'Oceana', *Works*, p. 90.

means whereby she sets them to it, is EDUCATION, the plastic art of government.[91]

The primary importance of education for Harrington was civil: 'the formation of the citizen in the womb of the commonwealth is his education'. This both extended the definition of education and gave it its utopian purpose. If a parent had only one son, he was allowed to direct his education, otherwise the claims of the state came first. The operative principle then was that 'The education. . .of a man's own children is not wholly to be committed or trusted to himself.'[92] The provision of six forms of education was envisaged in *Oceana*: schools, mechanics, universities, inns of court, travel and military discipline. For the male children of those with more than one son, education was compulsory between the ages of nine and fifteen. When necessary this was free and Harrington saw this as a great boon to the needy. It removed the expense of their children when they were unable to make much economic contribution to the family and restored them when they were. These free schools were to be set up in every tribe and to be regularly inspected by the censors, 'to the end there be no detriment or hindrance to the scholars upon case of removing from one to another'.[93] In other words the system was to be national and uniform. At the age of fifteen the children left school and were either apprenticed or sent to the universities or inns of court, according to their abilities or inclinations. 'This with the multitude must be to the mechanics, that is to say, to agriculture of husbandry; to manufactures, or merchandise.' Harrington's hope was that husbandry would predominate, as this produced both a well fed and a militarily capable populace.[94] At eighteen, unless this were deferred by the county authorities, the child joined the order of the youth and was eligible for military service. The militia of Oceana provided what Harrington described as the main education of the youth. It was the school of valour, discipline and public spirit. There was some attempt to indoctrinate the populace in the constitution and the ideas behind it by a system of public lectures held on every Tuesday. These also gave scope for the training of office holders in oratory.[95] Similarly Harrington believed that, by dispersing experience of office, the

---

[91] *Ibid.*, p. 159. Harrington's main discussion of education is to be found *ibid.*, pp. 159–61, 164–6. See also, W. A. L. Vincent, *The State and School Education 1640–1660 in England and Wales* (London, 1950), pp. 90–1.

[92] 'Oceana', *Works*, pp. 164, 159–60. Commenting on the compulsory element in Harrington's scheme, J. W. Adamson has drawn attention to the provision by the General Court of Connecticut that every settlement of fifty families should maintain a schoolmaster and the stipulation that those who neglected to send their children should be deprived of them. Adamson, *Pioneers of Modern Education 1600–1700* (Cambridge, 1905), p. 262.

[93] 'Oceana', *Works*, p. 160.

[94] *Ibid.*, p. 165.   [95] *Ibid.*, pp. 148–9.

system of rotation would educate the people in political responsibility.[96] Above all he saw a state-controlled religion as a useful tool for social control: 'it has bin a maxim with legislators not to give checks to the present superstition, but to make the best use of it, as that which is always the most powerful with the people'.[97]

Harrington's Oceana does give the impression of being a much more open system than most utopias, particularly on the legislative side. This impression is accurate up to a point. There was an operative legislature, which many utopias do not provide for, but the degree to which that legislature opened Oceana up to change should not be exaggerated. There was considerable provision for fixity of law within the constitution. The land settlement, the religious establishment, education, and distribution of office were all seen as permanently provided for. Moreover, Harrington offered a system whereby, at the end of a period of eleven years, taxation could be abolished and the state left self-financing.[98] In this way one of the major legislative preoccupations as well as a source of constitutional friction was removed. Harrington saw the adoption of his model as leading very rapidly to the disappearance of parties and conflicting interests. 'If your commonwealth be rightly instituted, seven years will not pass, ere your cluster of parties, civil and religious, vanish not through any force, as when cold weather kills flies, but by the rising of greater light, as when the sun puts out candles.'[99] In this atmosphere of general agreement and reconciliation of interests, the scope for legislative activity would rapidly diminish.

Outside the constitution itself Harrington left scattered suggestions for the maintenance of public morality. Prostitutes, wastrels and a vaguely general category of the immoral were to be privately warned, and, after six months, if unreformed, they could be reproved before the Council of Religion or the censors. If after a further six months their behaviour remained unimproved they could be forbidden to appear publicly.[100] There was also some provision for theatrical censorship, but, in the main, Harrington offered no detailed criminal code and no social welfare system. He said nothing, for example, on the subject of poor relief. Perhaps it was because he accepted the systems already operative in England. At all events, he remained indifferent to these problems. His concern was political instability, and he traced this neither to the masses nor to the poor. The source of political instability was always, for Harrington, propertied groups who had been denied power. The equal commonwealth was

---

[96] 'The Prerogative of Popular Government', *Works*, p. 299.
[97] 'Oceana', *Works*, p. 196.
[98] *Ibid.*, pp. 150–1.
[99] 'A Discourse upon this Saying', *Works*, p. 574.
[100] 'Oceana', *Works*, p. 206.

designed to prevent these frustrations and their consequences. Nevertheless there is in *Oceana*, as in other utopias, a sweeping limitation of men's liberties. Wastrels, divines, physicians, lawyers and bachelors all suffered loss of civil rights.[101] Political discussion was prohibited outside the senate,[102] and refusal of public service could result in servitude.[103] Parental control over the education of children was restricted. The right to property was conditional. Those holding a surplus of land were liable to have it seized by the state.[104] Harrington took a dismal view of men's capacities for individualism both in politics and religion. Most men would, he believed, accept leadership in political, moral and spiritual matters. His constitution sought to use leadership without letting it become a threat to social harmony.

'The people is in no wise to be trusted with their liberty, but by stated laws or orders.' Harrington believed that he had created a closed system, where men could 'have no other motion than according unto the order of their commonwealth'.[105] In *A Discourse Upon This Saying* he drew an analogy between his commonwealth and a cats' kitchen. The cats were so harnessed into the machine that their instinctive movements operated the machine and prepared the food. To Harrington, at least, Oceana was a self-contained system capable of harnessing men's natural behaviour into a harmonious social whole. Its great merit was its 'entireness'. It answered every possibility. It was a total, a utopian solution. 'Security of government must be from entireness of form; and entireness of form must be from soundness or rightness of foundation.'[106] Nevertheless he was, as Pocock has exhaustively demonstrated, the self-conscious apostle of the classical republican tradition, and that tradition stressed participation and the moral openness of the *vivere civile*.

There remained consequently a tension in his *Oceana* and subsequent writings which remained unresolved. The classical republican who believed that a moment had arrived in England when citizens might rule themselves, also believed that the legislator must presume all men wicked. His obsession with permanence, with immortality as well as perfection, led him to see the participation of citizens in a free republic as a ritualised performance, no more than the participation of its various components in the functioning of a machine, like the 'Cats and Kitlings' tied into an extraordinary frame. The difference was almost that between the moral effort which would give meaning to the republic and the republic which could give meaning to moral effort. Both these elements are in tension in

---

101 *Ibid.*, pp. 78, 169.   102 *Ibid.*, pp. 90, 158.   103 *Ibid.*, p. 163.
104 *Ibid.*, p. 95.
105 'A Discourse upon this Saying', *Works*, pp. 568, 569.
106 'A Sufficient Answer to Mr. Stubb', *Works*, p. 585.

the republican tradition springing from civic humanism and especially its Machiavellian development. But, whereas that tradition remained liberal, in the sense at least that it sought to use institutional balances to enable men to face the choice of moral action (and hence exposed the republic constantly to the danger of corruption; the other face of men's fallibility in the pursuit of civic virtue), the utopian is too sceptical of men's capacity for civic morality to allow citizens freedom of choice. The republic, in the hands of the utopian, becomes not so much participatory as restraining and constraining. Freedom from corruption, immortality, is purchased hereby at the price of civic virtue, for men without choice are neither citizens nor capable of virtue, as their society is incapable of corruption. But, it is a dead society, a human machine, programmed forever for the repetitious performance of the same functions; the epitome of the totalitarian state. These polarities are in tension against one another in Harrington's perfect and immortal commonwealth.

Harrington saw problems which emerged in secular time according to intelligible principles as resolvable in secular time and, if the circumstances were right, as resolvable for all time. The perfection of the citizen and his performance in the new order, however, arise not out of his assumed moral capacities – it is the duty of the legislator to presume all men wicked – but out of constraints, limitations and patterns imposed on his behaviour by constitutional machinery, procedures and laws. So there may be no discussion of politics outside the senate. The casting of votes is a secret, non-public, rite. Offices must be vacated at set times and for set periods. There are limits set on the accumulation and transference of property. Those who propose legislation may not decide on it. There is discrimination between one type of citizen and another and prescribed limitations on their relationships. By the operation, not of divine providence, but of secular constitutional contrivances, applied at the appropriate moment in secular time, the equal commonwealth is maintained. In secularising and ruralising the classical republic Harrington also utopianised it and thereby made it incorruptible, immortal. In the process he risked the individual moral worth of his citizens. The *zōon politikon* could be reduced by analogy to 'Cats and Kitlings'. The explanation for this may well be because, while the Florentines were habituated to republics, the second nature of Englishmen had been shaped to the customary uses of the ancient constitution and therefore required more radical moulding.

The neo-Harringtonians had two alternatives open to them. They could drop the utopian scaffolding in the name of human virtue and thus, compromising with a world of human choice, grapple with and become preoccupied with the problem of corruption. Alternatively, they could retain the utopian structure and go on elaborating the dehumanised political machinery of which Harrington was ambivalently the author. We must now turn to consider some of those who took this second path.[107]

[107] John Pocock has dealt decisively with the first group in various writings. The second group, the utopian neo-Harringtonians dealt with in the next chapter, have been largely neglected. For reasons of space a third group, the colonial utopians influenced by Harrington, are not dealt with in this book.

9

The Harringtonians

Here Cooks Reports and Bridgemans are
Useless; our Laws are shorter far;
Here we permit no long delays
Which after Cases sundry walout
Heres *Magna Charta* full in view:
Here every free-man hath his due:
Here's no encouragement for knaves,
Whom fittest 'tis to use as slaves.

Anonymous, Chaos (1659)

... till the Ax be laid to the root of every evil and corrupt interest, we may not expect to reap any great fruit or success by our Reformation, for all flesh is corruptible, and every man a lie, nor is he that marches in the Rear any better able to resist the Temptation, or avoid the snares of his place then he that fell before him.

William Sprigge, A Modest Plea,
For An Equal Commonwealth (1659)

Wealth is a very turbulent thing, and the occasion of great disorders, when it hath not Authority and Preferments answerable.

Anonymous, The Free State of
Noland (1696/1701)

The odd notion that Harrington, at least in England, had no followers and founded no school,[1] is now no longer viable. He was undoubtedly the most important of the first generation of English republicans, because, by his theories, he undermined both the historical and the legal bases of the doctrine of the ancient constitution.[2] Professor Zagorin has felt it no exaggeration to describe him as 'the creator of republican theory'.[3] But the neo-Harringtonian adaptation of his theories, as described by John Pocock, saw some far-reaching and substantial changes.[4] Harrington's rejection of the ancient constitution as anachronistic and unstable was replaced by its defence with particular stress on the place of a hereditary House of Lords as a bulwark against a packed Commons and a standing army. In conjunction with this, the Gothic balance and its feudal under-pinnings, condemned by Harrington as inherently unstable, were to be nostalgically revered as virtuous and free, uncorrupted by the menace of standing, mercenary armies or the rise of the monied interest. It was a transformation gaining way in the 1670s and 1680s and completed in the Augustan period. In the process the constitutional innovations of *Oceana* – the functionally differentiated bicameralism, the ballot and rotation, the agrarian law – quietly sank into desuetude.

[1] See for example, T. W. Dwight, 'Harrington and his Influence upon American Political Institutions and Political Thought', *Political Science Quarterly*, 2:1 (1887), p. 1.

[2] J. G. A. Pocock, *The Ancient Constitution and the Feudal Law: A Study of English Historical Thought in the Seventeenth Century* (Cambridge, 1957), Chapter 7; Pocock, ' "The Onely Politician": Machiavelli, Harrington and Felix Raab', *Historical Studies*, 12 (1966), pp. 265–96; Pocock, 'James Harrington and the Good Old Cause: a Study of the Ideological Context of his Writings', *Journal of British Studies*, 10:1 (1970), pp. 30–48.

[3] Perez Zagorin, *A History of Political Thought in the English Revolution* (London, 1954), p. 155.

[4] J. G. A. Pocock, *The Machiavellian Moment: Florentine Political Thought and the Atlantic Republican Tradition* (Princeton, 1975), Chapters 12–14; Pocock, 'Machiavelli, Harrington and English Political Ideologies in the Eighteenth Century', *William and Mary Quarterly*, 3rd series, 22:4 (1965), pp. 549–83; *The Political Works of James Harrington*, ed. Pocock (Cambridge, 1977), pp. 128–52.

Amongst Harrington's followers there was perhaps almost bound to be a utopian bias, as contrasted with the perfect moral commonwealth bias of the defenders of monarchy.[5] This arose out of the nature of the republican attack, directed largely at the dependence of monarchy on the particular qualities of individual kings. Following Harrington, they contrasted the empire of men and the empire of laws. In some cases, for example that of Henry Neville in the early 1680s, an attempt was made to reconcile the form of the ancient constitution with the institutions of a republic. The result was an inevitable movement away from the utopianism implicit within the Harringtonian tradition.[6] There can be little doubt that the majority of those influenced by Harrington after the Restoration leaned in this direction. Nevertheless there were those who, responding to the pressures of polemic, pushed their belief in the superiority of an empire of laws to an ideal. Out of these Harringtonian republicans, the polarising tendencies of political debate made utopians.

At least three utopias, heavily indebted to the Harringtonian school, were devised in the second half of the seventeenth century and it is on these that this chapter concentrates. Two of them were published in that *annus mirabilus* of Harringtonian expectation, 1659. The first, an anonymous work, entitled significantly *Chaos*, presented 'a Frame of Govern-

---

[5] This contrast may be seen, for example, in Thomas Goddard's attack on Henry Neville's *Plato Redivivus* (1681). Goddard saw clearly that, whereas he believed that social perfection could only come through the moral effort of individual men, Neville placed his reliance in forms of government and administrative institutions. See Goddard, *Plato's Demon: Or, the State-Physician Unmaskt* (1684), pp. 16–18.

[6] Neville has been quite commonly described as a utopian. See, for example, the catalogue of utopias in R. W. Gibson, *St. Thomas More: A Preliminary Bibliography of his Works and of Moreana to the Year 1750* (New Haven and London, 1961), pp. 372–3. For a discussion of *The Isle of Pines*, see above Chapter 1. Neville's *Plato Redivivus* (1681) is not a utopia and indeed is barely republican. In it Neville followed Harrington's historical analysis but modified Harrington's proposals to provide a moderate solution to the problems of 1680–1. He proposed that the king exercise his prerogatives in relation to war and peace, the militia, appointments, and expenditure only through four committees elected by Parliament. In addition laws were to be passed providing for annually elected Parliaments, and for peers only to be made with the approval of Parliament. Neville offered his scheme as a defence of the legitimate succession and at least one of his critics accepted it as such. (See W.W., *Antidotum Britannicum: Or, A Counter-Pest Against The Destructive Principles of Plato Redivivus* (1681), Preface.) For Neville's authorship of *Plato Redivivus* see Anthony A. Wood, *Athenae Oxonienses*, edited by P. Bliss, 4 vols. (London, 1813–20), vol. IV, p. 410; Anna Maria Crino, 'Lettere inedite italiane e inglesi di Sir Henry Neville', in *Fatti e Figure del Seicento Anglo-Toscana*, Biblioteca dell'Archivum Romanicum, 48 (Florence, 1957), pp. 203–4. The most convenient text of *Plato Redivivus* is now in Caroline Robbins (ed.), *Two English Republican Tracts* (Cambridge, 1969).

ment by way of a Republique, wherein is little or no danger of miscarriage, if prudently attempted and thoroughly prosecuted by Authority'.[7] The second, *A Modest Plea, For An Equal Commonwealth, Against Monarchy*, was written by William Sprigge, who had been a protégé of Oliver Cromwell's, recommended by him to a fellowship at Lincoln College, Oxford (1652) and one of the first fellows of the college at Durham established by Cromwell. In 1696, a third Harringtonian utopia, again anonymous, appeared. It was entitled, *The Free State of Noland: or, The Frame and Constitution of That Happy, Noble, Powerful and Glorious State. In which all Sorts and Degrees of People find their condition Better'd*. A revised and expanded version of it was published in 1701.[8] Separated by a period of forty years these utopias may yet be linked by their debt to Harrington and their dependence both on his theory of the balance of property and on his constitutional devices.

George Thomason, the London bookseller, recorded on the title page of his copy of the anonymous tract *Chaos* the date of its appearance, 18 July 1659. Two months previously, in May, Richard Cromwell had resigned. The Protectorate with its trappings of monarchy and two chamber legislature had collapsed. The commonwealth had been re-established with the recall of the Rump. England was once more a republic ruled by a single chamber. But the republicans' triumph was not yet. The Rump offered no stable basis of government and was at loggerheads with the army commanders. It was in this atmosphere that Harrington and his followers pressed their designs to rescue England from disorder. Three weeks before the full version of *Chaos* was published, an eight page prospectus taking the form of the first eight pages of the final work was issued.[9] This emphasised the chaotic and dangerous state of England and the need for a legislator capable of establishing a basis for social stability, and outlined the proposals which were to be dealt with in detail in *Chaos* when it finally appeared. The procedure of issuing such a prospectus indicates the seriousness with which its anonymous author viewed his self-appointed task.

He pointed with some justification to 'the lacerate and torn condition' of England's 'ruinous Fabrick'. He adopted the name 'Chaos' in referring to her. The public faith, he held, after so many convulsions, reversals, treacheries and engagements broken, was bankrupt. The social order and its values had been stood on its head: 'as if Fortunes Wheel were turned

---

[7] Anon., *Chaos* (1659), title page. The shelf-mark of the British Museum's copy is E989 (28).

[8] I have used the 1701 text of *The Free State of Noland*, from a copy held in the Bodleian Library, Oxford.

[9] Also entitled *Chaos*. British Museum shelf-mark E988 (22). Dated by Thomason 28 June 1659.

upside down we may seem to be in the first condition of things again...
The Tail commands the Head, and all things are out of course; insomuch
as a Solon was never anywhere more needful.'[10]

Convinced that 'nothing we do savours of safety or relishes like a
Republique', the author offered himself as the lawgiver capable of reducing chaos to order. If his own design was insufficient for the task, he more
modestly suggested that at least it might encourage others to undertake
the work.[11] He divided the reorganisation of English government and
society into six phases, or, as he described it, into 'six days work'. First,
comparable to the creation of light, was the establishment of general
principles and a common interest. Second, a system of parochial, provincial and national registers would be set up. Third, associated with these
registers, was a series of registerial courts. The fourth phase was concerned with elections to and the transactions of Parliament. In the fifth
phase, taxation and the poor law were dealt with, and finally, trade and
husbandry, the militia, the church and education were provided for.

The author described the first day's work as 'the Balancing of Interests,
and reducing each piece to its proper place'. He proposed, somewhat
vaguely, 'that one Common Interest be erected whereof each member
shall share, as well in receiving protection from, as giving contribution to;
and to be so incorporated as no variant opinion, either in Religion or
Policie, shall be able to weaken the whole'. What this amounted to in fact
was what the author described as 'one Law, and one Registry' for Britain.
Within eight months a system of registries, each with its own court and
officers, was to be set up in all parishes, sub-provinces, provinces and at a
national level. All existing civil suits were to be wound up and no new
ones started until the system was complete. The registries would then take
jurisdiction over all civil disputes which, it was confidently anticipated,
would be both less costly and less numerous.[12]

The author of *Chaos* certainly gave most of his attention to the system
of registries and their courts. He dealt with their duties, staffing, and
finance in assiduous and exhaustive detail. The initial function of the
registries was to record all titles to land, all income from land and all
leases and inheritances of land. In addition they were responsible for
registering all marriages, births, deaths, wills, all contracts and apprenticeships, and the conditions under which every servant was hired. The effect
of the system was to provide a complete picture of the economic life of the
nation and an official record of the ownership and conditions of use of all
real property. These functions were divided between the various levels of
registry on a financial basis. Thus all title to ownership or use of land
worth up to £10 per annum or debt of up to £10 had to be registered in
the parish register. Every 'Wapentake, Hundred, Lathe or Rape' was to

[10] *Chaos*, Preface, p. 1.   [11] *Ibid*., Preface, p. 3.   [12] *Ibid*., pp. 4–6.

have a sub-provincial register. Here records were kept of land worth £10 to £100 per annum and debts between £10 and £100. The provincial or county registers dealt with land worth £100 to £1000 per annum and debts between £100 and £1000. Items of over £1000 in debt or landed income had to be recorded with the National Registry at Westminster. The information so collected was communicated both up and down the system so that each registrar had available to him a full record of all landed income and indebtedness within his area of responsibility. The certificates under the seals of the various registries were to be binding at law. They had to be renewed every three years but it was held that their possession would remove the uncertainties which gave rise to litigation and social friction. The system was extended to cover all bargains and particular attention was directed to the registrar's responsibilities at markets and fairs. Entries were to be made of all cattle sold with 'known Vouchers who shall attest the sale'. Some pains were taken to provide that this bureaucratic apparatus, which would extend down from Westminster to every parish in the land, should be free from corruption. The fees that officers at various levels were entitled to were set out in explicit detail. Tables of these fees were to be hung up in each registry. It was also provided that any fraud or neglect by officers of the registry, causing damage to clients, should be compensated for by the fraudulent party or he should be dismissed. The registrars themselves were to be appointed by Parliament and subject to such oaths as Parliament should impose. The registrars were to appoint their own clerks and should be responsible for their behaviour. The attorneys employed by the registries would be expected to give security for their good behaviour.[13]

The author saw the advantages of this system as numerous. All public assessments and taxes might be equally borne. All persons 'who shall have responsible Estates fit to undergo any Imployment fore the Republique' would be known. There would be little danger of anyone being defrauded by false title, consequently the level of litigation would be reduced and social justice preserved. The estates of any person assisting in or causing an insurrection would be known and could therefore be easily confiscated. Civil disorder would thereby be deterred. Greater knowledge gave greater control. Against those who objected to the cost and trouble of erecting such a system, the author pointed out the fiscal benefit to the republic, through the elimination of evasion and the accuracy of assessments. The

---

[13] *Ibid.*, pp. 7–22. For seventeenth-century anxieties about the open market and preference for controlled markets see Alan Everitt, 'The Marketing of Agricultural Produce', in Joan Thirsk (ed.), *The Agrarian History of England and Wales*, vol. IV, 1500–1640 (Cambridge, 1967), pp. 466–592. For discussion of land registries by the Rump Parliament in 1652–3 see K. H. D. Haley, *The First Earl of Shaftesbury* (Oxford, 1968), pp. 69–70.

ordinary citizen would benefit through the reduction in the amount of litigation, and through the reduction in his legal costs as a result of the proximity of the registries.[14]

Associated with this system of registries was to be a hierarchy of registerial courts which were to form the main judicial apparatus of the new society.[15] In each parish there was to be a parochial court consisting of the registrar, the minister of the parish, the parish constable and the churchwardens. For the court to function, the registrar and at least two others had to be present. The court was normally to meet every two weeks and grant a preliminary hearing to all cases of slander, trespass, murder, manslaughter, rape, theft, robbery, fraud, breach of the peace and filial disobedience. The parochial magistrates were not allowed to exceed a punishment of £10 fine and therefore had to refer all the more serious cases to a higher court. The author, however, set out penalties for various crimes. Murder, manslaughter and rape were capital offences. In cases of theft, robbery and fraud the guilty were to make triple restitution, once to the victim, once to the common stock of the town and once to the constable for repair of the highways. If he were incapable of making such restitution, he was to be condemned to the workhouse where a third of what he produced should go to the common stock, the rest to his own maintenance. Breaches of the peace and of contract between master and servant were also subject to compensation for the victims. False accusation was to be punished immediately with no appeal. There were to be heavy punishments for disobedience on the part of servants, apprentices and children. Disobedient servants were to work a double year for one year's wages. Disobedient apprentices would find the term of their indenture doubled by the courts. 'No son or daughter vilifying or slighting their Parents, or either of them, shall be capable of inheriting any thing from either father or mother after their respective deaths.' Clearly, household discipline could not be left to the heads of households.

As a court was attached to the parish register, so too each sub-province had a court composed of the registrar, his assistant, the minister of the parish where the court was and the sheriff's deputy. In different cases the justices of the peace might be called in. Sub-provincial courts were to meet every three weeks. Above them were the provincial courts which met once a month, and consisted of two judges appointed by Parliament and the provincial registrar. Finally, twelve judges were appointed by Parliament to attend the court of the National Registry. All great cases came up to them. Any three of them with the registrar or one of his assistants had the authority to hear any case. They were to enjoy only two vacations (1 December to 10 February and 31 May to 1 September) and in the summer vacation the judges were to ride circuits hearing complaints

[14] *Chaos*, pp. 23–4.   [15] *Ibid.*, pp. 30–8.

against any registrar and dealing with any outstanding cases. The rest of the year was divided into two long terms and the procedural timetable for these terms was set out in considerable detail. The author clearly believed that he had set down a system capable of guaranteeing speedy and inexpensive justice for all. There was no mention of juries, which were frequently criticised by legal reformers in the seventeenth century as vulnerable to the pressure of men of influence.

The old system of justices of the peace was maintained but with a completely new function. The author of *Chaos* proposed 'That one or more persons of quality in every sub-province be and execute the place of Justices of the Peace'. They were to hold monthly sessions as often as necessary and quarter sessions at which they would be joined by the sheriff or deputy sheriff of the county, constables or their deputies and one or more churchwardens from every parish. The function of these sessions was to hear complaints against the various registries and the justices were empowered to act in order to check abuses. The author was thus proposing to replace an apparatus of justice administered by unpaid amateurs of local standing with a system of full-time, professional bureaucratic administration. At the same time he wished to preserve the amateur system to act as a check upon the professionals.[16]

Supervising the whole arrangement was, of course, Parliament, which it was proposed would be a single chamber assembly, elected annually.[17] All those with estates entered in the register, that is those with land worth £5 per annum or above, or with over £100 in money, were entitled to vote. As in Harrington's *Oceana*, however, the election of representatives was a very indirect process. The voters in each parish were to meet each January and by secret ballot to choose five persons to be 'the Representees of that Parish, in all publique elections and transactions for that year'. These parish representatives were then to meet in sub-provinces and elect two sub-provincial representatives. The sub-provincial representatives were to sit for their area in Parliament. Only those with land or property on the sub-provincial register were eligible to be so elected.[18] The sub-provincial representatives then met by counties or provinces and elected four provincial representatives for each county, except for Yorkshire which had six. Only those with an income of £1000 per annum in land (that is, according to the rules laid down by the author af *Chaos*, knights) were

---

[16] *Ibid.*, pp. 28–9. For the fulfilment of some of these functions by contemporary grand juries see J. S. Morrill, *The Cheshire Grand Jury 1625–1629*, University of Leicester, Department of English Local History Occasional Papers, Third Series, Number 7 (Leicester, 1976).

[17] *Ibid.*, pp. 38–44.

[18] That is to say were possessed of estates worth £10 to £100 per annum. Unfortunately the author did not indicate how many sub-provinces he envisaged for the country as a whole.

eligible for election as county representatives. The county representatives, or knights, would be men of great wealth and the system was tipped in their favour. They were each allowed a double vote in Parliament and the sub-provincial representatives, who had one vote each, only served for six months so that each sub-province only had one representative serving at one time. What began in the parish with a fairly wide franchise ended up in Parliament with a strong bias in favour of plutocracy. This was the author's alternative to Harrington's reconciliation of empire and authority on a bicameral basis.

Detailed regulations were laid down covering elections and the service of M.P.s. Non-residents were not eligible for election, nor were those involved in suits at law, nor those who had been elected in either of the two previous Parliaments. Canvassing disqualified. No one was forced to serve in Parliament but those who refused candidacy were expected to pay £20 towards the cost of the next election. M.P.s were to receive moderate salaries, the aim being that none should serve the public at their own charge but equally that none should be moved to serve purely for profit. Absence from Parliament without leave was subject to heavy fines.

Parliament was possessed of sole power to make laws and conduct foreign policy. Four committees of Parliament were established to direct this work. The first, a Committee of Grievances, was to be appointed within a week of Parliament's first sitting. Great stress was laid upon the speedy answer of all petitions of grievance, 'for it ill becomes a free State to shut the doors, eyes or ears of Justice, to any suppliant'. A Council of State of forty M.P.s was also to be elected on a rotating basis, such that twenty of its members retired every six months. On a similar basis the Council of State was to select from its members a committee of twelve to manage the army and navy. This committee would be directly responsible to Parliament. Finally, six M.P.s, three elected by Parliament and three by the Council of State, were to manage the receipt and expenditure of public monies. The personnel of central government were hereby changed annually and consequently the rotational system was more vigorous and offered less continuity than that suggested by Harrington.

The author of *Chaos* proposed a simple system of honours based purely on the possession of landed wealth. Those of estates worth over £10 000 per annum should be deemed capable of Lordship conferred by Parliament. Persons with over £1000 per annum should become knights and from these alone could provincial representatives be chosen. Lastly those with over £300 per annum should bear the title of Esquire. All of them were to carry arms.

This distribution of titles and the provision relating to the selection of knights (i.e. those with over £1000 per annum) run into apparent difficulties when placed alongside the author's proposals for an agrarian law.[19] 'All former precedent Customs notwithstanding', he wrote, 'let one Law be through the whole Nation, whereby the Publique Interest may be best supported, and each private moderately provided for; and that one Prodigal Riotous person may not consume the patrimony of a whole Family, neither any one lord it over his brethren'. Primogeniture was abolished in favour of multiple inheritance, although under a system of preferences whereby elder received priority over younger, sons over daughters and uncles or cousins of the whole blood over those of the half blood. In the inheritance of estates not exceeding £100 per annum each son was to receive two parts and each daughter one part, the eldest son having the first choice and so on. Where estates exceeded £100 per annum, the eldest son was to receive £100 per annum, the rest to be distributed as before. It was provided, however, that the eldest son should never inherit more than half the estate, except where there were only two sons, when he should not receive more than two-thirds. The wife of the deceased was to be provided for in accordance with contemporary practice with a third of the estate for life. This is clearly a much more drastic agrarian law than Harrington's. Whereas the latter's proposal did not interfere with estates of less than £2000 per annum, this reached right down to estates of under £100 per annum. The agrarian law proposed here raises a fundamental paradox. On the one hand, as we have seen, the political system leaned in the direction of plutocracy, favouring those with estates of over £10 000 per annum with special honours. On the other hand, the agrarian proposals make it difficult to see how such estates could be maintained. The problem here was that of creating a broad citizenry of independent property owners while reconciling it with the political leadership of a powerful wealthy élite.

Despite the paradoxical implications of the author's attempts to reconcile the few and the many, his preference for a republic based in a broad and numerous independent citizen class was clear. To ensure their independence he proposed means of reducing the influence of the great landlords. All copyhold estates were to be made freehold at reasonable composition.[20] All reliefs and heriots were also to be compounded for. Manor and baron courts and courts leet were to be discontinued, although those who had profited from them were to be compensated out of the immediate profits of the registry. Similarly, hundredal courts were abolished but in this case no mention was made of compensation. Services to lords of manors were to cease but rents, provided they were certificated through the registry, were

---

[19] For the agrarian laws see *Chaos*, pp. 24–5.

[20] *Chaos*, p. 26. For the general appeal for conversion of copyhold to freehold see Margaret James, *Social Problems and Policy during the Puritan Revolution 1640–1660* (London, 1930), pp. 94–7; H. N. Brailsford, *The Levellers and the English Revolution* (London, 1961), pp. 436–43.

still to be paid. The author thus proposed a plutocracy while cutting the threads of the plutocrats' influence and undermining the basis of their wealth.

The revenue of the state was to be collected through yet another hierarchy of officials.[21] Parliament was to appoint in each province or county a sheriff. In turn, subject to the approval of the provincial registerial court, the sheriff was to appoint a deputy to each sub-province. Initially in each parish a constable was to be elected, but thereafter the outgoing constable was to propose three persons from whom the sub-provincial registry would select one to succeed him. Each of these offices – sheriff, deputy, constable – was tenable for one year and the holder on retirement was ineligible for re-election for seven years. All taxes, excise and commonwealth rents were to be collected by the constables and the amounts collected entered in the parish register. The deputies then collected from the parishes and entered the amounts in the sub-provincial register. The sheriffs collected from them all the revenue from the province, entered the total in the provincial register and handed it over to the committee of six appointed by Parliament to control the treasury. Taxes were to be imposed annually by Parliament on the annual value or rent of land, on stock in husbandry and trade, and on usury.

One great assessment was to be made to provide a system of relief for those poor capable of working but without employment. Out of this capital a stock was to be set up in every parish to provide work for poor men, women and children. The parochial registries were to appoint a master or governor of the poor to manage the stock and its employment. 'Whereby if vigilance and industry be used', the author confidently predicted, 'a small stock will in short time increase to a great inheritance, whereby the poor shall be equally provided for, to the best and richest of every Parish: so there shall be no crying out, nor complaining in our streets.' A workhouse was to be established, in which the poor would be taught such trades as metalworking and clothmaking. In every workhouse there was to be a smith, a shoemaker and a tailor. All children over seven years old, not otherwise provided for, were to be apprenticed at the workhouse. The poor were to have four-fifths of the profit, the remainder going to the common stock. The inmates of the workhouse could, if licensed by the master, take work outside, but in this case four-fifths of their wages should go to the common stock. The workhouse poor would also form a reserve pool of labour at such times as harvest. The impotent poor were to be set to work in the workhouse in so far as their condition allowed. Women were to be employed in appropriate work under female supervision. By these means, not only the poor would be helped, but it was optimistically anticipated that the nation and its merchants would be made

[21] *Chaos*, pp. 27–8, 45, 46.

rich. The relief of the incapable poor fell under the administration of the churchwardens. Each parish was to elect the customary number of church-wardens. They were to be responsible for the maintenance of the church fabric, furnishings and equipment, for the repair of roads, the relief of 'such poor as shall not be able to help themselves', and for sending beggars to the workhouse. Local rates were to be raised to pay for these things but the parish constables were to be responsible for the monies.[22]

The author of *Chaos* made a number of economic proposals. He wished to see the wastes and commons enclosed and proposed that one-quarter of such land should go to landlords sponsoring the enclosure, a quarter to the poor and the rest to the common people. Where two-thirds of the lords, tenants and owners of land agreed to the enclosure of waste and commons they should have their way. Moreover, those who resisted would be punished for obstructing 'a common good'. Perhaps he was influenced by Samuel Hartlib when he insisted that everyone enclosing lands must plant at least one ash, oak, beech or elm tree on every pole of land and where appropriate plant fruit trees.[23] One of his most interesting proposals was for a policy of urban specialisation. In areas where wood was plentiful coopers were to congregate in one town, carpenters in another, wagonmakers in another and so on. The same was to apply for trades employing flax and hemp. Unfortunately he made no recommendations for the improvement of transport by means of which such a policy might have been made possible. In each sub-province the tradesmen were to form 'a particular society or corporation' for every trade. They were to meet once a month and pass laws amongst themselves for the benefit of the whole. Fishing was to be encouraged by government action. All persons were to bring up their sons in apprenticeship to some trade from the age of fourteen to twenty-one. Under these provisions agriculture was to be regarded as a trade which 'none shall follow who with his own Team shall not Till every year twenty Acres of Land or upwards, as a Master Husbandman'.[24]

In every parochial town there was to be a schoolmaster paid £10 a year. He would teach all children between the ages of seven and fourteen to read and write and to cast accounts. Children from the workhouse were also to attend his lessons. At the age of ten those children who were destined for scholarship were to attend one of the grammar schools set up in every sub-provincial or market town. In addition to the normal grammar school curriculum, a scrivener was to be employed to teach handwriting and the casting of accounts. The boys would also be taught music

[22] *Ibid.*, pp. 45–9, 29–30.
[23] *Ibid.*, pp. 46–7, 49. Cf. Samuel Hartlib, *A Designe for Plentie* (London, 1652).
[24] *Chaos*, pp. 48, 50, 54.

by a qualified master for half a day a week.[25] The universities were to be purged of Popism and all graduates to be subject to an oath to be administered by the judges. No one was to be admitted to the universities under sixteen years old, nor take a degree before the age of twenty-one, nor be admitted to preach publicly before they were twenty-six. The cathedral or chief church in every province was to be restored and an endowment of £400 per annum set up for the ministers and staff. Similar endowments were to be made for sub-provincial churches in market towns. Benefices were to be augmented to a minimum income of £60 per annum. No 'quarellers, railers or State-Incendiaries' were to be admitted to any benefice. The gospel was to be taught from the scriptures. 'Let every Province be a classis.' Seditious and scandalous ministers were to be sent to the workhouse. The details of church government were left to Parliament to devise but strict observance of the Sabbath was insisted upon. It was incumbent upon the civil magistrate to bring contentious clerics to obedience and conformity.[26]

In true Harringtonian fashion the bearing of arms was seen as an inalienable adjunct of citizenship, its mercenary practice a threat to the public interest. Accordingly the existing armies were to be dispersed amongst the county militia which was to be put on a pre-war footing. All the disaffected were to be disarmed and no officer of the militia was allowed to sit as an M.P.[27]

The author of *Chaos* believed that his scheme could be adopted rapidly and perfected in seventy days. Once established it would be invulnerable: 'if any shall endeavour a breach, he shall break himself'. It was as necessary as it was desirable.

The eyes of all the Nation are upon our Governours expecting it; our intestine divisions advise it; the confederacies of Europe require it, and our own safety commands it, to be speedily undertaken and vigorously prosecuted: which if private interests be laid aside (by the doers) will be easily perfected; And the more durable it shall be, the more honour it shall be to the doers . . .[28]

Chaos possessed none of the constitutional sophistication of *Oceana*, but the attempt to establish some kind of agrarian law, the use of indirect election, the ballot, rotation of office, the definition of parochial, sub-provincial, provincial and national levels of government were all reminiscent of Harrington. Political privilege and social distinction were offered to men of wealth but neither their wealth nor their privilege were in any way protected. Harrington's bicameralism was rejected. On the other

---

[25] *Ibid.*, p. 51. On mid-seventeenth-century grammar schools see, W. A. L. Vincent, *The State and School Education 1640–1660 in England and Wales* (London, 1950), Chapter 1, p. 91.
[26] *Chaos*, pp. 52–3, 56.   [27] *Ibid.*, p. 52.
[28] *Ibid.*, title page and p. 55.

hand the author of *Chaos* reached beyond Harrington in his concern for provision for the poor and the regulation of the economic life of the nation.

In September 1659, two months after the publication of *Chaos*, the hold of the republic appeared even more tenuous. In August a royalist insurrection had had to be suppressed, but even the activities of the old common enemy had not healed the breach between the Rump and the military commanders. The future of the republic was uncertain. People were beginning to talk of the restoration of the Stuarts.

It was against such a threat that William Sprigge directed *A Modest Plea, For An Equal Commonwealth, Against Monarchy*.[29] Sprigge was determined to combat the threat of restoration by attacking the social apparatus that underpinned the ancient constitution – the personal dependence of monarchy; the titled, aristocratic society integral to it; the territorial, tithe-gathering clergy who preached monarchy for hire; the fat lawyers, parasitic on a system of privilege; above all, the tyranny of the elder brother. It was an exercise which remained close in spirit and substance to Harrington's teachings and, like them, was embodied in a utopia designed to reconcile all dissident interests.

Sprigge was born most probably some time in the early 1630s, in or near Banbury in Oxfordshire, the younger son of William Sprigge, steward of New College, Oxford.[30] His elder brother, Joshua, became a servant to Sir Thomas Fairfax, as well as a preacher of advanced religious views and vigorous enthusiasm for the parliamentary cause.[31] William,

---

[29] The work appeared anonymously in September 1659. According to Sprigge the work was in an advanced state of preparation before the royalist outbreak of August 1659. See *A Modest Plea, For An Equal Commonwealth, Against Monarchy*, 'To the Right Honourable, The High Court of Parliament'. Sprigge's authorship was attested by Anthony A. Wood, a personal friend of his. See Wood, *Athenae Oxonienses*, vol. IV, pp. 560–1. For comment on Sprigge and *A Modest Plea*, see Richard L. Greaves, 'William Sprigg and the Cromwellian Revolution', *Huntington Library Quarterly*, 34:2 (197), pp. 99–113; H. F. Russell Smith, *Harrington and his Oceana: A Study of a Seventeenth Century Utopia and its Influence in America* (Cambridge, 1914), pp. 94–5; Zagorin, *History of Political Thought*, pp. 155–6; C. Robbins (ed.), *Two English Republican Tracts*, p. 40.

[30] This would seem probable from the date of his matriculation at Oxford University, 2 October 1652. Unless otherwise stated the details of Sprigge's life are taken from Wood, *Athenae Oxonienses* and *Dictionary of National Biography*.

[31] See Wood, *Athenae Oxonienses*, vol. IV, pp. 136–8 and *Dictionary of National Biography*. Joshua Sprigge preached against the execution of Charles I in 1649, and for the release of James Nayler in 1656. For his part in the army debates see A. S. P. Woodhouse, *Puritanism and Liberty* (London, 1949). For his affinities with the early Quakers see Theodor Sippell, 'The Testimony of Joshua Sprigge', *Journal of the Friends Historical Society*, 38 (1946), pp. 24–8; Henry J. Cadbury, 'Joshua Sprigge on the Continent', *Journal of the Friends Historical Society*, 45 (1953), pp. 60–3. In 1673 he married the widow of James, Lord Say. He died in 1684.

the younger, matriculated at Oxford in October 1652 and received his
B.A. ten days later. In December of the same year he was elected a fellow
of Lincoln College, on the recommendation of Oliver Cromwell, who was
chancellor of the university. He was awarded the degree of M.A. in June
1655. While at Lincoln College he became a member of the Oxford
Experimental Philosophy Club, in which John Wilkins, Christopher
Wren, Robert Boyle, John Locke, William Petty, Thomas Sprat, Robert
Hooke, Seth Ward and many future members of the Royal Society were
prominent. In 1657 Sprigge was elected as one of the first fellows of
Cromwell's new college at Durham. Two years later, on the dissolution of
that college, he was incorporated at Cambridge.[32] Because of his junior
status and his associations with Cromwell, the Restoration may well have
ended his hopes of academic preferment within the universities. Certainly
after 1660 he devoted himself to legal studies. He had already been admitted to Gray's Inn in November 1657 and in early 1664 he was called to
the bar.[33] Even then his prospects of success as a lawyer in England were
limited and he decided to move to Ireland. Here he worked as a barrister[34]
and in 1669 was appointed as Recorder to the borough of Galway.[35] On
his brother's death in 1684 he inherited the family estate at Crayford in
Kent. The management of his new responsibilities may have made it
difficult for him to continue with his work as Recorder, and in 1686 he
resigned the position. His connections with the borough, however, remained strong and even as late as 1701 the name 'William Sprigge,
Esquire, Barrister att Law' reappeared on the Common Council list. We
have no knowledge of the date of his death.

Sprigge published three known works. The first, *Philosophicall Essayes
With Brief Advisos Accomodated to the Capacity of the Ladyes and
Gentlemen, sometime students of the English Academy, lately erected at
London*, appeared in 1657. In these conventional academic pieces Sprigge
attacked the techniques of professional logicians, praised natural science,
in particular chemistry and anatomy, and condemned Galenist physicians.

[32] J. Foster (ed.), *Alumni Oxonienses: The Members of the University of Oxford
1500–1714*, 4 vols. (London, 1891–2), vol. IV, p. 1401; Charles Webster, *The
Great Instauration: Science, Medicine and Reform 1626–1660* (London, 1975),
pp. 168, 234, 237, 531. Sprigge may well form one of the links between Harringtonianism and the Baconianism of the Hartlib circle. For the latter see below,
Chapter 11.

[33] J. Foster (ed.), *The Register of Admissions to Gray's Inn, 1521–1889* (London,
1889), p. 284; R. J. Fletcher (ed.), *The Pension Book of Gray's Inn*, 2 vols.
(London, 1901–10), vol. II, p. 1, n. 1. In November 1680 Sprigge was listed
amongst the Grand Company of Ancients, *ibid.*, vol. II, p. 63.

[34] Wood, *Athenae Oxonienses*, vol. IV, p. 560.

[35] Archives of the Town of Galway preserved at Queen's College Galway, *Historical
Manuscripts Commission Reports*, 10th Report, vol. I, pp. 503–7, 513.

He preached moderation and virtue on the part of students and a balance between the authorities of church and state. Two years later, in *A Modest Plea*, his moderation was dropped. His tone was urgent and passionate. He struck out against the prospect of the restoration of 'a National Clergie, Hereditary Nobility and Mercenary Lawyers'. With his own career threatened he bitterly bewailed the lot of younger brothers. His final work, *The Royal and Happy Poverty*, published in 1660, was a meditation on the Gospel of St Matthew, chapter 5 verse 3.

In the 'Epistle to the Reader' prefacing *A Modest Plea*, Sprigge suggested that, despite the numerous constitutional experiments, the country's grievances were now worse than ever. He pointed to the 'deadness of trade', the unemployment, the 'knavery in every shop', the fraud and deceit in every profession and the multiplication of thieves and beggars. It was decidedly not safe to leave these ills for time to heal. Worse might well be to come and the most devious manifestation of this, to Sprigge's mind, would be a restored monarchy. To the proof of this proposition he devoted the first part of his work. Monarchy was 'no other then the more gentle or civil expression of tyranny'. It was 'diametrically opposite to, and inconsistent with, the true liberty and happiness of any people'. Sprigge even argued that the term 'king' was derived from the word 'cunning', which was an attribute of the devil.[36] The accidents of hereditary monarchy exposed men to the rule of women and children. Partly because of this weakness, most monarchies were in fact oligarchies.[37] If perfect monarchy could be guaranteed then, Sprigge protested, he would become an advocate of monarchy, but monarchs were fallible like other men. Moreover, they were exposed to unique pressures: 'they stand on slippery places, & their dignities, their interests, their parasites, their flatterers, are snares to great for them to retain their integrity'. King's were God's scourges. When the Israelites wanted a king, God saw it as a rejection of himself. To limit monarchy was a remedy worse than the disease, 'for to divide the soveraignty, is to lay a scene of blood, to sow the seed of a perpetual civil War, and intail ruine on our selves and posterity'. Sprigge found no virtue in the conventional defences of monarchy. Though it was familiar, it was anachronistic. Sprigge urged his readers to consider how the 'Ballance of lands altered since these last Centuries'.[38] His version of Harringtonian historiography laid the responsibility for the decline of royal fortunes at the door of Henry VIII. In alienating church revenues and ex-monastic lands, the king had robbed himself and his descendants of the possibility of controlling a third of the land of England and hence of wielding overwhelming political power.

---

[36] *A Modest Plea*, pp. 11, 5, 8.
[37] *Ibid.*, p. 7. Sprigge followed Harrington here.   [38] *Ibid.*, pp. 9–10, 11, 15, 19.

It was 'a Maxime of truth, placed beyond all hazard of Contradiction, That no Government can be fixed in this Nation, but according to the Ballance of Land'. The Henrician sale of church lands had set up many thousands of families without dependence on the Crown and, as the numbers of freeholders increased, the nation developed a natural tendency towards a commonwealth. This had been illustrated in the rise of the House of Commons. When a prince was not able to balance the people either by his own property or by the public purse he had become in effect a tenant-at-will. Since the church lands had been sold, only a foreign or mercenary army could provide security for the Crown. Wherein, then, connoted the subject's safety under a restored monarchy? Sprigge thus used conventional Harringtonian theory to undermine the conservative defence of monarchy. The basis of a long-lived monarchy had been removed and it had become dangerous and unstable. He was equally contemptuous of what Professor Greenleaf has called the order theory of monarchy. Argument from analogy with the order of the universe, heaven or the body was 'trite, bald and slight'. One might equally well prove the necessity of the rule of a triumvirate from the nature of the Godhead. Monarchy might as well be compared with the princedom of the devil as with the kingdom of God. Secrecy, speed, unanimity could indeed be seen as conveniences associated with monarchy but they did not offset its inconveniences. Moreover, Harrington in his *Oceana* had demonstrated how in an emergency a commonwealth might enjoy these conveniences through the device of the dictator.[39]

Only three groups, Sprigge felt, could be said to have an interest against that of a free state. They were the hereditary nobility, the divines and the lawyers.[40] Harringtonian theory had not yet reached the stage of seeing the nobility as a bulwark against a standing army. Sprigge's case against a hereditary nobility was based on the weakness of the hereditary principle. 'Could they transmit their vertues as well as names into their posterity, I should willingly become the Advocate of such a Nobility...'[41] Those who had raised themselves by their own merits were more worthy of respect than those who merely enjoyed the privileges of birth. The interest of such people was bound to be contrary to that of a free republic and accordingly it would be better if they were removed completely.[42] Lawyers, if anything, presented an even more potent threat. They had become men's

---

[39] *Ibid.*, pp. 15–22.
[40] *Ibid.*, p. 25. It is noteworthy that Harrington excluded three professions from political life in *Oceana*: clerics, lawyers and physicians. The first two Sprigge saw as incompatible with a stable commonwealth. The last he condemned elsewhere. See, *Philosophicall Essayes* (London, 1657), pp. 41–2.
[41] *A Modest Plea*, p. 103.
[42] *Ibid.*, pp. 104, 100–1; *Philosophicall Essayes*, pp. 77–9.

lords and masters through their capacity to interpret the law, and they had proved willing to sell English liberties to tyranny.

The Professors of which mystery of iniquity that live upon the sins of the people, are of late grown so numerous, that like Locusts, or an Egyptian plague, they cover the face of our Land, and are thriven to such vast Estates, that whereas heretofore the Church and Clergy being in possession of two-thirds of the best lands throughout the Realm, gave birth to the statute of Mortmain for the security of the rest: We may justly fear, unless some prudent care be taken for prevention of their future purchases, lest this Pack, &C by their Querks &C. instate themselves in our inheritances, and ingross the wealth and Revenues of the whole Nation unto themselves, &C.[43]

Sprigge rejected the distinction between clergy and laity and doubted the wisdom of forcing men into subscription to an established church.[44] But his defence of freedom of conscience was argued from a peculiar point of view. Whereas others who advocated toleration urged the separation of church and state, allowing the civil magistrate no authority over religion, Sprigge would not admit that church and state were distinct authorities. The functions of priest, prophet and king had been combined by the patriarchs, just as Henry VIII was head of both church and state.[45] He desired, however, that this should be reflected rather in the godly magistrate than in religious uniformity.

As we have had a successful experience that our battels were best fought, and wars manag'd, by a praying Army; so I am persuaded, our commonwealth would best thrive and prosper in the hands of a Religious and Preaching Magistracy...though I am not of opinion, that every Saint is fit to have the conduct of armed troops, or a place at the Helm of State Affairs; yet I think it desirable, and to be endeavoured, that whosoever hath the conduct of Troops, or a place at the Helm of a Christian Commonwealth, should be a Saint...[46]

But, as Richard Greaves has summarised Sprigge's position, 'The function of magistrate and minister were to be combined in the same officials though not to the extent that religious doctrines were enforced by civil power.'[47] While the law of the land should rest on the law of God, Sprigge would not allow the magistrate the power of compulsion in matters of faith. The magistrate might instruct; indeed it was incumbent upon him to send itinerant ministers to evangelise the 'dark corners of the Land'. Everyone, nevertheless, should enjoy the free exercise of their spiritual gifts. All those were to be tolerated who kept 'themselves within the pales

[43] *A Modest Plea*, pp. 94–5.
[44] *Ibid.*, pp. 26–32.
[45] *Ibid.*, pp. 33–6. Cf. *Philosophicall Essayes*, pp. 49–52.
[46] *A Modest Plea*, pp. 42–3. See also his remarks on the Nominated Assembly, *ibid.*, pp. 31–2.
[47] Greaves, 'Sprigg and the Cromwellian Revolution', p. 104.

of the Law, and the bounds of moderation and moral honesty'. On the other hand, the magistrate was charged to rouse up those asleep in carnal security and to punish vice and prophanity.[48]

The established clergy had, in his view, little to recommend them. Their multiplication was a product of the unwillingness of men to accept the simplicity of the gospel. As recent events had shown, they could not even keep faith with one another. Within Sprigge's anticlericalism was a strong element of social resentment. 'It is not a small thing will satiate the ambition of the English Clergie, who many of them, though taken from the meanest of the people, usually so much forget their Original, that they think the best preferments below their merits and capacities.' These were the men who were prepared to buy and sell the values of religion for ecclesiastical preferment.[49] Tithes were a cause of dissension, diverted from their original purpose which he conceived to be provision for the poor. They were condemned both by the people of God and by covetous worldlings. Parliament should follow its mandate and abolish them by sale or composition, the proceeds going to the state. In this way Parliament could discharge its debts, pay the arrears owing to the army and expect the people to pay their taxes more cheerfully in future. More particularly he believed that ecclesiastical incomes could be redistributed to provide means of relieving the poor.[50]

At one time, Sprigge claimed, he had been 'strongly possessed with a fond opinion of the indifferency of all Forms of Government'. It had seemed to him that all governments were 'alike subject to corruption and oppression'. Consequently resistance or opposition to the existing form of government had seemed 'ill Manners, or a peevish kind of Morosity'. Malcontents would be ill-disposed under any form of government, 'unless their ambition were gratified with a share and interest in the administration and management thereof'. 'The consideration whereof rendered me very neutral in reference to State Affairs, supposing Faction and Ambition to bear greater sway than Religion, in byassing mens propensities, and ruling their inclinations, as to things of this nature...' He had tended, so he said, to sympathise with rulers on the grounds that there would always be those who would malign them. But the 'late Troubles and Changes' had opened his eyes 'to a clearer discerning of that wherein the true interest of our liberties and felicity is wound up'. 'I cannot but acknowledge some Government more pure, refined, and less prone to corruption, then others...'[51]

Whereas the author of *Chaos* had provided a detailed scheme, Sprigge tended to make statements of principle which were to be followed up elsewhere, but he was equally indebted to Harrington and equally convinced

[48] *A Modest Plea*, pp. 44–8.

[49] *Ibid.*, pp. 39–40, 57–8, 125.   [50] *Ibid.*, pp. 49–51.   [51] *Ibid.*, pp. 1–4.

that the political fluidity of the times opened the way for the adoption of a Harringtonian utopia. 'God hath put the Nation like wax into your hands', he informed the recalled Rump, 'that you may mould and cast it into what form you please: We are now *Rasa Tabula* and your Honours may write what you please upon us, I hope it will be Holiness to the Lord, that we may for the future be truly term'd a Holy Commonwealth, and Royal Priesthood unto God.'[52] The work of the present statesmen must be to prevent monarchy, oligarchy and anarchy, and 'to settle a Free-State upon such just and righteous foundations as cannot be moved'. However, 'they may not deceive themselves, or the Nation, by thinking to patch up a sorry half patch'd Commonwealth, upon the old crazy, and rotten foundations of Monarchy as heretofore'.[53] Sprigge therefore offered a platform of principles upon which his 'Holy Commonwealth' might be erected.

Influenced both by Harrington and the Kentish custom of gavelkind with which he was familiar because of his family background, the first thing that Sprigge offered for consideration was the necessity of an agrarian law.[54] All lands, he suggested, should be held at one tenure, 'the most free and absolute that can be devised'. This would wipe away a major cause of litigation. At the same time, primogeniture should 'be abated and moderated' and a system of gavelkind or multiple inheritance instituted. In order to clear himself of any charge of 'levelling', and 'for keeping up a Gentry fit for management of the most important affairs of the Nation', Sprigge suggested that eldest sons might be allowed a double portion and the personal estate of the deceased. Taxes would be levied on the estates of those who sought to evade these provisions 'till their estates be crumbled down to the common standard or due proportion, and that the State or Commonwealth may be declared heir, and to inherit whatever beyond the just proportion of the fixed Agrarian, any man shall leave unto his heir or posterity'. Sprigge saw this system as providing a check on men's covetousness but, far more important, he saw in it a means of undermining that political deference to men of wealth which had nullified all attempts at change.

We have had great disputes and sharp controversies; first, about a House of Lords, and since a Senate: But, in my apprehension, not worth a bul-rush; for the case is the same, whether Lords or not Lords, when as the great landlords in each Country, shal be constantly chosen by their tenants, to be our Legislators...is it not then all one, whether we have an everlasting *Parliament*, or successive, if elections are but a new choyce of the same men, and that it be not difficult to prick a *Parliament*, before the writs are gone forth?

[52] *Ibid.*, 'To the Right Honourable, The High Court of Parliament'.
[53] *Ibid.*, pp. 23–4, 109.
[54] *Ibid.*, pp. 73–5, 112–16.

The operation of the agrarian law would moderate the inequalities of wealth so 'that men may be esteemed qualified, not so much by their Estates, as Religion and Virtue of bearing the chief offices of trust in the Commonwealth'. But, in the election of officers of state, the recognition of such qualities was not to be left to chance. The qualities desired should be set out in such a way that the unworthy were barred access to office. Sprigge himself attempted to sum up what those qualities might be: 'the interest of a Commonwealth is to employ such as are less flegmatick and more mercurial, of greater spirit, prudence and activity for the management of their several Trusts and Provinces, then are usually found among such as have had the advantage of no better Education then their trades, or known no other Academy then their Shops or Exchange'. No one should be trusted with more power than they could wield with integrity. Once chosen, it was necessary to guard against the progressive corruption of officials. Rotation of office was the answer. By it, 'all that are capable may alike taste of Rule as well as subjection: By reason that fixed powers, like standing waters, are apt to corrupt and stink in the Nostrils of the people'.[55]

Once the new system of government was operative it should embarke on a programme of legal reform. Sprigge hoped that the laws would 'be rendered so facil and easie, that the meanest capacity may conceive them, at least so far as he is concern'd therein'. There would be no recognised legal profession. Every man would plead his own cause or have any friend to do it. Justice would be free. Sprigge also wished to see 'Registers in each County' but what exactly these were he neglected to explain. The main advantage of them seems to have been that people would no longer have to journey down to London in pursuit of their legal rights.[56] He expected not only that magistrates would suppress prophanity and vice but that English law would be amended in accordance with the laws of God. Distinctions between moral and legal offence would count for nothing in the simple legal code that he envisaged.

Law is or ought to be nothing but pure Reason founded on the Word of God, or such clear and natural inferences and deductions as unbyast reason shall make from the Morale Law, and then what need would there be of those many Books and large Volumes of so many Reports, Cases, Presidents, Comments &C with which the World is crouded.[57]

In line with this Sprigge sought to give institutional expression to a Christian concern for the plight of the poor.[58]

I know not of what temper other men may be that can relish the pleasures of

---

[55] *Ibid.*, pp. 117–19.   [56] *Ibid.*, pp. 96–7.
[57] *Ibid.*, p. 128. Cf. also pp. 48–98.
[58] For his treatment of poverty see *ibid.*, pp. 54–6.

their plentiful and luxuriant Estates, when so many of their own flesh lie stinking in the streets, and are clothed with rags and misery: I am sure it much abates the content of my small fortunes, to see any one stand in need of the bread I eat. . .Certainly the deafness of this uncharitable age to the cryes of the poor, is one of the crying sins of this Land. . .

But the concern of his proposals was primarily with the employable poor. Holland, he believed, had set the example of conquering poverty by encouraging industry. Even the Turks were admired in his *Philosophicall Essayes* for they gave every man a trade 'as an Antidote against idlenesse, the root and seed of all evil'.[59] He therefore proposed the abolition of tithes, the annexation of glebe-hands to workhouses, the raising of a 'stock' and the setting of the poor to work. It was better, Sprigge believed, in this way to nourish industry than by indiscriminate charity to feed idleness. Moreover out of the profits of the scheme an itinerant ministry might be maintained. All this was typical of Sprigge: a crude approach to the problem, a solution vaguely proposed, and optimistic results anticipated. Nevertheless his is the institutional approach of the utopian.

Sprigge's educational proposals were mainly confined to the field of university education.[60] He found the universities wanting in most respects. They were badly governed, and sited, taught the wrong subjects and were unco-ordinated with the needs of society: 'how dissonant a key of discipline to the Government of a Commonwealth', he wrote, 'they are at present strung and tun'd'. The statutes of the colleges were Popish in origin and fit for repeal as 'monarchick, monkish and pedantick'. The heads of colleges were examples of monarchy triumphing still. They governed, like King James I, by fomenting faction. Under them the colleges were little better than courts.[61] The convenience of the nation had not, in Sprigge's view, been considered in the siting of colleges. Their concentration at Oxford and Cambridge diminished their economic and social value to the country as a whole. He wished to see a dispersal of the facilities for higher education and suggested that Chelsea might be a good place to site a new college.[62] In addition, he believed that the universities still retained too much of the character of seminaries, concerned with the training of priesthood. Instead they should become 'Schools of Education and Humane Literature for the training up the youth of the Gentry in Learning and good manners'. French, Italian, Spanish, History, Politics, Civil and Common Law should be included in the curriculum as should riding, fencing, vaulting, dancing and military exercises. He wished to see laboratories for chemical and anatomical experiments replacing 'those

[59] *Philosophicall Essayes*, pp. 70–1.
[60] For a discussion on Sprigge's views on education see Greaves, 'Sprigg and the Cromwellian Revolution'; Webster, *The Great Instauration*, pp. 238–9.
[61] *A Modest Plea*, pp. 59–60, 66, 72.   [62] *Ibid.*, pp. 64–5, 66–7, 67–8.

many fruitless wrangling Disputations in which Scholars are trained up, that tend to nothing but strife, and rendring men factious, morose, and troublesome in the Commonwealth'. Drawing, painting, carving and engraving might be taught to gentlemen as leisure pursuits. Commerce and husbandry would make fitter subjects than logic. Every college should send out one or two fellows every year to take parties of young gentlemen on continental tours. Such reforms would render learning more pleasant to the gentry and hence be a means of supplying the nation with a learned gentry.[63]

These suggestions owe a great deal to Bacon and in particular to *The Advancement of Learning*, but Sprigge took one of Bacon's ideas and made out of it a major theme. The idea was that the country was over-stocked with free schools and colleges 'for the proportion of its preferments'. This had two effects. The first was that 'mean mens sons' were educated only to become a danger to the nation 'by overstocking it with persons elated by their Education, and discontented for want of employment suitable thereto, & therefore desirous of change and innovations'.[64] The second effect was that on the younger sons of the gentry, excluded from the patrimony by the system of primogeniture but endowed with a liberal education. To their cause Sprigge devoted a whole section of his book.[65] To account for the present parlous position of younger brothers, Sprigge returned once more to his version of the Harringtonian historical analysis. Under the pre-Henrician constitution, the arrangement whereby the eldest sons received the whole inheritance while the younger sons received a liberal education was neither imprudent nor unjust. Primo-geniture was appropriate to monarchy as long as public revenues were ample and the church well endowed so that younger brothers could make their fortunes in the service of church or state. These arrangements, 'whatever their other faults, they were not injurious to younger Brethren, till after the sale of Church-lands, and the abrogating those many preferments that were their former inheritance'. But the impoverishment of the church and the alienation and depreciation of the wealth of the Crown had brought this to an end. 'A generous education was then a sufficient portion, which is now for want of a suitable employment become a curse instead of a blessing...' Sprigge disclaimed any intention of criticising the ecclesiastical reformers. He wished only that 'since the reason and circumstances of our Laws are quite altered, we might not still build on old foundations, and intail the whole Land on a few Proprietors or Elder Brethren, to the exclusion and utter ruine of the greatest part of the

---

[63] *Ibid.*, pp. 65, 68–72.   [64] *Ibid.*, pp. 65–66.
[65] *Ibid.*, pp. 76–93. See also, 'An Epistle to the Reader'. W. K. Jordan, *Philanthropy in England 1480–1660* (London, 1959), p. 212; Joan Thirsk, 'Younger Sons in the Seventeenth Century', *History*, 54 (1969), pp. 358–77.

Nation, and contrary to the interest of a Free State or Commonwealth'. The education of younger sons was valuable to the nation only so long as they were provided with opportunities to benefit from it. However, 'the unnatural, though usual divorce, that is at this day found between Wit and Money, renders both useless, if not pernitous to the Commonwealth'. Younger sons were both numerically stronger than their elder brothers and endowed with their natural share of abilities: 'that which arms their discontent with fit weapons for revenge, and renders them more formidable in their generous education'; 'knowledge makes men proud and factious, especially when they conceive their fortunes and employments are not correspondent to the grandure of their birth and education'. It would have been more logical, as well as more conducive to peace, to have taken away the younger son's facilities for education as well as his opportunities for preferment. But Sprigge was not prepared to recommend this. He wished to provide opportunities, not to destroy education, and opportunities could be provided if the younger sons of gentlemen as well as the elder were provided with capital through a system of multiple inheritance. If gavelkind were instituted, he wrote, 'we shall stand in need of no other devices for keeping out of poverty, then the setting industry on work according to the opportunities plentiful occasions will administer in an equal Commonwealth'. All the able gentleman needed was a stock to start him off.

Recently somewhat exaggerated claims have been made for Sprigge as a potential philosopher to the Cromwellian Revolution.[66] The banality, the generality, of his thought surely robs him of any such title. The same characteristics make his hold on the designation 'utopian' tenuous at best. Sprigge sketched in outlines for others to populate with detail. 'I have not presumed to Chalk out any particular modell, referring that to the wisdom of our Senators'; 'My design being only to propose some Fundamental things, that may lay a firm Basis for an equal Common-wealth to be founded in...' He certainly believed that he was providing a basis for 'the best and most happy of all Governments'.[67] His means, such as we know of them, were institutional, legal and educational, but his work is pervaded by an indolence or a haste which inhibited him from providing the detail through which we could see how his ideal government could operate. He owed something to the study of Bacon but much more to a knowledge of *Oceana*. It is indeed his Harringtonianism which gives some backbone to his claim to be considered a utopian. Like Harrington, he had rejected the ancient constitution. But, while Harrington saw the value of an aristocracy in a popular commonwealth, Sprigge was not so sure. His suspicion is reflected in an agrarian law far more severe in its

66 Cf. Greaves, 'Sprigg and the Cromwellian Revolution'.
67 *A Modest Plea*, pp. 120–1.

operations than Harrington's and in a preference for the political leadership of the gentry rather than of aristocrats. He wished to make the
economic independence basic to independent citizenship more widely
available by protecting the interests and aspirations of younger brothers.
In his educational welfare concerns, Sprigge reflected the attitudes of the
Baconian reformers of the 1640s and 1650s. Indeed he may form one of
the links between these two reforming groups. His was a neo-Harring-
tonianism accommodated to younger sons with Baconian/Hartlibian
aspirations.

In the last decades of the seventeenth century the Financial Revolution
and the growth of a standing army were associated with the rise of an
ideology of opposition which, in its neo-Harringtonian aspects, was preoccupied with the threat of corruption stemming from an ever-expanding
bureaucracy.[68] Yet, as the century died, there appeared a third Harringtonian utopia, *The Free State of Noland* (1696; expanded second edition,
1701),[69] which attempted to reconcile republican virtue with bureaucratic
expansion. Like William Sprigge, the anonymous author was fascinated
by a bureaucratic system's capacity for absorbing the loyalties of large
numbers of people simply through offering them employment, and he
pursued the ramifications of this notion through immense detail in a
utopia of startling complexity.

Nowhere is the classical republican's preoccupation with systems of
mixed government[70] better exemplified than in the pages of *Noland*.
Indeed it is there almost carried to an extreme, where nearly all features of
government are held in balance by their antithesis. Thus, within the same
institutional framework, career-open-to-talents is combined with plutocracy, elective with hereditary office holding, appointment on merit with
sale of office, permanent with temporary status, and an almost federal
system of decentralisation is combined with an emphasis on centralised
unity. The combination and attempted reconciliation of these things could
hardly be achieved in any but a complex way and *Noland* is nothing if not

[68] *Political Works of Harrington*, ed. Pocock, pp. 133–7.
[69] All references in this chapter are to the second edition. For discussion of the
work see, J. Max Patrick, 'The Free State of Noland, A Neglected Utopia from
the Age of Queen Anne', *Philological Quarterly*, 25 (1946), pp. 79–88; V.
Dupont, *L'Utopie et le Roman Utopique dans la Littérature Anglaise* (Toulouse,
1941), pp. 249–51. Patrick has suggested the authorship of John, Lord Somers
(1651–1716) as a possibility. There is no direct evidence to support such an
ascription. Patrick, 'Free State of Noland', p. 81.
[70] Cf. Zera S. Fink, *The Classical Republicans: An Essay in the Recovery of a
Pattern of Thought in Seventeenth Century England* (Evanston, 1945; 2nd
edition 1962), Chapter 1. See also Chapter 3 for mixed government theory in
Harrington.

complex. In the second edition the author added a brief appendix describing how the government of Noland was set up. It will be convenient to follow the order laid down there rather than work through the seventy-nine laws fundamental to the constitution in sequence.

With *Noland* we return to the fictional utopian tradition of More, Bacon, and Harrington. Utopia is an ideal England transposed in time and space.

This Country is Situate beyond the Line, being part of the great Southern Continent, or *Terra Australia incognita*. Which Continent, tho it be little known to the rest of the World, (by reason of the Mists and Fogs, which be almost continually before the Coast, and forbid our approaches to it): yet the People have found means to know the World well: being also well skill'd in all the Arts and Learning of Europe.[71]

Noland much resembled England in soil, climate, religion, language and laws. Until recently its government had been exactly like the monarchy of England. 'But the Royal Line wholly falling, they are now a Free State.' The last king had died suddenly without heirs and in an interval between Parliaments. On the death of their sovereign, the Lords met 'with all speed at their usual place' and summoned the Commons to meet also. Together they chose a new king, Aristaeus. 'He was a Person most accomplish'd in every respect: And had been the Late Kings chief Minister and Favourite, to the great Satisfaction and Delight of the whole Kingdom. So that now they Elected him their King without any difficulty.'

Aristaeus, however, refused the crown and advised the two Houses to set up a free state in accordance with a scheme prepared by himself and the late king. It was to be

A Government wherein all Sorts and Degrees of People shall find their Account, and feel their Condition better'd: Shall be enriched, advanc'd and adorn'd with the spoils of the Monarchy; and shall have those Advantages shared amongst them, which in a Monarchy are engross'd and swallowed up by one man. Where the Peers will be in greater Splendor and Honour, where the Gentlemen will have a mighty Increase of Dignity, and where Trade and the Learned Professions will have high Encouragement. Where also the meaner Sort, by their Right of Suffrage in Elections, will oblige the Great Ones (who are the Candidates) to treat them kindly, and without any appearance of Insolence or Oppression.

But the most immediate benefit of the Free State would be its strength against external enemies: 'the neighbouring Idolaters (who were furiously bent to destroy the Christians) were exceeding Potent: Especially one over-

---

[71] Anonymous, *The Free State of Noland: or, The Frame and Constitution of That Happy, Noble, Powerful, and Glorious State. In which all sorts and Degrees of People find their condition Better'd* (London, 1701), p. 1.

grown absolute Monarch, that was ready to devour all that part of the World'.[72] Aristaeus was allowed six months to complete the plans for a republic and a method for its adoption. Meanwhile the country was administered by a council of Lords and Commons. At the end of the six months, the joint assembly which adopted the scheme was kept in being for a further twelve months while the country continued to be administered by a council of the two Houses and the scheme was implemented.[73]

The country was first divided into five provinces and in each a town or city was designated as provincial capital. Each of the provinces was divided into twelve counties, making sixty counties in all. This involved some reorganisation in Wales and in the larger English counties. 'Most of the Counties continue as they were under Kingship, or with some small Alterations. But in one Mountainous part, Thirteen Counties do now make but Four: and those not of the full midling value. Seven or Eight great ones are divided into ten hundreds, which in turn were composed of ten to twenty parishes.' The parishes were reorganised to approximate to a common standard of annual income in the range of £1000 to £2000.[74] One sees here the rigorous application of a rational common standard, ignoring all claims based on historical continuity.

Obviously in order to implement this scheme assessments had to be made of the yearly income of all areas and new assessments were made for the whole country every five years. The annual value of land was relatively easy to reckon. All other 'Personal Estates are reckon'd as the Quantity of Land they will purchase. So that where Land is at twenty Years purchase, a Hundred Pound, (or the Value of it in Stock or Goods) is reckon'd as Five Pound a Year.' 'In regard of Casualties and Decays, Houses are assessed at a third part less, than the Rent they do or may yield.'[75] These calculations were crucial to both the fiscal and representational systems of Noland. It is no exaggeration to say that the whole structure of government rested upon them. Never has a form of government been designed more closely to represent property. *Noland* gave ultimate institutional expression to the Harringtonian proposition that property is the basis of empire.

Six commissioners were chosen for each county: three from the joint assembly of Lords and Commons, and three from amongst the residents of the county. Their function was to set up the structure of governmental institutions within the county. In each parish they organised the election of a council or moot. 'Every housekeeper that Pays Taxes' was entitled to vote and the parish was allowed one councillor for every £50 per annum

---

[72] *Ibid.*, pp. 1–3. There is an obvious reference here to Louis XIV.

[73] *Ibid.*, p. 4. For the implementation of the scheme see the Appendix, *ibid.*, pp. 47–61.

[74] *Ibid.*, pp. 16, 21, 24, 48. [75] *Ibid.*, pp. 14–15.

taxable income in the parish. Half the parish moot – the Vestry – managed the affairs of the parish on a day-to-day basis. For elections and the levying of local rates the authority of the whole moot was required.[76] In this way a standard and fairly wide franchise was combined with representation proportional to property. The commissioners then organised the election of deputies for the Assembly of the hundred. One deputy was allowed for every £200 per annum of taxable income in the hundred. They were elected for a triennial term on a rotational basis and were not allowed to stand for successive terms. Election was by the parish moots using a secret ballot. In addition to the elected deputies, provision was made for life deputies who were to bear the title of 'Esquire'. The Esquires numbered half the triennial deputies or made up one-third of the total Assembly. Half the positions of Esquire were filled by election from the whole Assembly. The other half were filled by sale, the proceeds going to finance bridge and road building and other public works. Out of the Esquires the whole assembly chose the Bench, a senate or court of aldermen, numbering one-fifth of the total of the Assembly. Half of the Bench were chosen for life, the rest were on triennial rotation. It was the function of the Bench to debate and make proposals on all issues of concern to the hundred. The Assembly itself did not debate but merely resolved on these issues.[77]

'A Hundred (or precinct, or Barony) is a Corporation, or a small Republick; governed by a Warden, two Associates, Bench and Assembly.' Its laws stood good unless revoked by a higher power. Each hundred had a Warden and two Associates. The Warden was chosen by the county council and was usually chosen from another hundred, as this was held to promote unity within the county. In the same way the chief magistrate of each county was chosen by the Grand Council of the Nation and need not be resident in that county. The Associates of the Warden and all other officials of the hundred were chosen by the Assembly of the hundred. Amongst these other officials were a Recorder, Marshall, Head Surveyor of Highways, Head Overseer of the Poor, Stewards of the Court of Conscience, and Chamberlain or Receiver. Each hundred had a court of conscience held on a daily basis by two stewards. Here cases involving less than £5 and disputes over servants' or labourers' wages were heard. Appeal could be made to the hundred court, held every fortnight by the Warden, his Associates and the Recorder. This dealt in the first instance with cases involving between £5 and £50. All common law cases had to be tried before a jury and appeal might be made from here to the county court. Finally, each hundred had a Dean who was also rector or minister of the chief town in the hundred. He was 'elected or presented by the Assembly'.[78]

The commissioners then organised the election of a shire or county council. The Assembly of each hundred elected one delegate for every

[76] *Ibid.*, p. 49.   [77] *Ibid.*, pp. 16–18, 50–3.   [78] *Ibid.*, pp. 16, 18–20.

£1000 per annum of taxable income in the hundred. The delegates were elected for a three year term, one-third of them retiring every year. In addition to these, there existed a class of knights, equal in number to about a third of the elected delegates, who were members of the Shire Council for life. They were recruited partly by election and partly by sale, but the author requested his readers to note, 'That where places are sold, they are Places in the Popular Councels, who barely give their Votes without debating: And not such Places, as require Personal Abilities and Qualifications.' Besides triennial councillors and councillors for life there were also hereditary councillors called Knights Baronets. These numbered about half the life councillors. They formed 'the Peerage of their Respective Counties' and were chosen 'out of the best and richest Families, and the most deserving Men'. In the election of knights and baronets, precedence was given to those who enjoyed these titles under the old system. On the same basis as the Assembly and Bench of the hundred, county government was divided between senate and council; the senate proposing, the council resolving. The administration of the county was headed by a Lord Steward appointed by the Grand Council of the Nation. He, two adjutants, and a sergeant-at-law held a county court every four weeks, hearing and dealing with all cases involving between £50 and £500 and appeals from the hundred courts. 'In every County there is a Lord Bishop, assisted by two Suffragans, and in greater things by a Synod. Of which Synod the Deans are the constant Members: beside a like number of other Clergy-men, annually chosen by the Clergy of the Diocese or County.' Bishops were appointed by the Grand Council of the Nation, suffragans elected for a biennial term by the Shire Council.[79]

In addition to the counties there were thirty to forty free cities and about twice as many boroughs, the difference between them being one of size rather than privilege. They were organised on the same basis as counties but their government was, for the encouragement of trade, in the hands of tradesmen. In addition the cities and boroughs were allowed £100 000 a year out of the revenue of customs and excise to support their government and trade. For the purposes of parliamentary representation they were organised on a provincial basis to form one county. The exception was the capital city which formed both a county and a province of itself.[80]

The Grand Council of Noland was elected by the Shire Councils on the basis of one representative for every £20 000 per annum of taxable income. The representatives were elected on a rotating triennial basis. Since the author computed the national taxable income to be about £12 000 000 per annum[81] there would be a total of six hundred elected representatives.

---

[79] *Ibid.*, pp. 20–3, 53–5.   [80] *Ibid.*, pp. 24–6.
[81] Cf. Harrington's estimate of £10 000 000 per annum.

To these were added a further six hundred life members (who would be recruited in the first instance from the members of the existing House of Commons). Half of these barons, as they were to be called, would be replaced by election, half by sale. In addition there were a further three hundred hereditary members to be known as counts or earls, chosen in the first instance from the existing peers but subsequently replaced by election and sale. Finally there were sixty archbishops and bishops eligible to sit. The Grand Council therefore numbered about 1560 members, entitled to sit on a number of different grounds. The author of *Noland* believed that this would ensure the continuity of the body. If, for example, the barons desired to be hereditary, rather than life members, the knights and peers would combine to oppose and defeat such a move. Again, 'where a Soverain Assembly is all in rotation or temporary they may be both able and willing to perpetuate themselves, and to engross and exclude: But where it is partly in rotation and partly permanent, there is no such danger.' Privilege would work to maintain balance. The Grand Council represented the nation and was its supreme legislative body. It appointed the country's chief magistrates, it judged and punished great offences against the state and acted as last court of appeal. Its members were salaried and their expenses paid by the state.

Out of the Council, and a part of it, was chosen the senate, for the Grand Council could only resolve what was debated, prepared and resolved by the senate. The senate numbered one hundred and fifty members, fifty of them peers and one hundred commoners (twenty knights and eighty barons). Half of those senators chosen out of the earls and barons were appointed for life, the other half on triennial rotation. Knights chosen as senators were elected on an annual basis. Members of the senate were given special titles and precedence over all other ranks. As well as preparing matter for resolution in the Grand Council, the senate had supreme executive authority which, in part, it delegated to specialist committees. The Chief Magistrate or Regent of Noland[82] was assisted by six palatines, who together made up the Signiory. Offices in the Signiory rotated triennially, and were subject to election by the whole of the Grand Council.[83]

As already noted Noland was divided into five provinces, initially for judicial purposes: 'That wretched, scambling, chargeable and vexatious way of Terms and Circuits, which they had formerly in imitation of England, being now cast off.' In the capital city of each province a Provincial Court was set up to deal with all appeal cases from below and with disputes involving sums of over £500. These last cases might be

---

[82] The author rejected the name 'Protector' as a title disgraced by 'a Villainous Usurper'.
[83] *Noland*, pp. 23–4, 32–40.

heard on appeal by the High Court of Appeals in London, or in extraordinary circumstances by the Grand Council itself. The officials of
Provincial Courts and the High Court of Appeals were chosen by the
Grand Council and served on a rotating basis. This was the initial design
for the provinces, acting solely in a judicial capacity, but it was decided
that 'their condition as Provinces would be slavish'. Consequently they
were allowed a share in the nomination of provincial officials and moreover the counties in each province were to choose a Provincial Convention
on the same basis of choice as for the Grand Council. Together the Convention and Grand Council chose the Provincial Officers. The main
functions of the province were judicial, fiscal and military.

The Legislator judg'd it a great Evil in the Late Government, that all the Law-
Business of the whole Nation was then brought to one Place. And that all the
Money of the Nation was also then brought to one Place, that is, the whole
Publick Revenue; he judg'd a great Evil likewise. To both these Evils he hath
now given a Remedy.

Provincial Conventions appointed all officers of the militia below the
Lords Marshall and the Major Generals and organised annual musters of
the militia. The provincial capitals were built up as centres of government,
commerce and culture rivalling the capital of Noland itself. They were to
be the centres of provincial life, the meeting place of the Convention; the
residence of the Lord Marshall, the archbishop of the province and the
bishop of the diocese. They were to be the location of a treasury, a
Heralds' Office, a post office, printing press, theatre, mint and bank.[84]

This is a much simplified account of a system for whose complexity
there is no space to do justice. The author laid down salaries for all his
major officials, provided a whole range of titles of honour, attempted to
show how the system could be financed and devised a separate system of
government for Scotland, Ireland and the colonies. At the end of the
work he confessed that his scheme was unfinished and promised additional detail on administration, the laws and justice, the militia, transport
and the poor. Like most utopians he had found the total scheme not quite
within his grasp.

In the design of Noland, its author believed that he had adhered to
twelve principles or rules.[85] First the state was to be a mixed government,
a mixture of aristocracy and democracy, or as he preferred to call it 'an
unexclusive Aristocracy'. Secondly, the government was to be representative, 'a firm, as well as a lofty Pyramid, whose Basis and Foundation is as
large as the whole People'. The problem arose, however, as to whether
the representatives were to be temporary or permanent. Both had advantages but the one was too 'Democratical', the other too 'Aristocratical'.

---

[84] *Ibid.*, pp. 24–31.   [85] See *ibid.*, pp. 4–13.

Therefore, the third rule was an extension of the first, mixing aristocracy and democracy, and provided part 'of the Representatives to be Temporary and in rotation, and part to be Constant and Permanent'. The advantages of this in regard to the temporary part were that the people were in constant use of their franchise and the deputies gained 'a fresh sense of their Duty to those that intrust them, and may more modestly use an Authority which they must shortly lay down'. More men would have hopes of office and consequently behave in a public-spirited way, while those in office would be restrained by the 'due Vicissitude of Commanding and Obeying'. On the other hand, the advantages of the permanent part were

That Persons of Merit, and above the Common Rate of People, and that have given sufficient tryal of themselves, may have a Port which they at last may rest in. Exempted from the irksome indecency of being always Candidates, and from the bitterness of Repulses: And settled in a more elevated Station, from whence they may direct their Thoughts and Hopes yet higher. A Community that hath nothing fixt and stable, but is all in rotation, is like a Windmill without a Post.

As Harrington in the 1650s had been concerned with the threat of self-perpetuating oligarchy, so, in the 1690s, the anonymous author of *Noland* was concerned with the indecencies of electoral politics. His fourth principle was that 'tho the State in the main be Representative, yet some part of it, and some Members of the Soverain Council may be Hereditary'. This was both to increase stability and to conciliate the existing peerage, who, in fact, would gain, since under monarchy they had a king over them but in a free state 'have nothing to top them'. Nevertheless, it was provided that they should nowhere be in a position of majority. On the representative side of government, the ruling principle and the fifth in the author's series was that the number of representatives 'must be proportionate to the Estates, of those that choose or send them'. The author pointed to ancient parallels in support of this and claimed that de Witte in Holland and Cromwell in his first Parliament had aimed at it: 'all Real Estates, (as Land, Houses, and the like) should Pay Taxes and have suffrages, according to the Rent which they do or may yield. And that Estates Personal should be regarded as they are equivalent to land. . . .' The sixth principle was that 'as the whole State is a Grand Corporation, so the Constituting Parts of it (that is, the Counties and Hundreds) must be Corporations likewise; having a neer Analogy to the Great one'. This was a classic expression of the federative approach to English politics implicit within Harringtonianism and of the identification of freedom with local independence which was such an important element in the Country/Whig tradition. When he spoke of corporations, the author pointed out, he was not referring to provinces, which were only corporations to some extent, but to counties and hundreds. 'In these the People have the Government among themselves: With Laws and Orders of their own making and Magistrates of their own choosing. Which is the Summ of Civil Liberty.' 'The Excellent Legislator held it unreasonable that while the whole was free, the Parts should be in Servitude: And that the Gentlemen and Yeomen should not have the same priviledges in the Counties and Hundreds, which the Tradesmen have in the Cities and Towns.' But he was careful to point out that this high decentralisation was tempered by the subordination of hundreds to counties, and of counties to the Grand Council. The important point about local independence, or the appearance of it, was that, while some men satisfied their ambitions in the management of affairs of state, others could satisfy them in local self government. Even more directly influenced by Harrington, the seventh principle provided that in all corporations or communities there should be both 'a greater or Popular Councel' and 'a lesser Councel or Senate'. 'The greater doth resolve and determine, but without Debate: The lesser both debate, and prepare and propose.' He acknowledged that Harrington had provided the best exposition of this principle but rejected his application of it: 'his Modell is meerly Democraticall: A Levelling sordid Democracy. For he chiefly aims at Equality, which in plain *English* is Levelling.' In the design of Noland the bicameral division of function was so applied as to embrace hereditary and life, as well as elective, membership of the legislature. Thus the balancing antitheses, of democracy and aristocracy, enabled *Noland* to enjoy the advantages of Harrington's utopia, without what the author saw as its disadvantages.

The last five of the twelve principles were all concerned with the distribution of offices, their rewards, titles of honour, the perks and prerequisites which do so much to sustain political ambition. Like Sprigge, the anonymous author of *Noland* believed that men in every condition should have something to aspire to, and he believed it to be incumbent upon the state, in the cause of social peace, to provide both the sources of aspiration and the means of satisfaction. Thus the eighth principle laid down was 'That all Publick Offices, Employments, and Charges, (from the highest to the lowest) should be made Beneficial and Desirable. And that their Number should not be sparing.' He emphasised the political as opposed to the administrative purposes of office. The ready availability of state employment would 'infinitely promote the Industry, exalt the Genius, and refine the Manners of the Nation'. People must be content to bear the charges for this in order to protect their liberty. Yet the author was sensitive to the problem of the cost of maintaining a large bureaucracy and a system of honours for political rather than administrative purposes. He pointed to the economies to be made with the disappearance of the royal court, and argued that the financing of a bureaucracy, like a lottery, was a means of redistributing wealth.

But suppose some money must be advanced: Yet it returns both soon and sure. People will have it back, by partaking of those Offices which it is given to maintain. It will be like the putting Money into a Lottery: But with this difference; that whereas there the Benefits come by chance, here they come according to each Man's Industry and Merit.

Nevertheless his ninth principle provided that 'as he would have plenty of Beneficial Places, so on the other side he would have their profits to be moderate'. He explained that this was acceptable in a free state, both because men were serving their own interests in serving the state and because the office holder's satisfaction was increased by the knowledge that he owed his position to merit. Once again the author was concerned with the influence of office on those who held and aspired to it rather than with its administrative significance. His tenth principle provided that the rewards of office should be proportionate to the importance of the position.

As men frustrated of office were a potential cause of social disorder, so special consideration had to be given to the wealthy, simply because the rich were capable of causing more trouble than the poor. The eleventh principle therefore recommended 'that a due and fair regard be had to Riches'. 'Wealth is a very turbulent thing, and the occasion of great disorders, when it hath not Authority and Preferments answerable.' In a deferential social order this was almost naturally taken account of: 'where Dignities are conferr'd by Popular suffrage, Men of Estates must rise: there is no keeping them down'. To provide, however, for the exceptional cases where men of wealth did not rise by the suffrage, offices were available for purchase: 'in these or the like cases, he may make short and sure work with his money. Very honourable Ranks and Degrees (but such as require not Personal Abilities) being thus attainable.' Supplementary to this, the final principle provided that titles of honour should be bestowed with liberality: 'in *England* we are too sparing in this kind'. All officers and magistrates were to be accorded the title of 'Lord'.

Like *Oceana*, *Noland* was concerned with the problem of balanced or mixed government. In many ways the latter was the more complex of the two precisely because it sought to combine more disparate elements. Thus, whereas Harrington made both houses of the legislature entirely elective, *Noland* attempted to combine elective, hereditary and life membership in the same institution. As far as the elective part of the system was concerned, the model of *Oceana* with its system of indirect elections, of interlocking pyramids, was fairly closely adhered to. The widest franchise was at the parish level and it is perhaps significant that here there was no provision for a secret ballot. Every taxpaying householder had the right to vote in the election of the parish moot, but the hundred Assembly was elected by the moot itself. Similarly the Assembly elected the Shire Council, and the Council elected both Provincial Convention and Grand Council.

The Grand Council was far removed from the votes of every taxpaying householder. This indirectness of election plus the sale of office has given substance to the claim that the free state of Noland was, in fact, an oligarchy representative of the upper middle classes, a plutocracy.[86] The restrictive nature of this has, however, to be set against the dramatic multiplication and dispersal of office in Noland. The effect is quite striking even when consideration is limited to elected and rotating offices. There were to be 240 000 parish councillors, 60 000 deputies elected to the hundred Assemblies, 12 000 county representatives and 600 elected knights on the Grand Council.[87] When the effects of rotation and vacation from office are taken into account, this produced a scale of office holding which would have reached far down into the social strata. There can be no doubt that this is what the author had in mind. The dispersal of office was a means of reconciling all interests and committing them to the maintenance of the new order. It was as he claimed, 'A Government wherein all Sorts and Degrees of People shall find their Account, and feel their Condition better'd: Shall be enriched, advanc'd and adorn'd with the Spoils of the Monarchy; and shall have those Advantages shared amongst them, which in a Monarchy are engross'd and swallowed by one Man.'[88]

All three of these utopians were indebted to some aspect of Harrington's thought: to his historiography, to his theories of balance, to his principles of an agrarian law or rotation of office, to his constitutionalism, to his attempt to wed empire and authority, or to his belief in the possibility of a strong, decentralised state. The debt is so clearly marked that it is the changes of emphasis which interest, rather than the similarities. One sees this particularly in their approach to land ownership and its significance. It is surprising how little attention the utopians of the sixteenth and seventeenth centuries gave to that central feature of early modern social and political life, land tenure. The Harringtonians certainly attempted to make up for that neglect. Harrington himself saw a direct relationship between land tenure and political power, command over men, and this relationship was central to his theory of politics and history. With the author of *Chaos* the emphasis shifted. Land for him was not primarily a source of power but a source of litigation and the social friction which went with it. His registries were designed to eliminate doubt over land tenure (amongst other things) and so reduce litigation. William Sprigge,

[86] Dupont, *L'Utopie et le Roman Utopique*, p. 251; Patrick, 'Free State of Noland', p. 84.
[87] The key information here is the estimate of gross taxable income at £12 000 000 p.a. *Noland*, p. 24. Since all elected offices are based on a taxable income figure their numbers can be worked out from this.
[88] *Ibid.*, p. 2.

on the other hand, saw land as primarily a launching pad, a source of opportunity for opportunity-starved younger brethren. What these three had in common was that they saw social instability as closely related to the disposition of land tenure. In the cause of social stability, therefore, they were all prepared to interfere with the existing form of tenure of land. They were all exponents of an agrarian law. The author of *Noland*, however, was not. He made no provision for an agrarian law. Indeed, he accepted the existing form of land tenure as justified by its very existence. He did not adjust the tenure of land to accord with a desired system of government. On the contrary his ideal system of government represented property rather than people. It was built on to the existing forms of land tenure. In many ways the author of *Noland* was more ambitious and more daring than Harrington. He assumed that he could leave land tenure untouched and achieve a balanced commonwealth by constitutional devices. In this way he contributed to the process by which Harrington's constitutionalism was divorced from his theory of the balance of property and so domesticated to the needs of rural English gentlemen, but, unlike other neo-Harringtonians, he saw the proliferation of office, bureaucratic expansion, not as corrupting but as a means of absorbing aspirations which might otherwise clash and hence jeopardise social harmony.[89]

This change of emphasis between the works of the three thinkers may also be noted in other areas. Sprigge, the least utopian, was also the most radical, condemning the hereditary principle, lawyers and the clergy. The most conservative, in so far as these terms have meaning, was the author of *Noland*, who emphasised the satisfaction of all interests rather than their elimination or reorganisation. Like all great seminal thinkers, Harrington moulded men who ultimately walked in different directions.

[89] Cf. Pocock, 'Machiavelli, Harrington and English Political Ideologies', pp. 549–583.

Royalism and utopia

The people of *Bensalem* have it as a received Maxim among them, *That their Solomona neither can nor will do them any injury, they being the members of that body whereof he is the head.*

R.H., *New Atlantis. Begun by the*
Lord Verulam, Viscount St. Albans:
And Continued by R. H. Esquire (1660)

... dangerous Revolutions must needs be incident to humane Rule that cannot expeditely provide, by inflictions or condign Reproach, to avert the delinquencies of evil Principles from the souls and practice of men.

Anon., *Antiquity Reviv'd: or the Government*
of a Certain Island Antiently call'd
Astreada (1693)

One of the possible assumptions of monarchist theory is that men are incapable of sustaining the morally demanding rôle of free citizens and must be subjected to the rule of one in authority over them. For their own good – or inevitably because of their own lack – men must be subject to an authority descending on them.[1] Close to the utopian in seeing people as subjects rather than citizens, the royalist who visualises a perfect monarchy must nevertheless grapple with the personal dependence of the system which he endorses. The perfect prince is indispensable to the perfect monarchy. A system premised in the fallibility of men must, at this level, assume some men infallible.

Where its exponents stressed the vulnerability of men to wickedness and corruption, the republican ideal, that men should rule themselves, encountered severe difficulties. Those who sought a way out in utopian constructs only succeeded, as we have seen, in adding a further twist to the dilemma. No more successful, however, were those of their opponents who endeavoured to solve the problem of the idealisation of monarchy in the same way. Monarchy could be justified as purely and solely legitimate, independent of its efficiency, effectiveness or justice. One had only to demonstrate the legitimacy of monarchy and the impossibility of any other system's being legitimate. This was the burden of Sir Robert Filmer's case: monarchy was the *only* legitimate form of government. But for those who sought to defend monarchy as not only legitimate but in some sense perfect, or capable of perfection, how could the problem of the personal dependence of the system be overcome? And how could the continuity, the stability of the system's perfection be guaranteed given its reliance on the personal qualities and integrity of successive individuals? Should one assume a series of acts of grace bequeathing perfect princes to the system,

---

[1] On the descending thesis of authority see Walter Ullmann, *A History of Political Thought: The Middle Ages* (Harmondsworth, 1965); Francis Oakley, 'Celestial Hierarchies Revisited: Walter Ullmann's Vision of Medieval Politics', *Past and Present*, 60 (1973), pp. 3–48. For a recent discussion of some of the themes arising out of monarchy in a sinful world see Robert Eccleshall, *Order and Reason in Politics: Theories of Absolute and Limited Monarchy in Early Modern England* (Hull and Oxford, 1978).

or, alternatively, the heroic moral capacities of a given royal line? Or should one hedge the royal personage around with institutional constraints against his personal fallibility – the utopian solution? But, what then was left of monarchy?

Whatever the inherent difficulties, the attempt was made. Twice in seventeenth-century England, the principle of legitimist hereditary monarchy was successfully challenged. On both occasions royalist utopias defending that principle were published. The first, R.H.'s continuation of Bacon's *New Atlantis*, was published in 1660 after the Interregnum and offered a model of government to the restored Stuarts. The second, the anonymous *Antiquity Reviv'd* (1693), appeared after the Glorious Revolution and offered a platform, if a somewhat unusual one, to the Jacobite cause.

The notion of a royalist or absolutist utopia is bound to be an ambivalent one. Royalism stresses the advantages of personal rule, rule by one man – speed, secrecy, unity, human sympathy, insight and flexibility. Utopianism, on the other hand, tends to be suspicious of the human personality and its weaknesses, seeking always to nullify its effects, to create the perfectly impersonal system. Utopianism restricts freedom to the point of denying it altogether. Absolutism grants one man absolute freedom in the exercise of absolute power. It is accordingly the monarch in an absolutist utopia who sets the critical problem. As we shall see both R.H. and the anonymous author of *Antiquity Reviv'd* had difficulty in solving it. Nevertheless the contrast between royalism and utopia is not complete. There are points of contact or overlap between the two modes of thought. Both royalism and utopianism place an extremely high priority on social and political unity. Both remain suspicious of pluralistic societies. Both seek an arrangement of institutions whereby private interest becomes the pursuit of communal interest. For the royalist this was relatively simple. On the head/body analogy he argued that the welfare of the people must logically and politically be the interest of the king. If he were to be strong, rich and glorious, so must his people be vigorous, prosperous and happy. For the utopian the reconciliation of personal and communal interest is more complex but his means, like the royalist's, remain institutional. There can, however, be no doubt that the utopian mode is a peculiar, if not irregular means of defending the claims of monarchy. The royalist utopia is by no means a common form of royalist literature, but in many ways it is its most ambitious variety. For whereas the royalist will often accept that kings are not always what they should be, the utopian royalist claims to have created a perfect monarchy, sound now and forever. Both the works considered in this chapter were influenced by Filmer. But, while Filmer could place all his reliance on legitimacy, accepting even a bad monarchy provided only that it was legitimate, neither of our authors could do that. For them, although the moral claim of monarchy rested in its legitimacy, it also had to be justified on utilitarian grounds and on its capacity to reconcile all interests.

On 15 October 1660 Samuel Hartlib wrote to Dr John Worthington, 'I suppose you have heard of a Nova Atlantis in print, by way of Supplement to that of Lord Verulam's. And although it be far inferior to his grave and judicious contrivances, yet such as it is it would make a noble alteration, if it were practiced in all human affairs.'[2] The tract to which he referred had appeared the previous month as a continuation of Bacon's *New Atlantis*, 'wherein is set forth A Platform of Monarchical Government with A Pleasant intermixture of divers rare Inventions, and wholsom Customs, fit to be introduced into all KINGDOMS, STATES, and COMMON-WEALTHS. Nunquam Liberatas gratior extat Quam sub rege pio.'[3] The only description given of the author was that of 'R.H. Esquire'.[4] He dedicated his work to the memory of 'that glorious Martyr', Charles I, and to Charles II in the hope that he might 'really become our Solomona, our second Justinian and Glorious Restouratour of our almost-lost Laws and Liberties'. The events of the last two decades had torn in shreds the conventions by which a stable society had been held together: 'here hath been such an Inter-regnum of tyranny and oppression, that all laws both divine

---

[2] James Crossley (ed.), *The Diary and Correspondence of Dr. John Worthington*, 3 vols. (Chetham Society Remains, XIII, XXXVI, CXIV (1874–86)), vol. I, pp. 213–214. It is interesting that Hartlib, one of the so-called philosophers of the Puritan Revolution, should have been prepared to recommend such an overtly royalist scheme as that of R.H. Cf. H. R. Trevor-Roper, 'Three Foreigners: The Philosophers of the Puritan Revolution', in Trevor-Roper, *Religion, the Reformation and Social Change* (London, 1967), pp. 237–93.

[3] *New Atlantis. Begun by the Lord Verulam, Viscount St. Albans: And Continued by R. H. Esquire* (London, 1660) title page. George Thomason's copy was dated by him September, 1660. (B.M. shelf-mark E1797 (2)).

[4] 'R.H.' has remained elusive. I have examined a number of possible users of the initials, including Robert Harris, Richard Hawkins, Robert Heath, Richard Harris and Henry Robinson, for all of whom there is some possible claim but also some possible objection. Sir Robert Harley, the second son of Sir Robert and Lady Billiana Conway, used the initials R.H. in his account of his doings on behalf of Charles II in the last days of the Interregnum. He was no doubt an ardent royalist but no direct connection can be establishd between him and the R.H. we seek. (*Historical Manuscript Commission Reports*: Portland, vol. VIII (1907), pp. 8–14.) The same must be held true of the claim on behalf of Robert Hooke, the author of *Micrographia* (1665), advanced by Frank E. Manuel. See Manuel, 'Pansophia, A Seventeenth Century Dream of Science', in *Freedom from History* (New York, 1971), p. 107. I am grateful to Professor Manuel for his correspondence on this matter. See also Edmund Freeman, 'A Proposal for an English Academy in 1660', *Modern Language Review*, 19 (1924), pp. 291–300; Geoffrey Keynes, *A Bibliography of Dr. Robert Hooke* (Oxford, 1960), pp. xi, 2–4.

and humane, have lain dead, at least fast asleep amidst these Alarms. Every Enthusiast in this Par-le-bra hath done both in Church and State (as when there was no King in Israel) what was right in his own eyes.'[5]

The reins of legitimate government had been allowed to fall, and so profound did R.H. find the effect to be that he felt it necessary to begin again, building from the bottom. Before he could demonstrate the perfect monarchy, therefore, he had to show the necessity both of government and of monarchy. Without government, he claimed, 'no man's person or propriety had been safe'. Without external discipline men were incapable of the self-restraint and moral behaviour necessary to harmonious social life. They were not capable of a perfect moral commonwealth. Left to themselves, they were more likely to produce a Hobbesian nightmare of social brutishness.

It were to be wished indeed that men might live without any Law, that is that men would be so just that St. Pauls word might be verified now of us; *The Law is not made for a righteous man, but for the lawlesse and disobedient &c.* But such hath ever been the fraielty of humane nature (which is still more to evil than to good) that there was a necessity of bridling that enormous disposition, and by severe discipline to restrein and compel, where Religion, Conscience and Reason would not lead. Good laws and Fences were therefore made and set: but the irregular inconstant people not willing to be confined, brake or plukt them up. *Hinc illae lacrymae.* They after a time grew lawlesse and disobedient; endeavouring to wrest that sword they had put into their legislatours hand, and by sinister pretences to resume that Liberty which they had parted with before...when by evil example the contagion spreads, they then grew masterlesse: then will becomes a law, Treason, reason; then liberty justles Praerogative, and sometimes even thrusts it out of doors. By wholsom laws then so to regulate the enormous ambition of the Noblesse, with the seditious gainsayings of the ever-querulous people, that the whole may be preserved without subdividing into factions or fractions, i.e. to govern securely; hath ever been the skill and artifice of *political prudence.*[6]

Political prudence therefore demonstrated the necessity of law and government but it also revealed that law in itself was not enough. What was required was an agency by means of which 'Wholsom laws' could be used to balance the interests of different social groups and reconcile them to a communal interest. That agency had to be monarchy. R.H. admitted that the English experience of monarchy had not been happy.

It is a received *Maxim in Politics*, that all Law and Government should be fitted to the humour and temper of the climate and people. Now in general we may observe, that all the Northern People, and particularly the British, have ever been more jealous of their Kings, and lesse of their wives then those of *France, Spain, Italy*, &c:...

[5] R.H., *New Atlantis*, preface. [6] *Ibid.*

But this did not mean that R.H. was moving on to the recommendation of mixed monarchy. A reference to Filmer's *Anarchy of a Mixed Monarchy*, he felt, was sufficient to dispose of that.[7] Filmer had shown that monarchy was the only legitimate, as well as the most natural, form of government. For R.H. also, kings were comparable to the head commanding the body, the pilot navigating a ship, and God ruling his universe.[8] But monarchy remained for R.H., rather more than for Filmer, an agency, a means of solving a problem rather than an object of veneration.

The gubernative power being then allowed in all ages and places, except in a few sickly and distempered German republics, to be safeliest rested in one single person, both for speed and secrecy: Besides it having been the first, and ever since accounted the best form; since the hatred of a State (which never pardons) is more mortal then the generous spleen of a Monarchy: It remained only to be provided that the Laws and rules be also few and good, by which this as well as any other form of Government whatsoever must necessarily be upheld and maintained.[9]

This statement of the grounds upon which R.H. endorsed monarchy is of some importance to the consideration of his utopianism. It was safest because most quick and secret; most legitimate because most ancient; most just because most human. It remained, however, an agency, an institutional device to be seen within the context of other institutions. Like any other form of government it was insufficient without good laws. R.H. took upon himself, as designer of an ideal society, the provision of those laws. In this way his royalism fell short of absolutism and remained compatible with a utopian model.

He had chosen to continue Bacon's *New Atlantis*, so he confessed, because it was monarchical.[10] The Baconianism of his works was, however, more profound than this and it was probably this aspect of it which inspired Hartlib's sympathetic remarks. In the dedicatory preface R.H. reprinted a Latin ode by George Herbert in praise of Bacon, which had been delivered at Cambridge in 1621.[11] Like Bacon, he was interested in the codification of law and more particularly in the systematisation of scientific knowledge.[12] He also was preoccupied with the utilitarian application of knowledge and with the process of invention. He shared with Bacon a conservative royalism. However, an even more considerable influence upon the features of his utopian design was that of Robert

---

[7] *Ibid.*   [8] *Ibid.*, pp. 20–2.   [9] *Ibid.*, preface.   [10] *Ibid.*

[11] For the ode, *Quis iste tandem*, see F. E. Hutchinson (ed.), *The Works of George Herbert* (Oxford, 1953). It is interesting perhaps that Bacon's letter of advice to George Villiers was printed in 1661 for R.H. and H.B. See Spedding, Ellis and Heath (eds.), *The Works of Francis Bacon*, 14 vols. (London, 1868–90), vol. XIII, p. 26.

[12] R.H., *New Atlantis*, pp. 18, 42–3, 53–70, 79–83, 92.

Burton's utopia. From Burton he borrowed attitudes, devices and even phrases. In the punishment of crime, in the regulation of markets, in the desire to involve the gentry in urban government, in the treatment of usury, in the insistence on plaintiffs' sureties in civil cases, in the provision of free schools in each provincial city, and in the planned exploitation of economic resources; in all these things R.H. recalled Burton. His 'Providorans' were merely Burton's 'Supervisors' under another name, and there was direct verbal plagiarisation in his proposals for city government.[13] Bacon and Burton did not, however, exhaust his sources. He was one of the most eclectic of utopian writers adopting ideas from Hobbes, Milton, Chamberlen, Petty, Harrith and others. His eclecticism is again reminiscent of Burton.

The laws of R.II.'s *New Atlantis* were digested into 'ten small codes' comparable to the Mosaic law or Justinian code. 'They be not many, but those easy, plain, and all writ in our native Language, and were first framed by that prudent Solomona, the first Law-giver of this Island.' Revision of the laws goes on and they had been generally revised by Solomona Politicus, Solomona's fourteenth successor. Periodically men were sent abroad from the 'grand Seminary of Students in the Law' to survey the law of other countries with a view to adopting what was best and practical. If what they proposed was agreed, it was merely promulgated by the king with the sacrifice of a lamb and so became law. 'This we think a quicker way then by assembling the heads of the peoples Election, since these many times, when convened, are either factious or dilatory...' R.H. had little good to say of representative assemblies. In Europe, he declared, 'Parliaments of late have been looked on as fatal, and almost sleighted: and in the latter it is doubted they will not long continue, at least in that authentic power and praetended priviledg which they have arrogantly assumed, if not too magisterially usurped.'[14] In New Atlantis the monarch had every appearance of sovereign legislative power, but R.H. still saw the exercise of this power as limited rather than absolute. In the first place the king worked within terms of a body of received law. Secondly, there was an assumed identity of interests between ruler and subject. 'The people of *Bensalem* have it as a received Maxim among them, *That their* Solomona *neither can nor will do them any injury, they being the members of that body whereof he is the head.*'[15] Finally the

[13] *Ibid.*, p. 44. Cf. Burton, *The Anatomy of Melancholy*, edited by Holbrook Jackson, 3 vols. (London, 1932), vol. I, p. 100. For comment on his borrowings see V. Dupont, *L'Utopie et le Roman Utopique dans la Littérature Anglaise* (Toulouse, 1941), pp. 233–5. H. R. Russell Smith, *Harrington and his Oceana: A Study of a Seventeenth Century Utopia and its Influence in America* (Cambridge, 1914), p. 15. Smith's view that R.H. plagiarised More has little to recommend it.

[14] R. H., *New Atlantis*, pp. 18–22.   [15] *Ibid.*, p. 20.

monarch always sought the advice of 'his ancient and prime Nobles' whom he called his 'copartners'. For 'it was much fitter that he should embrace the faithful advice of such and so many judicious friends (for so he called all his Counsellours) then that they all should follow and submit to his single will'.[16] Even so the king of New Atlantis remained 'a puissant monarch', head of both church and state and maintaining a standing militia at his own expense, 'without any tax or charge on the subject'. The apparatus, if not the will and practice, of absolutism existed. The king was the pinnacle of an hierarchical society, both secular and ecclesiastical. There were 'many degrees of Nobility' distinguished from the blood royal down. The lesser nobility were limited in number and their status, which was not always hereditary, was accorded on grounds of merit rather than wealth. Supporting this structure was 'a solid kind of heraldry', not to be confused with European heraldry which 'Any Fool may buy and wear for his money'. A complex system recorded the virtues and services of potential candidates for honours.[17]

The church was organised on a similarly hierarchical, an episcopal, basis. The clergy were 'modest, but yet austere, serious, grave and holy'. But no one was admitted to holy orders until they had attained the age of thirty and had demonstrated their learning and good character. Clerical marriage was allowed but was a bar to high office. Of the clergy, 'only the chiefest were permitted to entermedle in the civil power and publicly to advise when called thereto, or act in Secular or State Affairs, least they should neglect their Spiritual'. R.H. rejected any element of voluntarism on the part of his parishioners. Only infant baptism was allowed and the church was strictly a territorial church. There were about twelve hundred parishioners to each church and these were forbidden 'to gad elsewhere, or have any subordinate Lecturers to officiate under their proper pastours, but in case of sickness only; and only such *curatores animarum* set over them as the universities and peculiar Archiepiscopan shall approve off [*sic*]'. From every city an episcopan, or bishop, controlled church discipline. Clerical misdemeanours were first reviewed by the church and then the guilty were passed over to the state for punishment. Excommunication was never used lightly.[18] There were severe laws to keep the Jesuits out, presumably because of their views on resistance to monarchs, but R.H.,

---

[16] *Ibid.*, p. 88. For a discussion of the subject of conciliar consultation in seventeenth-century English government see Clayton Roberts, *The Growth of Responsible Government in Stuart England* (Cambridge, 1966); Donald W. Hanson, *From Kingdom to Commonwealth: The Development of Civic Consciousness in English Political Thought* (Cambridge, Mass., 1970).

[17] R.H., *New Atlantis*, pp. 22–3, 36.

[18] On the church's over-exploitation of excommunication in the early seventeenth century see Christopher Hill, *Society and Puritanism in Pre-Revolutionary England* (London, 1966), Chapter 10.

like Bacon and Harrington, recognised the Jews as a peculiar problem. 'We have a Law inhibiting all forein rank Jews to live in this Island, or any to have converse or commerce with them when ever they land.' Any Jews entering the country and remaining obstinate were crucified. More moderate provision was made for Jews to be housed on an offshore island where they underwent religious instruction in the hope of conversion to Christianity preliminary to their permanent settlement in New Atlantis. Nothing was then allowed to disturb the state-controlled religious uniformity of R.H.'s utopia.[19]

New Atlantis was divided into fifteen provinces, each with a capital town, and to the planning of these and other townes R.H. gave great attention. The city of Bellatore, for example, which was next in importance to the city of Solomona's residence, was of regular shape, having twelve gates and twenty-four towers. As in all other cities the buildings lining the streets were of uniform construction. Each trade conducted in the city was located in a different street, as R.H. believed it to be in Algiers. All 'offensive Trades', unwelcome because of smell or noise, were restricted to the suburbs. At the centre of each town or city was a large, square market place. On one side of this stood a House of Correction and Armouries, which also contained fire-fighting equipment. Opposite were 'Courts of Justice, publick Halls for all Societies and Companies, Free Schools, and publick schools (if it be an Universitie) we having three in three of the chiefest cities'. On the third side of the square were 'Theaters, common Granaries, Amoscadoes or Lumbars, the Burse or Exchange (if it be a Provincial Citie) and the Artillerie Gardens'. On the fourth side were hospitals for the old, sick, crippled, orphans and lunatic. Each city had a cathedral and twelve churches, all built in imitation of the Church of St John the Baptist in Florence. Only coastal cities were fortified and with this exception the appearance of the cities of New Atlantis must have been strikingly uniform.[20] In the middle of each civic square was a Common Council House 'where the richer and wiser inhabitants assemble to consult of the politic Government of the Citie'. Amongst the civic officials were 'publick Tresorers, Ediles, Quaestors, Overseers of the poor Pupils and Orphans Goods'. In each city there were also two 'justiciers of the Market' who checked that dealings were just, and severely punished false measure. R.H. gave only the sketchiest picture of the functioning of these officials and their tenure of office. They were obliged to give an annual account of their service and a full account on the expiration of their term. Like Burton, R.H. hoped that the gentry would reside, at least for part of the

---

19 Cf. Harrington's proposals for the settlement of Jews in Ireland. Harrington's motives were, of course, economic not religious. For the religious arrangements discussed see R.H., *New Atlantis*, pp. 24–5, 29, 30–1, 46–7.
20 *Ibid.*, pp. 29, 35, 36–8, 74–5.

year, in the towns and take a full part in municipal affairs. 'These Magistrates are not elected out of the Plebeians, Tradesmen or Mechanicks only; but out of the Noblesse and Gentry, who are to reside in these Cities, at such times and seasons especially, we thinking it not dishonourable for Noble persons to govern in the City as well as in the Country.'[21]

Each provincial city had a 'Surveyour General', who planned public works for the province, and a 'Providoran Council' to ensure that the provincial granaries were well stocked and kept in good repair. The officers of these councils, the Providorans, were given a wide responsibility in ensuring the maximum exploitation of the productive resources of the province. They were clearly based on Burton's supervisors and their objectives recalled the economic objectives of Hartlib's *Macaria*. 'These *Providorans* suffer not any Commons... nor any Wasts, Bogs, Forests, Fens, Marishes, Desarts, Heaths, or Parks (but some few only for our *Solomona*'s pleasure) but by inclosures or draining improve all to the best advantage for the public good.' They attempted to keep prices stable and to prevent the engrossing of grain. They supervised the laws for the improvement of lands and woods. No one was to cut down a tree without planting ten and special encouragement was given for the planting of fruit trees. It was obligatory upon landlords to offer preferential leases to those who would improve decayed farm land. They were to ensure the maximum return from the human, as well as the physical, resources of the country.

Providorans have a power to summon all whom they please to suspect, before them once a year, to give an account by what trade or occupation they get their livelyhood. If such cannot give a good accompt, they are sent immediately to the *Corrigidorans*, who either finds them work, or lets them forth the next Market day either to the Husbandmen or Vignerons.

Complementary to this attempt to increase national output and productivity was a policy of transport improvement. R.H. envisaged a national transport system of post-horses, wagons and coaches, and a highly developed network of canals and schools of navigation in the principal maritime cities.[22]

While throwing great emphasis on increasing production by regulation, planning and state encouragement, R.H. was unwilling to accept that distribution should take place in an unplanned or uncontrolled way. He remained highly suspicious of the free market. At the heart of his economic proposals lay a concern with the collective problem. It was not

---

[21] *Ibid.*, pp. 37–8, 44. Cf. Burton, *Anatomy of Melancholy*, vol. i, pp. 98–101.

[22] *Ibid.*, pp. 39–41, 50, 52. Cf. Gibson's comment on R.H. as attempting 'the fullest exploitation of available resources of men and material'. R. W. Gibson, *St. Thomas More: A Preliminary Bibliography of his Works and of Moreana to the Year 1750* (New Haven and London, 1961), pp. 355–6.

sufficient to produce abundance if the distribution of utilities placed all goods in the hands of a few. Like More, he believed that this was the situation in contemporary Europe and that it was a situation productive of theft and crime:

you suffer great Men in office, first to rob, spoil and oppress the Common People, and when such depraedatours have made them poor, and in want, if they steal but a sheep or the like (which they are often necessitated to do to save themselves from starving) then you either hang them, if the theft be above such a value, or in some places send them to the mines or Gallies to enslave them more, and where through extream want and converse with one another, they learn more roguery.

Unlike More, R.H. did not choose communism as the solution but preferred a supervised market, the prevention of engrossing and unfair practice, the maintenance of fair prices. Itinerant markets and fairs were not permitted. 'For the first do but beggar Cities, and the last only disgrace them; and abuse the Countrey in the vending of bad and unwarrantable Merchandise.' In the same spirit, R.H. adopted Burton's suggestions for the regulation of usury and the prevention of extortion. Municipal pawnshops replaced 'private brokage' and public guest houses replaced 'Inns or cut-throat harbours'. To prevent frauds in the sale, mortgage and conveyancing of land, '*Escrivons* or *Notaries*' were appointed in every city to record all transactions and deeds. As in the case of the registries in *Chaos* their records might be consulted for a fee.[23]

The officials who staffed these offices formed 'a faithful, learned, judicious and uncorrupt Magistracie'. They were all over the age of thirty and received their positions 'for their deserts and not money'. Plebeians were not excluded from office provided their merits and industry justified their appointment. All officials were appointed 'during the Monarchs pleasure' but he only removed those guilty of misdemeanour or corruption and the normal age of retirement was seventy. Reversions were not permitted as they interfered with the king's privilege of advancement on merit and because they discouraged younger officers from meritorious performance. Corruption was regarded as an extremely serious offence. Guilty officials were suspended from their offices, suffered the loss of both eyes and the forfeiture of all their goods. The punishment of those who sought to bribe or corrupt them was to have their right hand bored with a red-hot iron and to lose half their estate.[24]

Partly in order to produce qualified officials at every level and partly to

---

[23] R.H., *New Atlantis*, pp. 16, 35, 45, 49. On market supervision and the problem of the open market cf. Alan Everitt, 'The Marketing of Agricultural Produce', in Joan Thirsk (ed.), *The Agrarian History of England and Wales*, vol. IV, *1500–1640* (Cambridge, 1967), pp. 466–592.

[24] R.H., *New Atlantis*, pp. 26, 51.

supplement his economic proposals, R.H. devised a complete educational system. Free schools were to be established in each provincial city to teach languages, singing, dancing, fencing, riding and writing. Here he thought it useful if pupils practised on a device such as had been suggested by Sir William Petty: 'an Instrument we have made to write two Copies at once, at one and the same motion, for dispatch'.[25] The governors and masters of these schools were to be chosen every three years by the members of the Academy. This last institution was modelled on the French Academy established by Richelieu. It existed 'to reform all errors in books, and then to license them'; to purify the language by establishing standard usages; to publish dictionaries establishing proper and undisputed meanings; and to translate the best foreign authors. The three universities of New Atlantis taught a much broader, Baconian curriculum than was current in the English universities. 'We have in the three Universities, Colledges (besides those for Divinity, Law and Philosophy) for Mathematicians, Historians, Poets, Musicians, Stage-players, Alchymnists, Florists, Herbalists, Chirurgions, Anatomists, and Physitians also. Unto the last are adjoyning large Physic Gardens, Theaters and Schools.' Students at the universities were obliged to specialise and were not allowed to change from 'that study and art they first undertake'. At the chief university a Historiographus Regius was appointed 'who hath a great pension allowed him for supervising all History that shall be put out . . . his province is to correct the History: that posterity may judge right of all praeceeding actions, and not be wronged by any sinister practices or false glosses'. But there can be little doubt that for R.H. the primary function of the universities was to be agricultural and horticultural research and the practical application of the knowledge thus gained.[26] The main element of R.H.'s Baconianism was his preoccupation with the winning and application of practical knowledge. In New Atlantis the concealment of knowledge discovered was made a civil offence. Those who had made inventions or discoveries of public benefit were publicly honoured and an elaborate pageant in honour of successful inventors was described in great detail.[27] R.H. made considerable effort to imagine the benefits that such a technologically oriented society might enjoy. These included a powder capable of preventing the ignition of gunpowder; an engine to drive ships without oars and against the wind and tide;[28] flying chariots; an invention to prevent chimneys from smoking; the submarine; 'the Revielleirs, which

[25] For Petty see Charles Webster, *The Great Instauration: Science, Medicine and Reform 1626–1660* (London, 1975), p. 164. R.H. did not mention Petty.

[26] R.H., *New Atlantis*, pp. 39, 42–4.

[27] *Ibid.*, pp. 53, 56–63.

[28] Cf. Peter Chamberlen's navigation device. See below Chapter 11 and *Commons Journals*, vol. x, pp. 103, 108.

at the same instant sound the alarm, strike fire, light the candles & of making the tenth part of fire serve for brewing, by placing the Cauldron and making the furnace exactly'; and a sympathetic powder, 'the most salubrious balsam in the world, and cures all wounds that are not mortale, in a very short time, at distance'.[29]

R.H. saw six threats to monarchy and to society in general. They were criminals, indigent persons, ambitious men, luxury, revenge and malice. Against each of these threats, he offered safeguards. To deal with criminals he offered good laws and incorruptible magistrates. At the beginning of his continuation of Bacon's work he described an incident of theft and its sequence in order to illustrate the inexorable operation and severity of the law in New Atlantis: 'all concealers are looked on as Accessories, and all injured persons are bound to prosecute the suspected, and in no wayes to compound it'. The penalty for theft from a stranger was a spell in the pillory, an apology and three years' work in a House of Correction. After that the thief was condemned permanently to wear a bell and brazen collar. Theft from a native was not punished so severely but the thief was obliged to work for his victim until he had earned for him compensation worth twice his loss. Since, however, there was little want in New Atlantis, R.H. claimed that theft was an infrequent occurrence. Adultery and murder were punished with death; sacrilege with the loss of both hands; false witness and perjury with the loss of the tongue. Slanderers were deprived of their lower lip, and common liars of the upper. The penalty for swearing was six months in a brass collar. If at the end of the period the culprit had not reformed, a bell was attached. If at the end of the year there was still no improvement, his tongue was bored with a hot iron. There was a similar pattern of punishment for convicted drunkards. At first they were fined. Subsequently they were refused all liquor for a year.[30] The common denominator in R.H.'s treatment of crime was the use of severe, disabling punishment and a retributive inflexibility. The law had to be seen *always* to take its course.

The threat of the poor to social stability was in good measure alleviated by the positive economic involvement of the state and the general level of prosperity in New Atlantis. It remained necessary, nevertheless, to provide for those who could not or would not work. In every city there were Houses of Charity to care for the old, infirm and incapable as well as orphans, and Houses of Correction where the idle were compelled to work for their sustenance. Special programmes existed to equip children for a life of industry and self-maintenance. Every artisan and tradesman was obliged to teach children his trade, to read, to 'shoot flying' and to swim. Even the children of nobles were taught a manual trade partly for the encouragement of others and partly to ensure against the decay of their

[29] R.H., *New Atlantis*, pp. 57, 65–6, 69.   [30] *Ibid.*, Preface and pp. 10–16, 46.

family fortunes. Great emphasis was placed on swimming as a means of aiding the digestion, hardening the body and enuring it to 'strong labours'. For this purpose two swimming pools (one for males the other for females) were built in every city and twelve public instructors appointed to each. Similar attention was given to archery and an 'Arcubalistory' was built in every city so that the skill might be taught. R.H. even went so far as to suggest that skill in archery was the true cause of plenty amongst the poor because it formed the basis of their hunting skill, and certainly by the game laws of New Atlantis hunting was reserved for peasants on foot.[31]

Yet another means by which the poor were saved from indigence was the control of marriage. None were to marry 'till of ripe age'; in the case of a man, twenty-one years old; of a woman, eighteen. No man was to marry 'after his Climacteric', nor woman after the age of fifty-three. There was no divorce, except for adultery, for which, in any case, the penalty was death. A widow was not permitted to remarry without special leave from the archbishops and only then after a year's mourning. On the other hand, a widower might marry only six months after the decease of his wife. Registers were kept in every parish to ensure the observation of these regulations. R.H. borrowed from Bacon the idea of a proxy naked viewing of the betrothed prior to marriage. He maintained a curiously ambivalent attitude towards pre-marital sex. On the one hand, the New Atlantans did not force 'two young sinners' to marry, although R.H. claimed that 'that obscoenity' seldom happened. On the other hand, they were punished if they did not marry, and a child conceived out of wedlock had no rights of inheritance. Sexual intercourse for a pregnant woman or even her public appearance was felt to be unfitting. Dowries were little or none, because of the serious economic effect of the dowry system on fathers. Probably for the same reason extravagant funerals and monuments were forbidden. R.H.'s treatment of inheritance was somewhat obscure but he seems to have favoured a system of multiple partition, with the eldest male receiving a double portion and the girls receiving an equal share with the other brothers. If a girl's father had not arranged a marriage for her before she reached the age of eighteen, she was entitled to claim her portion and arrange her own marriage.[32]

The zeal and energy of ambitious men were contained and harnessed by the judicious distribution of honours and by a system of privilege based

---

[31] *Ibid.*, pp. 26–8, 94. On contemporary attitudes to swimming see Michael West, 'Spenser, Everard Digby and the Renaissance Art of Swimming', *Renaissance Quarterly*, 26:1 (1973), pp. 11–22. Henry Robinson also believed that all children should be taught to swim. See W. K. Jordan, *Men of Substance: A Study of the Thought of Two English Revolutionaries: Henry Parker and Henry Robinson* (Chicago, 1942), p. 227.

[32] R.H., *New Atlantis*, pp. 32–4. On dowries see Alan Macfarlane, *The Family Life of Ralph Josselin* (Cambridge, 1970), pp. 93–5.

on merit. The enervating effects of luxury, however, had to be dealt with by legislation. This was particularly so with respect to dress. 'We allow no excesse in attire of embroideries or wearing Gold or Silver laces upon wearing apparel: Every Nobleman, Magistrate, Merchant or Tradesman, with their Wives respectively, being distinguished with decent attire suitable to his Calling or Profession, and that fashion not to be altered.' Only a few privileged persons were allowed to wear swords.[33] The anti-social forces of revenge and malice were dealt with on two different levels. As a threat to the Crown, R.H. believed that they were best defeated by the virtue and innocence of the monarch. As the socially divisive activities of 'schismatical men', he sought their suppression and containment. To this end religious and political uniformity were the rule, property claims were clearly established through a land registry and unnecessary legislation was discouraged. In a civil case the plaintiff was obliged to advance a bond equal in value to the size of his claim. It was forfeit if he was found to have sued 'maliciously and wrongfully'. Where a criminal charge was not proven the accuser was made to suffer the penalty that would have been inflicted on the accused if he had been found guilty. If he had 'maliciously and wrongfully' brought the charge, he was to be beheaded or shot.[34]

The fundamental paradox of R.H.'s continuation of the *New Atlantis* was the paradox of all royalist utopia. He rejected a perfect moral commonwealth because of 'the fraielty of humane nature', but built his own model around the most personal of all governmental forms, hereditary monarchy. Although men were not to be trusted, R.H. had to trust one man.[35] Yet, while it was indispensable, that trust was not enough. It was not sufficient to list the virtues of Solamona and his court.[36] There had to be legal, educational and institutional provision which in its all-embracing character was typically utopian. The island was a closed community, uniform in civic planning, building and dress, whose language, historiography and literature were controlled by the state.[37] The scope of state authority extended from the conditionality of property rights on adherence to state policy, to directions for the nursing of children.[38] In his preface, R.H. described the two hinges upon which government turns as the Legislative and Coercive. Despite his talk of legal research and review, the law was essentially provided in ten compact folio volumes and outlined by R.H. himself.[39] Again, despite his talk of the flexibility of monarchy, he had devised a coercive machine of harsh and irrevocable punishments administered by an incorruptible magistracy. In him the

[33] R.H., *New Atlantis*, pp. 23–4, 26, 41–2. [34] *Ibid.*, p. 48.
[35] See, for example, his grounds for dispensing with elected assemblies, *ibid.*, p. 20.
[36] *Ibid.*, pp. 88–9. [37] *Ibid.*, pp. 17, 41–2, 42–3. [38] *Ibid.*, pp. 46, 83, 33.
[39] *Ibid.*, Preface, p. 18.

royalist and the utopian were equally strong, and they marred each other. As a royalist, R.H. implicitly admitted the impossibility of monarchy as a self-sufficient ideal. As a utopian, he opened his system to corruption and collapse by placing his trust in one man chosen only by the process of heredity.

The anonymous work, *Antiquity Reviv'd: or the Government of a Certain Island Antiently call'd Astreada, in Reference to Religion, Policy, War and Peace. Some hundreds of Years Before the coming of Christ*, which was published in 1693, was basically a vehicle for Filmerian royalism directed against the usurpation of the Stuarts by the House of Orange.[40] In so far as it was a utopia, it was, therefore, a Jacobite utopia.

The form adopted by the author was that of the dialogue and the setting was classical. After Alexander the Great's conquest of Greece 'a Senator, a Philosopher, and a person of Sacerdotal Function' had fled Athens with the intention of taking refuge in Persia. They had, however, been blown off course on to an island named Astreada after the 'Tutelar Deity of Piety and Justice'. The island was 'of large Extent, if not great and powerful, both in Number, Grandeur, and Valor of Inhabitants, and Opulency of Soil, and Conveniency of Scituation, preferable in most Respects, if compar'd with other Neighbouring Dominions; and had not visibly deviated, in any known Age, from requisite Greatness or Virtue'. The principality was 'so happy, as neither the Imputation of Tyranny in their Monarchs, or detestable Sedition and Rebellion of their People, had any sanguine Records amongst them'.[41] The strangers were courteously received on the island and introduced to two officials: a Fidefendon who examined their religious views and explained the religious policy of Astreada; and a Jussinedos, or principal magistrate, who explained the laws and form of government of the island. About a third of the work was devoted to the issue of religion; a third to a defence of hereditary monarchy and an attack on social contract theory, which was heavily dependent on, and in places a direct plagiarisation of, Filmer; and a final third to the description of the government and law of Astreada.

Like Bacon, the unknown author gave precedence to the issue of religion in the discussions between the strangers and the inhabitants of the utopia. Although the work was set 'Some hundreds of years before the coming of Christ', there is no doubt that the author subscribed to the anti-clerical rationalism put forward by the Fidefendon. He was a deist rather than a Christian and expressed scorn at the reliance of traditional religion

---

[40] I have consulted two copies of the work, both of which are severely marred by a poor type face. They are the British Museum copy (shelf-mark 8005 c 5) and the Yale University Library copy.

[41] Anon., *Antiquity Reviv'd* (1693), pp. 1–3.

on scriptural authority. Nevertheless the form of religion was a crucial factor in the social and political stability of Astreada. Uniformity of religion was indispensable to harmony. It was the Fidefendon's function 'to examine Strangers, and take care that no Religion differing from theirs should be diffus'd within the Island of Astreada'.[42] To this end he engaged them in religious debate, treating their beliefs kindly because they had absorbed them in their upbringing, but, nevertheless, hoping that they would discern their errors.

The Fidefendon began by rejecting the teaching of any authority unsupported by any 'visible Fact, or universal Manifestation'. The physical harmony of the universe proved the existence of a deity, a providence which founded and maintains the universe. This being, he argued, must have been spiritual and not physical.

It being impossible that Religion should be so nearly ally'd to Mortality, or be oblig'd to a Founder of Human Denomination. And if the World was govern'd by a visible and constant Providence, there was no Reason to doubt that Religion was deducible from thence, and no less manifest and perpetually extant to Sense, as palpably as we behold the Sky and Stars above our Heads.

This position raised two problems. How can a spiritual being control a physical universe, and how can man, a physical being, worship a spirit?[43] In response, the Fidefendon claimed, the only appropriate reaction was one of suspended judgement. Like the Athenians, the natives of Astreada admitted to belief in an unknown god.

We Astreadans, after the rational form of Worship profess'd by us, attribute to the denomination of Providence, an Omnipotency or Divine Conservator and Disposer of the total World, as it is either compos'd of whatever we behold, or of what we do neither discern or apprehend: And yet we do not definitively infer from any of these Expressions, the Essential Nature or Modality of Existence in reference to the Supreme Power which we devoutly celebrate.[44]

The result could be summarised in three maxims: 'nothing is in the Intellect of Man, but was first in the Senses'; 'a Spiritual Being cannot be in any kind the object of the Understanding or Senses'; and following from these, 'a Supreme Cause may be visibly existent in the Effects it produceth; yet so, as not to be otherwise defin'd or apprehended'. Thus although it was possible to conclude the existence of a sublime being from its physical effects, for example, the order of the universe, it was not possible to go further. Judgement on the character and intentions of the deity had to remain suspended. Divine inspiration could never be proven. Consequently, in Astreada, providence was adored without giving it the name of a deity. Worship took the form of the sensibility and acknowledgement of the effects and benefits of the operation of providence,

[42] *Ibid.*, pp. 3–4, 87–8.   [43] *Ibid.*, pp. 6–11, 24–6.   [44] *Ibid.*, p. 15.

gratitude for bounty from an unknown hand. The very vagueness, the undoctrinal nature, of this religion was its strength. Since there were no forms, rules or hair-splitting distinctions to be fought over, religious controversy was removed as a threat to social stability.[45]

The same spirit informed the Astreadans' attitude to the immortality of the soul. They were, for want of evidence, in a state of suspended judgement. The low-key undogmatic, rationalist approach to religious questions was both most logical and safest in social terms. However, in approaching the social problem of religion in the ideal society, the author of *Antiquity Reviv'd* stumbled against a number of problems. On the one hand, sin was seen in legal terms as a civil offence. On the other hand, religion was seen as outside the sphere of state activity: 'their Religion did effectually disown all subordinate dependency on traditions and Precepts of State'. Conflicts between church and state were thereby averted and the church freed from the effects of alternation of government. The religious disposition of the country owed nothing to compulsion, custom or indoctrination but represented the mature choice of independent minds.[46] Nevertheless the primary factor guaranteeing the stability of Astreada was its uniformity of religion. Diversity of belief was seen as the main cause of civil disturbance: 'the grand corruption of States, have generally emerg'd from the Silliness of their Creeds: by which their Devotion and civil obedience is highly impaired'. But how was this uniformity of religious belief achieved if not through the coercive power of the state? The Jussinedos, taking over from the Fidefendon, suggested that it was based purely on the clarity and rationality of its tenets.[47] However, this confidence in the ability of enlightened men to accept disinterestedly the clear and rational is not evinced by the Astreadans in other respects. Moreover, with the unenlightened multitude the problem was even more intractable. The Jussinedos was contemptuous of the gullibility of the masses and of their capacity for superstitious belief.[48] The confidence behind the author's belief that a rational religious position could command universal acceptance accords badly with the rest of his work.

He certainly entertained no such confidence in the capacities of men by their individual efforts to sustain a perfect moral commonwealth. It appeared wonderful to him

that man by the prerogative of reason should impose Subjection on all other Creatures; and yet with the best of his capacity not sufficiently compleated to give Law to himself, in reference to subordinate duty; which enormous and pernicious mistake ariseth from no other source of evil, than the natural depravity of man, in being too pronely averse and contumacious of the benefits

---

[45] *Ibid.*, pp. 16–20, 33.   [46] *Ibid.*, pp. 32–3, 46–8.   [47] *Ibid.*, pp. 87–90.
[48] *Ibid.*, pp. 79, 57.

of orderly Tranquility. This irregular defect and inclination of the humane mind, too often bypass'd and enhans'd by worldly Advantage and Interest; can have no proper Remedy, unless by a rational cure whereby we may discern the useful Integrity, and happy Obedience, that ought to be paid to Secular Dominion.[49]

The difficulty was in apprehending the true form and basis of Secular Dominion.

The middle section of *Antiquity Reviv'd* was devoted to this problem and the attempt to prove that hereditary monarchy was the only legitimate form of government. The argument was heavily indebted to Sir Robert Filmer's *Patriarcha* both in substance and in presentation. Large sections of it were unacknowledged direct plagiarism.[50] Like Filmer, the author of *Antiquity Reviv'd* rejected contract theory, mixed monarchy, any concession to popular or representative government. His basic proposition was the Filmerian one that 'all Kings that have, or ever had Dominion, are, or were Fathers of their People, or the Heirs of such Fathers, or Usurpers of the paternal Right of Soveraignty'.[51] This position raised the problem of royalist utopianism in its most crucial form. To Filmer legitimacy of title was all. Once it was acknowledged, obedience could not rightfully be withheld. The power of the patriarchal monarch was absolute, limited only by the monarch's own interpretation of his responsibility as father of his people and as a creature of God.[52] But such reliance on the rule of one individual leads out of utopianism into the Mirror of Princes tradition. The author of *Antiquity Reviv'd* expressed the Filmerian theory but backed away from the practical implications.

The government which he envisaged for Astreada was 'perfectly Monarchical, with all the requisites incident to Soveraignty'. Its success, its endurance and its unchanging character were dependent on the quality with which successive monarchs had ruled: 'it had continued uninterrupted in the due course of lineal succession beyond their records of Ages; yet so establish'd as by the excellency of Rule, there was no deviation in

[49] *Ibid.*, p. 54.
[50] See e.g. *ibid.*, pp. 58–62. Cf. Sir Robert Filmer, 'The Anarchy of a Limited or Mixed Monarchy', in *Patriarcha and Other Political Works*, edited by Peter Laslett (Oxford, 1949), pp. 285–7.
[51] Anon., *Antiquity Reviv'd*, p. 56. Cf. Filmer, 'Patriarcha' and 'Anarchy of a Limited or Mixed Monarchy', in Laslett (ed.), *Patriarcha*, pp. 60, 288. For patriarchalist theory in the later seventeenth century see Gordon J. Schochet, *Patriarchalism in Political Thought* (Oxford, 1975), Chapter 11; J. P. Kenyon, *Revolution Principles: The Politics of Party 1689–1720* (Cambridge, 1977), especially Chapter 5. The most committed Filmerian of the period was Charles Leslie but there is no evidence to connect him directly with *Antiquity Reviv'd*.
[52] Filmer, 'Patriarcha', Chapter 22 in Laslett (ed.), *Patriarcha*, pp. 95–6; Cf. *Antiquity Reviv'd*, pp. 83–6.

King and People from the Original Integrity annex'd to the most primitive constitution of their nation'. What this 'primitive constitution' was remained unclear. The language, adherence of king and people, was expressive of contract theory but this had been dismissed elsewhere. On the other hand if the primitive constitution were simply the patriarchal authority of kings, monarchs were left with little to adhere to but their own wills. Rather than either of these, the correct interpretation would appear to be that the argument used here was not so much patriarchalist as in terms of the theory of the ancient constitution. However sweeping their original powers the kings of Astreada were seen as bounded and limited by a historically acquired constitution, so integral a part of the system as to be considered immemorial and unchangeable. Thus any king who endeavoured to change the Astreadan constitution would have been, according to the Jussinedos, considered a fool and a tyrant.[53] The area of the monarch's legitimate behaviour was bounded by a pre-defined constitution.

As the author of *Antiquity Reviv'd* drew back from the implications of Filmer's patriarchalism in this respect, so in another area he went far beyond it. Not only were titles of honour purely hereditary in Astreada, so was the ignominy and shame of crime. Faction, sedition and crime were the work of families, just as much as loyalty and virtue. Men were 'too propensely disposed and interested in adhering to the crimes of their nearest Kindred and Acquaintance'. They took pride in the fame of their ancestors even if it stemmed from iniquity. 'Nor is anything more manifest, than that the most pernitious attempts against Principalities and States have proceeded from the conspirations and Facts of Hereditary Traitors.'[54] Since families were bound to own the deeds of their members, however nefarious, it was of little use to punish the guilty individuals alone. The shame of crime and sedition had to be visited not only on the actual offenders but on their kindred and posterity as well. Accordingly the Astreadans had set up a Court of Renunciation to punish families for the misdeeds of their members. There were no executions even in cases of murder: 'our Government has rather thought fit to impress a visible disgrace on the persons of men, than to terminate their Lives by legal execution'. The guilty were condemned to wear plates of steel (emblazoned with the letter 'R') upon their chests, and this punishment was visited on the whole family and their descendants. Consequently, 'Families gave a check to themselves. . .' Moreover it was socially effective because the families of the great were already concerned with their honour and it was they who swayed the careless multitude. The family was thus institutionalised as a major source of social order and an agency for law enforcement.

[53] *Antiquity Reviv'd*, pp. 52, 94–5.
[54] *Ibid.*, pp. 96–7, 101–11.

By this device, faction was killed and the corruption of the people stopped. It was 'the Phoenix of civil Regiment'.[55]

The magistrates who were to carry through this process of condemning whole families to shame had clearly to be carefully trained and selected. All candidates for positions of magistracy or public trust had to 'pass the Inquiry and Test of their publick Integrity', under supervisors appointed by the Crown. They had to give assurance of loyalty and diligence and an indenture to refund any bribes or selfish gains. Their corruption would be punished by the disgrace of themselves and their kinfolk through the Court of Renunciation. Lawyers in Astreada were expected to act not for profit but in the public interest. This was interpreted as meaning that they should not thrive on the ruin of the law by successfully defending criminals. Such an offence could be punished by the death penalty or by permanent shame. The law was frequently read to the youth of the country in an attempt to produce a legally educated society.[56] By these means it was expected that the corruptions of the law would vanish.

Apart from this it was felt that there were two main, and related, causes of civil unrest. These were ambition and 'the boundless desire of dominion'. These were not to be contained, but exhausted, not by war but by populating the uninhabited areas of the world. The Astreadans had never had to fight a religious war because of the nature of their religion. They were never involved in aggressive alliances and they managed defensive warfare so as to give the aggressor cause for repentance.[57]

The institutional apparatus of Astreada was at best rudimentary but it did exist. In the nebulous constitution, in the Court of Renunciation and in the conditions governing the service of lawyers and magistrates an attempt was made to contain the socially damaging tendencies of men by legal and institutional means. But the very vagueness of the provision testifies to the strength of Filmer's influence on the author. If absolute royal authority was the only legitimate form of government it was useless to lay down detailed conditions for its exercise. On the other hand, he sought to escape the personal dependence of Filmer's patriarchalism by stressing its importance on a social level other than that of monarchy. In Astreada the family, through the operation of the Court of Renunciation, became both the epitome and the fundamental apparatus of the state.

[55] *Ibid.*, pp. 98–9, 101–3, 104, 106–10, 110–11.
[56] *Ibid.*, pp. 93, 97, 112–13, 114.
[57] *Ibid.*, pp. 115, 118–19, 121–2.

The full-employment utopia of seventeenth-century England

... there was not a foot of soil to be seen which was not under cultivation or in come way put to use for mankind.

J. V. Andreae, Christianopolis (1619)

If I should intend to lay open the Mischievousnesse of Disorderliness and Confusion, I might fill a volume, it is either the root or the effect of all the evils of this world...

Samuel Hartlib, *A Discovery for Division or Setting Out of Land* (1653)

MAN ONELY MAKES MAN MISERABLE

Peter Chamberlen, *A Scourge for a Denn of Thieves* (1659)

Industry brings Plenty. The Sluggard shall be cloathed with Raggs. He that will not Work, shall not Eat.

John Bellers, *Proposals for Raising a Colledge of Industry* (1696)

But Men seem to be ignorant both of the Publick Interest and of the Duties of Charity; for instead of going about to enrich the Publick, and contriving to make every one live easily and plentifully, they take all manner of ways to render themselves incapable of being helpful to others indulging a thousand unreasonable Appetites, and sacrificing all they have to their Pleasure and Vanity, so that instead of being Rich and able to do much good, they are always Poor and can scarce supply their own contrived wants.

Anon., *Annus Sophiae Jubilaeus* (1700)

II

In his search for social order and harmony, the designer of utopia has necessarily to devise an economic system which will satisfy the legitimate wants of his utopians. Two approaches to this problem may be distinguished. On the one hand are those, like Sir Thomas More, who would define 'legitimate wants' in an austere and narrow fashion. Production here can be limited in step with limited demand.[1] The approach with which we are concerned in this chapter, on the other hand, emphasises not limited, but maximised production through the full employment of all the community's economic resources and the elimination of waste. Those who espouse this approach begin with production, and only through it confront the problem of total demand and the difficulty of defining 'legitimate wants'.[2]

The concern with waste and the desire to exploit resources efficiently is a common theme of utopian literature. In *Utopia* itself there is no 'license to waste time, nowhere any pretext to evade work'.[3] Robert Burton, as we have seen, insisted on the exhaustive use of all available land, in the context of a managed and planned economy.[4] Likewise, Winstanley urged all men to labour on what would otherwise have remained uncultivated land.[5] The full-employment theme is not unique to

[1] For a seventeenth-century French example of this genre, full employment in frugality, see François de Salignac de la Mothe-Fénelon, *Salentum* (1699), in Frank E. and Fritzie P. Manuel (eds.), *French Utopias: An Anthology of Ideal Societies* (New York, 1966).

[2] Glenn Negley and J. Max Patrick, *The Quest for Utopia* (New York, 1952), p. 292. 'The main theme of Utopias from 1500 to 1850 was advocacy, explicit or implicit, of the fullest possible, efficient utilization of the available resources of men and materials in a given society.' This judgement seems to mar their recognition of an important theme by exaggerating its importance.

[3] *Utopia*, edited by Edward Surtz, S. J. and J. H. Hexter, in *The Complete Works of St. Thomas More*, vol. IV (New Haven and London, 1965), p. 147.

[4] Robert Burton, *The Anatomy of Melancholy*, edited by Holbrook Jackson, 3 vols. (London, 1932), vol. I, pp. 100–1; cf. V. Dupont, *L'Utopie et le Roman Utopique dans la Littérature Anglaise* (Toulouse, 1941), pp. 162–3; see also Luigi Firpo's comments on Kaspar Stüblin's *De Eudaemonensium republica* (1553), in Firpo, 'Kaspar Stiblin, Utopiste', in Jean Lameere (ed.), *Les Utopies à la Renaissance*, Travaux de l'Institut pour l'Etude de la Renaissance et de l'Humanisme (Paris and Brussels, 1963), p. 115.

[5] See above, Chapter 7.

those considered in this chapter but it is their special concern. Their primary preoccupation is the avoidance of waste through the full employment of all the available factors of production. Their emphasis is on efficient and thorough utilisation of the community's resources.

It is only in the twentieth century that the notion of the state's responsibility for the maintenance of full employment, in terms of the full employment of labour and other resources, has come to be widely accepted. There is a tendency, by comparison, to regard early modern man as fatalistic in his approach to economic problems. The state's responsibility for the economic life of the community, well before the influence of laissez faire doctrines in the nineteenth century, is seen as slight. The spasmodic economic intervention of early modern government arose from fiscal preoccupations, a concern for law and order or the desire to satisfy the appetites of important political groups, not from any aspiration to exercise a function of overall economic management. For the early modern period, it has become almost habitual for historians to deny that governments had any concept of economic policy 'in the modern sense'.

Indeed, there are periods and circumstances in which early modern government seemed to be concerned to restrain rather than maximise economic output,[6] in particular to control the effects of technical innovation.[7] Such concern as it appeared to have for employment was related to labour rather than to the other factors of production, and arose out of its fear of social unrest emanating from distress caused by unemployment amongst those who were at best on, or near, the level of subsistence. As a consequence, employment was only fitfully a government concern, rising in priority in periods of slump and fading into the background in periods of relative prosperity.[8] On the whole, beyond ineffectively implemented legislation, policy amounted to makeshift efforts to cajole employers into maintaining employment in economic adversity by ignoring the profit motive and responding to the social dangers inherent in slump conditions. The public provision of labour employment that there was, through public workhouses and stocks or, perhaps quantitatively more important, through private philanthropy, tended to emphasise charity and restraint rather than rehabilitation and continuing employment.[9]

[6] See, for example, F. J. Fisher, 'Commercial Trends and Policy in Sixteenth Century England', *Economic History Review*, 10 (1940), pp. 112–16.

[7] See, for example, Sir George Clark, *Science and Social Welfare in the Age of Newton* (2nd ed., Oxford, 1949), Chapter 4.

[8] Fisher, 'Commercial Trends', pp. 104, 110, 111–12.

[9] The existence of exceptions to this must be noted. Some of them will be discussed below. Nevertheless the overall picture seems to be borne out in the literature. See, Sidney and Beatrice Webb, *English Poor Law History: Part I, The Old Poor Law* (London, 1963); E. M. Leonard, *The Early History of English Poor Relief* (Cambridge, 1900); Dorothy Marshall, 'The Old Poor Law, 1662–1795',

Such a situation accords with the general economic scene as we have come to understand it. Early modern England was a basically agrarian society, handicapped by low productivity, heavy emphasis on cereals and a low state of farming technology, vulnerable to climatic fluctuations, hampered by market restrictions and transport limitations. A chronically underemployed labour force existed on or just above subsistence level and was consequently incapable of developing as a steadily growing mass consumer market. Inevitably, therefore, the manufacturing sector consisted of small-scale, low capital, low technology and low productivity enterprises. Against this background it is not surprising to read in the histories of economic thought that those who theorised about economic matters tended to concentrate on issues such as foreign trade and currency manipulation, and assumed the continuance of a traditional subsistence economy, inflexible in its upper levels of demand and production, and of governmental incapacity to change it.

Nevertheless, it would be a mistake to accept this as the total picture. There were individuals in the seventeenth century concerned with economic management and the maximisation of output, who sought ways of eliminating waste and achieving full employment. Their overall conception of economic society has been neglected because (when not patronisingly dismissed as 'cranks') they have too often been identified with poor relief; as individuals in 'a series of reformers and philanthropists' concerned with the problem of the poor and their 'profitable employment'.[10] It was, of course, impossible to approach any social problem in early modern Europe without encountering large numbers of the poor, the basis of subsistence society.[11] In this light, almost any social policy would appear to have connections with poor relief policy, in one way or another. More-

in E. M. Carus-Wilson (ed.), *Essays in Economic History*, 3 vols. (London, 1954–62), vol. 1, pp. 295–305; Margaret James, *Social Problems and Policy During the Puritan Revolution 1640–1660* (London, 1930); A. L. Beier, 'Poor Relief in Warwickshire 1630–1660', *Past and Present*, 35 (1966), pp. 77–100; J. P. Cooper, 'Social and Economic Policies under the Commonwealth', in G. E. Aylmer (ed.), *The Interregnum: The Quest for Settlement 1646–1660* (London, 1972), pp. 121–42; L. A. Clarkson, *The Pre-Industrial Economy in England 1500–1750* (London, 1971), Chapter 7; Peter Clark and Paul Slack (eds.), *Crisis and Order in English Towns 1500–1700* (London, 1972), Chapters 1 and 5; John A. Garraty, *Unemployment in History: Economic Thought and Public Policy* (New York and Toronto, 1978), Chapters 1–3. For some anticipation of a revisionist view see the important essay by Valerie Pearl, 'Puritans and Poor Relief: The London Workhouse, 1649–1660', in D. Pennington and K. Thomas (eds.), *Puritans and Revolutionaries: Essays in Seventeenth Century History Presented to Christopher Hill* (Oxford, 1979), pp. 206–32.

[10] Webb, *English Poor Law History, Part I*, pp. 101–2, 158.

[11] A point made by Fernand Braudel, *The Mediterranean and the Mediterranean World in the Age of Philip II*, translated by Siân Reynolds, 2 vols. (London, 1972), vol. 1, pp. 453–9.

over, it is true that the full-employment reformers of this chapter were desirous of reducing unemployment amongst the poor and to that extent sought the relief of the poor. But it was a release from idleness in the name of work, as much as a release from indigence in the name of sustenance. Equally, they wanted to improve the work discipline of the poor, and to this end sought their moral reform. The children of the poor should be educated in such a way as to prevent the evils of idleness amongst them. However, these attitudes to the poor must be set in the context of a more comprehensive programme for the fuller exploitation of all natural resources – land, minerals, fisheries, talent and time – as well as the relief of poverty through the provision of work.

The rôle of philanthropic concern in these attitudes was limited. The oft-stated notion that a combination of philanthropy and profit motive became one of the keynotes of social thought in seventeenth-century England is difficult to maintain simply because so often the philanthropy is lacking.[12] John Locke, with his proposals to whip soundly all pauper children, impress vagrants into the navy, and confine beggars to three years' hard labour in the house of correction, is scarcely any less philanthropic or sympathetic than many of his contemporaries.[13] To those concerned with full employment, poor relief by employment was rarely motivated by a simple philanthropic endeavour to alleviate the plight of the poor. It is better seen, in this context, as but one aspect of a demand for the full employment of all resources. The object was greater output, the means full employment, and the removal of poverty a possible by-product. As seen, for example, in proposals to set the poor to work on 'sea fisheries' or linen manufacture, the concern is to increase national wealth by bringing two unexploited resources together and proceeding to exploit them; to work towards full employment in the sense of optimum utilisation of all resources and facilities rather than merely, or even primarily, to alleviate the conditions of the poor.[14]

---

[12] Cf. Sir George Clark, *The Later Stuarts 1660–1714* (Oxford, 1961), p. 53: 'the prevailing opinion, in which Locke shared, was that with better organisation, philanthropy could be not merely economical, but could even be made to pay'. Note Clark's difficulties in reconciling Locke's savagely repressive proposals for dealing with the poor in his famous report to the Board of Trade in 1697, with his supposed philanthropy. *Ibid.*, pp. 52–3. Cf. R. H. Tawney, *Religion and the Rise of Capitalism* (London, 1938), pp. 262–3, 269–70.

[13] Webb, *English Poor Law History, Part I*, pp. 109–11; compare, for example, Samuel Hartlib, *Londons Charity Inlarged* (1650). Hartlib proposed sending beggars to the house of correction, the galleys, or the plantations. It was Hartlib who coined the phrase 'the obstinate, ungodly poor'. See also, D. C. Coleman, 'Labour in the English Economy in the Seventeenth Century', in Carus-Wilson (ed.), *Essays in Economic History*, vol. II, p. 291; James, *Social Problems and Policy*, p. 345.

[14] See, for example, James Puckle, *Englands Path to Wealth and Honour, in a*

The insistence that idleness and waste are social evils which must be eradicated by no means originated in the early modern period.[15] It must, however, be distinguished from the view that what was inhibiting the development of a just or good society was the failure to exploit economic resources and opportunities, the crippling problem of poverty, its association with moral degeneration, social conflict and general misery. Where the object was the individual moral improvement which could be produced, or at least assisted, by the abolition of idleness and the provision of employment, a piecemeal, pragmatic approach to the problem tended to result, frequently consisting of little more than an impassioned emphasis on the implementation of the existing laws or a rehashing of them.[16] Where the end was full employment itself, utopia could result in either of two ways. Full employment might be seen as a prerequisite of the ideal society, providing a flow of satisfactions and work which were seen as necessary to a harmonious and moral society. On the other hand, a utopian social structure might be seen as the prerequisite to full employment, providing the discipline which made full employment possible and eliminating the habits which impeded it.

What do we mean by 'full employment'? It was not, as far as I know, a term used in the seventeenth century. In popular political and economic discussion today it tends to have a narrow, somewhat imprecise, meaning relating to the unemployment of labour. The imprecision arises in part because, even in its restricted labour application, full employment is used in a non-literal sense. Frequently reference is being made only to registered labour, rather than all labour. No western economist would suggest that zero percentage unemployment would be either desirable or possible.

Dialogue between an Englishman and a Dutchman (1700), reprinted in *Somers Tracts*, edited by Sir W. Scott, 13 vols. (1809–15), vol. II, pp. 371–86; Richard Haines, *A Profitable Method Compiled for the Benefit of All Indigent People* (London, 1679). This broader concern with full employment requires a detailed treatment which cannot be afforded it here, where we must restrict ourselves to its utopian expressions. Equally, no claim can be made to have placed the utopian works selected accurately and exhaustively in their correct context. Both the topic of full employment and its expression in ideal-society forms are topics worthy of further research. Despite its dogmatic tone, the present chapter should be regarded as a speculative essay.

[15] Helen C. White, *Social Criticism in Popular Religious Literature of the Sixteenth Century* (New York, 1944), Chapter I. An important work relevant to many of these issues which came too late for me to make extensive use of is Joan Thirsk, *Economic Policy and Projects: The Development of a Consumer Society in Early Modern England* (Oxford, 1978).

[16] See, for example, Anonymous, *Stanleyes Remedy: Or, The Way How to Reform Wandring Beggers, Theeves, High-Way Robbers and Pick-Pockets* (1646); T[homas] L[awson], *An Appeal to the Parliament Concerning the Poor, That There May Not Be A Beggar in England* (1660).

'Full employment', therefore, tends to be taken to mean a statistically low percentage of registered unemployment of labour. Again, there tends to be no distinction of underemployment as part of the full-employment problem. So part-time work is seen as an acceptable question of individual choice. Overmanning, or 'featherbedding' as it is sometimes called, is seen as a problem of labour relations, as time wasting by employees is seen as a result of poor management or poor labour attitudes, rather than in the context of an unemployed labour resource. These issues are seldom related to the problem of full employment. Similarly, 'qualitative unemployment', the misuse of talents, is rarely discussed in the context of full employment. It is salutary, perhaps, to be reminded that all these issues come within the scope of the full employment utopians of seventeenth-century England.

The narrow view of full employment, as a high percentage of the registered labour force being indiscriminately in work, has persisted from the heyday of classical economics into the post-war period. Lord Beveridge's well-known definition sums it up: 'Full employment means having more vacancies than workers seeking vacancies. It does not mean having no unemployment at all.'[17] Although Keynesian theoretical economics should have produced a broadening of the concept, political rhetoric and social attitudes have sustained a rather narrow, if sometimes confused, view of full employment.[18] In referring to full employment in the seventeenth century the term will be used in its broadest possible context. It will be taken to mean the full productive utilisation of all available resources of land, labour, capital and time and the avoidance of waste in respect of each.

However, that in itself is not a sufficient clarification. The term 'full employment' still retains connotations – some very widely held; connotations of policy attitudes. We define the problem, partially at least, in terms of how we see it being solved. For example, to the Keynesian economist, the maintenance of full employment is seen very much in terms of investment levels and monetary policy. It is a problem soluble in these terms and hence will be defined as such. For Beveridge, to take another example, unemployment was a product of the overpricing of labour and/or market imperfections. Government should, in his view, attempt to remove or ease market imperfections by devices such as labour exchanges and unemployment insurance. But, if Beveridge had had his way, governments would not have subsidised otherwise uneconomic jobs

[17] W. H. Beveridge, *Full Employment in a Free Society* (2nd edition, London, 1960), p. 1, see also p. 18.
[18] For Keynes' definition of full employment see, John Maynard Keynes, *The General Theory of Employment, Interest and Money* (London, 1960), pp. 15–16, 303.

because of the distorting effect that this would have on the supply of and demand for labour. Adjustments in the price mechanism, rises and falls in the price level of labour (i.e. wage adjustments), were the means of maintaining full employment.[19]

Clearly, however, this latter concept of full employment has little relevance to the conditions of seventeenth-century Europe. Large-scale unemployment and underemployment were coupled with already depressingly low earnings; a subsistence level existence which inhibited the development of a mass consumer market capable of sustaining expanding employment opportunities.[20] What might be described as the deficiency of demand in this situation could hardly be remedied by depressing wages still further. Consequently it seems inappropriate to talk about overpriced labour in these circumstances. Similarly, to describe unemployment as a product of 'market imperfections' implies the desirability of a national open market in labour, but it may be doubted not only whether such a market was desired in the seventeenth century, but also whether it was possible.[21] In order to complete a definition of full employment applicable to the seventeenth century, it will therefore be necessary to look at the nature of the unemployment problem in the early modern period. If it is accepted that the contemporary view of both full employment and unemployment were broad in character, the problem is essentially the same as explaining the generally low level of economic activity and of living standards in the period. Obviously no more than a sketch can be attempted here.

Seventeenth-century England was possessed of a predominantly

---

[19] See, for example, W. H. Beveridge, *Power and Influence: An Autobiography* (London, 1953), pp. 48, 83, 327; Beveridge, *Unemployment: A Problem of Industry* (London, 1930). In his own exercise in utopian thinking, Beveridge carried his 'market forces' analysis of labour value and opportunities a step further by arguing that, in his ideal society, people would be scarce and consequently governments would place a high humanitarian value on them. Beveridge, *Planning under Socialism and Other Addresses* (London, 1936), Chapter 22, 'My Utopia'.

[20] See Coleman, 'Labour in the English Economy'. For general descriptions of the early modern European economy see Pierre Goubert, *The Ancien Regime*, translated by Steve Cox (London, 1973); Fernand Braudel, *Capitalism and Material Life 1400–1800*, translated by Miriam Kochan (London, 1973); Carlo M. Cipolla, *Before the Industrial Revolution: European Society and Economy, 1000–1700* (London, 1976); Hermann Kellenbenz, *The Rise of the European Economy 1500–1750* (London, 1976). Specifically on England see, for example, Charles Wilson, *England's Apprenticeship 1603–1763* (London, 1965); Clarkson, *Pre-Industrial Economy in England*.

[21] Coleman, 'Labour in the English Economy'; Alan Everitt, 'The Marketing of Agricultural Produce', in Joan Thirsk (ed.), *The Agrarian History of England and Wales*, vol. IV, *1500–1640* (Cambridge, 1967), pp. 466–592.

agrarian, low technology, subsistence economy. The majority of the population, living at a comparatively low level of subsistence, generated little demand for secondary products. The basic small-scale farming unit was handicapped by low seed yields, low-level technology, and the severe limitation of the area a given labour unit was capable of farming. Typically, the small family farming unit was barely feeding itself and had little capacity for surplus. This was exacerbated by the uncertainties of weather, epidemic disease, war, migratory movements of population and so on. Throughout the century but particularly in the depressed decades 1620–50 it was possible to find many 'whose labour is not sufficient to yield them maintenance'.[22] The smallness and vulnerability of surplus, as well as the dependence of many on charity in times of dearth, all tended to depress effective demand and hence restrict employment opportunities. Market imperfections aggravated this problem. Both glut and dearth tended to be intensely localised, so that a local surplus could have little value because of plummeting local prices. This unstable situation was reflected in uncertainty about demand and employment in the secondary sector. The background to this, of course, was set by major transport problems and restrictive marketing practices.

The result of this general economic dependence on a backward agrarian sector was a low capacity for surplus above subsistence and a surplus which was itself extremely vulnerable to sharp fluctuations within the economy. The impact on manufacturing and commerce was overwhelming. Enterprises tended to remain small and investment low. Their dependence on a localised rural region for labour, supplies of materials and markets tended to make them cautious and conservative in the face of the known tendency of the fortunes of those regions to fluctuate widely. Once again, practical difficulties, in particular the uncertainty and general deficiency of effective demand, militated against any steady expansion of employment opportunities in this area.

Finally, such surplus as there was in this pre-industrial economy of the early modern period is seen as typically diverted so as to prevent a steady growth in mass consumption and thence in mass employment. For, through taxes and rents, the surpluses produced were diverted into war, the support of a leisured class and their conspicuous consumption. This is obviously a highly simplified picture, and all too often the secondary income effects of these uses of surplus are underestimated or neglected. After all, war expenditure creates a kind of mass market for both labour and for some of its products, as does conspicuous consumption. The artists

---

[22] Lawson, *An Appeal to the Parliament Concerning the Poor*, p. 2. On the related problem of underemployment see [Thomas Firmin], *Some Proposals for the Imploying of the Poor, Especially In and About the City of London* (1678), pp. 18–19. Coleman, 'Labour in the English Economy'.

and craftsmen, who supply a cultivated market, themselves distribute wealth in the form of their own consumer and investment demand.

The initial problem of the full-employment utopian in the early modern period was, therefore, to devise a system which would furnish an effective demand for the flow of goods and services which would be produced by a fully employed society. For, in many ways, the critical problem of the early modern economy can be reduced to a deficiency of effective demand. Society as a whole could not generate the level of effective demand capable of sustaining the full exploitation of all its resources.[23] Whereas successive governments and private philanthropists concerned themselves with symptoms rather than with causes, with poverty, vagrancy and wild price fluctuations, ironically the full-employment utopians recognised the superficiality and impracticality of the approach of the men of affairs. They recognised the need for a more radical approach. Consequently, their attention focussed on means of increasing total output and with it the absolute quantity of surplus available for distribution in such a way as to stimulate growth in demand and hence in employment. To this end they advocated more intensive labour usage; improved techniques, crops or technology; and the integration of the functioning of the primary and secondary sectors of the economy. In some cases they were prepared to suggest a rediversion of existing surpluses or a reallocation of existing resources. Almost all sought to improve the efficiency of the secondary sector, and, in particular, to create a more disciplined workforce.

First in time, if not in importance, of our selected full-employment utopias must come the unlikely tract by Rowland Vaughan, *Most Approved and Long Experienced Waterworks* (1610). This work has often been noted by historians of agriculture along with Vaughan's contributions on flooding meadows and land drainage.[24] Yet it is his community scheme, usually passed over in silence, with which Vaughan is most concerned. In his prefatory address to the Earl of Pembroke, he claims that his system of

---

[23] For a mid-seventeenth-century discussion of the problem of deficient demand see William Goffe, *How to Advance the Trade of the Nation, and Employ the Poor* (n.p., n.d.), reprinted in *The Harleian Miscellany* (London, 1745), vol. IV, pp. 366–70. Goffe, a regicide and thoroughgoing Cromwellian, recognised that expanding total production must be met by an expansion of effective demand. He proposed to shift demand for imports into demand for domestic goods and so support increases in domestic output and employment. See also the discussion in N. G. Pauling, 'The Employment Problem in Pre-Classical English Economic Thought', *Economic Record*, 27 (1951), pp. 52–65.

[24] Thirsk (ed.), *Agrarian History*, vol. IV, pp. 100–1, 181–2; Clarkson, *Pre-Industrial Economy in England*, p. 57; see also B. Kirkman Gray, *A History of English Philanthropy: From the Dissolution of the Monasteries to the Taking of the First Census* (London, 1905), pp. 55–7.

flooding or floating meadows is already a success. What he is appealing for in this pamphlet is support for his 'mechanical undertakings', central to his vision of an ideal society.

By his own account, Vaughan, a nephew of Elizabeth I's old servant, Blanche Parry, had spent his early years at court and had served in the wars in Ireland for three or four years. After settling in Herefordshire he had spent many years in experiments with drainage and irrigation projects. By 1601 he seems to have had an irrigation scheme working to his satisfaction, and he then began to turn his attention to the wider social problems of the area in which he lived. Rather enigmatically he wrote,

I propose to raise a golden world (for Commonwealth) in the Golden Vale of Herefordshire...being the richest yet (for want of imployment) the plentifullest place of poor in the Kingdome, yielding two or three hundred-folde, the number so increasing (Idleness having gotten the upper hand;) if Trades bee not raised; beggary will carry such reputation in my quarter of the country, as if it had the whole to halves.[25]

The potential of the Golden Vale, however, stood in marked contrast to its actuality, as Vaughan saw it. There was enormous waste of land, both in areas uncultivated and in poor cultivation. Vaughan's drainage scheme alone, he claimed, could profit the kingdom by two million pounds per annum.[26] More particularly, the overpopulation already referred to had compounded the problems of underemployment and unemployment in the Golden Vale. The rest of the problem, as Vaughan saw it, lay in the organisation, or perhaps disorganisation, of rural life. There were, in his estimation, five hundred households within a one-and-a-half mile radius of his house, 'whose greatest meanes consist in spinning Flax, Hempe, and Hurdes'. They were underemployed and lived dangerously close to subsistence, forced frequently into beggary. Their lives were dogged by financial incapacity, their time wasted by the social inconveniences attendant upon poverty. Not one in ten had five shillings to buy a bale of flax. They were forced to run to Hereford to borrow money to set up in their trade. There they would buy a bushel of corn and be obliged to waste more time waiting for it to be ground at the mill. When their flax was spun they would spend a day with the weaver waiting for it to be woven. Then followed the effort to sell a finished product: 'many journeys to markets and honest mens houses'. 'And thus many dayes were mispent in most miserable manner.' Such irrationality in the

---

[25] Rowland Vaughan, *Most Approved and Long Experienced Water-Works* (London, 1610), pp. L1–L4, E3. Vaughan should not be confused with the Welsh royalist and poet of the same name for whom there is an entry in *Dictionary of National Biography*.

[26] *Ibid.*, pp. Q2, Q4.

expenditure of time and effort resulted in an annual cycle of indigence and near criminality. In May, June and July, Vaughan's poor neighbours were to be found begging round the locality for whey, curds and butter-milk. In August, September, and October they gleaned the cornfields after the harvesters. In November, December and January they were stealing fruit and vegetables and begging once more. February, March and April, when food was scarce anyway, were for them months of long fasting and little prayer.[27]

This vicious cycle of indigence Vaughan sought to break by the setting up of a fully employed, self-sufficient community. This would provide work and security for the occupants, eliminating the waste of time, effort and resources which typified their present existence. At the same time, for those who subscribed the necessary finance, the facilities of a gentleman's club would be made available.

Sufficient land would be needed to provide grazing for three hundred cattle and three thousand sheep, as well as arable land and resources of brick and stone. A watermill would be built for the grinding of corn and next to it buildings to house the 'Mechanicals', artisans and craftsmen drawn to the community. There was to be only one member of each trade accompanied by his assistants and Vaughan set out a detailed list of them – maltmaker, chandler, baker, turner, cobbler, currier, scythe and sickle maker, nailer, cooper, mercer, cutler, hosier, fletcher, tailor, hatter and so on down to 'a noise of Musitians with the Greene-Dragon and Talbot'. Twenty broad looms, ten narrow looms and ten fustian looms and some silk looms were to be set up.[28]

Vaughan envisaged a total of two thousand workers or more. All, except carders and spinners, were to live and eat within the community. 'They shall never loose an houres time to provide for such *meanes* as the backe or belly requires...' No women, children or apprentices were to be made free of the establishment. Members were in fact to be carefully selected, 'Journey-men of the best ability of body and Arte that may be had'. Fifty habitations with shops, chambers, chimneys and cisterns were to be provided for them in the community. The 'Clarke, Recorder of the Company' was to fix rates of exchange within the community but trading with outsiders was to be free and open. Again the emphasis in all of this was on the avoidance of wasted time and effort: 'that neither *Clothiers*,

---

[27] *Ibid.*, p. E3. On underemployment and the critical concern with it in a situation of overpopulation see Coleman, 'Labour in the English Economy'; on the prob-lem of rural by-employments and underemployment see Alan Everitt, 'Farm Labourers', in Thirsk (ed.), *Agrarian History*, vol. IV, pp. 396–465. According to Kirkman Gray, Herefordshire was an area poorly endowed with charitable be-quests to assist the poor (*History of English Philanthropy*, p. 56).

[28] Vaughan, *Water-workes*, pp. K3, E3, F2.

Weavers, Pyckers of Woll, Quill-Winders, Spinners and *Carders*, shall ever loose an houres labour'.[29]

The community represented a careful attempt to balance agricultural and manufacturing activities in such a way as to maximise the utilisation of the resources of members' skill and effort. There was inherent in it an attempt at comprehensive self-sufficiency but also a leaning towards textiles. It had the atmosphere of an unspecialised factory, yet it reached out to offer a total, utopian community concerned for the soul as well as the body. A chapel and a preacher were to be maintained within the community. The preacher was to be paid £50 per annum and his curate £20. Vaughan was concerned with what he regarded as the desperate lack of preaching in his neighbourhood. 'There were not', he wrote with undoubted exaggeration, 'Two Sermons in the *Golden-Vale* this 500 yeares.' Within his ideal community the artificers were to attend morning and evening prayer daily in the chapel. An inspector bearing the ominous title 'The Visitor of the *Negligencers* Attendant' was to report misdemeanours such as non-attendance at church, swearing, drunkenness and 'swaggering'. A first offence was to be met with a warning, a second with unspecified punishment and a third with expulsion. Once again the issue was drawn back to wasted time and effort, the economic consequences of undisciplined life. '*Pleasures* that tickle our senses, make us but spoile Pretious-time, while they betray our *Reason*, that should rule rebellious affections that ought to obey. The sooner these enemies to mans dignity, are shaken off from the *Minde*, the sooner will the *Minde* advance the Body to dignity.'[30]

The fruits of this discipline and organisation were to be found in the greater security and stability as well as dignity which the members of the community were to enjoy. In addition almshouses for the aged, lame, blind and needy were to be maintained.[31] More spectacularly, however, benefits were to redound to the subscribers of the scheme, who Vaughan visualised as drawn primarily from the aristocracy and gentry.[32] For their reward, a dining-room, with elaborate supporting facilities, was to be perpetually furnished to entertain forty of them daily. Every artificer was to show deference and humility to every contributor. A sentinel was to keep watch for the arrival of any contributors, whose entry was to be greeted by an appropriate fanfare on drums or trumpets. Well furnished rooms, good fires, music and lavish meals were to await them. One

---

[29] *Ibid.*, pp. F1, 13. Vaughan appended a sketch plan of the community to his tract as well as a map of one of his irrigation schemes.

[30] *Ibid.*, pp. F4, 13, F3, K, K4.   [31] *Ibid.*, p. F4.

[32] As well as the Earl of Pembroke, Vaughan hoped to enlist the Earl of Montgomery and various 'Lords Spiritual and Temporal' as subscribers. See, *ibid.*, pp. E1, E3, g.

hundred artificers could volunteer for service at the contributors' table and earn the reversionary right to their office by doing so.[33] The contributors therefore enjoy the benefit not only of a good conscience, but also of a good gentleman's club with the deferential attention of those whom they have enabled to be fully employed.

In the end Vaughan is somewhat hazy about the means whereby agrarian and manufacturing activities are to be harmonised and stabilised at a level of full employment. His intention is, nevertheless, clear enough. Initially he was concerned with the instability of employment and the lack of by-employment amongst his poorer neighbours. It was part of his general abhorrence of waste. What impelled him to visualise a community was his concern with wasted time and effort, that is, his concern with the maximisation of benefit from those resources, with full employment. But as a vision of a full-employment utopia, Vaughan's retains its conservative elements. The gentry with their prescriptive social right to idleness cannot be integrated into a society the basic purpose of which is to eliminate idleness. This is the seed of radicalism inherent in the full-employment notion if it is seen as an absolute or universal ideal. Vaughan, in his conservatism, is concerned that his community should not make the leisured gentlemen appear completely irrelevant, particularly as he needed their financial contributions. Hence his provision of the gentleman's club and his insistence on social deference, on keeping the tradesmen in their place. Their activities were still to be carefully regulated and the consumption of their surplus product was still to fall, in part at least, to the gentlemen.[34]

Whereas Vaughan had been concerned with limited problems of rural by-employment, the rôle of the tradesman in provision of that employment, and the relationship between this and the maintenance of gentry status, the author of *A Description of the Famous Kingdome of Macaria* (1641) was concerned to throw the problem of full employment on to the broader canvas of the nation as a whole. Where Vaughan sought to resolve what he saw as an intensely local problem by means of a privately sponsored, withdrawn community, the author of *Macaria* urged the solution to a national problem by means of publicly responsible institutions.[35]

---

[33] *Ibid.*, pp. E3, K1–K2.

[34] Vaughan recalled how he had to upbraid a joiner, who claimed credit for the invention of his irrigation scheme, that 'the ambition of soldiers would not indure society with men of Mechanicall *trades*'. *Ibid.*, p. 14.

[35] I have used the copy of the first edition of *Macaria* in the British Library's Thomason collection (shelf-mark E173(28)). The work was reprinted in *The Harleian Miscellany*, vol. I, (London, 1744), pp. 564–9 and vol. IV (London, 1808), pp. 380–7, and more recently in Charles Webster (ed.), *Samuel Hartlib and the Advancement of Learning* (Cambridge, 1970), pp. 79–90.

Until very recently, *Macaria* had been thought of as the work of 'the great Intelligencer', Samuel Hartlib. It has now been argued with some force that the author may have been Gabriel Plattes, although a degree of collaboration with Hartlib is seen as probable.[36] Whatever its immediate authorship, and it seems likely, although there is no direct evidence, that Plattes did have a hand in its preparation, the tract has to be seen as a product of the circle of scientific and religious thinkers associated with Samuel Hartlib, and it will be treated as such here. The group around Hartlib certainly saw themselves as engaged in a collaborative effort. In their writings they commented on, advertised and amplified each other's work. For many of them, the group and its common objectives were more important than individual recognition. It is not surprising to find, therefore, that Hartlib's *Considerations Tending to the Happy Accomplishment of Englands Reformation in Church and State* (1647), published two years after Plattes' death, reads almost as an appendix to *Macaria*.[37]

The activities of that group and their intellectual development have been comprehensively dealt with in Charles Webster's magisterial study, *The Great Instauration: Science, Medicine and Reform 1626–1660* (London, 1975). The ramifications of these activities are immense, running across many of both the well-known and the esoteric currents of scientific, religious, educational and political thought of the early modern protestant world. *Macaria* stands, in some respects, in a central position relative to those activities. Unfortunately it is impossible, in a work of this length, to deal with it exhaustively in that context. Here it will have to be looked at, somewhat narrowly, as a full-employment utopia. The general background will be commented on only as it appears relevant to an understanding of *Macaria*'s utopianism and its full-employment themes.

Webster's achievement in the study of the Hartlib circle has been to demonstrate the comprehensiveness and integration of their collective programme and to set it all firmly in a religious context. Bringing together a revival of learning, along paths sketched principally by Bacon and Comenius, and a millenarian eschatology, the friends and collaborators of Hartlib sought a recovery of man's lost dominion over nature, the Great

---

[36] Charles Webster, 'The Authorship and Significance of *Macaria*', *Past and Present* 56 (1972), pp. 34–48.

[37] Relatively little is known about Gabriel Plattes beyond his interest in agricultural improvement, metallurgy and mining technology. His patrons included William Engelbert, inventor and drainage engineer, and Hartlib, who may have seen him as a practical complement to the theoretical contributions of Comenius (Charles Webster, *The Great Instauration: Science, Medicine, and Reform 1626–1660* (London, 1975), p. 359). Plattes died in the winter of 1644–5 (*ibid.*, p. 472). A note on the inside title page of the British Library copy of Plattes, *A Discovery of Subterraneall Treasure* (1639), reads, 'The Author of this booke died of meer want in the year 1644 in London.'

Instauration, a return to the pre-lapsarian state.[38] Comenius, in his *Via Lucis*, looked forward to 'Light, Peace, Health...and that golden age which has ever been longed for'.[39] One can perhaps speak of a vague ideal-society notion surrounding the Hartlib circle and extending to figures like Peter Chamberlen and Peter Cornelius Plockhoy, at whom we shall be looking later. In it, the various types of ideal society were seldom distinguished and disentangled. So we find visions of a pre-lapsarian arcadia, an anticipated millennium, and a utopia of human effort doing business together in the writings and thought of the group. It is arguable that the full-employment concerns of the group, which are to be seen strongly reflected in *Macaria*, represent the most utopian characteristics of the group's vision. Full employment depended necessarily on continuous human effort, organisation, management, legal and institutional arrangements. Other aspects of the programme could be visualised as arising in other ways. Scientific knowledge, for example, could be thought to arise from divine inspiration or as a reward for moral conduct, as well as resulting from sustained human effort. Plattes saw God inspiring technological innovation whenever serious overpopulation crises threatened.[40] John Beale, another associate of Hartlib, believed that personal holiness would be rewarded with knowledge.[41]

Macaria, however, was placed self-consciously within a utopian tradition. In a prefatory address (dated 25 October 1641) to the reassembling Long Parliament, the author announced his intention to set out his message 'in a Fiction, as a more mannerly way, having for my pattern Sir Thomas Moore, and Sir Francis Bacon once Lord Chancellour of England'.[42] As well as keeping a watching brief on such contemporary utopian writings as those of Chamberlen and Plockhoy and R.H.'s continuation of Bacon's *New Atlantis*, the group were naturally interested, through their connection with Comenius, in the writings of Andreae. In 1647 they published at Cambridge an English translation of Andreae's *Christianae Societatis Imago* (*A Modell of a Christian Society*) and *Christiani Amoris Dextera Porrecta* (*The Right Hand of Christian Love Offered*).[43] In

---

[38] For Bacon on this see above Chapter 5, pp. 124–5. Also Webster, *The Great Instauration*, Chapter 1. See also Katharine R. Firth, *The Apocalyptic Tradition in Reformation Britain 1530–1645* (Oxford, 1979), pp. 225–8, 242–5.

[39] Quoted in Webster, *The Great Instauration*, pp. 26–7. *Via Lucis* was circulated in manuscript from 1642 but was not published until 1668.

[40] Gabriel Plattes, *A Discovery of Infinite Treasure* (London, 1639), Preface.

[41] Webster, *The Great Instauration*, p. 328.

[42] *Macaria*, 'To the High and Honourable Court of Parliament'.

[43] See G. H. Turnbull, 'Johann Valentin Andreae's *Societas Christiana*', *Zeitschrift für Deutsche Philologie*, 73 (1954), pp. 407–32 and 74 (1955), pp. 151–85. See also Frank E. Manuel, 'Pansophia, A Seventeenth century Dream of Science', in Manuel, *Freedom from History* (New York, 1971), Chapter 5; Charles

March of the same year, John Hall wrote to Hartlib about plans to publish a translation of Andreae's *Christianopolis*. Those plans came to nothing. Similarly Hall's work on 'an Idea of a Commonwealth and Colledge in a Romance' to be called Lucenia, on which he was busy in February 1647, was thwarted when a friend borrowed the manuscript and never returned it. In some ways 1647 was a year of intense preoccupation with the utopian mode. Hartlib wrote of his recognition of Robert Burton as a utopian and in February engaged Jeremy Collier to work on a translation of Campanella's *Civitas Solis*.[44]

It is possible to distinguish three waves of ideal-society expectation in the group's activities of the 1640s and 1650s. They were points at which what Webster has called the group's 'enthusiasm for institutionalism' could spill over into utopian schemes, but also times of optimism when utopianism jostled with other forms of ideal-society aspiration, in particular the millennial.[45] The first of these came in 1640-1 and culminated in the visit of Comenius to England and, in a sense, in the publication of *Macaria* itself. However, that tract has to be seen as embodying only one aspect of the lofty ambivalences of 'Pansophism' and the 'Great Instauration' with its dreams of universal knowledge, powerful societies of Christian intellectuals, and a quasi-millenarian recovery of the pre-lapsarian state of dominion in innocence.[46] The second wave came in about 1647 and lasted until about 1653. It followed on the parliamentary victory over the royalist forces and was exhausted by the failure to wring achievement out of the Rump and the crushing of hopes with the dispersal of the Nominated Assembly. It centred on the Office of Address scheme, announced in Hartlib's *Considerations Tending to the Happy Accomplishment of Englands Reformation in Church and State* (1647), and the

---

Webster, 'Macaria: Samuel Hartlib and the Great Reformation', *Acta Comeniana*, 26 (1970), pp. 147-64; Webster, *Samuel Hartlib and the Advancement of Learning*, Introduction; A. Rupert Hall, 'Science, Technology and Utopia in the Seventeenth Century', in P. Mathias (ed.), *Science and Society 1600-1900* (Cambridge, 1972), pp. 33-53.

44 G. H. Turnbull, 'John Hall's Letters to Samuel Hartlib', *Review of English Studies*, 4:15 (1953), pp. 221-4.

45 Webster, *The Great Instauration*, p. 366.

46 This is not the place to enter into the vexed question of Rosicrucian and hermetic influences on the Hartlib circle, yet some note must be made of Frances Yates, *The Rosicrucian Enlightenment* (London, 1972), pp. 175-81. Charles Webster has dismissed these claims; see *The Great Instauration*, pp. 329-33, 516 n. 40 and 'Macaria: Samuel Hartlib and the Great Reformation', p. 149. This is a difficult and very complex area in which, despite Miss Yates' undoubted erudition and brilliance, speculation has outstripped learning. We must await more exhaustive and cautious research, but in the meantime I am inclined to side with the scepticism of Webster.

projects of economic and educational reform associated with it.[47] The Office of Address was in its full form to consist of two sections, Accommodations and Communications. The Office of Accommodations was envisaged as a clearing house for economic information and as a kind of labour exchange, while the Office of Communications was to further the advancement of learning by acting as a clearing house for matters of religion, learning and 'all Ingenuities'.[48] Millenarian hopes also attracted the group's attention at this time, as typified in Hartlib's publication of an English translation of Joseph Mede's *Clavis Apocalyptica* in early 1651.[49]

Again in the late 1650s, with the collapse of the Protectorate, members of the group turned their minds to prophetic schemes[50] and to notions of both intellectual fraternities and ideal communities. There was, however, a tiredness, scepticism and disillusion about their discussion.[51] What is of more immediate interest, in terms of the themes of this chapter, are John Beale's strictures of 1659 that the group should turn its attentions from national designs, as in *Macaria*, to small withdrawn communities, 'the Buildings of Christian Societies in Small Models', which he is not afraid to compare with the monasteries of old.

O that all the religious houses of the Christian world were reformed into true societies, or that our English monasteries could be thus restored! But it seems we men are prompt and skilful enough to pull down, and then leave it to God to plant, build, and reform, whilst we talk big of reforming laws and making whole nations Churches, and of erecting the Kingdom of Christ all over the world.

It was a shift in focus from the national scheme which *Macaria* repre-

---

[47] For the Office of Address see Webster, *The Great Instauration*, Chapter 2, section vi. As well as *Considerations Tending*, the following are relevant: Hartlib, *A FurtherDiscoverie of the Office of Publick Addresse for Accomodations* (1648); Hartlib, *Cornucopia: A Miscellanium* (1652?); William Petty, *The Advice of W.P. to Mr. Samuel Hartlib* (1648).

[48] Hartlib, *Considerations Tending*, p. 45; see also, *ibid.*, pp. 37–58.

[49] It was at Comenius' urging that the work of translation was undertaken. See Hartlib, *Clavis Apocalyptica: Or, A Propheticall KEY* (1651), p. 1. Discussion of the publication of Mede's works went on into the 1650s, see, for example, Hartlib to Worthington, 12 December 1655, James Crossley (ed.), *The Diary and Correspondence of Dr. John Worthington*, 3 vols. (Chetham Society Remains, XIII, XXXVI, CXIV, 1847–86), vol. I, p. 66.

[50] Comenius' *Lux in Tenebris* was published in 1657 and may have provided the stimulus here. See Webster, *The Great Instauration*, pp. 86–87.

[51] For the discussion on these themes see, e.g., Crossley (ed.), *Worthington Correspondence*, vol. I, pp. 153, 156, 163, 194–5, 211, 238–41, 244, 342; Robert C. Winthrop (ed.), *The Correspondence of Hartlib, Haak, Oldenburg and Others of the Founders of the Royal Society with Governor Winthrop of Connecticut 1661–1672*, Proceedings of the Massachusetts Historical Society (Boston, 1878), p. 12; *The Works of the Honourable Robert Boyle*, edited by Thomas Birch, 6 vols. (London, 1772), vol. VI, pp. 121, 132.

sented to the small, selected, full-employment community which Plockhoy was in process of envisaging at this very time.[52]

The concern with full employment and the elimination of waste was a persistent and frequently voiced preoccupation of the Hartlib circle. Gabriel Plattes claimed that by following the advice in *The Profitable Intelligencer* (1644) 'all the inhabitants of England will recover the wealth of the kingdom now so miserably wasted'. The naked would be clothed, the hungry fed, virgins married and the sick cared for. All this could be achieved by the more intensive cultivation of the land and the elimination of waste.[53] Nine years later, in his edition of a collection of writings on agricultural improvement and the avoidance of wasteful farming practices, Hartlib was writing,

and except all concur to order themselves aright both within themselves, and towards each other, we cannot be thoroughly happy or settled in any course successfully, because it is in Humane societies almost as a Watch; except all the Wheels be not only sound and well settled upon their own axle-trees; but fitly ordered to correspond with each other, there can be no Universall Motion because the disorderliness of one will disturbe many from acting in their Spheres; so it falls out in most matters of Humane Society...

But the moral of this observation was still directed at both a utopian and a full-employment conclusion.

For if Husbandry, and Trade at home and abroad be well regulated; all hands may be Employed, and where all hands are at work, there the whole strength of a Nation, doth put forward its endeavours for its own advantage, which if it can be directed to do in an Orderly way; and with a joynt Concurrence of all parts to one and the same effect; it is not to be imagined how successful such an undertaking may be...[54]

In part, of course, the Office of Accommodation was designed to help produce such a 'joynt Concurrence' and to put government in a position to direct it. Designed 'to accomplish the effect of a well-ordered Society', it would be 'the onely Proper Remedy and Help to that disorderly and confused condition of Life wherein we may lye for want of profitable Contrivements begetting sociable encounters and communications'. Magistrates would find the Office useful in many things, 'but chiefly in that of a healthful Reformation: because it may be in his hand (if we will

---

[52] See Hartlib to Worthington, 20 July 1659 in Crossley (ed.), *Worthington correspondence*, vol. I, pp. 157–8; for a reference to Plockhoy, see *ibid.*, pp. 211–12.

[53] Gabriel Plattes, *The Profitable Intelligencer* (n.p., n.d.), title page. Thomason in his usual annotation gave the date as June 1644. (British Library shelf-mark E52(I))

[54] Samuel Hartlib (ed.), *A Discovery for Division or Setting Out of Land* (1653), 'To the Reader'. In this collection Cressy Dymock complained of the waste of land in England because of poor surveying and land division.

make use of it) an Engine to reduce all into some Order which is confused; and to discover what the Chief Inconveniences of the Subjects are,
which are to be remedied, which Two Things are the Pillars of an Outward Reformation'.[55]

Naturally, full-employment attitudes came out clearly in the group's
attitude to the poor. What was needed was 'a godly and politick government; that the godly and laborious poore may be countenanced and
cherished, and the idle, and wicked poore supprest'.[56] The distinction
between the honest and the vicious poor was one constantly maintained.
The former should be provided with work, the latter driven to it, even if
hunger had to be the whip.[57] Poor children should also be set to work
before habits of idleness set in and as a resource to be exploited, like any
other, for national benefit. 'By the work and labor of the children, every
Parish is like to be eased, and plenty of all things flow in upon the
Nation...'[58]

John Dury approached education and the school day in a similar frame
of mind: 'no time of the day is to be lost without some teaching exercise',
and nothing was to be taught but what was useful to society.[59] William
Petty's proposals for 'literary workhouses', providing literacy and training
for work, are well known.[60] These attitudes were not brought on by the
deepening of the economic depression of the 1640s nor by the 'subsistence
crises' of the last years of the decade, but arose with a renewed interest in
economic planning evident at the end of the 1630s. As Charles Webster

[55] Hartlib, *Considerations Tending*, pp. 37, 40, 44–5. The Office of Address was
to some extent inspired by the Bureau d'Adresse which Théophraste Renaudot
had been running in Paris since 1631. John Pell had suggested a mathematical
intelligence office in the 1630s (Webster, *The Great Instauration*, p. 354). In
1657 the foundation of an Office of Public Advice with eight branches in London was announced. Two weekly information sheets attempting to perform a
similar function appeared in the streets of London, also in 1657. See Keith
Thomas, *Religion and the Decline of Magic* (London, 1971), p. 651. However,
in 1660 Thomas Lawson was still calling for the setting up in the capital of
'a Poor Mans Office' to act as a labour exchange. Lawson, *An Appeal to the
Parliament Concerning the Poor*, pp. 2–3.
[56] Samuel Hartlib, 'The Parliament Reformation' (1646) in Webster (ed.),
Samuel Hartlib and the Advancement of Learning, p. 122. On their general
attitude to employing the poor see Webster, *The Great Instauration*, Chapter 5,
section v. For Hartlib's connection with the London Corporation of the Poor see
Pearl, 'Puritans and Poor Relief', pp. 217–22.
[57] See, for example, Hartlib, *Londons Charity Inlarged*, pp. 2, 19.
[58] Samuel Hartlib, *Londons Charity, Stilling the Poore Orphans Cry* (1649), p. 5.
In the same tract Hartlib bemoans the waste of food in London, 'the abundance
of salt beef broth, and pottage thrown down the sinks'.
[59] John Dury, 'The Reformed School' (1650) in Webster (ed.), *Samuel Hartlib
and the Advancement of Learning*, p. 148.
[60] Webster, *The Great Instauration*, pp. 210–11.

has observed, 'Reformers wished to promote an ordered economy, which would ensure efficiency and guarantee adequate rewards, but prevent degeneration into uncontrolled monopolies.'[61]

Whatever his involvement with the writing of *Macaria*, Gabriel Plattes illustrates these attitudes very well. Despising waste, he sought to follow the example of Christ who, feeding the five thousand, preserved everything from loss to the benefit of great numbers.[62] Plattes deplored the excesses of 'our hot *Apocalypse* men', 'sure in their own conceit, that they have such divine revelations, that they cannot possibly be deceived'. The majority of people wanted peace, and the application of sound, experimental knowledge could help them to realise its benefits. The hive of bees was a model of a well ordered commonwealth, in two points excelling men: industry and commitment to the general good. In *A Discovery of Infinite Treasure*, he recalled:

And one of the principall Motives which mooved me to put out this Booke was a greife of mind to see some indifferent well disposed persons, to lye and shift even as a thiefe that stealeth a Sheepe for very hunger: with whom I have conferred about it, and found that they could get no convenient implyment, at least answerable to their nature and education.

And yet there was plenty to be done if only men could be set to work and Plattes' proposed improvements in agriculture, mining and metallurgy be implemented to sustain demand for the product of their efforts. He was against labour-saving devices, because there was already a surplus of labour, but when his suggestions had been adopted there would be a shortage of labour and labour-saving devices could be encouraged. The whole community would benefit from fully employed labour, efficiently exploited natural resources and the elimination of waste: 'there is nothing wanting but willing mindes to make this Countrey the Paradise of the World'.[63]

The choice of the name 'Macaria' was a gesture of identification with an early modern utopian tradition and the use of the term by such authors as Thomas More in his *Utopia*, and Kaspar Stüblin in his *De Eudae-monensium republica*. But 'Macaria' was also a kind of code word used by Hartlib and his circle in reference to their dreams of social and intellectual reform, and it persistently cropped up in Hartlib's correspondence over a period of twenty years.[64] Like many other works in the utopian literary genre, *Macaria* took the form of a dialogue, this time between a traveller and a scholar. The dialogue was addressed to Parliament in the

[61] *Ibid.*, pp. 370, 355–60.
[62] Plattes, *A Discovery of Subterraneall Treasure*, dedicatory epistle.
[63] Plattes, *A Discovery of Infinite Treasure*, Preface, pp. 75–6.
[64] H. Dircks, *A Biographical Memoir of Samuel Hartlib* (London, 1865), pp. 44–5.

confidence 'that this Honourable Court will lay the Corner Stone of the worlds happinesse before the final recesse thereof'. In that intention Parliament had encountered some hindrances and the traveller therefore offered his account of Macaria to assist them in making 'a good reformation'.[65]

The description of Macaria begins with an outline of the attributes of that kingdom which are then treated in turn and in detail: 'the King and Governours doe live in great honour and riches, and the people doe live in great plenty, prosperitie, health, peace, and happinesse, and have not halfe so much trouble as they have in these European Countreyes'.[66] Kings are rich in Macaria because of the careful management of their estates. They are honoured because they seldom tax the people, they fight few wars and are generally careful of the welfare of their people. They rule well and hence their subjects are willing to keep the royal coffers full. The key to sound government is seen to lie in conciliar consultation and firm control of ministers and state officials. Central to this is a Great Council similar to the Parliament of England, which sits briefly every year but confines itself to hearing complaints against 'Ministers of State, Judges and Officers', punishing them if necessary. Its legislative functioning is not made clear.[67]

Legislation is delegated, if that is the correct term, to five 'under Councels', one each for husbandry, fishing, trade by land, trade by sea and new plantations or colonies. It is significant that they are all concerned with economic activities. How they are chosen we are not told. Like the Great Council they sit briefly every year, hearing complaints, punishing malefactors, rewarding benefactors and making new laws 'not repugnant to the lawes of the Great Councel'.[68] While it is not entirely clear, it appears that legislative power has been substantially vested in under councils, concerned largely with economic affairs, and that Parliament, or the Great Council, has become a body primarily devoted to judicial review and administrative supervision. The under councils were chiefly responsible for the plenty and prosperity of Macaria and some examples of their legislation were given to illustrate this achievement. The under council for husbandry, for example, had passed laws to stimulate the maximum exploitation of agricultural resources: 'the twentieth part of every mans

---

[65] *Macaria*, 'To the High and Honourable Court of Parliament', pp. 2–3.
[66] *Ibid.*, p. 2.   [67] *Ibid.*, pp. 3, 8–9.
[68] *Ibid.*, p. 3. Cf. Francis Bacon on government by commission in a memorandum of January 1620 to King James I, see James Spedding, *The Letters and the life of Francis Bacon*, 7 vols. (London, 1874), vol. VII, pp. 70–2. In his manuscript notes William Petty outlined a scheme for government by the king and four councils. After liberty of religion their principal concerns were to be economic development. *The Petty Papers: Some Unpublished Writings of Sir William Petty*, edited from the Bowood Papers by the Marquis of Lansdowne, 2 vols. (London, 1927), vol. I, pp. 5–7.

goods that dieth' was to be employed improving lands, roads and bridges, 'by which meanes the whole kingdome is become like to a fruitful Garden'.

if any man holdeth more land than he is able to improve to the utmost he shall be admonished, first, of the great hinderance which it doth to the commonwealth. Secondly, of the prejudice to himselfe; and if he do not amend his Husbandry within a yeares space, there is a penalty set upon him, which is yeerely doubled, till his lands be forfeited, and he banished out of the Kingdome, as an enemy to the commonwealth.

The rights of private property and citizenship do not here extend to a freedom to waste.[69]

The operation of the other under councils in pursuit of full employment was dealt with even more sketchily than this. For fishing, laws were established 'whereby immense riches are yeerly drawne out of the Ocean'. The under council for 'Trade by Land' showed awareness of the problem of integrating primary and secondary sectors of the economy, by trying to adjust the numbers employed in manufacturing and hence the supply of manufactured goods. Laws were passed by them 'so that there are not too many Tradesmen, nor too few, by enjoyning longer or shorter times of Apprenticeships'. Least satisfactory of all, the under council for 'Trade by Sea' simply provided that 'all Traffick is lawfull which may enrich the kingdom'. Lastly the under council for 'New Plantations' pursued a forward policy of colonial development, sending a number of colonists out every year and providing public support for them until they were able to 'subsist by their own endevours'. Care was taken to relate the numbers going to the overall population.[70]

The goal in all this, a high level of economic activity or full employment, is clear enough, even though the means of its realisation may be somewhat obscure. Similarly the peace attributed to Macaria is clear but its maintenance remains shrouded in generality. The Macarians are militarily strong and seize the territory of any aggressive prince. In other words anticipatory aggression, the exercise of might, is the path of peace. A rather more careful explanation is offered of the health of Macaria: 'they have an House, or College of Experience, where they deliver out,

---

[69] *Macaria*, p. 4. Robert Burton had in some ways anticipated *Macaria's* willingness to menace private property rights in the name of economic efficiency. See above Chapter 5 and *Anatomy of Melancholy*, vol. 1, pp. 100–1. For other examples of contemporary criticism of the waste of deer parks and chases see Brian Manning, *The English People and the English Revolution* (London, 1976), p. 188.

[70] *Macaria*, pp. 4–5. See also Mildred Campbell, ' "Of People Either Too Few or Too Many": The Conflict of Opinion on Population and its Relation to Emigration', in W. A. Aiken and B. D. Henning (eds.), *Conflict in Stuart England* (London, 1960), pp. 171–201.

yearly such medicines as they find out by Experience; and such as shall be able to demonstrate any Experiment, for the Health or *Wealth* of Men, are honourably rewarded at the publick charge, by which their skill in Husbandry, Physick, and Surgery is most excellent'.[71] The knowledge so gained is dispersed and made effectual by having the parson in every parish double as a physician, caring for both body and soul. This was not an uncommon suggestion amongst the members of the Hartlib circle but it is interesting to see the scholar in *Macaria* approving the suggestion because it would enable the clergy to govern the people. This point brings the dialogue on to the discussion of religion in Macaria and in particular to the absence of religious friction. The non-denominational Christianity of the Macarians is obviously linked to the ecumenical concerns of Hartlib and his friend John Dury.[72] 'Their Religion consists not in taking notice of severall opinions and sects, but is made up of infallible tenets, which may be proved by invincible arguments.' Since there is no diversity of religious opinion it is thought easier to ensure that the clergy are men of learning. The penalty for public heresy is death but men are allowed to dispute new opinion privately before the Great Council. Their decision as to its truth or falsity has to be accepted as final. Like Hobbes, the Macarians believed that for the sake of social stability it was necessary to accept the magistrate's arbitration in matters of opinion.[73]

Key figures in the operation of this managed and well-disciplined economy are the public officials. It is their assiduous and public-spirited administration which keeps the whole enterprise operating to maximum advantage. They resemble the Christian magistrate, depicted elsewhere by Hartlib, whose 'Care and Duty should be not onely to rule Men, so as he doth finde them, but he should looke upon their wayes, to order them, so as they should be, to become partakers of that Happinesse which this life doth afford, whereunto he is bound to give them addresse'.[74] Bribery and corruption is unknown amongst the officials of Macaria, who are subject to rigorous scrutiny by both the Grand Council and the under councils. In

[71] *Macaria*, p. 5. The parallel with Salomon's house in Bacon's *New Atlantis* is obvious. For the Hartlib circle's general interest in medicine see Webster, *The Great Instauration*, Chapter 4. Note also Webster's point that seen within the context of a pre-industrial, subsistence society, agriculture and medicine appear as vital aspects of scientific activity. *Ibid.*, p. 505.

[72] *Macaria*, pp. 6–7; Samuel Hartlib, *A Briefe Relation of That Which Hath Been Lately Attempted to Procure Ecclesiasticall PEACE amongst PROTESTANTS* (1641); Hartlib, *A Faithfull and Seasonable Advice* (1643); Hartlib, *The Necessity of Some Nearer Conjunction and Correspondency Amongst Evangellicall Protestants* (1644).

[73] *Macaria*, p. 7. Thomas Hobbes, *Leviathan*, edited by C. B. MacPherson (London, 1968), pp. 365–6.

[74] Hartlib, *Considerations Tending*, p. 21.

addition they receive large incomes 'for that, in case they doe not their dutie, in looking to the kingdomes safety, for conscience sake, yet they may doe it for feare of loosing their own Estates'. Nevertheless, the officials are left as shadowy figures. We know nothing of their recruitment nor of their precise functions. It is in general difficult to see *Macaria*, in this as other respects, as a comprehensive programme of reform.[75]

Predictably the dialogue ends with the scholar announcing his approval of the Macarian system of government. A millenarian objection that such a reformation cannot come before the day of judgement is brusquely put aside: the great need is seen as that of persuading others but confidence is expressed that with the aid of the printing press this would be soon accomplished. 'I doubt not but we shall obtaine our desires, to make England to bee like to *Macaria*...and though our neighbour Countreys are pleased to call the English a dull Nation, yet the major part are sensible of their owne good, and the good of their posterity, and those will sway the rest; so wee and our posterity shall bee all happie...'[76]

The outstanding aspect of *Macaria* from the point of view of full employment is the author's determination to put responsibility firmly in the hands of the state and its agencies. Unlike many other utopias concerned with economic integration and efficiency, in *Macaria* planning is not vested in a private corporation or withdrawn community, but in national, public institutions. Almost all of the Hartlib circle's schemes were in fact addressed to the state, rather than, as in the case of Rowland Vaughan, to private patrons. Offices of Address, educational reforms, poor relief, improvements of all kinds were seen as the responsibility of central government or Parliament. Hartlib himself expressed very marked distrust of private enterprise, preferring public control, for the adoption and implementation of improvements. In reference to the management of agricultural resources, he wrote, 'And I could wish, that God would put it in the heart of those Worthies that manage the Publique Trust, that by their Influence and Arthority, these and such like meanes of Industry, may not be left wholly to the uncertaine, disorderly, and lazy undertakings of private men...' The profit motive itself could not be relied upon: 'In respect to the known untowardness of the Major part of the People; who being wonderfully wedded to old customes, are not easily won to any new course, though never so much to their own profit...' Accordingly, he

---

[75] *Macaria*, pp. 8–9. On the relationship between salaries and corruption amongst seventeenth-century officials see G. E. Aylmer, *The King's Servants: The Civil Service of Charles I, 1625–1642* (London, 1961); Aylmer, *The State's Servants: The Civil Service of the English Republic, 1649–1660* (London, 1973). On *Macaria* as a comprehensive programme of reform see Webster, 'Authorship and Significance', p. 36.

[76] *Macaria*, pp. 10–15.

urged public supervision of husbandry and woods, both for preservation and increase.[77]

Nevertheless, while showing this faith in public authority, *Macaria* has to be seen as a curiously limited vision in terms of the enormous aspirations of Hartlib and his associates. Even its status as a utopia is only tenuously held.[78] Its vagueness and imprecision enable it to evade many of the more obvious social problems inherent in the pursuit of a fully employed society. Chief amongst these, because of its political importance, must be the implications of such a goal for the leisured upper classes. While their right to property, or at least their freedom not to exploit their parks and chases, is called into question, what of their right to leisure?

Macaria remains in substance little more than a call for administrative and legislative reorganisation and redirection, as a means of achieving radical economic expansion. But the happiness, peace and prosperity of this ideal society are only sketchily conceived. In respect to the composition, organisation and effectiveness of the crucial under councils of state, the author is alarmingly vague. There is a naivety about the whole work which makes it politically unsatisfying even in the context of other ideal-society schemes. The Hartlib group may have foisted the utopian mode upon Plattes, but, if he indeed wrote *Macaria*, they did not equip him with the political skill and insights of his forbears in that tradition. *Macaria* remains an essay in aspirations rather than a comprehensive programme of social and economic reform or a contribution to political and social ideas. Yet those aspirations are of some significance in the present context. The idea of a society whose resources were fully managed and exploited was given dramatic, if imprecise, expression within the utopian literary tradition. Moreover, Macaria was conceived as a national, state-run economy. After its failure to produce any reaction from Parliament in the 1640s, others in pursuit of the full-employment ideal moved away from the state to smaller and more voluntaristic associations and institutions.

One who did not make this move, however, was that rather extraordinary figure Dr Peter Chamberlen, who seems to have hovered on the fringe of the Hartlib group. Chamberlen's *The Poore Mans Advocate* (1649) is perhaps not strictly a utopia. It neither proposes a perfected society nor does its projected society offer a total community. Rather, it should be seen

---

[77] Samuel Hartlib (ed.), *Samuel Hartlib His Legacie* (1651), 'To the Reader'.
[78] Note Webster's uncertainty here. On the same page he describes *Macaria* as both a 'utopian sketch' and a 'reform tract'. Webster, of course, uses the term 'utopia' consistently in the broad sense of ideal society. Webster, *The Great Instauration*, p. 259.

as a scheme for the employment of large numbers of the poor, made possible by the resources available for redistribution in the aftermath of civil war and revolution, and to the relief of the taxpaying classes. Nevertheless, it is worth looking at because in it a number of themes are drawn together. On the one hand, the tract follows the Hartlib circle's approach to full employment as a problem to be solved on a national level by public institutions. On the other hand, Chamberlen's solution comes surprisingly close to that of Winstanley's, with its emphasis on parallel societies and the utilisation, if not of what Winstanley called 'commonwealth's land', then of something very close to it. Finally, Chamberlen crystallises yet another aspect of the problem of rich and poor as it confronts those committed to the realisation of full employment.

Peter Chamberlen was born in London in 1601, son of another Peter, who was a member of the Barber Surgeons' Company, and great-grandson of William Chamberlen, a French protestant who took refuge in England in Elizabeth I's reign.[79] The family had a virtual monopoly of the use of the short forceps which gave them a considerable and influential practice in midwifery. Both Peter's father and uncle practised as barber surgeons, running into considerable opposition from the Royal College of Physicians. Peter himself became a member of the Royal College but friction did not thereby cease, as we shall see.[80]

Peter was baptised at the French church in Threadneedle Street and educated at the Merchant Taylors School. At the age of fourteen he entered Emmanuel College, Cambridge, where by his own account he 'piddled in Chyrurgery'.[81] From there he went on to Heidelberg and Padua where, still only eighteen years old, he received a doctorate in medicine in 1619.[82]

[79] There is an inadequate entry on Peter Chamberlen in *Dictionary of National Biography* as well as entries on several other members of the family. Both Peter's father and his uncle were also called Peter, a frequent source of confusion. For Peter's own account of his background and early life see Peter Chamberlen, *A Voice in Rhama: or, The Crie of Women and Children* (London, 1647), p. 22.

[80] On the background of the family and for much biographical information see J. H. Aveling, *The Chamberlens and the Midwifery Forceps* (London, 1882). On the conservatism of the Royal College of Physicians and the problems of medical licensing and control in the period see Sir George Clark, *A History of the Royal College of Physicians of London*, 2 vols. (Oxford, 1964–6); R. S. Roberts, 'The Personnel and Practice of Medicine in Tudor and Stuart England', *Medical History*, 6:4 (1962), pp. 363–82 and 8:3 (1964), pp. 217–34; Webster, *The Great Instauration*, Chapter 4, sections 2 and 3.

[81] Chamberlen, *Voice in Rhama*, p. a2. Emmanuel may have been something of a puritan centre; see Webster, *The Great Instauration*, p. 37.

[82] For the superiority and economy of a continental medical education in the seventeenth century see Phyllis Allen, 'Medical Education in Seventeenth Century England', *Journal of the History of Medicine*, 1:1 (1946), pp. 115–43.

He was incorporated in that degree at Oxford in 1620 and a year later in Cambridge. His admission to the Royal College of Physicians and then two years later, in 1628, his election as a Fellow of the College, marked not only his entry to a medical élite but also a substantial rise in social status and image. Membership of the College was severely limited; the number of fellowships even more restricted. Election carried with it not only legal privileges and gentle status of a relatively high standard, but also an aura of cultivated intellect and literary endeavour ranging far beyond the confines of medicine.[83] From the beginning, the Royal College found Chamberlen difficult to deal with and royal patronage of the Chamberlens' midwifery practice can only have compounded the difficulty. On his election as a Fellow, he was admonished concerning his style of dress.[84] From 1634 onwards he was engaged in a project to gain royal authority for an incorporation of midwives. This had already been suggested by his father and uncle in 1616 and there was clearly a case for improving the training and licensing of midwives. The Royal College, while accepting the need for improved training, opposed the idea of an incorporation.[85] About this time, and certainly before 1643, Chamberlen published a textbook on midwifery which was reprinted in various editions throughout the seventeenth century.[86]

In 1648 he engaged in another project which brought him into even more heated conflict with the College of which he was a Fellow. This time he was petitioning Parliament for support for the erection of public baths as a means of combating infection and improving public health generally. The Royal College was inflexibly opposed to the scheme and a bitter debate ensued in which the scheme was associated with immorality, profiteering and insanity. At least on this occasion Chamberlen had the satisfaction of some official support. In early 1649 the House of Lords, before its own demise, sent an ordinance on public baths down to the

[83] James L. Axtell, 'Education and Status in Stuart England: The London Physician,' *History of Education Quarterly*, 10:2 (1970), pp. 141–59; Clark, *Royal College of Physicians*, vol. 1, pp. 14–17.

[84] William Munk, *The Roll of the Royal College of Physicians of London*, 2 vols. (2nd edition, London, 1878), vol. 1, p. 194.

[85] Thomas R. Forbes, 'The Regulation of English Midwives in the Sixteenth and Seventeenth Centuries', *Medical History*, 8:3 (1964), pp. 235–44; Munk, *Roll of the Royal College*, vol. 1, p. 195; Clark, *Royal College of Physicians*, vol. 1, pp. 253–4, 262.

[86] Like other well-used textbooks, the work is now comparatively rare. I have used the copy of the 1665 edition in the Hunterian Museum, Glasgow. Peter Chamberlen, *Dr. Chamberlain's Midwifes Practice* (London, 1665). Donald Wing records an 'enlarged' edition of 1643 which suggests that the original edition must have been published before that date. Donald Wing, *A Gallery of Ghosts: Books Published between 1641–1700 Not Found in the Short-Title Catalogue*, Modern Language Association of America (New York, 1967), p. 44.

Commons, but there is no record of further proceedings with it there.[87] Like many other schemes, it was swallowed up in the Rump's backward shuffle from revolution following the establishment of the English republic. Perhaps, nevertheless, the progress achieved with this scheme encouraged Chamberlen to put forward the more ambitious vision of *The Poore Mans Advocate* in the same year.

Chamberlen had become a Baptist in 1648 and this involved him in three controversies in the 1650s: in 1650 on lay preaching, in 1654 on ordination and in both 1650 and 1658 on baptism.[88] In the crisis of 1659 he wrote three pamphlets arguing for a return to Christian magistracy and recalling the proposals of *The Poore Mans Advocate*.[89] On 23 November of the same year he was deprived of his fellowship by the vote of his colleagues, according to Munk for 'repeated acts of contumacy' and according to Sir George Clark under the absenteeism clause of the rules of fellowship.[90] Despite this, on the restoration of Charles II he was appointed Physician-in-Ordinary to the king. He did not, however, abandon his concern for projects of various kinds.

In 1662 he published a remarkable and, in places, powerful plea for liberty of conscience, addressed to the Lords and Commons at the very

---

[87] For the controversy over public baths see Peter Chamberlen, *A Paper Delivered ... Together with an Answer Thereunto* (1648); Chamberlen, *A Vindication of Publick Artificiall Baths & Bath-Stoves* (1648); Chamberlen, *To the Honourable House of Commons assembled in Parliament* (1649); Philalethes [George Starkey], *An Answer to Doctor Chamberlanes Scandalous and Faslse Papers* (1650). It is unfortunate that so great an authority as Sir George Clark should have attributed insanity to Chamberlen on the basis of his advocacy of this scheme (see Clark, *Royal College of Physicians*, vol. 1, p. 282 n. 4). This is to accept the hostile and vituperative attacks of George Starkey [Philalethes] at face value. Through Clark and others the charge of insanity or eccentricity against Chamberlen has become fairly widely accepted. It has no foundation of fact nor of implication in Chamberlen's later writings, where he frequently appears as mild, moderate and rational by contrast with the hysteria of some of his opponents. On the contemporary interest in balneotherapy see Webster, *The Great Instauration*, pp. 298–9.

[88] See, Thomas Bakewell, *The Dippers Plunged in A Sea of Absurdities* (1650); Chamberlen, *Master Bakewell's Sea of Absurdities... Driven Back* (1650); Chamberlen, *A Letter to Mr. Braine* (1650); Thomas Bakewell, *Doctor Chamberlain Visited with a Bunch of His Own Grapes* (1650); Chamberlen (ed.), *The Disputes Between Mr. Cranford and Dr. Chamberlen* (1652); John Graunt, *The Shipwrack of All False Churches* (1652); Chamberlen (ed.), *A Discourse Between Cap. Kiffin, and Dr. Chamberlain, About Imposition of Hands* (1654); Chamberlen, *To My Beloved Friends and Neighbours of the Black-Fryers* (1658?); for his conversion to Baptism see Munk, *Roll of the Royal College*, vol. 1, p. 195.

[89] *The Declaration and Proclamation of the Army of God* (1659); *A Scourge for a Denn of Thieves* (1659); *Legislative Power in Problemes* (1659).

[90] Munk, *Roll of the Royal College*, vol. 1, p. 194; Clark, *Royal College of Physicians*, vol. 1, p. 288.

time that they were preparing the Act of Uniformity. A broadsheet published by him in the same year sought to vindicate his various activities and set out the broad economic benefits which would have accrued to the nation had his proposals been adopted.[91] He became absorbed in the mid 1660s with a project for propelling both sea and land vehicles by sail in a straight line whatever the wind direction. In 1669 Chamberlen managed to get a bill, to grant him the patent for such devices, read in the House of Commons, though it seems to have died at the committee stages.[92] A few years later he was involved with a scheme for phonetic writing, an idea of some interest to Baconians and philosophers of the seventeenth century. In 1672 he received a royal grant of exclusive benefit from his inventions in phonetic writing for fourteen years.[93]

The last great cause to which he devoted himself was that of Christian unity and the conversion of the Jews in preparation for the apocalypse. By 1682 he seems to have despaired of the Roman Catholic Church which now became identified with the 'Triple-Crowned-Little-Horn', and his warnings against it can be seen as a rather individual contribution to the Exclusion controversy.[94] He died in December 1683 and his will recalled the words of Hythlodaeus early in Book 1 of More's *Utopia*. Chamberlen left all to his wife on the grounds 'that I have already advanced all my children in the world...and given them considerable porcons of my estate'.[95]

In his call for full employment, the aspect of underemployment that Chamberlen concentrated on was the unemployment or underemployment of labour. His hope as recorded in *The Declaration and Proclamation of the Army of God* was 'To indeavour all the Poor may be imployed and maintained, without injury to any mans Propriety'.[96] But how was this to be done? The answer appeared to be that England in 1649, faced by one of the worst years economically of the century, was also presented by the revolution with one of its greatest opportunities. The immediate priority was to 'keep whol the publique stock'.[97] This, as envisaged by

[91] Chamberlen, *A Speech Visibly Spoken* (1662); Chamberlen, *The Sober Man's Vindication* (1662).

[92] Aveling, *The Chamberlens*, pp. 90–101; *Commons Journals*, vol. IX, pp. 103, 108; *Historical Manuscripts Commission Reports*, 78 Hastings II, p. 315. For Chamberlen's earlier interest in the idea see Hartlib to Boyle, 19 April 1659, Birch (ed.), *The Works of Robert Boyle*, vol. VI, p. 121.

[93] Aveling, *The Chamberlens*, p. 101.

[94] *Ibid.*, pp. 113–20; Chamberlen, *England's Choice* (1682); Chamberlen, *The Sons of the East* (1682).

[95] Aveling, *The Chamberlens*, pp. 121–2.

[96] Chamberlen, *Declaration and Proclamation of the Army of God*, pp. 4–5.

[97] Chamberlen, *The Poore Mans Advocate* (1649), p. a2. I have used the copy in the John Rylands Library, Manchester (shelf-mark R94716).

Chamberlen, consisted of all property and income which had fallen to the commonwealth as a result of civil wars and revolutions to come as well as those completed. It included royal and ecclesiastical property, made available by the abolition of monarchy and episcopacy, the remains due on public accounts, commons and wasteland, 'drowned lands', unworked mines (subject to the owners' prior agreement), all parish collections and abused charities, and the revenue from three years of tithes after which the tithe system would be abolished. In addition the public stock was to retain a property in all improvements made by working these resources.[98] In respect to royal and ecclesiastical lands, commons and wasteland, Chamberlen's 'publique stock' has close affinities with Winstanley's 'Commonwealths land'. It does, of course, include more types of resource and sources of income but there is the same insistence on not invading legitimate private property and the same belief that these 'public' resources can be used to provide employment and support for the propertyless and unemployed. They differ markedly, however, over the use of the fruits of that employment.

'...the only riches of a Common-wealth is, by employing the poore, and making such industrious as are not'. But the benefit to the nation from the utilisation of the public stock, the elimination of waste and the employment of the unemployed is to accrue particularly to the taxpaying classes in the form of the relief of taxation and the paying off of public debt. Indeed the problem of taxation is a major theme of Chamberlen's argument. The tract opens with a letter to the House of Commons in which Chamberlen analyses the influence of fiscal problems in recent English history. 'None more fond of a King then the English, yet they departed from him to ease their purses and their consciences.' The struggle against financial tyranny had escalated, however, into a nightmare in which public debts rose faster than taxes: 'shall not you and we all by tyed up at last in a Usurers bag'. Now, in 1649, the challenge of heavy debt, an army in arrears, and a crushing level of taxation was clear. At the same time the deepening problem of poverty had taken on menacing proportions. 'Provide for the poor, and they will provide for you. Destroy the poor and they will destroy you. And if you provide not for the poor, they will provide for themselves.'[99]

To Chamberlen, at least, the answer to the challenge was clear, even if he did not make it equally clear to his readers. The unemployed poor should be set to work on the public or 'Joint Stock'. If two hundred thousand were engaged in this way, he calculated, and if they only produced twenty pounds each in the first year, that would give an annual product worth four million pounds from the enterprise. What wonders

---

[98] *Ibid.*, pp. 3–4.   [99] *Ibid.*, pp. 14, 4, title page, a2, 19, 1–3.

could not such a device perform? The 'Joint Stock' and those working on
it could, as well as feeding and supporting themselves at no public charge,
undertake to provision the army; to join it when occasion required; to pay
off the army's arrears within five years; to receive all idle poor, set them
to work, feed and clothe them; to care for the sick; to place poor children
in schools; to take off all taxes within a year except customs which were
to be used to encourage domestic manufacturers and discourage the
export of raw materials; to pay all public debt within ten years at six per
cent interest, and the late king's debts within twenty years; to erect a
'public banke' and to maintain an academy; and, finally, to maintain a
fleet for the defence and preservation of the nation.[100]

Like the Hartlib group, Chamberlen believed that schemes of this kind
should be run on a national level by public officials. He proposed that
general administration should be in the hands of a well-qualified, annually
elected 'Trustee or Aumner'. Such work was better in the hands of one
man, as, according to Chamberlen, the failure of commissions in the past
testified. Beneath him would be subtrustees or governors, also elected, one
for each house or section of the scheme. The poor, apparently, were to be
allowed to decide for themselves whether they would work the land in
common, as in Winstanley's scheme, or at rent. Full records were to be
kept and accounts were to be submitted every quarter by the Trustee
General.[101]

For Chamberlen this scheme could become fused with a millenarian
vision of Christ's coming rule on earth.

The Saints shall Reign on EARTH. God's will shall be done on EARTH. No more
shall Apolluon Abaddon, Scorpionize Men. No more shall Beasts arise out of
the Sea or Earth to Stygmatize men. Then shall the Oppressor cease, and no
more complaining be heard in the streets. Taxes should be no more, And Trade
and industry should abound more than in our Neighbours blessed Bee-hive.
The poor should have bread and the Army no more in Arrears, Prison doors
should be open, and Debtors satisfied without Arrests. The youth and flower
of our Nation instead of being infected with the Crabbed nonsensical study of
the Lawes, or drawing streight lines by crooked Rules, raise up their noble
Fancy to the Wisdom of Arts and Arms, the Depths of Nature and knowledge
of the whole world, to the Honour of God and themselves, and not imbesling
but enriching of their Estates and Posterity; then Peace and safety, plenty and
prosperity should overflow the land.[102]

His persistence[103] with the ideas set out in *The Poor Mans Advocate* never
resulted in utopia, because Chamberlen was neither prepared to integrate

---

[100] *Ibid.*, pp. a2, 23–4.   [101] *Ibid.*, pp. 35–45.
[102] Chamberlen, *Legislative Power in Problems*, p. 8. The 'Neighbours Blessed Bee-
hive' refers to Holland. Cf. *ibid.*, p. 4.
[103] He was still pressing them in 1662. See, *The Sober Man's Vindication*.

the whole community around the focus of full employment, nor form a parallel but separate society for the poor working the 'Joint Stock', as, in a sense, Winstanley did.

Nevertheless, he kept alive the Hartlib circle's view of full employment as a national, public responsibility. Moreover, he illustrates once more the difficulty for seventeenth-century full-employment theorists of the propertied leisure class. Like Winstanley, he attempted to reassure them by offering to solve the problems of poverty and unemployment without touching their property. But he went far beyond Winstanley in offering them inducements based on the use of the profits of employing the poor to reduce taxation.[104] For the rich, Chamberlen promised the end of fears that the poor would rise against them, reduction of taxation, and both without threat to their leisure or private property. For the poor came the opportunity to work and to sustain themselves at a limited level of material comfort, in the knowledge that such surplus as they produced would be used for national purposes and to the relief of the rich.

Ten years later a Dutch Mennonite writing in English and addressing himself to an English situation, as he saw it, escaped the problem of the rich and leisured by the simple expedient of withdrawing his full-employment community from society at large. In *A Way Propounded to Make the Poor in these and other Nations happy* (1659), Peter Cornelius Plockhoy proposed the setting up of integrated economic communities based on the model of the regulated, rather than joint-stock company.[105]

[104] There was nothing new in the idea of employing the poor *en masse* for profit although it has been argued that, with the exception of the London Corporation for the Poor (1647–9), 1640–60 was a barren period as far as schemes for the provision of work are concerned. Webb, *English Poor Law History, Part I*, pp. 101–2; W. K. Jordan, *The Charities of Rural England 1480–1660* (London, 1961), p. 285; William Letwin, *The Origins of Scientific Economics: English Economic Thought 1660–1760* (London, 1963), pp. 59–60; E. Lipson, *The Economic History of England*, 3 vols. (London, 1947), vol. III, pp. 294–318; Paul Slack, 'Poverty and Politics in Salisbury 1597–1666', in Clark and Slack (eds.), *Crisis and Order in English Towns*, pp. 164–203. On the Corporation and its general significance see Pearl, 'Puritans and Poor Relief'.

[105] Considerable confusion has surrounded not only Plockhoy's authorship but also his name. Pieter Cornelisz(on) Plockhoy was accustomed, as was common with his compatriots, to use Christian name and patronymic, omitting his surname. As this has caused some confusion I have elected to follow English practice and used his surname. The confusion over Plockhoy's authorship begins untypically with an error by George Thomason, the London bookseller, when a copy of *A Way Propounded* came into his possession on 28 May 1659. Thomason already possessed, since the previous March, a copy of Plockhoy's *The Way to the Peace and Settlement of these Nations* (1659) which he had attributed to 'Hugh Peter's man Cornelius'. (British Library shelf-mark E972 (16).) Naturally the two pamphlets were seen as associated and at some later date an unknown hand

Plockhoy was from Zierickzee, a commercial centre in Zeeland, itself one of the economically most advanced areas of seventeenth-century Europe. In Amsterdam in the 1640s he was associated with the Mennonites and in particular with a group of Mennonite reformers led by Galenus Abrahams de Haan and known as the Collegiant movement. The Mennonites emphasised adult baptism, inner religion and the separation of church and state. They rejected military service and oaths and adopted a rôle of passive obedience in relation to government. In their sectarian communities they strove to achieve a primitive Christianity based on scriptural authority and the Sermon on the Mount, simplicity in life and dress. The Collegiants grafted on to this a concern for religious freedom expressed in the form of open discussions at interdenominational meetings, almost as an alternative to sectarian worship. All these themes may be found reflected in Plockhoy's writings.[106]

Attracted by what he saw as opportunities for religious reform, Plockhoy arrived in England shortly before Cromwell's death and attempted, apparently with some success, to interest him in a Collegiant approach to the problem of religious toleration in England.[107] On the Protector's death, however, his hopes in this direction lapsed and he turned his attention to social and economic issues, perhaps encouraged by the speculation on radical social possibilities which was again rife in 1659.

wrote on p. 19 of Thomason's copy of *A Way Propounded*, 'I believe this pamphlet was made by Mr. Hugh Peters: who had a man named *Cornelius Glover*.' (British Library shelf-mark E984(7).) Peters did have a servant of that name but, as he turned royalist and betrayed his master in 1660, it is not certain that he was still with him in 1659. See R. P. Stearns, *The Strenuous Puritan, Hugh Peter 1598–1660* (Urbana, 1954), p. 335. However, the ascription has been followed by some recent authorities, for example, W. K. Jordan, *Philanthropy in England 1480–1660* (London, 1959), pp. 214–215. Plockhoy's authorship of *A Way Propounded* is clearly shown by references in a pamphlet, *Kort en Klaer Ontwerp*, published by him in Amsterdam in 1662. See Leland and Marvin Harder, *Plockhoy from Zurick-Zee: The Study of a Dutch Reformer in Puritan England and Colonial America*, Mennonite Historical Series, no. 2 (Newton, Kansas, 1952), p. 2. The Harders provide good editions and translations of Plockhoy's work and the best account of his life, although their book is difficult to obtain. Their edition of *A Way Propounded* supersedes the selection edited by John Downie in *Peter Cornelius Plockboy: Pioneer of the First Cooperative Commonwealth 1659* (n.p., n.d. [1934?]). As can be seen Plockhoy's name took on yet another shape in Downie's hands. I have used the British Library copy of *A Way Propounded*. For a more recent study of Plockhoy which closely follows the Harders' work, see Jean Seguy, *Utopie Coopérative et Oecuménisme: Pieter Cornelisz Plockhoy van Zurik-Zee 1620–1700* (Paris, 1968).

106 Harder, *Plockhoy from Zurick-Zee*, Chapter 2.
107 Plockhoy, *The Way to Peace and Settlement*; Harder, *Plockhoy from Zurick-Zee*, pp. 24–30.

Plockhoy began *A Way Propounded* in a way familiar amongst utopians, with a denunciation of the world around him.

Having seen the great inequality and disorder among men in the World, that not only evil Governours or Rulers, covetous Merchants and Tradesmen, lazie idle and negligent Teachers, and others, have brought all under slaverie and thraldom: But also a great number of the common handy-craft-men, or labourers (by endeavouring to decline, escape or cast off the heavy burthen) do fill all things with lyes and deceipt, to the oppressing of the honest and good people, whose consciences cannot bear such practises, therefore have I... designed to endeavour to bring four sorts of people, whereof the World chiefly consists out of several sects into one Familie or Household-government, viz. Husbandmen, Handycrafts people, Mariners and Masters of Arts and Sciences, to the end that we may better eschue the yoke of the Temporall and Spirituall Pharaohs, who have long enough domineered over our bodies and souls, and set up again (as in former times) Righteousnesse, love and Brotherly Sociableness, which are scarce anywhere to be found for the convincing of those that place all greatnesse only in domineering, and not in well-doing.[108]

Here all the major themes of Plockhoy's utopia are announced, pre-eminent amongst them that of equality. Disorder and inequality, associated with the wickedness innate in men, conspire to make goodness hard, even for those honestly disposed. Like More, Plockhoy saw social pressures warring against conscience. But unlike More he did not see the answer in a comprehensive, totally withdrawn communism but in the withdrawal of those for whom there was some hope, those who had not been contaminated by power and wealth and those who had not been degraded by poverty, the middling sort, husbandmen, artisans and teachers. It is 'a fit, suitable and qualified' people who will be brought together in his community. In the first edition of his work Plockhoy listed seventy-two types of craftsmen who were accepted, in the second seventy-seven.[109] Their common Christianity should hold them in harmony but, as we shall see, it could not be relied upon. Careful selection was, of course, a means of ensuring order; a type of discipline through prior elimination, an attempt to avoid the awkwardness of expulsion by anticipating its necessity.

if we be insufferable to the World, and they be incorrigible, or unbetterable, as to us, then let us reduce our friendship and society to a few in number...that we might truely be distinguished from the life of the Barbarous and Savage people, not by bookes, nor by Titles of honour, nor by universitys but by such morality as Christian philosophy doth prescribe.[110]

108 Plockhoy, *A Way Propounded*, p. 3.
109 *Ibid.*, title page, pp. 18–19; Harder, *Plockhoy from Zurick-Zee*, pp. 36–7. Cf. *Kort Verhael van Nieuw Nederlandts* (Amsterdam, 1662), reprinted in *Plockhoy from Zurick-Zee*, p. 199.
110 Plockhoy, *A Way Propounded*, pp. 31–2, see also p. 23.

Men would be willing to enter the withdrawn communities which Plockhoy proposed because of the oppressive disorder of the world about them. 'Many finding no rest in their present estate and condition, and being wearied with all the differences in spiritual, as in worldly matters, will be ready to come in to us.' For 'no painfuller or miserabler thing can be thought on, than that life which a man lives according to the course of this world'. Yet, to those to whom Plockhoy would be prepared to select for his community, he is careful to indicate that the critical obstacles to a loving harmony amongst men are precisely those inequalities which oppress them. They are the honours and dignities, the riches and estates of the idle wealthy. For the artisans Plockhoy hoped to recruit, his community offered an escape from the oppressions and ensnaring vanities of the rich, and thereby the possibility of a harmonic society amongst men equal in status, skill and aspiration.[111] The escape from inequality was focal to building a new society, but, as we shall see, Plockhoy's success in this regard was not unqualified.

A beginning must be made, Plockhoy thought, with some able man raising a stock and buying land 'whereupon the Husbandman, handy Craftsmen, Tradesmen, Marriners, and others...may be secured'. Two houses would be established, a city warehouse and, close to a river, a country community centre. The city warehouse had to be big enough to provide accommodation for twenty or thirty families and Plockhoy seems to have thought of this as the initial development, moving on to the rural community only when manufacturing and marketing in the city were well established. The careful integration of rural and manufacturing activities was, in fact, a vital aspect of the whole exercise, hence the well-considered lists of craftsmen.[112]

At first recruitment would be confined to unmarried persons, 'that with laying out little money may presently be on the getting hand'. Their trade should increase because, with living costs low, their prices would be attractive and their profits would go back to the common good. As their activities expanded, Plockhoy saw them moving into vertically and horizontally integrated enterprises: weaving, bleaching and dying, sheep and cattle farming; corn, flax and hemp growing and gardening. By the time rural activities were underway, the community would begin to consist of *families*. The country house was

to be built after a convenient manner, with public and private places, for freedom and conveniency a chamber and a closet for every man and his wife with

---

[111] *Ibid.*, pp. 14, 24, 25–26.
[112] *Ibid.*, pp. 5–7. Eduard Bernstein, *Cromwell and Communism: Socialism and Democracy in the Great English Revolution*, translated by H. J. Stenning (London, 1930), Chapter 15. Bernstein emphasises integration between primary and secondary sectors in Plockhoy's social thought.

a great Hall, to lay all things ready made in order, a place to dress victuals, another to eate together, a third for the children, also cellars to keep meate and drink in, a place for the sick, one for the Physitians and Chyrurgeons furniture and medicines, one other for all kinds of usefull (as well natural as Spirituall) Books, Maps, and other Instruments belonging to the Liberal Arts and Sciences, several places for Scholars, a place for strangers, who intending to stay any long time, shall do some work, or pay for their lodging and diet.

Once the country house was complete, the city house was to become almost entirely a warehouse but physicians, surgeons, apothecaries and merchants would be maintained there on a roster basis.[113]

The community was seen as operating on the basis of a regulated company. Members were to make an investment on entry. No interest would be paid, but, when they left or died, their contribution would be repaid with an appropriate share of the accrued profits. There was no distinction possible, as in the joint-stock company, between investors and working members. It is therefore quite incorrect to see Plockhoy's proposal as a joint-stock company. Equally it is mistaken to see it as a poor relief proposal. Plockhoy's intention was not to admit the undifferentiated poor, but well qualified artisans, tradesmen, husbandmen and professional men.[114]

Members of the society were to work six hours a day for six days each week. Hours could be adjusted to allow for time off but leisure time should be used 'for the refreshing of their bodies, and profitable exercises of the mind'. Outsiders, 'being not fit to be of our society', might be employed for wages but should work for twelve hours each day and their working times were carefully set out. Teachers and doctors of medicine provided services, not only for members of the community, but also for those outside the community who were able to pay for them. Here again Plockhoy has to confront the perennial problem of the full-employment utopia, the problem of the idle rich. Children of rich outsiders who come to the community 'to be instructed in Arts, Sciences and Languages' must not be allowed to jeopardise the equality which the society offered its members. They would, in addition to their studies, have to work for three hours a day six days a week, 'to the end they may allwaies in case of losse and want get their living without being necessitated to fall upon such courses...as may prove hurtfull to their souls and bodies'. They were only to be taught 'usefull trades' so that whatever the vicissitudes of the market they might continue in employment.[115]

113 Plockhoy, *A Way Propounded*, pp. 6–8.
114 *Ibid.*, pp. 5–6; cf. Bernstein, *Cromwell and Communism*, p. 223; Harder, *Plockhoy from Zurick-Zee*, p. 35.
115 Plockhoy, *A Way Propounded*, pp. 4–5, 7, 12. Medical services would be provided to the poor outside the society free of charge, *ibid.*, p. 7.

Every six months or year the accounts were to be rendered and the surplus distributed amongst the members. Three of the 'uppermost' men were to have the keys of the treasury, and no single one was to open it without the others present. No one was to enjoy office in the society for longer than a year, 'least he domineer in his office and others seeking his favour play the Hippocrites'. The chief officer or Governor of the society was to be chosen annually, 'everyone giving his voyce for him, that he judgeth to be fit'. The governor was to rule in accordance with the orders of the community, except in small matters, and was to be chosen for his wisdom, not for riches. Men and women appointed overseers of food and drink, and the like, were to be replaced every six months so that everyone had experience of the work. Maids were to be appointed to deal with housework and the care of children but were also to learn a trade in case they should leave the society. As regards the wider society, members were to pay taxes and regard themselves as subject to the civil law 'under all humane Ordinances, which are not contrary to the will of God'.[116]

The communities Plockhoy hoped to establish were seen as offering numerous advantages over existing society. Many of these related to economy of cost and effort. The problem of demand for the fully employed society's products would be solved by the competitiveness of its costs and prices. Whereas in a hundred separate households, a hundred women would be engaged in housework, here only twenty-five would be absorbed. Similarly, in a hundred households, a hundred fires must be maintained for heating and cooking. Here only four or five were necessary. Subsistence would cost less not only because of a degree of self-sufficiency but because the community could buy such supplies as it needed in bulk. Indeed the benefit to society at large is seen to inhere in the competitive effect of the community's low costs and prices, which would force others to reduce prices to the benefit of the poor. However, Plockhoy offers no explanation of how other producers would be able to reduce costs. When they joined, artisans would be assured of a ready-made market within the community, and reassurance in the knowledge that old age, sickness, and children are all provided for by the community. From this too follows economy: 'every one shall be able quietly to do his work, because none shall have more than one single work to mind'.[117]

Religious provision was to follow the Collegiant pattern. Christ and the Gospels were to be accepted by all members, otherwise they should enjoy freedom of conscience. A debating and lecture hall was to be built in the community where members could expound their knowledge, read and debate scripture in an atmosphere of tolerance.[118]

Nevertheless, harmony could not be assumed. Plockhoy was caught

[116] *Ibid.*, pp. 9–10, 12.   [117] *Ibid.*, pp. 10–14.   [118] *Ibid.*, pp. 15–16.

repeatedly in the tension between his voluntarism, the hope that he has chosen good men, and his utopianism, the fear that all men are wicked. It expressed itself in the desire to have few laws and yet to make them effective against innate selfishness, to allow freedom and yet prevent it being abused. 'Our Rules and Laws being few, are to be only for necessity, not to take away any ones liberty, leaving them alwaies open to the tryall of all rationale men, that so self-seeking (to be more or above others, in natural or spirituall matters) may be discovered and excluded.' Liberty does not extend to the choice of seating at communal meals. Dress should be convenient but, having said that, ambivalences abound. There was to be no compulsion as regards fashion, but unnecessary trimmings were to be avoided. Any desiring clothes finer than others could, however, in one final twist, add a sum, equal to the extra cost, to the sums set aside for the poor.[119]

Many young men and women, Plockhoy argued, would be glad to find in the community an escape from the pressures of the world: 'they are often times stirred up and provoked (by reason of hard, strict, severe Masters and Mistresses) to wicked and desperate resolutions'. But the question remained as to whether the removal of those pressures to evil was enough, or had countervailing pressures to be erected? Was liberty possible in a good society? Plockhoy never succeeded in resolving the issue. 'Covetousness, excesse, lying and deceit, together with all the evils that spring up out of riches, or poverty, will be excluded from us who maintain equality. . .' Drunkenness, whoredom, adultery are eliminated from the society but, in the end, he is not able to tell us how.[120]

Similarly because, in order to sustain full employment, his society has to have a market wider than itself, Plockhoy has still to encounter the problem of the rich and their corrupted tastes. What will be done when rich customers, buying from the city warehouse, demand all sorts of luxuries or unnecessary ornamentation? It is a difficulty with which Plockhoy clearly felt uncomfortable. The city warehouse existed, he wrote,

especially to serve every one as there shall be occasion, making all things for sale without unnecessary trimmings unless, that any buying of us would have any trimming upon them, those we shall endeavour to give content, if they bring to us those necessary T[r]immings, which we ourselves have not, doing our endeavour to keep their custom that so in time they may be convinced of their folly, being better with us, who give them reasons for alterations, than with others who bolster them up in pride and excesse.

But he goes on worrying for another page. If unnecessary things are sinful, should all of them be destroyed? Children employed in manufacturing vanities should be taken from those trades, but to do what? Perhaps, to

---

[119] *Ibid.*, pp. 10, 11.   [120] *Ibid.*, pp. 14, 33.

prevent the children of the community serving worldly people, they should be kept always at home.[121]

Plockhoy's plain anxiety in the face of this problem stems straight from the dilemma of his utopian strategy. The withdrawn community is a way of avoiding the confrontation between leisure, as a right claimed by the wealthy, and the demands of the full-employment ideal. At the same time two problems stem from this. The poor must also be excluded, if for no other reason than because the resources of the middling sort were inadequate to set them all on work, and they have, by definition, no resources of their own to contribute. Secondly, the demand generated by a low-surplus agriculture within the community must be supplemented by outside demand if its manufacturing activities are to be sustained, and here once more one encountered the rich and their influence; the rich as consumers whose tastes can generate the very pressures of inequality and the corruption of luxury which Plockhoy's society is designed to escape. Hence his ambivalence over luxury production, the necessity of rich pupils working and the membership of the rich. Like Winstanley, he is prepared to allow rich persons to reside in the community without working, provided they pay for all the facilities which they enjoy, but the concession undermines the much vaunted equality of his society.[122]

A few years later, with the approval of the burgomasters of Amsterdam, Plockhoy was able to try out a variation of his programme in an area of what was then the Dutch colony of the New Netherlands, south of the Delaware River. Set in the wilderness, the emphasis had to shift much more strongly to agriculture and a comprehensive criminal code had to be worked out. Otherwise, Plockhoy's colonial scheme bears marked similarity to *A Way Propounded*.[123] Unfortunately, the experiment, set on foot in July 1663, was abruptly terminated in the following year by English military occupation of the colony. Almost twenty years later, in 1682, Plockhoy appeared in Lewes, Delaware where he was granted the use of a piece of land and English citizenship. Twelve years later still, he and his wife arrived in the recently established Mennonite settlement of Germantown. Plockhoy was blind and destitute and the settlers accepted him as a public charge. He may still have been alive in 1700 but his final days are shrouded in obscurity.[124]

Comfortable to the end and never without hopes that his schemes might be realised, John Bellers nevertheless showed marked similarities to Plock-

---

[121] *Ibid.*, pp. 8–9.   [122] *Ibid.*, pp. 4–5.
[123] For the colonial experiment and the documents associated with it, see, Harder, *Plockhoy from Zurick-Zee*, Chapter 4 and pp. 174–204. There is not space in this work to deal with what is essentially a Dutch colonial utopia.
[124] *Ibid.*, pp. 62–66.

hoy. A Quaker of some importance, Bellers shared many of the religious attitudes of Plockhoy. Like him, too, he proposed to establish his full-employment ideal in a self-sufficient, withdrawn community. But he came much closer than Plockhoy to finding a solution to the problem of the rich outsider, by conceiving a full-employment utopia not as a regulated company, but as a joint-stock company whose profits would accrue to rich investors.

John Bellers was born in 1654.[125] His father, Francis, was a prosperous 'Grocer and citizen of London' and became an active and important member of the Society of Friends. John was trained as a cloth merchant and brought up as a Quaker, possibly taking over many of his father's religious responsibilities on his death. He was arrested and fined for his religious activities, twice in 1684 and once in 1685. On 2 September 1686 Bellers married Frances Fettiplace at the Cirencester meeting house. His father-in-law, Gyles Fettiplace, was the head of an old and influential Gloucestershire county family with a family seat at Coln St Aldwyn.[126] Despite his active Quakerism, Fettiplace retained both his political influence in the country and his style as a gentleman, driving to Friends' meetings at Cirencester in a coach and six.[127] Soon after his marriage, if not before, Bellers began to live the life of a country gentleman. From 1690 to 1701 he occupied the Grange, Chalfont St Peters and, on his father's death in 1701, moved to Coln St Aldwyns where he lived for the rest of his life. He died in 1725, a wealthy man, possessed of lands in Wiltshire, Warwickshire, Oxfordshire, Berkshire, Middlesex, Pennsylvania and West New Jersey, as well as of a considerable library and a collection of instruments and maps.[128]

125 For Bellers' life see A. Ruth Fry, *John Bellers 1654–1725, Quaker, Economist and Social Reformer: His Writings Reprinted with a Memoir* (London, 1935); Charles R. Simpson, 'John Bellers in Official Minutes', *Journal of the Friends Historical Society*, 12:3 (1915), pp. 120–7 and 12:4 (1915), pp. 165–71; Karl Seipp, *John Bellers, Ein Vertreter des frühen Quäkertums* (Nuremberg, 1933). The article in *Dictionary of National Biography* is now inadequate. Bernstein's essay remains one of the most comprehensive studies of Bellers. Bernstein, *Cromwell and Communism*, Ch. XIV.

126 Cf. Richard T. Vann, *The Social Development of English Quakerism 1655–1725* (Cambridge, Mass., 1969). Vann has argued that gentry and wholesale traders were prominent amongst early Quakers. If this is so, Bellers' background and marriage reflect both elements in early Quakerism.

127 Ruth G. Burtt, 'Records from Cirencester: Fettiplace and Bellers', *Journal of the Friends Historical Society*, 35 (1938), pp. 82–6 and 'Records from Nailsworth', *ibid.*, 37 (1940), p. 32.

128 See Bellers' will, a copy of which is held in the Friends House Library, mss. collection, Box L.2.4. See also 'The Will of John Bellers', *Journal of the Friends Historical Society*, 12:2 (1915), pp. 103–8; 'John Bellers and John Cheyney', *ibid.*, 20:2 (1923), p. 94. The will was drawn up on 5 March 1725, Bellers died in the following April and the will was proved in August of that year.

Not only was Bellers a prominent Quaker, acquainted with Fox, Penn and Isaac Pennington, but he engaged in far-reaching activities as intellectual, publicist and philanthropist. He wrote extensively on economic matters,[129] on trade, colonial development, education, electoral reform, penal reform and medicine. In 1710 he proposed a system of annual European congresses as a means of guaranteeing international peace and stability.[130] Like Peter Chamberlen at the end of his life, Bellers sought to persuade the anglican hierarchy to consider ways of reconciling men of different persuasions on basically accepted religious truths and of finding a *modus vivendi* between non-conformity and the national church.[131] His eldest son, Fettiplace Bellers, was elected a Fellow of the Royal Society in 1711, and Bellers senior followed him in 1718.[132]

The central project of his life, however, and the one with which we are concerned here was his full-employment utopia, the 'Colledge of Industry'. He first published his *Proposals for Raising a Colledge of Industry* in 1695.[133] Twenty-nine years later, in the year before his death, he was still urging the same scheme.[134] There can be little doubt that two influences predominated in the emergence of this scheme in Bellers' thought. The motive arose out of his own experiences in trying to cope with the problem of the Quaker poor. The solution, to a many-sided problem, arose out of the joint-stock company promotion boom of the 1690s.

From the age of nineteen, Bellers had worked with the Quaker Committee of the Meeting for Sufferings, endeavouring to relieve persecution amongst Friends. In 1679 he was made a treasurer for a fund set up by

---

[129] The only systematic study of Bellers' economic thought is Philip S. Belasco, 'John Bellers', *Economica*, 5 (1925), pp. 165–74.

[130] Bellers, *Some Reasons for an European State* (1710), reprinted in Fry, *John Bellers*, pp. 89–103.

[131] Bellers, *To the Arch-Bishop, Bishops and Clergy, of the Province of Canterbury* (n.p. n.d. [1711/12?]), Friends House Library 27 (18): *Some Considerations as an Essay towards Reconciling the Old and New Ministry* (1712), Friends House Library 27 (19).

[132] 'Friends and the Learned Societies', *Journal of the Friends Historical Society*, 7:1 (1910), pp. 30–1. For Fettiplace Bellers see Fry, *John Bellers*, p. 17. John Bellers was a friend and correspondent of Sir Hans Sloane; see, for example, Bellers to Sloane, 5 August 1724, Friends House Library Mss., Box 5, 19 (a photocopy of a letter from the Sloane Mss. in the British Library).

[133] I have used here the slightly fuller edition of 1696 (Wing B1829) held by the Friends Library. It was reprinted anonymously in 1790 and again in John Morton Eden, *The State of the Poor* (1797). Robert Owen also reprinted it in *A New View of Society* (1817).

[134] Bellers, *An Abstract of George Fox's Advice and Warning to the Magistrates of London* (1724). See also, *To the Lords and Others Commissioners Appointed by the Queen to Take Care of the Poor Palatines* (1709); *An Essay for Imploying the Poor to Profit* (1723).

Friends for employing poor Quakers.[135] In 1660 he was supplying cloth to Quaker women's Box Meetings to be used to make clothes for the poor. Relief of the poor, especially their employment, remained, throughout his life, an aspect of Bellers' activities within the organisation of the Society of Friends. In August 1695, the London Six-Weeks Meeting, which had since 1693 been administering a stock for the poor, agreed to consider some proposals of Bellers' relating to the poor. At its next meeting those proposals were read and Bellers asked that they should be considered in each Monthly and Quarterly Meeting, so reaching the regional organisation of the Quakers. The committee decided, however, that, if this were to be done, it should be left to Bellers' initiative and expense. Possibly out of this arose Bellers' readiness to have his scheme published in a wider form. Moreover, the apparent necessity for a legal incorporation drove him to address his *Proposals* to Parliament.[136] Hence arose the publication of *Proposals For Raising a Colledge of Industry*, which, although it was offered as a non-sectarian scheme, never lost in Bellers' mind its special relevance for Quakers.

In March 1697, the great annual conference of Friends, the Yearly Meeting, considered the scheme and recommended it to be considered on a regional basis.[137] In at least some areas the proposal was greeted with enthusiasm and offers of contributions were forthcoming.[138] But two difficulties seem to have stood in the way. One was that it appeared that legislation would be required and how were Quakers to get it? The second problem was that of selecting the poor, an issue which had bedevilled Quaker welfare activities from the beginning.[139] By the time the issue of legality had been resolved, the proposal had become one clearly restricted to Friends and the children of Friends and its emphasis was moving in an

---

[135] Simpson, 'Bellers in Official Minutes', pp. 121–2. According to Richard Vann, after 1670 Quakerism tended to recruit members from a lower social plane than originally, although in the seventeenth century few of the really poor joined. It is difficult to know whether the poor Quakers, with whom Bellers was so concerned were poor before they became Quakers, possibly attracted by Quaker welfare concern, or were Quakers who became poor, possibly because of persecution. Vann, *Social Development of Quakerism*, pp. 73, 78.

[136] Friends House Library Mss., Minutes of the Six-Weeks Meeting, London, vol. VIII (1692–8), pp. 82, 118, 133; Simpson, 'Bellers in Official Minutes', pp. 123, 165–6; G. W. Edwards, 'The London Six Weeks Meeting', *Journal of the Friends Historical Society*, 50:4 (1964), pp. 233–4, 242.

[137] Friends House Library Mss., Minutes of the Yearly Meeting, vol. II (1694–1701), pp. 185, 187; Sundry Ancient Epistles, case 51, vol. 47, pp. 154–8.

[138] For example, Friends House Library Mss., Wandsworth Meeting of Friends Minute Books (1695–1789), 2 January 1698; 6 February 1698.

[139] Vann, *Social Development of Quakerism*, p. 143. In 1696 the Six-Weeks Meeting was trying to restrict assistance to poor and genuine Friends. Minutes of the Six Weeks Meeting, London, vol. III (1692–8), p. 141.

educational direction.[140] Out of it all came the establishment of the Friends' Workhouse at Clerkenwell which ultimately became the Friends' School at Saffron Walden.[141]

Just as his experience as a member of a non-conformist minority under persecution may have influenced him to envisage a withdrawn community, so the background of the joint-stock boom of the 1690s influenced Bellers in choosing the form of its organisation. Between 1689 and 1695 the paid up capital of British joint-stock companies expanded from about £630 000 to about £3 500 000, the number of companies rising from eleven to about a hundred. There existed 'a stock market... overloaded with investment capital'. Partly because of war, partly because of the limitations of investment in overseas trading companies, pressure from investors was pushing joint-stock company formation into domestic manufacturing and trading fields. The obvious ease with which money could be raised and the popularity of the form of joint-stock companies clearly influenced Bellers. He certainly found it necessary to provide arrangements should the stock in his College of Industry be oversubscribed.[142] Bellers himself, like many Quakers, was a holder of stock.[143] Again, it is possible that, towards the end of the seventeenth century, poor law administration was moving to the provision of workhouses, not only under the existing law, but also in the form of incorporated workhouses which bore some resemblance to both factories and joint-stock companies.[144]

---

[140] Friends House Library Mss., Minutes of the Yearly Meeting, vol. II (1694–1701), fo. 5, 258–9, 315–17; Simpson, 'Bellers in Official Minutes', pp. 169–71.

[141] David W. Bolam, *Unbroken Community: The Story of the Friends School Saffron Walden 1702–1952* (London, 1952). In his will Bellers left £100 to the 'Friends Workhouse' provided his heirs could have the nomination of one child there.

[142] Bellers, *Proposals for Raising a Colledge of Industry* (1696), p. 10; H. J. Habakkuk and M. Postan (eds.), *Cambridge Economic History of Europe*, vol. VI (Cambridge, 1966), part 1, p. 3; W. R. Scott, *The Constitution and Finance of English, Scottish and Irish Joint Stock Companies to 1720*, 3 vols. (Cambridge, 1911), vol. I, p. 328; K. G. Davies, 'Joint Stock Investment in the Later Seventeenth Century', in Carus-Wilson (ed.), *Essays in Economic History*, vol. II, p. 281; K. G. Davies, *The Royal African Company* (London, 1957), pp. 38, 48–56.

[143] In 1705, for example, he held twenty £50 shares in the newly constituted London Lead Company which was largely financed by Quakers. Arthur Raistrick, *Two Centuries of Industrial Welfare: The London (Quaker) Lead Company, 1692–1905* (London, 1938), p. 138. Theodore Rabb has found that early-seventeenth-century investment came predictably from just those social groups which provided the Quakers with the main sources of their early membership. Theodore K. Rabb, *Enterprise and Empire: Merchant and Gentry Investment in the Expansion of England* (Cambridge, Mass., 1967).

[144] Webb, *English Poor Law History: Part I*, pp. 101–110; Gray, *History of English Philanthropy*, pp. 105–14, 216.

The joint-stock company model did not appeal to someone like Bellers, however, simply because it was popular, nor, more seriously, because it offered an attractive way of financing the project in the 1690s. Rather it seemed to offer solutions to a number of the perennial problems facing the full-employment utopian. In the first place, investors and workers could be kept completely separate. The leisured rich could play their part – indeed they could retain control – simply by investing money. They need not be made to appear irrelevant, as in Winstanley's vision, nor need they be challenged by the full-employment ethic. Moreover, they could be reassured in their leisure by the prospect of rentier profits. Secondly, the joint-stock model could fit a selective approach to the full employment problem like a glove. It was eminently compatible with a withdrawn community. Hence, under its aegis, Bellers could concentrate in a selective way on the industrious or Quaker poor. Lastly, the joint-stock model enabled him to solve the economic problem of sustaining a full-employment society when the tacit assumption was that total demand was inelastic. The college did not have to sustain its increased production by expanding its own demand. It merely had to grab a larger share of the national market by lower prices and costs. In other words, the colleges could adopt a mercantilist policy towards the greater society within which they existed.

It is not surprising that the introduction to *Proposals For Raising a Colledge of Industry* reads like the prospectus for a joint-stock company, offering profits and other inducements to potential shareholders. The three things, Bellers proclaimed, which the scheme was aimed at were, in order: 'Profit for the Rich, (which will be Life to the Rest), plenty for the poor, and a good Education for Youth'. Profit was, he admitted, a necessary incentive.

For what Sap is to a Tree, that Profit is to all Business, by increasing and keeping it alive; so imploying the Poor, excells the barren keeping them, in the first, the increase of the Poor is no Burthen, (but Advantage) because their Conveniences increase with them; but in the latter, there is no strength or relief but what they have from others, who possibly may sometimes think they have little enough for themselves.[145]

So two things followed. The rich would be saved the expense of maintaining the idle poor. The more industrious poor there were, the richer would the rich become. 'The Labour of the Poor being the mines of the rich.' Indeed it was folly on the part of the rich not to encourage 'honest Labourers' to marry and so increase their numbers. Without the labour of the poor, the rich could not exist. It followed in self-interest, as well as natural justice, that the rich should encourage an industrious and *temperate*

[145] Bellers, *Proposals for a Colledge*, pp. 1–2.

lower class. The poor, in this scheme, were not to be made affluent consumers but industrious, godly and temperate workers who, *by their own efforts*, could provide a secure, anxiety-free and comfortable subsistence for themselves and be an example to others. 'The Regular Life in the Colledge with abatement of Worldly Cares, with an honest Labour, and Religious Instructions, may make it a Nursery and School of Vertue... a Community something like the example of Primitive Christianity.'[146] The suggestion of letting the poor receive the profits of their efforts in the scheme was explicitly rejected. Not only would this make money difficult to raise but the scheme was designed to assist the rich as well as the poor, and the former could not exist without the labour of the latter. So no one could reasonably suggest it 'except they turn Levellers, and set the Rich to work with the Poor'. And that apparently was unacceptable, or, at least, it was incompatible with the objects of the exercise. The poor were to be relieved only of dire want and insecurity in order to become 'Regular People'.[147]

The alternative to this pursuit of self-interest by the rich was clear, stark and traditional. To leave the poor idle, promiscuous and undisciplined was to risk instability in their own lives as well as in society generally: 'except we make those Poor our Friends, which we may and ought to take care of: Such Poor may come to be a vicious and distrest Mobb, and ready Instruments in the Hands of our Enemies to bring much sufferings upon us'. Without employment, Bellers asked, 'What can awe the Misery of Starving?'[148]

All this could be calculated to appeal to potential shareholders in terms of their interests, but Bellers also hoped to tap wider values in their consciousness by appealing for a reformed and a fully employed nation. The reformation of society might well begin with the poor and the young because they were not only the majority but also the most pliable and dependent.[149] Basic to Bellers' computations on the fuller economic exploitation of England's resources was the estimate that a third of what efficiently employed workers produced was surplus to their subsistence and hence could become profit. 'Two hundred of all Trades I suppose sufficient to find necessaries for three hundred, and therefore what manu-

---

[146] *Ibid.*, pp. 2–3, 12–14. Cf. this with the wants of the poor which will be met. Bellers, *Essays about the Poor, Manufactures, Trade, Plantations & Immorality* (1699), p. 4; *An Abstract of George Fox's Advice*, p. 10. 'My Proposal is not more to feed the Poor, than to imploy them with Profit, and by that Opportunity to Reform them.'

[147] Bellers, *Proposals for a Colledge*, pp. 23–4, 26.

[148] *Ibid.*, p. 1; *An Abstract of George Fox's Advice*, p. 9; *Essays about the Poor*, To the Lords and Commons in Parliament Assembled (n.p., n.d.).

[149] *Proposals for a Colledge*, p. 4; *An Abstract of George Fox's Advice*, pp. 3–4.

factures the other hundred make, will be Profit to the Founders.'[150] This seemed to him to be borne out in the national economy, 'where I suppose not above Two Thirds, if one half of the Nation, are Useful Workers; and yet all have a Living'.[151] In addition, within the self-sufficient colleges which he proposed there would be savings on all forms of wasted time, activity and resource. Shopkeepers, useless trades and lawyers would disappear, as would bad debts, dear bargains, underemployment, beggars, much housework, houseroom, fetching and carrying, and curiously, damaged clothes. Even the present occupants of hospitals and almshouses could be enlisted in the general effort: 'the Blind or Lame being able to do something, and everybody but Sucklings & Bed-rid is capable of doing little or much towards a living'.[152]

Within his colleges the existence of an integrated community of artisans and husbandmen would facilitate further improvements of agriculture. The nightsoil of tradesmen as well as husbandmen could be used on the land. More cattle would be kept to feed the community and hence more dung would be produced to fertilise the land. So agricultural production could be pushed beyond the possibilities of the landlord/tenant relationship.[153] So convinced was he of the advantages of the system he proposed that he could envisage a form of internal colonisation with his colleges settling and cultivating vast areas of wasteland, especially in the northern counties:

in 58 Years time such a Body as our present idle Poor, if they were imployed about it, would be able to turn all our wast and unimproved Lands (which some think may be near a quarter Part of the Lands in the Kingdom) into fruitful Fields, Orchards, and Gardens, and their mean Cottages into Colleges, and fill our Barns with Plenty of Bread, and our Store-houses with Manufactures, which would greatly incourage the Increase of our People, and the Strength, and Riches of the Nation.[154]

In the same spirit Bellers believed that every encouragement should be given to discoveries in 'the Mechanicks and Husbandry'. He was absolutely opposed to legislation against labour-saving inventions or devices.

[150] *Proposals for a Colledge*, p. 5.

[151] *Ibid.*, p. 7. For other calculations of the national loss through unemployment see, *To the Lords and Commons in Parliament Assembled*, p. 1; *Essays about the Poor*, pp. 5–6, 7–8; *To the Lords and Others Commissioners*, p. 4.

[152] *Proposals for a Colledge*, pp. 7, 20. One of the reasons why Bellers favoured an end to capital punishment was that it wasted labour. *Essays about the Poor*, p. 18. See also *To the Criminals in Prison* (n.p., n.d.), Friends House Library Broadsides A/63.

[153] *Proposals for a Colledge*, pp. 7–8; on the manure problem see Joan Thirsk, 'Farming Techniques', in Thirsk (ed.), *Agrarian History*, vol. IV, pp. 167–8.

[154] Bellers, *An Essay for Imploying the Poor*, p. 6; *Essays about the Poor*, pp. 4–5.

Laws against shortening of Labour are as unreasonable, as to make a Law that every labouring Man should tye one Hand behind him, that two men might be imploy'd in one Body's Work, which would be to make the Rich poor, by doubling their Charge, and the Poor miserable for the same Reason whilst they would earn less, or must pay double for all their Necessaries of Life.[155]

The flywheel for this vision of an England fully employed, exploiting all its resources and wasting nothing was, of course, the College of Industry. To begin with Bellers proposed raising a capital of £18 000[156] with which land and stock would be acquired, and buildings erected to set up an integrated manufacturing and farming community. The minimum shareholding was to be twenty-five pounds, and every fifty or a hundred pounds invested would entitle the holder to one vote in choosing officers or making laws. No one, however, was to have more than five votes. Twelve or more of the investors were to be chosen 'a Committee, as Visitors to Inspect, and Counsellors for Advice, for the Governours and Workmen to apply to, as there may be occasion'. There was to be an annual valuation and distribution of the profit which could be reinvested. Stock-jobbing was forbidden. Investors wishing to sell their shares had to offer them to the other investors. In other words, it operated as a private joint-stock company. Investors also enjoyed other rights. They might take part of their profits in the form of the produce of the college. They, amongst others, might enter and live in the college under its rules and 'lay up the Profit of their own Estates'. Alternatively anyone giving land worth fifteen pounds a year or three hundred pounds in cash could keep one person in the college without working.[157]

The model Bellers described was a college of three hundred inhabitants. Eighty-two of them would be women and girls. Twenty-four men would work the college farm and forty-four were listed as officials or specified tradesmen. The greater the variety of trades, however, the better. If possible, Bellers wanted one representative of every useful trade. The governors and officials would be unsalaried, enjoying only the same rewards as the other collegians.[158]

Bellers recognised that much depended on the quality of the workpeople recruited for his colleges. It would be necessary to scour the nation for good, exemplary workmen to set the tone and train the youth up

[155] Bellers, *An Essay for Imploying the Poor*, p. 8. Sir George Clark is quite wrong in identifying Bellers as an opponent of labour-saving devices. Sir George Clark, *Science and Social Welfare*, pp. 114 n. 1.

[156] £10 000 to buy land worth £500 p.a.; £2000 to stock the land; £3000 for stock to set up several trades, and £3000 for buildings. Bellers, *Proposals for a Colledge*, p. 8.

[157] *Ibid.*, pp. 7–8, 8–9, 10, 11.

[158] *Ibid.*, pp. 5–6, 8–9.

well.[159] He recognised, however, that it would not be easy. Dealing with possible objections to his scheme, he returned several times to this problem. Good men were always hard to find but the prevailing recession was a good time to look for them, since in prosperous times only the worst sort lack work. However carefully workers were selected, the confinement and discipline of the college would, he admitted, be necessary to keep them at work. 'Neither would the Poor work, if there were not greater Inconveniences; that is, Starving, or Robbing, and that's Hanging.' Moreover, the founders would ensure industry because their profits were at stake. Nevertheless Bellers was uneasily caught between a discipline which he was afraid would introduce 'Monkery' and the suspicion that it would be impossible to prevent selfish men entering the colleges.[160]

In the end reliance could not be placed in the moral character of the collegians. Discipline had to be maintained and punishment provided. Colleges and hospitals in England and Holland should be visited, Bellers suggested, to adopt from them any useful rules. All sorts of tradesmen should be consulted to determine a reasonable day's work for a man, so that the college rules could be adapted accordingly. There would be rules covering not only hours of work, but also dress, eating, sleeping and working arrangements.

If we improve our Land, multiply our People, increase our Treasure, and have all the Rules (of Pollicy) for Government and of Trade in the greatest perfection, that we could live with half the Labour we do, and might seem invincible in Strength, and abound with Plenty and Grandeur; if Virtue be not encouraged, and Vice suppressed, it will make us but the more open Enemies to Heaven, and bring us the Nearer Step to Ruin; for as the Plains of *Sodom* were the richest Land of the Country, so it sooner ripened their Pride, Idleness and Lust that destroyed them.

The sanctions on Virtue were ultimately punitive but Bellers preferred 'corrections to be rather abatements of Food &c. than stripes'. For those who deserved greater punishment that form of civil death, expulsion, was the penalty.[161]

Education was to play a vital part but in a rôle subordinate to the ends of discipline and morality. If a child's will were kept in constant submission to the will of another, the mature adult would be more ready to submit his will to God. In this sense, a good education was better than a good estate. Yet it was 'a Vertuous Industrious Education' which was the

---

[159] *Ibid.*, p. 9. Note, however, that he regarded the Quaker poor as more amenable to discipline. Bellers, *To the Children of Light, In Scorn called Quakers* (1695?).
[160] Bellers, *Proposals for a Colledge*, pp. 21–22, 25, 26–7.
[161] *Ibid.*, pp. 9, 14–15; *Essays about the Poor*, pp. 15–16; see also *To the Lords and Other Commissioners*, p. 2; *An Abstract of George Fox's Advice*, pp. 3–4.

goal, for temperance and industry were more important, both to society and the individual, than book-learning.

beyond Reading and Writing, a multitude of Scholars is not so useful to the Publick as some think; the Body requiring more Hands and Legs to provide for, and support it, than Heads to direct it; and if the Head grows too big for the Body, the whole will fall into the Rickets. It's Labour sustains maintains and upholds, tho' Learning gives a useful Varnish.[162]

Eight hours a day was far too long for children to spend in desk-bound study. A good proportion of their time should be given up to working at a craft or trade. Bellers saw this as one of the reasons why rich people might pay to have their children boarded and educated in the college, for they would imbibe habits of industry and providence from the atmosphere around them. Moreover, they, like others in the community, 'will be more under the Eye-sight of one Master or another, than in a private Family; and consequently prevented of more Folly'. Constant supervision, constant industry and constant discipline are the watch-words of the utopian life.[163]

Other schemes had failed, Bellers claimed, because they had not been self-sufficient, integrated economies, combining the production of all necessaries for their members. Only such a community could offer its members the security and freedom from the uncertainties of the market, which would be to them the compensating advantages for the hard discipline of collegiate life. The college would, for example, be free of the fear of famine because, being self-sufficient, it would be under no compulsion to sell in times of plenty and so could lay up a store of agricultural produce against years of dearth.[164] Part of the exercise was to produce an integrated economy in which agricultural and manufacturing activities balanced and supported each other. A stable farming sector was necessary to provide sustenance and a stable level of demand from the products of the artisans and tradesmen. The college would assume the responsibility for 'Proportioning our Labourers' to produce this stability, and by cutting out middlemen would remove the speculative factor in market uncertainty. It was, furthermore, recognised that agriculture and manufacturing could only grow in co-ordination.[165]

Bellers was confident enough of the possibilities of these integrated, self-sufficient communities to be able to envisage problems of expansion, specialisation and surplus profit. Though his original model was for a

---

[162] *Proposals for a Colledge*, pp. 17–19.   [163] *Ibid.*, pp. 12, 16, 19.
[164] *Ibid.*, pp. 12–14, 22–3, 25, 27. Cf. *Essays about the Poor*, p. 2.
[165] Bellers, *To the Lords and Commons in Parliament Assembled*, p. 2; *Essays about the Poor*, pp. 9–10, see also pp. 8–9 for underemployment; Cf. *An Essay for Imploying the Poor*, p. 5.

community of three hundred members, there might be three thousand or more. New colleges could be set up; at Colchester for 'Bayes and Perpetu-antoes'; at Taunton for serges; at Stroud and in Devonshire and so on. Several could be established on the sea coast for fisheries. Where surplus profit was produced it could be distributed to the shareholders or re-invested.[166]

Clearly, in order for this expansion to be maintained demand had to keep pace with output. Bellers, like most of his contemporaries, assumed that total demand was relatively inflexible.[167] The growth, or rather extension, of demand which sustained the expansion of the colleges repre-sented in fact their growing share of what Bellers conceived to be a basically static national market. Like Plockhoy, then, Bellers found the withdrawn community a useful way of solving the full-employment utopians' problem of growth in the face of an assumed inelasticity of demand. At the same time, the joint-stock model, with its distribution of profits, enabled him to have growth in production as a result of full employment without the corrupting effects of affluence or luxury.

In a postscript to *Proposals For Raising a Colledge of Industry*, Bellers admitted that it was a difficult thing to reconcile the interests of the rich and the poor. Many of the things he said on the subject of labour could be taken to imply the irrelevance of the rich. As we have seen, he calcu-lated in one passage that two-thirds of the people of England laboured to support both themselves and the non-labouring third: 'and if the one third which are not Labourers, did not spend more than the two thirds which are Labourers, one half of the People or Families Labouring could supply all the Nation'. It was in this sense not only the idleness of the wealthy which was a burden, but their standard of living too. What was the justifi-cation for their leisured wealth? The rich could not exist without labourers. Masters were in a sense dependent on their servants. Why should they exist at all? It was, after all, 'Regular People', the industrious poor, who were 'the Life and Perfection of Treasure, the Strength of Nations, and Glory of Princes'. But, although he came close to it, Bellers never put these questions, never saw the implications for leisured wealth that the modern eye might detect in his theory of labour. Accordingly, he never felt the necessity to justify the position of the idle rich. Their rôle should be one of stewardship in relation to their wealth, and the demands of this, as well as self-interest, could best be met by providing employment for the poor. Where better than in Colleges of Industry?[168] The joint-stock

---

[166] Bellers, *Proposals for a Colledge*, pp. 10–11.
[167] Joyce Appleby, 'Ideology and Theory: The Tension between Political and Economic Liberalism in Seventeenth Century England', *American Historical Review*, 81:3 (1976), pp. 499–515.
[168] Bellers, *Proposals for a Colledge*, pp. 2, 20, 28; *Essays about the Poor*, pp. 5–6, 8.

model had thus solved for Bellers the problem of the leisured rich. They could be kept separate from the labouring poor, assigned a rôle, their property secured and augmented, without the awkward implications of his labour theory being explored.

Like Vaughan, Bellers wished to win the support of the rich, not to threaten them. He was prepared to offer them the surplus product of the industrious poor to get it. This is what sets him irremediably apart from Winstanley.[169] Like Plockhoy, influenced by his sectarian religious position, he could visualise the full-employment ideal within a withdrawn community, which in the joint-stock form solved at a blow the problems of the leisured rich, the selected poor and the assumed inelasticity of general demand. This resolution was assisted by the fact that, unlike Hartlib and his followers, Bellers had no faith in public enterprises, preferring always private enterprise and the profit motive. 'Private stock are better than public stock for employing the poor as being better husbanded as experience has shown; while the interests of the undertakers will oblige them to more care in managing the stock; and besides constant overseers will be much better than annual ones.'[170]

What Bellers' colleges resembled more than anything else were the factories beginning to emerge in the late seventeenth century. For those factories were not marked by technological innovation, division of labour, specialisation of function, but by the attempt to tackle the problems of scale in terms of detailed regulation and organisation of space and time. The pre-industrial factory, to coin a rather unlikely term, was using familiar and traditional modes of production on a new scale, and it was the problems of scale which obliged its devisers to innovate. Their innovation took the form of a striving after organisational perfection. The institutions, rules and procedures which they adopted were designed to impose time, work and organisational disciplines upon pre-industrial man, to make him a functioning part of a human machine.[171] It is not surprising then that we

---

[169] It is impossible to find support for Margaret James' supposition that Bellers was influenced by Winstanley and the Diggers. James, *Social Problems and Policy*, pp. 29, 340.

[170] Quoted by Belasco, 'John Bellers', p. 173. See also, Bellers, *Essays about the Poor*, To the Lords and Commons in Parliament Assembled, p. 2. I see little evidence to support Charles Webster's assertion that Bellers was developing reform projects covering almost the same ground as Hartlib. See Webster (ed.), *Samuel Hartlib and the Advancement of Learning*, pp. 72, 111.

[171] Cf. Lewis Mumford, 'Utopia, the City and the Machine', *Daedalus* (1965), pp. 271–92, reprinted in Frank E. Manuel (ed.), *Utopias and Utopian Thought* (Boston, Mass., 1966), pp. 3–24. See also Keith Thomas, 'History and Anthropology', *Past and Present*, 24 (1963), pp. 11–12; E. P. Thompson, 'Time, Work-Discipline, and Industrial Capitalism', *Past and Present*, 38 (1967), pp. 56–97; Neil McKendrick, 'Josiah Wedgwood and Factory Discipline', *Historical*

may observe a convergence between the utopian attempt to organise a fully employed community and the factory owners' attempt to create an organisation which would ensure a disciplined workforce and maximised output.[172] These utopian elements within the emergent factory can best be illustrated by examining the experiments of Sir Ambrose Crowley and his son, John, at their Winlaton and Swalwell ironworks in northeast England.

Like Bellers, Ambrose Crowley was brought up a Quaker.[173] Despite his training as apprentice to a London draper, Crowley followed his father and grandfather in the ironware industry, but unlike them he was not prepared to accept the restrictions of the trade as it operated in the Black Country. The iron industry in seventeenth-century England consisted of small dispersed units dependent on scattered fuel supplies and limited by poor transport. Crowley's innovation arose from his realisation that the manufacture of ironware from bar-iron need not be bound by these restrictions. By placing his ironware works in the Newcastle area he availed himself of the following: plentiful supplies of coal; bar-iron, available locally or by import from Sweden; and good, cheap transport between the northeastern coalfields and London. The major limitations on scale were organisational problems and the quality of labour. The Crowley's *Law Book* was devised to overcome both limitations.

In the early 1690s Crowley opened a nailworks at Winlaton near Newcastle, maintaining his headquarters in London so as to handle warehousing, distribution and contracts for the sale of finished goods. The Winlaton works rapidly developed to production of many other kinds of ironware besides nails. Benefiting from naval contracts in the 1690s and 1700s, the business expanded. Rolling and slitting mills, furnaces, a plating forge, smiths' shops, workmen's houses and offices were built. In 1707 Crowley bought out a rival establishment at Swalwell and this became the main centre of his activities. At his death in 1713 it was, according to

Journal, 4:1 (1961), pp. 30–55. Even for Adam Smith economic progress was associated with organisational development rather than with technological innovation. See, Phyllis Deane, *The Evolution of Economic Ideas* (Cambridge, 1978), p. 12.

[172] Cf. Peter Laslett, *The World We Have Lost* (London, 1965), Chapter 7. Laslett associates the emergence of the factory with poverty and destitution through municipal workhouses. One should also note Laslett's point that the joint-stock company represented a first break with traditional society. For an example of a poor relief scheme approximating to a factory see Thomas Firmin, *Some Proposals for the Imploying of the Poor*. Firmin was a Congregationalist. See, H. W. Stephenson, 'A Seventeenth Century Philanthropist: Thomas Firmin (1632–1697)', *Transactions of the Unitarian Historical Society*, 6 (1936), pp. 130–47.

[173] For Crowley's life, background and the history of his business see M. W. Flinn, *Men of Iron: The Crowleys in the Early Iron Industry* (Edinburgh, 1962). See also M. W. Flinn (ed.), 'The Law Book of the Crowley Iron Works', *Publications of the Surtees Society*, 167, (London, 1957). Hereafter cited as *Law Book*.

M. W. Flinn, the largest industrial undertaking outside the naval dock-yards in England. It was the largest business controlled by one man in the country. In 1702 Winlaton alone employed 197 workers and in the second quarter of the eighteenth century the Crowley firm was employing over a thousand workers altogether.[174]

Employing such relatively great numbers involved problems of recruit-ing and discipline. Agents were sent on recruiting tours of Yorkshire and the Midlands and workers were imported from as far afield as Liège.[175] Within the establishment, however, there was virtually no change in methods of work, in techniques of production or in the end product. Work was still done in small units or shops, using traditional methods. Master workmen often employed their own assistants. The Crowley works were, as has been pointed out, a combination of factory and domestic system. Workers had to respond to the factory buildings and the factory day, to a different concept of space and time, but the processes of manufacture remained virtually unchanged.[176] What innovation there was arose out of an attempt to control an extraordinarily large manufacturing complex over a long distance in an age of poor communications. Such remote con-trol made necessary a framework of rules and administrative procedures, but in Crowley's hands it was the idealisation of organisation and the profound faith in its procedures which brought the *Law Book* of the Crowley ironworks close to a utopian vision.

'It hath always been the practise of wise and experienced masters at the settlement of any factory to lay such foundamentals for the members thereof to be ruled as might tend to the satisfaction of the one and the peace and tranquillity of the other.' Over the years of their establishment's development Crowley and his son, John, set about this task with a vengeance. Laws and instructions followed one another until they amounted to a prodigious, and bulky, written constitution under which the firm operated. Crowley himself was a kind of absentee monarch to whom all owed allegiance and whose decision was final. The immediate recipients of his instructions in the factories were the members of the Council. They were appointed by Crowley and swore an oath to serve his best interests and conform to his orders. A 'comptrol' or committee of the Council was set up to expedite day-to-day administration. Beneath the Council came a host of committees and officials responsible to it, and beyond it to Crowley. Their functioning and organisation were set out in elaborate detail.[177]

---

[174] Flinn, *Men of Iron*, pp. 54, 61, 75, 252.　　　[175] *Ibid.*, pp. 40, 236.
[176] Flinn (ed.), *Law Book*, p. xxiv; cf. Maurice Dobb, *Studies in the Development of Capitalism* (London, 1963), pp. 147–8. See also Flinn, *Men of Iron*, pp. 192–3, 206–7, 252–3.
[177] *Men of Iron*, pp. 195–201; *Law Book*, pp. xiv–xx, 8.

The main purpose of the organisation was, of course, to maintain and control a *flow* of materials through manufacturing processes to finished goods and profitable sale. Major concern therefore centred around control of materials, time and officials supervising the flow. Each week, accredited workers were issued with a stock of raw material for which they had to account at the end of the week, either as finished goods or raw material in hand. Stock, however, remained a subject under constant supervision and renewed efforts at control, a problem never finally solved. The same difficulty occurred with tools issued by the firm until finally workers were made to buy them.[178]

The standard working week which Crowley expected of his men was a six-day, eighty-hour week. Finding, however, that some employees did not do what he considered a fair day's work, nor make the firm's interest their own, he characteristically introduced a new official, the Monitor or time-keeper, and a set of regulations covering his functions. The Monitor was to sleep on the premises and keep strict account of each worker's entry and exit. He was to deduct time spent in drinking, smoking or conversation. Other officials were warned against wasting workers' time, or slowness in despatch of articles ready for shipping. Severe penalties were laid down for altering the timekeeper's clock, and informing against loiterers was encouraged.[179]

The lynchpin of the whole system was clearly the local, managerial bureaucracy which Crowley hoped would implement his instructions and guarantee the running of the business in accordance with his wishes. Like utopians before and after him, he found it necessary to strain after disinterested and efficient bureaucracy if his organisation was to work perfectly. It was not an easy achievement. Amongst the officials and foremen there was clear division of labour, but Crowley found it necessary to add detailed regulations, cross-checks and fines for non-performance or abuse. Officials were found acting unilaterally, defrauding workers, accepting bribes, showing bias, engaging in private deals, neglect, drunkenness and outright felony. Check was added to check, law to law. The corruptability of managers predisposed Crowley to work through committees, but their delay and caution, in turn, obliged him to elaborate yet more detailed regulations. Out of all this struggle with organisation and training did come efficient and honest managers such as John Hanmer, John Bannister, Abraham Alleyne and Isaiah Millington, who ran the firm through the eighteenth century and made its interests their own.[180]

Although new recruits to the firm were scrupulously examined, not only as to trade experience but also in moral character, nothing was taken

[178] *Men of Iron*, pp. 203–4; *Law Book*, pp. 98–9.
[179] *Law Book*, pp. 6, 88–97, 115, 119, 133.
[180] *Ibid.*, pp. xxvi, 11, 22–5, 30; *Men of Iron*, pp. 84–5, 194–5.

for granted. For an impressive range of offences, fines were collected. Informers were rewarded and failure to inform on a law-breaking colleague became itself an offence. Orders were at all cost to be made effective; discipline at all cost to be established. 'I had better any order had never been made', read Order Number 80, 'provided it be not put into practice, and the not inflicting the penalties upon the offenders doth not only destroy the intent of the order but weakens all other orders.' The cashier, an official on whom much depended, was to take the following oath on entry to office: 'And in case the devil shall have so much ascendant over me that I shall break any of these promises I own myself to be a lying impostor, a destroyer of my own safety, and a treacherous false villain to John Crowley Esqr., and deserve a halter more than his favour.'[181]

The design was ultimately to prevent abuse by removing choice. Something might be achieved by persuading the individual worker and official to internalise the firm's values. 'Be sure you perfectly print in your mind all laws wherein your office is concerned, and with steady resolution to keep them; and upon no terms adhere to those that shall propose or put you in methods to break your laws, or any ways evade the true intent and meaning of them.'[182] But this conscientious spirit could not be relied upon and as the Crowleys reached out to embrace every eventuality, to offset every risk, they came close to the detailed totality so familiar in the utopian. As M. W. Flinn has observed, 'Crowley's determination to avoid administrative chaos led him to prescribe every detail.'[183] Not only were gambling, drinking, swearing, smoking and fighting forbidden on pain of fines, but precise rules were laid down as to how letters should be folded or bags labelled.[184] 'Every jest or jocque' at Council meetings was to be fined a penny.[185]

Men could be outlawed, demoted, fined or discharged in punishment for offences. Perhaps the most significant effort to restrain waste and abuse was to lay the charge for it against the fund set up for the general welfare of the workers and their dependants and contributed to by both the workers and Crowley. It was, in a sense, an attempt to use the pressure of community feeling against waywardness. And Crowley thought of himself as building a complete community.[186] Religion was provided for by the appointment of a chaplain to conduct regular services. Similarly, medical facilities were provided although regulations were carefully framed so as to prevent their abuse. The workmen's children were to receive regular instruction in basic literacy and the catechism of the established church. Some housing was provided and other lodgings sub-

---

[181] *Men of Iron*, pp. 239–40; *Law Book*, pp. 2, 26, 35, 46–47, 127–9.
[182] *Law Book*, p. 69. Cf. *ibid.*, pp. 66, 87, 159.   [183] *Men of Iron*, p. 124.
[184] *Law Book*, pp. 5–6, 32, 39, 60–1, 117, 156.   [185] *Ibid.*, p. 32.
[186] Cf. *Men of Iron*, p. 219.

sidised. Sickness benefits, funeral expenses and relief in dire poverty were provided out of what amounted to an employee–employer insurance scheme.[187] Of course, there are respects in which this can be regarded as a means of producing labour stability in the economic interests of the firm. That should not detract from the overall effect. To control a large-scale enterprise the Crowley's were obliged to conceive a comprehensive community with utopian dimensions.

Vaughan to a slight extent, Plockhoy to a greater and Bellers to the greatest degree had, in projecting their full-employment utopias on to withdrawn communities, almost necessarily anticipated the factory as it was to become known at the end of the seventeenth century. 'Necessarily' because what distinguished the factory at the end of the seventeenth century was not differentiation of process, not division of labour or technological innovation, but differentiation in space – the factory building or complex – and differentiation in time – the factory day.

By a convergent process Sir Ambrose Crowley, in elaborating his factory, came near to a utopian solution because in order to overcome the fearful complexities of organising men, without the discipline of the machine or the punitive resources of the state, he had to devise structures of organisation and administration which could produce a disciplined sense of time, space, flow and property essential to what remained labour-intensive, large-scale industry. It would be tempting therefore to see the history of the seventeenth-century full-employment utopia as a movement away from national solutions, with their problems of leisured classes and levels of demand, towards the withdrawn community of the joint-stock factory. But the publication of two anonymous tracts as the century waned adds one last twist to the story.

In 1698 and 1700 two essays in utopian thought by the same anonymous author appeared in London. They were, in a sense, extensions of, or commentaries upon, each other. The first, *An Essay Concerning Adepts* written by a 'Philadept', raises the question of whether 'Adepts', that is, those who possess knowledge of the philosopher's stone and transmutation, do exist. That they do, Philadept believes is evident, just as 'the Principles of the *Hermetick Philosophy*' have been established beyond question. The problem then raised is that, if they exist, why do the Adepts not reveal themselves and use their power to benefit and transform society? The answer is 'the perverse disposition of the generality of men'. The Adepts cannot show themselves or reveal their knowledge because in a corrupt and wicked society there is no guarantee that the knowledge revealed, and the power it represents, will not be used for evil ends. Adepts will reveal

[187] *Law Book*, pp. 141, 154–86.

themselves when they see 'Reason, Justice and Moderation prevail among Men'. In order for it to be possible for mankind to share this knowledge a good society must be created, and one must begin by knowing what a good society is. Philadept, therefore, begins his essay by sketching an ideal society at the level of village communities, although he goes on to sketch a *minimum* programme of reform such as might satisfy the Adepts.[188] In the second work, *Annus Sophiae Jubilaeus, The Sophick Constitution: or, The Evil Customs of the World Reform'd*, a dialogue takes place between Philadept and 'a Citizen'. The theme is the same, but this time Philadept sketches out his ideal society at the level of national government, and in terms of general social welfare and town planning.[189] The two works are therefore complementary and together form a comprehensive picture of an ideal society.

That picture echoes a number of themes of the utopian genre. The Adept is seen as a man of knowledge, an innocent who can only be sure that his power will be used innocently in a just and good society. He is a pre-lapsarian Adam, still possessed of his dominion over nature, who is trying to find a home in the fallen world.[190] The problem of the nature of that dominion raises the question of what rôle the author is adopting in the rivalry of late-seventeenth-century scientific ideologies, and the place of hermeticism at this late stage.[191] Again, the author raises the problem of the scientific utopia, on which Bacon's ideal-society aspirations foundered. On the one hand, scientific knowledge may only be thought safe in a perfect society. On the other hand, can the possessors of scientific knowledge be restrained within virtue in the good society, and can the knowledge which they possess be prevented from changing the *perfect* society? To a degree, the author here evades some of the issues by concentrating on a pre-scientific ideal society – the society in which science will be safe – and ignoring the issue of the later impact of science upon that society. In an old utopian dodge, he justifies his evasions by suggesting

---

[188] [Philadept], *An Essay Concerning Adepts* (1698), pp. 6, 7–8, 9. I have used the Cambridge University Library copy: shelf-mark Bb°12.45³(G): Wing S.T.C. E3279.

[189] *Annus Sophiae Jubilaeus: The Sophick Constitution: or, The Evil Customs of the World Reform'd* (1700). Again the Cambridge University Library copy has been used: shelf-mark Bb12.2"(F): Wing S.T.C. A3248.

[190] Cf. *Annus Sophiae Jubilaeus*, pp. 4, 10, 17.

[191] On the place of hermeticism in the 1650s see Webster, *The Great Instauration*, pp. 305, 391–2. Webster sees transmutation as a long-term objective in *Macaria*; *ibid.*, p. 332. Frances Yates in *Rosicrucian Enlightenment* has raised a number of questions and possibilities regarding the rôle of hermeticism and the Rosicrucian ideology in seventeenth-century thought, but we still lack a serious examination of these themes for the seventeenth century as a whole, and for the later seventeenth century in particular.

that, whatever else, the exercise is useful as a means of discovering and reforming evil customs.[192]

In *An Essay Concerning Adepts* the author describes the kind of college-like communities that the Adepts would prefer men to live in. An estate worth four hundred pounds a year should, he argued, be able to support four parishes (or a town). The income from the land should be distributed in the proportions of one-quarter to the landlord, three-quarters to the populace. From this point on the landlords' existence becomes quite detached. They live in their manor houses with their servants, the rest of the populace live in college communities, dining together, doing without money, each man equal in his share of the land and working it by his own labour. The inhabitants of the parishes annually choose three magistrates for each parish, and twelve together from four associated parishes make a Parliament to decide, 'with the Approbation and confirmation of their Lord', the affairs of the community.[193]

In each parish the inhabitants live in a square or college. Dominating the square is a central hall, with adjoining butteries and kitchens, for communal dining, worship, education and meetings. Around the other sides of the square 'a little House for every family' is built. These, although uniform, are described in great detail. Another square is comprised of barns, workshops, magazines, stables, pigsties, a gaol, henhouses, wash-houses and dairies. The author says he will give no more detail but then goes on to describe the orchards, water supply and sanitation of the community.[194]

Four of these parishes are joined to form one self-sufficient town. Everyone is to have a particular skill but also to join in the general work of husbandry. The working day is set out in extraordinary detail for every-one. Each person is to work five hours each day on public projects. One hour may be devoted to private enterprises. Three hours are given over for devotion and instruction in religion and a further three for meals and conversation. Two hours are spent each evening at a public reading of history, law, physic or similar studies, 'but let Romances be utterly banished'. Two hours are allowed for play or recreation and one hour may be 'lost in preparing for Work, and in putting up the Instruments after the work, &c.'. After these seventeen hours of designated activity, seven hours are left for sleep.

On some days the young men were to be allowed time for fencing and shooting practice as preparation for war. Young people, however, were to be constantly supervised and boys and girls were not allowed to play

---

[192] *Annus Sophiae Jubilaeus*, p. 20. The examination of the two works in this chapter, which is restricted to the full-employment aspects, makes no claim to a comprehensive treatment.

[193] *An Essay Concerning Adepts*, pp. 12–14.   [194] *Ibid.*, pp. 14–17.

together. Children were to live in their parents' or guardians' house until the age of seven when they would enter service in other men's houses, if necessary in another parish. Here they would work until marriage or the age of thirty, when they would have a house, servants and full civic rights allowed to them. Men were expected to marry at the age of twenty-six and women at twenty-three. Those who married much before or remained unmarried much after these ages were 'liable to some punishment'.

Masters were not to work as long hours as their servants and their burdens were eased with age. The old were honoured as senators, giving counsel and acting as an inspectorate to check the work of others and the general condition of the town. Elderly women and men sat as sentinels at each gate of the town and watchmen patrolled the streets day and night.

The aldermen and mayor were to change every year, 'that everyone may have his turn'. Each parish was to maintain a schoolmaster and a divine. The first day of each week was set aside for rest, devotion and thanksgiving. These local officials had to supervise a battery of regulations, presumably produced by a king and Parliament which are merely mentioned in passing. The highest punishments were reserved for fornicators, adulterers, the unclean and those who married without the approval of a majority of the governors. Imprisonment was the penalty for theft or riot. Prisoners, chained by the feet, were to do hard labour for ten hours a day.[195]

There were to be no unnecessary occupations. Painting, engraving and the making of ribbon or lace were prohibited. Music and dancing were not to be anyone's sole means of employment and there were to be no songs about love or drinking and no dancing of men and women together. People had to wear a plain, uniform dress. Food was to be plain and wholesome, sufficient but not excess. Sauces and tobacco were not allowed. Standard meals were set out in some detail. Pullets, partridges and small birds were reserved for the sick and infirm. 'For to do as we would be done to is the law of Reason and the Dictate of the Wisdom of God.' Pigeons, geese, swans, as well as superfluous dogs and horses, might not be kept because of the damage they did.[196]

This was the ordered life of a well-disciplined community as captured in the author's description of a routine day.

The first thing that shall be done in the morning (after our People have washed

---

[195] *Ibid.*, pp. 17–20. For the correspondence of the family arrangements advocated here with contemporary practice see, Laslett, *The World We Have Lost*, Chapter 4; Philippe Ariès, *Centuries of Childhood* (London, 1962) Chapter 1; Alan Macfarlane, *The Family Life of Ralph Josselin* (Cambridge, 1970), Chs. 5, 6; John R. Gillis, *Youth and History* (New York, 1974), Chapter 1; David Hunt, *Parents and Children in History* (New York, 1972).

[196] *An Essay Concerning Adepts*, pp. 20–2.

and are ready, and have been at their private Devotions, which shall be done at Six of the Clock, there being an hour allowed for that and their dressing, being called up to rise at five of the clock at farthest; then just at six of the Clock, a Bell having tolled) they shall repair to the Common Hall, where there shall be made a Publick Prayer, and one Chapter shall be read in the new Testament, after which every one shall receive the portion allowed for his Breakfast. After that every one also shall prepare for Work, and shall Work three or four hours or more, as it shall be best determined. Then the Bell shall toll again, and every one shall wash and clean himself; and all things being disposed of, and the last signe of the Bell being giving, all shall repair to the Hall again, where the whole Service shall be read, and after that, a portion of some Book of Devotion. Then will follow the Dinner, before and after which, Grace shall be said. And after some Conversation after Dinner, there shall be Song a Spirituall Hymn, before they return to work. And thus they shall spend their time...They may dine about one, and sup about seven. Immediately also before Supper, the service shall again be read. And at Night, the last thing that shall be done in Publick before they part, shall be to Worship God by Prayer and Devotion.[197]

The discipline is that of a religious community where work and worship are the organising principles of life. The author acknowledged that only by disciplined employment and controlled consumption could the lavish community buildings which he envisaged be supported. All ought to work and the problem of the leisured rich could be avoided by leaving them out of the central community. In this sense all men were equal and, if this could only be acknowledged, 'All men would have enough, and would Bless, and Help, and Comfort one another.'[198]

Yet, the author conceded, this standard of perfection might be seen as too high. Perhaps science could flourish in a society less perfect. Nevertheless the list of required improvements, even in a situation of compromise, was impressive. Selfish designs should be set aside, provision be made for the poor and their instruction, prices be fixed, the law be reformed, justice and medicine be made free to all, soldiers not be left idle, crime and immorality be punished, luxury be suppressed, the church be reformed and revived and Parliament be kept busy finding remedies for all disorders.[199] The author recognised that to make this reformed, rather than ideal, society acceptable to the Adepts involved men limiting their aspirations. In this sense there was more of an atmosphere of the perfect moral commonwealth about it than the utopian parish communities described earlier. 'May God in His infinite Mercy inspire every one in his Station with what he is to do, and what every one in particular shall answer for at

[197] *Ibid.*, p. 23.
[198] *Ibid.*, pp. 24–5, 27–8, 30. See also p. 34 for an acknowledgement of the monastic parallel.
[199] *Ibid.*, pp. 37–42.

the great Day of Judgement.'[200] Like Winstanley, the author assumed in this tract that the gentry could be left alone – although this time with their servants – and forgotten. Two years later, when his focus was national rather than parochial and on demand rather than leisure, he did not find the problem of a wealthy, leisured class so easy to shelve.

Annus Sophiae Jubilaeus demonstrates this national rather than parochial focus from the beginning by concentrating on the question of the terms upon which an Adept would be prepared to enter a national government. Given that Adepts were protected and maintained in full liberty in a college to be built, furnished and supplied with servants in the metropolis, they would be prepared to enter government in an advisory rather than administrative rôle. The government, however, should not be on an arbitrary basis but consist, in variation on the Polybian theme, of king, Adepts and a senate. These three would swear oaths of reciprocal loyalty. The senate would be composed partly of nobles, 'partly of a certain number of the most Expert, the most Judicious, and the most Vertuous among the People, chosen and nominated by the People themselves'. It should control its own assembly and meetings, and share in the nomination of officers of state. Conflict between the three elements of the constitution – king, Adepts and senate – should be resolved by a committee of arbitrators consisting of all the judges and twenty men of virtue. Treating and bribery in elections were regarded as serious offences punishable by imprisonment.[201]

More particularly, the Adepts were seen as wanting an informed, worshipping, protestant society. The basic, common principles of Christianity should be made clear and adherence to them insisted upon. Otherwise there should be toleration, although no one would be allowed to live irreligiously. The parochial structure would be renewed so that all parishioners could be accommodated in their parish church building. This obviously meant that many parishes would have to be divided and new churches built. Four services of worship would be held each day of the year and attendance at two each day was compulsory for everyone. Parishioners were to be constantly catechised until the age of thirty or until they could expound their faith satisfactorily. Several sorts of catechisms would be devised for different age groups. In the smaller parishes the minister should know each member of his congregation well. He was to spend at least an hour every month with every parishioner as well as organising two hours' instruction every day for the catechumens. Hence the idleness of the clergy, subject to episcopal supervision, would be avoided. Ministers were to meet regularly in associations of parishes to confer on problems and to set up lectureships. A godly nation was clearly a reading, studying and listening nation.

[200] *Ibid.*, pp. 41–2.   [201] *Annus Sophiae Jubilaeus*, pp. 21–3, 33–6.

When he moved on to parochial church affairs, the author demonstrated his utopian preoccupation with detail. More ministers would be needed to serve the greater number of parishes. A fifth of their incomes should be laid up for their widows and children. New church buildings would also be needed and they should be carefully designed. There should be galleries where women and girls could be placed behind glass to prevent the immodest regarding of either sex by the other during the services. No pictures, carvings, funeral monuments or tombs were to be allowed in the building and seating was to be without respect of person. The vestibulum and chancel were to be small so that the congregation might easily be kept warm in the winter when it would be spending six sabbath hours in devotion. Communion was to be taken every first Sunday of the month and elaborate detail of its ordering was laid down. Public fasts and thanksgivings were treated with great seriousness. Breach of a fast was in fact a capital offence. Like the Quaker botanist, Thomas Lawson, the author wanted the 'heathenish names' of the days and months to be changed to something more 'Christian-like'.[202]

The main theme of the social and economic aspects of the society described in *Annus Sophiae Jubilaeus* was equality. Government was expected to undertake the provision of full employment at reasonable rewards. This meant a system of minimum wages. A man should be entitled to a minimum of eighteen pence per day 'all the Year round, throughout the nation'. Similarly a woman should get at least a shilling a day, and a child of seven to fifteen years threepence, fourpence or fivepence. 'By this means there should be some equality (more at least, than is ordinary in this wicked and unjust World,) every one being able to live comfortably and conveniently according to his condition.'[203] Equality in this context then meant comfort in one's station in life. Later, however, the author suggests that 'all fit Means should be used to render every Man Rich, and make him live plentifully and comfortably'. But there is a distinction between comfort as security from want, and comfort as affluence or expanding consumption. The former is favoured, the latter discountenanced. While people should enjoy a comfortable equality, frugality and temperance were regarded as socially essential, 'indispensibly necessary Vertues'. It is a bad failing in parents to bring their children up effeminately and accustomed to superfluity; rather they should be hardy and temperate. All unnecessary trades should be abolished, unnecessary expenses spared. There should be no 'Fringe, Lace, Imbroidery, nor the Like'. Men were to be exhorted against delicacies and gluttony. Tobacco

---

202 *Ibid.*, pp. 23–33. Cf. the manuscript by Thomas Lawson, *Adam Anatomized*, Friends House Library Mss., Box c, no. 2. See also his *Dagon's Fall Before the Ark* (1679). See also Keith Thomas, *Religion and the Decline of Magic*, p. 360.
203 *Annus Sophiae Jubilaeus*, pp. 38–39.

and snuff should be abolished, feasting and treating forbidden, excess in dress a punishable offence.

For Moderation, Industry and Charity are always necessary in order to present and future Happiness. Men should then in some Measure, bear one another's Burdens; concur, in their several Stations, to do the affairs of the Society, carefully and diligently, according to their several Capacities; and deny themselves those Things which would be prejudicial to the Felicity of the whole Body.[204]

The notion of expanding consumer demand as a way of promoting full employment was firmly rejected. The author recognised it in the form that it would take in Bernard Mandeville's 'private vices, public benefits' formulation.[205] The argument that excess provided employment for thousands of artisans assumed a situation which, to him, was unacceptable in a Christian society. Of course, restraining consumption in temperance and frugality merely exposed the other side of the problem, that of disposing of the surplus produced by a fully employed society, but we shall see how the author dealt with this shortly.[206]

The theme of equality was pursued into areas such as fiscal policy, everyone paying something, however little: 'if it were but a Penny in the Pound, and an Equal Poll, according to every one's Ability, tho' it were never so little'. Limits were suggested to the possessions in land of each man, 'that those that had too large a share should distribute part of them to some of their Family and Kindred, and should sell some part to the Adepts, for the use of the Publick'.[207] As in *An Essay Concerning Adepts*, law and medicine were to be equally available to all. All were to work, 'to exercise some Calling, or Employment useful to the Society'. All parks, commons and wasteland were to be cultivated and all land improved to its maximum advantage. Even prisoners were not to live in penal idleness but were to be seen labouring hard in 'Schools of Repentance and Vertue'. All likewise were to receive a hard and disciplined education: 'they should set private observators over them, to watch to all their Actions; and for every Immorality, they should be punished more than for any other Fault: These Rules should be observed in all Schools, great and small'.[208]

There was to be public provision for the poor, especially in the form of work. No matter how little they were able to do, all conditions of men, women and children should be provided with work. 'It is then, visibly,

[204] *Ibid.*, pp. 58–60, 62.
[205] Bernard Mandeville, *The Fable of the Bees: or, Private Vices, Publick Benefits*, edited by F. B. Kaye, 2 vols. (Oxford, 1924); M. M. Goldsmith, 'Public Virtue and Private Vices', *Eighteenth-Century Studies*, 9:4 (1976), 477–510.
[206] *Annus Sophiae Jubilaeus*, pp. 62–3.   [207] *Ibid.*, pp. 36–7, 40–1.
[208] *Ibid.*, pp. 39–49, 57. Space forbids a more thorough examination of the detailed provisions for education, defence and so on.

horridly, shameful to have Beggars in a Commonwealth. It is a sign that there is little Charity and Christianity, little Prudence and Order...' The cause of the present neglect was that men were habituated to thinking in terms of inequality.

A merchant, a Nobleman, a rich Cardinal think abundance of things necessary to their well being, without which they would account Life a perfect misery. But a poor, honest Artizan, that worketh hard perpetually for the Society, they think is well provided for, if he can get six Pence a day for his maintenance, and that of a Wife and several Children.

The remedy was that 'such constitutions should be made, that those whose living depends upon their labour, might live agreeably and comfortably, as well as they that possess the Lands, and keep the purse'.[209]

So the author returns to the theme of equality and just rewards, but he deals rather unsatisfactorily with the problem of the leisured rich, evading both the question of their idleness and their wealth in vague talk of Christian charity. However, the problem of surplus production in a fully employed society is much more directly dealt with. The surplus is seen as channelled towards the Adepts who use it for building churches, hospitals, fortifications, for paving highways and for repairing and rebuilding towns and cities. Half the masons and carpenters of the land were to be employed on public works and teaching soldiers their trades so they might be likewise employed. This permitted the author, who two years previously had sketched out his ideal village, to engage in a town planning exercise. Cities and towns were to be 'built square, all the Streets straight, broad and equal; so that there should be no Lanes nor Allies, but the Streets should be alike'. All houses were to be built to the same pattern. Traffic was to be carefully controlled. Sanitation, waste disposal, provision of open spaces, industrial zoning were all provided for. Living in a city would become a privilege and not a right. 'All unnecessary Persons should be obliged to remove to some other place.'[210] These planned and beautiful cities were but the epitome of a public works programme made possible in a full-employment society, and in turn providing a means of absorbing its surplus product without producing either a more unequal society or one corrupted by luxury.

Just as the public works programme absorbed the surplus of a successful economy, so the Adepts with their capacity to transmute base metal to gold were seen as underwriting that economy against failure. In emergency the Adepts would provide for the poor or meet the needs of the national treasury. To prevent men from depending too greatly on the Adepts' skills and falling into idleness, however, it was necessary to disguise them behind trading operations, run by the Adepts, with the Indies. As the

[209] *Ibid.*, pp. 49–51.   [210] *Ibid.*, pp. 54–5.

Adept solves the problem of the utopian moment and the need for a moral giant, a lawgiver who can lead men from a world gone wrong into an ideal society, so also the Adepts' powers sustain that society once in being.[211]

In this version of the full-employment utopia, the labouring classes are to enjoy at least a minimum income and full employment. But this is not seen as leading to expanding consumer demand and a generally rising level of economic activity, self-sustaining growth. Rather the concern is to limit the effects of affluence on consumption – preventing wasteful consumption and the evils of excess, which are still seen as both morally corrupting and taking out of the mouths of others. Hence the importance of the Adepts' underwriting the economy with gold, the quasi-magical panacea, whenever culturally and legally limited demand causes production to flag. In *An Essay Concerning Adepts* the problem of the leisured wealthy is solved by setting them aside with their servants, and the writer concentrates on local organisation. Here, where the focus is national, there is an ambivalence between talk of equality and the existence of disparities, which produces appeals to Christian charity and a certain tension between utopian and perfect moral commonwealth elements.

It has recently been argued that there existed in the last decades of the seventeenth century a number of economic thinkers in England who did begin to see that demand could be a dynamic, expansive factor in economic growth, and that steadily expanding demand in an autonomous market could be the best guarantee of economic strength.[212] Consumption, in this framework, could be seen as creating full employment of itself, if only the level of demand were high enough. None of the full-employment utopians studied here appear to have accepted the dynamic demand analysis. They assumed the inflexibility of the total level of effective demand. Indeed, not to have accepted it would have been to emphasise a supply/demand relationship which saw market autonomy as the most effective mode of growth, and this left no room for utopian planning. Rather they sought an integrated economy stabilised at a level of comfortable frugality. The surplus produced by full employment and the elimination of waste could be dealt with in a variety of ways. It could be diverted to investors who themselves lived outside the full-employment community; a solution adopted by both Rowland Vaughan and John Bellers. It could be invested and absorbed in public works, as in *Annus Sophiae Jubilaeus* or, to a degree, in *Macaria* and *The Poore Mans Advocate*. Finally it could be

---

[211] *Ibid.*, pp. 22, 36, 37, 53.

[212] Appleby, 'Ideology and Theory'; 'The Social Origins of American Revolutionary Ideology', *Journal of American History*, 64:4 (1978), pp. 935–8. For a fuller treatment see Appleby, *Economic Thought and Ideology in Seventeenth Century England* (Princeton, 1978).

used in reducing costs to undercut competitors' prices at 'home' or
abroad. To the withdrawn community the national market is, in a sense,
an external market of which the community can design to seize a greater
share by lower pricing and costs. The fact that the withdrawn community
can ignore problems of total demand is a great pressure in its favour, given
the underlying assumption of inflexible total demand. Both problems of
demand and of surplus were amenable to solution from the base of the
withdrawn community.

A more critical problem still, judging by the difficulties it caused, was
that of a leisured class, the comfortably unemployed in a full-employment
society. Where all other resources were busily employed, they would stand
out in their idleness. Their existence challenged the equal obligation of all
to work productively which was central to the full-employment ethic.
There was always thus a radical potential about the full-employment
aspiration. In the 1690s Sir Dalby Thomas argued, like Bellers, that
people are the wealth of a nation, but only 'laborious and industrious
people; and not such as are wholly unemployed, as gentry, clergy, lawyers,
serving men and beggars, etc.'. The lumping together of gentility and
mendicancy as burdens on society was a disturbing point of view. Earlier,
Sir William Petty had argued for a transfer of wealth by taxation 'from
the Landed and Lazy, to the Crafty and the Industrious'.[213] Gerrard
Winstanley had seen his programme of labour withdrawal forcing the
gentry and aristocracy to put aside their pride and work their estates with
their own hands.[214]

Even earlier Sir Thomas More had approached the problem by redefin-
ing the leisured class. In a society which gave all men equal claims to the
community's property, men were to be released from the obligations of
communal work on the basis of intellectual distinction rather than wealth.
Riches could not justify inequality of work in *Utopia*, but wisdom could.
James Harrington, a century and a half later, had sought to defend an
aristocracy on a more nearly traditional basis. In *Oceana* and elsewhere,
he had presumed an identity between wealth, leisure and political prudence
which might justify the continuance of a privileged class, but he never
systematically examined the relationship between the three attributes.

The full-employment utopians studied here all demonstrate an ambivalence towards the leisured class and this is no doubt associated with the
fact that the ruling class and the leisured class were one and the same. To

---

[213] Appleby, 'Ideology and Theory', p. 500, n. 4. See also Thomas Scott, *The
Belgicke Pismire* (1622) for an even earlier insistence on the duty of all, including nobles, to work. For other criticism of the idle upper classes and their waste
of resources in such things as deer parks see Brian Manning, *The English People*,
pp. 188, 282.
[214] See above, Chapter 7.

make them irrelevant or to threaten their existence might well appear reckless in the extreme. On the one hand, the full-employment utopian asserts the equality of all in their obligation to work. On the other, he admits the possibility of leisured wealth. The easiest solution to the dilemma was to move from a national society to a withdrawn community, as did Vaughan, Plockhoy and Bellers. The rich could be excluded and hence the problem of their idleness be avoided, and moreover, they could be offered a rôle as both investors and consumers of surplus. Since the appeal to charity was uncertain, the offer of a profit income in return for their investment completed the picture. John Bellers' joint-stock utopia, in this sense, represents the culmination of a long struggle with the problem.

In addition the withdrawn community solution had two other aspects. First, it made possible a shift from harnessing the promiscuous poor for continual labour to providing security for a select group of workers. Plockhoy, for example, was not thinking of recruiting unemployed workers at all. Bellers seems to have thought in terms of a morally refined selection of Quaker poor. The Crowleys, faced with severe problems of labour recruitment, might be thought to have had little choice, but it is interesting to note that they restricted citizenship to piece workers, that is to those who were selling the product of their labour, rather than those, simply wage labourers, who were selling their labour itself.[215] The former, as self-proprietors, could still act as moral agents.

Secondly, the evolution of a withdrawn community response to the problems of the full-employment utopia may be associated with waning confidence in the will or capacity of the state to tackle the problem. Not only had the traditional apparatus proved ineffective, but the opportunity of reform in the 1640s and 1650s, such as it was, had never been taken. Certainly there is evidence that members of the Hartlib circle were, by the end of the 1650s, thinking in terms of small community alternatives to national reform. The Act of Settlement of 1662 must have looked like an abandonment of the problem at a national level. Every parish was to shift for itself.

Traditionally, poor law legislation provided, at its best, an emergency relief system only. W. K. Jordan has shown the massive importance of private charity in the effort to fill the gap, but the problems of the able bodied poor and of unemployment were never tackled convincingly. Partly this was because of 'moral decadence' amongst the poor, partly because of the difficulty of distinguishing honest from ungodly poor and partly because of the sheer scepticism of donors.[216] The full-employment utopians

[215] Flinn (ed.), 'Law Book', p. 9.
[216] W. K. Jordan, *Philanthrophy in England; The Charities of London 1480–1660: The Aspirations and Achievement of the Urban Society* (London, 1960); *The Charities of Rural England.*

sought to resolve all these difficulties in their vision of a total community environment, but increasingly it was based on the sectional solution of a withdrawn community.

In so far as one can simplify to this point, it seems that by the end of the seventeenth century two alternative solutions to the problems of the full-employment utopia existed. One, as in *An Essay Concerning Adepts* and *Annus Sophiae Jubilaeus*, was to maintain a national vision and underwrite it with magical infusions of gold, absorbing any surplus produced in massive public works schemes. The second was the joint-stock factory of Bellers and the Crowleys. From this one excluded the leisured class and so confronted neither their idleness nor their power. Having not alienated them, one could aspire to tap their wealth available for investment and reward them with profits, so solving the community's difficulties with the moral problems of surplus.[217]

217 Cf. this with George Orwell's solution on a national basis in *Nineteen Eighty-Four*. Full employment could be balanced with unremitting scarcity if the state pursued endless war. See, Martin Kessler, 'Power and the Perfect State', *Political Science Quarterly*, 72 (1957), p. 575.

Conclusion

There is no other way for escaping these ills than to give the city institutions that can by themselves stand firm.

Machiavelli, *A Discourse on Remodelling the Government of Florence* (c. 1520)

Utopian thought is dominated by a 'rage for order'. A strong utopian impetus is to save the world from as much of its confusion and disorder as possible. Utopia is a dream of order, of quiet and calm. Its background is the nightmare of history.

George Kateb, *Utopia* (1971), Introduction

The new society cannot be brought about by a number of partial reforms within the existing framework. The utopian approach expresses its aspirations by projecting a new totality.

Martin G. Plattel, *Utopian and Critical Thinking* (1972)

So that prisons should vanish forever, we built new prisons. So that all frontiers should fall, we surrounded ourselves with a Chinese Wall. So that work should become a rest and a pleasure, we introduced forced labour. So that not one drop of blood be shed anymore, we killed and killed and killed. In the name of the Purpose we turned to means that our enemies used.

Andrei Siniavski, *On Socialist Realism* (1965)

What then is utopia? It is a mode of visualising social perfection which is best defined by distinguishing it from alternative modes of social idealisation. The utopian mode is one which accepts deficiencies in men and nature and strives to contain and condition them through organisational controls and sanctions. The Land of Cockaygne presumes no deficiencies in nature but an abundance distinguished by the capacity to satisfy the grossest appetite, leaving all men replete. Arcadia is a world of natural beneficence and human benevolence, where the deficiencies of both man and nature are made good in an atmosphere of calm and gentle fulfilment. The perfect moral commonwealth presupposes a continual and successful moral striving by everyone, a moral heroics, such that the wilfulness and occasional hostility of nature is contained and subordinated in social harmony. Man is assumed perfectible and perfect in performance. Finally, the millennium assumes a coming state of redeemed and perfected men, restored to their pre-lapsarian command over nature, but such things cannot come from fallen man himself, only from a *deus ex machina*.

Contemporary writing about utopia in the West tends to fall into two schools. On the one hand are those who see utopia as a threat to liberal, democratic society – in Karl Popper's phrase to the 'open society' – or as a threat to the essential humanity of man as a moral agent.[1] On the other side are those who believe that without utopian vision man may lose control of his future, that even social engineering must be designed around a comprehensive and integrated vision of what future society will be.[2] This ambivalence has been paralleled in the Soviet Union, where utopia has been regarded with suspicion as non-scientific and pre-Marxian, but Soviet planning has almost necessarily involved some uneasy flirtation with

[1] Karl Popper, *The Open Society and Its Enemies*, 2 vols. (London, 1961); Popper, 'Utopia and Violence', *Hibbert Journal*, 46 (1947–8), pp. 109–16; F. A. Hayek, *The Road to Serfdom* (London, 1962); Thomas Molnar, *Utopia: The Perennial Heresy* (New York, 1967).
[2] Andrew Hacker, 'In Defense of Utopia', *Ethics*, 65 (1955), pp. 135–8; Martin G. Plattel, *Utopian and Critical Thinking*, translated by H. J. Koren (Pittsburg, 1972). Rudolf Moos and Robert Brownstein, *Environment and Utopia: A Synthesis* (New York, 1977). Charles J. Erasmus, *In Search of the Common Good: Utopian Experiments Past and Future* (New York, 1977).

utopian designs.[3] To some degree this uncertainty has been obscured by a tendency to confuse utopia with other forms of ideal society. We must begin by being clear about utopia's distinctness.

From a study of early modern utopianism one derives perhaps a certain scepticism about some forms of broad generalisation. What impresses even in the narrow selection of utopias studied here is a variety which militates against simple identification of utopianism with aspects of class, freedom, the city, degrees of seriousness or psychological states.[4] Nevertheless some general observations on early modern utopianism may be made and in the main they stem out of utopia's distinctness as a form or type of ideal society.

The utopian mode is distinguished by its pursuit of legal, institutional, bureaucratic and educational means of producing a harmonious society. Since nature and man have proved inadequate, artifice must be tried.[5] Moreover, the devices to be used – legal, educational, bureaucratic, and institutional – must not follow nature, since nature itself is deficient. Rather they must discipline man and nature to conform to them. Men must be made to conform to the law and not *vice versa*. The fault of English policy in Ireland, Richard Beacon wrote in 1594, was that you 'framed your lawes to the subiect and matter, and not the matter and subiect unto your lawes, as sometimes Lycurgus did in his reformation of Sparta'.[6] Essential to the exercise, therefore, was the setting up of such an apparatus of social control as would not be corrupted by the deficiencies inherent in men and nature. It is not surprising in this context to find so many of the early modern utopians drawn to the monastic model, for the monastery in its discipline, structures, rituals and rule of life had sought to subdue sinful nature in servitude to a perfect or holy commonwealth.[7]

---

[3] See, Jerome M. Gilison, *The Soviet Image of Utopia* (Baltimore and London, 1975).

[4] On the psychological issue, for example, see Frank E. Manuel, 'Towards a Psychological History of Utopias', *Daedalus* (1965), pp. 293–322; Frank E. Manuel and Fritzie P. Manuel (eds.), *French Utopias: An Anthology of Ideal Societies* (New York, 1966), p. 5, where utopias are held to become really serious only in the eighteenth century.

[5] This involves rejecting the view that early modern utopianism was in essence a return to nature (cf. J. O. Hertzler, *The History of Utopian Thought* (London, 1923), p. 126) and the view that utopians reduced the rôle of the law (Cf. Paul Foriers, 'Les Utopies et le Droit', in Jean Lameere (ed.), *Les Utopies à la Renaissance*, Travaux de l'Institut pour l'Etude de la Renaissance et de l'Humanisme (Paris and Brussels, 1963), p. 234).

[6] Richard Beacon, *Solon His Follie, or A Politique Discourse, Touching the Reformation of Common-weales Conquered, Declined or Corrupted* (Oxford, 1594), p. 6.

[7] Cf. Max Weber, *The Protestant Ethic and the Spirit of Capitalism*, translated by Talcott Parsons (London, 1930), pp. 119–21.

It has been argued that, in the Christian framework, primacy could only be attached to politics at the risk of blasphemy or heresy.[8] If secular time, which must be the dimension of politics' operation, is seen as little more than a meaningless flux – the realm of *fortuna* and contingency in which men, to survive, must act in an amoral and self-centred fashion – it may be the duty of Christian man to direct his attention outside of time to the universal and eternal. The classical republican, like the utopian, defied the meaninglessness of secular time by offering a construct of agencies and institutions which could restrain anti-social behaviour and open to participating citizens the opportunity to choose the path of civic virtue, giving meaning to that choice. The risk always was, as the history of classical republicanism shows, that the freedom which choice and participation imply might not be used well and wisely and that corruption and collapse would follow. It was the long-term risk of impermanence and instability, a risk which utopianism was not prepared to take, and freedom, participation and politics pay the price for that unwillingness. As politics, with its potential for the pursuit of sectional interests, its irreconcilable value clashes, may represent man at his most selfish, perverse and deficient, unable to elevate his social nature above his egoism, so one of the utopian's deepest urgings is to end politics. Just as utopian fiction is a way of escaping the deadlock of values, which political debate can end in, by visualising the implications of one set of those values, by engaging in a thought experiment,[9] so in reality utopia seeks to end the social debate, the struggle over sacrifice and reward, over opportunities and restrictions, over the distribution of justice, which is politics. In utopia, as Ralf Dahrendorf has pointed out, there can be no conflict over values or institutions.[10] So both in social intent, and in its operation as fiction, utopia's greatest enemy is pluralism. This thread runs, for example, through Benjamin Zablocki's deft and perceptive study of one of America's most successful utopian communities, the Bruderhof. In their communities no sub-groups are permitted and factionalism is regarded as a sin. The smallest of sub-groups, the individual self, is identified with evil, the collective self with good. 'Unity is the highest value in Bruderhof life' – just as it was in Plato's *Republic*. To some degree, Bruderhof success as an ideal com-

[8] J. G. A. Pocock, *The Machiavellian Moment: Florentine Republican Thought and the Atlantic Republican Tradition* (Princeton, 1975), p. 552. Even where early modern thinkers stress civic participation, one has to ask whether in fact they are according *primacy* to politics or if primacy in this context has any real meaning for them.

[9] Cf. Elizabeth Hansot, *Perfection and Progress: Two Modes of Utopian Thought* (Cambridge, Mass., 1974), pp. 30, 4–5, 38, 90–1.

[10] Ralf Dahrendorf, 'Out of Utopia: Toward a Reorientation of Sociological Analysis', *American Journal of Sociology*, 64:2 (1958), p. 116. Reprinted in George Kateb (ed.), *Utopia* (New York, 1971).

munity has rested on breaking the separateness of the smallest of sub-groups and so preventing the emergence of others. Not only are individual members forbidden to share confidential information between one another, but 'The Bruderhof socialization process is designed to make it torment to withhold information about oneself on any matter.'[11]

Like any other writer, the utopian must begin by visualising his audience. It is his first fiction.[12] To visualise and project a reconstructed society he must visualise an audience with shared values. Hythlodaeus so assumes that his hearers, and by extension perhaps the readers of More's *Utopia*, will recognise and share his values. Such shared values are the precondition of appreciating his critique of contemporary society and for accepting the 'perfection' of his utopian ideal.[13] In a Christian society which, nominally at least, shared or aspired to many common values, the utopian writer might visualise his audience as the entire community and weigh his design in seriousness and possibility accordingly. In a world of secular pluralism, on the other hand, the utopian writer may find it diffi-cult to visualise his audience and particularly so should he address himself to remodelling his whole society, rather than a withdrawn segment of it.

Another aspect of this same phenomenon is the desire to end what I have called moral inefficiency, and this too finally results in the end of politics. The danger that besets the utopian is that it may after all, in a social sense, appear reasonable for deficient man to pursue selfish aspira-tions if the inefficiency of the connecting chain between intention, deed and result is such that no moral purpose, however zealously pursued, can be *guaranteed* to obtain its objective. The problem, serious as it is, can be intensified if we allow that not only may good not flow from good inten-tions, but that, such is the perversity of things, bad itself may flow from the desire for and pursuit of the good. When we add to this the relativism of moral values in a pluralistic world, society begins to appear like a moral sieve. The utopian is engaged in stopping all the holes. Not only must a pluralism of values cease, but an efficient connection between moral inten-tion, deed and result must be established, and the accidental must be diminished, if not eliminated. To adapt Friedrich Meinecke's terminology, empirical necessity must reinforce supra-empirical obligation, or, in Gaetano Mosca's terms, the gap between collective illusion and social reality must be closed.[14] The dramatisation of this is the order/disorder

---

11 Benjamin Zablocki, *The Joyful Community* (Baltimore, 1971), pp. 156, 158, 209, 225.
12 Walter J. Ong, 'The Writers' Audience is Always a Fiction', *P.M.L.A.*, 90:1 (1975), pp. 9–21.
13 Hansot, *Perfection and Progress*, p. 77.
14 Freidrich Meinecke, *Machiavellism: The Doctrine of Raison d'Etat and its Place in Modern History*, translated by Douglas Scott (London, 1957); Gaetano Mosca, *The Ruling Class*, edited by Hannah D. Kahn (New York, 1939).

dichotomy with which the utopian sustains his vision. 'The choice is no longer between Utopia and the pleasant ordered world that our fathers knew. The choice is between Utopia and Hell.' It is 'Utopia, or else'.[15] To escape hell, the nightmare of history, a moral chaos, men must accept that only by submitting their whole lives can life be made whole. Totality of control is the answer to the order/disorder dichotomy. As Berdyaev says, 'utopia is always totalitarian, and totalitarianism in the conditions of our world is always utopian'.[16] Even the self-defining, intentional communities of the 1950s felt drawn to define their purpose as 'establishing a whole way of life'.[17] In Fénelon's *Salentum* of 1699, 'Magistrates must be appointed to superintend the conduct, not of every family only, but of every person.'[18] It is a point which has been exemplified repeatedly in this study. Freedom always carries the possibility of disorder. In offering choice, it enables one to choose wrongly, foolishly and wastefully, and not only well, wisely and to good effect. In removing the threat of disorder, one removes freedom. The ultimate totalitarianism is to remove one's freedom as a biological or intellectual organism. Aldous Huxley in *Brave New World* was satirising a utopian view of eugenics which had been taken seriously since Campanella and before. In B. F. Skinner's *Walden Two*, motivations, which utopians have always sought to condition, are simply treated more scientifically and systematically.

The utopians of early modern Europe could address themselves to a society imbued with common Christian values and shaped by common material realities. In its social organisation it was, however, complex, confused, irregular, riddled with exceptions, exemptions and privileges, with overlapping jurisdictions. It was a corporative society, an organic amalgam of privileged and competing groups loosely held into a hierarchical frame, a society without uniformity, rationality or equality, to which the early modern utopian gave his challenge. In place of the organic, pluralistic, corporative society of his age he offered a rational and uniform construct based on a single set of principles and embodying them. The irony is perhaps that the would-be utopian of today faces a world of growing uniformity and standardisation, but one in which all values have become relative. His opportunity arrived at the very moment that his audience fragmented. Hence today it is easier to find a public audience for the dystopia than for the utopia itself. All anti-utopias to date – *Nineteen*

---

[15] W. H. Beveridge, *Power and Influence: An Autobiography* (London, 1953), p. 355; René Dumont, *Utopia or Else...* (London, 1974).

[16] *Slavery and Freedom*, quoted in Robert C. Elliott, *The Shape of Utopia: Studies in a Literary Genre* (Chicago, 1970), pp. 89–90; cf. Fred L. Polak, *The Image of the Future*, 2 vols. (Leyden, 1961), vol. I, p. 432.

[17] Zablocki, *Joyful Community*, p. 19.

[18] Manuel and Manuel (eds.), *French Utopias*, p. 79.

Eighty-Four, Brave New World, We and the others – have been written from the point of view of the miscreant, the criminal. He represents our relativism, our desire for self-affirmation, the pressure to pluralism, and he also represents the other limb of the paradox. The unorthodoxy of the rebels is what gives them their critical capacity but it also gives them their underlying weakness, their general sense of being unsatisfactory. For the utopian's answer to the miscreant's action is to point to his ignorance, ignorance of the conditions of pre-utopian life. The rebel's criticism can only be understood in terms of a selfish ignorance which stems from its anti-social nature. All anti-utopianism hitherto is profoundly anti-social.

Both the challenge and the threat implicit within utopianism remain profoundly disturbing despite the difficulty which faces the utopian in search of an audience. For he asks two questions which the post-industrial world, with its dispersal of power, its *arcana* and mysteries of specialised technological advancement and its relentless dependence on continued economic growth, faces and evades every day. How seriously do you take social values? How negotiable is individual liberty? As long as affluence maintains this least bad of all possible worlds, these questions can be shirked, but nevertheless a vague unease persists.

Amongst the ways used to dismiss or at least diminish utopia have been those of questioning its relevance or its seriousness of purpose. Utopia, it has been said, not without reason, would be a dull and boring place to be, with the peaks and troughs of existence flattened out,[19] one where man could not be happy. The answer to this, of course, is that the utopian's prior value is not happiness but *order*, and, while he may go on to consider the happiness that might be built on that order, this is not necessary. A second charge is that utopia, like all forms of ideal society, is unreal, unrelated to time and space as we know it. This is a charge easily exaggerated. In so far as utopia deals with what ought to be rather than what is, it seems unreasonable to judge it by the standard of the latter. But this may not be entirely fair. The utopian is concerned with the links between is and ought. As our analysis of him in terms of the collective problem showed, he distinguished himself from other types of ideal-society thinker precisely by his unwillingness to abandon the problems of the real world, the deficiencies of man and nature. For a number of reasons it simply will not do to assert that utopia is outside time, ahistorical. The utopian's visualisation straddles two spheres. He projects something which has not been realised, but his selection of it relates to the world of here and now. 'Utopia transcends the given reality; it is not transcendental in a metaphysical sense.'[20] In a similar fashion, the conclusion has too often been

[19] For a recent discussion in these terms see Kateb (ed.), *Utopia*, Introduction.
[20] M. I. Finley, 'Utopianism Ancient and Modern', in Finley, *The Use and Abuse of History* (London, 1975), pp. 180–1. Cf. François Bloch-Lainé, 'The Utility of

drawn that, because a common purpose of utopias is to satirise existing society, this necessarily precludes them from serious consideration as political thought, that they are purely material for literary study. All satire operates from a point of view or reference to which the satirist owes allegiance and from which he finds existing society wanting. The attack on what is elucidates the nature of what should be, just as the vision of what should be arises out of an appreciation, an analysis, of what is.[21] What may more precisely be meant by the challenge that utopia is unrealistic is that it possesses no notion of means by which the ideal should be made real. It is not so much the content of the utopian vision which is seen as unrealistic here,[22] but the absence of any programme of action. Compared with millenarianism, for example, utopia has no theory of change, no 'transfer mechanisms'.[23] There is validity in this criticism. It is difficult to see how the utopian can move from present reality to utopian perfection, given his belief in the necessity and inevitability of environmental conditioning. If men are perverse and corrupted by the world in which they live, how can they rise above it to achieve a better society? It is a problem most clearly revealed in considering the utopian lawgiver – Utopus, Solamona, Olphaeus Megaletor, the 'Cromwell' to whom Winstanley appeals and the rest. These lawgiver heroes are presented with an opportunity which they exploit with perfect wisdom, disinterestedness and morality. In allowing that man can rise to this moment, the utopian comes dangerously close to admitting the case of the perfect moral commonwealth, that man can perform with perfect morality. Since all change implies choice and all choice implies moral alternatives, the moment of transfer from now to utopia is fraught with difficulties for the utopian, and it is not surprising that he evades them.

It might be argued that all ideal societies are outside of time – notime, as well as nowhere. But in relation to the Christian framework, the background against which early modern utopias were written, time was the working out of the consequences of sin, the fall of man and God's redemptive process. Most ideal societies in the European tradition were related to that concept of the flow of time. Arcadia was a vision of the pre-lapsarian Eden; the perfect moral commonwealth, society in process of redemption;

Utopias for Reformers', *Daedalus* (1965), p. 422; Polak, *Image of the Future*, vol. I, pp. 24–6; on Raymond Ruyer's theory of utopia as a play on parallel possibilities see Roger Mucchielli, 'L'Utopie de Thomas Morus', in Lameere (ed.), *Les Utopies à la Renaissance*, p. 101.

[21] On the theme of satire and utopia see Elliott, *Shape of Utopia*.

[22] On realism in this context see David Riesman, 'Some Observations on Community Plans and Utopia', in Riesman, *Individualism Reconsidered and Other Essays* (Glencoe, ill., 1954), pp. 70–98.

[23] Dahrendorf, 'Out of Utopia', p. 116. Cf. the discussion in Harold V. Rhodes, *Utopia in American Political Thought* (Tucson, Ariz., 1967), Chapter I.

the millennium, society redeemed; utopia, 'perfection' is a state of sin – the best possible in the fallen world. In this sense, utopia is the closest of all forms of ideal society to history as the story of the fall, because it accepts the consequences of sin and the continuity of the problem of sin. Within the framework of his utopian vision the utopian writer can build a sense of time, of history, and this may in fact be very important to him. In *The History of the Kingdom of Antangil*, a French utopia of the early seventeenth century, it is recorded how two thousand two hundred years previously the state had been founded on its present basis in order to bring continual warfare to an end.[24] Of course, this is a historical myth, but in what sense are the historical myths of utopia different from the historical myths of the real world? Are not all our perceptions of our place in time artificial? What looks like a world without history, the world of utopia, is a world without politics. Only if we assume a rather narrow identification of history with politics can utopia be seen as a world without history. As William Morris pointed out, history in the ideal society is important as a warning of what otherwise might be.[25]

In recent writing the relationship between utopia and history has been used as a means of categorising utopia or of distinguishing phases of its development. Judith Shklar has argued that classical utopia existed no-where in time, as well as in space, that its function was to erect an unchanging moral standard. As soon as projects have the objective of change, as soon as they become action-minded, they cease to be utopian.[26] Building on this, Elizabeth Hansot divides utopias into the classical, which by portraying a fixed moral standard seek only to change the individual and are not concerned with social realisation, and the modern, which are activist, seek to incorporate change and are designed for realisation. The change from classical to modern utopias is seen as taking place during the seventeenth and eighteenth centuries. Unfortunately, this sort of *schema* just does not fit the evidence of early modern utopias. It is nonsense to say that More and Andreae 'downgrade the importance of society' or that their efforts are directed at 'man's flawed moral nature rather than the

---

24 Anonymous, *The History of the Kingdom of Antangil* (1616) in Manuel and Manuel (eds.), *French Utopias*, p. 37. Cf. the histories of Utopia and New Atlantis. In Utopia 'Their annals, embracing the history of 1760 years, are preserved carefully and conscientiously in writing.' *Utopia*, edited by Edward Surtz, S. J. and and J. H. Hexter, *The Complete Works of St. Thomas More*, vol. IV (New Haven and London, 1965), p. 121. Cf. pp. 113, 219–23, 386, 520–6. Bacon, *New Atlantis* (1627), pp. 10–11, 14–18.

25 William Morris, *News From Nowhere*, edited by G. D. H. Cole (London, 1948), p. 138.

26 Judith Shklar, 'The Political Theory of Utopia: From Melancholy to Nostalgia', *Daedalus* (1965), pp. 367–81; Shklar, 'Rousseau's Two Models: Sparta and the Age of Gold', *Political Science Quarterly*, 81:1 (1966), pp. 25–51.

institutional arrangements that later utopians were to emphasise'.[27] Basic
to the difficulties here is a confusion between perfect moral commonwealth
and utopia. The utopian's prior assumption has always been that man's
deficient moral character could not be changed by example alone but that
its deficiencies must be supplied by social sanctions and arrangements. In
these terms the utopian type of ideal society has been unchanging through
history.

Perhaps the three most important legitimating devices of early modern
English political thought were ancient constitutionalism, order theory,
and patriarchalism.[28] Utopianism cut across all three. However much
utopian writers might play with historical myths for their utopias, they
never imagined their ideal societies as immemorial. Indeed such an
assumption would have imperilled their view of man as naturally deficient.
The ideal state had to be seen as an artifice, created in time, precisely in
order to overcome human and social deficiencies as recorded in history. In
the same way patriarchal authority could not simply be accepted as legitimate on the basis of its antecedents or origins. In Sir Robert Filmer's
hands this had been a means of legitimating obedience to bad and even
wicked government but the utopian was interested in good government
alone. Utopians thereby rejected both the claims of fundamental law as
purveyed by ancient constitution theory and of fundamental authority as
embodied in patriarchalism. Similarly, the concept of order and corre-
sponding planes, and argument by correspondence, which Greenleaf sees
as integral to the political theory of order, played no great part in utopian
thinking. All three forms of political justification precluded change other
than renovation, but the utopians' critique of contemporary society and its
ills was too radical to permit of such compromise with human and natural
deficiencies. Whereas for patriarchalists, ancient constitution and order
theorists models could be found, notionally at least, in history or nature,
for the utopian history was a nightmare and nature a wilderness.

Utopia represented an image of triumph over *fortuna*, over the endless
play of accident and fate in the lives of men. But as in other ideal societies,
that triumph is represented as social rather than individual. In a world
wedded to traditionalism and suspicious of innovation, utopia offered a
new society, remade from top to bottom. Its weaknesses by comparison
with the other great theory of social plasticity available to the early modern
world, millenarianism, were that it was not possessed of a theory of change

[27] Hansot, *Perfection and Progress*, pp. 56, 49.
[28] For a discussion of these traditions see J. G. A. Pocock, *The Ancient Constitution and the Feudal Law* (Cambridge, 1957); W. H. Greenleaf, *Order, Empiricism and Politics: Two Traditions of English Political Thought 1500–1700*
(Oxford, 1964); Gordon J. Schochet, *Patriarchalism in Political Thought*
(Oxford, 1975).

and that it placed its trust in human design rather than divine power. It represented changed states but offered no process or dynamic of change.[29] By contrast, the millenarian, as we have seen, had difficulty in envisaging the changed state which the processes upon which he dwelt would bring about. The classical republican also saw a means, through a balanced constitution, of creating a moment – which John Pocock has called 'the Machiavellian Moment' – when men might be freed from the play of *fortuna* to exercise civic virtue and realise their full humanity as citizens. As I have argued earlier, what distinguishes the utopian from the classical republican is the latter's *desiderata* of freedom and participation. The utopian wishes to produce a society of order, goodness and stability, triumphant over *fortuna*, but he attaches no primacy to participation and freedom. Through the manner in which he brings time under control (makes of it a rational order) he is made incapable of depicting the confrontation between virtue and corruption and therefore sets himself outside the Machiavellian Moment. This leaves the problem of Harrington. Was he, as Pocock argues, confronting that moment in English history and thereby dependent on grace, a millenarian? Or was he a utopian and therefore evading the confrontation between *fortuna*, civic virtue and corruption and so not engaging grace? The central issue here is the nature of the participatory republic in Harrington's *Oceana* and what it is that the citizens in that republic might be said to participate in doing, a problem which I have tried to examine in Chapter 8.

What has to be acknowledged is the surprising capacity of early modern thinkers to see society as a system of interrelated parts which might be based on a common, even a single, set of principles, as evidenced by the utopian writers of this period. This is a capacity which has often been denied them by later commentators. We may illustrate this quite simply in terms of civic consciousness. According to Donald Hanson, 'civic consciousness refers to the elementary perception that there is a public order, that the social order is in part a network of shared problems and purposes, and to the installation of that recognition at the centre of political ideas and conduct'.[30] All three elements in this definition are present in utopian thought and it is all the more surprising that the development of civic consciousness in the early modern period can be so often discussed without reference to utopianism. One aspect of utopianism's

---

[29] Cf. R. J. W. Evans' characterisation of the court of Rudolph II in Prague as 'the delicate combination of a fatalism about action and a striving for ideal solutions'. Evans, *Rudolph II and His World: A Study in Intellectual History, 1576–1612* (Oxford, 1973), p. 274.

[30] Donald W. Hanson, *From Kingdom to Commonwealth: The Development of Civic Consciousness in English Political Thought* (Cambridge, Mass., 1970), p. 1, see also pp. 12, 26.

relevance to the development of civic consciousness is as a commentary on the inadequacy of the governmental and administrative power and effectiveness of the early modern state. The pretensions of government in this period are often barely distinguishable from the totalitarian range of utopian social controls.[31] Dress, work, wages, morals, opinions, property and time were all seen as fit subjects for legislation, but scarcely anywhere was policy effectively implemented. 'How many proclamations thereof have been divulgate and not obeyed? How many commissions directed and not executed? (Mark well here, that disobedient subjects and negligent governors do frustrate good laws.)'[32] The weakness and ineffectiveness of central government in the early modern European state, which has been stressed in so many recent historical studies, is highlighted by the utopian's vision of well-ordered, effectively governed and efficiently administered societies. The lynchpin of that vision was, of course, the impersonal, state-serving bureaucrat who developed so painfully and slowly out of the *ancien régime*. For him to emerge it was necessary to break the notion of public office as a property to be exploited for private gain and class or sectional advantage, a notion which held considerable sway in early modern administration.[33] The utopians prefigured this development in their images of ideally administered states and in their emphasis on the capacity of impersonal bureaucracy, law, education and fit institutions to mould social performance. They stand at the fountainhead of a fateful development. Usurers, monopolists, property owners, lawyers, clergy, officials, soldiers, merchants, and courtiers – all these on

---

[31] For a recent exemplification of this theme see G. Benecke, 'Labour Relations and Peasant Society in North West Germany, *c.* 1600', *History*, 58 (1973), pp. 350–9.

[32] Sir Thomas Elyot, *The Book Named the Governor*, edited by S. E. Lehmberg (London, 1962), p. 119.

[33] Cf. G. E. Aylmer, *The King's Servants: The Civil Service of Charles I, 1625–1642* (London, 1961); Aylmer, *The State's Servants: The Civil Service of the English Republic, 1649–1660* (London, 1973); Joel Hurstfield, *Freedom, Corruption and Government in Elizabethan England* (London, 1973), Parts III and IV. Enlightened despotism, as exemplified by both Frederick William I of Prussia and Joseph II of Austria, was engaged with the definition of the ideal bureaucrat. Frederick William: 'an intelligent, assiduous and alert person who after God values nothing higher than his King's pleasure and serves him out of love and for the sake of honour rather than money and who in his conduct solely seeks and constantly bears in mind his King's service and interests, who, moreover, abhors all intrigues and emotional deterrents'. Joseph II in 1781 instructed all state servants that 'they must not act purely as useless copyists, not simply devote their backsides to sitting and their hands to signing for the State', but 'must sacrifice the powers of their souls, their reason, their wills and their whole strength to such work, and thus without considering the hours, the days, the manner, try zealously to keep it in good condition'. E. N. Williams, *The Ancien Regime in Europe: Government and Society in the Major States 1648–1789* (London, 1970), pp. 316, 427.

occasion may fear the utopian dispensation, but never does the bureaucrat share this fear. Utopia is ever welcome to him. It means the end of un-certainty, confusion, change of heart – indeed the end of governmental change in general. Utopia leaves the bureaucrat with a given, unvarying order. It focusses all attention on his primary rôle, the implementation and efficient operation of a given system. By extension, decentralisation, where it was advocated, was not a recognition of the claims of communal diversity or human individuality but an attempt to buttress the authority of institutions over men. The early modern utopians knew that, given the state of communications, the smaller region was likely to be a more effective disciplinary and administrative unit than the larger.

Intertwined in the history of western political thought are two notions of liberty – the participatory and the defensive.[34] In the former men are only free when as citizens they participate, in some sense, in governing themselves. Defensive liberty, on the other hand, consists of those forms of freedom from the incursions of other men and from the arbitrary action of public authority, the quiet enjoyment of personal rights, which can only exist under the protection of the law in a stable civil society. These two notions are not antithetical, although the language in which they are sometimes expressed by extremists would make this appear to be the case. The utopian is, in this sense, an extremist. He sees participatory freedom as always involving risks too great to be sustained and his pessimistic view of the nature of man reinforces that attitude. Men will choose wickedly, selfishly and foolishly. They will reduce society to chaos and disorder, or their fecklessness will allow evil and corrupt tyrannies to flourish. The utopian frees man from the consequences of this kind of participatory freedom and erects many barriers of defence against it. Freedom in utopia is therefore freedom from disorder and moral chaos, freedom from moral choice altogether.[35] This was not difficult to accommodate to a common early modern definition of freedom as expressed, for example, in Guicciardini's famous dictum 'a prevalence of law and public decrees over the appetites of particular men'. Or in Locke's formulation 'where there is no *law*, there is no Freedom'.[36] It was to this concept of freedom that Comenius appealed when he diagnosed the utopian view of man. 'There-

---

[34] See J. H. Hexter's comments in this vein in his review of Pocock's *Machiavellian Moment*, in *History and Theory*, 16:3 (1977), pp. 331–6.

[35] Cf. Molnar, *Utopia: The Perennial Heresy*, p. 16.

[36] John Locke, *Two Treatises of Government*, edited by Peter Laslett (Cambridge, 1970), p. 324. Cf. p. 302: 'Freedom of Men under Government, is to have a standing Rule to live by, Common to every one of that Society, and made by the Legislative Power erected in it; A Liberty to follow my own Will in all things, where the Rule prescribes not; and not to be subject to the inconstant, unknown, Arbitrary Will of another Man.'

fore man is not badly defined as the *disciplinable animal*; deprived of discipline, he fails to become man.'[37]

The malaise which commentators have so often noted as afflicting utopian thought in the second half of the twentieth century in fact extends to all forms of ideal-society thinking. Arcadia, for example, becomes difficult to imagine once the myth of the noble savage has been rejected and the findings of modern anthropology and psychology substituted for it. To create arcadia in the post-industrial world becomes a revolutionary task rather than a passive acceptance of Eden discovered. The Dark Satanic Mills must be swept away. This is essentially what has happened in the England of William Morris' *News from Nowhere*. The cities have disappeared. Nature has been restored and man finds society natural. But we know too much about the aftermath of revolution to be satisfied with such a vision of post-revolutionary arcadia. The alternative has been to imagine arcadia as emerging from a further and long drawn out process of evolution, in which a new and noble version of man, who can harmonise with nature, has emerged.[38] It is a far distant prospect.

Despite such movements as moral rearmament, the perfect moral commonwealth has become even harder to envisage, even more naive in appearance. Partly this is a result of what are seen as the dramatic and inescapable moral failures of twentieth-century man, in terms at least of the Judaic-Christian tradition and its values. Two world wars, genocidal anti-semitism, the crimes of imperialism and Stalinism, racialism and nuclear horror: these things rob us of optimism in the moral capacities of man. Moreover, in a world conscious of itself through modern communications systems as a massive labyrinth, in which individual will and action pale in significance, where complexity, accident and pluralism reduce moral certainty, we find it difficult to regard ourselves as moral agents with any potency. These fears set up a number of pressures which push away from the perfect moral commonwealth towards utopia.[39] Since it is 'only within stable situations that intentions can be adequately expressed in actions and actions freed of unintended and undesirable consequences',[40] utopian restructuring of society tends to be the result. Man, his actions and their consequences must be made predictable in order to create the predictable society which turns out to be utopia and not the

[37] Quoted in J. W. Adamson, *Pioneers of Modern Education 1600–1700* (Cambridge, 1905), p. 58.
[38] The classic example is E. Bulwer-Lytton, *The Coming Race* (London, 1886). For a discussion on this theme see Richard Gerber, *Utopian Fantasy: A Study of English Utopian Fiction since the End of the Nineteenth Century* (New York, 1973).
[39] In Cabet's *Icaria*, for example, there is a law forbidding accidents to pedestrians by horses and vehicles. Elliott, *Shape of Utopia*, pp. 105–6.
[40] Hansot, *Perfection and Progress*, pp. 49, 52.

perfect moral commonwealth.[41] However, not only has the concept of history as a nightmare been revived, but the city too, once a symbol of hope and achievement, has been identified as a place of nightmare and torment.[42] Its problems are urgent, complex, unwieldy and in appearance intractable.

Even the last hope of an arcadian existence (or at least of a shared moral effort), the small commune appears to set demands not easily met without utopian structures. Judson Jerome's exploration of what he calls 'the new anarchism' provides a useful contemporary example. According to Jerome, the new anarchism sees nature as essentially good and humanity as a part of nature.[43] The new society carries a promise 'not of chaos but of the supreme orderliness and dependable rhythm of nature'.[44] But its coming is dependent on 'a revolution in consciousness', an 'I-Death', 'a change in human nature' which does not come easily.[45] Social mechanisms may have to be established to trigger such conversions; discipline implemented, institutions established and privacy proscribed in order to maintain them.[46] There is a feeling of ineluctable shift through arcadia, to perfect moral commonwealth, to utopia. Moreover, the societies which Jerome describes have a low survival rate compared with those which accept from the start a need for laws, institutions, bureaucracy and education.[47]

The last ideal-society alternative, the millennium, aspired to in the West by groups as disparate as the Jehovah's Witnesses and Charles Manson's Family, is being played out in a disillusioning way in the world of Soviet Marxism. Marxism was the most potent millenarian theory of a secular age. Man was to be saved and society perfected, not by efforts of will or imagination – these were stigmatised by Marx as he found them in the 'utopian socialists' – but by a force beyond himself: the impersonal force of history. Today the Soviet Union struggles with that inheritance in

41 See Andrew Hacker, 'The Specter of Predictable Man', *Antioch Review*, 14:2 (1954), pp. 195–207; Hacker, 'Dostoevsky's Disciples: Man and Sheep in Political Theory', *Journal of Politics*, 17:4 (1955), pp. 590–613; Rosabeth Moss Kanter, *Commitment and Community: Communes and Utopias in Sociological Perspective* (Cambridge, Mass., 1972), p. 39.

42 Constantinos A. Doxiadis, *Between Dystopia and Utopia* (London, 1968), Lecture 7.

43 Judson Jerome, *Families of Eden: Communes and the New Anarchism* (London, 1975), pp. 234, ix, 58.

44 *Ibid.*, p. 271.

45 *Ibid.*, pp. 4, 239, 250–251, Chapter 7.

46 *Ibid.*, pp. 180–1, 184, 257.

47 Kanter, *Commitment and Community*; see also her articles, 'Communes', *Psychology Today*, 4:2 (1970), pp. 53–7, 78; 'Commitment and Social Organisation: A Study of Commitment Mechanisms in Utopian Communities', *American Sociological Review*, 33:4 (1968), pp. 499–517. Zablocki, *Joyful Community*, Chapter 7.

its approach to the future communist state, uncertain whether to wait 'until the happy future descends on them from the heavens' or to create it with their own hands.[48] If writers consider the specific details of the emerging society too closely, they are in 'danger' of 'utopianism', as indeed are all economic planners.[48] Yet it is generally accepted by Soviet thinkers that communism is only possible in conditions of material super-abundance and that this superabundance must be achieved artificially. Consequently, planning and social controls can be seen as essential pre-requisites of the communist state. 'Under Communist conditions, all production will function like a single co-ordinated mechanism. Thus communism will finally conquer spontaneity in the development of society.'[50] This is virtually indistinguishable from the utopian view of society as a co-ordinated machine.

It is not, therefore, surprising that the last few decades have witnessed many calls for a revival of utopian thinking,[51] even when those calls have not been distinguished by clarity as to what the utopian type is and what its implications are.[52] Utopia does not evade the problems of man, nature and history in its reach for the ideal society. The willingness to accept its forms of 'authoritarian control' is shown repeatedly and is a marked feature of those recent community experiments which have survived for long periods.[53] But a number of serious problems bedevil the utopian imagination in the post-industrial world. Whereas, in early modern writing, utopianism represented sophistication, elaboration and innovation

---

[48] Gilison, *Soviet Image of Utopia*, p. 59. I am well aware that there is, of course, much more to Marxism than a facile, and in some quarters popular, identification with religious millenarianism.

[49] *Ibid.*, pp. 101, 119.

[50] A. Kovalev in *Kommunist* (1962), quoted in Gilison, *Soviet Image of Utopia*, p. 119.

[51] For example, Plattel, *Utopian and Critical Thinking;* Matthew Murray, 'The English Utopians', *Twentieth Century*, 174 (1966), pp. 12–15; W. E. Moore, 'The Utility of Utopias for Reformers', *American Sociological Review*, 31:6 (1966), pp. 765–72.

Herbert Marcuse has been in the rather curious position of demanding a vision of the new society while denying that it will be utopian on the grounds that it will be possible. See, Herbert Marcuse, 'The End of Utopia', in *Five Lectures: Psychoanalysis, Politics and Utopia*, translated by Jeremy J. Shapiro and Shierry M. Weber (London, 1970), pp. 68–82.

[52] See, for example, Plattel's confusion over the totalitarian aspirations of utopia; Plattel, *Utopian and Critical Thinking*, pp. 26, 55.

[53] Robert V. Hine, *California's Utopian Colonies* (New Haven and London, 1966), p. 169; Peyton E. Richter (ed.), *Utopias: Social Ideals and Communal Experiments* (Boston, 1971), pp. 20–3; Ed Schwartz, 'Why Communes Fail', in Richard Fairfield (ed.), *Utopia U.S.A.* (San Francisco, 1972), pp. 220–3; Kanter, *Commitment and Community*, pp. 33, 39, 129–30; Philip Abrams and Andrew McCulloch, *Communes, Sociology and Society* (Cambridge, 1976).

in terms of organisation, should it now move towards simplification?[54] The very success of man's modes of dominating nature and exerting social control may be seen as a dark and sinister threat rather than as a liberating force. All three of the classic dystopias of the early twentieth century – Zamiatin's *We*, Huxley's *Brave New World*, Orwell's *Nineteen Eighty-Four* – start with the assumption that the problems of production, distribution and social order have been solved.[55] On the other hand, given modern communications and global economic relationships, it is difficult to visualise the small, self-sufficient utopia. Few communes, for example, would lay any claim to self-sufficiency. Rather there seems to be a pressure towards a global utopia.[56] The problem therefore appears intractable. Simplicity, interdependence, massive scale and complexity are juxtaposed in apparent deadlock. Moreover, the generally held conception of freedom in the West is no longer compatible with utopian order. We tend to see freedom not as life under a law common to all men, but as an absence of external restraints including those of the law. We are, in this sense, Hobbesians rather than Lockeians. As, however, the problems of mixed economies, committed to policies of full employment and social welfare which are acceptable, if not obligatory, in representative democracies, have been revealed, the necessity for planning has been borne in upon us. It has frequently, and with force, been argued that large-scale planning is a human impossibility without compulsory limitation of choices, because no planner can know enough to do the job if choice remains free.[57] But in the name of what shall freedom be curtailed? What shall be the ends and justifying values of our planning? What world shall we create? Can social engineering itself be given meaning without utopian vision?[58] Against complexity, technology, the capacities of record and information retrieval systems and accumulated knowledge might be set the demands

[54] Cf. Northrop Frye, 'Varieties of Literary Utopias', *Daedalus* (1965), p. 342; Plattel, *Utopian and Critical Thinking*, p. 23.

[55] Martin Kessler, 'Power and the Perfect State', *Political Science Quarterly*, 72 (1957), pp. 565–77; cf. Lewis Mumford's warning in this context of the danger of impersonal social forces, of what he calls 'the Invisible Machine', Lewis Mumford, 'Utopia, the City and the Machine', *Daedalus* (1965), pp. 290–2.

[56] W. W. Wagar, *The City of Man, Prophecies of a World Civilization in Twentieth Century Thought* (Boston, 1963). Moos and Brownstein, *Environment and Utopia*, pp. 234, 274.

[57] Riesman, 'Observations on Community Plans and Utopia', p. 76; Hayek, *The Road to Serfdom*.

[58] Polak, *Image of the Future*, vol. 1, pp. 401–8; George Woodcock, 'Utopias in Negative', *Sewanee Review*, 64 (1956), p. 82. Cf. also the difficulties of integrating sociological and economic models in planning. Mancur Olson, 'Economics, Sociology and the Best of All Possible Worlds', *The Public Interest*, 12 (1968), pp. 96–118; Roland L. Warren, 'Toward a Non-Utopian Normative Model of the Community', *American Sociological Review*, 35:2 (1970), pp. 219–28.

of human individuality and its less fortunate concomitants, muddle, uncertainty and, ultimately, evil. Even the resort to small community experiments, as we have seen, does not solve the fundamental tension between freedom and social organisation. Indeed the substitution of happiness or self-fulfilment for order as the primary objective of ideal community, which is often associated with such experiments, has only exacerbated the problem. The exhaustion of such concepts as the 'General Will', 'Common Good' or 'Utilitarian Calculus' which our day has seen leaves us with a relativism or pluralism of standards which reduces choice to that between the private pursuit of satisfaction or greater social control. Both are negations of *communities of self-fulfilling, free individuals*.

The issue might then be presented as utopia or freedom, and it is hardly surprising that in this context utopias and dystopias appear to be barely distinguishable.[59] The rebel in dystopia – Winston Smith in *Nineteen Eighty-Four*, D-503 in *We* – represents freedom, but it is a freedom which is condemned to be anti-social, concerned only with personal satisfaction or worth. Man lives in a fragmented world. The utopian seeks to integrate it. In the process freedom is destroyed. The rebel, who strikes for freedom, must also embrace fragmentation. Freedom may well be, as the Grand Inquisitor in Dostoevsky's *The Brothers Karamazov* has it, a burden which men can only be happy without,[60] but the question of freedom and happiness is secondary to that of freedom and evil. The utopian impetus, as Morelly defined it with peculiar emphasis in his *Code de la Nature* (1755), is 'TO FIND A SITUATION IN WHICH IT WOULD BE ALMOST IMPOSSIBLE FOR MAN TO BE DEPRAVED, OR WICKED, OR AT LEAST WHERE THERE WOULD BE AS LITTLE EVIL AS POSSIBLE'.[61] More recently, B. F. Skinner has asked whether automatic goodness is something we desire, for he believes that behavioural conditioning and cultural engineering are capable of producing just that.[62] We may, however, while allowing the possibility that some men are capable of conditioning others to automatic responses, question whether this is the same as potential for 'automatic goodness'. For goodness is a pattern of choice, not a pattern of behaviour. Holy poverty is holy precisely because it is chosen poverty. We act well when we could have chosen to act badly. When we take away choice we take away morality. There can be no such thing as 'automatic goodness'. The most appalling threat of utopianism may not be in its potentiality for

[59] Eugen Weber, 'The Anti-Utopia of the Twentieth Century' in Kateb (ed.), *Utopia*, pp. 81–9; see also Kateb's introduction, *ibid.*, p. 9.

[60] Fyodor Dostoevsky, *The Brothers Karamazov*, translated by Constance Garnett (London, 1912), pp. 259–68. Cf. Elliott's discussion of this in *Shape of Utopia*, pp. 89–98.

[61] Manuel and Manuel (eds.), *French Utopias*, p. 100.

[62] B. F. Skinner, 'Freedom and the Control of Men', in Kateb (ed.), *Utopia*, pp. 70–1, 74.

violence,[63] but in its capacity to destroy man as a moral agent. Not only is utopia the negation of possessive individualism,[64] the denial that the individual has rights in his own person, it is also the denial of the individual's claim to any irreducible moral responsibility. Candidates for the Bruderhof are asked, 'Are you ready to put yourself completely and utterly at the disposal of the Church-Community of Christ to the end of your life – and with yourself, all your faculties and the whole strength of your body and soul, as well as your entire property, both that which you now possess and that which you may later inherit or earn?' The demand is for both outward and inward conformity and ultimately perfect predictability. If necessary, motivations, appetites and desires will be conditioned to that end.[65] In utopia one is not free to hate, to be conceited, to be extravagant, to commit an infinity of offences great and small. We remember that what Andreae admired about Geneva was the appearance that the authorities enquired 'even into the slightest transgressions of the citizens'.[66] The distinction between good man and good citizen has been obliterated. Just as the full-employment utopia seeks to eliminate waste of effort as well as waste of all other resources, so the utopian generally seeks to eliminate the waste of moral effort. He wants to forge strong links between intention and result so far as moral activity is concerned. The madness of the world he sees around him, the nightmare which impels his utopian construct, is the absence of any such links, the prevalence of moral anarchy. The paradox is that in giving moral certainty to life, in reconciling intention and result, he destroys morality itself.

Perhaps this brings us back to the ultimate conundrum which utopian studies can at least help us to focus. In the West we are now dependent upon legislative machinery, institutions, bureaucracies, technology, which would once have been considered utopian. But change and freedom, planning, complexity and morality seem inescapable and incompatible. Both complexity and the attempt to control it through utopian planning threaten morality. It is a baby-and-the-bath-water dilemma. In the communist world the dependencies are much the same but they have to cope too with a chosen tradition of millenarian vision. Liberal, humane writers of the last twenty or so years have repeatedly warned us either that utopia is evil or that it is necessary. Like a shirt of Nessus it threatens to destroy us and yet we cannot put it aside. The growth in complexity of our society

---

[63] Cf. Popper, 'Utopia and Violence'.

[64] For possessive individualism and its associations with the liberal tradition see C. B. MacPherson, *The Political Theory of Possessive Individualism: Hobbes to Locke* (Oxford, 1962).

[65] Zablocki, *Joyful Community*, p. 327. Cf. ibid., pp. 156–8, 169, 209, 223, 238, 248, 250; Kanter, *Commitment and Community*, p. 16.

[66] F. E. Held (ed.), *Christianopolis* (New York, 1916), pp. 27–8.

and economy, much more the dispersal of power within that society, has made planning both necessary and inevitable. But in terms of what goals, what ultimate values is the planning to be? Progress over the last two hundred years has meant the development of an 'Invisible Machine', an autonomous, extremely powerful and rapidly changing social organism, whose welfare we can no longer entrust to some benign Invisible Hand. The dark side of that organism is its capacity for waste, conflict, destruction and alienation which evokes a bleak and unprepossessing prospect of the future. Man in his freedom can choose to choke the human race in a sea of pollution, to destroy and squander those resources on which human life upon this planet depends, to create societies where material values have devalued human dignity and respect for truth. The utopians will offer to save us from any or all of these fates but only at the price of freedom of choice. To retain order, and whatever values are selected, the freedom to create confusion, muddle, to make mistakes or to do the wrong thing must be eliminated and in the process man as a moral agent, a possessive individual, ceases to exist. Much more immediately, any planning which we undertake to mitigate or prevent the evils surrounding or threatening us must be done, in an open society, in the name of some better and therefore ultimately ideal reference point. There will always be those who press this to the point of utopianism.

The problem of utopianism, its threat and its necessity is no easy one to solve. It may even be the kind of intractable dilemma with which we have to learn to live. But awareness is clearly vital. We must recognise what utopianism is and what its implications are, and we must remember that it is but one type of ideal society.

Bibliographies

SELECT BIBLIOGRAPHY OF PRIMARY SOURCES

Place of publication is London unless otherwise mentioned.

Andreae, Johann Valentin, *Christianopolis* (1619), edited by F. E. Held (New York, 1916)

Christianae Societatis Imago, Christiani Amoris Dextera Porrecta, and *In Nomine Dei Omnipotentis*, in G. H. Turnbull, 'Johann Valentin Andreae's *Societas Christiana*', *Zietschrift für Deutsche Philologie*, 73 (1954), pp. 407–32; 74 (1955), pp. 151–85

A Modell of a Christian Society and *The Right Hand of Christian Love Offered*, translated by John Hall in *Of the Advantageous Reading of History* (1647)

The Hermetick Romance: or the Chymical Wedding. Written in High Dutch by Christian Rosencrentz, translated by E. Foxcroft (1690) with a critical commentary, in J. W. Montgomery, *Cross and Crucible: Johann Valentin Andreae (1586–1654), Phoenix of the Theologians*, Archives Internationales d'Histoire des Idées 55, 2 vols. (The Hague, 1973), vol. II

[Anonymous: 'Philadept'], *Annus Sophiae Jubilaeus: The Sophick Constitution: or, The Evil Customs of the World Reform'd* (1700)

An Essay Concerning Adepts . . . With Some Resolutions Concerning the Principles of the ADEPTISTS; And a Model, Practicable and Easy, of Living in Community (1698)

[Anonymous], *Antiquity Reviv'd: or the Government of a Certain Island Antiently call'd Astreada* (1693)

[Anonymous], *Chaos: Or, A Discourse, Wherein is Presented . . . a Frame of Government by Way of a Republique* (1659)

[Anonymous], *The Free State of Noland: or, The Frame and Constitution of That Happy, Noble, Powerful, and Glorious State. In which all Sorts and Degrees of People find their condition Better'd* (1696; enlarged edn 1701)

[Anonymous], *A Modest Reply, In Answer to the Modest Plea, For an Equal Commonwealth* (1659)

[Anonymous], *A Paradox, Proving the Inhabitants of the Island called Madagascar or St. Lawrence (in Things temporal) to be the happiest People in the World*, in *The Harleian Miscellany* (1744), vol. I, pp. 256–262

[Anonymous], *Publique Bathes Purged: Or, A Reply to Dr. Chamberlain* (1648)

[Anonymous], *Stanleyes Remedy: Or, The Way How to Reform Wandring Beggers, Theeves, High-Way Robbers and Pick-Pockets* (1646)

Archer, Henry, *The Personall Reign of Christ Upon Earth* (1642)

Aspinwall, William, *A Brief Description of the Fifth Monarchy, or Kingdome, That shortly is to come into the World* (1653)

Bacon, Sir Francis, *The Works of Francis Bacon*, edited by James Spedding, Robert Leslie Ellis, Douglas Denon Heath, 14 vols. (1868–90)

New Atlantis: A Worke Unfinished in *Sylva Sylvarum: Or A Naturall History in Ten Centuries* (1627)

Bakewell, Thomas, *Doctor Chamberlain Visited with a Bunch of His Own Grapes* (1650)

The Dippers Plunged in a Sea of Absurdities (1650)

Barclay, John, *Argenis, Translated out of Latine into English. The prose upon his Majesties Command: by Sir Robert Le Grys, Knight: And the Verses by Thomas May, Esquire* (1628)

Barrow, Humphrey, *The Relief of the Poore: and Advancement of Learning Proposed* (1656)

Beacon [or Becon], Richard, *Solon His Follie, or A Politique Discourse Touching the Reformation of Common-weales Conquered, Declined or Corrupted* (Oxford, 1594)

Beale, John, *Herefordshire Orchards: A Pattern For All England* (1657)

Bellers, John, *An Abstract of George Fox's Advice and Warning to the Magistrates of London in the year 1657* (1724)

An Epistle to Friends Concerning the Education of Children (1697)

An Epistle to Friends . . . Concerning the Prisoners, and Sick, in the Prisons, and Hospitals of Great-Britain (1724)

An Epistle to the Quarterly Meeting of London and Middlesex (1718)

An Essay for Imploying the Able Poor (1714)

An Essay for Imploying the Poor to Profit, Humbly Dedicated and Presented to the Lords and Commons of Great Britain, In Parliament Assembled (1723)

An Essay Towards the Ease of Elections of Members of Parliament (1712).

Essays About the Poor, Manufactures, Trade, Plantations, & Immorality (1699)

Proposals for Raising a Colledge of Industry (1695, 1696)

Some Considerations as an Essay towards Reconciling the Old and New Ministry (1712)

Some Reasons for an European State (1710)

To the Arch-Bishop, Bishops and Clergy, of the Province of Canterbury (n.p., n.d. [1711/12?])

To the Children of Light, In Scorn called Quakers (n.p., n.d., 1695?)

To the Lords and Commons in Parliament Assembled: A Supplement to the Proposal for a Colledge of Industry (n.p., n.d., 1696?)

To the Lords and Others Commissioners Appointed by the Queen to Take Care of the Poor Palatines (1709)

Watch unto Prayer: Or, Considerations, For All Who Profess They Believe in the Light (1703)

Bernard, Richard, *The Isle of Man, or the Legall Proceedings in Man-Shire against SINNE* (1626; 10th edition 1635)

Blith, Walter, *The English Improver Improved* (1653)

Boyle, Robert, *The Works of the Honourable Robert Boyle*, edited by Thomas Birch, 6 vols. (1772)

Burton, Robert, *The Anatomy of Melancholy* (1621, sixth edn 1651), edited by Holbrook Jackson, 3 vols. (London, 1932)

Campanella, Tommaso, *The Defense of Galileo* (1622), translated and edited by Grant McColley, *Smith College Studies in History*, 22:3–4 (1937)

    A Discourse Touching the Spanish Monarchy, [translated by Edmund Chilmead], (1654)

    Thomas Campanella, An Italian Friar and Second Machiavel: His Advice to the King of Spain, translated by Edmund Chilmead (1660)

Cavendish, Margaret, *The Description of a New World, called the Blazing World* (1666)

Chamberlen, Peter, *The Declaration and Proclamation of the Army of God* (1659)

    A Discourse between Cap. Kiffin, and Dr. Chamberlain, About Imposition of Hands (1654)

    Dr. Chamberlain's Midwifes Practice (1665)

    Englands Choice (1682)

    Legislative Power in Problemes (1659)

    A Letter to Mr. Braine...Concerning an Administrator of Water-Baptisme (1650)

    Master Bakewell's Sea of Absurdities...Driven Back (1650)

    A Paper Delivered in by Dr. Alston, Dr. Bates, Dr. Hamens, Dr. Micklethwaite on Monday the 16 of October, 1648 Together with an Answer Thereunto (1648)

    Plus Ultra (1651)

    The Poore Mans Advocate (1649)

    A Scourge for a Denn of Thieves (1659)

    The Sober Man's Vindication (1662)

    The Sons of the East (1682)

    A Speech Visibly Spoken (1662)

    To My Beloved Friends and Neighbours of the Black-Fryers (n.p., n.d., 1658?)

    To the Honourable House of Commons...The Humble Petition of Peter Chamberlen, Doctor in Physick (n.p., n.d., 1649)

    A Vindication of Publick Artificiall Baths & Bath-Stoves (1648)

    A Voice in Rhama: or, The Crie of Women and Children (1647)

D.I., *A Cleare and Evident Way for Enriching the Nations of England and Ireland, And for Setting Very Great Numbers of Poore on Work* (1650)

Day, Robert, *Free Thoughts in Defence of a Future State* (1700)

Dury, John, *Considerations Tending to the Happy Accomplishment of England's Reformation* (1647)

    Israels Call to March out of Babylon unto Jerusalem (1646)

    A Motion Tending to the Publick Good of this Age (1642)

The Reformed School (1650)

Some Proposalls Towards the Advancement of Learning (1653)

Dymock, Cressy, *An Invention of Engines of Motion Lately Brought to Perfection* (1651)

Elyot, Sir Thomas, *The Book Named The Governor*, edited with an introduction by S. E. Lehmberg (London, 1962)

Erasmus, Desiderius, *The Colloquies of Erasmus* (1527), translated by Craig R. Thompson (Chicago, 1965)

The Education of a Christian Prince (1516), translated and edited by L. K. Born (New York, 1965)

The Epistles of Erasmus, translated and edited by F. M. Nichols, 3 vols. (New York, 1901)

The Praise of Folly (1511), translated and edited by Hoyt H. Hudson (Princeton, 1941); translated by Betty Radice with an introduction by A. H. T. Levi (London, 1971)

Fennor, William, *The Compters Commonwealth* (1617)

Filmer, Sir Robert, *Patriarcha and Other Political Works*, edited by Peter Laslett (Oxford, 1949)

[Finch, Sir Henry], *The Worlds Great Restauration or The Calling of the Jewes* (1621)

Firmin, Thomas, *Some Proposals for the Imploying of the Poor, Especially In and About the City of London* (1678)

Floyd, Thomas, *The Picture of a Perfit Commonwealth* (1600)

Forset, Edward, *A Comparative Discourse of the Bodies Natural and Politique* (1606)

A Defence of the Right of Kings (1624)

Goddard, Thomas, *Miscellanea* (1661)

Plato's Demon: Or, The State-Physician Unmaskt (1684)

Goffe, William, *How to Advance the Trade of the Nation, and Employ the Poor* (n.p., n.d.) in *The Harleian Miscellany* (1745), vol. IV, pp. 366–70

Goodwin, Francis, *The Man in the Moone* (1638)

Nuncius Inanimatus in Utopia (1629)

[Goodwin, Thomas], *A Glimpse of Syons Glory: Or, The Churches Beautie Specified* (1641)

Gott, Samuel, *The Divine History of the Genesis of the World. Explicated and Illustrated* (1670)

An Essay of the True Happiness of Man. In Two Books (1650)

Novae Solymae. Libri Sex (1648)

Nova Solyma: The Ideal City; or Jerusalem Regained: An Anonymous Romance written in the Time of Charles I. Now first drawn from obscurity and Attributed to the Illustrious John Milton, translated and edited by the Rev. Walter Begley, 2 vols. (1902)

Graunt, John, *The Shipwrack of All False Churches* (1652)

Hall, Joseph, *The Works of Joseph Hall* (1628)

Mundus Alter et Idem, translated by John Healey, edited by Huntington Brown (Cambridge, Mass., 1937)

Harrington, James, *The Oceana and Other Works, with an account of his life by John Toland* (1771)
    The Political Works of James Harrington, edited with an introduction by J. G. A. Pocock (Cambridge, 1977)
Hartlib, Samuel, *A Briefe Relation of That Which Hath Been Lately Attempted to Procure Ecclesiasticall PEACE amongst PROTESTANTS* (1641)
    Clavis Apocalyptica: Or, A Propheticall KEY (1651)
    Considerations Tending to the Happy Accomplishment of Englands Reformation in Church and State (1647)
    A Continuation of Mr. John Amos-Comenius School Endeavours (n.d.)
    Cornucopia: A Miscellanium (n.p., n.d., 1652?)
    The Correspondence of Hartlib, Haak, Oldenburg ... with Governor Winthrop, edited by Robert C. Winthrop (Boston, 1878)
    A Description of the Famous Kingdome of Macaria (1641) [ascribed to Plattes]
    A Designe for Plentie (1652)
    A Discovery for Division or Setting Out of Land, As to the Best Form (1653)
    Englands Thankfulnesse (1642)
    A Faithfull and Seasonable Advice (1643)
    A Further Discoverie of the Office of Publick Addresse for Accommodations (1648)
    Londons Charity, Stilling the Poore Orphans Cry (1649)
    Londons Charity Inlarged (1650)
    The Necessity of Some Nearer Conjunction and Correspondency Amongst Evangellicall Protestants (1644)
    The Parliaments Reformation (1646)
    A Rare and New Discovery...For the Feeding of Silk-worms (1652)
    Samuel Hartlib His Legacie (1651)
Haywood, Eliza, *Memoirs of a Certain Island Adjacent to the Kingdom of Utopia* (1725)
Howard, Edward, *The Six Days Adventure, Or The New Utopia* (1671)
Lupton, Thomas, *Sivqila: Too Good to be True* (1580)
    The Second Part and Knitting Up of the Boke Intituled, Too Good to be True (1581)
    A Persuasion from Papistrie (1581)
    The Christian Against the Jesuite (1582)
    A Dreame of the Divell and Dives (1589)
    A Moral and Pitieful Comedie, Intituled, All For Money (1578)
Manley, Mary, *Secret Memoirs...From the New Atlantis* (1709)
More, Sir Thomas, *The Correspondence of Sir Thomas More*, edited by Elizabeth Frances Rogers (Princeton, 1947)
    A Dialogue of Comfort Against Tribulation (1553), in *Utopia and a Dialogue of Comfort*, edited by John Warrington (1951)
    The History of King Richard III (1543), edited by Richard S. Sylvester, in *The Complete Works of St. Thomas More*, vol. II (New Haven and London, 1963)

The Latin Epigrams of Thomas More (1518), edited by L. Bradner and C. A. Lynch (Chicago, 1953)

Translations of Lucian, edited by Craig R. Thompson, in *The Complete Works of St. Thomas More*, vol. III, part 1 (New Haven and London, 1974)

Utopia (1516), edited by Edward Surtz, S. J. and J. H. Hexter, *The Complete Works of St. Thomas More*, vol. IV (New Haven and London, 1965)

[Nedham, Marchamont], *The Excellencie of a Free-State: Or, The Right Constitution of a Commonwealth* (1656)

Neville, Henry, *Discourses Concerning Government* (1698)

An Exact Diurnall of the Parliament of Ladyes (1647)

The Isle of Pines (1668), edited by W. C. Ford (Boston, 1920)

The Ladies, A Second Time, Assembled in Parliament (1647)

Newes from the New Exchange (1650)

Plato Redivivus (1681), in *Two English Republican Tracts*, edited by Caroline Robbins (Cambridge, 1969)

Shufling, Cutting and Dealing in A Game at Picquet (1659)

The Works of the Famous Nicholas Machiavel, Citizen and Secretary of Florence, [edited and translated by Henry Neville] (1695)

Norwood, Robert, *A Pathway Unto England's Perfect Settlement* (1653)

An Additional Discourse Relating unto a Treatise lately published by Capt. Robert Norwood (1653)

Petty, Sir William, *The Advice of W.P. to Mr. Samuel Hartlib for the Advancement of some particular parts of Learning* (1648)

The Petty Papers: Some Unpublished Writings of Sir William Petty, edited from the Bowood Papers by the Marquis of Lansdowne, 2 vols. (1927)

Plattes, Gabriel, *A Discovery of Infinite Treasure, Hidden Since the Worlds Beginning* (1639)

A Discovery of Subterraneall Treasure (1639)

The Profitable Intelligencer (n.p., n.d., 1644?)

Plockhoy, Peter Cornelius, *A Way Propounded to Make the Poor in these and other Nations happy* (n.d., 1659?)

The Way to the Peace and Settlement of these Nations (1659)

R.H., *New Atlantis. Begun by the Lord Verulam, Viscount St. Albans: And Continued by R.H. Esquire* (1660)

Robinson, Henry, *Certain Proposals in Order to a New Modelling of the Lawes and Law Proceedings* (1653)

Englands Safety in Trades Encrease (1641)

Sadler, John, *Olbia: The New Iland Lately Discovered* (1660)

Salkeld, John, *A Treatise of Paradise And The Principall Contents Thereof* (1617)

Sprigge, William, *A Modest Plea, For An Equal Commonwealth, Against Monarchy* (1659)

Philosophicall Essayes (1657)

Starkey, George [Philalethes], *An Answer to Doctor Chamberlanes Scandalous and Faslse Papers* (1650)

Vaughan, Rowland, *Most Approved and Long Experienced Water-Workes* (1610)

W. W., *Antidotum Britannicum: Or, A Counter-Pest Against the Destructive Principles of Plato Redivivus* (1681)

Wallace, Robert, *Various Prospects of Mankind, Nature and Providence* (1761)

Warwick, Sir Philip, *A Discourse of Government* (1694)

White, John, *The Troubles of Jerusalems Restauration or the Churches Reformation* (1646)

Wilkins, John, *Mathematical and Philosophical Works* (1708)

Winstanley, Gerrard, 'Englands Spirit Unfoulded' (1650), edited by G. E. Aylmer, *Past and Present*, 40 (1968), pp. 3-15

   Winstanley: The Law of Freedom and Other Writings, edited by Christopher Hill (1973)

   The Works of Gerrard Winstanley with an Appendix of Documents Relating to the Digger Movement, edited by G. H. Sabine (New York, 1941; reprint 1965)

Worthington, John, *The Diary and Correspondence of Dr. John Worthington*, edited by James Crossley in *Chetham Society Remains*, volumes 13, 36, 114 (1847-86).

SELECT BIBLIOGRAPHY OF SECONDARY SOURCES

Abercrombie, Patrick, 'Ideal Cities. No. 1: Christianopolis', *Town Planning Review*, 8 (1920), pp. 99-104

Abrams, Philip and Andrew McCulloch, *Communes, Sociology and Society* (Cambridge, 1976)

Adams, Robert P., *The Better Part of Valor: More, Erasmus, Colet and Vives on Humanism, War and Peace 1496-1535* (Seattle, 1962)

   'Designs by More and Erasmus for a New Social Order', *Studies in Philology*, 42 (1945), pp. 131-45

   'The Philosophic Unity of More's *Utopia*', *Studies in Philology*, 38 (1941), pp. 45-65

   'The Social Responsibilities of Science in *Utopia, New Atlantis* and After', *Journal of the History of Ideas*, 10 (1949), pp. 374-98

Adamson, J. W., *Pioneers of Modern Education 1600-1700* (Cambridge, 1905)

Aldridge, A. Owen, 'Polygamy in Early Fiction: Henry Neville and Denis Veiras', *P.M.L.A.*, 65 (1950), pp. 464-72

Allen, J. W., *English Political Thought 1603-1644* (London, 1938)

   A History of Political Thought in the Sixteenth Century (London, 1960)

Allen, Peter R., '*Utopia* and European Humanism: The Function of the Prefatory Letters and Verses', *Studies in the Renaissance*, 10 (1963), pp. 91-107

Allen, Phyllis, 'Medical Education in Seventeenth Century England', *Journal of the History of Medicine*, 1:1 (1946), pp. 115-43

Alsop, James, 'Gerrard Winstanley's Later Life', *Past and Present*, 82 (1979), pp. 73-81

Ames, Russell, *Citizen Thomas More and his Utopia* (Princeton, 1949)

Anderson, Fulton H., *Francis Bacon: His Career and His Thought* (Calif., 1962)

The Philosophy of Francis Bacon (Chicago, 1948)

Appleby, Joyce Oldham, *Economic Thought and Ideology in Seventeenth Century England* (Princeton, 1978)

Arblaster, Anthony and Steven Lukes (eds.), *The Good Society: A Book of Readings* (London, 1971)

Armytage, W. H. G., 'The Early Utopists and Science in England', *Annals of Science*, 12 (1956), pp. 247–54

Heavens Below: Utopian Experiments in England 1560–1960 (London, 1961)

Yesterdays Tomorrows: A Historical Survey of Future Societies (London, 1968)

Aveling, J. H., *The Chamberlens and the Midwifery Forceps: Memorials of the Family and an Essay on the Invention of the Instrument* (London, 1882)

Avinieri, Shlomo, 'War and Slavery in More's *Utopia*', *International Review of Social History*, 7 (1962), pp. 260–90

Axtell, James L., 'Education and Status in Stuart England: The London Physician', *History of Education Quarterly*, 10:2 (1970), pp. 141–59

Aylmer, G. E., *The King's Servants: The Civil Service of Charles I, 1625–1642* (London, 1961)

The State's Servants: The Civil Service of the English Republic, 1649–1660 (London, 1973)

(ed.), 'Gerrard Winstanley's, *England's Spirit Unfoulded*', *Past and Present*, 40 (1968), pp. 3–15

(ed.), *The Interregnum: The Quest for Settlement 1646–1660* (London, 1972)

Babb, Lawrence, *Sanity in Bedlam: A Study of Robert Burton's Anatomy of Melancholy* (Michigan, 1959)

Baldry, H. C., *Ancient Utopias* (Southampton, 1956)

Baumann, F. L., 'Sir Thomas More: A Review Article', *Journal of Modern History*, 4:4 (1932), pp. 604–15

Baumer, Franklin le Van, 'The Conception of Christendom in Renaissance England', *Journal of the History of Ideas*, 6:2 (1945), pp. 131–56

Beer, M., *A History of British Socialism* (London, 1919)

Belasco, Philip S., 'John Bellers', *Economica*, 5 (1925), pp. 165–74

Bell, Susan Groag, 'Johan Eberlin von Günzburg's *Wolfaria*: The First Protestant Utopia', *Church History*, 36:2 (1967), pp. 122–39

Bensly, Edward, 'Some Alterations and Errors in Successive Editions of *The Anatomy of Melancholy*', in F. Madan (ed.), 'Robert Burton and *The Anatomy of Melancholy*', *Oxford Bibliographical Society Proceedings and Papers*, 1, part 1 (1922–6), pp. 198–215

Berdan, John M., 'Doni and the Jacobeans', *P.M.L.A.*, 22 (1907), pp. 291–7

Berens, L. H., *The Digger Movement in the Days of the Commonwealth as Revealed in the Writings of Gerrard Winstanley* (London, 1961)

'A Social Reformer in the Days of the Commonwealth', *Westminster Review*, 164:3 (1905), pp. 273–85

Berneri, Marie Louise, *Journey Through Utopia* (London, 1950)

Bernstein, Eduard, *Cromwell and Communism: Socialism and Democracy in the Great English Revolution*, translated by H. J. Stenning (London, 1930; reprint 1963)

Beveridge, W. II., *Full Employment in a Free Society* (London, 1944, 2nd edition 1960)

'My Utopia', in *Planning Under Socialism and Other Addresses* (London, 1936), pp. 130–42

Power and Influence: An Autobiography (London, 1953)

~~*The Price of Peace* in *A Problem of Industry* (London, 1930)~~

Bevington, David M., 'The Dialogue in *Utopia*: Two Sides to the Question', *Studies in Philology*, 58 (1961), pp. 496–509

Bierman, Judah, 'Science and Society in the *New Atlantis* and other Renaissance Utopias', *P.M.L.A.* (1963), pp. 492–500

Blitzer, Charles, *An Immortal Commonwealth: The Political Thought of James Harrington* (New Haven, 1960)

(ed.), *The Political Writings of James Harrington: Representative Selections* (New York, 1955)

Bloch-Lainé, François, 'The Utility of Utopias for Reformers', *Daedalus* (1965), pp. 419–36; reprinted in Frank E. Manuel (ed.), *Utopias and Utopian Thought* (Boston, 1966)

Blodgett, Eleanor Dickinson, 'Bacon's *New Atlantis* and Campanella's *Civitas Solis*: A Study in Relationships', *P.M.L.A.*, 46 (1931), pp. 763–80

Bloomfield, P., *Imaginary Worlds or the Evolution of Utopia* (London, 1932)

Blum, Irving D., 'English Utopias from 1551 to 1699: A Bibliography', *Bulletin of Bibliography*, 21:6 (1955), pp. 143–4

Boas, George, *Essays on Primitivism and Related Ideas in the Middle Ages* (Baltimore, 1948)

Bolam, David W., *Unbroken Community: The Story of the Friends School Saffron Walden 1702-1952* (London, 1952)

Bonansea, Bernardine M., 'The Political Thought of Tommaso Campanella', in John K. Ryan (ed.), *Studies in Philosophy and the History of Philosophy*, vol. II (Washington, 1963), pp. 211–48

Tommaso Campanella: Renaissance Pioneer of Modern Thought (Washington, 1969)

Born, L. K. (ed.), *Erasmus – The Education of a Christian Prince* (New York, 1965)

'The Perfect Prince: A Study in 13th and 14th Century Ideals', *Speculum*, 3:4 (1928), pp. 470–504

'Some Notes on the Political Theories of Erasmus', *Journal of Modern History*, 2 (1930), pp. 226–36

Bouwsma, William J., 'Lawyers in Early Modern Culture', *American Historical Review*, 78:2 (1973), pp. 303–27

Bowen, Catherine Drinker, *Francis Bacon: The Temper of a Man* (London, 1963)

Brailsford, H. N., *The Levellers and the English Revolution* (London, 1961)

Brink, Andrew, 'Gerrard Winstanley', *Journal of the Friends Historical Society*, 49:3 (1960), pp. 179–80

Brinton, Crane, 'Utopia and Democracy', *Daedalus* (1965), pp. 348–66

Brown, Louise Fargo, *The Political Activities of the Baptists and Fifth Monarchy Men in England during the Interregnum* (London, 1911)

Brzezinski, Zbigniew, 'America in the Technetronic Age', in George Kateb (ed.), *Utopia* (New York, 1971)

Bullough, Geoffrey, 'Bacon and the Defence of Learning', in B. Vickers (ed.), *Essential Articles for the Study of Francis Bacon* (Hamden, Conn., 1968)

Burke, Peter, *Popular Culture in Early Modern Europe* (London, 1978)

Burtt, Ruth G., 'Records from Cirencester: Fettiplace and Bellers', *Journal of the Friends Historical Society*, 35 (1938), pp. 82–6

Bush, Douglas, *English Literature in the Early Seventeenth Century 1600–1660* (Oxford, 1945; 2nd edition, 1962)

Butterfield, H., *The Origins of Modern Science 1300–1800* (London, 1958)

Cadbury, Henry J., 'First Publishers of Truth in Lancashire', *Journal of the Friends Historical Society*, 31 (1934), pp. 3–19
 'Joshua Sprigge on the Continent', *Journal of the Friends Historical Society*, 45 (1953), pp. 60–3

Capp, B. S., 'Extreme Millenarianism', in Peter Toon (ed.), *Puritans, the Millennium and the Future of Israel: Puritan Eschatology 1600–1660* (Cambridge, 1970), Chapter 4
 The Fifth Monarchy Men: A Study in Seventeenth-Century English Millenarianism (London, 1972)

Cardwell, D. S. L., *Turning Points in Western Technology: A Study of Technology, Science and History* (New York, 1972)

Carmichael, Montgomery, 'The Utopia: Its Doctrine of the Common Life', *Dublin Review*, 383 (1932), pp. 173–87

Cawley, R. R., 'Shakespeare's Use of the Voyagers in the Tempest', *P.M.L.A.*, 41 (1926), pp. 688–726

Chambers, R. W., *Thomas More* (London, 1963)
 'The Saga and the Myth of Sir Thomas More', *Proceedings of the British Academy*, 12 (1926), pp. 179–225

Chesneaux, Jean, 'Egalitarian and Utopian Traditions in the East', *Diogenes*, 62 (1968), pp. 76–102

Child, Harold, 'Some English Utopias', *Transactions of the Royal Society of Literature*, 3rd series, 12 (1933), pp. 31–60

Christianson, Paul, *Reformers and Babylon: English Apocalyptic Visions from the Reformation to the Eve of the Civil War* (Toronto, 1978)

Clark, David, *Basic Communities: Towards an Alternative Society* (London, 1977)

Clark, Sir George, *A History of the Royal College of Physicians of London*, 2 vols. (Oxford, 1964–6)

Science and Social Welfare in the Age of Newton (2nd edition, Oxford, 1949; reprint 1970)

Clark, Peter and Paul Slack (eds.), *Crisis and Order in English Towns 1500–1700* (London, 1972)

Clark, Stuart, 'Bacon's Henry VII: A Case-Study in the Science of Man', *History and Theory*, 13:2 (1974), pp. 97–118

Clarke, I. F., *The Pattern of Expectation 1644–2001* (London, 1979)

Clouse, R. G., 'The Rebirth of Millenarianism', in P. Toon (ed.), *Puritans, the Millennium and the Future of Israel: Puritan Eschatology 1600–1660* (Cambridge, 1970), Chapter 3

Cohn, Norman, 'Medieval Millenarism: Its Bearing on the Comparative Study of Millenarian Movements', in Sylvia T. Thrupp (ed.), *Millennial Dreams in Action* (The Hague, 1962), pp. 31–43

  The Pursuit of the Millennium (London, 1962)

  'The Ranters', *Encounter*, 34 (1970), pp. 15–25

Cole, Alan, 'The Quakers and the English Revolution', *Past and Present*, 10 (1956), pp. 39–54

Coleman, D. C., 'Labour in the English Economy in the Seventeenth Century', *Economic History Review*, 2nd series, 8 (1955–6), pp. 280–95; reprinted in E. M. Carus-Wilson (ed.), *Essays in Economic History*, 3 vols. (London, 1954–62), vol. II

Coles, Paul, 'The Interpretation of More's "Utopia"', *Hibbert Journal*, 56 (1958), pp. 365–70

Colie, Rosalie L., 'Cornelis Drebbel and Salomon de Caus: Two Jacobean Models for Salomon's House', *Huntington Library Quarterly*, 18:3 (1955), pp. 245–60

Cooper, J. P., 'Social and Economic Policies under the Commonwealth', in G. E. Aylmer (ed.), *The Interregnum: The Quest for Settlement 1646–1660* (London, 1972), Chapter 5

Coulton, G. G., *Medieval Panorama* (Cambridge, 1943)

Crane, Ronald S., 'The Relation of Bacon's *Essays* to his Program for the Advancement of Learning', in *The Schelling Anniversary Papers* (New York, 1923); reprinted in B. Vickers (ed.), *Essential Articles for the Study of Francis Bacon* (Hamden, Conn., 1968)

Crino, Anna Maria, *Il Popish Plot Nelle Relazioni Inedite dei Residenti Granducati alla Corte di Londra (1678–1681)* (Rome, 1954)

  'Lettere inedite italiane e inglesi di Sir Henry Neville', in *Fatti e Figure del Seicento Anglo-Toscana*, Biblioteca dell'Archivum Romanicum, 48 (Florence, 1957)

Croce, Benedetto, 'History and Utopia', in *History as the Story of Liberty*, translated by Sylvia Sprigge (London, 1941), pp. 256–61

Crowther, J. G., *Francis Bacon, The First Statesman of Science* (London, 1960)

Curtis, Mark H., *Oxford and Cambridge in Transition 1558–1642* (Oxford, 1959)

Dahrendorf, Ralf, 'Out of Utopia: Toward a Reorientation of Sociological

Analysis', *American Journal of Sociology*, 64:2 (1958), pp. 115–27; reprinted in George Kateb (ed.), *Utopia* (New York, 1971)

Dallison, A. R., 'Contemporary Criticism of Millenarianism' in P. Toon (ed.), *Puritans, the Millennium and the Future of Israel: Puritan Eschatology 1600–1660* (Cambridge, 1970), Chapter 6

Davidson, Morrison, *The Wisdom of Winstanley the Digger* (London, 1904)

Davies, H. Neville, 'Bishop Godwin's "Lunatique Language" ', *Journal of the Warburg and Courtauld Institute*, 30 (1967), pp. 296–316

' "Symzonia" and "The Man in the Moone" ', *Notes and Queries*, new series, 15 (1968), pp. 342–5

Davies, K. G., 'Joint Stock Investment in the Later Seventeenth Century', *Economic History Review*, 2nd series, 4 (1952), pp. 283–301; reprinted in E. M. Carus-Wilson (ed.), *Essays in Economic History*, 3 vols. (London, 1954–62), vol. II

The Royal African Company (London, 1957)

Davis, J. C., 'Gerrard Winstanley and the Restoration of True Magistracy', *Past and Present*, 70 (1976), pp. 76–93

'More, Morton and the Politics of Accommodation', *Journal of British Studies*, 9:2 (1970), pp. 27–49

'Utopia and History', *Historical Studies*, 13:50 (1968), pp. 165–76

Dean, Leonard F., 'Sir Francis Bacon's Theory of Civil History Writing', in B. Vickers (ed.), *Essential Articles for the Study of Francis Bacon* (Hamden, Conn., 1968)

Debus, Allen G., *The Chemical Dream of the Renaissance*, Churchill College Overseas Fellowship Lecture no. 3 (Cambridge, 1968)

'Renaissance Chemistry and the Work of Robert Fludd', in Allen G. Debus and Robert P. Multhauf, *Alchemy and Chemistry in the Seventeenth Century* (Los Angeles, 1966)

Science and Education in the Seventeenth Century: The Webster–Ward Debate (London, 1970)

Dell, Edmund, 'Gerrard Winstanley and the Diggers', *Modern Quarterly*, new series, 4 (1949), pp. 129–41

Derrett, J. Duncan M., 'The Trial of Sir Thomas More', *English Historical Review*, 79 (1964), pp. 449–77

Dickens, A. G., 'A New Prayer of Sir Thomas More', *Church Quarterly Review*, 124 (1937), pp. 224–37

Dircks, H., *A Biographical Memoir of Samuel Hartlib* (London, 1865)

Ditz, G. W., 'Utopian Symbols in the History of the British Labour Party', *British Journal of Sociology*, 17 (1966), pp. 145–8

Dobb, Maurice, *Studies in the Development of Capitalism* (London, 1963)

Donner, H. W., *Introduction to Utopia* (Uppsala, 1945)

Doxiadis, Constantinos A., *Between Dystopia and Utopia* (London, 1968)

Dubois, C. G., *Problèmes de l'Utopie*, Archives des Lettres Modernes (Paris, 1968)

Dudok, Gerard, *Sir Thomas More and his Utopia* (Amsterdam, 1923)

Duff, Edward Gordon and F. Madan, 'Notes of the Bibliography of the Oxford editions of the *Anatomy*', in F. Madan (ed.), 'Robert Burton and

The Anatomy of Melancholy', *Oxford Bibliographical Society Proceedings and Papers*, 1, part 1 (1922–6), pp. 191–7.

Duhamel, P. A., 'The Medievalism of More's Utopia', *Studies in Philology*, 52 (1955), pp. 99–126

Duke, H. E. and B. Campion, *The Story of Gray's Inn* (London, 1950)

Dumont, René, *Utopia or Else...*(London, 1974)

Dupont, V., *L'Utopie et le Roman Utopique dans la Littérature Anglaise* (Toulouse, 1941)

Dwight, T. W., 'Harrington and his Influence upon American Political Institutions and Political Thought', *Political Science Quarterly*, 2:1 (1887), pp. 1–44

Eliott, Dean 'The Tempest: Rebellion and the Ideal State', *Shakespeare Quarterly*, 16 (1965), pp. 161–73

Eccleshall, Robert, *Order and Reason in Politics: Theories of Absolute and Limited Monarchy in Early Modern England* (Hull and Oxford, 1978)

Edwards, G. W., 'The London Six Weeks Meeting', *Journal of the Friends Historical Society*, 50:4 (1964), pp. 228–45

Elliott, Robert C., *The Shape of Utopia: Studies in a Literary Genre* (Chicago, 1970)

Elmen, Paul, 'The Theological Basis of Digger Communism', *Church History*, 23:3 (1954), pp. 207–18

Elton, G. R., 'An Early Tudor Poor Law', *Economic History Review*, 2nd series, 13 (1953), pp. 55–67

'Sir Thomas More and the Opposition to Henry VIII', *Bulletin of the Institute of Historical Research*, 41 (1968), pp. 19–34

Emerson, Roger L., 'Utopia', in Philip P. Weiner (ed.), *Dictionary of the History of Ideas*, 4 vols. (New York, 1973), vol. IV, pp. 458–65.

Eurich, Nell, *Science in Utopia: A Mighty Design* (Cambridge, Mass., 1967)

Evans, Bergen, *The Psychiatry of Robert Burton* (New York, 1944)

Fairfield, Richard (ed.), *Utopia U.S.A.* (San Francisco, 1972)

Farrington, B., *Francis Bacon, Philosopher of Industrial Science* (London, 1951)

The Philosophy of Francis Bacon: An Essay on its Development from 1603 to 1609 with New Translations of Fundamental Texts (Liverpool, 1964)

Ferguson, Arthur B., *The Articulate Citizen and the English Renaissance* (Durham, N.C., 1965)

Fink, Zera S., *The Classical Republicans: An Essay in the Recovery of the Pattern of Thought in Seventeenth Century England* (Evanston, 1945; 2nd edition 1962)

Finley, M. I., 'Utopianism Ancient and Modern', in Finley, *The Use and Abuse of History* (London, 1975), pp. 178–92

Firpo, Luigi, 'Kaspar Stiblin, Utopiste', in Jean Lameere (ed.), *Les Utopies à la Renaissance* (Paris and Brussels, 1963), pp. 107–33

Firth, C. H., 'A Puritan Utopia', *Church Quarterly Review*, 57 (1903), pp. 101–30

Firth, Katherine R., *The Apocalyptic Tradition in Reformation Britain 1530–1645* (Oxford, 1979)

Fish, Stanley E., *Self-Consuming Artifacts: The Experience of Seventeenth Century Literature* (Los Angeles, 1972)

Fleisher, Martin, *Radical Reform and Political Persuasion in the Life and Writings of Sir Thomas More*, Travaux d'Humanisme et Renaissance, 132 (Geneva, 1973)

Flinn, M. W. (ed.), 'The Law Book of the Crowley Iron Works', *Publications of the Surtees Society*, 167 (London, 1957)

　Men of Iron: The Crowleys in the Early Iron Industry (Edinburgh, 1962)

Fogarty, Robert S., *American Utopianism* (Itasca, Ill., 1972)

Forbes, Thomas R., 'The Regulation of English Midwives in the Sixteenth and Seventeenth Centuries', *Medical History*, 8:3 (1964), pp. 235–44

Ford, Worthington Chauncey, *The Isle of Pines 1668: An Essay in Bibliography* (Boston, 1920)

Foriers, Paul, 'Les Utopies et le Droit', in Jean Lameere (ed.), *Les Utopies à la Renaissance* (Paris and Brussels, 1963)

Francastel, Pierre (ed.), *Utopie et Institutions An XVIIe Siècle: Le Pragmatisme des Lumières* (Paris, 1963)

Frank, Joseph, *The Levellers* (New York, 1969)

French, Peter J., *John Dee: The World of an Elizabethan Magus* (London, 1972)

Fry, A. Ruth, *John Bellers 1654–1725, Quaker, Economist and Social Reformer: His Writings reprinted with a Memoir* (London, 1935)

Frye, Northrop, 'Varieties of Literary Utopia', *Daedalus* (1965), pp. 323–47; reprinted in Frank E. Manuel (ed.), *Utopias and Utopian Thought* (Boston, 1966)

Fussner, F. Smith, *The Historical Revolution: English Historical Writing and Thought 1580–1640* (London, 1962)

Fuz, J. K., *Welfare Economics in English Utopias: Francis Bacon to Adam Smith* (The Hague, 1952)

Gabrielli, Vittorio, 'Giovanni Pico and Thomas More', *Moreana*, 4:15/16 (1967), pp. 43–57

de Gandillac, Maurice, 'Le Realisme Politique de Thomas More', in *Utopie, Kritiek en Verlichting* (n.p., 1973–4)

Gardiner, Judith Keegan, 'Elizabethan Psychology and Robert Burton', *Journal of the History of Ideas*, 38 (1977), pp. 373–88

Gardner, J. E. G., *Tommaso Campanella and his Poetry: The Taylorian Lecture 1923* (Oxford, 1923)

Garraty, John A., *Unemployment in History: Economic Thought and Public Policy* (New York and Toronto, 1978)

George, C. H., 'Gerrard Winstanley: A Critical Retrospect', in C. Robert Cole and Michael E. Moody (eds.), *The Dissenting Tradition* (Athens, Ohio, 1975), pp. 191–225

Gerber, Richard, *Utopian Fantasy: A study of English Utopian Fiction since the End of the Nineteenth Century* (New York, 1973)

Gibson, R. W., *Francis Bacon: A Bibliography of his Works and of Baconiana to the Year 1750* (Oxford, 1950)

Francis Bacon: A Bibliography of his Works...Supplement. (Privately issued typescript, 1959)

St. Thomas More: A Preliminary Bibliography of his Works and of Moreana to the Year 1750, compiled by R. W. Gibson with a bibliography of Utopiana compiled by R. W. Gibson and J. Max Patrick (New Haven and London, 1961)

Gilison, Jerome M., *The Soviet Image of Utopia* (Baltimore and London, 1975)

Goldsmith, M. M., 'Public Virtue and Private Vices: Bernard Mandeville and English Political Ideologies in the Early Eighteenth Century', *Eighteenth Century Studies*, 9:4 (1976), pp. 477–510

Golffing, Francis and Barbara, 'An Essay on Utopian Possibility', in George Kateb (ed.), *Utopia* (New York, 1971), pp. 29–39

Gooch, G. P., *English Democratic Ideas in the Seventeenth Century* (2nd edition, Cambridge, 1927)

Gough, J. W., 'Harrington and Contemporary Thought', *Political Science Quarterly*, 45:3 (1930), pp. 395–404

Gove, Philip Babcock, *The Imaginary Voyage in Prose Fiction. A History of its Criticism and a Guide for its Study, with an Annotated Check List of 215 Imaginary Voyages from 1700 to 1800* (New York, 1941)

Grace, William J., 'The Conception of Society in More's "Utopia" ', *Thought*, 22 (1947), pp. 283–96

Grant, Douglas, *Margaret the First, A Biography of Margaret Cavendish Duchess of Newcastle 1623–1673* (Toronto, 1957)

Graus, F., 'Social Utopias in the Middle Ages', *Past and Present*, 38 (1967), pp. 3–19

Gray, B. Kirkman, *A History of English Philanthropy: From the Dissolution of the Monasteries to the Taking of the First Census* (London, 1905)

Graziani, René, 'Non-Utopian Euthanasia: An Italian Report, c. 1554', *Renaissance Quarterly*, 22 (1969), pp. 329–33

Greaves, Richard L., 'The Early Quakers as Advocates of Educational Reform', *Quaker History*, 58 (1969), pp. 22–30

'Gerrard Winstanley and Educational Reform in Puritan England', *British Journal of Educational Studies*, 17:2 (1969), pp. 166–76

'The Ordination Controversy and the Spirit of Reform in Puritan England', *Journal of Ecclesiastical History*, 201 (1970), pp. 225–41

'Puritanism and Science: Anatomy of a Controversy', *Journal of the History of Ideas*, 30 (1969), pp. 345–68

'William Sprigg and the Cromwellian Revolution', *Huntington Library Quarterly*, 34:2 (1971), pp. 99–113

Greenleaf, W. H., *Order, Empiricism and Politics: Two Traditions of English Political Thought 1500–1700* (Oxford, 1964)

Grendler, P. F., *Critics of the Italian World (1530–1560): Anton Francesco Doni, Nicolo Franco and Ortensio Lando* (Madison, Wis., 1969)

'Utopia in Renaissance Italy: Doni's New World', *Journal of the History of Ideas*, 26:4 (1965), pp. 479–94

Grillo, F., *Tommaso Campanella in America: A Supplement to the Critical Bibliography* (New York, 1957)

Grimble, Ian, *The Harington Family* (London, 1957)

Gunn, J. A. W., *Politics and the Public Interest in the Seventeenth Century* (London, 1969)

Hacker, Andrew, 'Dostoevsky's Disciples: Man and Sheep in Political Theory', *Journal of Politics*, 17:4 (1955), pp. 590–613
  'In Defense of Utopia', *Ethics*, 65 (1955), pp. 135–8
  'The Specter of Predictable Man', *Antioch Review*, 14:2 (1954), pp. 195–207

Hall, A. Rupert, 'Science, Technology and Utopia in the Seventeenth Century', in P. Mathias (ed.), *Science and Society 1600–1900* (Cambridge, 1972), pp. 33–53

Haller, William, *Foxe's Book of Martyrs and The Elect Nation* (London, 1963)

Hanson, Donald W., *From Kingdom to Commonwealth: The Development of Civic Consciousness in English Political Thought* (Cambridge, Mass., 1970)

Hansot, Elizabeth, *Perfection and Progress: Two Modes of Utopian Thought* (Cambridge, Mass., 1974)

Harbison, E. Harris, 'Machiavelli's *Prince* and More's *Utopia*', in William H. Werkmeister (ed.), *Facets of the Renaissance* (New York, 1963), pp. 41–71

Hardacre, Paul H., 'Gerrard Winstanley in 1650', *Huntington Library Quarterly*, 22 (1958–9), pp. 345–9

Harder, Leland and Marvin, *Plockhoy from Zurick-Zee: The Study of a Dutch Reformer in Puritan England and Colonial America*, Mennonite Historical Series, no. 2 (Newton, Kansas, 1952)

Harington, Henry (ed.), *Nugae Antiquae* (London, 1804: reprint, New York, 1966)

Harrison, John L., 'Bacon's View of Rhetoric, Poetry, and the Imagination', in B. Vickers (ed.), *Essential Articles for the Study of Francis Bacon* (Hamden, Conn., 1968)

Hayes, T. W., 'Gerrard Winstanley and Foxe's "Book of Martyrs"', *Notes and Queries* (1977), pp. 209–12
  Winstanley the Digger: A Literary Analysis of Radical Ideas in the English Revolution (Cambridge, Mass., 1979)

Healey, Robert M., 'The Jew in Seventeenth-Century Protestant Thought', *Church History*, 46 (1977), pp. 63–79

Heath, T. G., 'Another Look at Thomas More's "Richard"', *Moreana*, 19–20 (1968), pp. 11–20

Heiserman, A. R., 'Satire in the "Utopia"', *P.M.L.A.*, 78 (1963), pp. 163–74

Hertzler, J. O., *The History of Utopian Thought* (London, 1923)

Hexter, J. H., 'The Loom of Language and the Fabric of Imperatives: The Case of *Il Principe* and *Utopia*', *American Historical Review*, 69:4 (1964), pp. 945–68
  More's Utopia: The Biography of an Idea (2nd edition, New York, 1965)
  Reappraisals in History (London, 1961)

'Thomas More: On the Margins of Modernity', *Journal of British Studies*, 1 (1961), pp. 20–37

'Utopia and Geneva', in T. K. Rabb and J. E. Seigel (eds.), *Action and Conviction in Early Modern Europe, Essays in Memory of E. H. Harbison* (Princeton, 1969), pp. 77–89

The Vision of Politics on the Eve of the Reformation: More, Machiavelli and Seyssel (London, 1973)

Hill, Christopher, *Antichrist in Seventeenth Century England* (London, 1971)

Puritanism and Revolution (London, 1962)

'The Radical Critics of Oxford and Cambridge in the 1650s', in John W. Baldwin and Richard A. Goldthwaite (eds.), *Universities in Politics: Case Studies from the Late Middle Ages and Early Modern Period* (Baltimore, 1972), pp. 107–32

'The Religion of Gerrard Winstanley', *Past and Present Supplement* 5 (1978)

Society and Puritanism in Pre-Revolutionary England (London, 1966)

(ed.) *Winstanley: The Law of Freedom and Other Writings* (London, 1973)

The World Turned Upside Down: Radical Ideas during the English Revolution (London, 1972)

Hine, Robert V., *California's Utopian Colonies* (New Haven and London, 1966)

Hollis, Christopher, *St. Thomas More* (London, 1961)

Holloway, Mark, *Heavens on Earth: Utopian Communities in America 1680–1880* (2nd edition, New York, 1966)

Holmes, Martin, 'Evil May-Day: The Story of a Riot', *History Today*, 15:9 (1965), pp. 642–50

Houghton-Evans, W., *Planning Cities* (London, 1975)

Hudson, W. S., 'The Economic and Social Thought of Gerrard Winstanley', *Journal of Modern History*, 18:1 (1946), pp. 1–21

'Gerrard Winstanley and the Early Quakers', *Church History*, 12 (1943), pp. 177–94

Hurstfield, Joel, *Freedom, Corruption and Government in Elizabethan England* (London, 1973)

Jackson, Holbrook (ed.), *Robert Burton, The Anatomy of Melancholy*, 3 vols. (London, 1932)

James, Margaret, *Social Problems and Policy during the Puritan Revolution 1640–1660* (London, 1930)

Jenkins, Michael, 'Arakchev and the Military Colonies in Russia', *History Today*, 19 (1969), pp. 600–7

Jerome, Judson, *Families of Eden: Communes and the New Anarchism* (London, 1957)

Johnson, Francis R., *Astronomical Thought in Renaissance England: A Study of English Scientific Writings from 1500–1645* (Baltimore, 1937)

Johnson, Robbin S., *More's 'Utopia': Ideal and Illusion* (New Haven and London, 1969)

Jones, Rufus M., *Mysticism and Democracy in the English Commonwealth* (New York, 1932)

Jones, Stephen K., 'The Authorship of *Nova Solyma*', *Library*, 3rd series, 1:3 (1910), pp. 225–38

Jordan, W. K., *The Charities of Rural England 1480–1660: The Aspirations and the Achievements of the Rural Society* (London, 1961)
 The Charities of London 1480–1660: The Aspirations and Achievement of the Urban Society (London, 1960)
 Philanthropy in England 1480–1660. A Study of the Changing Pattern of English Social Aspirations (London, 1959)

de Jouvenel, Bertrand, 'Utopia for Practical Purposes', *Daedalus* (1965), pp. 437–53

Juretic, George, 'Digger No Millenarian: The Revolutionising of Gerrard Winstanley', *Journal of the History of Ideas*, 36:2 (1975), pp. 263–80

Kaminsky, Howard, 'The Free Spirit in the Hussite Revolution', in Sylvia L. Thrupp (ed.), *Millennial Dreams in Action* (The Hague, 1962), pp. 166–186

Kanter, Rosabeth Moss, *Commitment and Community: Communes and Utopias in Sociological Perspective* (Cambridge, Mass., 1972)
 'Commitment and Social Organization: A Study of Commitment Mechanisms in Utopian Communities', *American Sociological Review*, 33:4 (1968), pp. 499–517
 'Communes', *Psychology Today*, 4:2 (1970), pp. 53–7, 78

Kateb, George (ed.), *Utopia* (New York, 1971)
 Utopia and Its Enemies (New York, 1963)
 'Utopias and Utopianism', in David L. Sills (ed.), *International Encyclopaedia of the Social Sciences* (n.p., 1968), vol. xvi, pp. 267–75

Kaufman, M., *Utopias; or, Schemes of Social Improvement from Sir Thomas More to Karl Marx* (London, 1879)

Keller, A. G., *Societal Evolution: A Study of the Evolutionary Basis of the Science of Society* (London, 1931)

Keniston, Keith, 'Alienation and the Decline of Utopia', *American Scholar*, 29 (1960), pp. 161–200

Kenyon, J. P., *Revolution Principles: The Politics of Party 1689–1720* (Cambridge, 1977)

Kessler, Martin, 'Power and the Perfect State', *Political Science Quarterly*, 72 (1957), pp. 565–77

Khanna, Lee Cullen, 'No Less Real than Ideal: Images of Women in More's Work', *Moreana*, 55–6 (1977), pp. 35–51

King, Bruce, ' "The Mower against Gardens" and the Levellers', *Huntington Library Quarterly*, 33 (1970), pp. 237–42

Klein, Robert, 'L'Urbanisme Utopique de Filarete a Valentin Andreae', in J. Lameere (ed.), *Les Utopies à la Renaissance* (Paris and Brussels, 1961), pp. 209–30

Kocher, Paul H., 'Francis Bacon on the Science of Jurisprudence', *Journal of the History of Ideas*, 19 (1957), pp. 3–26; reprinted in B. Vickers (ed.), *Essential Articles for the Study of Francis Bacon* (Hamden, Conn., 1968)

Korshin, P. J. (ed.), *Studies in Change and Revolution: Aspects of English Intellectual History 1640–1800* (Menston, Yorks., 1972)

Küng, Hans, *Freedom in the World: St. Thomas More*, translated by Cecily Hastings (London, 1965)
Freiheit in des Welt (Einsiedein, 1964)

Laidler, H. W., *Social-Economic Movements: An Historical and Comparative Survey of Socialism, Communism, Co-operation, Utopianism; and Other Systems of Reform and Reconstruction* (London, 1949)

Lakoff, Sanford A., *Equality in Political Philosophy* (Cambridge, Mass., 1964)

Lameere, Jean (ed.), *Les Utopies à la Renaissance*, Travaux de l'Institut pour l'Etude de la Renaissance et de l'Humanisme (Paris and Brussels, 1963)

Lamont, William, *Godly Rule: Politics and Religion 1603–1660* (London, 1969)

Lasky, Melvin J., 'The Novelty of Revolution: A Study in Seventeenth-Century English Ideology', in Jean-Claude Casanova (ed.), *Science et Conscience de la Société*, vol. 1 (Paris, 1971), pp. 251–80
Utopia and Revolution (London, 1977)

Laslett, P., 'Market Society and Political Theory', *Historical Journal* 7 (1964), pp. 150–4
The World We Have Lost (London, 1965)
Family Life and Illicit Love in Earlier Generations (Cambridge, 1977)

Lawton, H., 'Bishop Godwin's Man in the Moon', *Review of English Studies*, 8 (1931), pp. 23–55

Leonard, E. M., *The Early History of English Poor Relief* (Cambridge, 1900)

Letwin, William, *The Origins of Scientific Economics: English Economic Thought 1660–1760* (London, 1963)

Levine, Joseph M., 'Ancients, Moderns and History: The Continuity of English Historical Writing in the Later Seventeenth Century', in P. J. Korshin (ed.), *Studies in Change and Revolution: Aspects of English Intellectual History 1640–1800* (Menston, Yorks., 1972)

Lewis, C. S., *English Literature in the Sixteenth Century* (Oxford, 1954)

Liljegren, S. B., 'Harrington and the Jews', *K. Humanistiska Vetenkapssamfundet i Lund Arsberättelse*, 4 (1931–2), pp. 65–92
(ed.), *James Harrington's Oceana* (Heidelberg, 1924)
Studies on the Origin and Early Tradition of English Utopian Fiction (Uppsala, 1961)

Lodge, David, 'Utopia and Criticism, The Radical Longing for Paradise', *Encounter*, 32:4 (1969), pp. 65–75

McColley, Grant, 'The Date of Godwin's Domingo Gonsales', *Modern Philology*, 35 (1937), pp. 47–60
'Francis Godwin. The Man in the Moone and Nuncius Inanimatus. For the first time edited, with introduction and notes, from unique copies of the first editions of London, 1629 and London, 1638', *Smith College Studies in Modern Languages*, 19 (1937)
'The Pseudonyms of Francis Godwin', *Philological Quarterly*, 16 (1937), pp. 78–80
'The Third Edition of Francis Godwin's "The Man in the Moone"', *Library*, new series, 17 (1937), pp. 472–5

McConica, James Kelsey, *English Humanists and Reformation Politics under Henry VIII and Edward VI* (Oxford, 1965)

McCutcheon, Elizabeth, 'Thomas More, Raphael Hythlodaeus and the Angel Raphael', *Studies in English Literature*, 9 (1969), pp. 21–38

McGregor, J. F., 'Ranterism and the Development of Early Quakerism', *Journal of Religious History*, 9 (1977), pp. 349–63

MacPherson, C. B., *The Political Theory of Possessive Individualism: Hobbes to Locke* (Oxford, 1962)

Madan, F. (ed.), 'Robert Burton and *The Anatomy of Melancholy*: Papers by Sir William Osler, Professor Edward Bensly and others', *Oxford Bibliographical Society Proceedings and Papers*, 1, part 1 (1922–6), pp. 159–246

Mannheim, Karl, *Essays in the Sociology of Knowledge* (London, 1952)
Ideology and Utopia (London, 1960)
'Utopia', in *Encyclopaedia of the Social Sciences*, ed. E. R. A. Seligman and A. Johnson (London, 1935)

Manning, Brian, *The English People and the English Revolution* (London, 1976)

Manuel, Frank E., *Freedom from History* (New York, 1971)
(ed.), *Utopias and Utopian Thought* (Boston, 1966)

Manuel, Frank E. and Fritzie P. (eds.), *French Utopias: An Anthology of Ideal Societies* (New York, 1966)

Marc'hadour, Germain, *L'Univers de Thomas More: Chronologie critique de More, Erasme, et leur epoque (1477–1536)* (Paris, 1963)

Marcuse, Herbert, 'The End of Utopia', in *Five Lectures: Psychoanalysis, Politics and Utopia*, translated by Jeremy J. Shapiro and Shierry M. Weber (London, 1970), pp. 62–82

Marshall, Dorothy, 'The Old Poor Law, 1662–1795', *Economic History Review*, 8 (1937–8), pp. 38–47; reprinted in E. M. Carus-Wilson (ed.), *Essays in Economic History*, 3 vols. (London, 1954–62), vol. 1

Massó, Gildo, *Education in Utopias* (New York, 1927)

Mazzeo, Joseph Anthony, *Renaissance and Revolution: The Remaking of European Thought* (London, 1967)

Mead, Margaret, 'Towards More Vivid Utopias', in George Kateb (ed.), *Utopia* (New York, 1971), pp. 41–56

Meinecke, Friedrich, *Machiavellism: The Doctrine of Raison D'Etat and its Place in Modern History*, translated by Douglas Scott (London, 1957)

Merchant, W. M., 'Bishop Francis Godwin, Historian and Novelist', *Journal of the Historical Society of the Church in Wales*, 5 (1955), pp. 45–51

Merton, R. K., *Social Theory and Social Structure* (Glencoe, Ill., 1951)

Mesnard, Pierre, 'L'Utopie de Robert Burton', in Jean Lameere (ed.), *Les Utopies à la Renaissance* (Paris and Brussels, 1963), pp. 73–88

Miles, Leland, 'The Literary Artistry of Thomas More: *The Dialogue of Comfort*', *Studies in English Literature*, 6 (1966), pp. 7–33
'Persecution and the *Dialogue of Comfort*: A Fresh Look at the Charges against Sir Thomas More', *Journal of British Studies*, 5 (1965), pp. 19–30

'The Platonic Sources of *Utopia*'s "Minimum Religion"', *Renaissance News*, 9 (1956), pp. 83–90

'Thomas More: Disenchanted Saint', in Bernice Slate (ed.), *Literature and Society* (Lincoln, Nebr., 1964), pp. 65–84

Molnar, Thomas, *Utopia: The Perennial Heresy* (New York, 1967)

Monro, T. K., *The Physician As Man of Letters, Science and Action* (2nd edition, London, 1951)

Montgomery, J. W., *Cross and Crucible: Johann Valentin Andreae (1586–1654) Phoenix of the Theologians*, Archives Internationales d'Histoire des Idées 55, 2 vols. (The Hague, 1973)

Moore, W. E., 'The Utility of Utopias for Reformers', *American Sociological Review*, 24 (1966), pp. 765–72

Moore-Smith, G. C., 'The Date of the *New Atlantis*', *The Athenaeum*, 3771 (1900), pp. 146–8

Moos, Rudolf and Robert Brownstein, *Environment and Utopia: A Synthesis* (New York, 1977)

Morgan, Arthur E., *Nowhere was Somewhere: How History Makes Utopias and How Utopias Make History* (Chapell Hill, 1946)

Morton, A. L., *The English Utopia* (London, 1952)

'Utopias Yesterday and Today', *Science and Society* (Spring 1956), pp. 258–63

Mucchielli, Roger, 'L'Utopie de Thomas Morus', in Jean Lameere (ed.), *Les Utopies à la Renaissance* (Paris and Brussels, 1963), pp. 99–106

Mueller, William R., *The Anatomy of Robert Burton's England* (Berkeley and Los Angeles, 1952)

Mulligan, Lotte, John Graham and Judith Richards, 'Winstanley: A Case for the Man as He Said He Was', *Journal of Ecclesiastical History*, 28:1 (1977), pp. 57–75

Multhauf, Robert P., 'Some Nonexistent Chemists of the Seventeenth Century: Remarks on the Use of the Dialogue in Scientific Writing', in Allen G. Debus and Robert P. Multhauf, *Alchemy and Chemistry in the Seventeenth Century* (Los Angeles, 1966)

Mumford, Lewis, *The Culture of Cities* (London, 1938)

'Utopia, the City and the Machine', *Daedalus* (1965), pp. 271–92

Murphy, Walter F., 'The Political Philosophy of Gerrard Winstanley', *Review of Politics*, 19 (1956), pp. 214–38

Murray, Matthew, 'The English Utopians', *Twentieth Century*, 174 (1966), pp. 12–15

Nadel, George H., 'History as Psychology in Francis Bacon's "Theory of History"', *History and Theory*, 5:3 (1966), pp. 275–87. (Also in B. Vickers (ed.), *Essential Articles for the Study of Francis Bacon* (Hamden, Conn., 1968))

Nagel, Alan F., 'Lies and the Limitable Inane: Contradiction in More's *Utopia*', *Renaissance Quarterly*, 26:2 (1973), pp. 173–80

Nef, John U., *Cultural Foundations of Industrial Civilisation* (London, 1958)

'The Genesis of Industrialism and of Modern Science (1560–1640)', in

Norton Downs (ed.), *Essays in Honor of Conyers Read* (Chicago, 1953), pp. 200–69

Negley, Glenn (ed.), *Utopia Collection of the Duke University Library* (Durham, N.C., 1965)

  Utopian Literature: A Bibliography with a Supplementary Listing of Works Influential in Utopian Thought (Lawrence, Kansas, 1977)

Negley, Glenn and J. Max Patrick, *The Quest for Utopia* (New York, 1952)

Nelson, William, 'Thomas More, Grammarian and Orator', *P.M.L.A.*, 58 (1943), pp. 337–52

  (ed.), *Twentieth Century Interpretations of 'Utopia'* (Englewood Cliffs, N.J., 1968)

Nicholson, Marjorie H., *Voyages to the Moon* (New York, 1948)

  'A World in the Moon: A Study of the Changing Attitude Toward the Moon in the Seventeenth and Eighteenth Centuries', *Smith College Studies in Modern Languages*, 17 (1937)

Novak, Maximilian E., 'Robinson Crusoe and Economic Utopia', *Kenyon Review*, 25 (1963), pp. 474–90

Nozick, Robert, *Anarchy, State and Utopia* (Oxford, 1974)

Oakley, Francis, 'Celestial Hierarchies Revisited: Walter Ullmann's Vision of Medieval Politics', *Past and Present*, 60 (1973), pp. 3–48

Olson, Mancur, 'Economics, Sociology and the Best of All Possible Worlds', *Public Interest*, 12 (1968), pp. 96–118

Ong, Walter J., 'The Writer's Audience is Always a Fiction', *P.M.L.A.*, 90:1 (1975), pp. 9–21

Osborne, Harold (ed.), *Bacon 'New Atlantis'* (London, 1937)

Osler, Sir William, 'Robert Burton – The Man, His Book, His Library', in F. Madan (ed.), 'Robert Burton and *The Anatomy of Melancholy*', *Oxford Bibliographical Society Proceedings and Papers*, 1, part 1 (1922–6), pp. 163–90

  'Creators, Transmuters and Transmitters', in *ibid*., pp. 216–18

Parrington, Vernon Louis, *American Dreams: A Study of American Utopias* (Providence, R.I., 1947)

Patrick, J. Max, *Francis Bacon* (London, 1961)

  'A History of Utopianism in England in the Seventeenth Century' (Oxford, D.Phil. Thesis, 1952)

  'The Literature of the Diggers', *University of Toronto Quarterly*, 12 (1942), pp. 95–110

  '*Nova Solyma*: Samuel Gott's Puritan Utopia', *Studies in the Literary Imagination*, 10:2 (1977), pp. 43–55

  'Puritanism and Poetry: Samuel Gott', *University of Toronto Quarterly*, 8:2 (1939), pp. 211–26

  'Robert Burton's Utopianism', *Philological Quarterly*, 27:4 (1948), pp. 345–58

  '*Scydromedia*, a Forgotten Utopia of the 17th Century', *Philological Quarterly*, 23:3 (1944), pp. 273–82

  'William Covell and the Troubles at Enfield in 1659, A Sequel to the

Digger Movement', *University of Toronto Quarterly*, 14 (1944–5), pp. 45–57

'Why Men Write Utopias', *Emory University Quarterly*, 4 (1948), pp. 110–121

Pauling, N. G., 'The Employment Problem in Pre-Classical English Economic Thought', *Economic Record*, 27 (1951), pp. 52–65

Pearl, Valerie, 'Puritans and Poor Relief: The London Workhouse, 1649–1660', in D. Pennington and K. Thomas (eds.), *Puritans and Revolutionaries: Essays in Seventeenth Century History Presented to Christopher Hill* (Oxford, 1979)

Penney, N. (ed.), *Extracts from State Papers Relating to Friends 1654 to 1672* (London, 1913)

The First Publishers of Truth (London, 1907)

Pineas, Rainer, 'More versus Tyndale: A Study of Controversial Technique', *Modern Language Quarterly*, 24 (1963), pp. 144–50

'Thomas More's Use of the Dialogue Form as a Weapon of Religious Controversy', *Studies in the Renaissance*, 7 (1960), pp. 193–206

'Thomas More's Use of Humor as a Weapon of Religious Controversy', *Studies in Philology*, 58 (1961), pp. 97–114

Plattel, Martin G., *Utopian and Critical Thinking*, translated by H. J. Koren (Pittsburg, 1972)

Pocock, J. G. A., *The Ancient Constitution and the Feudal Law: A Study of English Historical Thought in the Seventeenth Century* (Cambridge, 1957)

'Custom and Grace, Form and Matter: An Approach to Machiavelli's Concept of Innovation', in M. Fleisher (ed.), *Machiavelli and the Nature of Political Thought* (New York, 1972), pp. 153–74

'Early Modern Capitalism: The Augustan Perception', in E. Kamenka and R. S. Neale (eds.), *Feudalism, Capitalism and Beyond* (London, 1975), pp. 62–83

'James Harrington and the Good Old Cause: a Study of the Ideological Context of his Writings', *Journal of British Studies*, 10:1 (1970), pp. 30–48

'Machiavelli, Harrington and English Political Ideologies in the Eighteenth Century', *William and Mary Quarterly*, 3rd series, 22:4 (1965), pp. 549–83

The Machiavellian Moment: Florentine Republican Thought and the Atlantic Republican Tradition (Princeton, 1975)

'Modes of Political and Historical Time in Early Eighteenth Century England', in R. C. Rosbottom (ed.), *Studies in Eighteenth Century Culture*, vol. v (Madison, Wis., 1976)

Obligation and Authority in Two English Revolutions (Wellington, 1973)

' "The Onely Politician": Machiavelli, Harrington and Felix Raab', *Historical Studies*, 12 (1966), pp. 265–96

Politics, Language and Time: Essays on Political Thought and History (London, 1972)

'Political Thought in the Cromwellian Interregnum', in G. A. Wood and P. S. O'Connor (eds.), *W. P. Morrell: A Tribute* (Dunedin, 1973)

Polak, Fred L., *The Image of the Future*, 2 vols. (Leyden, 1961)

Popper, K. R., *The Open Society and Its Enemies*, 2 vols. (London, 1945, 1961)

　The Poverty of Historicism (London, 1960)

　'Utopia and Violence', *Hibbert Journal*, 46 (1947–8), pp. 109–16

Prest, Wilfrid R., 'The Art of Law and the Law of God: Sir Henry Finch (1558–1625)', in D. Pennington and K. Thomas (eds.), *Puritans and Revolutionaries: Essays in Seventeenth Century History Presented to Christopher Hill* (Oxford, 1979)

　The Inns of Court under Elizabeth I and the Early Stuarts 1590–1640 (London, 1972)

Prior, Moody E., 'Bacon's Man of Science', in B. Vickers (ed.), *Essential Articles for the Study of Francis Bacon* (Hamden, Conn., 1968)

Raab, Felix, *The English Face of Machiavelli: A Changing Interpretation 1500–1700* (London, 1964)

Rabb, Theodore K., *Enterprise and Empire: Merchant and Gentry Investment in the Expansion of England, 1575–1630* (Cambridge, Mass., 1967)

　'Francis Bacon and the Reform of Society', in T. K. Rabb and J. E. Seigel (eds.), *Action and Conviction in Early Modern Europe: Essays in Memory of E. H. Harbison* (Princeton, 1969), pp. 169–93

Raistrick, Arthur, *Two Centuries of Industrial Welfare: The London (Quaker) Lead Company 1692–1905* (London, 1938)

Ratiere, Martin N., 'More's *Utopia* and *The City of God*', *Studies in the Renaissance*, 20 (1973), pp. 144–68

Raven, C. E., 'Thomas Lawson's Note Book', *Proceedings of the Linnean Society of London*, 160 (1947–8), pp. 3–12

Reiner, Thomas A., *The Place of the Ideal Community in Urban Planning* (Philadelphia, 1963)

Reynolds, E. E., *The Field is Won: The Life and Death of St. Thomas More* (London, 1968)

　(ed.), *Lives of Sir Thomas More*, by W. Roper and N. Harpsfield (London, 1963)

　'Which Thomas More? A Retraction', *Moreana*, 4:13 (1967), pp. 79–82

Rhodes, Harold V., *Utopia in American Political Thought* (Tucson, Ariz., 1967)

Richter, Peyton E. (ed.), *Utopias: Social Ideals and Communal Experiments* (Boston, 1971)

Riesman, David, 'Some Observations on Community Plans and Utopia', in Riesman, *Individualism Reconsidered and Other Essays* (Glencoe, Ill., 1954), pp. 70–98

Righter, Anne, 'Francis Bacon', in B. Vickers (ed.), *Essential Articles for the Study of Francis Bacon* (Hamden, Conn., 1968)

Ritter, Gerhard, *The Corrupting Influence of Power*, translated by F. W. Pick (Hadleigh, Essex, 1952)

Roberts, R. S., 'The Personnel and Practice of Medicine in Tudor and Stuart England', Part I: 'The Provinces', *Medical History*, 6:4 (1962), pp. 363–382; Part II: 'London', *Medical History*, 8:3 (1964), pp. 217–34

Robertson, D. B., *The Religious Foundations of Leveller Democracy* (New York, 1951)

Rogers, P. G., *The Fifth Monarchy Men* (London, 1966)

Rood, Wilhelmus, *Comenius and the Low Countries* (Amsterdam, 1970)

Roscoe, T., *The Italian Novelists*, 4 vols. (London, 1825), vol. III

Rosen, George, 'Left-Wing Puritanism and Science', *Bulletin of the History of Medicine*, 15 (1944), pp. 375–80

Rosenau, Helen, *The Ideal City: Its Architectural Evolution* (2nd edition, London, 1974)

Ross, H., *Utopias Old and New* (London, 1938)

Rossi, Paolo, *Francis Bacon: From Magic to Science*, translated by Sacha Rabinovitch (London, 1968)

Rostenberg, Leona, *Literary, Political, Scientific, Religious and Legal Publishing, Printing and Bookselling in England 1551–1700: Twelve Studies*, 2 vols. (New York, 1965)

Rowntree, B. Seebohm and Bruno Lasker, *Unemployment: A Social Study* (London, 1911)

Russell, R. (ed.), *The Utopian*, second series, 1 (1911); 2 (1912); 3 (1912)

Russell Smith, H. F., *Harrington and his Oceana: A Study of a Seventeenth Century Utopia and its Influence in America* (Cambridge, 1914)

Rutt, J. T. (ed.), *Diary of Thomas Burton, Esq. Member in the Parliaments of Oliver and Richard Cromwell from 1656 to 1659*, 4 vols. (London, 1828)

Salmon, Vivian, 'Problems of Language-Teaching; A Discussion Among Hartlib's Friends', *Modern Language Review*, 59 (1964), pp. 13–24

Saulnier, V. L., 'Mythologies Pantegrueliques L'Utopie en France: Morus et Rabelais', in Jean Lameere (ed.), *Les Utopies à la Renaissance* (Paris and Brussels, 1963), pp. 135–62

Schenk, W., *The Concern for Social Justice in the Puritan Revolution* (London, 1948)

Schochet, Gordon J., 'The Family and the Origin of the State in Locke's Political Philosophy', in John W. Yolton (ed.), *John Locke: Problems and Perspectives: A Collection of New Essays* (Cambridge, 1969)
  Patriarchalism in Political Thought: The Authoritarian Family and Political Speculation and Attitudes Especially in Seventeenth-Century England (Oxford, 1975)

Schoek, R. J., 'More, Plutarch and King Agis: Spartan History and the Meaning of Utopia', *Philological Quarterly*, 35 (1955), pp. 366–75

Schwoerer, Lois G., *'No Standing Armies!' The Anti-Army Ideology in Seventeenth Century England* (Baltimore and London, 1974)

Seaver, Paul S. (ed.), *Seventeenth Century England: Society in an Age of Revolution* (New York, 1976)

Seguy, Jean, *Utopie Coopérative et Oecuménisme: Pieter Cornelisz Plockhoy van Zurik-Zee 1620–1700* (Paris, 1968)

Seipp, Karl, *John Bellers, Ein Vertreter des frühen Quäkertums* (Nuremberg, 1933)

Sharp, Andrew, 'Edward Waterhouse's View of Social Change in Seventeenth Century England', *Past and Present*, 62 (1974), pp. 27–46

'The Manuscript Versions of Harringtons *Oceana*', *Historical Journal*, 16 (1973), pp. 227–39

Sharp, Isaac, 'John Bellers, Lost and Found', *Journal of the Friends Historical Society*, 12 (1915), pp. 117–19

Shepperson, George, 'The Comparative Study of Millenarian Movements', in Sylvia L. Thrupp (ed.), *Millennial Dreams in Action* (The Hague, 1962), pp. 44–52

Shklar, Judith, 'Ideology Hunting: The Case of James Harrington', *American Political Science Review*, 53 (1959), pp. 662–92

'The Political Theory of Utopia: From Melancholy to Nostalgia', *Daedalus* (1965), pp. 367–81; reprinted in Frank E. Manuel (ed.), *Utopias and Utopian Thought* (Boston, 1966)

'Rousseau's Two Models: Sparta and the Age of Gold', *Political Science Quarterly*, 81:1 (1966), pp. 25–51

Simpson, Charles R., 'John Bellers in Official Minutes', *Journal of the Friends Historical Society*, 12:3 (1915), pp. 120–7 and 12:4 (1915), pp. 165–71

Sippell, Theodor, 'The Testimony of Joshua Sprigge', *Journal of the Friends Historical Society*, 38 (1946), pp. 24–8

Skinner, B. F., 'The Design of Experimental Communities under Utopianism', in David L. Sills (ed.), *International Encyclopaedia of the Social Sciences* (n.p., 1968), vol. xvi, pp. 267–75

'Freedom and the Control of Men', in George Kateb (ed.), *Utopia* (New York, 1971), pp. 57–75

'Visions of Utopia', *The Listener* (5 Jan. 1967 and 12 Jan. 1967)

Walden Two (New York, 1962)

Skinner, Quentin, *The Foundations of Modern Political Thought*, 2 vols. (Cambridge, 1979)

'More's Utopia', *Past and Present*, 38 (1967), pp. 153–68

Spencer, Theodore, 'The History of an Unfortunate Lady', *Harvard Studies and Notes in Philology and Literature*, 20 (1938), pp. 43–59

Stark, W., *The Sociology of Knowledge* (London, 1958)

Stephenson, H. W., 'A Seventeenth Century Philanthropist: Thomas Firmin (1632–1697)', *Transactions of the Unitarian Historical Society*, 6 (1936), pp. 130–47, 6 (1937), pp. 222–45, 6 (1938), pp. 354–78

Stimson, D., 'Hartlib, Haak and Oldenburg: Intelligencers', *Isis*, 31 (1940), pp. 309–26

Stone, Lawrence, *The Crisis of the Aristocracy 1558–1641* (Oxford, 1965)

The Family, Sex and Marriage in England 1500–1700 (London, 1977)

Straka, Gerald M., 'Revolutionary Ideology in Stuart England', in P. J. Korshin (ed.), *Studies in Change and Revolution* (Menston, Yorks., 1972)

Strauss, Gerald, 'Success and Failure in the German Reformation', *Past and Present*, 67 (1975), pp. 30–65

Surtz, E. L., 'Interpretations of *Utopia*', *Catholic History Review*, 38 (1952), pp. 156–74

'The Link between Pleasure and Communism in *Utopia*', *Modern Language Notes*, 70 (1955), pp. 90–3

'More's "Apologia Pro Utopia Sua" ', *Modern Language Quarterly* (1958), pp. 319–24

The Praise of Pleasure: Philosophy, Education and Communism in More's Utopia (Cambridge, Mass., 1957)

The Praise of Wisdom: A Commentary on the Religious and Moral Problems and Backgrounds of St. Thomas More's Utopia (Chicago, 1957)

'The Setting for More's Plea for Greek in Utopia', *Philological Quarterly*, 35 (1956), pp. 353–65

'Thomas More and Communism', *P.M.L.A.*, 64 (1949), pp. 549–64

Sylvester, R. S. (ed.), *St. Thomas More: Action and Contemplation* (New Haven, 1972)

Sylvester, R. S. and G. M. Marc'hadour (eds.), *Essential Articles for the Study of Thomas More* (Hamden, Conn., 1977)

Talmon, J. L., 'Utopianism and Politics', in George Kateb (ed.), *Utopia* (New York, 1971), pp. 91–101

Tawney, R. H., 'Harrington's Interpretation of his Age', *Proceedings of the British Academy*, 27 (1941)

Thirsk, Joan (ed.), *The Agrarian History of England and Wales*, vol. IV, *1500–1640* (Cambridge, 1967)

'Younger Sons in the Seventeenth Century', *History*, 54 (1969), pp. 358–77

Economic Policy and Projects: The Development of a Consumer Society in Early Modern England (Oxford, 1978)

Thomas, Keith, *Religion and the Decline of Magic: Studies in Popular Beliefs in Sixteenth and Seventeenth Century England* (London, 1971)

'Another Digger Broadside', *Past and Present*, 42 (1969), pp. 57–68

Thompson, Max, 'James Harrington (1611–77) An Aristocratic Radical', *History Today*, 2 (June 1952), pp. 406–11

Thrupp, Sylvia L. (ed.), *Millennial Dreams in Action*, Comparative Studies in Society and History, Supplement 2 (The Hague, 1962)

Tierney, Brian, *Medieval Poor Law: A Sketch of Canonical Theory and Its Application in England* (Los Angeles, 1959)

Tihany, Leslie C., 'Utopia in Modern Western Thought: The Metamorphosis of an Idea', in Richard Herr and Harold T. Parker (eds.), *Ideas in History: Essays Presented to Louis Gottschalk by his Former Students* (Durham, N.C., 1965)

Tod, Ian and Michael Wheeler, *Utopia* (London, 1978)

Toon, Peter (ed.), *Puritans, the Millennium and the Future of Israel: Puritan Eschatology 1600–1660* (Cambridge, 1970)

Traugott, John, 'A Voyage to Nowhere with Sir Thomas More and Jonathan Swift: *Utopia* and *The Voyage to the Houyhnhnms*', *Sewanee Review*, 69 (1961), pp. 534–65

Trevor-Roper, H. R., *Religion, the Reformation and Social Change* (London, 1967)

Turnbull, G. H., *Hartlib, Dury and Comenius: Gleanings from Hartlib's Papers* (London, 1947)

'Johann Valentin Andreae's *Societas Christiana*', *Zeitschrift für Deutsche Philologie*, 73 (1954), pp. 407–32; 74 (1955), pp. 151–85

'John Hall's Letters to Samuel Hartlib', *Review of English Studies*, 4:15 (1953), pp. 221–33

Samuel Hartlib: A Sketch of his Life and his Relations to J. A. Comenius (London, 1920)

'Samuel Hartlib's Acquaintance with John Aubrey', *Notes and Queries*, 195 (1950), pp. 31–3

Tuveson, E. L., *Millennium and Utopia: A Study in the Background of the Idea of Progress* (Berkeley and Los Angeles, 1949; Gloucester, Mass., 1964 and 1972)

Ulam, Adam, 'Socialism and Utopia', *Daedalus* (1965), pp. 382–400

Underwood, T. L., 'Early Quaker Eschatology', in P. Toon (ed.), *Puritans, the Millennium and the Future of Israel: Puritan Eschatology 1600–1660* (Cambridge, 1970), Chapter 5

Vann, Richard T., 'From Radicalism to Quakerism: Gerrard Winstanley and Friends', *Journal of the Friends Historical Society*, 49:1 (1959), pp. 41–6

'Quakerism and the Social Structure in the Interregnum', *Past and Present*, 43 (1969), pp. 71–91

'The Later Life of Gerrard Winstanley', *Journal of the History of Ideas*, 26:1 (1965), pp. 133–6

Vincent, W. A. L., *The State and School Education 1640–1660 in England and Wales, A Survey based on Printed Sources* (London, 1950)

Wagar, W. W., *The City of Man, Prophecies of a World Civilisation in Twentieth Century Thought* (Boston, 1963)

Wallace, Karl R., 'Discussion in Parliament and Francis Bacon', in B. Vickers (ed.), *Essential Articles for the Study of Francis Bacon* (Hamden, Conn., 1968)

Francis Bacon on Communication and Rhetoric or: The Art of Applying Reason to Imagination for the Better Moving of the Will (Chapel Hill, N.C., 1943)

Walzer, Michael, 'Puritanism as a Revolutionary Ideology', *History and Theory*, 3 (1963), pp. 59–90

The Revolution of the Saints (Cambridge, Mass., 1965)

Warren, Roland L., 'Toward a Non-Utopian Normative Model of the Community', *American Sociological Review*, 35:2 (1970), pp. 219–28

Weber, Eugen, 'The Anti-Utopia of the Twentieth Century', in George Kateb (ed.), *Utopia* (New York, 1971), pp. 81–9

Weber, Max, *The Protestant Ethic and the Spirit of Capitalism*, translated by Talcott Parsons with a forward by R. H. Tawney (London, 1930)

Webster, Charles, 'The Authorship and Significance of *Macaria*', *Past and Present*, 56 (1972), pp. 34–48

'English Medical Reformers of the Puritan Revolution: A Background to the "Society of Chymical Physitians"', *Ambix*, 14 (1967), pp. 16–41

The Great Instauration: Science, Medicine and Reform 1626–1660 (London, 1975)

(ed.), *The Intellectual Revolution of the Seventeenth Century* (London, 1941)

'Macaria: Samuel Hartlib and the Great Reformation', *Acta Comeniana*, 26 (1970), pp. 147–64

(ed.), *Samuel Hartlib and the Advancement of Learning* (Cambridge, 1970)

Weinstein, Donald, 'The Savonarola Movement in Florence: Millenarianism in a Civic Setting', in Sylvia L. Thrupp (ed.), *Millennial Dreams in Action* (The Hague, 1962), pp. 187–203

Wells, H. G., *A Modern Utopia* (London, 1905)

West, Michael, 'Spenser, Everard Digby and the Renaissance Art of Swimming', *Renaissance Quarterly*, 26:1 (1973), pp. 11–22

Westfall, Richard S., *Science and Religion in Seventeenth Century England* (New Haven, 1958)

Wheeler, Harvey, 'The Constitutional Ideas of Francis Bacon', *Western Political Quarterly*, 9 (1956), pp. 927–36

Whitaker, Virgil K., *Francis Bacon's Intellectual Milieu* (Los Angeles, 1962)

White, Helen C., *Social Criticism in Popular Religious Literature of the Sixteenth Century* (New York, 1944)

White, Howard B., *Peace Among the Willows: The Political Philosophy of Francis Bacon* (The Hague, 1968)

'Political Faith and Francis Bacon', *Social Research* (1956), pp. 343–66

White, Lynn, Jr, 'The Iconography of *Temperantia* and the Virtuousness of Technology', in T. K. Rabb and J. E. Seigel (eds.), *Action and Conviction in Early Modern Europe* (Princeton, 1969), pp. 197–219

Medieval Technology and Social Change (Oxford, 1962)

Wilkinson, R. S., 'The Hartlib Papers and Seventeenth Century Chemistry', part I, *Ambix*, 15 (1968); part II, *Ambix*, 17 (1970)

Winthrop, Robert C. (ed.), *The Correspondence of Hartlib, Haak, Oldenburg and Others of the Founders of the Royal Society with Governor Winthrop of Connecticut 1661–1672*, Proceedings of the Massachusetts Historical Society (Boston, 1878)

Wolfe, D. M., *Milton in the Puritan Revolution* (London, 1941)

Woodcock, George, 'Utopias in Negative', *Sewanee Review*, 64 (1956), pp. 81–97

Worsley, Peter, *The Trumpet Shall Sound* (London, 1957)

Yates, Frances A., *The Art of Memory* (London, 1969)

'Foxe as Propagandist', *Encounter*, 27 (1966), pp. 78–86

Giordano Bruno and the Hermetic Tradition (London, 1964; reprint 1971)

The Rosicrucian Enlightenment (London, 1972)

Theatre of the World (London, 1969)

Zablocki, Benjamin, *The Joyful Community* (Baltimore, 1971)

Zagorin, Perez, *A History of Political Thought in the English Revolution* (London, 1954)

Index